THE INFLUENTIAL 1000
WHO'S WHO IN IRELAND

PLUS 200 RISING STARS

EDITED BY
MAUREEN CAIRNDUFF

AGA KHAN IV, H. H. Prince Karim; SPIRITUAL LEADER, BLOODSTOCK BREEDER; *b* 1936; *educ* le Rosey, Switzerland; Harvard (U.S.), BA; *m* Sarah Frances Croker-Poole (*m dis*); *2s* 1 *da;* succeeded to title on the death of his grandfather, Sir Sultan Mohamed Shah, Aga Khan III; founder of various cultural, academic and charitable institutions and trusts; recipient of numerous international honours and decorations; owner of three of Ireland's most prominent stud farms Gilltown Stud (Stallions *Darshaan, Kahyasi),* Sallymount Stud, Sheshoon Stud; although not resident in Ireland plays a major role in the country's bloodstock industry. Contact: Sheshoon Stud, The Curragh, Co. Kildare. Tel: 045 441080. Fax: 045 481687.

AGNEW, Robert Francis; EXECUTIVE DIRECTOR BELFAST FESTIVAL AT QUEENS; *b* 1944; *educ* Campbell College, Belfast; Trinity College Dublin, BA; *m* Amy McGrehan; *2s* 1 *da;* working in Germany on book exhibitions and teaching; Sales Director, John Compton Ltd., Armagh, 1967-80; Publicity and Marketing Manager, Grand Opera House, Belfast, 1980-85; Assistant Director, Belfast Festival at Queens, 1985-90, Executive Director, 1994 to date; the strong leader of an outstanding Arts Festival; member, Advisory Panel for Drama, Northern Ireland Curriculum Council, 1991 to date. Hobbies, theatre, music and travel. Contact: Belfast Festival at Queens, 25 College Gardens, Belfast BT9 6BS, Northern Ireland. Tel: 080 1232 667686. Fax: 080 1232 663733.

AGNEW, Robert Francis

AHERN, Bertie; TAOISEACH; *b* 1951; *educ* St. Patrick's National School, Drumcondra; St. Aidan's Christian Brothers School; College of Commerce, Rathmines; University College Dublin; *married;* 2 *da;* Accountant, Mater Hospital, 1974; elected Fianna Fail Deputy for Dublin Finglas, 1977, and each subsequent election; Asst. Chief Whip, 1980-81; spokesman on Youth Affairs, 1981; Govt. Chief Whip and Minister of State at Departments of Taoiseach and Defence, 1982; Minister for Labour, 1987-91; Minister for Finance, 1991-94, Leader of Opposition, 1994-97; Lord Mayor of Dublin, 1986-87; member, Board of Governors IMF, World Bank, EIB (Chairman, 1991-92) 1991-94; recipient, Grand Cross, Order of Merit with Star and Sash (Germany), 1993; a media friendly, popular politician who enjoys personal inter-action with the public. Hobbies, sports and reading. Contact: Office of the Taoiseach, Merrion Street, Dublin 2. Tel: 01 662 4888.

AHERN, Bertie

AHERN, Dermot; POLITICIAN, SOLICITOR; *b* 1955; *educ* Marist College, Dundalk; University College Dublin; Incorporated Law Society; member, Louth County Council, 1979-91; elected Fianna Fail Deputy for Louth, 1987; Assistant Government Whip, 1988-91; Minister of State at the Department of the Taoiseach with special responsibility as Government Chief Whip and Minister of State at the Department of Defence, 1991-92; Minister for Social, Community and Family Affairs, 1997 to date; member, Oireachtas Joint Committee on Commercial State Sponsored Bodies, 1987, Special Oireachtas Committees on Judicial Separation and Child Care, Foreign Adoptions and the Solicitors' Bill, Dáil Select Committee on Legislation and Security; member, British-Irish Parliamentary Body since 1991 (Co-Chairman since 1993). Contact: Department for Social, Community and Family Affairs, Aras Mhic Dhiarmada, Store Street, Dublin 1. Tel: 01 874 0954.

AIKEN, James, "Jim"; PROMOTER; *b* 1932; *educ* St. Patrick's College, Armagh; St. Patrick's College, Maynooth, BA; St. Mary's Training College, Belfast, NT; *m* Anne McGovern; 1 *s* 4 *da*; Teacher 1956-65; Promoter 1966 to date. Honorary Life Member, R.D.S. Dublin, Board Member, Investment Belfast Ltd., Ex Board Member, Arts Council (NI) and National Concert Hall, Dublin. Promoter of major concerts in Ireland including Neil Diamond, U2, Rod Stewart, Diana Ross, Bruce Springsteen and Garth Brooks. Also, organiser of major events, including Smurfit Shamrock Classic and Elton John at Stormont. Enjoys horse racing, GAA, travelling, especially if associated with business. Contact: Aiken Promotions Ltd., Marlborough House, 348 Lisburn Road, Belfast. Tel: 0801 232 381047. Fax: 0801232 682091.

AL-HUSSEIN, Yayha Mohammad; IMAM AND DIRECTOR, ISLAMIC FOUNDATION OF IRELAND; *b* 1950; *educ* University of Khartoum, B.Sc. (Agri); *m* Nawal Al-Haj; 2 *s* 1 *da*; Inspector, Rahad Agricultural Corporation, 1980-83; Imam and Director, Islamic Foundation of Ireland, 1983 to date. Hobbies, reading. Contact: Islamic Foundation of Ireland, 163 South Circular Road, Dublin 8. Tel: 01 453 3242. Fax: 01 453 2785.

ALLEN, Bert; MANAGING DIRECTOR SLANEY FOOD GROUP, HOTELIER; *b* 1935; *educ* Newtown School, Waterford; *single;* Farmer, Livestock Dealer, Meat Processor and Exporter; established Slaney Meats in the '70s (processors and exporters) and Slaney Cooked Meats, (now Slaney Food Group); has a number of hotels in Ireland and Scotland, including Bewleys Hotel at Newlands Cross. Recognised as a tough, shrewd businessman. Contact: Slaney Food Group, Ryland, Bunclody, Co. Wexford. Tel: 054 77155.

ALLEN, Colm; SENIOR COUNCIL; b 1951; *educ* Marian College, Lansdowne Road; UCD and Kings Inns; *m* Amanda Grieve; *2s*; called to the Irish Bar 1978; UK Bar 1981; Inner Bar 1992; member, Council of the Arthritis Foundation of Ireland; Joint Patron of Cartoon Ball. Clubs, St. Stephen's

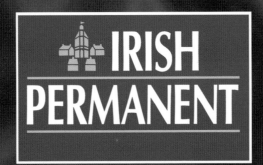

Green, Fitzwilliam Tennis Club, Rathsallagh Golf Club. Hobbies, hill walking, wine and food. Contact: The Law Library, 158-59 Church Street, Dublin 7. Tel: 01 804 5005. Fax: 01 804 5151.

ALLEN, Darina

ALLEN, Darina; née O'Connell; COOKERY SCHOOL OWNER/AUTHOR/TV PRESENTER; *b* 1948; *educ* Dominican Convent, Wicklow; College of Catering, Cathal Brugha Street, Dublin, Dip. Hotel and Catering Mgmt; *m* Tim Allen, Farmer; 2*s* 2 *da;* Cook Ballymaloe House, Cork, 1968; Owner/Principal, Ballymaloe Cookery School, 1983 to date; publications include articles in *Sainsburys Magazine, House & Garden* and *Food & Wine*; eight *Simply Delicious* Cookbooks (Gill & Macmillan), and eight *Simply Delicious* Cookery series for RTE; twenty six part TV series for Carlton Food Network, based on her book *A Year at Ballymaloe Cookery School;* other books include, *The Festive Food of Ireland* and *Irish Traditional Cooking;* Certified Teacher, Certified Culinary Professional and Food Professional, International Association of Culinary Professionals; member, IACP and Euro Toques, Guild of Food Writers and Irish Organic Centre; a top class teacher and Ireland's leading culinary expert due to highly rated TV series; an outspoken critic of GM foods. Hobbies, gardening, reading, walking and tennis. Contact: The Ballymaloe Cookery School, Shanagarry, Co. Cork. Tel: 021 646785. Fax: 021 646909.

ALLEN, Padraic

ALLEN, Elizabeth, "Liz"; CRIME CORRESPONDENT, THE SUNDAY INDEPENDENT; b 1969; educ Stanhope Convent, Stoneybatter, Dublin; Queen's University Belfast, ; *m* Andrew Hanlon; 1 stepson; started freelancing at the age of fourteen for the *Evening Herald*; Correspondent, *Evening Herald*, Tallaght Edition, 1986-88, Freelance Journalist, 1988-92; Freelance Journalist, *Irish Independent*, specialising in investigative pieces, 1992-96; was prosecuted under the Official Secrets Act for investigation of the Brinks Allied Robbery, 1995; Crime Correspondent, *The Sunday Tribune*, 1996; Crime Correspondent, *The Sunday Independent*, 1996 to date; continues to investigate drugs and crime rackets in Ireland; hobbies, horse riding, writing; Contact: The Sunday Independent, Middle Abbey Street, Dublin 1.

ALLEN, Padraic; VICE PRESIDENT DELL PRODUCTS EUROPE; *b* 1957; *educ* in Co. Meath; *married;* children; Production Manager, Leaf Chewing Gum, Co. Kildare, 1978; Production Manager, N.E.C. Ballivor, 1978-80; joined Apple Computers in Cork, Materials Manager, Managing Director, 1980-98; Vice President, Dell Products Europe, Middle East and Africa (EMEA) 1998 to date; Dell are the world's second largest makers of personal computers with an Irish workforce in excess of 3,500 in Cork and Limerick; a highly valued member of the computer industry, seen as a media shy manager, an excellent delegator and communicator. Contact: Dell Computer Corporation, Raheen Industrial Estate, Limerick. Tel: 061 304091.

ANDREWS, David

ALLEN, Paul; PUBLIC RELATIONS CONSULTANT; *b* 1962; *educ* Rosmini College, Drumcondra; College of Commerce, Rathmines; *single;* worked with CBS Records, Murray Consultants, RTE TV News, Slattery PR, formed Paul Allen & Associates PR Ltd., Managing Director, 1992 to date; member, Marketing Institute of Ireland, Public Relations Consultancy Association; featured in *Who's Who in Ireland People of Tomorrow 1991.* Hobbies, reading, American and domestic politics and flying. Contact: Paul Allen & Associates, 4 Upper Mount Street, Dublin 2. Tel: 01 676 9575. Fax: 01 676 9518.

ANDREWS, David; POLITICIAN, BARRISTER; *b* 1936; *educ* Colaiste Mhuire, Parnell Square; St. Joseph's College, Roscrea; University College Dublin, BCL; Kings Inns, BL; *m* Annette Cusack, Musician; 2 *s* 3 *da*; elected Fianna Fáil Deputy for Dun Laoghaire, 1965; Parliamentary Secretary to the Taoiseach, Minister for Defence and Chief Whip, 1970-73; Minister of State, Foreign Affairs and Justice, 1977-80; Minister for Foreign Affairs, 1992-93; Minister for Defence & the Marine, 1993-94; Fianna Fáil Spokesman on Tourism & Trade, 1995-97; Minister for Defence, June-October 1997; Minister for Foreign Affairs, October 1997 to date; A patrician figure within the Fianna Fáil party, regarded as representing the core values of the Party. Hobbies, fishing and walking. Contact: Dáil Eireann, Leinster House, Kildare Street, Dublin 2. Tel: 1890 337889.

ANISSIMOV, Alexander; CONDUCTOR; *b* 1947; *educ* St. Petersburg and Moscow Conservatories; 1*s* 2 *da;* appointed Director of the Bolshoi Theatre of Opera and Ballet in Minsk, Belorussia 1980; appointed Principal Guest Conductor, National Symphony Orchestra of Ireland, 1995, Principal Conductor, 1998; has conducted opera in some of the most famous opera houses in the world including Kirov Opera, Fenice of Venice, Bastille Opera in Paris, Lyceum in Barcelona, San Fransisco Opera and Teatro Colon in Buenos Aires; also at the Wexford Festival and Opera Ireland; worked with orchestras in many countries including the Moscow Philharmonic, St. Petersburg Philharmonic, Rotterdam Philharmonic, Radio Symphony Orchestra of the Netherlands, Monte Carlo Philharmonic, and Orquesta Filharmonica de Buenos Aires; also records with Naxos/Marco Polo; awards include: Orchestra of St Cecilia baton of Leonard Bernstein; named "Conducted of the Year" by "Musikalnaya Elita". Hobbies, travelling, walking, cooking and chess. Contact: R.T.E., Donnybrook, Dublin 4. Tel: 01 208 3111.

APPLEBY, John M.

ASHE, Alan Scott

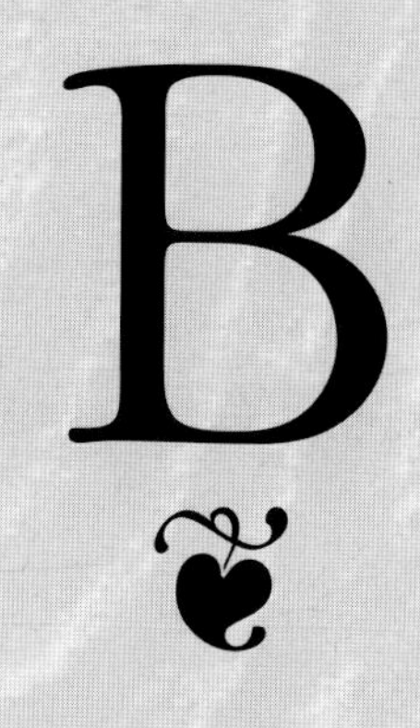

APPLEBY, John M; MANAGING DIRECTOR ORACLE CORPORATION; *b* 1962; *educ* St. Michael's College, Ailesbury Road; Gonzaga College, Ranelagh; Royal College of Music, London; *m* Sarah McDonnell; 2*s* 1*da;* worked with IBM Ireland, 1983-94; moved to Sun Microsystems, 1994-98; Managing Director; Oracle Corporation, 1998 to date; Oracle are the second largest software company in the world and market leaders in data technology; the Irish operation currently has 650 employees. Hobbies, country pursuits and music. Contact: Oracle House, Herbert Street, Dublin 2. Tel: 01 803 1000. Fax: 01 803 1951.

ARNOLD, Bruce; WRITER; *b* 1936; *educ* Kingham Hill School, UK; Trinity College Dublin; *m* Mavis Cleave, Writer; 2 *s* 1 *da;* freelance Journalist throughout the sixties with *The Irish Times, The Sunday Press, The Sunday Independent, Hibernia* and Editor, *The Dubliner,* Correspondent, *The Guardian,* (1962-1968); frequent contributor to U.K. newspapers, magazines and journals and radio and television broadcaster; Political Commentator and Parliamentary Correspondent, *Irish Independent* 1972 into the eighties, twice winning awards for Outstanding Contributor to Journalism; London Editor, *Irish Independent,* 1986-87; Literary Editor and Political Commentator, *Irish Independent,* 1987 to date; publications include: *A Concise History of Irish Art, Orpen: Mirror to an Age, What Kind of Country, Margaret Thatcher: A Study in Power,* and four novels: *A Singer at the Wedding, The Song of the Nightingale, The Muted Swan, Running to Paradise;* recent publications include: *An Art Atlas of Britain and Ireland, William Orpen ,The Scandal of Ulysses, Mainie Jellett and the Modern Movement in Ireland* and *Jack Yeats;* has made four films on artistic and literary subjects: *The Scandal of Ulysses, Images of Joyce, To Make it Live: Mainie Jellett;* librettist for opera, *A Passionate Man,* 1995; produced an exhibition on Swift (the subject of the opera), National Library, 1999; published catalogue in book form; currently writing biography on Dean Swift. A cultured, witty man; a colourful dresser; recognised as an astute political correspondent (so astute that his telephone was tapped during the serious bugging crisis in 1982); a prolific writer, a literary editor with little tolerance of the second rate. Contact: Irish Independent, 90 Middle Abbey Street, Dublin 1. Tel: 01 705 5333.

ASHE, Alan Scott; CHIEF EXECUTIVE STANDARD LIFE ASSURANCE COMPANY, IRELAND; *b* 1942; *educ* Christian Brothers College, Cork; Gormanston College, Co. Meath; Trinity College Dublin, MA, BBS, FCMA; *m* Rosemarie Hennessy; 1 *s* 2 *da;* Financial Analyst, Ford Motor Company, UK, 1966-70; Financial Controller, Crown Controls Ltd. Galway, 1970-1976; General Manager Finance, TSB Dublin, 1976-88; Chief Executive, Standard Life Assurance Company, Ireland, 1988 to date; President, Insurance Institute of Dublin, 1993; President, Irish Insurance Federation, 1994; Chairman, Insurance Ombudsman of Ireland, 1992-1995; Board Member, Rotunda Hospital; member, Fitzwilliam Lawn Tennis Club, Carrickmines Lawn and Croquet Club, Old Conna Golf Club. Hobbies, theatre, arts, tennis, golf. Contact; Standard Life, 90 St. Stephen's Green, Dublin 2. Tel: 01 475 7411. Fax: 01 475 4047.

BAILEY, Michael; MANAGING DIRECTOR BOVALE DEVELOPMENTS LTD.; b 1953; *educ* Ballintubber National School, Co. Roscommon; *m* Teresa ____; 5 children; one of the country's leading builders in both commercial and domestic development with warehousing and over 2,000 houses in the greater Dublin area. Contact: Bovale Developments Ltd., St. Patrick's House, South Circular Road, Dublin 8. Tel: 01 453 7598. Fax: 01 453 7615.

BALLAGH, Robert; ARTIST; *b* 1943; *educ* St. Michael's College, Blackrock; College of Technology, Bolton Street; *m* Elizabeth Carabini; 1 *s* 1 *da*; professional musician with a showband; moved on to painting after assisting Michael Farrell with his murals at the National Bank on College Green; recognised for his hyper-realistic paintings; has exhibited extensively in Ireland and abroad, mainly in Lund, Warsaw, Moscow, Sophia and Varna; has executed many important commissions from portraits, murals, posters and graphic designs to stamps, book covers and a series of banknotes for the Central Bank of Ireland; in recent years has turned increasingly towards stage design including *I'll Go On, The Importance of Being Ernest, Salome, The Tramway End, Romeo and Juliet* (all for the Gate Theatre) and *Riverdance*; *The Wake* was winner of a Fringe First at the Edinburgh Festival 1990; has been the subject of numerous bibliographies, including *Robert Ballagh* (1986) by Ciaran Carthy; member, Aosdana; Honorary President, International Association of Art (a UNESCO affiliate); Fellow, World Academy of Arts and Science. A talented artist whose radical chic masks an ability to move through the multi-layered art power structure, the financial rewards from *Riverdance* are a well deserved bonus. Contact: Aosdana, 70 Merrion Square, Dublin 2. Tel: 01 661 1840 Fax: 01 676 1302.

BALLARD, Ray S; GENERAL MANAGER AMERICAN POWER CONVERSION; *b* 1939; *educ* Bachelor of Industrial Engineering, Master of Engineering; *married;* 1*s* 1*da;* various manufacturing positions, 1962-75; Manufacturing General Manager, Modcomp Ft Laud, Florida, 1975-83; various management positions, Allied Signal, Ft Laud Florida, 1983-94; Plant Manager, APC,

classic cuts by armani

elegant eyewear by gucci

subtle scents by calvin klein

there's a world **in store**

desirable accessories by prada

timeless cotton by ralph lauren

Florida, 1994-97; General Manager, American Power Conversion, Galway, 1997 to date; the largest manufacturer of uninterruptable power supply units in the country with 800 employees in the West of Ireland. Hobbies, music, walks in the country, fishing and travel. Contact: APC, Ballybrit Business Park, Co. Galway. Tel: 091 702000.

BANOTTI, Mary

BANOTTI, Mary' née O' Mahony; MEMBER EUROPEAN PARLIAMENT; *b* 1939; *educ* Dominican Convent, Wicklow; Royal London Hospital, SRN; Hunter College, New York, Dip. Psych; *m* Dr. Giovanni Banotti (decd); 1 *da;* started career as bank official and, subsequently, trained as a nurse; brief, inglorious, show business career in America and worked in development in Kenya, 1966-67; brief broadcasting career on Vatican Radio; Industrial Welfare Officer, Irish Distillers, 1970-82; presenter, weekly television programme on social welfare rights; Senate candidate in 1982-83; By-Election candidate, 1983, and elected to the European Parliament in 1984, 1989 and 1999; Fine Gael candidate for Presidency of Ireland, 1997; The President of the European Parliament's Mediator for Transnationally Abducted Children; member, Board of Rutland Centre; Trustee, Christian Brothers Marino Institute of Education; membership of the Board of the International Centre for Missing and Exploited Children; nominated for European of the Year, 1991, 1992, 1994, 1995 and 1996; Selected European of the Year, 1997; Honorary UN Ambassador for Population Control; a poll topper in the 1999 elections; a compassionate hard working M.E.P.; comes from a family with a history of service to the State, grand-niece of General Michael Collins and sister of former Minister for Justice, Nora Owens. Hobbies, friends, travel, cinema, above all reading, walking. Contact: 43 Molesworth Street, Dublin 2. Tel: 01 662 5100. Fax: 01 662 5132.

BANVILLE, John; AUTHOR, WRITER; *b* 1945; *educ* Christian Brothers School, Wexford; St. Peter's College, Wexford; *m* Janet Dunham; 2 *s*; Literary Editor, *The Irish Times* 1988 to 1999; Novels include: *Kepler* (1980), *The Newton Letter* (1983), *Mefisto* (1987), *The Book of Evidence* (1989), *Ghosts* (1993), *Athena* (1995), *The Untouchable* (1997); recipient of AIB Literary Award, Guardian Fiction Award, Guinness Peat Aviation Award, Premio Ennio Flaiano (Italy 1991); member of Aosdana. A highly regarded Irish writer with an international reputation. Contact: Aosdana, 70 Merrion Square, Dublin 2. Tel: 01 661 1840. Fax: 01 676 1302.

BARNES, Ben; ARTISTIC DIRECTOR, *Abbey Theatre*; *b* 1956; *educ* St. Peter's, Wexford; University College Dublin, BA; *m* Julia Lane; 1*da;* Resident Director, Abbey Theatre, 1982-86; Artistic Director, Opera Theatre Company, 1986-89; Director, Groundwork, 1989-96; Director, National Youth Theatre, 1984 & 1988; Director, Gaiety Theatre, 1993-1996; productions include 45 productions and revivals at the Abbey Theatre, 16 productions and revivals at the Gate Theatre; international work seen in Tokyo, Wellington, Adelaide, Athens, Glasgow, London, New York, Moscow, St. Petersburg, Montreal; Council Member, Dublin Theatre Festival; recipient, Harveys Irish Theatre Awards, Best Director, 1987, *Irish Times* /ESB Award, Best Director, 1998, *Sunday Tribune* Arts Award Nomination, 1987 & 1988, Harveys Irish Theatre Awards Nomination, 1981; appointed Artistic Director, Abbey Theatre, July 1999; Hobbies, reading, tennis and Cistercian Abbeys. Contact: Abbey Theatre, 26 Lower Abbey Street, Dublin 1. Tel: 01 874 8741. Fax: 01 874 6507.

BARNES, Eamonn

BARNES, Eamonn; DIRECTOR OF PUBLIC PROSECUTIONS; *b* 1934; *educ* National School, Ballymote; Franciscan College, Multyfarnham. St. Nathan's College Ballaghaderreen; University College Dublin; Kings Inns; *m* Dolores Walsh; 3 *s* 2 *da*; called to the Bar 1958, built up a practice on the Western Circuit; served as Legal Assistant, Office of the Attorney General; Director of Public Prosecutions, since the founding of the office, 1975 to date; President, International Association of Public Prosecutors since 1996; regarded as an independently minded man, with a sharp edge; a lawyer who prefers to maintain a low personal profile in a high profile office. Hobbies, family, music, reading, travel, food and drink, good conversation; Clubs, Woodbrook GC, Bohemians Musical Society. Contact: Director of Public Prosecutions, 14-16, Merrion Street, Dublin 2. Tel: 01 678 9222. Fax: 01 661 8116.

BARR, The Hon. Mr. Justice Robert; JUDGE OF THE HIGH COURT; *b* 1930; *educ* Belvedere College; Clongowes Wood College; Trinity College Dublin; King's Inns; *married*; 4 *s* 1 *da*; called to the Bar, 1957; called to the Inner Bar, 1972; elected a Bencher of King's Inns, 1984; had a broadly based legal practice covering common law, arbitration and criminal matters; regular Prosecutor in the Special Criminal Court; appointed High Court Judge, 1985; Presiding Judge, The Special Criminal Court, 1987 to date. Contact: The Four Courts, Morgan Place, Dublin 7. Tel: 01 872 5555.

BARRETT, J. Brendan; MANAGING DIRECTOR ASCON LTD., ROHCON LTD; *b* 1948; *educ* Christian Brothers School, Tralee; University College Dublin, BE (CEng); INSEAD, Paris, A.M.P; *m* Carmel Mulvihill; 1 *s* 1 *da*; Executive Engineer, Kerry County Council, 1971-73; joined Ascon Ltd. (major building and civil engineers operating in Ireland and overseas) as Engineer in 1973, Contracts Manager 1978, Director 1982, Managing Director since 1986; Managing Director, Rohcon

BARRETT, J. Brendan

Ltd., since 1992; these two companies comprise Ireland's second largest construction group and the largest public works contractor; Fellow of Institute of Engineers of Ireland. Member: Irish Academy of Engineers, K Club, Naas Golf Club, R.C.Y.C. Hobbies, golf, sailing, reading, walking. Contact: Ascon Ltd., Kill, Co. Kildare. Tel: 045 866 400. Fax: 045 877 264.

BARRETT, Roy; STOCKBROKER; *b* 1963 *educ* Blackrock College, Dublin, University College Dublin BCL, MBS; *m* Susie Lynch 1 *s* 1 *da*; Equity Analyst with Warburg Securities 1987-89, Banker with Paribas 1989-90, Director, International Equities, NCB Group Ltd., 1990-95, Head of Equities, Goodbody Stockbrokers, 1995-97, Managing Director, Goodbody Stockbrokers, 1997 to date; Director, Irish Stock Exchange, Tilman Asset Management. An exceptionally young head of a major stockbrokerage, a powerbroker to watch. Hobbies, soccer and horse racing. Contact: Goodbody Stockbrokers, 122, Pembroke Road, Dublin 4. Tel: 01 667 0400.

BARRINGTON, Colm; INVESTMENT BANKER; *b* 1946; *educ* Gonzaga College, Dublin; National University of Ireland, MA in Econ; Institute of Public Administration, Diploma in Public Administration; *m* MaryRose Callaghan; 2 *s* 1 *da;* joined Aer Lingus Teoranta, 1967-73; OMNI Hotels Corporation, 1974-80; GPA Group plc, 1981-93; GE Capital Aviation Services Ltd., 1993-94; Babcock & Brown Ltd., 1994 to date; specialists in aviation finance and aircraft leasing; has published papers on aircraft leasing; member Royal Irish Yacht Club, Bray Sailing Club, Powerscourt Golf Club, Druids Glen Golf Club; winner of Round Ireland Yacht Race, 1992 & 1999, course record holder in Round Ireland Yacht Race, 1998; Winner, Britannial Cup & New York Yacht Club Trophies, (Cowes), 1995. Hobbies, yacht racing, golf, skiing and shooting. Contact: Babcock & Brown, Oracle House, Herbert Street, Dublin 2. Tel: 01 661 6505. Fax: 01 661 6506.

BARRINGTON, Edward John "Ted"; AMBASSADOR OF IRELAND TO THE UK; *b* 1949; *educ* University College Dublin; *m* Clare O'Brien; 1*s*: entered the Department of Foreign Affairs as a Third Secretary, 1971; Third Secretary, European Communities Division, September, 1971; First Secretary, European Communities Division, 1973; First Secretary, Permanent Representation to the European Communities, Brussels, 1975; First Secretary, Press Section, Headquarters, 1980; Counsellor, Political Division, Headquarters, December, 1980; Assistant Secretary General, Administration Division, Headquarters, 1985; Assistant Secretary General, European Communities Division, Headquarters, 1989; Assistant Secretary General, Political Division, and Political Director, Headquarters, 1991; Deputy Secretary General, 1995; Ambassador to London, 1995 to date; one of Ireland's senior diplomats who has had a notable success at all levels, as Ambassador to Britain. Contact: Department of Foreign Affairs, 80 St. Stephen's Green, Dublin 2. Tel: 01 478 0822.

BARRON, Henry Denis; JUDGE OF THE SUPREME COURT; *b* 1928; *educ* St. Columba's College, Dublin; Trinity College Dublin, BA LLB; *m* Rosalind Barron (decd); 2*s* 2 *da;* called to the Irish Bar (King's Inns), 1951; called to the English Bar (Middle Temple), 1953; called to the Inner Bar (S.C.), 1970; appointed High Court Judge, 1982; appointed Visitor to Dublin University, 1983; appointed Supreme Court Judge, 1997 to date; recognised as being highly efficient and practical with an eye for detail; the first member of the Jewish faith to be appointed to the High and Supreme Courts; member, Kildare Street and University Club. Hobbies, travel, bridge and golf. Contact: The Four Courts, Morgan Place, Dublin 7. Tel: 01 872 5555.

BARRY, Anthony "Tony"; CHAIRMAN CRH PLC; *b* 1935; *educ* Christian Brothers School, Cork; University College Cork, BEng (Civil); *m* Delia Greaney; 2*s; 2da;* Civil Construction Engineer, Cementation Ltd., U.K., Sierra Leone, India, Tasmania and New Zealand; joined Binnie and Partners (UK), Civil Engineer in Pakistan; worked briefly with C.I.E. and Cavan County Council before joining John A. Woods (Cork), General Manager, 1967; Managing Director, Roadstone Wood Group, 1978; Chief Executive, Cement Roadstone Holdings, 1988-94; Chairman, CRH plc, 1994 to date; Fellow, Institute of Engineers (London), Fellow, Institute of Engineers of Ireland; former President, I.B.E.C; Director, Greencore plc, D.C.C.; one of the most respected figures in Irish industry. Contact: CRH plc, Belgard Castle, Dublin 22. Tel: 01 404 1000.

BARRY, Anthony "Tony"

BARRY, Frederick John "Fred"; MANAGING DIRECTOR JACOBS ENGINEERING LTD.; *b* 1951; *educ* University College Dublin, BE; Trinity College Dublin, Dip Mgmt; King's Inns, BL; *m* Elaine Fitzpatrick; 2 *s* 1 *da;* worked with Jacob Engineering Ltd. in Canada, Africa and California, where he set up offices in Sacramento; currently Group Managing Director for Jacobs companies in Ireland and the U.K.; projects designed and built include Wyeth Medica, Coca Cola, Loctite, Smithkline Beecham. Fellow, Institution of Engineers; member, Royal St. George Yacht Club; Glen of the Downs Golf Club; Irish Cruising Club; Regent Bridge Club. Hobbies, sailing, golf and bridge. Contact: Jacobs Engineering Ltd., Knellys House, 17 Addiscombe Road, Croydon, CRO 6SR, England. Tel: 0044 181 667 0852.

BARRY, Gerald; COMPOSER; *b* 1952; *educ* University College Dublin, M.A., BMus; Amsterdam

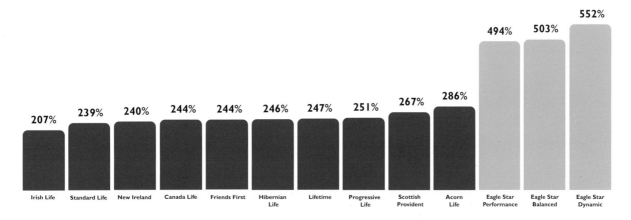

Muzieklyceum; Cologne Musik Hochshule; Vienna Musikhochshule; studied composition with Stockhausan, Kagel, Schat and Cerha, organ with Gerard Gillen and Piet Kee; recipient of State scholarships from Ireland, Australia, Germany and Holland; many of his works have been commissioned by the BBC, including *Chevaux-de-Frise, Hard D* for Orkest de Volharding and *The Conquest of Ireland*; his opera *The Intelligence Park*, commissioned by the London Institute of Contemporary Arts was premiered at the Almeida Festival, 1990, his second opera *The Triumph of Beauty and Deceit* was written for British Channel 4; a new work was commissioned for Frankfurt Radio Symphony Orchestra, 1997; his music has been played at all the prestigious international festivals; has worked with numerous ensembles, including, Ensemble Modern, Speculum Musicae, Kew Music Ensemble (New York), Array Music (Toronto), New Juilliard Ensemble, Capricorn, The Arditti Quartet, the St. Ives Ensemble; many of his works have been used for dance; regarded as a strikingly original composer; a distinctive voice in music capable of blending 18th and 20th century together. Contact: Oxford University Press, 70 Baker Street, London, W1M 1DJ. Tel: 0044 171 616 5900.

BARRY, Gerard; CHIEF PARKS SUPERINTENDENT DUBLIN CORPORATION; *b* 1950; *educ* St. Joseph's Convent, Kilbeggan, Co. Westmeath; Warrenstown Horticultural College; University College Dublin, B.Agr.Sc., M.Agr.Sc.; *m* Phyllis Boland, 3 *s* 1 *da;* Lecturer in Horticulture, National Botanic Gardens, 1975-77; Parks Superintendent, responsible for the control and management of municipal parks in Dublin city, including street trees, Dublin Corporation, 1977 to date; member, Irish Landscape Institute (past President). A creative talent who has literally transformed the face of Dublin. Hobbies, gardening and golf. Contact: Dublin Corporation, Wood Quay, Dublin 8. Tel: 01 672 2222.

BARRY, Sebastian; WRITER; *b* 1955; *educ* Catholic University School, Dublin; Trinity College Dublin, B.A. (Mod); *m* Alison Deegan; 2 *s* 1 *da*; writer since 1997; began to write for the theatre in 1986, with *Boss Grady's Boys* at the Abbey; has written six plays since, produced variously by the Abbey, Gate, Royal National Theatre, Royal Court and world-wide; other publications include *The Steward of Christendom* (1995), play, *Our Lady of Sligo* (1998), play, *The Whereabouts of Eneas McNulty* (1998), novel, translated into 4 languages; Shareholder, Abbey Theatre, member, Greystones Tennis Club; recipient, London Critics' Circle Award, 1995; British Writers' Guild Award, 1995; Lloyd's Playwright of the Year Award, 1996; Ewart-Biggs Memorial Prize, 1997; Ireland Funds Literary Prize, 1997; Writer Fellow, Trinity College, 1995-96; Ansbacher / Abbey Theatre Writer-in-Association, 1989-90. A gifted, original and emotional writer who portrays the undertones of the Irish psyche. Hobbies, fly-fishing, tennis, old houses. Contact: The Agency, (London). Tel: 0044 171 727 1346.

BATES, Ray

BATES, Ray; NATIONAL LOTTERY DIRECTOR; *b* 1947; *educ* O'Connells Christian Brothers School; Trinity College Dublin, BSc (Comp), MEcon Sc; *m* Mary Elliot; 1*s* 1*da;* Civil Servant, Department of Agriculture, Finance and Public Service, 1965-80; Head of Division, OECD (Paris) 1980-83; Civil Servant, Department of Finance and Social Welfare, 1987-89; Systems Manager in setting up Lotto, National Lottery, 1987-89; Chief Executive, National Lottery, 1989 to date. Hobbies, music, theatre and bridge. Contact: National Lottery, Abbey Street, Dublin 1. Tel: 01 836 4444. Fax: 01 836 6034.

BEGGS, Mark Patrick; GENERAL MANAGER INDIGO; *b* 1965; *educ* O'Connells School, Dublin; Rathmines College of Commerce ACCA; currently studying MBA with IMI; *m* Anne Marie Nolan; 1*s* 1*da;* Assistant Chief Accountant STA Travel (UK) 1987-89; Internal Auditor, Colonial Mutual Insurance (UK), 1989-90; operated own business 121 Bookkeeping Financial Services, 1990-94; Marketing Manager, Shay Moran, 1994-96; General Manager, Indigo, 1996 to date; member, AAT, IMI. Hobbies, walking, reading and holidays. Contact: Indigo, B2 Eastpoint Business Park, Fairview, Dublin 3. Tel: 01 604 6901. Fax: 01 667 2698.

BENNETT, Mary

BENNETT, Mary, née O'Donoghue; COMPANY DIRECTOR; *b* 1938; *educ* Boston National School, Co. Clare; Convent of Mercy, New Ross, Co. Wexford; Convent of Mercy, Gort, Co. Galway; *m* Eddie Bennett, Company Director; 1 *s* 2 *da*; Hotel Management Trainee, Great Southern Hotel, 1956-62; established fashion and gift shop in Galway 1966, Chairman, Managing Director, Treasure Chest (an emporium specialising in fashion, china and crystal) 1966 to date; Chairman, Galway City & Co. Enterprise Board, 1994 to date; Chairman, Tourism 2000, 1997 to date; Director, Aer Lingus, 1990-1996; Director, Galway / Boston Ventures; Irish Goods Council, 1988-96; Director, Ireland West Tourism (formerly Chairman); director, Bord Failte, 1980-85; former President, Skal Club of Galway and National President (1985); former President, Galway Chamber of Commerce, President of Chambers of Commerce of Ireland (1989-91). Runs a highly successful business in Galway; deeply involved in local communities; a player also on the national stage. Contact: Treasure Chest, William Street & Castle Street, Galway. Tel: 091 563862. Fax: 091 567757.

BERGIN, Joan; DESIGNER; *b* 1943; *educ* Dominican Convent Cabra; Sisters of Charity, Kings Inn Street; Scholarship from Swedish Arts Council to study Furniture Design in Scandanavia; long term relationship; travelled worldwide in 70s promoting Irish product design; established Bergin Designs, 1978; interior design projects include Guinness pubs and boardrooms, houses for Noel Pearson and Daniel Day Lewis, night clubs include Lillies Bordello; as a costume designer film credits include *My Left Foot, In the Name of the Father, Dancing at Lughnasa;* television credits include *Sunday Night at the Olympia* (RTE), *Sweeny Todd* (HBO), *A Bright Shining Tie* (HBO) filmed in Thailand; theatre credits include all the Noel Pearson musicals, work in all the major theatres, particularly the Gate; Fellow of the Chartered Society of Designers (UK), first woman Vice President, 1990. An innovative talent, recognised at home and abroad as one of Ireland's foremost professional designers. Hobbies, theatre, good food and Connemara. Contact: Joan Bergin, 52 Edenvale Road, Ranelagh, Dublin 6. Tel: 01 497 5895. Fax: 01 667 2698.

BERHERY, Michael; GENERAL SECRETARY IRISH FARMERS ASSOCIATION; *b* 1948; *educ* Monmouthshire College of Agriculture (UK), Dip. Animal Production; *m* Mary Delaney; 1*s* 2 *da* worked in the UK and Denmark; Secretary of the IFA Pigs Committee and Animal Feeds Committee, 1977-84; General Secretary of the Irish Farmers Association, 1984 to date; member of numerous EU Farming Bodies and Associations; probably the most influential figure in Irish agriculture; has a unique knowledge of the intricacies of dealing with the EU and with Irish bureaucracy. Contact: Irish Farmers Association, Irish Farm Centre, Bluebell, Dublin 12. Tel: 01 450 0266. Fax: 01 455 1043.

BEWICK, Pauline

BEWICK, Pauline; ARTIST; *b* 1935; *educ* Douris National School, Kenmare; St. Catherine's School, Bristol; National College of Art, Dublin; *m* Patrick Melia, Medical Doctor; 2*da;* began artistic career singing and dancing in Dublin reviews; worked as a set designer, Pike Theatre; freelance artist, has exhibited in various groups and solo exhibitions in Ireland, UK, Germany, Italy, France, Belgium, Canada and USA; retrospectives of her works, Guinness Hop Store, 1985, RHA Gallagher Gallery, 1996; a noted book illustrator, tapestry designer and stained glass artist (Bewleys' Cafes); publications include *Pauline Bewick's Ireland: An Artist's Year;* has written and illustrated *Ireland and Artist's Year,* 1990, *The Yellow Man,* 1995, *The South Seas and a Box of Paints,* 1996; subject of a biography by Dr. James White *Pauline Bewick: Painting a Life;* and of a documentary *A Painted Diary* by David Shaw Smith. A talented artist, illustrator and writer; a charismatic woman with a gift for attracting media attention. Contact: Taylor Galleries, 16 Kildare Street, Dublin 2. Tel: 01 676 6055.

BINCHY, Maeve; WRITER; *b* 1940; *educ* Holy Child Convent Killiney; University College Dublin, BA; *m* Gordon Snell, Children's Author; Teacher of History and Latin in Dublin schools 1960-68; *Irish Tmes* Journalist 1968 to date; publications include: *Light a Penny Candle, Echoes, Firefly Summer, Silver Wedding, Circle of Friends, Evening Class* and *Tara Road*; recipient of Honorary DLitt from NUI 1990. Immensely popular media figure and best selling author who tops bestseller lists in Ireland, U.K. and U.S.A. Some of her works have been adapted for television. Hobbies, reading and travel. Contact: Agent - Christine Green, 40 Doughty St., London WC IN 2LF.

BIRD, Charlie Brown; CORRESPONDENT RTE NEWS; *b* 1949; *educ* University of Life; 2 *da;* Library Assistant, *Irish Times,* 1971-73; Researcher, RTE Current Affairs, 1974-80, Journalist, RTE News, 1980, Chief Reporter, RTE News, Special Correspondent RTE News to date; as the RTE Correspondent has been involved in covering most of the major political stories in Ireland over the past 20 years; Co-Author (with George Lee) *Breaking The Bank* , The Story of NIB; Presenter, Scriptwriter of two major RTE TV documentaries on President Mary Robinson; former Chairman, Dublin Broadcasting Branch, NUJ; Journalist of the Year, 1998 (with George Lee); has travelled extensively for RTE News, the release of Fr. Niall O'Brian, Phillipines, early 80s, covered famine in Africa, including Sudan, Somalia, covered Gulf War for RTE. Hobbies, hill walking, reading and watching Reports of 'Politics'. Contact: RTE, Donnybrook, Dublin 4. Tel: 01 208 3111. Fax: 01 208 2620.

BINCHY, Maeve

BLACK, Frances Patricia; SINGER; *b* 1961; *m* Brian -------; lead singer with Black Family, 1986-88; Arcady, 1988-91; Kieran Goss, 1991-93; commenced solo career 1993 to date; recordings include *The Black Family* (The Black Family) 1986, *Time for Touching Home* 1989, *After The Ball* (Arcady) 1991, *Francis Black and Kieran Goss* 1992, *Talk To Me* 1994, *The Sky Road* 1995, *The Smile on Your Face* 1997, *Don't Get Me Wrong* 1998; recipient, Lord Mayor's Award 1997, IRMA Award - Best Irish Female Artist 1995, IRMA Award - Best Album by Irish Female 1997, National Entertainments Award - Best Newcomer 1994, Irish World Awards - Best Solo Artist 1995, Irish World Awards - Best Album 1996. Hobbies, walking, cinema and travel. Contact: Pat Egan Sounds Ltd., 2 Merchants Quay, Dublin 8. Tel: 01 679 770. Fax: 01 679 7495.

BLACK, Mary; SINGER; *b* 1955; *educ* St. Louis Convent, Rathmines; *m* Joe O'Reilly; played first gig, aged fourteen, with brother Terence's folk band; recorded first album with brother Shay, and his band, General Humbert, 1975; toured extensively with bothers and sister, recorded two albums under the title, *The Black Family* 1986; replaced Dolores Keane in De Danaan 1983-86; released solo debut album *Mary Black* under Dara Records label 1983 (a company set up with husband / manager Joe O'Reilly); albums released include *No Frontiers* 1989 (double platinum), *Babes in the Wood* 1991 (sold 500,000 copies), *The Holy Ground* 1993 (platinum), *Circus* 1995 (featured in U.K. charts), *Shine* 1997; collaborates with guitarist / producer Declan Sinnott. Contact: Dara Management, Unit 4, Great Ship Street, Dublin 8.

BLAKE, Bruce St. John; LAWYER/SOLICITOR; Knight of Honour and Devotion of the Order of Malta; *b* 1936; *educ* Colaiste Iognaide S.J., Galway; Glenstal Abbey School, Co. Limerick; University College Galway, BA, LLB: Solicitor; Alumnus of Salzburg Seminar in American Studies; *m* Mary Grace Hanna, Lawyer/Solicitor; 3*s* 5*da;* Chief of the Blake Family, one of the famous Tribes of Galway; Founder/Principal of Bruce St. John Blake and Company Solicitors; President of the Incorporated Law Society of Ireland, (1976-77); Council member, International Bar Association; has served on two Government Commissions - The Commission on Industrial Relations (1978-81) and The Commission on Safety and Health and Welfare at Work - The Barrington Commission (1980-83); an eminent lawyer. Clubs, Galway County Club, Hibernian United Services Club, Connemara Golf Club, Lansdowne R.F.C., Past President Galwegian R.F.C., President, University College Galway Rugby Football Club. Hobbies, rugby, soccer, GAA sports, swimming, skiing, horse racing, shooting and fishing. Contact: Bruce St. John Blake & Company Solicitors, Serpentine Court, Dublin 4. Tel: 01 660 3122. Fax: 01 660 3381.

BLACK, Frances Patricia

BLAKE, Rhona Elizabeth; PUBLIC RELATIONS EXECUTIVE; *b* 1961; *educ* Mount Anville; University College Dublin, B.A.; P.R.I.I., Diploma in Public Relations; *m* Charles Murless; 1 *s* 1 *da*; Account Manager, Pembroke Public Relations, 1985-90; Account Director and Partner, Fleishman-Hillard Saunders, 1990 to present; member, Irish Horseracing Authority Tote Ireland Ltd., Public Relations Institute of Ireland. A woman of great style and a networker *extraordinaire* - the perfect PR executive. Hobbies, horseracing, theatre, current affairs. Contact: Fleishman-Hillard Saunders, 15 Fitzwilliam Quay, Dublin 4. Tel: 01 618 8444. Fax: 01 660 2244.

BLACK, Mary

BODLEY, Seoirse; COMPOSER, CONDUCTOR; *b* 1933; *educ* Colaise Mhuire; High School of Commerce; Royal Irish Academy; State Music School Stuttgart, Dr. D. Mus., LTCL; *separated*; 2*s* 3 *da;* awarded Arts Council Prize in musical composition 1956, also University College Dublin Macauley Fellowship; currently Emeritus Professor of Music, University College Dublin; compositions include *Ceol* (a choral symphony); *A Concert Mass,* Symphony No. 3, 4 and 5 (no. 3 was played at inauguration of the National Concert Hall, 1981); *Fraw Musica*, premiered Schlosskirche, Torgau 1996; *Pax Bellumque* (text Wilfred Owens and Thomas MacGreevy) premiered National Concert Hall, 1997; *News from Donabate* (50 mins Piano Solo) commissioned RTE, 1999; Orchestral work commissioned for National Youth Orchestra for Year 2000 (in progress); work for Voice and Orchestra (for Bernadette Greevy) commissioned by Duchas for Year 2000; *Piano Concerto 30*, in progress; also composer of song cycles and film scores; former Chairman, Association of Irish Composers; Chairman, Irish Folk Music Society; member, Aosdana; recognised as a champion of contemporary music in Ireland, both through his teaching and writing; seen by many as the thinking man's Sean O'Riada. Hobbies, canoeing and camping in North America. Contact: Music Department, University College Dublin, Belfield, Dublin 4. Tel: 01 706 7777.

BLAKE, Rhona Elizabeth

BOLAND, Eavan; POET; *b* 1944; *educ* Holy Child Convent, Killiney; Trinity College Dublin, BA; *m* Kevin Casey; 2 *da*; Lecturer, Trinity College Dublin 1967-68; Fellowship, International Writing Programme, Iowa University 1979-80; Fellow of Trinity College Dublin 1989-90; Writer in Residence, University College Dublin 1990-91; currently Professor of English, Head of the Creative Writing Department, Stanford University, California; awarded Macauley Fellowship, Irish-American Cultural Award 1983, Jacobs Award for Radio Broadcasting 1978; member, Irish Academy of Letters; publications include: *New Territory, The War Horse, In Her Own Image, Night Feed, The Journey, Selected Poems, Outside History, Object Lessons, The Lost Land.* Recognised as an outstanding poet and critic. Hobby, patchwork. Contact: c/o Carcanet Press, Corn Exchange, Manchester. Tel: 0044 61 834 8730

BOLAND, Frank; MANAGING DIRECTOR FRANK BOLAND LTD.; *b* 1938; *educ* Christian Brothers School, Cork; *m* Judy Lane; 3*s* 1 *da;* Managing Director, Frank Boland Ltd., 1960 to date (major commercial vehicle distributors in Southern Ireland); Chairman, B&I Lines; Director, Beamish & Crawford, Cork Communications Ltd.; former Director, Aer Lingus; Vice-President, Cork Chamber of Commerce; Chairman, Cork Enterprise Board; member, Cork Harbour

Commissioners; a popular and influential figure in the Cork commercial world. Hobby, boating. Clubs, Cork Golf Club, Royal Cork Yacht Club. Contact: Frank Boland Ltd., Mallow Road, Cork. Tel: 021 303271.

BOLGER, Dermot; AUTHOR, PUBLISHER; *b* 1959, *educ* St. Canice's School, Finglas, Beneaven College, Finglas; *m* Bernadette Clifton, nurse; 2 *s;* Factory Hand, Unidare, Finglas; Library Assistant, Dublin County Council; Founder and General Editor, Raven Arts Press, 1977-92; Co-founder and Executive Editor, New Island Books, 1992 to date; recipient of A.E. Memorial Award, The Macauley Fellowship and *The Sunday Tribune* Arts Award, among others, for his six novels, *Night Shift, The Woman's Daughter, The Journey Home, Emily's Shoes, A Second Life* and *Father's Music.* Edited and devised the collaborative novels, *Finbar's Hotel* and *Ladies Night at Finbar's Hotel.* Received the Samuel Beckett Award, the BBC Stewart Parker Prize and two Edinburgh Fringe First Awards for his plays that include *The Lament For Arthur Cleary, Blinded By the Light, In High Germany, The Holy Ground, One Last White Horse, April Bright* and *The Passion of Jerome.* Author of six collections of poetry including *Taking My Letters Back* - New & Selected Poems. Editor of various anthologies, including *The Picador Book of Contemporary Irish Fiction.* Former member of the Arts Council of Ireland, Member of Aosdana; A radical publisher and a prolific writer. Hobbies, soccer and golf. Contact: New Island Books Ltd., 2 Brookside, Dundrum Road, Dublin 14. Tel: 01 298 9937.

BOLGER, Jim; RACEHORSE TRAINER AND BREEDER; *b* 1941; *educ* Oylegate National School; Enniscorthy Christian Brothers School; College of Commerce, Rathmines; *m* Jackie Foley, 2 *da*; Accountant/General Manager, Motor Business 1963-74; took out Trainers Licence 1976, recipient, S.P. Graham Award 'Young Trainer of the Year' 1979, RTE/Ballygowan Horse Racing Award 1990, Texaco Sports Star of the Year Horse Racing, 1990 and 1991; Holds all time Irish record for winers on the Flat in a season - 125 in 1990; Trained European Champion *St. Jovite* to win the Irish Derby in record time, 1992; One of the country's leading trainers, recognised as being both astute and outspoken. Hobbies, hurling, football and racing. Contact: Glebe House, Coolcullen, Co. Kilkenny. Tel: 056 43150. Fax: 056 43256.

BOLGER, Jim

BOOTH, Paul Clifford; MANAGING DIRECTOR McDONALDS IRELAND; *b* 1961; *educ* public school; *married;* 2 *s* 1 *da;* joined McDonald's as Trainee Manager, 1983, Restaurant Manager, 1987, Operations Manager E. Midlands, 1992, Managing Director, Romania, 1994, Director of Operations, Hungary, 1998, Managing Director, Ireland, 1999 to date; awards include Flacara Award for Management, Romania, 1997 (the national management award). Hobbies, travel, reading, swimming and badminton. Contact: McDonald's Restaurants, Block 7, Richview Office Park, Clonskeagh, Dublin 14. Tel: 01 208 0020.

BOOTH, Richard; FARMER; *b* 1954; *educ* Rockwell College; *m* Mary Buggy; 1*s* 3*da;* took over family farm in 1981; engaged in tillage, commercial cattle and sheep farming; member, I.F.A. (National Council); former Chairman, National Livestock, former member, Bord Bia, former Chairman, EU Meat Advisory Committee. Hobby, reading. Contact: The Heath, Portlaoise, Co. Laois. Tel: 0502 46512.

BOUCHIER-HAYES, Timothy; SOLICITOR; b 1953; educ St. Conleth's College; UCD, BCL; Law Society, Solicitor; *m* Sinead Phelan; 2*da*; Solicitor with Max Abrahamson Solicitors, specialising in construction law and arbitration, 1974-91; Partner, McCann Fitzgerald Solicitors – Head of Construction Law Group, 1991 to date; member, Law Society of Ireland (former Vice Chairman of Arbitration Committee); Fellow, Chartered Institute of Arbitrators; member, Irish Amateur Fencing Federation Executive Committee (former Hon. Sec.); holder of several national titles in fencing, 1969-84 and represented Ireland at junior and senior world championships 1969-81. Clubs, Milltown Golf Club, Monkstown Tennis Club. Hobbies, fencing, tennis and golf. Contact: McCann Fitzgerald, 2 Harbourmaster Place, Dublin 1. Tel: 01 829 0000. Fax: 01 829 0010.

BOURKE, John Oliver PAGET; CHAIRMAN IRISH PERMANENT PLC; *b* 1937; *educ* Clongowes Wood College; University College Dublin, BCL; Kings Inns, BL; K.P.M.G. FCA; Harvard SMP; *m* Margaret Passrath; 2 *s* 2 *da*; Director, E.K.O'Brien Ltd., 1963-68; Managing Director, Bank of Ireland, 1968-83; Managing Director, Power Securities Ltd., 1984-85; Chairman and Chief Executive, TSB Group (London), TSB Commercial Holdings, 1985-93; Chairman, Irish Permanent, 1993 to date; Chairman Major Events Organisers Committee (world body for major sailing events); ex President, Irish Sailing Association; ex Chairman Off Shore Racing Council; member, Royal St. George Yacht Club (ex Commodore), Royal Ocean Racing Club (ex Commodore), Royal Cork Yacht Club, Royal Thames Yacht Club, Royal Yacht Squadron, Carrickmines Croquet and L.T.C., Kilmashogue Golf Club. Contact: Irish Permanent plc, 56-59 St. Stephen's Green, Dublin 2. Tel: 01 661 5577. Fax: 01 661 5828.

BOOTH, Paul Clifford

BOURKE, Jonathan 'Jay'; MANAGING DIRECTOR SHERLAND ENTERTAINMENTS LTD.; b 1966; educ St. Columbas College, Rathfarnham; Trinity College Dublin, BA Econ; *m* Sarah Harte; 1*s* 1*da*; started meteoric career with Wolfman Jacks (restaurant) Rathmines; opened The Globe and Rí Rá 1992; Odessa and Front Lounge 1994; Eden (restaurant) and Bodega (Cork) 1997; The Garavogue (Sligo), The Roundy House (Cork), The Long Hall (London) 1999, also The Eating Rooms (Cork) and G.U.B.U. in Capel Street (Dublin); recognised as an exceptional operator with his finger on the pulse of the young achievers, drinkers and eaters. Contact: Sherland Entertainment Ltd., 37 Drury Street, Dublin 2. Tel: 01 677 4835.

BOURKE, John Oliver

BOURKE, Siobhan; FILM PRODUCER; *b* 1959; *educ* Presentation Convent, Thurles, Co. Tipperary; University College Dublin, BA, MA; *m* Jobst Graeve; Executive Producer, Rough Magic Theatre Company, 1984-98; Lecturer, Arts Administration Studies, UCD, 1992 to date Producer, Theatre Shop, 1994 to date; Film Producer, Rough Magic Film Productions 1998 to date; publications include *Rough Magic: First Plays* (ed) published by New Wland / Methuen Drama 1999; Board member, Rough Magic Theatre Company, Dublin Theatre Festival; Committee member, Cultural Relations Committee. Hobbies, drama, film, reading and gardening. Contact: Rough Magic Film Productions Ltd., 7 South Great Georges Street, Dublin 2. Tel: 01 672 5464. Fax: 01 670 4275.

BOWE, Mary

BOWE, Mary, née Murphy; HOTELIER; *b 1936; educ* Loreto Abbey, Rathfarnham; Shannon College of Hotel Management, Dip. Hotel Mgmt; *m* Raymond Bowe, Farmer, Director of Slaney Meat Packing Company; 2 *da*; Management Trainee, Europaischer Hof (Heidelberg); Savoy Hotel (London); Manager, Woodbrook Golf Club 1959-63; opened 'Esker Lodge' Restaurant in family home at Curracloe, Co. Wexford; acquired the historic Marlfield House, home of the Earls of Courtown 1978; converted it into one of Ireland's leading hotels and restaurants, management being taken over by daughter Margaret; Marlfield House Hotel, Gorey is a member of the prestigious Relais & Chateaux Hotel Group and Ireland's Blue Book; recipient of Best Worldwide Breakfast Award from Relais & Chateaux 1990, U.D.T. Endeavour Award for Tourism 1986, Andrew Harper "Best 25 Hideways in the World" 1982 and 1986, overall National Garden Award Bord Failte 1986, Bord Failte Award for Excellence (13), Three Red Stars and Three Red Rosettes from Automobile Association (4), The Good Hotel Guide Cesar Award 1996, Egon Ronay Hostess of the Year 1995, Johansen's Best Country Hotel Award 1997, numerous other national and international awards; Fellow, Irish Hotel and Catering Institute. A dedicated, meticulous hotelier, constantly upgrading the already top-class establishment; a vivacious woman whose warm approach has gained the hotel international acclaim. Hobbies, gardening, antique and art collecting and travel to keep abreast of international hotel industry trends. Contact: Marlfield House, Gorey, Co. Wexford. Tel: 055 21124. Fax: 055 21572.

BOWLER, Gillian; TRAVEL AGENT; *b* 1952; *educ* in England; *m* Harry Sydner; 1 stepdaughter; worked with Greek Island Holidays (London) 1969-71; founded Budget Travel 1971; Joint Managing Director with Harry Sydner, Budget Travel (part sold to Granada plc., September 1987, remaining stake sold, Thomson Group, 1996). Formerly served on many State Boards, currently director Irish Life & Permanent plc., Grafton Group plc., More Group Ireland, Thomson Holidays, Thomson Travel Group Ireland, Riordans, Clifton Converse, Irish Cancer Society, Sonaco Travel Club Ltd., Vice President, Institute of Directors. Elected Fellow, Irish Marketing Institute, May 1995, Fellow, Irish Management Institute, March 1990; Awarded Doctor of Law Honoris Causa, February 1989. A successful businesswoman noted for astute financial skills. Hobbies, modern art, country weekends, theatre and reading.

BOWLER, Gillian

BOYD, Dermot Gordon Mahon; ARCHITECT; *b* 1967; *educ* St. Andrew's College, Dublin; Trinity College Dublin; Dublin Institute of Technology, B.Arch Sc. (TCD); Dip Arch (DIT); Member of the Royal Institute of Architects of Ireland, MRIAI 1997; *single* ; joined Ahrends Burton and Koralek (U.K.), 1987; Alberto Campo Baeza (Spain) 1988; Scott Tallon Walker, 1990; John Pawson (U.K.), 1991-92; Shay Cleary, 1993; McCullough Mulvin, 1994 to date; private practice 1993 to date; Tutor, Dublin Institute of Technology, 1996 to date, University of Strathclyde, Glasgow, 1997, University College Dublin, 1998; Projects include Higgins Apartment London, 1993; Viva Shop, Barcelona, 1995; Unlimited Shop Madrid, 1996; Anne McDevitt Clinic Dublin, 1996; Watson Loft, New York, 1997; Watson Apartment London, 1997; Nectar Juice Bar, Ranelagh, 1998; McDevitt House, 1999; President, Architectural Students Association DIT, 1988; Architectural Association of Ireland Committee, Vice President 1996, President 1997; Council of the Royal Institute of Architects of Ireland, 1998; Editorial board of the *Irish Architect*, 1999. Awards include first Prize, FIS Collaboration, 1996; RIAI Regional Award, 1998; AAI Special Mention 1999. Work was exhibited: Athlone Riverside Competition, 1993; 20/20 Chair Exhibition 1993; Tales from Two Cities 1994; FIS, 1996; Smithfield Competition, 1998; RIAI Regional Awards, 1998; AAI Awards, 1999. An architect for the twenty-first century; a young man of flair and talent. Hobby, beauty. Contact: 15 Upper Baggot Street, Dublin 4. Tel: 01 667 7277. Fax: 01 667 7278.

BOYLAN, Clare

BRADLEY, Stephen

BRADY, Kieran

BOYLAN, Clare; NOVELIST AND SHORT STORY winner; *b* 1948; *educ* St. Louis Convent, rathmines; *m* Alan Wilkes, Journalist; worked as a sales girl in book department of Easons & Sons Ltd.; Reporter, *Irish Press*, 1966-67; Editor, *Young Woman*, 1967-68; Editor, *Woman's Choice*, 1968-69; Features Writer, *Evening Press*; Editor, *Image*, 1980-84; frequent broadcaster on radio and television; book reviewer for newspapers and journals in Ireland, the UK and US; novels include: *Holy Pictures* (1983), *Last Resorts* (1984), *Black Baby* (1988), *Home Rule* (1992), *A Nail on the Head, Room for a Single Lady* (1997), *Concerning Virgins* (1993), *The Bad Woman* (1995), *The Stolen Child* (1996), *Another Family Christmas* (1997) Collected Stories; *The Agony and the Ego,* Literary Essays (ed.), 1993; *The Literary Companion to Cats* (ed.) 1994; film version of short story, *Making Waves*, was nominated for a Hollywood Oscar, 1988; former judge of Booker McConnell Literary Awards; Awarded, Spirit of Life Arts Award, 1997; Listed in *Debrett's People of Today, International Who's Who of Professional and Business Women*; Member: Aosdana, Groucho Club. A hard working and prolific writer; a petite, self effacing woman; a hard nosed professional journalist and an acclaimed novelist. Contact: Aosdána, 70, Merrion Square, Dublin 2. Tel: 01 661 1840. Fax: 01 676 1302.

BRADLEY, Stephen; FILM-MAKER; *b* 1965; *educ* Midleton College; Harrow School; Trinity College, L.L.B.; produced *Balcony Belles;* co-produced *Ailsa,* 1993; wrote and directed *Reaper,* 1994; co-produced *Guiltrip,* 1995; wrote, directed, produced, *Barabbas;1996;* wrote and directed *Sweety Barrett,* 1998. Contact: Temple Films, Shamrock Chambers, 1-2 Eustace Street, Dublin 2. Tel: 01 671 9313. Fax: 01 671 9323.

BRADSHAW, Lar; MANAGING DIRECTOR MCKINSEY IRELAND; *b* 1960; *educ* Rosmini College; St. Pats, Drumcondra; University College Dublin, BA, M.I.I.E.; IMD, MBA; *m* Claire Hession; 1*s* 1 *da;* held various positions in Guinness, 1977-83; joined McKinsey UK, 1985, Paris, 1986, New York, 1987, UK, 1987-94, opened Irish office, 1994, elected Director of McKinsey Inc, 1997; appointed Chairman, Dublin Docklands Development Authority, 1997. Hobbies, chess, golf and football. Contact: McKinsey & Co. Inc. Ireland, 65 St. Stephen's Green, Dublin 2. Tel: 01 478 5500.

BRADY, Conor; NEWSPAPER EDITOR; *b* 1949; *educ* Cistercian Abbey, Roscrea; University College Dublin, BA, MA; *m* Ann Byron, Teacher; 2 *s*; Reporter, *The Irish Times*, 1969-73; Editor, *Garda Review*, 1974-75; Reporter/Presenter, *RTE Radio News*, 1975-76; Features Editor, *The Irish Times*, 1977-79; Editor, *Sunday Tribune*, 1981-82; Deputy Editor, *The Irish Times*, 1985-86; Editor, 1986 to date; Editorial Director of The Irish Times Ltd., member, executive, World Editors Forum (Chairman 1995-99); member, Board of Directors, of the European Journalism Centre at Maastricht (Chairman Board of Counsellors), 1994-99; a polished strategist, who has confounded critics by maintaining and elevating the status of the newspaper; an editor effortlessly in control. Hobbies, reading, travel, golf. Contact: The Irish Times Ltd., 10-16, D'Olier Street, Dublin 2. Tel: 01 679 2022. Fax: 01 671 9407.

BRADY, Kieran Michael; VICE PRESIDENT, WORLDWIDE CHEMICAL DEVELOPMENT BRISTOL -MYERS SQUIBB; *b* 1955; *educ* University College Cork, B.Sc. (1976), PhD (1979); *m* Carol O'Leary; 3 *s*; Joined Bristol Myers Sqibb as Process Development Chemist, 1979; Appointed Director of Technical Operations, 1984; Joined Angus Fire Chemicals Ltd., Process Development Director, 1985; Rejoined Bristol Myers Squibb as Director of Chemical Development, 1987; Appointed Vice President, Irish Operations, 1996; Vice President, Worldwide Chemical Development with responsibility for Chemical Development sites in the U.S., Puerto Rico, Italy and Ireland, 1999. Member: The Royal Society of Chemistry, The Institute of Directors, I.M.I, Executive Committe of IBEC, Dublin Region; Holder of All Ireland Club Championship medal (1979), Munster Club Championship Medal (1978) and two Cork County Senior Football Championship medals (1977, 1978). Hobbies, all sports, cinema, photography, golf. Club, St. Margaret's Golf Club. Contact: Swords Laboratories, Watery Lane, Swords, Co. Dublin. Tel: 01 840 6611.

BRADY, Paul; SINGER/SONGWRITER; *b* 1947; *educ* Sion Mills P.E.S., Co Tyrone; St. Columb's College, Derry; University College Dublin; *m* Mary Elliot, Administrator; 1*s* 1*da;* left college to join *The Johnstons*; music group, group recordings for Transatlantic Records include: *The Barleycorn* 1968, *Bitter Green* 1969, *The Colours of Dawn* 1970, *If I Sang My Song* 1971, and others; later recordings: *Andy Irvine and Paul Brady* (Mulligan Records) 1976, *The Green Crow Caws* with John Kavanagh, 1979; recordings under own name include: *Welcome Here Kind Stranger* (Mulligan Records) 1978, *Hard Station* (WEA Records) 1981 - No. 1 Irish Charts, *True For You* (Polygram Records) 1983 - No. 2 Irish Charts, *Full Moon* (Polygram Records) live album 1984, *Back To The Centre* (MCA Records) 1987 - No. 2 Irish Charts, *Primitive Dance* (MCA Records)1987 - No. 1 Irish Charts, signed to Rykodisc 1999; recipient *Melody Maker Folk Album of the Year Award* 1987, STAG/HOT PRESS *Music Critics Award for Best Single* 1981, Best Song 1982, Best Songwriter 1985, Best Songwriter and Best Male Vocalist 1986, National

Entertainment *Opel Award* 1986, remains at the top of Hot Press Readers Poll since 1980; an Irish musician with a high profile abroad, especially in the UK. Hobbies, scuba diving, photography, gardening and theatre. Contact: ALK Management, 7 Seapoint Terrace, Irishtown, Dublin 4. Tel: 01 667 7607. Fax: 01 667 7608.

BRADY, Paul

BRAIDEN née Egan, Olive Carmel; DIRECTOR RAPE CRISIS CENTRE; *b* 1946; *educ* Colaiste Muire, Ballymote, Sligo; UCD, Social Science; *m* Sean Braiden; 3*s* 2*da*; lived abroad for a number of years; joined Dublin Rape Crisis Centre, 1983 as a volunteer, appointed Director of the Centre in 1990; initiated counselling training programmes in Croatia and Bosnia in 1993 to date; planning for similar programmes with Kosovar refugees in Albania; initiated unique study on 'Legal Process and Victims of Rape', 1998 (funded by Grotius Programme); member, Amnesty, Children Rights Alliance, Ireland Action for Bosnia, Unifem – United Nations Women's Organisation, Board member, Well Woman Centres, member, Board of the Irish Court Services Transitional Board (1998), Board of the Independent Radio and Television Commission (1998), The Judicial Appointments Advisory Board (1999); Irish delegate to EU Commission Expert Committee on Crime Victim's Issues (1998); member, RDS (Royal Dublin Society), Friend of the Hugh Lane Gallery, Friend of the National Concert Hall; nominated 'European Women of the Year' (1993), candidate European Parliament election (1994); also listed in The Expert Group on Child Abuse Guidelines – Dept. of Health (1998); The National Steering Committee on Violence against Women – Dept. of Justice (1998). Hobbies, current affairs, music (jazz in particular), theatre, cinema, cooking, family and friends. Contact: Rape Crisis Centre, 70 Lower Leeson Street, Dublin 2. Tel: 01 661 4911. Fax: 01 661 0873.

BRANAGAN, Peter F; DIRECTOR OF DIGITAL PLANNING RTE; *b* 1948; *educ* Oatlands College; College of Technology, Kevin Street, MIEE, CEng; *married*; 2*da*; thirty years in RTE, Manager, Network Projects, 1982-86, Head of Engineering, Design & Development, 1986-94, Director of Production Facilities & Engineering, 1994-97, Director of Technology, 1997-98; member, Institute of Electrical Engineers; Fellow, Royal Television Society. Hobbies, gardening, golf and fishing. Contact: RTE, Donnybrook, Dublin 4. Tel: 01 208 3111.

BRAZIL, Tony

BRANIGAN, Orla Moraid Angela; SENIOR VICE PRESIDENT MARKETING, FLEXICOM; *b* 1966; *educ.* M. Dip. International Hotel Management, Shannon College; Cornell University, New York, Post Grad. Dip Marketing & Finance; University of Ulster, M. Sc. Tourism Management; *single;* Project Manager, Medallion Hotel Group, Chicago 1986-88; Deputy General Manager, Adare Manor Hotel & Golf Course 1988-90; Management Development Consultant, CERT, 1990-93; Executive Vice President, Shorex International (Carribean tour operators based in the Cayman Islands and Miami) 1993-95; Director of Europe, Irish Tourist Board 1995-98; Senior Vice President Marketing, Flexicom (international software company) 1998 to date; Member, Irish Hotel & Catering Institute, Marketing Institute of Ireland; Awarded Monaghan Person of the Year 1998. Hobbies, sport, travelling, current affairs. Contact: Flexicom Ltd., 32 Lower Leeson Street, Dublin 2. Tel. 01 603 0000.

BRAZIL, Tony; MANAGING DIRECTOR LIMERICK TRAVEL; *b* 1943; *educ* St. James Christian Brothers School; University College Dublin, BComm; *m* Sheila McNamara; 3 *s*; Assistant Regional Manager, Shannonside Tourism, 1966-69; Marketing Manager, Dan Ryan Rent-a-Car Ltd., 1969-71; Managing Director/Owner, Limerick Travel, 1971 to date; member, Marketing Institute; Honorary Spanish Consul (Clare / Limerick); President, Irish Travel Agents Association, 1990-92; Director, Bord Failte, 1974-88; Aer Rianta, 1985-89. As owner of the largest travel agency in the West of Ireland and competent Director of Operations for Budweiser Irish Derby (since 1986), maintains a high national profile. Hobbies, reading and rotary. Contact: Limerick Travel, Bedford House, Bedford Row, Limerick. Tel: 061 204444. Fax: 061 204455.

BREATHNACH, Paddy; FILM DIRECTOR; *b* 1964; *educ* Scoil na Leanbh, an Rinn, Co Port Lairge; Sallynoggin Community School; University College Dublin, BA Phil and Pol.; *single;* first worked as a director on *Exploring the Landscape*, a natural history series with Eamon de Buitlear; directed *A Stone of the Heart* (writer, Joseph O'Connor, producer, Robert Walpole), 1991; founded Treasure Films, with Robert Walpole, 1992; directed, *The Road to America*, 1993; *Ailsa* (producer Ed Guiney, writer Joseph O'Connor), 1994, won Euskal Media Award, San Sebastian Film Festival; directed *WRH* a six part documentary for R.T.E.; *A Long Way Home* (writer Joseph O'Connor), 1995; other director credits include *I Went Down* (producer Robert Walpole, writer, Conor McPherson) which won New Director's Prize, Jury Prize, Best Screen Play Award, Special Mention from Fipresci Jury, San Sebastian Film Festival, 1997, Silver Disc Award, Bogota, also Best Director Award, Thessaloniki Film Festival 1997, selected for World Cinema section at Sundance Festival 1998 and premiered New York, 1998; produced *South Paw* (director Liam McGrath) with Robert Walpole, 1998, selected for Sundance Festival, 1999; other awards include Special Jury Prize for *A Stone of the Heart*, Cork 1991; member, Board of Directors, Dublin Film Festival. The director/producer partnership with Walpole makes this duo leaders in the new wave of Irish cinema.

Contact: Treasure Films, Shamrock Chambers, 1-2 Eustace Street, Dublin 2. Tel: 01 670 9609. Fax: 01 670 9612.

BRENNAN, Francis

BRENNAN, Francis; HOTELIER; *b* 1953; *educ* Westland Row Christian Brothers School; C.U.S. Leeson Street; Dublin College of Catering, HDip H&C Mgmt; Trinity College Dublin, BSc (Man.); *single;* Front Office Trainee, Jury's Hotel, Dublin 1976-77; Assistant Manager, Great Southern Hotel, Parknasilla 1977-79; Deputy Manager, Victoria Hotel, Cork 1979-80; Managing Director, Park Hotel Kenmare 1980-84; Proprietor 1984 to date; awarded, Eoin Sheey Skeffington Scholarship 1978, Billy Kelly I.H.F. Award 1987, Egon Ronay Hotelier of the Year in UK and Ireland 1988; Condé List 1998, '99; the only hotel in Ireland awarded a Michelin Star, RAC Blue Ribbon; Director, Shannon Castle Banquets and Heritage; Vice Chairman, Small Luxury Hotels of the World; member, Relais & Chateaux, Ireland's Blue Book; member, Soc. Incentive Travel Execs., Hotel Sales Management Association, International Hotel Association; runs one of the most internationally renowned hotels in Ireland. Hobby, work. Contact: Park Hotel, Kenmare, Co. Kerry. Tel: 064 41200. Fax: 064 41402.

BRENNAN, Michael J.

BRENNAN, Michael Joseph; MANAGING DIRECTOR EAGLE STAR; *b* 1952; *educ* London School of Economics, BSc; Fellow, Institute of Actuaries; Associate of the Society of Actuaries, America; *m* Clare Millet; 1 *s* 1 *da*; Irish Life Assurance Company, 1973-77; Eagle Star Life Assurance Company of Ireland, 1977 to date, Company Actuary and first employee, 1977, Director and General Manager, 1986, Managing Director, 1989 to date; Managing Director, Eagle Star European Life Assurance Company, 1995 to date; President, Irish Insurance Federation, 1989-90; President, Society of Actuaries in Ireland, 1991-93; National Committee for Mathematics of the Royal Irish Academy, 1992-95; Executive Committee of the Financial Services Industry Association, 1994 to date; member, Carrickmines Croquet and Lawn Tennis Club, Woodbrook Golf Club and National Yacht Club. Hobbies, golf, sailing, classical music and art. Contact: Eagle Star, Eagle Star House, Frascati Road, Blackrock, Co. Dublin. Tel: 01 283 1301. Fax: 01 283 1578.

BRENNAN, Seamus

BRENNAN, Seamus; POLITICIAN; *b* 1948; *educ* St. Joseph's School, Galway; University College Galway, BComm, BA; University College Dublin, MComm; *m* Anne O'Shaughnessy; 2*s* 4 *da*; qualified as an Accountant; has worked in Management Consultancy; General Secretary, Fianna Fail 1973-80; Taoiseach's (Jack Lynch) nominee to the Seanad 1977-81; elected Dáil Deputy for Dublin South 1981 to date; Minister of State for Trade and Marketing 1987-89; Minister for Tourism and Transport 1989-91; Minister for Tourism, Transport and Communications 1991-92; Minister for Education 1992-93; Minister for Commerce & Technology 1993-94; Front Bench Spokesperson on Transport, Energy and Communications 1994-97; Minister of State at the Department of the Taoiseach and Defence and Government Chief Whip 1997 to date. Clubs, Grange GC and Riverview Tennis and Fitness Club. Contact: Department of the Taoiseach, Government Buildings, Upper Merrion Street, Dublin 2. Tel: 01 662 4888.

BRENNAN, Stephen Denis Patrick; ACTOR; *b* 1955; *educ.* Terenure College; *partner;* 1 *s* 3 *da*; has played in *Joseph and His Amazing Technicolor Dreamcoat,* 1974; *Jesus Christ Superstar,* 1975; with Abbey Theatre Company - over fifty leading and supporting roles including title role in *Hamlet,* 1976-83; with Royal National Theatre, London, 1984; starred in Gate Theatre productions including *Private Lives, Waiting for Godot, Tartuffe, Cyrano de Bergerac;* T.V. includes *El Cid* and *Ballykissangel;* films include *Eat the Peach;* member Irish Actors Equity; The Theatrical Cavaliers Cricket Club. Hobbies, painting, gardening, songwriting, interior decorating, drinking and women. Contact: Aude Powell, Brunskill Management, Suite 8A, 169 Queensgate, London S.W.7. Tel: 0044 171 581 3388.

BRETT, James "Jim"; MANAGING DIRECTOR BRETT GROUP; *b* 1952; *educ* Windgap National School; Christian Brothers School, Callan; University College Dublin, BAgr.Sc.; *m* Frances Minogue, Speech and Drama Teacher; 2*s*; Radio Producer/Presenter, R.T.E., 1975-80; Assistant Editor, *The Farmer,* 1979-81; Director, Brett Group, Kilkenny based family agribusiness, 1980, Managing Director since 1989; Fianna Fail supporter, member of Kilkenny County Council since 1985; Board member and former Chairman, Radio Kilkenny; member, former Chairman, South East Regional Authority; member, E.U. Committee of the Regions, The Society of Feed Technologists, A.S.A.; a regular contributor to journals and radio; has written and delivered a number of graveside orations at old I.R.A. funerals; Clubs, Mount Juliet Golf and Country, Callan Golf Club; a strong business, political and media force in Co. Kilkenny. Hobbies, reading and tennis. Contact: Brett Brothers Ltd., Callan, Co. Kilkenny. Tel: 056 25140. Fax: 056 25353.

BREWER, Stephen James

BREWER, Stephen James; CEO EIRCELL (IRELAND) LTD.; *b* 1947; *educ* St. Martin's London, Marketing and Distribution; *m* Christine ----; 1 *s* 1 *da;* Sales & Marketing Director, Apple Computer Inc, 1982; Marketing Director, MBS plc, 1985; Sales & Marketing Director, Cellnet (London), 1989; Commercial Director, France Telecom (Paris), 1993, CEO, Eircell (Ireland), 1995 to date; Fellow, Royal Institute (UK); member, Druids Glen Golf Club. Hobbies, family, golf and reading. Contact: Eircell, Richview Office Park, Clonskeagh, Dublin 14. Tel: 01 203 7701. Fax: 01 260 0991.

BRITTON, David A.; ART GALLERY OWNER; *b* 1963; *educ* Sligo Grammar School; Trinity College Dublin, BBS, ACA; *m* Karen Reihill; 1 *s* 1*da;* articled with Stokes Kennedy Crowley; joined family hotel business in Co. Donegal, Sand House Hotel, 1988-90; joined Adam & Sons, 1990-92; established, with wife Karen, The Frederick Gallery, Dublin, 1992, specialists in Irish art from 1880-1980. Clubs, St. Stephen's Green, RIAC. Hobbies, weekend gardener, wine and food. Contact: The Frederick Gallery, 24 South Frederick Street, Dublin 2. Tel: 01 670 7055. Fax: 01 670 4900.

BRODER, Gavin; CHIEF RABBI OF IRELAND; *b* 1963; *educ* Council of National Academic Awards, BA (Hons); University of London, MA; Rabbinic Diploma; *m* Daniella ----; 4*s;* Rabbi of Staines & District Synagogue, Middx, England, 1988-90; Rabbi of Newbury Park Synagogue, Essex, England, 1990-96; Chief Rabbi of Ireland, 1996 to date. Hobbies, reading, music, squash and tennis. Contact: Herzog House, Zion Road, Rathgar, Dublin 6. Tel: 01 492 3751. Fax: 01 492 2599.

BROGAN, Patrick; MANAGING DIRECTOR P. G. BROGAN & CO. LTD.; *b* 1962; *educ* St. Mary's Primary School, Moynalta; Christian Brothers School, Kells, Co. Meath; *m* Kay Sheridan; 2 *da;* Production Assistant, R&J Emmet Ltd., 1982-84, Research & Development Controller, 1984-86, Laboratory Controller, 1986-89, Production Controller, 1989-97; Founder, Managing Director, P .G. Brogan & Co. Ltd., 1997 to date; researched, formulated, developed and produced *Brogans Irish Cream Liqueur;* distributes to USA, Canada, Central & South America, UK, mainland Europe and the Middle East; the brand has gained premium recognition world-wide and is seen as a serious contender for category leader. Hobbies, golf and horse-riding, competes in national horse-ploughing competitions. Contact: P.G. Brogan & Co. Ltd., Carlanstown, Kells, Co. Meath. Tel: 046 46000. Fax: 046 46100.

BROMLEY, John Joseph

BROMLEY, John Joseph; NEWSPAPER EDITOR; *b* 1956; *educ* De La Salle College, Ballyshannon; *m* Frances O'Dowd; 1*s* 1 *da;* joined *Donegal Democrat* 1973 as a journalist, Editor, 1989 to date; member, National Union of Journalists, Ballyshannon Athletic Club. Hobbies, reading, walking, cinema, sport. Contact: Donegal Democrat, Donegal Road, Ballyshannon, Co. Donegal. Tel: 072 51201. Fax: 072 51945.

BROPHY Mary

BROPHY Mary, EDITOR, CHECKOUT IRELAND MAGAZINE; *b* 1942; *ed* Holy Faith Convent, Glasnevin; University College Dublin; Dublin City University; BA, H.Dip in Ed. Graduate Diploma in Journalism; *m* Edward Brophy, accountant; 3*s* 2*d.* Secondary School Teacher, career change to journalism in mid-1980s. Assistant Editor Smurfit Publications, 1986-1989; Freelance Journalist in national media 1989-1994; Editor *Checkout Ireland* 1994. *Checkout Ireland* is described as the 'Bible of Irish Grocery', an industry now valued at £4.5 billion, and the premier Irish trade journal. Hobbies, good conversation and heated debate, mostly with family and book club friends around a dinner table, avid reader, gardener. Addicted to exercise. Contact: Checkout Ireland, 1-3 Dungar Terrace, Dun Laoghaire, Co. Dublin. Tel: 01 2300322 Fax: 01 2300629.

BROPHY, Michael; MANAGING DIRECTOR SUNDAY WORLD; *b* 1949; *educ* Marian College Ballsbridge; Dublin Institute of Technology; *m* Eileen Noonan; 1*s* 1 *da;* Night Editor, *Irish Independent*, 1980; Editor, *Evening Herald*, 1985; Editor and Director of Independent Star Limited, 1990; Managing Director, Sunday World and Terenure Printers, 1995 to date; the powerhouse behind the success of the *Sunday World*; one of the Independent Group's brightest editors now thriving in senior management; member, DLSP Rugby Club, Riverview Racquet Club, Roundwood Golf Club. Contact: Sunday World, 18 Rathfarnham Road, Dublin 6. Tel: 01 490 1980.

BROSNAN, Denis; MANAGING DIRECTOR KERRY GROUP PLC; *b* 1940; *educ* St. Brendan's College, Killarney; University College Cork, MSc.; *m* Joan McNamara; 2*s* 2*da;* worked as a detergent salesman before joining Golden Vale as Production Manager; General Manager, North Kerry Milk Products,1972; prime mover in the co-operative movement among Kerry farmers, formed Kerry Co-operative, 1974, within three years turnover had trebled; masterminded the flotation of Kerry Co-Op, now Kerry Group 1986; acquired Beatreme Foods and a move into the US market; acquired for £250 million, DCA Food Industries 1994; acquired for £394 million Dalgety plc; Kerry Group are now one of the major players worldwide in the speciality foods industry; Brosnan is regarded as one of the most hard working, low key and successful industrialists in the country; a keen race horse owner and breeder who has played a key role in the Irish horse industry and the development of racetracks; Chairman, Irish Horseracing Authority, 1994 to date. Hobbies, GAA sports (Kerry Group sponsor county team), soccer, racing and golf. Contact: Kerry

Group plc, Princes Street, Tralee, Co. Kerry. Tel: 066 718 2000.

BROSNAN, Joseph; CHEF DE CABINET TO COMMISSIONER FLYNN; *educ* Maynooth, B.A.; Kings Inns, BL; *m;* 1 *s* 1 *da;* Administrative Officer, Department of Local Government, 1967-73; Assistant Principal Officer, Department of Justice, 1973-1980, Principal Officer, 1980-81; Research Counsellor Law Reform Commission, 1981-1985; Assistant Secretary, Department of Justice, 1985-91; Secretary to the Department of Justice, 1991-93; Chef de Cabinet to European Commission for Employment and Social Affairs, 1993 to date. Hobbies, reading, cinema, sport, music, current affairs. Contact: European Commission. Fax: Brussels 295 5503.

BROWNE, Matthew John; CHAIRMAN AND MD, HOECHST ROUSSEL VET LIMITED *b* 1942 *educ* B.Sc. (Pharm) 1965; M.P.S.I. 1966; Fellowship (Pharmaceutical Society) 1993; *m* Joan Bernie; 2 *s* 3 *da*; Lived and worked for two years in Germany with Hoechst; Joined Hoechst Ireland Limited 1967; Director, Hoechst Ireland Limited 1976; Managing Director, Hoechst Ireland Limited, 1984-97; Chairman and MD, Hoechst Roussel Vet Limited 1997 to date; Former President, Pharmaceutical Society of Ireland, Former President, Federation of Irish Chemical Industries. A keen sportsman, played All Ireland hurling for Wexford and University and Ireland selections in the 60s and early 70s. Hobbies, hurling, football, rugby and golf. Contact: Hoechst Roussel Vet Ltd., Cookstown Industrial Estate, Dublin 24. Tel: 01 451 1544. Fax: 01 451 1906.

BROWNE, Vincent

BROWNE, Vincent; BARRISTER, BROADCASTER AND JOURNALIST; *b* 1944; *educ* National School, Broadford, Co. Limerick; Colaiste na Rinne, Co. Waterford; St. Mary's Drumcologher, Co. Limerick; Castleknock College, University College Dublin, Kings Inns, BA, BL; *m* Jean Learmond; 2 *da;* Researcher/ Reporter, RTE; Correspondent for *The Irish Times* in Prague, 1968; Editor, *Nusight*, 1969-70; Northern News Editor, The Irish Press Group, 1970; *Sunday Tribune*, 1983-94; columnist, *The Irish Times* since 1994; relaunched *Magill*, 1997 and sold it in 1998; Broadcaster with RTE since 1996 on *Tonight with Vincent Browne* and *The Midnight Court*; called to the Bar, 1997. Ireland's foremost investigative journalist has been re-invented as a popular broadcaster - with bite. Contact: The Irish Times, 11 D'Olier Street, Dublin 2. Tel: 01 679 2022.

BRUTON, John; POLITICIAN, FARMER; *b* 1947; *educ* St. Dominic's College, Cabra; Clongowes Wood College, Co. Kildare; University College Dublin, BA Econ and Pol.; King's Inns, Barrister-at Law; *m* Finola Gill; 1 *s* 3 *da;* National Secretary, Fine Gael Youth Group, 1966-68; Elected Fine Gael Deputy for Meath 1969; Parliamentary Secretary to the Minister for Education, 1973, to the Minister for Industry and Commerce 1975-77; Fine Gael Spokesperson on Agriculture 1972-73 and 1977-78; Minister for Industry and Energy 1982-83; Minister for Industry, Trade, Commerce 1983-86; Minister for Finance 1986-87; Minister for Public Service January-March 1987; Spokesperson on Industry and Commerce 1987-89, on Education 1989-90; Elected Leader of Fine Gael 1990; Member of Parliamentary Assembly of the Council of Europe 1989-91; Member British-Irish Parliamentary Body 1993-94; Elected Taoiseach 1994-97, his administration was a three party coalition government with Labour and Democratic Left; Publications include, *Reform of the Dáil* (1980), *A Better Way to Plan the Nation's Finances* (1981), *Real Issues or Mock Battles* (Furrow Magazine 1996); Elected Vice President, CDI, 1998; Vice President, EPP, 1999; Member of the Council of State; seen as a strong leader, well in control of the big issues but lacking the common touch; a well respected politician, a second term as Taoiseach looks unlikely. Hobbies, reading history. Contact: Dáil Eireann, Leinster House, Kildare Street, Dublin 2. Tel: 01 618 3000.

BUCKLEY, Leslie

BUCKLEY, Leslie; MANAGING DIRECTOR L.F. BUCKLEY & ASSOCIATES; *b* 1944; *educ* Presentation College, Cork; University College Cork, BSc, MSc; *m* Carmel Mackey; 2 *s* 1 *da*; worked in various management positions with leading Irish companies, including the Jefferson Smurfit Group and Waterford Crystal; established own consultancy company, L.F. Buckley and Associates 1990; has been retained on various key appointments including the restructuring of Waterford Crystal and Aer Lingus; appointed Acting Chief Executive of Irish Steel which was successfully sold to a suitable partner 1994; carried out major review on Irish Rail 1996; appointed Acting CEO Esat Telecom Ltd. 1996; appointed to the National Commission on Nursing by Minister of Health 1997; Director, Fexco, Rennicks, IMOS, National Utilities Ltd., Esat Telecommunications Ltd., Esat Digifone Ltd., Radio 2000, 98FM Classic Hits, Esat Telecom Group plc. Totalnet Ltd., Eunet Ireland Ltd., Cork Internet Services Ltd., Bridgecom Ltd., Bridgecom Group Ltd., Bridgecom Technologies Ltd., Bridgecom Networking Ltd., Bridgecom Munster Ltd.; recognised as one of the shrewdest and toughest negotiaters in business today. Hobbies, marathon running, wind surfing, hill walking and swimming. Contact: 5 Rocklands, Harbour Road, Dalkey, Co. Dublin. Tel: 01 602 6390.

BUDD, The Hon. Mr. Justice, Declan; JUDGE OF THE HIGH COURT; *b* 1943; *educ* St. Stephen's School, Dublin; Radley; Trinity College Dublin, Classical Exhibition 1962, Foundation Scholarship, History and Political Science; Mod. 1964, LLB 1968; King's Inns, BL; *m* Ann Lawson;

1*s* 3 *da;* called to the Bar 1968; called to the Inner Bar 1981; appointed Judge of the High Court, 1991; as a member of the Leinster Circuit had a broadly based practice; member of the Tribunal with the Railways Inspector in both the Buttevant and Cherryville Rail Crash Inquiries; Co-author with Ross Hinds *The Hist and Edmund Burke's Club;* a sportsman of note, former Irish squash and international and interprovincial hockey player. Contact: The Four Courts, Morgan Place, Dublin 7. Tel: 01 825 5555.

BUDDEN, Richard Gordon; MANAGING DIRECTOR WELLMAN INTERNATIONAL LTD; *b* 1947; *educ* BA; *m* Lynne ----; 1 *s* 1 *da;* ICI Fibres (in U.K.), 1968-87; Coats Viyella (in U.K.), 1987-94; Managing Director, Wellman International Ltd., 1995 to date. Hobby, golf. Contact: Wellman International Ltd., Mullagh, Kells, Co. Meath. Tel: 046 80200.

BUDDEN, Richard G.

BUGGY, Niall Michael; ACTOR; *b* 1948; *educ* St. Patrick's, Drumcondra, Sandymount High School, Dublin; joined Abbey Theatre; has appeared in numerous productions in Ireland and abroad, including, *Uncle Vanya* (Gate Theatre), *Give me Your Answer Do* (Hampstead), *Aristocrats* (Hampstead and New York), *The Misanthrope* (Young Vic), *Juno and the Paycock* (Abbey Theatre), *The Rivals, Love for Love, Threepenny Opera* (RNT), *Travesties* (Liverpool Playhouse), *The Cherry Orchard, The Seagull* (Abbey Theatre); television credits include: *Upwardly Mobile, Father Ted, Red Roses for Me, The Butchers Boy;* awards include: Olivier Award for Best Comedy Actor, Regional Theatre Awards, Obie Award, New York Drama Desk Award, Time Out Award, Harvey Award, *Irish Times* Award; with intelligent casting - an actor of international standing. Contact: ICM, The Barracks, 76 Irishtown Road, Dublin . Tel: 01 667 6455.

BUGGY, Niall Michael

BUNN, Michael "Mike"; PHOTOGRAPHER; *b* 1942; *educ* St. Olivers and St. Xaviers, London; Camberwell Art School, figure drawing; *partner* Betty Wall; busked in streets of Europe and travelled the world as ship's steward; worked in restaurant business in Spain; self taught photographer, first major assignment was to sell Irish travel shots to Aer Lingus; moved into fashion photography and has featured in all major international magazines, a pioneer in Irish fashion photography; currently one of the leading Irish photographers; creative works include, *Ireland, the Taste and the Country,* (script and photographs); has illustrated many books; recipient, I.C.A.D. Award, Satzenbrau Fashion Photography Award, *Sunday Independent* Arts Award. Hobbies, fanatical fly fisher and country pursuits. Contact: Tel: 071 65255.

BURGESS, William J; MANAGING DIRECTOR IBM IRELAND LTD.; *b* 1946; *educ* The High School, Dublin; Trinity College Dublin, BA. BAI (Production Engineering); *m* June Smith; 1 *s* 2*da;* joined IBM as a Systems Engineer, 1967; responsible for the development of IBM's computer business and the building of the Authorised Dealer Network, 1984-86; General Manager of Channel Strategy and General Manager in charge of Nordic Operations, IBM European Headquarters, Paris, 1987-88; Executive in charge of Sales, Customer Support, Customer Service, Internal Information Systems, 1989-91; Managing Director, IBM Ireland, July 1991 to date; Board Member, IMI; member, Marketing Institute of Ireland, CII, Dublin Chamber of Commerce, American Chamber of Commerce. Contact: I.B.M. Ireland Ltd., 2 Burlington Road, Dublin 4. Tel: 01 660 3744. Fax: 01 660 0638.

BURKE, John; CHIEF EXECUTIVE AER RIANTA; *b* 1945; *m* Rosemary-----; 4 children; joined Aer Lingus, 1964; moved to Aer Rianta, 1969; has held various positions within the organisation, currently Chief Executive; Aer Rianta has a 20% (£75m) stake in Birmingham and Dusseldorf airports; with the loss of duty free and the lobbying for a second airport for Dublin, winds of change are sweeping through the industry. Hobbies, swimming and computers. Contact: Aer Rianta, Dublin Airport. Tel: 01 814 1111.

BURKE, Joseph "Joe"; MUSICIAN; *b* 1939; *educ* Kilnadeema National School; *m* Ann Conroy Burke, musician; started out as a farmer moving gradually into full time career in music; gave first public performance 1955; has been performing and recording for the past forty years; record labels include Gael Linn, Outlet, Shanachie, now records exclusively for Green Linnet Records; classical solo albums have sold worldwide; has performed at Carnegie Hall (New York), Royal Albert Hall, (London), Unuesque Hall (Paris), American Musical Hall (San Francisco); has given workshops and master classes worldwide; regarded as a master accordionist who started a major revival of interest in the instrument; voted Traditional Musician of the Year (R.T.E.), 1970; awarded, *Hall of Fame* (Rostrevor), 1990; A.I.B. *Traditional Musician of the Year* Award, 1997; has represented Ireland at Montmagny International Accordion Festival (Quebec) and has toured with various prestigious musicians. Hobbies, music, history and Gaelic Games. Contact: Kilnadeema, Loughrea, Co. Galway. Tel: 091 842419.

BURROWS, Richard; CHAIRMAN, CHIEF EXECUTIVE IRISH DISTILLERS GROUP PLC; *b* 1946; *educ* Wesley College, Dublin; *m* Sherril Dix; 1*s* 3*da;* Assistant to Managing Director, Edward

Dillon & Company Ltd. (wine merchants) 1970-72; General Manager, Fitzgerald & Company, 1972; Managing Director, "Old Bushmills" Distillery Company, 1972; General Manager, Irish Distillers Ltd., 1976; Managing Director Irish Distillers Group plc, 1978, Chairman, Chief Executive, 1991 to date; member, Institute of Chartered Accountants. A self effacing man who heads up the Irish whiskey industry, with distilleries at Bushmills, Co. Antrim, and Middleton, Co. Cork; employing over 1,000. Irish Distillers Group plc is one of Ireland's largest industrial concerns. The company is now a member of Groupe Pernod Ricard; Chairman, Irish Sailing Olympic Committee; President, I.B.E.C.. Hobbies, rugby and sailing. Contact: Irish Distillers Group plc, Bow Street, Dublin 1. Tel: 01 872 5566. Fax: 01 872 3109.

BURROWS, Richard

BUTLER, Jean; DANCER; *b* 1971; *educ* Birmingham University, U.K., BA, Theatre Studies; *single*; born and raised in New York, first attended dance classes at the age of four; trained in ballet and tap, won consecutive regional, national and world championships; during University acted in productions of *Women Beware Women, Hamlet, Crimes of the Heart, All My Sons, Beside Herself, Fool for Love*; has worked with The Chieftains, touring throughout America, Canada, Europe and Japan, performing for former President Mary Robinson in Mayo, and appearing on the new Chieftains album alongside Mick Jagger; performed for Princess Diana at the Royal Premiere of *Far and Away*, and represented Ireland at the Expo '92 in Seville, Spain; choreographed and starred in *Riverdance* during Eurovision '94, subsequently enjoying huge success with *Riverdance The Show* in Dublin, Belfast, Cork, London, New York, Los Angeles; recently completed her first screen role in *The Brylcreem Boys*. Contact: The Agency, 47, Adelaide Road, Dublin 2. Tel: 01 - 6618535. Fax: 01 - 6760052.

BUTLER, Jean

BUTLER, John; CHIEF EXECUTIVE SCAFFORM; *b* 1944; *educ* Blackrock College, Dublin; University College Dublin, BComm; *m* Breidi Prendergast (*m dis*); 1*s* 1 *da;* founded Scafform Ltd. 1964 (the largest scaffolding operation in Ireland), also Scafform Ltd. (Australia) and Scafform Inc. (US); Co-owner, Avenue Restaurant, Dublin, Construct Sales Ltd. (manufacturers of equipment for the building industry), Alto Seatting Systems (UK), Westlands Hotel (Cumbria, UK); Director, other private companies in Ireland, U.S. and U.K.. Hobbies, motor racing, sailing and travel. Contact: Scafform Ltd., Killeen Road, Dublin 10. Tel: 01 626 6601.

BYRNE, Catherine; ACTRESS; *b* 1954; *educ* Holy Faith Convent; *m* John Olahan; 2 *s;* window and interior design display artist, Arnotts, for four years; trained at Abbey School of Acting; member, Irish Theatre Company and The Abbey Theatre Company; has starred in numerous productions including, *Yerma* (Peacock Theatre), *Whistle in the Dark* (Abbey Theatre), *Da* (Abbey Theatre), *The Field* (Abbey Theatre), *Dancing at Lughnasa* (Abbey Theare, London and New York), *Wonderful Tennessee* (Abbey Theatre and New York), *Give me Your Answer Do* (Abbey Theatre and New York), *Plough and the Stars* (Gaiety Theatre), *Factory Girls* (Druid Theatre), *Choke my Heart* (Red Kettle), *A Month in the Country* (Gate Theatre), *Old Times* (Gate Theatre), *Molly Sweeney* (London and New York); television and film work include *Fair City* (RTE), *Kidnapped* (Disney), *Upwardly Mobile* (RTE), *Eat the Peach* (film); recipient, Harvey Award for Best Actress. Hobbies, film, music and sculpts in spare time. Contact: First Call Management, 29-30 Dame St., Dublin 2. Tel: 01 679 8401. Fax: 01 679 8353.

BYRNE, Catherine

BYRNE, David Anthony; MANAGING DIRECTOR TNT; *b* 1965; *educ* MBA Business Studies, Diploma in Foreign Trade; General Manager Dublin, 1992-96, Sales and Marketing Director, 1996-98, Managing Director TNT, 1998 to date; member, Institute of Freight Forwarders, Chartered Institute of Transport, Sales Institute of Ireland, Swedish Business Association. Hobbies, golf and all sports. Contact: TNT, Corballis Wood, Dublin Airport. Tel: 01 806 7888. Fax: 01 806 7778.

BYRNE, David M; EUROPEAN COMMISSIONER; *b* 1947; *educ* Monasterevan CBS; Dominican College, Newbridge, Co. Kildare; University College Dublin, BA; King's Inns Dublin, Barrister-at-Law, *m* Geraldine Fortune; 2 *s* 1 *da;* Founder, Chairman Free Legal Advice Centre (FLAC) 1969-1970; called to the Bar in 1970 and Inner Bar in 1985; Member Bar Council 1974-1987 and Hon. Treasurer 1982-1983; Member Executive Committee Irish Maritime Law Association 1974-1992; Member National Committee of International Chamber of Commerce 1988-1997; Member of Government Review Body on Social Welfare Law 1989; Member of I.C.C. International Court of Arbitration, Paris 1990-1997; Fellow Chartered Institute of Arbitrators; Extern examiner for arbitration and competition law, Kings Inns 1995-1997; Member Barristers Professional Practices Committee 1995-1997; Member Constitution Review Group 1995-1996, Attorney General, 1997-99; Appointed European Commissioner, July 1999, Commissioner for Health and Consumer Protection; Member of the Council of State Low key legal man with a keen interest in the Arts. Member Royal Irish Yacht Club, Blainroe Golf Club. Contact: European Commission, 200 Rue de la Loi, Brussels 1049. Tel: 00 322 299 1111.

BYRNE, Gay

BYRNE, Gay; BROADCASTER; *b* 1934; *educ* CBS Synge Street; *m* Kathleen Watkins, Harpist,

Singer, Broadcaster; 2*da*; worked in insurance, cinema management, car hire and advertising before starting broadcasting; Newscaster, Reporter, Interviewer, Granada TV (Manchester) 1958; moved to BBC (London); returned to Ireland and RTE; Executive Producer and Presenter *Late Late Show* (TV) 1963-99; Presenter *The Gay Byrne Show* (radio), 1973-99; also presenter, *Jackpot, Pickin' the Pops, Film Night, Rose of Tralee, Housewife of the Year,* etc.; publications include *To Whom it May Concern, The Time of my Life;* contributor to magazines and newspapers including *The Sunday World*; his production company Gabra Ltd. has produced programmes for RTE, Channel 4 and corporate educational programmes; presented *People are Talking* WBZ TV (Boston) 1986-87; recipient, citations from Jacobs Award 1963, 1970, Golden Award 1971, 1976, 1978, Personal Broadcasting Award 1982, Publicity Club Award 1986, Hall of Fame Award 1996, Entertainer of the Year Award 1998, Medal from Public Relations Institute; awarded Freedom of the City of Dublin 1999; Charity Fundraising includes Gay Byrne Fund (raises approximately £100,000 a year), Anchor man for Telethon, raising millions for People in Need; Chairman, Fund Raising Committee, Irish Cancer Society; member, Executive Fund Raising Committee Our Lady's Hospital for Sick Children; Board member, Research Foundation of Crumlin Hospital; former Board member, RTE Authority; Director, Virgin Airlines; the most influential broadcaster in Ireland - ever. Hobbies, collecting jazz records, listening to music, cycling, walking and reading. Contact: RTE, Donnybrook, Dublin 4. Tel: 01 208 3111. Fax: 01 208 3098.

BYRNE, David M

BYRNE, Michael Patrick "Pat"; COMMISSIONER OF THE GARDA SIOCHANA; *b* 1946; *educ* St. Ronan's Secondary School, Dunmanway, Co. Cork; Graduate of FBI Academy, Quantico, Virginia, U.S.A; *m* Dolores Mahon; 2 *s* 2 *da*; Joined the Garda Siochana, 1965, served in Dublin 'A' District; Detective Garda 1972, Detective Sergeant, Special Detective Unit, 1978, Detective Inspector, 1985, Superintendent Tipperary District, 1988, Detective Superintendent (Security), 1989-91; Detective Chief Superintendent 1991; Assistant Commissioner (Personnel) 1992; Deputy Commissioner (Operations) 1994; Garda Commissioner, 1996 to date; recognised as open, gregarious and media friendly, and a man tough enough to tackle rising crime rates. Hobbies, golf, Gaelic sports, spectator rugby, soccer; Clubs, Portmarnock Golf Club, Royal Irish Automobile Club. Contact: Office of the Commissioner, An Garda Siochana, Phoenix Park, Dublin 8. Tel: 01 666 0000 Fax: 01 666 2013.

BYRNE, Michael Patrick

BYRNE, Pat; CHIEF EXECUTIVE CITYJET; *b* 1954; *educ* Presentation Brothers, Bray; *married;* 1 child; worked in banking on leaving school; founded, with partner, Savings & Investment (an insurance and investment brokerage), sold to Woodchester in the late '80s; left Woodchester 1991; formed CityJet 1994; a major £8m investment in CityJet is announced 1999; Air Foyle's £4m investment give them a 50.1% stake; Air France has invested £2m and the existing shareholders, including Yeoman International, invested a further £2m. Hobbies, flying light aircraft and running. Contact: CityJet Head Office, The Atrium, Level 5, Terminal Building, Dublin Airport. Tel: 01 844 5588.

BYRNE, Peter

BYRNE, Peter; SPORTS WRITER; *b* 1937; *educ* St. Macartan's College, Monaghan; O'Connell School, Dublin; *m* Tina McLoughlin, Accounts Executive; 1 *s* 2 *da*; Sports Writer, *Evening Mail*, 1955-62; Sports Writer, *Sunday Review*, 1962-63; Sports Writer (Olympic Games, Soccer and Athletics Correspondent), *Irish Times*, 1963 to date; recipient of Benson & Hedges Sports Journalist of the Year, 1973, 1977, 1980, 1981; Soccer Writer of the Year, 1975; publications include: *Irish Athletics Split* (1963), *My Part of the Day* (1980), *Jack Charlton's World Cup Diary* in association with Jack Charlton (1990), *Official History of the Football Association of Ireland* (1996); member, Board of Directors of St. Michael's House, 1978 to date (Chairman, 1986-89); A journalist with a thorough knowledge of his subject; recognised as one of the ablest sports commentators in the country. Hobbies, hill walking and swimming. Contact: Irish Times, D'Olier Street, Dublin 2. Tel: 01 679 2022.

CADEN, John Patrick; MEDIA CONSULTANT; *b* 1946; *educ* CBS Synge Street; *m* Julie Parsons; 1*s* 1 *da;* RTE Radio Producer 1980-98; Media Consultant, The Radio Centre, 1998 to date; Radio Critic, *Sunday Times,* 1998 to date; recipient, Jacob's Award for Production of *Gay Byrne Show*. Hobbies, sailing, the sea, the company of friends. Contact: The Sunday Times, Huguenot House, 35 St. Stephen's Green, Dublin 2. Tel: 01 602 8800. Fax: 01 602 8816.

CALLAGHAN, John; CHAIRMAN FIRST ACTIVE; *b* 1942; *educ* St. James' Christian Brothers School; College of Commerce, Rathmines; *m* Maureen Gibney; 2*s* 1 *da;* Trainee Accountant with Peter Kennedy & Co. 1960-65; Chief Accountant, Smith Motor Group, 1966-70; Manager, Corporate Finance, KPMG (formerly Stokes Kennedy Crowley), 1970-74, Partner, 1974, Personnel Partner, 1974-76, Corporate Finance Partner, 1976-83, Managing Partner, 1984-91; International Council Member KPMG/Peat Marwick 1984-91; Chief Executive/Director, Fyffes plc, 1991-93; Director, First Active, 1993, Chairman, 1999; Director, Esat Telecom Group plc; Director, Scottish Amicable International Assurance plc, Rabobank Ireland plc, Esat Digifone Ltd., Bupa Reinsurance,

Glanbia plc; Fellow, Institute of Chartered Accountants, Institute of Bankers, Institute of Directors (President, 1996/7, 1997/8); member, Institute of Taxation; regarded as one of the country's leading accountants. Club, St. Stephen's Green. Hobbies, golf and music. Contact: First Active plc, Skehan House, Booterstown, Co. Dublin. Tel: 01 283 1801. Fax: 01 288 5300.

CAMPBELL, Patrick

CAMPBELL, Patrick; CHAIRMAN, CAMPBELL BEWLEY GROUP; *b* 1942; *educ* Marlborough Street National School; Belvedere College; Marian College, Ballsbridge; College of Catering, Cathal Brugha Street, DipHotelMgmt; *m* Veronica Dolan; 3 *s* 2 *da*; Management Trainee, Ashford Castle (Cong), Piccadilly Meridien (London), Hotel Opalen (Gothenburg), 1963-65; Founder/Chief Executive, Campbell Catering Ltd., 1967-86; Chairman/Chief Executive, Campbell Bewley Group, 1986-96; Campbell Catering was initially involved in catering for school meals, functions and banquets; the company moved into contract catering and catering for offshore oil rigs worldwide before acquiring the legendary, but ailing, Bewley's; Campbell Bewley Group also acquired a number of contract catering companies in the U.K. between 1996 and 1999, and took over the Rebecca's Restaurant and Catering chain in Boston, U.S.A., in 1997. Recipient, Irish Distillers/*Irish Press* Business Person of the Year Award, 1989-90. An innovative, hard working businessman; controls 60% of the country's catering contracts and one of the most popular food retail chains. Hobbies, walking, running, skiing, art and sports. Contact: Campbell Bewley Group Ltd., 4, St. John's Court, Santry, Dublin 9. Tel: 01 862 0900. Fax: 01 862 0771.

CARBERRY, Paul; JOCKEY; *b* 1974; *educ* National School, Ratoath; Dunshaughlin Community College; *single;* obtained Jockey's Licence aged 16; rode winner in a Point-to-Point for Carberry family stables and winner for Jim Bolger in that first year; top apprentice jockey; highlights of winning rides include *Rhythm Section* (Cheltenham), *Squire Silk* (Newbury), *Unguided Missile* (Cheltenham), *Looks Like Trouble* (Cheltenham), *Bobby Joe* (Irish Grand National 1998, Aintree Grand National 1999). Hobbies, showjumping, hunting, hunter trials, and water skiing. Contact: Ballybin, Ashbourne, Co. Meath. Tel: 01 825 6272.

CARNEY, Paul

CARNEY, The Hon. Mr. Justice Paul; JUDGE OF THE HIGH COURT; *b* 1943; *educ* Gonzaga College, King's Inns, *m* Marjorie Young, Consultant Dermatologist; 3 *s*; 1 *da*; called to the Bar in Ireland, 1966; called to the Bar of England and Wales, 1969; called to the Inner Bar, 1980; Appointed Judge of the High Court, 1991; President of the Irish Association for the Protection of the Financial Interests of the European Community. A hard working, media friendly judge; Clubs, Kildare Street and University Club; Contact: The High Court, Dublin 7. Tel: 01 872 5555. Fax: 01 872 1620.

CARROLL, The Hon. Mr. Justice Mella; JUDGE OF THE HIGH COURT; *b* 1934; *educ* Sacred Heart Convent, Leeson Street, Dublin; University College Dublin; Kings Inns; *single;* called to the Bar 1957; called to the Inner Bar 1977; first woman Chairperson of the Bar Council 1979; Chairperson, Legal Aid Board; had a good general practice specialising in Conveyancing and Company Law in the Chancery Division of the High Court; appointed High Court Judge 1980; considered a painstaking and hard working judge, highly regarded by colleagues. Hobbies, travel, music, particularly opera. Contact: Four Courts, Morgan Place, Dublin 7. Tel: 01 872 5555.

CARROLL, Raymond "Ray"; CHIEF EXECUTIVE, THE KILDARE HOTEL & COUNTRY CLUB; *b* 1944; *educ* Christian Brothers School, Dundalk; Dublin College of Catering, DipHotelMngt; *m* Maura Tiernan; 4 *da*; Worked in various positions in the hotel industry, 1967-72; General Manager, Sandy Lane Hotel & Country Club, Barbados, 1974-78; General Manager, Grosvenor House, Park Lane, London, 1978-81; Owner Manager, Cashel Palace, Cashel, Co. Tipperary, 1982-93; Chief Executive, Kildare Hotel & Country Club, Straffan, Co. Kildare, 1991 to date; Fellow: Irish Hotel & Catering Institute; Recipient, Gilbeys Gold Medal Award for Excellence in Catering; Hobbies, golf, reading, walking, travel and football; Contact: The Kildare Hotel & Country Club, Straffan, Co. Kildare. Tel: 01 601 7300. Fax: 01 601 7399.

CARROLL, Thomas A; CIVIL SERVANT - SECRETARY GENERAL OF THE DEPARTMENT OF THE MARINE AND NATURAL RESOURCES; *b* 1948; *educ* Good Counsel College, New Ross, Co. Wexford, University College Dublin, Diploma in Public Administration; BA Econ (1st class Hons); *m* Kathleen Whelan, 3 *da;* joined Department of Finance as Administrative Officer in 1971; promoted First Assistant Principal, 1976, Principal Officer, 1985; main responsibilities included economic analysis, expenditure control, overall responsibility for the delivery of the annual budget and head of economic forecasting; served with the International Monetary Fund, 1984; promoted Assistant Secretary in the Department of the Marine, 1988, appointed as Secretary General Department of the Marine and Natural Resources, 1994 to date; responsibilities expanded in 1997 to include the mining, forestry and offshore oil and sea sectors; Fellow, Chartered Institute of Transport. Hobbies, hurling, golf and walking, economics, history and politics. Contact: Department of the Marine and Natural Resources, 4 Leeson Lane, Dublin 2. Tel: 01 678 9141. Fax:

01 661 3817.

CARTY, Jane; SENIOR PRODUCER, MUSIC, RTE; *b* 1936; *educ* Convent of the Sacred Heart, Dublin; Paris; Strasbourg, Italy, University College Dublin, BA (Modern Languages and Music); *single;* studied piano with Alice Bryan and Lily Huban; singing with Jean Nolan; cello at Municipal School of Music; managed own piano school, 1956-64; Teacher, Municipal School of Music, (now D.I.T.) 1957-64; Programme Assistant, Music Department, R.T.E. 1964, Producer 1968, Senior Producer 1976, Senior Producer in charge of Music, 1989 to date; Founder/Director Musician of the Future Competition 1976 to date; has presented and produced programmes covering all areas of classical music, including documentaries on international festivals and young musicians competitions; former Director, National Concert Hall, National Youth Orchestra; Chairman of jury for E.S.B. Veronica Dunne International Singing Competition since inception; Chairman of jury for Irish section of Guardian Dublin International Piano Competition, 1988, 1991, 1994, 1997 and 2000; Adjudication at numerous international competitions. Hobbies, promoting young musicians, travel, reading, gardening, swimming. Contact: RTE, Donnybrook, Dublin 4. Tel: 01 208 3111.

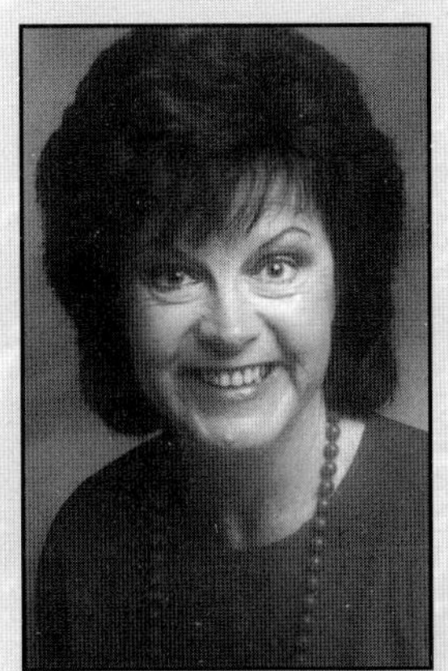

CARTY, Jane

CARTY, Paul; MANAGING Partner DELOITTE & TOUCHE; b 1940; *educ* O'Connell Schools; m Una Fitzpatrick; 1*s* 2*da*; joined Haughey Boland Chartered Accountants, 1967, Partner 1971, Managing Partner, 1980-86, merged with Deloitte Haskins & Sells, Managing Partner, 1986-91, Managing Partner, Deloitte & Touche Chartered Accountants, 1991 to date; Fellow of Institute of Chartered Accountants in Ireland; member, Institute of Taxation in Ireland; Fellow, Institute of Directors; member, Advisory Committee of the National Treasury Management Agency; Council Member of Dublin Chamber of Commerce. Hobbies, chess and golf. Contact: Deloitte & Touche, Deloitte & Touche House, Earlsfort Terrace, Dublin 2. Tel: 01 475 4433. Fax: 01 475 6622.

CASEY, John "Jack"; MANAGING DIRECTOR, NEW IRELAND ASSURANCE PLC; *b* 1942; *educ* Christian Brothers School, Cork; *m* Audrey Dillon; 1 *s* 2 *da;* Director, Rohan Group Ltd. 1970-78; Director, Cab Motor Company Ltd. 1978-82; Managing Director, Beamish & Crawford (Sales) Ltd. 1982-87; Managing Director, New Ireland Assurance 1987 to date; Director New Ireland Holdings plc, Greencore Group plc, Bon Secours Health System Ltd.; member, Marketing Institute of Ireland. Recognised as a dynamic leader. Contact: New Ireland Assurance plc., 9, Dawson Street, Dublin 2. Tel: 01 617 2000.

CASEY, John "Jack"

CASEY, Pierse; INVESTMENT BANKER AND INVESTOR; *b* 1955; *educ* Clongowes Wood College, 1967; University College Dublin, BComm; FCA, FCMA; *m* Judy Lynch, 2*s* 3 *da;* accountant with Price Waterhouse, Dublin, 1976-80; KMPG, Bermuda, 1980-82; DCC, Dublin & London, 1982-88, Director, 87-88; Chief Executive, Equity & Corporate Finance, London, 1988-89; Managing Director, Apax Partners, London & Dublin, 1998 to date; Apax, founded in the US, 1969, manages more than $3.9 billion for leading institutional investors around the world; Investor, 1991 to date; Director, Lamont Holdings; Joint owner with Ronald Wilson, Castlemere; member, FCA (Institute of Chartered Accountants); FCMA (Institute of Cost and Management Accountants); RAC Club, London; Moor Park Golf Club, London; Fitzwilliam LTC, Dublin; Druids Glen Golf Club; Biographical details also listed: *Directory of Directors*, London; London *Stock Exchange Yearbook.* Recognised as having a sharp eye and excellent timing in the investment market; described by the media as "the new Dermot Desmond". Hobbies, golf and chess. Contact: 10 Fitzwilliam Square, Dublin 2. Tel: 01 661 2671. Fax: 661 3057.

CASEY, Pierse

CASHMAN, Liam; BLOODSTOCK BREEDER; *b* 1937; *educ* Kilmagner National School; Salesian Agricultural College, Pallaskenry; *m* Catherine Beecher; 1*s* 1*da*; took over family Stud Farm, 1971; Rathbarry Stud, founded in 1935, has some fine horses, both flat and National Hunt; has bred *By the Way, Earth Stopper, Danish Knight, Alpride, Savage, Unconditional Love, Casque Blue, Locombe Hill, Liprandi, Lagado, Bajan, Humberts Landing;* stallions at stud include *Barathea, Charmwood Forest, Rainbow, For Life, Royal Abjar, Tagula;* an astute and dedicated member of the Bloodstock industry. Hobbies, horse racing, farming and GAA sports. Contact: Rathbarry Stud, Fermoy, Co. Cork. Tel: 025 36362. Fax: 025 36602.

CASSELLS, Peter; GENERAL SECRETARY ICTU; *b* 1949; *educ* St. Patrick's Classical School, Navan; Institute of Public Administration, DipAdmin; *single*; has held various positions in the Irish Congress of Trade Unions, 1973-89; General Secretary, 1989 to date; Member, Central Review Committee, National Economic and Social Council; Board member, European Trade Union Confederation. Considered by many to be the *eminence gris* of the trade union movement. Hobbies, Manchester United fan. Contact: Irish Congress of Trade Unions, 19 Raglan Road, Dublin 4. Tel: 01 668 0641. Fax: 01 660 9027.

CAVANAGH, Tom; CHAIRMAN CAVANAGH'S MOTOR GROUP; *b* 1931; *educ* Christian Brothers

CASSELLS, Peter

CAWLEY, Noel

School, Fermoy; University College Cork BComm, HDip.; *m* Marie O'Neill; 2*s* 2*da;* Teacher, Vocational Education Committee, Cork, 1952-53; joined family motor business in Fermoy, built business into one of the major family controlled firms in the South West, The Cavanagh Motor Group; company run by children, Tom Jnr, Conor and Marie; Cavanagh's are the main Ford dealers in the State; former director Allied Irish Bank; Chairman, Conrad Hotel; Patron, Cheshire Homes, Cork; Trustee, Multiple Sclerosis Society of Ireland; Trustee, Fermoy Golf Club; an influential figure at both county and national level; plays a major role in community welfare. Contact: Cavanagh of Fermoy, Ashe Quay, Fermoy, Co. Cork. Tel: 025 31211. Fax: 025 32345.

CAWLEY, Noel; MANAGING DIRECTOR, IRISH DAIRY BOARD, CHAIRMAN IRISH HORSE BOARD; *b* 1944 *educ* St. Nathy's College, Ballaghdeereen, University College Galway, B.Sc, University College Dublin, PhD; University of California, Berkeley, Post Doc. Fellow; *m* Anita Murphy; 2 *da*; Executive, Guinness U.K., 1972-73; Joined Bord Bainne, 1973; Executive Director, 1976; Managing Director, 1989 to date; Chairman, Irish Horse Board, 1993 to date; Member, National Council, IBEC; Life Member, R.D.S. A highly qualified and capable executive with a cool, low key approach; a dedicated bloodstock enthusiast; Hobbies, showjumping, racing, golf, Gaelic football. Contact: Irish Dairy Board, Grattan House, Mount Street Lower, Dublin 2. Tel: 01 661 9599 Fax: 01 661 2778.

CHADWICK, Michael; EXECUTIVE CHAIRMAN GRAFTON GROUP PLC; *b* 1951; educ Trinity College Dublin, BA, MSc; *married*; 1 *child*; appointed to the board of established family firm 1979; Executive Chairman 1985 to date. Contact: Grafton Group plc, Heron House, Corrig Road, Sandyford Industrial Estate, Dublin 18. Tel: 01 216 0600. Fax: 01 295 4470.

CLAFFEY, Úna; POLITICAL CORRESPONDENT RTE; *b* 1947; *educ* Mercy Convent, Mourne Rd, Drimnagh; Loreto High School Beaufort, Rathfarnham; University College Dublin, BA; Université D'Aix, Marseilles; *single;* Primary School Teacher, 1970-71; Studying and Community Politics, Boston, Mass, 1971-74; Organising Sec. Resources Protection Campaign, Dublin, 1975-77; Production Assistant, RTE, 1977-82; Presenter/Reporter, *Today Tonight*, 1982-90; Presenter, *Morning Ireland*, 1990-91; RTE Political Correspondent, 1991 to date; published *The Women Who Won*, best selling book on women elected to Dáil 1992; awards include Commendation, 1997 - AEJ Award for coverage of 50th Anniversary of VE Day in Moscow. Hobbies, food, travel, hurling and life. Contact: RTE, Donnybrook, Dublin 4. Tel: 01 208 3111.

CLANCY, Paddy; JOURNALIST IRISH SUN HEAD OF BUREAU; *b* 1943; *educ* Summerhill College, Sligo; *m* Bernadette Hanna; 1 *s* 2 *da;* Reporter, *Sligo Champion*, 1961-64; *Donegal People*, (South Donegal Staff Reporter), 1964-65; Reporter, *Irish Press*, 1965-67; Reporter, *Brighton Evening Argus*, 1967-68; Reporter, *Daily Telegraph*, London, 1968-74; Reporter, *Daily Express*, London, 1974-79; Founded Clancy News Service (Freelance Agency), Dublin, 1979-82; Founder and Senior Partner, Ireland International News Agency, Dublin, 1982-89; Editor, News and Sports, Century Radio, Dublin, 1989-91; Reporter, later Head of Bureau, *Irish Sun*, Dublin, 1992 to date; Presenter, *It Says in the Papers* , RTE Radio, 1992 to date; member, National Union of Journalists, (former Chairman of Dublin Freelance Branch); Republic of Ireland Representative on Freelance Industrial Council; club, Shelbourne Club. Hobbies, follows Sligo Rovers, Republic of Ireland Soccer Team. Contact: The Irish Sun, Huguenot House, 35-38 St. Stephen's Green, Dublin 2. Tel: 01 602 8866. Fax: 01 602 8869.

CLANDILLON, Margaret; PRINCIPAL AND GENERAL COUNSEL PEMBROKE GROUP LTD.; *b* 1960; *educ* Santa Sabina Convent, Sutton; Trinity College Dublin, BA Legal; Blackhall Place (Awarded First Prize and A.I.B. Award for Company Law); *m* John Mulcahy; 2*s*; apprenticed to Mason Hayes and Curran; joined G.P.A. as General Counsel 1985-93; co-founder, with Brian Goulding and Michael Dolan, Pembroke Group Ltd.; specialists in aircraft ownership and leasing and the provision of financial services to aviation; the company, since its inception, has acquired, owned and managed fleet of over 100 aircraft with a market value of over £2 billion; one of the new breed of high flying Irish business women; has looks, charm, and an exceptional legal/financial brain. Clubs, Powerscourt Golf Club, Mount Juliet Golf Club, Riverview Fitness Club. Hobbies, golf, reading and socialising. Contact: Pembroke Group Ltd., 33-41 Lower Mount Street, Dublin 2. Tel: 01 661 0900.

CLARKE, Darren Christopher; PROFESSIONAL GOLFER; *b* 1968; *m* Heather Tosh; 1*s*; turned professional in 1990 (Amateur handicap: plus 4); qualified for the PGA European Tour at the first attempt, at the 1990 qualifying school; PGA European Tour member, 1991 to date; during amateur career, represented Irish Boys and Youths and played on two Senior Teams (1985-90), won Spanish Open Amateur championship 1990, Irish Open Amateur Championship 1990; professional career includes representative, Ryder Cup 1997, Dunhill Cup 1994-98, World Cup 1994-96, victories include Alfred Dunhill Open 1993, German Masters 1996, B&M International Open 1998, Volvo

Master 1998, Irish Open PGA Championship 1994. Hobbies, all sports, films, reading, cars and fishing. Contact: ISM, Colshaw Hall, Stocks Lane, Knutsford, Cheshire, WA16 8TW. Tel: 0044 1565 722 755. Fax: 0044 1565 724 910.

CLARKE, The Rev. Martin Noel; COMMUNICATIONS OFFICER AND PRINCIPAL SPOKESPERSON FOR THE IRISH CATHOLIC BISHOPS CONFERENCE; *b* 1946; *educ* Blackrock College, Dublin; Bakersfield College, California (Rotary Scholarship); University College Dublin, BCL; Law Society; solicitor, 1970; *single*; joined Eugene F Collins & Sons, partner, 1972-76; studied for the priesthood, Holy Cross College, Clonliffe, BD, 1976-80; served as curate, Celbridge and Straffan, Co. Kildare; Director, Catholic Youth Council (providing a service in the greater Dublin area), President National Youth Council of Ireland, 1988-89; appointed Communications Officer and Principal Spokesperson for the Irish Catholic Bishops Conference, 1997 to date; member, Law Society of Ireland, Royal St. George Yacht Club, Blackrock College Union; regarded as a warm human cleric with a keen legal mind and a difficult task ahead. Hobbies, sailing and music. Contact: Communications Officer, Irish Bishop's Conference, 169 Booterstown Avenue, Blackrock, Co. Dublin. Tel: 01 208 4528. Fax: 01 283 4161.

CLARKE, Richard Lionel

CLARKE, Most Rev. Richard Lionel; BISHOP OF MEATH AND KILDARE; *b* 1949 *educ* Wesley College Dublin, Trinity College Dublin, BA, MA, PhD; King's College London, BD; *m* Linda Thompson; 1 *s* 1 *da*; Curate, Holywood, Co. Down, 1975-77; Curate, St. Bartholomew's and Leeson Park, 1977-79; Chaplain, Trinity College Dublin, 1979-84; Rector, Bandon Union of Parishes, Co. Cork, 1984-93; Dean of Cork, 1993-96; Bishop of Meath and Kildare, 1996 to date; Hobbies, music, travel - France in particular; Club, University and Kildare Street Club. Contact: Bishop's House, Moyglare, Maynooth, Co. Kildare. Tel: 01 628 9354. Fax: 01 628 9696.

CLEARY, Shay; ARCHITECT; *b* Cork 1951; *educ* De La Salle College Waterford; University College Dublin, BArch, 1969-7; *m* Lulu Lazar, Business Consultant; 2 *s* 1 *da*; Assistant Architect, Marcel Breuer, Candilis Josic & Woods Paris 1974-75; Assistant Architect, London Borough of Camden 1975-76; Partner, Grafton Architects 1977-80; Partner, Cleary & Hall 1981-86; Principal, Shay Cleary Architects 1987 to date; Director Group 91 Architects 1990-98; Visiting Professor, Princeton University Graduate School 1989; Design Tutor, University College Dublin 1977-1997; recipient: A.A.I. Award 1988, 1992, A.A.I. Downes Medal 1990, major projects include: Point Depot, Riverside Building, Irish Museum of Modern Art at R.H.K., Arthouse Multi Media Centre Temple Bar, The new Project Arts Centre Temple Bar, New Galleries RHK 1999, Queen St. Urban Renewal, Office Building Dawson Street, Temple Bar Framework Plan (Group 91), Redevelopment of Beggars Bush Barracks; publications include contributions to national and international architectural and design journals; has exhibited in Dublin, London and Zurich; noted for the quality of his restrained and thoughtful design; Fellow of the Royal Institute of Architects of Ireland. Contact: 19 Palmerston Park, Dublin 6. Tel: 01 497 3053. Fax: 01 497 3053.

CLIFFORD, His Grace Most Rev. Dermot; ARCHBISHOP OF CASHEL AND EMILY; *b* 1939; *educ* Clogher National School; St. Brendan's College, Killarney; Maynooth College, Co. Kildare, BSc.; Irish College, Rome, BD, STL; University College Cork, HDipEd; London School of Economics, MSc (Econ); Loughborough University of Technology, PhD; *single*; Dean of Studies, St. Brendan's College, Killarney 1964-72; Diocesan Secretary, Diocese of Kerry, 1974-86; Chaplain, St. Mary of the Angels Home for Special Children 1976-86; Co-adjutor Archbishop, Cashel and Emly 1986-88; Archbishop of Cashel 1988 to date; publications include: *The Social Costs and Rewards of Caring* (1990), and articles in *The Furrow*; Patron: G.A.A., St. Patrick's College, Thurles and Tipperary Rural and Business Institute (T.R.B.D.I.), Trustee of Bóthar (Third World Organsiation). An influential figure in the traditional, conservative mould. Hobbies, reading and walking. Contact: Archbishop's House, Thurles, Co. Tipperary. Tel: 0504 21512. Fax: 0504 22680.

COADY, Treasa née Ní Laoire; BOOK PUBLISHER; *b* 1951; *educ* Scoil Chaitriona, Eccles St., Dublin 7; qualified as an Occupational Therapist; *m* Jim Coady; 3*da*; Occupational Therapist in clinical practice, 1972-80; established Amach Faoin Aer Teo, to publish books on environmental matters with film-maker Éamon de Buitléar, 1981; established Town House and Country House Ltd., 1986, list broadened to include fiction, biography, illustrated non-fiction and occasional children's books; has published over 150 books to date including the works of David Bellamy, Frank Mitchell, Mary Lavin, Deirdre Purcell, Julie Parsons, Fergus Linehan, also *Lifelines*, 1, 2, 3, Brian Kennedy, Helen Dillon, Ulick O'Connor, John Hume, Mike Murphy; member CLÉ Irish Bookpublishers Association. Hobbies, choral singing, reading, yoga, family and friends. Contact: Town House and Country House, Trinity House, Charleston Road, Ranelagh, Dublin 6. Tel: 01 497 2399. Fax: 01 497 0927.

COCHRANE, Alfred

COCHRANE, Alfred; ARCHITECT, FURNITURE DESIGNER, M.I.D.I.; *b* 1948 (Beirut); *educ* Eton College; University of Rome (Dr.Arch.). In private practice since 1981; recipient of Europa Nostra

Awards for architectural conservation; has designed much published buildings at home, in the U.K., Europe and the U.S.A.; appears regularly in the media on matters of design; established Alfrank Designs Ltd. (with Frank Carroll), 1984, to create and manufacture contemporary upmarket furniture and accessories for home and export markets; now the leading brand of its kind in Ireland; son of the late Sir Desmond Cochrane and Yvonne Sursock; a prolific designer, trend setter and occasional party animal; member Institute of Designers in Ireland, Union Internationale des Architectes; recipient, Europa Nostra Award, for restoration of Mediaeval Castle, Italy, 1981 and for restoration of Royal Hospital, Kilmainham, 1983. Hobbies, painting and travelling. Contact: Alfrank Designs Ltd., Brickfield Lane, Dublin 8. Tel: 01 454 0209. Fax: 01 433 0209.

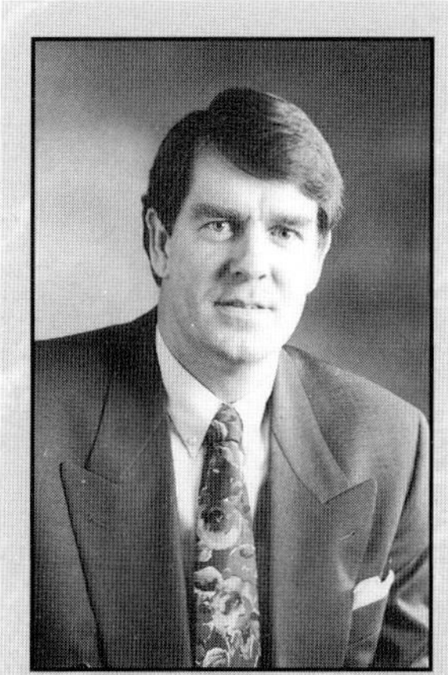

CODY, Patrick J.

CODY, Patrick J; PUBLISHER; *b* 1953; *educ* Cost Accountancy, 1 year; Marketing, 1 year; Business Development Programme, I.M.I. - 18 months; *m* Maura Byrne; 1*s* *1 da*; Trainee Accountant, Institute for Industrial Research and Standards, 1973-75, Marketing Executive, I.I.R.S., 1975-80; Sales Manager, (Publications) EOLAS, 1980-83, Sales and Marketing Manager, 1983-85; Managing Director and Co-Founder, Kompass Ireland, 1985 to date; Co-Founder, Kompass Internet, 1995 to date; member, Marketing Institute of Ireland, Irish Direct Marketing Association (Chairman, 1995), Irish Internet Association, (Founding Director, 1997); recipient, Irish Direct Marketing Award - Supreme Award, 1998; member, St. Margaret's Golf and Country Club; A man of vision and marketing skills; produced the first directory of Irish Web Sites and sponsored the first Irish Business Web Sites Awards. Hobbies, golf and travel. Contact: Kompass Ireland, Information House, Parnell Court, Dublin 1. Tel: 01 872 8800. Fax: 01 873 3711.

COLEMAN, Terence

COEN, Rynal; DIRECTOR COEN HOLDINGS LTD.; *b* 1934; *educ* Blackrock College; *m* Dairin Mathews; 3*s* 3 *da;* joined established family firm of builders providers in County Galway; Director, (former Chairman and Managing Director) Coen Holdings Ltd.; Director, various private companies; former Chairman, Galway Hospice; clubs, Lahinch Golf Club, Gort Golf Club, Portmarnock Golf Club, Gort and Galwegians R.F.C.s. Hobbies, golf, rugby (former interprovincial player). Contact: Coen Holdings Ltd., Station Road, Gort, Co. Galway. Tel: 091 631511. Fax: 091 631513.

COGLEY, Fred; SPORTS BROADCASTER AND COMMENTATOR; *b* 1934; *educ* St Mary's College, Rathmines; *m* Madeleine White; 2*s* 2 *da;* Sports sub editor, *Irish Times*, 1952-56; Sports Columnist, *Evening Herald*, 1956-60; Irish Sports Correspondent, *Sunday Telegraphy*, 1961-91; Freelance Sports Broadcaster, 1951-63; Radio and television sports broadcaster, RTE, 1963-72; Head of Sports, Radio and Television, RTE, 1972-99; Freelance Broadcaster and Commentator, June 1999 to date; member, Irish Golf and Rugby Writers Associations; publications include several rugby annuals; clubs, Grange Golf Club, European Golf Club. Hobbies, watching all sports, particularly cricket, golf and music. Contact: RTE, Donnybrook, Dublin 4. Tel: 01 208 3111.

COLGAN, Michael

COLEMAN, Terence; CHAIRMAN SCORPION GROUP; *b* 1943; *educ* University College Dublin BComm.; *m* Anita ----; 1*s* 3 *da;* Client Service Executive, AC Nielson of Ireland; Manager, North America, Irish Distillers; Chief Executive, The Process Company of the Jefferson Smurfit Group; Founder and Chairman, Scorpion Group; member, Fitzwilliam LTC; an imaginative and highly successful Irish businessman in the U.K. with an Irish base overlooking Killiney Bay - probably one of the most expensive houses to change hands in recent years. Hobbies, family pursuits, fly fishing, shooting, flying (possesses Commercial Pilots license and Instrument rating). Contact: Scorpion Group, Siemens Road, Northbank Industrial Estate, IRLAM, Manchester, M30 5BL. Tel: 0044 161 777 9666.

COLGAN, Michael; PRODUCER, DIRECTOR; *b* 1950; *educ* St. James's Christian Brothers School, Dublin; Trinity College Dublin, BA; *m* Susan FitzGerald, actress; 1 *s* 2 *da*; Director at the Abbey Theatre, 1974-77; Company Manager, Irish Theatre Company, 1977-78; Manager, Dublin Theatre Festival, 1978-81; Artistic Director, 1981-83; Director, Gate Theatre since 1984; Executive Director, Little Bird Films, 1986-95, Guest Director, Parma Festival, Italy, 1982; Member, Irish Arts Council, 1989-94; recipient *Sunday Independent* Arts Award, 1985 and 1987; recipient, National Entertainment Award, 1996 (Eamon Andrews Special Award for The Beckett Festival); Board member: Gate Theatre, Dublin Theatre Festival, Millennium Festivals Limited; Chairman, St. Patrick's Festival; Member, Governing Authority D.C.U.; founded Belacqua Film Company, 1998. An exceptional force in Irish theatre and all aspects of the performing arts; flies the Irish flag abroad with award winning Gate productions; noted for ability to charm sponsors and entertain friends. Hobbies, music, cinema, reading and conversation. Contact: Gate Theatre, Dublin 1. Tel: 01 874 4368. Fax: 01 874 5373.

COLLINS, Anthony E; SOLICITOR; *b* 1939; *educ* Xaviers School, Donnybrook; St. Gerards School Bray; Downside, Somerset (UK); Trinity College Dublin BA BComm; Incorporated Law Society; *m* Mary Deasy, Solicitor, now District Judge; 3*s* 1 *da;* Solicitor's Apprentice, Eugene F.

Collins, 1959, Partner, 1964, Senior Partner, 1978 to date; Director, Grafton Group plc, Deputy Chairman, 1995 to date; Chairman, Automobile Association (Ireland), 1987 to date; Director, Leinster Leader, 1972, Chairman, 1988 to date; publications include various legal articles; member, Strollers Club (President, 1988-91), Three Rock Rovers Hockey Club (Club Captain 1995-96), Incorporated Law Society of Ireland (President, 1984-85); Hon. member, Canadian Bar Association; a gregarious lawyer, highly respected in legal and business circles; heads up long established family law firm. Hobbies, sport of all kinds, a catholic taste in music. Contact: Eugene F. Collins, Temple Chambers, 3 Burlington Road, Dublin 4.

COLLINS, Finghin James

COLLINS, Bob; DIRECTOR-GENERAL RTE; *b* 1947; *educ* Christian Brothers, Adare; University College Dublin, BA, MBA; *separated*; 2*s*; Executive with Confederation of Irish Industry, 1968-71; Assistant to General Manager, Rehabilitation Institute, 1971-72; Assistant Secretary to College, Trinity College Dublin, 1972-75; joined Radio Telefis Eireann as Secretary to the Authority, 1975-80, Deputy Controller of Programmes Television, 1980-86, Director of Television Programmes, 1986-93, Director of Corporate Affairs, 1993-95, Assistant Director-General, 1995-97, Director-General, 1997 to date; numerous contributions to a variety of publications and specialist journals on broadcasting; President, Television Committee of European Broadcasting Union (EBU); Chairman, Celtic Film and Television Association (1991-94); Director, Merriman Summer School, (1981 and 1987). An erudite man with a low key approach. Hobbies, music, reading and Irish history. Contact: RTE, Donnybrook, Dublin 4. Tel: 01 208 2744. Fax: 01 208 3074.

COLLINS, Gerard

COLLINS, Con; RACEHORSE TRAINER; *b* 1924; *educ* Newbridge College, Co. Kildare; *m* Barbara Smith; 3*da*; joined father M.C. Collins in well known training establishment; obtained trainers licence, 1959; has won major races including with *Almaty* (Goodwood 1995), *Lady Alexander* (Goodwood 1997); a well established and respected figure in the Irish racing industry. Hobbies, shooting, fishing and golf. Contact: Conyngham Lodge, Curragh, Co. Kildare. Tel: 045 441239. Fax: 045 441605.

COLLINS, Finghin James; PIANIST; *b* 1977; *educ* Gonzaga College, Ranelagh; *single*; gained first place in Ireland in Music; is currently in final year of BA course in Music Performance under Dr. John O'Conor at Royal Irish Academy of Music; winner of numerous national and international awards and scholarships, including; Leeds International Pianoforte Competition, semi finalist 1996; Dublin International Piano Competition, semi finalist and Brennan Prize, 1997; *Vemes Rencontres de Jeune Pianistes*, Paris and Strasbourg, 1998, overall winner, 1998; National Entertainment Awards (Classical), Dublin, 1998; début recital, Wigmore Hall, London, April 1999;winner, Clara Haskil International Piano competition, Vevey, Switzerland, September 1999, winner, Clara Haskil International Piano Competition, Vevey, Switzerland, September 1999; one of the most exciting musical talents to emerge in Ireland in this century. Hobbies, opera, travel, foreign languages, literature. Contact: Royal Irish Academy of Music, 36, Westland Row, Dublin 2. Tel: 01 676 4412. Fax: 01 662 2798.

COLLINS, Gerard; MEMBER OF EUROPEAN PARLIAMENT; *b* 1938; *educ* Patrician College, Ballyfin; University College Dublin, BA; *m* Hilary Tattan; served as Fianna Fail Deputy for Limerick West 1967-97; member of Limerick County Council 1974-77; Minister of State, Industry and Commerce and the Gaeltacht 1969-70; Minister, Post and Telegraphs 1970-73; Opposition Spokesperson, Agriculture 1973-75, Justice 1975-77; Minister for Justice 1977-81 and 1987-89; Minister for Foreign Affairs 1982 and 1989-92; Co-Chairman, Anglo-Irish Conference 1988-92; Member, Fianna Fail Delegation New Ireland Forum, Consultative Assembly of Council of Europe 1973-77; Chairman, Parliamentary Committee on European Affairs; elected to the European Parliament 1994, Leader of Fianna Fail Group, Vice President of Union for Europe Group; Vice President of Parliament with responsibility for Budgetary Affairs 1998 to date; Co-ordinator of Policy, Regional Affairs Committee; substitute member, Foreign Affairs; Vice President Fianna Fail Party; a highly experienced politician. Contact: The Hill, Abbeyfeale, Co. Limeric. Tel: 068 31238.

COLLINS, Stephen

COLLINS, Sean M; VETERINARY SURGEON, STUD FARMER; *b* 1926; *educ* Blackrock College, Veterinary College of Ireland, M.R.C.V.S.; *m* Hanne Jorgensen; 3*s* 1 *da;* Veterinary Practitioner; Owner/Manager, Corbally Stud (Kildare), one of the major independent stallion stations in Ireland, stallions include *Desert Style, Paris House, Persian Bold* and *Priolo*; President and Founder, Irish Equine Centre (Johnstown/Kildare); Chairman, Irish European Breeders Fund; member, Irish Turf Club; former Chairman, Irish National Stud & Irish Thoroughbred Breeders Association; clubs, Hermitage Golf Club, Luttrellstown Golf and Country Club. Hobbies, fishing and golf. Contact: Corbally Stud, Celbridge, Co. Kildare. Tel: 01 628 8081. Fax: 01 627 3166.

COLLINS, Stephen; JOURNALIST; *b* 1951; *educ* Oatlands College, Stillorgan; University College Dublin, BA, MA, HDipEd; *m* Jean Wrigley; 1 *s* 2 *da;* Sub-Editor, *Irish Press*, 1975; Reporter, Irish

Press Group, 1976, Consumer Affairs Correspondent, 1982-84, Political Reporter, 1987; Political Correspondent, *The Sunday Press*, 1987-95, Political Correspondent, *The Sunday Tribune*, 1995 to date; Contributor on politics to radio and television; recipient, AT Cross Print Journalist of the Year Award, 1990; ESB National Media Award for Comment and Analysis, 1998; author of *The Haughey File*, 1992, *Spring and the Labour Story*, 1993, *The Cosgrave Legacy*, 1996. A low key professional; widely regarded as one of the finest political analysists in the country. Hobbies, reading and history. Contact: Sunday Tribune, 15, Lower Baggot Street, Dublin 2. Tel: 01 661 5555. Fax: 01 661 5302.

COLLINS, Steve

COLLINS, Steve; FORMER MIDDLEWEIGHT CHAMPION OF THE WORLD; *b* 1964; *educ* O'Connells School, Dublin; Colaiste Eanna; *m* Gemma Comiskey; 1*s* 1 *da;* Electrician with Guinness Brewery, 1981-86; moved to the U.S., worked in various positions before turning Professional Boxer; titles won include: U.S. and Irish Professional Middleweight Champion, Junior World Middleweight Champion, Middleweight Champion of the World, 1994, Super Middleweight Champion of the World, 1995, retired undefeated; now concentrates on his string of eleven horses, hunting and polo; also involved in media work, talk programmes and commentary; regarded as a true sportsman, talented, unassuming, gregarious and full of charm. Hobbies, anything to do with horses. Contact: P.O. Box 4000, Dublin 7.

COMISKEY, Most Rev. Brendan; CLERIC, BISHOP OF FERNS; *b* 1935; *educ* Annyalla National School; Castleblayney Boys School; St. Macartan's College, Monaghan; Sacred Heart Novitiate, Cootehill; Wareham, Massachusetts; Jaffrey Centre, New Hampshire; Catholic University of America; Lateran University, Rome, STL; Trinity College Dublin, MSc (1979); ordained in the Congregation of the Sacred Heart, Tanagh, Co. Monaghan 1961; Teacher, Dean at Damien High School, La Verne, California 1961-64; Lecturer, Chairman, Department of Moral Theology, Theological Union, Washington D.C. 1964-69; elected Provincial, Anglo-Irish Province of the Congregation of the Sacred Heart; Secretary General Conference of Major Religious Superiors 1974; Auxiliary Bishop of Dublin 1980; Bishop of Ferns 1984 to date; Chairman, Bishops' Commission for Communications; President, Catholic Communications Institute of Ireland; member, National Episcopal Conference, Bishops' Commissions for Ecumenism and Education and Commission for Youth; Founding member of Irish Churches' Council for Television and Radio Affairs; Patron, Wexford Opera Festival; Freeman of Wexford Town (1990), An outstanding pastor, a powerful media spokesman, a church leader in the modern mould. Contact: Bishop's House, PO Box 40, Wexford. Tel: 053 22177. Fax: 053 23436.

COMYN, Edward F

COMYN, Edward Frederick; SENIOR COUNSEL; *b* 1929; *educ* Belvedere College, University College Dublin, King's Inns; *m* Rosemary McGuire; 4 *da*; Called to the Bar, 1952; Called to the Inner Bar, 1975; Elected Bencher of King's Inns, 1992; Currently member, Superior Courts Rules Committee; Member: Royal Irish Yacht Club; Represents the State in constitutional, extraditional and criminal cases; noted as a meticulous and refined law man. Hobbies, fishing, reading, listening to music. Contact: The Law Library, Four Courts, Dublin 7. Tel: 01 872 0622. Fax: 01 872 0455

CONDRON-KING, Adèle "Twink"; ENTERTAINER; *b* 1951; *educ* Loreto, Beaufort, Rathfarnham; St. Louis Convent, Rathmines; St. Anne's School, Milltown; *m* David Agnew, Oboist, RTE Concert Orchestra; 2 *da*; embarked on singing career with Young Dublin Singers; vocalist, Jury's Cabaret; founded Maxi, Dick n' Twink; Lead female vocalist, Big 8 Showband (Las Vegas), 1970-75; radio and television performer/presenter (UK, Ireland and Turkey); star in annual Christmas pantomimes; has written and co-produced, *Sleeping Beauty Sort of,* (Point Theatre), *Rockinson Crusoe* and *Rockin Hood Prince of Thieves* (Olympia Theatre); also appears in straight theatre roles, *Country in Our Heads* (Andrews Lane), *Not I* (Gate); lead role in national tour, *Sive*; special guest on *The Perry Como Show* (US); recipient of numerous national and international awards including Jacobs and Montreaux Awards for television; one of the most popular and versatile entertainers in the country; currently studying Turkish language and culture at Trinity College Dublin. Hobbies, computers, sports, gym, tennis, squash, pets, needlework, scientific documentaries and many more. Contact: Carol Hanna, 57 Meadow Bank, Busy Park Road, Dublin 6. Tel: 01 490 9339.

CONNOLLY, Maura

CONNELL, His Grace the Most Rev. Desmond; ARCHBISHOP OF DUBLIN AND PRIMATE OF IRELAND; *b* 1926; *educ*; St Peter's National School, Phibsboro; Belvedere College, Clonliffe College;University College, Dublin B.A., M.A.; Maynooth B.D.; Louvain, Dr. Phil.; ordained at Clonliffe College Church, 1951; assistant professor Methaphysics 1972; appointed Dean, Dept. of Philosophy and Sociology 1983, re-elected 1986; granted title, Monsignor 1984; has served as chaplin to the Poor Clares and Carrmelites; awarded D.Litt (Hons), National University of Ireland 1981; Member, Irish Hierarchy's theological Commisson; a noted linguist and recognised authority on the 17th century French priest/philosopher, Nicolas Malebranche; a churchman of unusual intelectual acumen, widely regarded as a traditionalist. Hobbies, reading, walking and music. Contact: Archbishop's House, Drumcondra, Dublin 9. Tel: 01 837 3732 Fax: 01 836 9796

CONNOLLY, Donal; WATERFORD COUNTY MANAGER; *b* 1942; *educ* Member of the Chartered Institute of Administration and Secretaries; m Catherine Curran; 4*s* 4*da*; Clerical Officer, Waterford Co. Council, 1963-69; Staff Officer, Tipperary N.R. Co. Council, 1969-70; Staff Officer, Waterford Co. Council, 1971-72; County Accountant, Tipperary S.R. Co. Council, 1972-77; County Secretary, Westmeath Co. Council, 1977-80; Assistant Co. Manager, Tipperary S.R. Co. Council, 1980-85; County Manager, Roscommon Co. Council, 1986-94; Co. Manager, Waterford Co. Council, 1994 to date; compositions include, *The Role of Local Government in Community Development*; *Quality in Local Government*; *Local Partnerships* and *Social Innovation; Local Government in Ireland; Housing in the 1990's; Practicalities of SPC scheme- a Manager's Perspective.* Contact: Waterford County Council, Davitt's Quay, Dungarvan, Co. Waterford. Tel: 058 42822. Fax: 058 42911.

CONNOLLY, Maura; PROGRAMME EXECUTIVE RTE; *b* 1948; *educ* St. Louis High School Rathmines, Commercial Teachers Diploma; *m* Líam Mac Beagáin; Joined RTE as a Clerk/Secretary in the Accounts Department, almost immediately transferred to Light Entertainment; Secretary to the then Head of Light Entertainment, Adrian Cronin; started work on the *Late Late Show* 1969; is currently Programme Executive with RTE, working on the longest running (now in its 37th year), and most popular talk show on television worldwide (running on RTE, Tara Cable TV/U.K. and Celtic Vision/U.S.A.), originator and co-ordinator of both the popular Antiques Show and Fashion Awards and many others on the *Late Late Show*; Co-ordinator, Christmas Toy Show; has worked with Gay Byrne on Centra Homemaker of the Year, Telethon and one of Ireland's highest rating shows, *The Rose of Tralee.* Regarded as having a major input on Ireland's most influential media programme; the *Late Late Show* has reflected social change in the country over 37 years; a high powered executive who has preferred to remain out of the limelight. Hobbies, reading, theatre, travel, horse riding, swimming, interior design, painting and the lecture circuit. Contact: RTE, Dublin 4. Tel: 01 208 3111. Fax: 01 208 3098.

CONROY, Luke; CHIEF EXECUTIVE SUN MICROSYSTEMS IRELAND LTD.; *b* 1959; *educ* O'Connells Christian Brothers School, Dublin; Trinity College Dublin, B.A.I. Engineering, B.A.Maths; *single;* Engineer/Consultant Chace Computer Consultants 1980-85; Consultant, IKOSS GMBH, Germany 1985-87; Sales and Marketing Director, Manager Software Centre Siemens Ltd. 1990-95; General Manager, Sun Microsystems Ireland Ltd., 1995 to date. Member Irish Software Association, I.B.E.C., Naomh Fionbarra GAA Club, ESB Sportsco. Hobbies, GAA, hurling, chess, ham radio, walking. Contact: Sun Microsystems Ireland Ltd., East Point Business Park, Dublin 3. Tel: 01 819 9100.

CONSIDINE, Margaret; DIRECTOR SALES & MARKETING, ICON AT THE BAILEYS CENTRE, SNR. PARTNER SALES & MARKETING, UBIQUITY LTD; *b* 1965; *educ* Presentation Convent, Portarlington; Bolton Street, studied COBOL Programming; ABC College, MAAT; Irish Management Institute, BA (Mgmt); Trinity College (Dublin), currently studying for an MSc in Org. Behaviour; won the IMI 1997 award for excellence; Co-Wrote "Psychology and Work" in 1998 for the IMI; *m* to Hugh; has experience in national, european and worldwide, operational and sales & marketing roles in the following industries; Engineering, Construction, I.T., Recruitment, Precious Metals Dealing, Manufacturing, Distribution & Logistics, Fast Food and Hotel & Catering; Hobbies: Tennis, basketball, golf, Irish art and reading. Contact: Icon at the Baileys Centre, Leopardstown Road, Foxrock, Dublin 18. Tel: 01-2891000, Fax: 01-2891166.

COOKE, Richard; MANAGING DIRECTOR ESAT NET; *b* 1965; *educ* De La Salle College, Waterford; University College Dublin, B.E.; *m* Tara O'Reilly; 1 *da;* Sales Engineer, Alcatel Business Systems (formerly Technico Communications) 1989-93; Sales Manager, Lake Communications, 1993-97; Sales Manager, EUNet Ireland (now ESAT NET), 1997-98; Managing Director, ESAT NET, 1998 to date; recipient, Earl of Cork Scholarship, 1980. Hobbies, socialising, keep-fit, sport, history and film. Contact: Esat Net, The Ecentre, Dundrum Business Park, Dublin 14. Tel: 01 216 6300. Fax: 01 216 6399.

COONEY, Patrick; MANAGING DIRECTOR GLEESON GROUP; *b* 1947; *educ* Christian Brothers; Institute of Certified Accountants, FACCA; *m* Maria White, Public Relations Executive; 3*s* 2*da*; Audit Senior with Deloitte Plender Griffith, London 1970-74; Managing Director, Gleeson Group 1975 to date; the Gleeson Group incorporates such well known brands as Tipperary Natural Mineral Water (founded by Patrick and wife Maria), also Merry's Cream Liqueur and Brew No. 1 and many others; with employment figures of over four hundred and a turnover of over £80m it is a major player in Irish industry; club, St. Stephen's Green; a media friendly, gregarious and successful businessman. Hobby, social exchange. Contact: M&J Gleeson & Co. 15 Cherry Orchard Estate, Ballyfermot, Dublin 10. Tel: 01 626 9787. Fax: 01 626 0652.

COOPER, Matthew Joseph "Matt"; EDITOR THE SUNDAY TRIBUNE; *b* 1966; *educ* North Monastry, Fair Hill Cork; University College Cork, B.Comm.; Dublin City University, Graduate

CONROY, Luke

CONSIDINE, Margaret

COOPER, Matthew Joseph

COPELAND, Louis F.

CORR, Andrea

CORR, Caroline

CORR, Jim

Diploma in Journalism; *m* Aileen Hickie; 1 *da;* Reporter, *Business & Finance* (magazine), 1988-89; Reporter, *Sunday Business Post,* 1989-92, Assistant Editor, from July 1992; Business Editor, *Irish Independent,* 1993-1996, Associate Editor, 1995; Editor, *The Sunday Tribune,* 1996 to date; Presenter, *Marketplace,* Network 2, 1991-92; Presenter, *Start Me Up,* RTE 1, 1997; regular stand-in presenter, *The Last Word* and *Sunday Supplement,* Today FM, since August 1997; awards include: Young Journalist of the Year, 1991, Business Journalist of the Year, 1992, National Journalist of the Year, 1993; member, Sunday's Well Rugby Football Club (Cork), St. Judes AFC (Dublin), Lillies Bordello, Renards. Seen as well capable of filling his challenging role; a bright, imaginative editor not unhappy in the media spotlight. Hobbies, music, reading (fiction, newspapers and magazines), cinema, eating out, eating in, socialising (pubs and night clubs), watching sports (especially soccer, rugby, hurling, Gaelic football) live and on TV, playing soccer and tennis. Contact: The Sunday Tribune, 15 Lower Baggot Street, Dublin 2. Tel: 01 661 5555. Fax: 01 661 5302.

COPELAND, Louis F; MANAGING DIRECTOR, LOUIS COPELAND AND SONS; *b* 1949; *educ* St. Patrick's College, Drumcondra; College of Tailoring and Textiles, London City and Guilds for Tailoring; *m* Mary Murphy; 1 s 2 da; Apprentice Tailor, Two-Owls, 1965-67; joined established family business, Louis Copeland and Sons, Hand Craft Tailors and Menswear, 1967 to date; is currently Managing Director, Louis Copeland and Sons; Originator of the highly publicised awards Best Dressed Man of the Year, and Tie Person of the Year; President, Fashion and Footwear Federation; A gentleman's outfitter to top showbusiness, business personalities and politicians, revamped Bertie Ahern's image; a frequent radio and television guest; not one to underestimate the value of publicity; Retailer of the Year, Menswear, UK, 1998; a first for Ireland, described by the editor of FHM "he redefines what a menswear retailer should be capable of". Hobbies, walking, swimming and golf; Clubs, Riverview Racquet and Fitness Club. Contact: Louis Copeland, 39 Capel Street, Dublin 1. Tel: 01 872 1600. Fax: 01 671 7685.

CORCORAN, John; PLANT MANAGER NORTEL NETWORKS, GALWAY; *b* 1962; *educ* Cistercian College, Roscrea; University College Galway BE (Industrial); University College Dublin, M.I.E.; *m* Niamh Conroy; 1 *da;* Army Officer, 1980-89; Engineering Manager, Precision Steel Components, 1989-92; Operations Manager, Cabletron Systems Irl., 1992-95; Operations Director, Nortel Networks, Galway, 1995-97, Plant Manager, 1997 to date. Contact: Nortel, Mervue Industrial Estate, Galway. Tel: 091 757671.

CORR, Andrea; SINGER/SONGWRITER; *b* 1974; *educ* in Dundalk; *single;* Lead vocalist and tin whistle performer with celtic rock group, The Corrs, 1990 to date; spotted by Bill Whelan during a pub gig, met U.S. Ambassador Jean Kennedy Smith, invited to play in Boston; met David Foster while there, signed up by 143 Records (Atlantic Group); toured with various other bands such as The Rolling Stones; released album *Forgiven Not Forgotten* 1995, *Talk on Corners* 1997; film work includes *The Commitments, Evita* and a guest appearance on *Beverley Hills 90210* (TV); extraordinary international popularity and good looks have not changed down-to-earth image. Contact: Barry Gaster, Martello Terrace, Dun Laoghaire, Co. Dublin. Tel: 01 285 5321.

CORR, Caroline; MUSICIAN/SONGWRITER; *b* 1973; *educ* in Dundalk; *single;* vocalist and performer on drums, bodhran and piano with family celtic rock group, The Corrs, 1990 to date; a mini tour in the US led to signing with 143 Records (Atlantic Records); subsequent tours with other bands led to growing international popularity; albums, *Forgiven Not Forgotten* (1995) and *Talk on Corners* have reached platinum and gold sales worldwide; Group awarded Brit Award for Best International Act, 1999; film credits include *The Commitments* and a guest appearance on *Beverley Hills 90210* (TV). Contact: Barry Gaster, Martello Terrace, Dun Laoghaire, Co. Dublin. Tel: 01 285 5321.

CORR, Jim; MUSICIAN/SONGWRITER; *b* 1964; *educ* in Dundalk; *single;* performs on key board and piano with family celtic rock group, The Corrs, 1990 to date; following a gig in Boston (US) band were signed with 143 Records (Atlantic Records); have toured extensively; albums released, *Forgiven Not Forgotten* (1995) and *Talk on Corners* (1997) made Irish music history by becoming the first band to have albums in the No. 1 and No. 2 slots in UK in the same week; film credits include *The Commitments* and a guest appearance on *Beverley Hill 90210* (TV). Hobby, motor racing. Contact: Barry Gaster, Martello Terrace, Dun Laoghaire, Co. Dublin. Tel: 01 285 5321.

CORR, Sharon; MUSICIAN/SONGWRITER/SINGER; *b* 1970; *educ* in Dundalk; *single;* vocalist and violinist with family celtic rock group, The Corrs, 1990 to date; played in small gigs throughout Ireland, invited to Boston, signed up with 143 Records (part of Atlantic Records); have toured extensively; released two albums, both chart toppers in the UK on the same week, *Forgiven Not Forgotten* (1995) and *Talk on Corners* (1997); film credits include *The Commitments* and a guest appearance on *Beverley Hills 90210* (TV). Contact: Barry Gaster, Martello Terrace,

Dun Laoghaire, Co. Dublin. Tel: 01 285 5321.

CORR, Sharon

COSGROVE, Art; PRESIDENT UNIVERSITY COLLEGE DUBLIN; *b* 1940; *educ* Abbey CBS, Newry; Queen's University Belfast, B.A., PhD.; *m* Emer Sweeney; 5 *s* 4 *da;* Assistant Lecturer (1963-71), College Lecturer (1971-76), Department of Medieval History, University College Dublin; Visiting Professor, History Department, University of Kansas, 1974; Statutory Lecturer (1976-1990), Associate Professor (1990-93), Department of Medieval History, University College Dublin; Chairman, Combined Departments of History, 1991-93, Member of Governing Body of UCD, 1979-93; Member, Senate of National University of Ireland, 1986-93; President of University College since 1994; publications include, *Late Medieval Ireland 1370-1541* (Dublin, 1981), ed. *Marriage in Ireland* (Dublin, 1985), ed. *A new History of Ireland ii: medieval Ireland 1169-1534* (Oxford, 1987, 2nd impression, 1993); member, Royal Irish Academy; Fellow, Royal Historical Society; awards include L.L.D. honoris causa Q.U.B. 1995. Hobbies, sport, particularly horse-racing, music and reading. Contact: University College Dublin, Belfield, Dublin 4. Tel: 01 668 7227.

COSTELLO, Finbar; CHAIRMAN IRISH INTERNATIONAL GROUP; *educ* Clongowes Wood College; University College Dublin, BComm; *m* Josephine Murray; 2 children; Marketing Manager, Irish Glass Bottle Co. Ltd. 1962-75; joined Irish International Advertising and Marketing Ltd., 1975; Managing Director until 1995, currently shareholder and non-executive Chairman Irish International Group; Director, Software Vineyard; member, Friends of the Rotunda; Director, Royal Hospital, Donnybrook; President, Irish Universities RFC; former President, UCD Rugby Club; member, Fitzwilliam LTC, Carrickmines Croquet and Tennis Club, Milltown GC and Connemara GC; a prominent businessman and a gregarious host. Hobbies, golf and tennis. Contact: Irish International Group, 17 Gilford Road, Dublin 4. Tel: 01 260 2000.

COSGROVE, Art

COSTELLO, Victor Carton Patrick; PROFESSIONAL RUGBY PLAYER; *b* 1970; *educ* Blackrock College; University College Dublin; *single;* Ireland Schools International (Triple Crown), 1987-89; Ireland Under-21 International, 1989-91; Ireland Senior International - 19 caps to date - 1996-99; Athletics: Chosen to represent Ireland in Europa Cup at age 16, Shot Putt (youngest ever), 1986; represented Ireland on numerous occasions at friendly international and on Europa Cup Team (Track and Field), 1986-92; represented Ireland at Barcelona Olympics, 1992; a quiet, unassuming sportsman. Contact: St. Mary's, Templeville Road, Dublin 6. Tel: 01 492 3633.

COSTELLOE, Paul; DRESS DESIGNER; *b* 1945; *educ* Blackrock College Dublin; Chambre Syndical de la Haute Couture, (Paris); *m* Anne Cooper; 5 *s* 1 *da;* worked in design in Paris, Milan and New York; set up own design and manufacturing company in Dungannon, Northern Ireland, has offices in London and a retail department store in Brown Thomas, Dublin; also designs a range of Home Furnishings, tableware for Wedgwood, cutlery for Newbridge Cutlery, crystal for Cavan and an optical range for Cambridge. Recipient: Fil D'Or Award France (three times), Designer of the Year UK (two nominations), Designer of the Year Ireland, 1991. Internationally acclaimed designer; clothes are stocked in exclusive retail outlets worldwide. Hobbies, painting, theatre, cinema, golf, snooker and swimming. Contact: Paul Costelloe International Ltd., 27 Cheval Place, London, SW7 1EW. Tel: 0044 171 589 9484. Fax: 0044 171 589 9481.

COSTIN, John Joe; MANAGING DIRECTOR, COSTIN NURSERIES; *b* 1945; *educ* Mount Melleray, Cappoquin; Scoil San Nioclas, Ring; National Botanic Gardens; Agricultural College, Clonakility Gold Medallist; University College Dublin, BAgSc (Hort.), awarded Patrick Hogan Prize; *m* Betty Ryan; 2 *s* 3 *da*; Research officer, An Foras Taluntais, 1968-73; Managing Director, S.A.P. Nurseries Ltd., 1973-77; Managing Director, Costin Nurseries, 1977 to date. A leading plantsman and landscape designer, has displayed at International Garden Festival Glasgow (Gold Medal), 1988, Osaka (First Place) 1990, Chelsea Flower Show London (Silver Gilt), 1991; Commissioned for Bicentennial Commemerative Garden, St. Patrick's College, Maynooth, 1995; former President, International Plant Propagators Society, 1989. A top class horticulturist, fast gaining an international reputation. Hobbies, swimming, travel, music, and reading. Contact: Costin's Nursery, Portgloriam, Kilcock, Co. Kildare. Tel: 01 628 7237. Fax: 01 628 7934.

COULSON, Paul; CHAIRMAN YEOMAN INTERNATIONAL GROUP PLC; *b* 1952; *educ* Gonzaga College, Dublin; Trinity College Dublin, BBS; *m* Moya Wall; 2*s* 2*da*; Accountant with Price Waterhouse 1973-82; Chief Executive, Yeoman International Leasing, now known as Yeoman International Group plc, 1982-89, Chairman, 1989 to date; Yeoman International Group plc is an investment company, main investments include, Tipperary Crystal Design Ltd., Cityjet, Ardagh plc, Point Information Systems, Jupiter Telecommunications; member, Institute of Chartered Accountants in Ireland. Clubs, Fitzwilliam Lawn Tennis Club, Donnybrook Tennis Club, Portmarnock Golf Club. Contact: Yeoman International Group plc, Yeoman House, Richview Office Park, Dublin 14. Tel: 01 283 7388. Fax: 01 283 7323.

COVENEY, Simon

COVENEY, Simon; POLITICIAN; *b* 1972; *educ* Clongowes Wood College; University College Cork, BA Econ & Hist; Gurteen Agricultural College, Royal Agricultural College (UK), BSc Agriculture and Land Management; *single;* worked as a Land Management Advisor in Scotland and Farm Manager in Cork; lead the Sail Chernobyl Project, an around the world fundraising sail in aid of the Chernobyl Children's Project 1997-98; cut short the trip to stand for election in Cork South Central in a by-election caused by the sudden death of his father, Hugh Coveney; sporting interests include, Grade A Sailing Instructor and qualified Life Guard, played rugby for Ireland at college level, also captained college team and played with Garryowen and Cork Constitution. Contact: Dáil Eireann, Leinster House, Kildare Street, Dublin 2. Tel.: 01 618 3333.

COWEN, Brian; POLITICIAN, SOLICITOR; *b* 1960; *educ* Clara National School; Cistercian College, Roscrea; University College Dublin; Incorporated Law Society; *m* Mary Molloy; 2 *da;* formed legal partnership, O'Donovan & Cowen; elected Fianna Fail Deputy for Laois-Offaly (taking over seat of late father, Bernard Cowen), 1984 to date; Minister for Labour, 1992-93; Minister for Transport, Energy and Communications, 1993-94; Opposition Spokesperson for Agriculture, 1994-97, for Health, January-June 1997; Minister for Health and Children, 1997 to date; regarded as bright and eloquent, if cutting. Hobbies, reading and Gaelic Games. Contact: Department for Health and Children, Hawkins House, Dublin 2. Tel: 01 671 4711. Fax: 01 671 1947.

COX, Patrick "Pat"; MEP; *b* 1952; *educ* Ardscoil Ris Christian Brothers School, Limerick; Trinity College Dublin, MA; *m* Cathy Tighe; 2 *s* 4 *da;* Lecturer, Institute of Public Administration 1974-76; Lecturer, NIHE (now University of Limerick) 1976-82; Presenter / Reporter, RTE, 1982-86; General Secretary, Progressive Democrats, 1986-89; Elected MEP for Munster, 1989; Elected T.D. for Cork South Central 1992-94; Re-elected MEP for Munster, 1994 (non party); First Vice President ELDR European Group Parliament 1994-98; President, ELDR Group E.P. 1998 to date; Member, Economic and Monetary Affairs Committee; substitute member, Legal Affairs Committee of the European Parliament. A clear, cool and incisive administrator and politician; a successful director of elections for the PDs in the 1987 election; an even more successful candidate for Munster in the European Elections 1989, achieved the highest per capita first preference votes in the E.C. Hobbies, reading and walking. Contact: 21, Cook Street, Cork. Tel: 021 278488.

COYLE, Brian

COYLE, Brian; FINE ART AUCTIONEER, CHARTERED SURVEYOR; *b* 1934 *educ* Clontarf High School; St. Fintan's College, Sutton; University of Reading; *single;* qualified as a Chartered Surveyor and joined James Adam & Sons, Auctioneers and Estate Agents, Dublin; is currently Chairman, James Adam Salerooms; Lecturer in Fine Art at University College Dublin; frequent lecturer in U.S and U.K. Fellow: Irish Auctioneers and Valuers Institute (past President), Royal Institute of Chartered Surveyors (FRICS), Society of Valuers & Auctioneers (FSVA), President, Board of Visitors of National Museum of Ireland and National Botanic Gardens. Publications include various articles on furniture and art for international journals. Popular television spokesperson on art and furniture (*Late Late Show*); has organised seminars on Fine Art throughout the country. Hobbies, golf, art, reading, conversation, travel, food, wine and amateur dramatics. Contact: James Adam & Sons, 26, St. Stephen's Green, Dublin 2. Tel: 01 676 0261.

COYLE, Eveleen Mary; COMMISSIONING EDITOR GILL & MACMILLAN, BOOK PUBLICIST; *b* 1951; *educ* Miss Meredith's, Pembroke Road; Dominican Convent, Wicklow; Commercial Course, Rathmines; *m* Fergus Mulligan; 2*s* 1 *da;* Clerk, St. Luke's Hospital, 1971; Schooled horses and taught riding, Southern California, 1971-72; General Secretary, Creation Group, 1972-74; joined Gill & Macmillan Publishers as secretary to Publicity Department, 1974; appointed Head of Publicity on all their lists, 1978; left to form own company specialising in book marketing and publicity to major UK and Irish Publishers, promoting writers such as Roddy Doyle, Richard Ford, Margaret Atwood, Gay Byrne, John Banville, Brian Moore and PJ O'Rourke, 1985 to date; joined Gill and Macmillan editorial team as Commissioning Editor, 1992 to date; creative works include *The Irish Potato Cookbook,* 1997; member, IFC, Irish Glass Society, Irish Book Publishers Association. Hobbies, literature, swimming, riding, theatre. Contact: 44 Oakley Road, Ranelagh, Dublin 6. Tel: 01 497 1700. Fax: 01 497 1245.

COYLE, John

COYLE, John, BUSINESSMAN; *b* 1946 *educ* Coláiste Iognáid; Glenstal Abbey; University College Dublin, BA, MEconSc.; Collége d'Europe, Bruges, Dip. Hautes Etudes Europeenes; *m* Sally Doyle; 3 *s* 3 *da;* Management Trainee, CIE 1969-70; Work Study Operator, Battery Makers, 1970-71; Financial Controller, Renvyle House Hotel 1972-83; Currently Chairman, Hygeia Chemicals Ltd., Renvyle House Hotel, Steelforms Ltd., Galway Airport; Vice President, Eurochambres; Past President, Galway Chamber of Commerce, Chambers of Commerce of Ireland, Galway Civic Trust. Hobbies, sailing, shooting, walking, reading. Clubs, Galway Co. Club, Galway Bay Sailing Club, Corofin Fishing Association, The Amicable Society. Contact: Hygeia Chemicals Ltd., Carrowmoneash, Oranmore, Co. Galway. Tel: 091 794722.

COYLE, Patrick; CHIEF EXECUTIVE RYAN HOTELS PLC; *b* 1965; *educ* Rockwell College; University College Dublin, BComm; Institute of Chartered Accountants in Ireland; *m* Jean Ryan; Accountant with Ernest & Young, Dublin, 1986-91; Group Accountant, Ryan Hotels plc, 1991, Chief Financial Officer and Company Secretary, 1994, Director of Finance and Marketing, 1995, Chief Executive, 1999; Ryan Hotels plc are a major player in the hotel industry with, Gresham Hotel (Dublin), Royal Marine Hotel (Dun Laoghaire), Limerick, Galway, Killarney Ryans, Memphis Hotel (Amsterdam), Le Belson (Brussels), Carat (Hamburg); member, Institute of Chartered Accountants in Ireland. Clubs, Malahide Lawn Tennis Club, Fitzwilliam Lawn Tennis Club, Island Golf Club, Donabate. Hobbies, golf, sailing and tennis. Contact: Ryan Hotels plc, 23 Upper O'Connell Street, Dublin 1. Tel: 01 878 7966. Fax: 01 878 6032.

COYLE, Trevor Alwyn; SHOWJUMPER/TRAINER/DEALER; *b* 1958; *educ* Foyle College, Derry; Qualified Accountant; *m* Heather Gahan; 1*s* 1*da;* worked in family construction business; trained in showjumping with Paul Darragh; currently has 30 horses in yard; own showjumping winners include *Red Fox, Bank Strike, True Blue, Moloney's Error, Cruising;* member, Irish Nations Cup Team since early 80s; achievements include, placed 7th in European Championship, 1997, placed 8th in World Equestrian Games, Rome; placed 2nd World Cup Final, Gottenburg 1999; has won major Grand Prix in Europe and Canada; Chairman, International Riders Club Ireland; awarded Irish Field Showjumper of the Year, 1997 & 1998, Irish International Showjumper of the Year, 1997; represented Show Jump Assoc. or Ireland at Peace Forum, Dublin Castle, 1996; member S.J.A.I, S.E.I. Hobbies, golf, family and music - fromer rock band member. Contact: Chestnut Farm, Annaghmore, Co Armagh BT62 1LY; Tel: 0801 762851 569

CRAIG, Maurice; ARCHITECTURAL HISTORIAN; *b* 1919; *educ* Castlepark School, Dublin; Shrewsbury School, (U.K.); Cambridge; Trinity College Dublin; *m* Beatrice Hunt (*m dis*); 1*s* 1 *da; m* Jeanne Edwards (decd); *partner* Agnes Bernelle (decd); Inspector of Ancient Monuments with the Ministry of Works, London; worked with An Taisce and as a consultant with Foras Forbatha; publications include *Dublin 1660-1860* (1952), *Irish Bookbinding* (1954), *The Volunteer Earl* (1948), *The Elephant and the Polish Question* (memoirs), *The Architecture of Ireland, Mausolea Hibernia* in collaboration with his son, the illustrator Michael Craig; member, Maritime Institute of Architects in Ireland; Honorary Fellow of Trinity College Dublin and the Royal Institute of Architects in Ireland; member Royal Irish Academy; recognised as a leader in his field, a distinguished scholar, an adventurous traveller and a man of urbane wit and charm. Contact: Publishers, The Lilliput Press, 62 Sitric Road, Dublin 7. Tel: 01 671 1647.

CRANFIELD, Patrick Arthur; GENERAL OFFICER COMMANDING AIR CORPS; *b* 1940; *educ* Presentation College Blackrock; Cadet School, Military College; RAF Training College; Command and Staff Course, Military College; *m* Dara Murphy; 2*s* 3 *da;* Flying Instructor, Air Corps, 1960-68, Chief Flying Instructor, 1968-77, Station Commander Baldonnel Airbase, 1977-79, Station Commander Gormanston Airbase, 1979-80; Chief Operations Officer, 1980-83, Executive Officer Air Corps, 1983-84; Officer Commanding Air Corps Group 1984-89; General Officer Commanding Air Corps 1989 to date. Hobbies, music, sport; Clubs, Blackrock College Rugby Club (President, 1989-90), Vice President, Leinster Branch Irish Rugby Football Union (1999-00). Contact: Air Corps, Casement Aerodrome, Baldonnel, Dublin 22. Tel: 01 495 2493.

CRAWFORD, Leo

CRAWFORD, Leo; CHIEF EXECUTIVE, BWG FOODS LTD.; *b* 1959; *educ* St. Joseph's C.B.S. Fairview, Trinity College Dublin, Bachelor of Business Studies, 1976; *m* Adrienne McCabe; 2 *s*; Joined Irish Distillers as a trainee accountant, 1981; Sales & Marketing, 1981-85; Irish Distillers Finance Division, 1985-88; Pernod Ricard acquired Irish Distillers in 1988, appointed Finance Director, Irish Distillers, 1991; Joined BWG Foods, Managing Director, 1996: BWG Foods owns the SPAR franchise in the Republic of Ireland and operates 30 Value Centre Cash & Carry units; Appointed Chief Executive of BWG Ltd.,1999, responsible for all operating subsidiaries of BWG Ltd. in Ireland and the UK. BWG Ltd. has a turnover of 1.2 billion Euros and continues to seek acquisition opportunities in the wholesale and distribution sector. Fellow, Chartered Institute of Management Accountants. Hobbies, tennis, golf, football. Contact: BWG Foods Ltd., Greenhills Road, Dublin 12. Tel: 01 460 2153. Fax: 01 450 3660.

CREAN, Patrick Joseph; GROUP CHIEF EXECUTIVE MOORE PARAGON GROUP; *b* 1963; *educ* Patrician College; CIMA; *married*; 1*s* 2*da*; Member of Management Group, Clondalkin Group plc, 1980-91; Group Operations Director, Adare Printing Group plc, 1992-98; Group Chief Executive, Moore Paragon / Grenadier Holdings, 1998 to date. Hobby, walking. Contact: Moore Paragon SA, 144 Avenue Roger Salengro, 92370 Chaville, France. Tel: 33(10) 141 15 30 28. Fax: 33 (10) 141 15 32 55.

CRIMMINS, James "Séamus"; HEAD OF LYRIC FM; *b* 1953; *educ* Abbey Grammar School, Newry; Queen's University Belfast, BMus.; University of London Institute of Education, MTC;

Head of Music, Abbey Grammar School, Newry, 1977-80; P.A. RTE Television, 1981-84; Producer RTE Radio 1 and FM3, 1984-89; Commissioning Editor, FM3, 1989-98; Present Head, Lyric, FM, 1998 to date; former Board Member of Association of Irish Choirs and Opera Theatre Company; currently on Board of Directors of the National Chamber Choir and West Cork Chamber Music Festival; awards, Arts Council NI Bursary Award for Conducting Classes; also resuscitated Newry Choral Union, 1977; founded Dun Laoghaire Choral Society, 1981; conducted the Irish Chamber Orchestra, RTECO, Orchestra of St Cecilia, London Baroque, Sinfonia, Northern Chamber Orchestra, (UK) and OTC productions in London, New York, Melbourne, Lisbon, Prague, Salisbury and Dublin. Hobbies, hill walking, cooking. Contact: R.T.E., Donnybrook, Dublin. Tel: 01 208 3111. Fax: 01 208 3080.

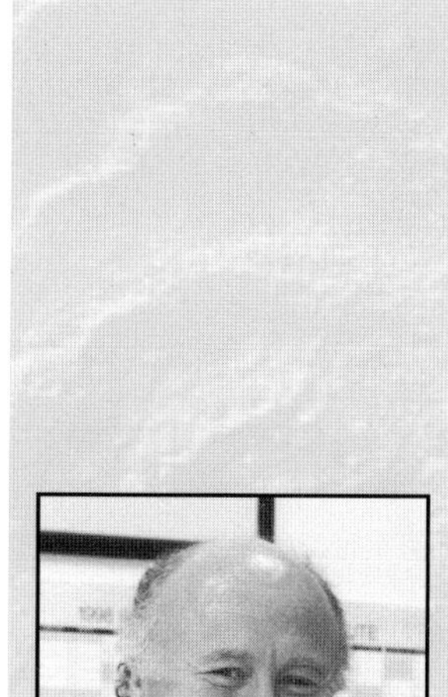

CROSBIE, Alan

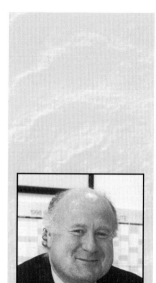

CROSBIE, Alan; CHIEF EXECUTIVE EXAMINER PUBLICATIONS; *b* 1954; *educ* Clongowes Wood College, Naas, Co. Kildare; Harvard Business School, OPM Programme; *m* Mary MacSweeney; 4 *s* 1 *da;* Advertising Sales, Courier Mail, Brisbane, Australia, 1980; Commercial Director, Examiner Publications (Cork) Ltd., 1981-93, Chief Executive, 1993 to date; President of European Newspaper Publishers, 1996-98. Chief executive of thriving family controlled newspaper; a noted sportsman, Irish National Dragon Champion, 1992. Hobbies, family & yacht racing. Contact: Examiner Publications (Cork) Ltd., PO Box 21, Academy Street, Cork. Tel: 021 272722. Fax: 021 275477.

CROSBIE, Henry "Harry"; PROPERTY OWNER; *b* 1946; *educ* Rockwell College, Co. Tipperary; Mount Sackville, Dublin; *m* Elizabeth Bethel (decd.); 1 *s*; 2 *da*; *m* Rita Fox; worked in family haulage business, Henry A. Crosbie; formed own tanker haulage company, Managing Director, Henry Crosbie Tankers; moved into the entertainment business with the purchase of The Point Depot (largest entertainment venue in the country with seating for 10,000); Opened Vicar Street, a radically new entertainment venue, 1998; Chairman, Spencer Dock Development Ltd., (an exciting new concept of an inner town within the city, a mixed new development designed by internationally renowned architect, Kevin Roche); hosted own TV Show, *Start Me Up*, 1996-97; developed Clarence Hotel, Dublin, with Bono and The Edge (from U2), 1997; a tireless entrepreneur, noted as a man of vision. Hobbies, rock music, walking, architecture and Georgian furniture. Contact: The Point Depot, East Link Bridge, North wall Quay, Dublin 1. Tel: 01 836 6777

CROSBIE, Thomas Edward; COMPANY DIRECTOR, EXAMINER PUBLICATIONS LTD; *b* 1931; *educ* Christian Brothers College, Cork; University College Cork, BSc(Chemistry); Post Graduate Studies, Sweden; *m* Gretchen Kelleher, (*decd.*) 3 *s* 3 *da*; member of Cork establishment family; joined family newspaper on leaving college; Maintenance Engineer, *Cork Examiner* 1953-63, Production and Projects Director 1963-80; Production and Projects Director, Harvey Printers 1969-82; Chairman, *Cork Examiner* 1976 and 1979; Chief Executive 1983-93; Executive Chairman 1993-97; Non Executive Chairman 1997 to date; publications include technical papers and lectures; Member, Cork Golf Club, Royal Cork Yacht Club (former Admiral), Cork Scientific & Historical Society; a yachtsman of international repute, Irish Helms Champion 1956; an innovative Press Baron, awarded Hall of Fame Print Awards 1997. Hobbies, sailing (racing and cruising), reading, model engineering and opera. Contact: PO Box 21, Academy Street, Cork. Tel: 021 272 722 Fax: 021 275 477.

CROWE, Paul; DIRECTOR OF GOLF AND DEPUTY CHIEF EXECUTIVE K CLUB; *b* 1964; *educ* St. Patrick's College, Cavan; qualified as ACCA (Certified Accountancy); *m* Caroline Egan; Senior Supervising Consultant at BCO Simpson Xavier, 1987-91; Financial Controller at the K Club, 1991-95, Director of Golf, 1996-97, Director of Golf and Deputy Chief Executive of K Club, 1997 to date; Fellow, Chartered Association of Certified Accountants. Hobbies, golf and horse racing. Contact: The Kildare Hotel and Country Club, Straffan, Co. Kildare. Tel: 01 601 7200. Fax: 01 601 7299.

CROWLEY, Brian; POLITICIAN; *b* 1964; *educ* Hamilton High School; University College Cork; *single;* worked as printer, auctioneer, local radio announcer, rock band singer; son of former Fianna Fail T.D. Flor Crowley; Taoiseach's nominee to the Senate 1993; elected to the European Parliament for Munster 1994, receiving the highest personal vote in the country; due to an accident in 1980 is paralysed from the hips down and confined to a wheelchair; member, Legal Affairs Committee, Rules and Procedures Committee and Social Affairs Committee; member, Council of State; was the subject of a recent biography *Against the Odds* (Bandon Books); a very bright and popular politician with a conservative outlook. Contact: 39 Sundays Well Road, Cork. Tel.: 021 394 598. Fax: 021 395 831.

CROWLEY, Frances Majella; HORSE TRAINER; *b* 1973; *educ* St. Brigid's College, Callan; University College Dublin, BComm. (Hons), Veterinary College, Post. Grad. Equine Sci; *single;* joined family training establishment; amateur champion rider, 1996, '97,'99; obtained Trainers Licence 1998; has trained over 50 winners including Grade I winner *Premalee*, listed and group placed *Golden Rule, Moscow Express* (8 races). Hobbies, sleeping and eating out. Contact: Eight Hills Stables, Owning, Piltown, Co. Kilkenny. Tel: 051 643 796.

CROWLEY, Patricia, "Pat" née Vernon; FASHION DESIGNER; b 1933; *educ* in various convents including the Faithful Companions of Jesus, Newtownbay, Bunclody; The Brendan Smith Academy of Acting; The Grafton Academy of Dress Designing; *m* Conor Crowley, businessman; 1 *s* 2 *da*; Aer Lingus Hostess, 1955-57; aide to dress designer Irene Gilbert, 1958-66; formed own couture fashion house, "Pat Crowley", in 1974; winner of Satzenbrau Award for leading Irish Designer, 1990. Her designs are worn by notable Irish women and American socialites; enjoys a prominent social and professional status on both sides of the Atlantic; a keen horsewoman, other hobbies include skiing, art and theatre. Contact: Pat Crowley, 3 Molesworth Place, Dublin 2. Tel: 01 661 5580. Fax: 01 661 2476.

CRUESS-CALLAGHAN, Frank; COMPANY DIRECTOR; *b* 1934; *educ* Glenstal Abbey; *m*; 1*s* 5 *da;* Articled Clerk, Craig Gardner & Company, 1951-57; Audit Clerk, Peat Marwick Mitchell (London) 1957-60; Consultant, Inbucon, 1960-72; Managing Director, Cruess-Callaghan & Associates, 1972-80; Managing Director, Pierse Engineering Ltd., 1980-83; Managing Director, Waterford Foundry Ltd (now Waterford Stanley Ltd.), 1983 to date; Fellow, Institute of Chartered Accountants in Ireland. An astute businessman; took over ailing Waterford Foundry and turned it around through innovative managerial and marketing strategies. Hobbies, golf, poker and horse racing. Clubs, St. Stephen's Green Club, Fitzwilliam LTC and Connemara Golf Club. Contact: Waterford Stanley Ltd., Bilberry, Waterford. Tel: 051 302 300.

CULLEN, Gary; CHIEF EXECUTIVE AER LINGUS; *b* 1945; *educ* Presentation College, Bray; University College Dublin, BComm; Trinity College Dublin MSc; *married;* 4 *children*; joined Aer Lingus over thirty years ago, Director of Operations, 1994-96, General Manager, Cargo, Project Manager (establishing Aer Lingus commuter services on British and Irish Routes); seconded as Commercial Manager with LIAT Airlines, Antigua, West Indies, 1984-87; Chief Operations Officer, Aer Lingus; Chief Executive, Aer Lingus, 1998 to date. Contact: Aer Lingus, Head Office, Dublin Airport. Tel: 01 705 2222.

CRYAN, Mary; HI-TECH BUSINESS ADVISOR; *b* 1957; *educ* St. Anne's, Milltown, Dublin; Presentation College, Carrick-on-Suir, Co. Tipperary; University College Dublin, BComm; *m* Jim Toomey; 1s 1da; Ollivetti Programmer, Bryan S. Ryan; Sales Executive, Wordplex; Software Advisor, Irish Trade Board, 1982-85; formed Cryan Consulting, 1985 to date; Cryan Consulting are the only specialist information technology strategic marketing, consultancy company in Ireland; author, *A Guide to Selling Software in the U.S.*; member, (former Chairperson) of the Irish Software Association. Clubs, member, Blackrock Tennis Club, Glen of the Downs Golf Club. Hobbies, sports and politics. Contact: Cryan Consulting, 40 Sydney Avenue, Blackrock, Co. Dublin. Tel. / Fax. 01 288 4897.

CULLEN, William, 'Bill"; CHAIRMAN RENAULT IRELAND; *b* 1942; *educ* St. Canice's School, Dublin; O'Connells Christian Brothers School, Dublin; *m* Rita Campbell (separated); 2 *da;* joined Walden Motor Company as messenger boy 1956; General Manager 1964-73; Managing Director, Fairlane Motor Company (Ford Dealership) 1974-86; acquired Smith Group from Waterford Glass, Chairman and Chief Executive, Renault Distributors 1986 to date; Chairman, Irish Youth Foundation. Steady rise through the ranks of the motor trade attributable to remarkable entrepreneurial flair and a thorough knowledge of all aspects of the trade. Hobbies, golf, tennis and squash. Contact: Renault, Kylemore Road, Dublin 10. Tel: 01 605 5000. Fax: 01 626 4978.

CUNNINGHAM, Liam; ACTOR; *b* 1961; *educ* St. Laurence O'Toole School; St. David's School, Artane; Institute of Technology, Kevin Street; *m* Colette Geraghty; 1*s* 1*da*; trained as an electrician; worked with the E.S.B. 1978-89; moved for three years to Zimbabwe to work on rural electrification; gave up the day job to join the Oscar School of Acting; professional debut in Wet Paint's production of *Lament for Arthur Cleary*; other theatre credits include, *A Streetcar Named Desire*, (Gate), As You Like It (RSC), The Herbal Bed (RSC), Poor Beast in the Rain (Bush Theatre), Away *Alone* (Peacock), *Studs* (SFX / Gaiety), *Goodnight Siobhan* (Royal Court Theatre); film credits include, *Into the West, War of the Buttons, The Little Princess, First Knight, Sweety Barrett*; television work include, *Cracker*, (nominated Best Actor RTS North West Awards), *Falling for a Dancer*. Hobby, motor racing. Contact: William Morris Agency (U.K.), Ltd., 1 Stratton Street, London W1X 6HB. Tel: 0044 171 355 8500.

CURRAN, Edmund

CURRAN, Edmund; EDITOR; *b* 1944; *educ* Royal School, Dungannon, Queen's University, Belfast (B.Sc. Dip. Ed); *m* Romaine Carmichael, (*m dis*) 2 *s* 2 *da; m* Pauline Beckett; Reporter, features writer, leader writer, *Belfast Telegraph*, 1966-74; Deputy editor, *Belfast Telegraph*, 1974-88; Editor, *Sunday Life* 1988-93; Editor, *Belfast Telegraph* 1993 to date; Member, Guild of Editors

Parliamentary & Legal Committee, Board member, Co-operation Ireland; Advisory board member, Salvation Army; Awarded UK Regional Editor of the Year, 1992. Hobbies, politics and sport. Clubs, Royal County Down and Belvoir Park Golf Club, Belfort Boat Club. Contact: Belfast Telegraph, 124-144 Royal Avenue, Belfast BT1 1EB, Northern Ireland. Tel: 08 01232 264000.

CURRAN, Maurice R.; SOLICITOR, NOTARY PUBLIC; *b* 1938; *educ* Blackrock College; University College, Dublin, BCL, LLB.; Law Society of Ireland, Solicitor, Silver Medalist, Overend Scholar, Findlater Scholar; *m* Noelle Anne Curran; 4 *da*; Assistant Solicitor, Walker Son & Mason, 1961-64; Partner, Walker, Mason & Curran, 1964; currently Senior Partner, Mason Hayes & Curran; President, Incorporated Law Society of Ireland, 1988-89; FIARB and International Arbitrator; Director of a number of private companies; Chairman of Solicitors Mutual Defence Fund Ltd. Clubs: Stephen's Green Club (former Chairman), Fitzwilliam LTC, Foxrock Golf Club. Contact: Walker Mason & Curran, 7, Fitzwilliam Square, Dublin 2. Tel: 01 661 1788.

DARDIS, John

DARDIS, John; SENATOR, JOURNALIST, FARMER; *b* 1945; *educ* Newbridge College, University College Dublin, B.Agr.Sc; *m* Beatrice Lane; 1 *s* 2 *da*; Advisor, Kildare County Committee of Agriculture, 1967-68; Tillage Editor, *Irish Farmers Journal*, 1968-89; Unsuccessful Progressive Democrat MEP Candidate, 1989 and 1995; Nominated to Seanad Eireann, 1989; Re-elected 1992, nominated 1997; Deputy Leader, Seanad Eireann, 1997 to date; P.D. Party Chairman, 1993-97; Party Spokesperson on Finance, 1997 to date; Member of Kildare County Council, and of Mid-East Regional Authority, 1991 to date; Member, All Party Oireachtas Committee on the Constitution; Life Member, Association of Referees, LB, IRFU; Past President, Old Kilcullen RFC; Chairman, North Kildare Anglers Association; Member, Guild of Agricultural Journalists; Member, R.D.S.; Awarded, Gold Medals for Debate, University College Dublin, 1965 and 1967; Ceres Gold Medal, University College Dublin, 1964; Agricultural Journalist of the Year, 1978; Best Dressed Politician, 1996; Highly regarded in farming and political circles; narrowly missed a Dáil seat in the 1998 elections, despite having the highest 1st count vote; Hobbies, angling, rugby, good food and good company, agriculture. Contact: Seanad Eireann, Leinster House, Kildare Street, Dublin 2. Tel: 01 618 3000.

DAWSON, Barbara; DIRECTOR HUGH LANE MUNICIPAL GALLERY OF MODERN ART; *b* 1957; *educ* Brigidine Convent, Tullow, Co. Carlow; University College Dublin, BA; Trinity College Dublin, HDipEd; *m* Paul McGowan; 1*s* 1 *da;* Research Assistant, later Administrator, National Gallery of Ireland; Exhibitions Officer, Hugh Lane Municipal Gallery of Modern Art, 1988, Director, 1991 to date; publications include: *Turner in the National Gallery of Ireland* and *Images & Insights Hugh Lane and the Origins of the Collection*, 1993; has also contributed papers and articles for art reviews and magazines; an active, energetic and attractive administrator, destined to make her mark in the Irish art world. Hobbies, horse riding, skiing and theatre. Contact: Hugh Lane Municipal Gallery of Modern Art, Charlemont House, Parnell Square, Dublin 1. Tel: 01 874 1903. Fax: 01 872 2182.

De BRUIN, Michelle, née Smith; ATHLETE; *b* 1969; *educ* Coláiste Chilliain, Clondalkin; University of Houston, Texas, USA; *m* Erik de Bruin; winner of two Gold and one Silver Medal - European Championships, Vienna, Austria, 1995; three Gold Medals and one Bronze - Olympic Games - Atlanta, USA, (400 Ind. medley; 400 Freestyle; 200 Ind Medley; Bronze, 200 Butterfly), 1996; two Gold Medals, and two Silver Medals, European Championships, Seville, Spain, 1997; broke European Record for 200 Butterfly, 1997; one of Ireland's most successful international athletes, banned from competitive swimming for four years by FINA 1999; Patron, Irish Guide Dogs for the Blind; Patron, Voice, Honorary Life Member, Mount Juliet Golf and Country Club. Hobbies, current affairs, journalism, history, gardening & DIY. Contact: John Givens, Media Sport & Leisure, 17 Gilford Road, Sandymount, Dublin 4. Tel: 01 260 2000.

De ROSSA, Prionsias; POLITICIAN; *b* 1940; *educ* Marlborough Street National School; College of Technology, Kevin Street; *m* Monica Kelly; 2*s* 1 *da;* while completing a Radio Officers course at Kevin Street Technology College, was arrested, 1956, and interned in the Curragh until 1959; worked in family wholesale potato business, Patrick Ross & Sons Ltd.; unsuccessful Dáil candidate, 1977 and 1981; elected Workers Party Deputy for Dublin North West, February, 1982, November, 1982, 1987 and 1989 (topped the polls); elected to Dublin City Council, 1984; elected President of the Workers Party, 1988; elected MEP, 1989; formed new party with five other Workers Party Deputies, became Leader of Democratic Left; spokesperson for Democratic Left on Department of Taoiseach, Foreign Affairs, Social Welfare, Defence, Marine and Arts, Culture and the Gaeltacht, 1993; Minister for Social Affairs (Rainbow Coalition), 1995-97; Democratic Left merged with Labour Party, 1999, President of Labour Party, 1999 to date; MEP 1999 to date; regarded as a thoughtful, professional politician and above all a survivor. Contact: Dáil Eireann, Leinster House, Kildare Street, Dublin 2. Tel: 01 618 3333.

de VERE WHITE, John F.

de VERE WHITE, John Frederick; AUCTIONEER; *b* 1949; *educ* St. Gerard's School, Bray; Glenstal Abbey, Limerick; *m* Miriam Kenny; 2*s* 2 *da;* worked with James Adam & Sons, circa 1970; established Fitzgerald & Partners with Alexis FitzGerald and Denis Bergin, c. 1973; established de Vere White & Smyth with Barry Smyth, c. 1982 to date; set up de Veres Art Auctions with Barry Smyth, 1988; member, MIAVI, Milltown Golf Club, Donnybrook Tennis Club, Dooks Golf Club, Kerry. Hobbies, art, wine, food and sport. Contact: 35 Kildare Street, Dublin 2. Tel: 01 676 8300. Fax: 01 678 8305.

DEANE, Seamus; ACADEMIC; *b* 1940; *educ* St. Columb's College, Derry; Queens University, Belfast, BA, MA; Cambridge University, PhD; *m* Marion Treacy, Teacher; 3 *s* 1 *da*; Visiting Fulbright Lecturer, Reed College, Oregon, U.S.A. 1966-67; Visiting Fulbright Lecturer, University of California, Berkeley 1967-68; Lecturer, University College Dublin 1968-77; Visiting Professor, Indiana, 1977-78; Professor of English, University College Dublin 1980 to 1993; Keough Professor of Irish Studies, University of Notre Dame, Indiana, 1993 to date; Visiting Professorships, Washington, Minnesota 1987, 1988, 1989; recipient of AE Award for Literature 1973, Ireland/America Award for Literature 1988, Guardian Fiction Prize 1997, *Irish Times* Irish Fiction Award 1998, *Irish Times* International Fiction Award 1998; Recent publications include: *The Field Day Anthology of Irish Writing* - three volumes (1991) (Ed.); *Reading in the Dark* (1996); *Strange Country* (Clarendon Lectures, Oxford), (1997); member, Royal Irish Academy; member, Aosdana; Director, Field Day Company. A highly respected scholar, poet, novelist and critic. Contact: Aosdana, 70 Merrion Square, Dublin 2. Tel: 01 661 1840. Fax: 01 676 1302.

DeBURGH, né DAVISON, Chris John; SINGER SONGWRITER; *b* 1948 *educ* Marlborough (UK); Trinity College Dublin, MA; *m* Diane Morley; 2 *s* 1 *da;* debut album, *Far Beyond These Castle Walls*, released 1975; has released twelve other albums; *Into the Light*, Number 1 in UK and US; single from that album, *Lady in Red*, achieved Number 1 status, US and UK; *Flying Colours* album also number 1, US and UK; has toured extensively worldwide; recipient of over eighty Gold, Silver and Platinum Discs, Berliner Award (Germany), Bambi Award (Germany), Midem International Trophy (France), ASCAP Award (America), IRMA Award (Ireland), 1985-90; Involved in various charitable fund raising events. Hobbies, swimming, scuba diving, golf, fine wine and antique furniture. Contact: Kenny Thomson Management Ltd. UK, 754 Fulham Road, London SW6 FS1T. Tel: 0044 171 731 7074. Fax: 0044 171 736 8605.

DEMPSEY, Gerald, Patrick; COMPANY DIRECTOR,CONSULTANT; *b* 1928; *educ* Glenstal Abbey, University College Dublin, BA Econ; Fellow, Institute of Chartered Accountants in Ireland; *m* Patricia McNally; 2 *s* 2 *da*; Joined Aer Lingus, 1954 to date; Assistant Chief Executive, Finance, 1968-74; Chief Executive, Ancillary Activities, 1974-86; Director, Waterford Wedgwood plc, 1986 to date; Director, Waterford Crystal, 1986 to date; Chairman, Design & Project Management Ltd., 1993 to date; Chairman, UNM Financial Services Ireland, 1995 to date; former President, Institute of Chartered Accountants in Ireland, American Chamber of Commerce in Ireland; former Vice Chairman, International Funds for Ireland, Fellow of the Irish Management Institute. Contact: 46 Upper Mount Street, Dublin 2. Tel: 01 676 2475. Fax: 01 676 2489

DEMPSEY, Matt; FARMER, CHIEF EXECUTIVE IRISH FARMERS JOURNAL; *b* 1948; *educ* Celbridge National School; Clongowes Wood College; University College Dublin, BAgrSc; *m* Mary O'Reilly; 3*s* 6*da;* Producer, Agricultural Programmes, RTE Radio 1969-73; Radio Presenter and EC Correspondent for *Irish Farmers Journal* 1973-78; Post-graduate Work (UCD) with EC Commission, 1978-79; EC Correspondent, *Irish Farmers Journal*, 1979-85; Chairman, ACOT - Agricultural Institute, 1985-88; Editor, *Irish Farmers Journal*, 1988 to date, Chief Executive, 1995 to date; member, Board of Management, RDS; member, Grasslands Association. Hobbies, tennis, swimming and horse riding. Contact: Irish Farmers Journal, Irish Farm Centre, Bluebell, Dublin 12 . Tel: 01 450 1166. Fax: 01 452 0876.

DEMPSEY, Noel

DEMPSEY, Noel; POLITICIAN; *b* 1953; *educ* St. Michaels CBS, Trim; University College Dublin; St. Patricks College, Maynooth (BA, HDipEd.); Diploma in Career Guidance, Diploma in Youth Leadership; *m* Bernadette Rattigan; 2*s* 2 *da*: worked as a career guidance counsellor; member Trim Urban District Council; elected to Meath County Council 1977-92 (Chairman 1986-87); former director, Dublin Eastern Regional Tourism Organisation; elected Fianna Fail Deputy for Meath 1987; Government Chief Whip 1992-94; Front Bench Spokesman on the Environment 1994-97; Minister of the Environment and Local Government 1997 to date. Contact: Department of the Environment and Local Government, Custom House, Dublin 1. Tel.: 01 679 3377. Fax: 01 874 2710.

DENHAM, The Hon. Mrs. Justice Susan, née Gageby; JUDGE OF THE SUPREME COURT; *b* 1945; *educ* Alexandra College, Dublin; Trinity College Dublin; Columbia University, New York; *m* Brian Denham, Paediatrician; 3 *s* 1 *da*; called to the Bar, 1973, member of Midland Circuit; called

to the Inner Bar 1987; Judge of the High Court, 1991-92; Judge of the Supreme Court 1996 to date; Pro-Chancellor, Dublin University, 1996 to date. Regarded as an expert on judicial reviews and extradition, acting for the State in various cases; former Vice-Chairman, Adoption Board. Hobbies, gardening and horses. Contact: Four Courts, Morgan Place, Dublin 7. Tel: 01 872 5555.

DENNEHY, John Joseph

DENNEHY, John Joseph; SECRETARY GENERAL, DEPARTMENT OF EDUCATION AND SCIENCE; *b* 1947; *educ* St. Michael's College, Listowel, Co. Kerry, St. Patrick's College of Education, Drumcondra, University College Dublin, Trinity College Dublin, Harvard University; *m* Deirdre____ 1 s (decd.); Primary Teacher, 1966-72; Principal Teacher, 1972-78; Schools Inspector, 1978-89; Assistant Chief Inspector, 1989-94; Assistant Secretary, Department of Education, 1994-98; Secretary General, 1998 to date; Chairman, National Youth Orchestra of Ireland; Author of a range of books and teaching manuals on the Arts; Commissioned Officer, F.C.A. Hobbies, art, music, DIY. Contact: Office of the Secretary General, Department of Education and Science, Marlborough Street, Dublin 1. Tel: 01 873 4700. Fax: 01 874 47013.

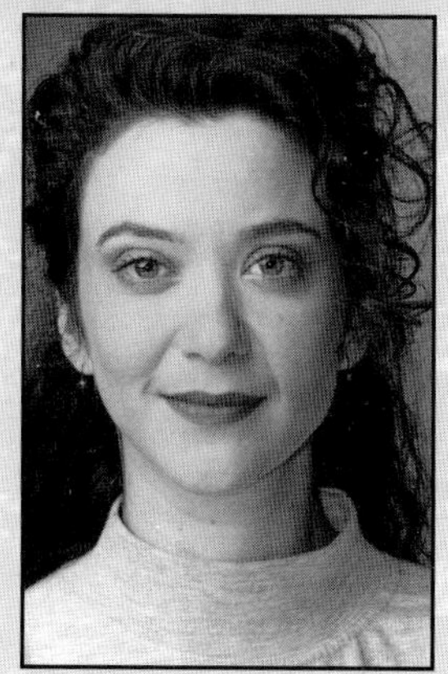
DENT, Donna

DENT, Donna; ACTRESS; *b* 1965; *educ* St. Nicholas Tolentine, Bronx, N.Y. City; St. Mary's Holy Faith Convent, Killester, Dublin; *m* Joe Gallagher; stage appearances include, leading roles in *Pride and Prejudice* (Gate) 1995; *A Woman of No Importance* (Abbey) 1996; *The Heiress* (Gate) 1998, *A Streetcar Named Desire* , 1998, *Uncle Vanya* 1998, *Cyrano de Bergerac,* 1998; Film and Television credits include: *Her Own Rules, The Fifth Province, The Bill, Fairy City, The Tree;* awards include: Nominee, Best Actress, 1997 and Winner Best Supporting Actress, 1998, *Irish Times* /ESB Theatre Awards; Actress of the Year, 1998, Ford/*Sunday Independent* Spirit of Life Award; *Sunday Tribune,* Actress of the Year, 1998. Regarded as one of the finest actresses on the Irish stage today. Hobbies, reading, horse riding, film, cards, playing pool and drinking champagne. Contact: The Lisa Richards Agency, 15 Lower Pembroke Street, Dublin 2. Tel: 01 662 4880. Fax: 01 662 4884.

DESMOND, Denis; CONCERT PROMOTER; *b* 1953; *educ* Presentation Brothers, Cork; University College Cork BEng (civil); *m* Caroline Downey; 2*s* 1*da;* after a brief engineering career in Hull moved back to Dublin and formed MCD in the early '80s; the company has grown to become one of the major concert promoters agencies in Europe; promotions include Feile Weekends (Thurles), concerts at the Point (Dublin), U2 at Lansdowne Road (Dublin), and Botanic Gardens (Belfast), *The Verve* concert at Slane Castle (Co. Meath); founded Solid Record Label, no Solid-Grapevine; Co-owner Olympia and Gaiety Theatres, owner SFX Hall; shareholder, TodayFM; recognised as a major force in the Irish entertainment business. Contact: MCD, 7 Park Road, Dun Laoghaire, Co. Dublin. Tel: 01 284 1747.

DESMOND, Dermot

DESMOND, Dermot; FINANCIER; *b* 1950; *educ* Good Counsel College, New Ross; *m* Pat Brett; 3 *s* 1 *da*; joined Citibank (Dublin); worked with the Investment Bank of Ireland, World Bank/United Nations; Consultant with Coopers and Lybrand; established NCB in 1981 and sold to Nat West Group in 1994; Chairman and Founder of IIU (International Investment & Underwriting Limited), established in 1994; Chairman, Baltimore Technologies Limited, Intuition Publishing Limited, Pembroke Capital Limited; Owner, London City Airport; Joint Owner, Sandy Lane Hotel, Barbados; Director, Celtic Football Club, plc; numerous other Directorships; Trustee of Chester Beatty Library; Board Member, UCD Foundation; Chairman of Respect. The man with the Midas Touch; the brains behind the International Financial Services Centre; now major investor in some of the world's most exciting businesses. Hobby, golf. Contact: IIU, IFSC House, Custom House Quay, Dublin 1. Tel: 01 605 4444 Fax: 01 605 4455.

de VALERA, Síle

de VALERA, Síle; POLITICIAN, MINISTER FOR ARTS, HERITAGE, GAELTACHT AND THE ISLANDS; *b* 1954; *educ* Loreto Convent, Foxrock; University College Dublin, BA, HDipEd, Dip Career Guidance, D Psych Sci; *single*, granddaughter of Eamon de Valera, former Taoiseach and President of Ireland; Fianna Fáil Dáil Deputy for Dublin mid County 1977-81; elected Fianna Fáil Dáil Deputy for Clare 1987 to date; Minister for Arts, Heritage, Gaeltacht and the Islands 1997 to date; member, European Parliament 1979-84; resigned Party Whip 1993, on Shannon stop-over issue; member, Oireachtas Joint Committee on Women's Rights 1987-92. Contact: Department of Arts, Heritage, Gaeltacht and the Islands, 43 Mespil Road, Dublin 4. Tel: 01 667 0788.

DILGER, David; CHIEF EXECUTIVE GREENCORE PLC.; *b* 1957; *educ* Clongowes Wood College, Co. Kildare; Trinity College Dublin, BA; Chartered Accountant; *m* Katherine Boylan; 1*s* 3 *da;* joined Stokes Kennedy Crowley, Manager, 1983; left to work with Craig McKinney in Woodchester Investments, 1983-88; Chief Executive, Food Industries plc, now Greencore Group plc, 1988 to date; Board member, I.B.E.C.; regarded as an excellent, if cautious, manager; there are rumours of a possible company merger. Hobbies, golf, rugby and skiing. Contact: Greencore Group plc, St. Stephen's Green House, Earlsfort Terrace, Dublin 2. Tel: 01 605 1000. Fax: 01 605 1100.

DILLON, Anne, née Audiat; SOTHEBY'S REPRESENTATIVE; *b* 1947; *educ* Institut St Dominique à Morte-Fountaine; Paris University; Degree in Public Relations; *m* William Dillon (decd.); *m* John Pierce Carrigan (decd.); 1 *s*; 1 *da*; ran Hibernian Antiques; co-owner with brother in law, Val Dillon of Dillon Antiques; currently representative for Sotheby's (U.K. Fine Art Auction House) in Ireland. A quiet force on the Irish antique scene. Contact: Sotheby's, Furness, Naas, Co. Kildare. Tel: 045 898 066. Fax: 045 898 071.

DILLON, John Myles; REGIUS PROFESSOR OF GREEK TRINITY COLLEGE DUBLIN; *b* 1939; *educ* St. Gerard's School, Bray; Downside School (UK); Oriel College, Oxford, BA, MA; University of California, Berkeley, PhD; *m* Jean Montgomery; 1*da*: Assistant Professor of Classics, University of California, Berkeley, 1969-72, Associate Professor, 1972-77, Professor of Classics and Chairman of University of California, Berkeley, 1977-80; Regius Professor of Greek, Trinity College Dublin, 1980 to date; publications include *The Middle Platonists* London 1977 (2nd ed. 1996), *A Classical Lexicon to James Joyce* (with Brendan O'Hehir), Berkeley, 1977, *Proclus Commentary on Plato's Parmenides* (with Glenn Morrow), Princeton, 1987, *The Golden Chain* (Collected Essays) Aldershot 1991, *The Great Tradition* (more Collected Essays), Aldershot, 1997; member, Royal Irish Academy (Council, 1987-88, 1990-94, 1997 to date); Fellow, Trinity College Dublin, 1982 to date; member, International Society for Neoplatonic Studies, Secretary for Europe, 1985 to date; recipient Gildersleeve Prize of the American Journal of Philology, 1989. Hobbies, tennis, golf, walking and chess. Contact: Trinity College, Dublin. Tel: 01 677 2941.

DILLON, Kevin

DILLON, Kevin; MANAGING DIRECTOR, MICROSOFT EUROPEAN OPERATIONS CENTER; *b* 1954; *educ* School of Law, Golden Gate University, LLM; University of Capetown, LLB, BComm, BA; *m* Jayne ----; 1*s* 1 *da;* Senior Manager, Price Waterhouse, Palo Alto, California, 1986-1989; Senior Manager, Price Waterhouse, London, 1990-91; Director, Finance, Europe, Microsoft, 1991-96; Managing Director, Microsoft European Operations Center, 1997 to date. Hobbies, golf, distance running. Contact: Microsoft EOC, Blackthorn Road, Sandyford Industrial Estate, Dublin 18. Tel: 01 295 3826. Fax: 01 295 3581.

DILLON, Michael; MANAGING DIRECTOR TORC GRAIN AND FEED LTD.; *b* 1951; *educ* St. Kieran's College, Kilkenny; Warrenstown Agricultural College, Co. Meath, Agri Diploma; *m* Joan Maher; 2*s* 4*da;* Commodity Trader, I.A.W.S. Ltd., 1970-78; Trading Manager, James Allen Ireland, Ltd., 1978-81; Managing Director, Torc Grain and Feed Ltd., 1981 to date; member, Luttrellstown Castle Golf and Country Club, Hermitage Golf Club. Hobbies, current affairs, family, Gaelic games and golf. Contact: Torc Grain and Feed Ltd., 47 Ranelagh Road, Dublin 6. Tel: 01 496 1600. Fax: 01 496 1180.

DILLON-LEETCH, John; SOLICITOR; *b* 1951; *educ* Castleknock College, Dublin; University College Dublin, BCL; *m* Elizabeth Spearman; 2*s* 2 *da;* Managing Partner, T. Dillon-Leetch & Sons, Ballyhaunis, Co. Mayo and Henry Comerford & Co. Galway; member, Chamber of Commerce of Ireland, (Hon Sec. 1990); member, Ballyhaunis Chamber of Commerce, (President 1987-88, '91); Life Member, Galway Chamber of Commerce; member, Ballyhaunis Golf Club (President 1998), Galway County Club. Hobbies, golf, tennis, sailing, The Life and Times of Percy French, classical music and opera. Contact: T. Dillon-Leetch and Sons, Ballyhaunis, Co. Mayo. Tel: 0907 30004.

DINEEN, Patrick J.; CHAIRMAN SEDGWICK DINEEN GROUP; *b* 1937; *educ* Presentation College, Cork; Harvard Business School, Boston (1986); *m* Colette Healy; 2 *s* 1 *da*; Formed Sedgwick Dineen Group 1965; currently Chairman, Sedgwick Dineen Group, Irish Pensions Trust Ltd., Bord na Mona, Gulliver InfoRes Services Limited, FEXCO (Foreign Exchange Company of Ireland), The Industrial Development Authority; former Chairman, Bord Gais 1984-89, former Executive Chairman, Irish Steel 1994-96. A notable cricketer, capped twenty five times for Ireland (1962-73). Hobbies, cricket, golf and tennis. Clubs, United Services Club, Killiney Golf Club. Contact: 55, South Mall, Cork. Tel: 021 271 449 Fax: 021 277 674.

DINEEN, Patrick J.

DIVILLY, Dermot Gerard; GROUP MANAGING DIRECTOR ALLEGRO HOLDINGS LTD.; *b* 1947; *educ* St. Nathy's College, Ballaghadereen; University College Dublin, BAgSc, M.B.A.; *m* Mary Campion; 2*s* 1 *da;* Chief Executive, Killeen Investments Ltd., 1983-86; Group Manager Director, CDL, 1986-90; Group Managing Director, Allegro Holdings Ltd., 1990 to date, one of the leading consumer/chemical companies in the State; member, K Club, Killiney Golf Club, Royal St. George Yacht Club. Hobbies, golf, walking, travel, sport and reading. Contact: Allegro Holdings Ltd., Sandyford Industrial Estate, Dublin 18. Tel: 01 206 8000. Fax: 01 206 8050.

DIXON, Padraic Martin; VETERINARY SURGEON; *b* 1950; *educ* CBS Kilkenny, Ballyhaise Agricultural College; University College Dublin, MVB, MRCVS; University of Edinburgh PhD in equine cardio-respiratory studies; *m* Ann Grace; 1*s* 3 *da;* Veterinary Surgeon, currently Reader and Head of Large Animal Surgery Services, Edinburgh University Veterinary School; recognised worldwide as an expert in equine respiratory and dental disorders; has published numerous papers and a book and lectures widely; awarded, *The Equine Veterinary Journal* Richard Hartley Clinical Prize (twice), the Open Award, Animal Health Trust Outstanding Veterinary Achievement Award 1998; partner with brother John in Scotland's largest antique dealers, Georgian Antiques, Edinburgh; partner, with brother David, Dixon Properties, Dublin, industrial property developers. Hobbies, gardening and golf. Contact: Veterinary School, University of Edinburgh. Tel: 00 44 131 650 1000.

DOHERTY, Kenneth; PROFESSIONAL SNOOKER PLAYER; *b* 1969; *educ* Westland Row, CBS, Dublin; *single*; Irish Under 16 Champion 1983-84, Irish Under 19 Champion 1985-86, Irish Amateur Senior Champion 1987-89; World Junior Champion 1989 (Iceland), World Amateur Senior Champion 1989 (Singapore), World Professional Champion 1997 (England), only person to hold all three titles; Guinness Book of Records - holder speed snooker potting six colours yellow to black in 23.4 seconds; winner of ten professional tournaments; recipient, Westland Row Past Pupils Award, Ballygowan Sports Personality Award 1997. Hobbies, soccer (Manchester United), golf, tennis, books, movies. Contact: Cue Masters, Kerse Road, Stirling, SK7 SG, Scotland. Tel: 0044 1786 46 26 34.

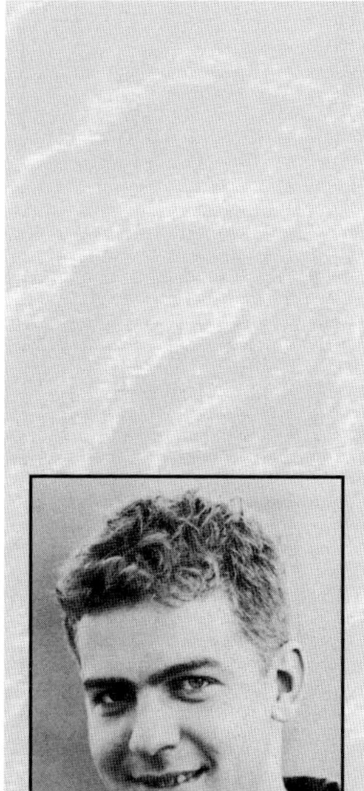
DONNELLAN, Michael

DOHERTY, Patrick; PROPERTY DEVELOPER; *b* 1942; *educ* National School, Buncrana, Co. Donegal; *m* Doreen Rayner; 4 *s* 1 *da;* worked in construction in the UK; is currently Chairman of Harcourt Developments, owner of shopping centres, office blocks and industrial estates in Ireland and the UK; Harcourt Developments is one of the most active developers in the country, it owns the Galway, Donaghmede, Dublin 13, Portlaoise, Letterkenny and Long Walk Shopping Centres as well as the New Park Business Centre off the Naas Road, the latter noted for its landscaping and collection of sculptures; a major fundraiser for Irish charities; gregarious amongst friends but prefers to keep a low profile for the media. Hobbies, racehorses and shooting. Contact: Harcourt House, 18-19 Harcourt Street, Dublin 2.

DONNELLAN, Michael; FOOTBALLER; *b* 1977; *educ* Ballinlass National School, Dunmore, Co. Galway; St. Jarlath's College, Tuam, Co. Galway; Institute of Technology, Tralee, Co. Kerry; *single*; currently working as sales representative; one of the country's leading sportsmen, a GAA star player, also plays soccer and represents Connacht at tennis; recipient, All Ireland Colleges Hogan Cup, 1994; Gigerson Cup, Institute of Technology, Tralee, 1998; Man of the Match, All Ireland Football Final, 1998; GAA Young Player of the Year, 1998; Texaco Football Player of the Year, 1998; Footballer of the Year, Galway Sports Awards; GAA Football All Star; Dunmore MacHales Clubman of the Year, 1998; Represented Connacht (under 14) Tennis, 1990; member, Clontarf Soccer Team, winner Roscommon Junior League, 1996; Member, GAA; Hon. member, Dunmore Demesne Golf Club, Tuam Golf Club. Hobbies, golf , tennis and television. Contact: GAA, 45, Dominic Street, Galway.

DONNELLY, Cornelius James; GROUP EXECUTIVE CHAIRMAN MOORE PARAGON GROUP; *b* 1953; *educ* Blackrock College; Trinity College Dublin, BBS; *married*; 2da; member of Management Group, KPMG Ireland, 1975-83; CEO, Firestone Group / Catoctin International – United States, 1984-90; Managing Partner, Donnelly & Partners (Corporate Finance) Ltd.; Group Executive Chairman, Grenadier Holdings Ltd. / Moore Paragon Group; Institute of Chartered Accountants, Fellow (1989), Associate (1979). Clubs, Fitzwilliam Lawn Tennis Club (former President Breakfast Club). Hobbies, swimming and travel. Contact: Moore Paragon SA, 144 Avenue Roger Salengro, 92370 Chaville, France. Tel: 33 (1) 141 15 30 28. Fax: 33 (1) 141 15 32 55.

DONNELLY, Joseph; BOOKMAKER; *b* 1947; *educ* Christian Brothers School, Cork; Rockwell College, Tipperary; *m* Marie O'Neill; 3*s* 1 *da;* joined family on-course bookmaking business; operates one of the major bookmaking businesses in the country; Director RESAM (private property investment company); Chairperson, Leopardstown Racecourse; member, Irish Horseracing Authority; member, International Council of the Tate Gallery (London); a soft spoken Corkman; a major player in Irish business and horseracing; a noted authority on contemporary art. Contact: 145 Lower Baggot Street, Dublin 2. Tel.: 01 676 2336.

DONNELLY, Marie, née O'Neill; CHAIRMAN IRISH HOSPICE FOUNDATION; *b* 1950; *educ* Presentation Convent, Youghal; *m* Joseph Donnelly; 3*s* 1 *da*; founder member Irish Hospice Foundation 1986; assisted with Hospice national fundraising campaign, Board member 1989, Chairman 1997 to date; an indefatigable fundraiser for the Hospice Foundation, launched *The Whoseday Book* 1999, national and international sales targeted at £2 million; Board member, Douglas Hyde Gallery, Chester Beatty Gallery; member, International Council of the Tate Gallery, London; a fashion conscious and innovative personality on the Irish social, artistic and community scene. Hobbies, reading, walking and art. Contact: Hospice Foundation, 9 Fitzwilliam Place, Dublin 2. Tel.: 01 676 5599.

DONNELLY, Patrick James; KILKENNY COUNTY AND CITY MANAGER; *b* 1938; *educ* St. Joseph's Christian Brothers Secondary School, Drogheda; Trinity College Dublin; Civil Service Training Centre and Institute of Public Administration; *m* Maura McAvinia; 2 *s* 1 *da*; Clerical Officer, Department of Finance, 1956; Executive Officer, Department of Local Government, 1959; Assistant Private Secretary to the Minister, 1960; Private Secretary to the Permanent Secretary of the Department of Local Government, 1964; Higher Executive Officer, 1965; Private Secretary to Minister, Department of Local Government 1967; Assistant Principal Officer, Department of Local Government, 1969; County Secretary, Meath County Council, 1973; Temporary Meath County Manager, 1974; County Manager, Kilkenny County Council, 1976 to date; Chairman, South Eastern Regional Water Laboratory, 1979 to date, Kilkenny Civic Trust 1988 to date, Kilkenny County Enterprise Board, 1993 to date; Vice Chairman of the Board of the Institute of Public Administration; Member, Board of National University of Ireland, Maynooth Kilkenny Outreach Campus, 1997 to date; Award from Quality Association of Ireland (South Eastern Branch) for work in relation to Conservation and Preservation in Kilkenny City, 1989, Honorary Degree of Master of Applied Science, University College, Dublin, Special Award as longest serving manager in Centenary Year of County Local Government, 1998. Trustee, Kilkenny Archaeological Society. Hobbies, gardening, reading and swimming. Conatct: Kilkenny County Council, John Street, Kilkenny. Tel: 056 52699. Fax: 056 63384.

DONNELLY, Patrick James

DONOGHUE, Bill

DONOGHUE, Bill; MANAGING DIRECTOR OF TRINITY COMMERCE; *b* 1965; *educ* St. Davids School, Artane; Irish Management Institute, BA; *single;* joined Quinnsworth, now Tesco Group, 1982; opened the Merrion Centre 1986, Manager, Quinnsworth largest branch in Artane 1990, Head of Technology Division; Managing Director, Trinity Technology, 1998-99; Managing Director, Trinity Commerce 1999; Telecom Eireann recently acquired a 51% stake in the company for £10 million; Trinity Commerce can supply Telecom with expertise on e-commerce and Internet integrated services. Contact: Trinity Group, Unit 4. Bracken Road, Sandyford Industrial Estate, Dublin 18. Tel: 01 206 1500

DONOGHUE, Denis; WRITER, CRITIC, ACADEMIC; *b* 1928; *educ* Christian Brothers School, Newry; University College Dublin, BA, MA, PhD; Cambridge University MA (ex officio); *m* Frances Ruttledge; 3*s* 5 *da;* Administrative Officer, Department of Finance; Assistant Lecturer in English, University College Dublin, College Lecturer, Professor of Modern English and American Literature; University Lecturer in English, Cambridge University, and Fellow of King's College, Cambridge; Henry James Professor of English and American Letters at New York University, University Professor; has taught semesters at several universities, including Princeton, UCLA; taught Harvard Summer School, Edinburgh Summer School; lecturerships in prestigious international universities; First Director of the Yeats International Summer School, Sligo; Fellow, Royal Society of Literature (London), ACLS Fellowship (University of Pennsylvania), National Humanities Center, Woodrow Wilson Center for International Scholars, Washington DC, Fellow of the American Academy of Arts and Sciences; awarded Hon Litt D (National University of Ireland) and Royal Irish Academy of Music; publications include, *The Third Voice : Modern British and American Verse Drama* (1959), *Jonathan Swift: A Critical Introduction* (1969), *Emily Dickinson* (1969), *Yeats* (1971), *Thieves of Fire* (1974), Editor, *Seven American Poets* (1975), *The Sovereign Ghost: Studies in Imagination* (1976), *The Arts without Mystery* (1983), *We Irish* (1986), Editor, *Selected Essays of R.P. Blackmur* (1986), *Reading America: Essays on American Literature* (1987), *Warrenpoint* (1990), *Being Modern Together* (1991), *The Pure Good of Theory* (1992), *The Old Moderns: Essays on Literature and Theory* (1994), *Walter Pater: Lover of Strange Souls* (1995), *The Practice of Reading* (Yale, 1998) (winner of the Robert Penn Warren-Cleanth Brooks Prize in Literary Criticism, 1998); *My T.S. Eliot,* and *Teaching Literature;* also essays and reviews; possibly the only modern Irish literary critic of international stature. Contact: New York University.

DOOLAN, Matthew; TEXTILE COMPANY MANAGING DIRECTOR; *b* 1936; *educ* St. Mary's College, Rathmines; Scottish College of Textiles, L.T.I., A.T.I; Trinity College Dublin; post graduate course, Org. Behaviour; *m* Patricia O'Kane; 2 *s* 3 *da;* pre and post textile education worked in design and management with Morrogh Bros. Cork, 1953-60; Designer/Manager of Handwoven Fabric Division, Magee & Co., Donegal, 1960-63; joined Irish Tapestry Company, Drogheda, 1963-81; established own company, Porterhouse Ltd., taking over Irish Tapestry Company, 1989; involved in the direction and design of serious design-led products for specific market sectors; Porterhouse Ltd. lead the export field in shop-at-home TV sales, the largest manufacturer in this area; member, Co. Louth Golf Club, Baltray (Captain, 1981), Seapoint Golf Club (President, 1996-7), Hibernian United Services Club. Hobbies, family, music, golf and walking. Contact: Porterhouse Ltd., Flax Mill Lane, New Field, Drogheda, Co. Louth. Tel: 041 37661.

DOORLEY, Thomas

DOOLEY, Patrick 'Pat'; CHAIRMAN DAN DOOLEY LTD.; *b* 1954; *educ* St. Munchen's College, Limerick; CBS Hospital, Co. Limerick; m Theresa Morrissey; 1*s* 2*da*; worked for a time as a barman in the Killiney Court Hotel and Kielys in Donnybrook, Dublin; returned to Limerick and joined motor company established by his father, Dan Dooley Ltd., currently Chairman of one of the largest motor companies in the South West, main Ford Dealers, car rental, car leasing and sale; former member, OTMI; member, ERDF 1994 to date; member, Killarney Golf Club. Contact: Dan Dooley Ltd., Knocklong, Co. Limerick. Tel: 062 53103.

DOORLEY, Thomas Christopher FitzGerald "Tom"; WINE AND FOOD CRITIC; *b* 1959; *educ* Belvedere College Dublin; Trinity College Dublin, BA Mod, H.Dip. Ed.; *m* Johann McKeever; 3*da*; Assistant Master and House Tutor, St. Columbas College, Rathfarnham, 1981-85; Features Writer, *Irish Independent*, 1985-89; Copy Writer, O'Connor O'Sullivan Advertising, 1989-91; Wine and Food Critic, *Sunday Tribune*, 1991 to date; publications include regular contributions to *The Field, Decanter, Checkout* and *Tom Doorley Uncorked* (On Stream 1996), *Best of Wine in Ireland* (A.A. Farmer 1998); television credits include, co-presenter, *Movable Feast*, RTE, 1996-98; presenter, *The Big Stew*, RTE, 1999; a witty and erudite writer and performer on food and wine; member, Kildare Street and University Club, Old Columbian Society. Hobbies, reading, gardening, (at 13, youngest ever member, of Royal Horticultural Society of Ireland). Contact: Sunday Tribune, 15 Lower Baggot Street, Dublin 2. Tel: 01 661 5555.

DORGAN, Sean; CHIEF EXECUTIVE, IDA; *b* 1951; *educ* St. Brendan's, Killarney; University College Dublin, B.Comm, MEconSc; *m* Mary Lennan; 4 *s*; joined the Civil Service, served in the Department of Post and Telegraphs, 1972-84; Assistant Secretary, Department of Industry and Commerce 1984-91; played a crucial role in shaping and implementing the Culliton Report, 1991; Secretary General, Department of Industry and Commerce, 1991-93; Secretary General, Department of Tourism and Trade, 1993-95; Chief Executive, Institute of Chartered Accountants in Ireland, 1995-98; Chief Executive of the IDA, January 1999 to date; the IDA is engaged in the promotion of Foreign Direct Investment into Ireland; Member, Board of Forfás. Contact: IDA Ireland, Wilton Park House, Wilton Place, Dublin 2. Tel: 01 603 4000. Fax: 01 603 4040.

DOUGLAS, Barry; CONCERT PIANIST; *b* 1960; *educ* Methody; Royal College of Music; a concert performer worldwide; recordings with BMG/RCA include: Tchaikovsky Concerto 1, Brahms Concerto 1, Liszt Concertos, Mussorgsky *Pictures at an Exhibition*, Beethoven *Hammerklavier* Sonata; appeared in *Madame Sousatzka* - starring Shirley McLaine; awards include 1986 Gold Medal at Tschaikovsky International Piano Competition, 1986 Hon. D. Music, Queens University, Belfast, RCM Dip. (Performance), ARCM, LRAM; worked with Berlin Philharmonic, Leipzig Gewandhaus, orchestras of Philadelphia, Chicago, and Los Angeles in the United States; the NHK and Tokyo Symphonies in Japan, the Israel Philharmonic and all the major London orchestras; the DSO Berlin, the Bayerischer Rundfunk, the Maggio Musicale in Florence, the Helsinki and Stockholm Philharmonics, the Orchestre Philarmonique de Radio France, the London Symphony Orchestra, the Cincinnati and Toronto Symphony Orchestras, San Franisco Symphony Orchestra, Frankfurt RSO, RAI Turin and Dresden Staatskapelle; one of the most succesful of today's pianists; an artist of talent and presence. Hobbies, driving, food, wine and reading. Contact: IMG Artists, Media House, 3 Burlington Lane, London, W4 2TH. Tel: 0044 181 233 5800. Fax: 0044 181 233 5801.

DOUGLAS, Julian Mark; BUSINESSMAN; *b* 1963; *educ* St. Gerards School, Bray, Co Wicklow; *single;* founder of Ireland's first Pizza Delivery Service - Pizza Pie Express, 1981-82; General Manager of Audio Engineering - the design of recording studios & professional recording equipment sales, clients include Rod Stewart, U2, Daniel Landis, Trevor Horn, 1985-94; founder of Big Bear Sound - recording studio design & professional recording equipment sales, current clients include Spice Girls, Riverdance etc.. 1995 to present; co-founder of Fusio Multimedia, co-founder of *Entertainment Ireland* - the first Irish based entertainment listings website, 1996 to present; Hobbies, golf, technology and music. Contact: Big Bear Sound, 20 Ringsend Road. Tel: 01 660 0746.

DOUGLAS, Roy

DOUGLAS, Roy; CHIEF EXECUTIVE, IRISH PERMANENT PLC; *b* 1944; *educ* St. Joseph's C.B.S., Fairview; University College Dublin, B.Comm, M.B.S; Alumnus Harvard Business School; Joined Central Bank of Ireland, 1963-74; Group Manager, Allied Irish Banks, (UK Division), 1974-91; Irish Permanent plc, 1991 to date; Chairman elect Irish Life & Permanent plc; Fellow, Institute of Bankers; Has brought the Irish Permanent into the 20th Century, how it will cope with the 21st Century has yet to be seen; Hobbies, golf, bridge, opera and theatre; Clubs, Portmarnock Golf Club, Island Golf Club. Contact: Irish Permanent plc., 56-59 St. Stephen's Green, Dublin 2. Tel: 01 661 5577 Fax: 01 661 5828.

DOWLING, Joseph "Joe"; ARTISTIC DIRECTOR, GUTHRIE THEATER, MINNEAPOLIS; *b* 1948;

educ Catholic University School, University College Dublin, BA; *m* Siobhan Cleary, Television Journalist; 1 *s* 1 *da*; Actor, Abbey Theatre, 1967; Founder, Young Abbey, 1970; Director, Peacock Theatre, 1973-76; Artistic Director, Irish Theatre Company, 1976-78; Youngest ever Artistic Director, Abbey Theatre, 1978-85; Founded Gaiety School of Acting, 1986; International Freelance Career in USA, Canada, Britain, 1988-95; Artistic Director, Guthrie Theater, Minneapolis, USA, 1995 to date; Publications include numerous newspaper articles, Essay in *Brian Friel*, edited by Alan Peacock; Awarded: Harveys Irish Theatre Awards, 1980 and 1986; *Sunday Independent* Award, 1986; *Sunday Tribune* Award, 1986; An innovator devoted to the performing arts; regarded as an able administrator and one of the finest directors that Ireland has produced. Hobbies, reading, travel, golf. Contact: Guthrie Theater, Vineland Place, Minneapolis, MN55403, Minnesota, USA.

DOWNER, Roger G. H.

DOWNER, Roger George Hamill; PRESIDENT, UNIVERSITY OF LIMERICK; *b* 1942; *educ* Methodist College, Belfast; Queens University Belfast, B Sc., M.Sc; University of Western Ontario, PhD.; Queens University Belfast, D.Sc.; *m* Jean Taylor; 1 *s* 3 *da*; University of Waterloo, Assistant Professor, 1970-78; Associate Professor, 1978-82; Professor, 1982-96, Chair of Biology, 1986-1989; Vice-President, 1989-1996; Asian Institute of Technology, President 1996-1998; University of Limerick, President, 1998 to date. Four edited books, one hundred and sixty chapters or referred journal articles; FEJ Fry Gold Medal 1990; ESC Gold Medal 1991; elected fellow of Royal Society of Canada 1992. Has been listed in *Who's Who in Canada* and *American Men and Women of Science;* member, Canadian Society of Zoologists (President, 1986); Canadian Council of University Chairs (President, 1989); Biological Council of Canada (Vice-President, 1988-91). Hobbies, reading, theatre, golf, rugby and walking. Contact: University of Limerick. Tel: 061 202 021. Fax: 061 330 027.

DOWNES, Margaret

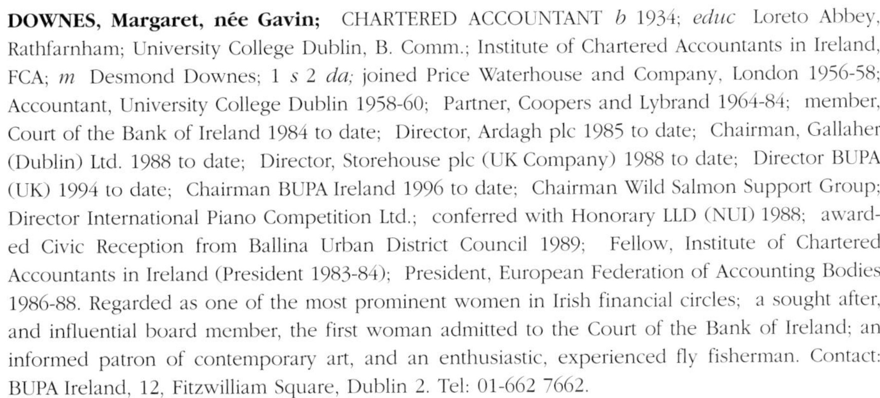

DOWNES, Margaret, née Gavin; CHARTERED ACCOUNTANT *b* 1934; *educ* Loreto Abbey, Rathfarnham; University College Dublin, B. Comm.; Institute of Chartered Accountants in Ireland, FCA; *m* Desmond Downes; 1 *s* 2 *da;* joined Price Waterhouse and Company, London 1956-58; Accountant, University College Dublin 1958-60; Partner, Coopers and Lybrand 1964-84; member, Court of the Bank of Ireland 1984 to date; Director, Ardagh plc 1985 to date; Chairman, Gallaher (Dublin) Ltd. 1988 to date; Director, Storehouse plc (UK Company) 1988 to date; Director BUPA (UK) 1994 to date; Chairman BUPA Ireland 1996 to date; Chairman Wild Salmon Support Group; Director International Piano Competition Ltd.; conferred with Honorary LLD (NUI) 1988; awarded Civic Reception from Ballina Urban District Council 1989; Fellow, Institute of Chartered Accountants in Ireland (President 1983-84); President, European Federation of Accounting Bodies 1986-88. Regarded as one of the most prominent women in Irish financial circles; a sought after, and influential board member, the first woman admitted to the Court of the Bank of Ireland; an informed patron of contemporary art, and an enthusiastic, experienced fly fisherman. Contact: BUPA Ireland, 12, Fitzwilliam Square, Dublin 2. Tel: 01-662 7662.

DOWNEY, Liam; DIRECTOR OF TEAGASC - THE AGRICULTURE AND FOOD DEVELOPMENT AUTHORITY; *b* 1937; *educ* North Monastry, Cork; University College Dublin, B.Sc., M.Sc; Reading University, PhD Research on Milk Enzymes; *m* June ----; 2*s* 2 *da;* Agricultural Research Institute, (Research milk and dairy products), 1960-74; National Science Council, (Science Policy), 1974-79; Chief Executive, An Foras Forbartha (The National Institute for Physical Planning and Construction Research); Director, An Chomhairle Oiliuna Talmhaiochta (ACOT) - The Council for Development in Agriculture, 1983-88; Director, Eradication of Animal Diseases Board (ERAD), 1988-92; Director, Teagasc, The Agriculture and Food Development Authority, 1994 to date; publications include wide range of research publications and *Food Quality and Nutrition*, 1977; member, Royal Society of Antiquaries of Ireland (RSAI), Friends of the Library, (Trinity College); awarded Doctor of Science (D.Sc) in recognition of international contribution of published research in milk and dairy products, UCD. Hobbies, archaeology, history and hurling. Contact: Liam Downey, Teagasc, 19 Sandymount Avenue, Dublin 4. Tel: 01 637 6000. Fax: 01 668 8023.

DOYLE, Avril

DOYLE, Avril, née Belton; MEMBER EUROPEAN PARLIAMENT; *b* 1949; *educ* Holy Child Convent, Killiney; University College Dublin, BSc Biochemistry; *m* Fred Doyle; 3*da*: was brought up with strong Fine Gael roots, father and grandfather were both members of the Oireachtas, grandfather, Paddy Belton, also served as Lord Mayor of Dublin; elected to Wexford County Council and Wexford Corporation, 1974; first woman Mayor of Wexford, 1976; elected Fine Gael Deputy for Wexford, 1982, 1989 and 1992-97; Senator and Fine Gael Leader in the Senate, 1989-92; Minister of State at the Department of Finance, 1986-87; ; Minister of State at the Departments of the Taoiseach, Finance and Transport, Energy and Communications, 1994-97; member of the Senate, 1997-99; regarded as a seasoned politician, articulate and well informed. Hobbies, all sports, particularly equestrian. Contact: European Parliment Offices, 43 Molesworth Street, Dublin 2. Tel: 01 605 7900 Fax: 01 605 7999

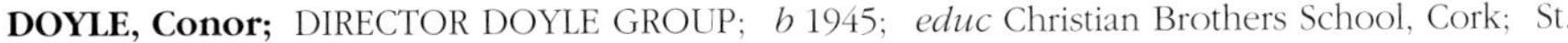

DOYLE, Conor; DIRECTOR DOYLE GROUP; *b* 1945; *educ* Christian Brothers School, Cork; St.

Gerard's, Bray; Glenstal Abbey; University College Dublin, BA; Kings Inns BL; *m* Mareta Cosgrave; 2*s;* Director since 1970 of established family firm, Doyle Group (shipping agents, warehousing, stevedoring etc.); Vice-Chairman Cork and Limerick Savings Bank, 1989-90; Chairman, Cork Harbour Commissioners, 1990-92; President, Cork Chamber of Commerce, 1997-99; Director, National Sculpture Factory, 1994 to date; Honorary Consul of Finland in Cork; member of old Cork family with long established links in commerce and sailing - one of Cork's merchant Princes; former Commodore, Kinsale Yacht Club and Chairman of International Dragon Association; clubs, Kinsale YC, Royal Cork YC, Kildare Street and University Club. Hobbies, tennis, skiing and yachting. Contact: D.F. Doyle and Co. Ltd., 1 Connell Street, Cork. Tel: 021 275 235. Fax: 021 276 418.

DOYLE, Niall; DIRECTOR OF MUSIC, RTE; *b* 1960 *educ* Mount Sion, C.B.S. Waterford, St. Patrick's College of Education, B.Ed; Trinity College Dublin, B.A. (Mod), *m* Catherine Breathnach; 2 *s*; Primary School Teacher, 1981-83; Professional Musician, 1983-92; Chief Executive, Music Network, 1992-98; Director of Music, RTE, 1998 to date; Member: European Cultural Foundation; Hobbies, family, music, music, music. Contact: RTE, Donnybrook, Dublin 4. Tel: 01 208 3111.

DOYLE, Niall

DOYLE, Roger; COMPOSER; *b* 1949; *educ* Sutton Park School, Co. Dublin; Scholarship to The Royal Irish Academy of Music; Dutch Government Scholarship to study at Institute of Sonology at Utrecht City University and The Hague Conservatory of Music; Finnish Government Scholarship to work at Finnish Radio Experimental Music Studio; *m* Mary Connolly; 1*s*; Teenage drummer in local pop group followed by drummer in the groups Jazz Therapy and Supply, Demand and Curv (early seventies); formed the Music Theatre Company Operating Theatre with actress Olwen Fouéré - productions for Dublin and tours abroad; Operating Theatre singles released by CBS Records and Mother Records (the latter produced by Bono of U2), 1986; since 1990 has been working on *The Babel Project*, a large scale musical structure, in which each piece of music is being thought of as a 'Room', 24 pieces of music have been composed, sections have been performed in an entire wing of the Irish Museum of Modern Art (1992); CD releases include, *Oizzo No, Thalia/ Charlotte Corday* (both 1992); *The Babel Project - Bitmac* (1994); *Rapid Eye Movements* (1995); *Under the Green Time* (1995, CD single); *Babel - Volume One* (1996); *Babel - Volume Two* (1997), all available from the Contemporary Music Centre, Dublin. Forthcoming: *Dance for me Salome* (music from the Gate Theatre production of *Salome*, directed by Steven Berkoff, 1999); Co-director of the newly reformed Operating Theatre; Co-director of Composers Ink; composed a 70 minute soundtrack for the film *Budawanny* (1987), directed by Bob Quinn; awards include, member, Aosdana, 1986; First Mention, Bourges International Electro-Acoustic Music Competition, France, 1981 (for *Rapid Eye Movements*) and 1991 (for *The Room of the Rhetoric);* winner of the Programme Music Prize at Bourges Competition, 1997, for *Spirit Levels 1-1V.* Hobbies, cycling, lost civilisations. Contact: The Contemporary Music Centre, 95 Lower Baggot Street, Dublin 2. Tel: 01 661 2105.

DOYLE, Vincent

DOYLE, Vincent; NEWSPAPER EDITOR; *b* 1938; *educ* St. Vincent's College, Glasnevin; *m* Gertrude Leech; 3 *s*; joined the *Irish Press* as a copyboy 1959, Film Critic and Feature Writer 1961-63; joined the *Sunday Independent* colour magazine (now defunct) 1963-64; freelance journalist U.K. 1964-67; Journalist, *Evening Herald* 1967-70, Assistant Editor 1970; Night Editor, *Irish Independent* 1973; Editor, *Evening Herald* 1976-81; Editor, *Irish Independent* since 1981. The consummate newspaperman in the mould of the traditional Fleet Street Editor; said to be a man's man. Hobby, the media. Contact: Independent Newspapers, 90, Middle Abbey Street, Dublin 1. Tel: 01 705 5333.

DREW, Joseph Ronald "Ronnie"; ENTERTAINER; *b* 1934; *educ* Christian Brothers School, Dun Laoghaire; *m* Deirdre McCartan; 1*s;* 1*da;* worked as an electrician, draper's assistant, dishwasher, telephone operator (Telecom) and English teacher in Spain; started musical career as a boy soprano; studied guitar and became interested in folk music and flamenco; Ronnie Drew Group, formed 1963 (following a chance meeting in O'Donoghues pub); group later called The Dubliners, comprising John Skeahan, Barney McKenna, Sean Cannon and the late Luke Kelly; a popular group who toured and recorded extensively; recordings include, *Celebration,* 1987, released to celebrate 25th anniversary of group; left Dubliners 1995; subsequent recordings include, *Dirty Rotten Shame,* Sony Records (with songs written by Christy Moore, Donal McDonald, Keith Donald, Elvis Costelloe, Bono, Simon Carmody, Shane McGowan); has recorded music and poetry with Jah Wobble; guested on records with Giles Servat, Antonio Breschi; appeared in one-man show *Ronnie I Hardly Knew You* (director, Derek Chapman) to widespread acclaim; a gravel voiced "Dub", the people's choice. Hobbies, reading, horses and racing.

DUDGEON, Vivian; DEPUTY MANAGING DIRECTOR ARNOTTS PLC; *b* 1934; *educ* Sligo Grammar School; IMI Courses; *m* Sheelagh McCullagh; 1*s* 1 *da;* Sales Manager, Arnotts plc, General Manager, currently Managing Director Arnotts plc; member, Rathfarnham Golf Club.

Hobbies, reading, rugby, caravaning, health and golf. Contact: Arnotts plc, 12 Henry Street, Dublin 1. Tel: 01 805 0400.

DUFFAUT, Eric; MANAGING DIRECTOR ORACLE DMD EMEA; *b* 1962; *educ* DECS, French Finance Degree; ESICI, French Business School; INSEAD, Advanced Management Program; *m* Nathalie ----, 1*s* 1 *da;* Account Manager, UNISYS France, 1987-90; Account Manager, ORACLE France, 1990-92, Branch Manager, South West of France, 1992-96, Director of DMD, France, 1996-97; Sales Director, ORACLE DMD EMEA (Dublin), 1997-98, Managing Director, 1998 to date. Hobbies, sports, arts (painting) and music. Contact: Oracle Corporation Ireland, Oracle House, Herbert Street, Dublin 2. Tel: 01 803 1000.

DUFFAUT, Eric

DUFFY, Joe; BROADCASTER; *b* 1956; *educ* Trinity College Dublin, B.Sc.; *m* June Meehan; 2 *s*, 1 *da;* Joined Arks Advertising 1973-76; President, T.C.D. Students' Union, 1982-84, Education Officer, U.S.I., 1982-84; President, U.S.I. 1983-84; Probation Social Worker, Department of Justice, 1984-88; joined RTE 1988, Producer, Reporter and Presenter to date; one of the most popular voices on RTE Radio; Represents for many the "True Dub"; Member, Fire Brigade Society of Ireland; Awards include, Jacobs Award 1995, National Media Award, 1998. Hobbies, swimming, walking, local public libraries and listening to good radio. Contact: RTE, Donnybrook, Dublin 4. Tel: 01 208 3111.

DUFFY, Martin; WRITER, FILM MAKER; *b* 1952; *single;* 2 *s* 1 *da;* worked as a labourer, shoe salesman, clapper loader and projectionist before career as a free lance film Editor and Staff Film Editor with R.T.E.; wrote and directed *The Boy from Mercury,* 1996; co-wrote and directed *The Bumble Bee Flies Anyway,* New York, 1998; directed *Testimony of Taliesin Jones,* Wales, 1999; other creative works include, film script of St. Patrick for TV (co-author), *Once Upon a Universe* (novel), *Mothership* (novel), *The Apollo* (radio play), *Poor Albert* (radio play), *Your Favourite Funny Man* (TV play), *Men of Consequence* (TV play), *Ygor* and *Henry Ford Killed my Father* (short plays); awards include, Jury Prize at Celtic Film Festival, 1997, Jury Prize at Hayange Film Festival (France), three prizes at Giffoni International Children's Film Festival (Italy), Special recommendation at Prix Europa (Berlin); member, Film Base (ex board member). Hobbies, aikido, popular science. Contact: Agent: Valerie Hoskins, 20 Charlotte Street, London W1P 1HJ. Tel: 0044 171 637 4490.

DUFFY, Michael William; CEO AN BORD BIA - THE IRISH FOOD BOARD; *b 1954; educ* C.B.C. Monkstown; University College Dublin, B. Sc.; Insead Business School, France, Executive Development Programme; *m* Jennifer Peart; 3 *s* 2 *da;* Research Physicist, Courtlands plc England, 1976-1978; Technical Manager, Courtlands plc, Ireland, 1978-81; Electronics and Pharmaceutical Manager, IDA Ireland, 1981-89; Head of Food and Agribusiness, IDA Ireland and Forbairt, 1989-94; CEO, An Bord Bia, The Irish Food Board, 1994 to date; Member, Institute of Directors, Institute of Marketing; Council Member, Institute of International Trade of Ireland. Hobbies, music, literature, hill walking, swimming. Contact: An Bord Bia, Clanwilliam Court, Lower Mount Street, Dublin 2 Tel: 01 668 5155.

DUFFY, Michael William

DUGGAN, John; FARMER, CHAIRMAN GLANBIA PLC; *b* 1938; *educ* Drangan National School; Christian Brothers School, Callan; *m* Breda McGrath, Nurse; 1 *s* 2 *da*; South Tipperary Chairman of Macra na Feirme 1961-63; Chairman, Tipperary County Macra 1963-64; Chairman, South Tipperary Farmers Co-operative 1970-73; Chairman, Glanbia Foods plc; Board member, Bord Bia, FBD Holdings, ICOS. A progressive and professional farmer; one of the most highly regarded figures in the Irish dairy industry. Hobbies, GAA, sports and dancing. Contact: Glanbia plc., Glanbia House, Kilkenny. Tel: 056 72200. Fax: 056 72222.

DUGGAN, Noel; CHAIRMAN NOEL C. DUGGAN LTD., MILL STREET HORSES LTD; *b* 1933; *educ* Millstreet National School; *m* Maureen Corkery; 2*s* 2 *da;* took over small hardware business on father's death, 1946; Executive Chairman of Noel C. Duggan, now one of the major hardware, builders providers and structural steelbuilding providers in the South West; Chairman and Managing Director, Mill Street Horses Ltd., a company involved in breeding, training and marketing the Irish Sport Horse throughout the world, currently involved in a £4 million Mill Street Horse Village with funding from IDA, Department of Agriculture and EC; Chairman, and Managing Director, Millstreet International Horse Show, an indoor and outdoor show, regarded as one of the most important equestrian events in Ireland; acclaimed for his whole-hearted commitment to the revitalisation of Millstreet, Cork. Hobbies, all sports, family and business. Contact: Noel C. Duggan Ltd., Main Street, MillStreet, Co. Cork. Tel: 029 70039. Fax: 029 70305.

DUIGNAN, Clare; HEAD OF INDEPENDENT PRODUCTIONS RTE; *b* 1936; *educ* Loreto Abbey, Dalkey; University College Dublin, B.A.; joined R.T.E. radio producer, features, current affairs, (including *Women Today*) 1977-80; Television Producer/Director, *Today Tonight, The Women's*

Programme, Late Late Show, 1980-86; Head of T.V. Features 1986-89, created *Head to Toe, Check Up, Saturday Live* etc.; Group Head, Features and Current Affairs, 1990-93, created *Would You Believe, Tuesday File* etc.; Head of Independent Productions 1993 to date, commissions 500 hours of programmes each year such as *Ear to the Ground, @ Last T.V., No Frontiers, Our House, The Joy, Drive;* Executive Producer (R.T.E.) *Amongst Women, I Went Down, Sweety Barrett;* member, EBU Documentary Group, Dun Laoghaire Institute of Art, Design and Technology (Governing Body), Educate Together; Shareholder, Abbey Theatre. Hobbies, media, film and theatre, reading - biography and contemporary fiction, gardening, food, family, education - especially multi-denominational sector. Contact: R.T.E., Donnybrook, Dublin 4. Tel: 01 208 3429. Fax: 01 208 2510.

DULLY, John T.

DULLY, John T.; CHIEF EXECUTIVE BORD FAILTE; *b* 1946; *educ* St. Mel's College, Longford; University College Dublin, BA, Ec, Eng Hist; M.Sc in Strategic Management (Public Sector); *separated;* 2 *s* 2 *da;* Economic and Commercial Counsellor, Irish Embassy, London, 1983-88, responsible for Bilateral Economic and Commercial Relations with Britain; Assistant Secretary responsible for Irish Trade Policy at the Department of Industry and Commerce and, later, the Department of Tourism and Trade, 1988-92; Assistant Secretary responsible for Irish Tourism policy at the Department of Tourism and Trade, 1993-98; Chief Executive, Bord Failte, 1998 to date. Hobbies, people, conversation, national issues, reading and sport. Contact: Bord Failte, Irish Tourist Board, Baggot Street Bridge, Dublin 2. Tel: 01 602 4000. Fax: 01 602 4100.

DUNGAN, Myles

DUNGAN, Myles; BROADCASTER; *b* 1954; *educ* St. Patrick's College, Cavan; University College Dublin, MA (History); Continuity Announcer, RTE Radio, 1977-82, Reporter, RTE Radio / TV Sports Presenter, 1982-88, Presenter *Today @ 5* and *5/7 Live* - RTE Radio, 1988 to date, Presenter, *Divided World,* RTE TV, 1994, Presenter, RTE Golf Coverage / RTE TV Sport, 1990; creative works include, *They Shall Grow Not Old - Ireland and the Great War,* 1997; *Preferred Lies* - Golf Anecdotes, 1996; *Irish Voices from the Great War,* 1995; *A Good Walk Spoiled* - Golf Quotes, 1994; *Distant Drums - Irish Soldiers in Foreign Armies,* 1993, *Snuff* (with Jim Lusby), a crime novel, 1992; awards include Jacobs Radio Award, 1998, New York Radio Award, 1994; member, Dublin Journalists Golf Society, Delgany Golf Club. Hobbies, drama, golf, music, Arsenal Football Club, running, cycling, swimming. Contact: R.T.E., Donnybrook, Dublin 4. Tel: 01 208 3111.

DUNNE, Aidan; WRITER ON VISUAL ARTS; *b* 1955; *educ* Crescent College Limerick; Templeogue College, Dublin; National College of Art and Design, Dip. Painting (ANCAD); *m* Helen Rock, Journalist; 1 step da; Art Critic, *In Dublin,* 1978-83; Arts Critic, *Sunday Press,* 1983-87; Art Critic, *Sunday Tribune,* 1987-98; Art Critic, *The Irish Times,* 1998 to date; publications include monographs on Barrie Cooke, Michael Mulcahy and Anne Madden, and numerous catalogue essays; a perceptive and thoughtful commentator on the visual arts. Contact: The Irish Times, D'Olier Street, Dublin 2. Tel: 01 679 2022.

DUNNE, Ben

DUNNE, Ben; DIRECTOR WESTPOINT HEALTH AND FITNESS LEISURE CENTRE; *b* 1949; *educ* Presentation College, Cork; *m* Mary Goodwin; 4 children; joined family chainstore/supermarket business founded by father, Ben Dunne; Managing Director, Dunnes Stores until 1993; following a buyout deal by the remainder of the family left Dunnes Stores and opened Westpoint Leisure Centre, Blanchardstown; member, Portmarnock Golf Club. Hobbies, golf. Contact; Westpoint Health and Fitness Leisure Centre, Blanchardstown Town Centre, Dublin 15. Tel: 01 822 1103.

DUNNE, Veronica "Ronnie"; MUSIC TEACHER; *b* 1927; *educ* Sacred Heart Convent, Mount Anville; *m* Peter McCarthy (*decd*); 1 *s* 1 *da*; Studied singing in Rome; made operatic debut, 1948; won first place, Concorse Lirico Milano, 1952, made Milan operatic debut in the same year; joined Covent Garden where she sang leading roles as well as giving numerous international recitals and recordings; joined teaching staff at College of Music, 1961; currently Director of Music, Leinster School of Music, Opera Studio; Teacher in Batchelor of Music and Masters Courses, Royal Irish Academy of Music; awarded Honorary Doctorate, University College Dublin; Honorary Membership, R.D.S.; Recognised internationally as the driving force behind young Irish singers; a powerful voice in music in Ireland; founder, The Veronica Dunne International Singing Competition. Contact: Royal Irish Academy of Music, 36, Westland Row, Dublin 2. Tel: 01 676 4412. Fax: 01 662 2798.

DUNPHY, Eamonn

DUNPHY, Eamonn; JOURNALIST / WRITER / BROADCASTER; *b* 1945; *educ* St. Patrick's National School, Drumcondra; Sandymount High School; *separated*; 1*s* 1*da*; represented Ireland in soccer at schoolboy, Under 23 and Senior Level, holds 23 international caps; played with Manchester United, York City, Millwall, Charleton, Reading, 1960-77; returned to Ireland, played and coached one season with Shamrock Rovers, won FAI Cup Medal; Soccer Correspondent, *Sunday Tribune* and frequent contributor to *Magill* magazine 1978-84; Columnist, *Sunday Independent,* 1984-97; Radio Broadcaster, mainly sport, RTE; Broadcaster (Radio Ireland) 1997, station now called Today

FM, Presenter, Editor, *The Last Word*, 1997 to date; Columnist, *The Examiner*, 1999 to date; publications include, *Only Again* (Memoir of playing years) Penguin 1976, *Unforgettable Fire* (U2 Biography) international best seller, 1985, *A Strange Kind of Glory* (biography of Sir Matt Busby) 1992; has provided radio audiences with the opportunity to listen to some of the most controversial thinkers in Irish society; one of the best known and sharpest journalists in the country; enjoys the limelight, unhampered by timidity. Hobbies, reading, travel – mainly in France, and sport. Contact: Today FM, 124 Upper Abbey Street, Dublin 1. Tel: 01 804 9000. Fax: 01 804 9099.

DWYER, William

DURCAN, Paul; POET; *b* 1944; *educ* Gonzaga College, Dublin; University College Cork, BA; *separated*; 2 *da*; Tutor in Archaeology and Medieval History, University College Cork 1979-80; gives frequent poetry readings in Ireland and abroad, Yogoslavia (1981), Soviet Union (1983, 1985, 1986), Saskatoon (1987), Toronto (1987, 1989), Rotterdam (1987), Montreal (1988), New Brunswick (1988, 1989), Nova Scotia (1988), Italy (1988), Paris (1988), Luxembourg (1988), Brussels (1988), Newfoundland (1989), Boston (1990), New York (1990), New Zealand (1992); Jerusalem (1993); Brazil (1995); Germany (1995); Prague (1996); Salzburg (1996); Lisbon (1997); Japan (1998); Resident Poet, Frost Place, New Hampshire 1985; Writer in Residence, Trinity College Dublin 1990; recipient of Patrick Kavanagh Poetry Award 1974; Creative Bursaries from the Arts Council / An Comhairle Ealaion 1976 and 1980, Irish American Cultural Institute Poetry Award 1989, Whitbread Poetry Prize 1990; Recent publications include *Crazy About Women* (1991); *A Snail In My Prime* (1993); *Give Me Your Hand* (1994); *Christmas Day* (1996); *Greetings To Our Friends In Brazil* (1999); member, Aosdána. A Ringsend resident without pretensions; a man of great warmth and one of Ireland's major contemporary poets. Hobbies, walking, movies, painting and music; Club, standing on the street corners of small towns in Ireland. Contact: Aosdána, 70 Merrion Square, Dublin 2. Tel: 01 661 1840 Fax: 01 676 1302.

DWYER, Michael; JOURNALIST; *b* 1951; *educ* CBS Tralee, Co. Kerry; St. Brendan's College, Killarney, Co. Kerry; Trinity College Dublin; Administrator, Federation of Irish Film Societies, 1978-82; Film Critic, *In Dublin*, 1980-83; Co-founder, Dublin Film Festival, 1985; Programme Director, Dublin Film Festival, 1985-91; Film Correspondent, *The Irish Times*, 1988 to date; member, NUJ; International Federation of Film Critics; awards include Arts Journalist of the Year, 1991; National Media Awards. Ireland's most prominent and expert commentator on the film industry, internationally and at home. Hobbies, cats (2 in particular, Ginger and Fred), media, books, politics, contemporary music, food and travel. Contact: Irish Times, 10-16 D'Olier Street, Dublin 2. Tel: 01 679 2022. Fax: 01 677 9181.

DWYER, William; ARMY GENERAL, DEPUTY CHIEF OF STAFF; *b* 1937; *educ* Military College - Command and Staff Course; United States Command and General Staff College Course, Fort Leavenworth, Kansas; *m* Breda Mackey; 1 *s* 5 *da;* joined Defence Forces, 1955; Cadet, 1955-57; 2Lt., 1957, Lieutenant, 1959, Captain, 1966, Commandant, 1976, Lt. Colonel, 1987, Colonel, 1991, Brig. General, 1994, Major General, 1996; United Nations medals include, ONUC (Congo) 1963, UNFICYP (Cyprus) 1965, UNIFIL (Lebanon) 1982 & 1989; Service Medals Defence Forces, Peace Medal Defence Forces; present appointment, Deputy Chief of Staff Defence Forces, formerly Adjutant General, 1996-98, General Officer Commanding Eastern Command, 1994-96. Hobbies, golf, all sport, choral singing, music. Contact: Parkgate, Dublin 8. Tel: 01 837 9911.

EAMES, Rev. Dr. Robert

EAMES, The Most Rev. Dr. Robert; ARCHBISHOP OF ARMAGH, PRIMATE OF ALL IRELAND; *b* 1937; *educ* Belfast Royal Academy; Methodist College, Belfast, Queen's University, Belfast, LLB, PhD; Trinity College Dublin; *m* Christine Daly, Lecturer; 2 *s*; Deacon, St. Clement's Belfast 1963; ordained Priest 1964, Dromore Cathedral; Curate at Bangor, 1963-66; Rector of Gilnahirk 1966-74; Rector at Dundela 1974-75; Bishop of Derry and Raphoe 1975-80; Bishop of Down and Dromore 1980-86; Archbishop of Armagh, 1986 to date; Select Preacher, Oxford University, 1987, Cambridge University, 1990, Edinburgh University, 1993; recipient of Honorary LL.D from Queens University, Belfast 1989; Awarded: Honorary LL.D Degree, Trinity College Dublin, 1992, University of Lancaster, 1994, Exeter University, 1999; Awarded Honorary DD Degree, Cambridge University, 1994, University of Aberdeen, 1997; An open and affable churchman; seen as a circumspect leader of the Church of Ireland in Ireland. Hobbies, reading, sport and sailing. Club, University and Kildare Street Club. Contact: The See House, Cathedral Close, Armagh, BT61 7EE, Northern Ireland.

EGAN, Dermot; CHAIRMAN NATIONAL CONCERT HALL; *b* 1934; *educ* St. Enda's College, Galway; University College Dublin, BA, HDip; Columbia University NY, MA.Psy.; *m* Noreen Smyth; 4*s* (1 decd); Industrial Psychologist, Aer Lingus, 1962-64; Management Specialist, IMI, 1964-70; joined Allied Irish Banks, 1970; General Manager Personnel, Director of Marketing, Human Resources and Technology; Deputy Group Chief Executive, AIB, 1990-94; Chairman, National Concert Hall, 1996 to date; Director, United Drug plc; Director, Project Management Ltd; Chairman, Insurance Council of Ombudsman; Chairman, Philately Advisory Committee; Adjunct

EGAN, Felim

Professor, Dublin City University; recipient of Honorary Doctorate, Trinity College Dublin; Life Fellow, Irish Management Institute; Companion, Institute of Personnel Development; member, Grange GC, Co. Louth GC, Seapoint GC, Aloha GC (Spain). Hobbies, golf, art, music, drama, walking and reading. Contact: National Concert Hall, Earlsfort Terrace, Dublin 2. Tel: 01 475 1572. Fax: 01 478 3797.

EGAN, Felim; ARTIST; *b* 1952; *educ* Ulster Polytechnic; Portsmouth Polytechnic, BA; Slade School of Fine Art, HDFA; *m* Janet Pierse, Painter; 3 *step-children*; represented Ireland at 'A Sense of Ireland', London 1980, Paris Biennale 1980, Contemporary Sculpture Verona 1989, Bienale de Sao Paulo 1995, Rosc 1984 Dublin, L'imaginaire Irelandais 1996; One-person shows since 1979 include, Douglas Hyde Gallery 1985, IMMA Dublin 1995; selected group exhibitions, Irland-Deutschland, Bonn 1989, New North, Tate Gallery Liverpool, (touring) 1990, Europaeisk Kunst '92, Holstebro Kunstmuseum, Denmark 1992, 29éme Festival International, Cagnes-sur-Mer; works hang in the major museums and collections in Ireland, Britain and Europe, as well as numerous private collections; major commissions, Temple Bar 1996, National Gallery of Ireland 1996, Conrad Gallagher restaurants 1998; member, Aosdána; recipient, Rome Scholarship, British School at Rome, 1979-80, premier UNESCO prize for the Arts, Paris 1993, premier award, Cagnes-sur-Mer, France 1997; publications include, *Squarings*, a handmade book with Seamus Heaney 1991, *Sandymount Strand*, with text by James Joyce and Seamus Heaney 1993; an established Irish artist who is making a strong impact abroad; Hobbies, walking on Sandymount Strand with his dogs, playing music, Irish musical festivals, Gardening, D.I.Y. Contact: Kerlin Gallery, Anne's Lane, Dublin 2. Tel: 01 670 9093.

EGAN, Patrick "Pat"; MUSIC MANAGER AND PROMOTER; *b* 1947; *educ* St. Patrick's Drumcondra, Colaiste Mhuire; *m* Margot Gernon (*m. dis.*); 1 *s* 1 *da*; *m* Caroline Foran, Managing Director, National Credit Ltd.; 1 *s* 1 *da*; Managing Director, Pat Egan Sounds Ltd.; Director, Irish Poster Advertising Ltd.; Manager of Frances Black, Sinead Lohan, Mary Coughlan, Eimear Quinn, The Nualas, Jimmy McCarthy; Major concert promoter, concerts in 1999 include Sarah Brightman and Sir George Martin; Former Director, Olympia Theatre, owner of Anglers Rest, Waterfront and Bad Bobs Backstage Bars; Former Partner with Oliver Barry in record retailing chain; Irish agent for Billy Connolly, Eric Clapton, Paul Merton, and football star Paul McGrath. Hobbies, cycling, premier collector of film and music memorabilia. Contact: Pat Egan Sounds Ltd., 24, Merchants Quay, Dublin 8. Tel: 01 679 7700. Fax: 01 679 7495.

ELLIOTT, Noel Patrick; CHAIRMAN, P. ELLIOTT CO. DUBLIN & CAVAN; *b* 1943; *educ* Marist St. Mary's Dundalk; *m* Katherine Smyth; 3 *s* 1 *da;* Joined family building company, P. Elliott & Co., Managing Director, 1969-97; Currently Executive Chairman; P. Elliott & Co. are a successful, Cavan based civil engineering and contracting company, operating mainly in large scale commercial construction. Hobbies, rugby, horse racing, opera. Contact: Patrick Elliott & Co., Church Street, Cavan. Tel: 049 31066. Fax: 049 31537.

ELLIS-KING, Deirdre; DUBLIN CITY LIBRARIAN; *educ* St. Louis Convent, Monaghan; University College Dublin, BA, Dip. Lib; University of Wales, M.Phil; *m* Roderick King; 1 *s;* Librarian, Dublin Corporation/County Council, 1971-78, Development Librarian, 1978-82, Deputy Dublin City and County Librarian, 1982-88; Dublin City and County Librarian, 1985-93; Dublin City Librarian, 1994 to date; responsible for Dublin City Public Libraries, City Archives, Museum and Cultural Services; publications include many contributions to national and international professional journals and monographs; President, Library Association of Ireland, 1991-93; Chairperson, Executive Board, Library Association of Ireland (LAI), 1991-93; Member, LAI; Committees, Dublin City Adult Education Board, 1988 to date; Chairperson, Dublin Heritage (Research) Group, 1989 to date; Board Member, The Library Council/An Chomhairle Leabharlanna, 1988 to date; Vice-Chairperson, International Impac Dublin Literary Award, 1995 to date; Board Member, Irish Genealogy Ltd.; Partner in European Union Assisted Research Projects; in distance education, contemporary literature, shared heritage and culture; Partner in Public Libraries Concerted Action in Europe, PubliCA; Member, Public Library Policy Team appointed by Minister for the Environment and Local Government, report *Branching Out: A New Public Library Service* published November 1998; Member, Working Party on Information Technology in Libraries, established by Local Government Computer Services Board, reported 1995; awards include Research Grant for the Investigation into the Practice of Community Librarianship - The Library Council, 1979. Contact: Dublin Corporation, Administrative Headquarters, Cumberland House, Fenian Street, Dublin 2. Tel: 01 661 9000. Fax: 01 676 1628.

EMPEY, The Most Rev. Walton Newcombe Francis; ARCHBISHOP OF DUBLIN AND BISHOP OF GLENDALOUGH; *b* 1934; *educ* Pretora Royal School; Trinity College Dublin, BA; Kings College, Halifax, Nova Scotia, Canada, BD; *m* Louisa Hall; 3 s 1 da; Assistant Curate, Glenageary 1958-60; Priest in Charge, Grand Falls (Canada) 1960-63; Rector, Edmunston (Canada) 1963-66;

Rector, Stradbally (Co. Laois) 1966-71; Dean, St. Mary's Cathedral (Limerick) 1971-81; Bishop of Limerick 1981-86; Bishop of Meath and Kildare, 1986 to 1996; Archbishop of Dublin and Bishop of Glendalough 1996 to date; Honorary Citizen of Madawaska, New Brunswick, Canada; member, General Synod of the Church of Ireland, Standing Committee of the Church of Ireland. A genial churchman; an influential ecumenist. Hobbies, reading, fishing and walking. Contact: The See House, 17 Temple Road, Milltown, Dublin 6. Tel: 01 497 7849. Fax: 01 497 6355.

FANNING, Aengus; NEWSPAPER EDITOR; b 1947; *educ* Christian Brothers School, Tralee; University College Cork; *m* Mary O'Brien; 3 *s*; worked as a Reporter under the editorship of his Uncle, the late James I. Fanning, on *The Midland Tribune* (Birr), a newspaper founded by his great grandfather in 1882; joined the Independent Group as a Reporter, 1969; Group Agriculture Correspondent, 1973-82; voted Agriculture Journalist of the Year, 1978; News Analysis Editor, *Irish Independent* 1982-84; Editor, *Sunday Independent*, 1984 to date; Recognised as an energetic and level headed editor; a good selector of top class editorial talent; *Sunday Independent* is the only Irish newspaper with over one million readers. Has impressive sporting credentials, having played minor and senior GAA football for Kerry, and rugby for University College Cork, Tralee and Birr. Hobbies, playing the clarinet, classical music, reading, jazz, opera, theatre and swimming. Contact: Sunday Independent, 90, Middle Abbey Street, Dublin 1. Tel: 01 705 5333. Fax: 01 705 5779.

FANNING, Aengus

FANNING, Dave; BROADCASTER; *b* 1955; *educ* Blackrock College; University College Dublin, BA, H.Dip; *m* Ursula Courtney; 2 *s*; worked briefly in a factory and as a teacher before moving into journalism as editor of *Scene Magazine*, 1977; Broadcaster, Radio Dublin, 1977, "Big D" 1978; joined R.T.E. Radio 1, 1979, Broadcaster of the five nightly music programme, *The Dave Fanning Show* 1979 to date; Rock Correspondent, *The Irish Times*, 1987-93; TV programmes include *Jobsuss* 1984, *Visual Eyes* 1986, *Rock Steady* (Channel 4) 1990, *Friday Night at the Dome* (Channel 4), *The Arts Express* (R.T.E); joined Virgin Radio (London) 1993-95; Writer/Presenter, *The Movie Show*, RTE Television, 1992 to date; *2 TV*, RTE Television and Radio music programme, 1995 to date; *Planet Rock Profiles* on night time I.T.V. (UK) and VHI across Europe and from Asia to South America, programme purchased by TnaG; Committee Member, Mercury Music Prize (UK); recipient, Jacobs Award, 1980; voted No. 1 DJ by *Hotpress* for twenty-one years in a row; a knowledgeable rock music commentator, highly respected in his field; worldwide contacts in the entertainment industry and one to one star interviews add to the entertainment value of the programmes. Hobbies, movies and music. Contact: R.T.E., Donnybrook, Dublin 4. Tel: 01 208 3111.

FANNING, Dave

FANNING, John; MANAGING DIRECTOR, McCONNELLS ADVERTISING; *b* 1944; *educ* Oatlands Christian Brothers School; University College Dublin, B.Comm; *m* Kaye Owens; 1 *s* 1 *da*; Research Executive, Gallup Poll 1965-69; Research Executive, Grey Advertising 1969-71; Advertising Sales, I.P.A. (Dublin) 1971-72; Account Executive, McConnells Advertising 1972-81; Managing Director, 1982 to date; past Chairman, Marketing Society and Marketing Institute; Director of the Abbey Theatre; Member of the Commission on the Newspaper Industry, 1996. The quiet power behind the largest advertising group in the country. Contact: McConnells Advertising, McConnell House, Charlemont Place, Dublin 2. Tel: 01 478 1544.

FANNING, John

FARRELL, Brian; ACADEMIC, BROADCASTER; *b* 1929; *educ* Colàiste Mhuire, Christian Brothers School, Dublin; Salesian Fathers, Ballinahill; University College Dublin, BA, MA; Harvard University; *m* Marie-Therese Dillon; 4 *s* 3 *da;* Associate Professor, Government and Political Science, University College Dublin, 1985-94; Broadcaster/Journalist, 1958 to date; Presenter of every Current Affairs series on RTE, *Seven Days, The Political Programme, Frontline, Today Tonight* and *Prime Time;* Anchorman for RTE election coverage, 1973 to date; Presenter/Reporter, RTE for major national events; recipient of two Jacobs Awards for public affairs broadcasting; frequent Visiting Lecturer UK and US universities; publications include: *The Founding of Dáil Eireann: Parliament and Nation Building, Chairman or Chief? Sean Lemass,* numerous articles for newspapers and political journals, contributing Editor to four books on the Irish Political and Social System; Chairman, Arts Council, 1998 to date; Director-General, Institute of European Affairs, Dublin, 1994-96; Vice-Chairman, IEA, 1996 to date; member, National Council of the Alzheimer Society of Ireland. A charming and urbane man, regarded as a fair minded Arts Council Chairman. Contact: R.T.E., Donnybrook, Dublin 4. Tel: 01 208 3111.

FARRELLY, James, "Jim"; JOURNALIST; *b* 1943; *educ* Gilson Endowed School, Oldcastle; St. Finian's College, Mullingar; Milltown Park Institute, Dip. Philosophy; University College Dublin, BA; Kings Inns, BL; *m* Joan Rice, choreographer; 2 *s* (*1 decd.*) 1 *da*; News Reporter, Independent Newspapers 1968-80; News Editor, *Sunday Tribune*, 1980-81; Deputy Editor/News Editor, 1981-82; Editor, *Daily News*, 1981-82; Investigative Specialist, *Irish Independent*, 1984-86; Features Editor, 1986-92; Managing Director, *Drogheda Independent*, 1992-97; Managing Director, *The Kerryman*, 1997 to date; Managing Director, Independent Provincial Newspapers Group, 1994 to date; Presided over development of Independent's 12 provincial titles, with sales now in excess

FARRELL, Brian

of 100,000 copies per week. Publications include: *Who's Who in Irish Politics - The Top 500* (first published 1989 and updated 1990). A genial newsman who brings an astute legal brain to editorial content. Hobbies, jogging and music. Contact: The Kerryman, Clash, Tralee, Co. Kerry. Tel: 071 45500. Fax: 071 28011.

FEARON, Ronan Joseph

FEARON, Ronan Joseph; CHAIRMAN, CHIEF EXECUTIVE COYLE HAMILTON GROUP; *b* 1937; *educ* C.U.S. Leeson St., Dublin; University College Dublin, BComm; Fellow of Chartered Institute of Management Accountants; *m* Kay McArdle; 2 *s;* 3 *da;* Trainee Accountant, Beecham Group, 1959-1961; Accountant, Brunswick Corporation, 1961-63; Accountant, Guinness, 1963-1969; Finance Director, Brunswick Corporation, 1969-1972; Group Finance Director, Coyle Hamilton Group, 1972-83, Chairman/Chief Executive, 1983 to date; member, Past President, Insurance Institute of Ireland, 1995; Past President Chartered Institute of Management Accountants, 1990; clubs, Fitzwilliam LTC, Carrickmines LTC, Edmonston Golf Club, Hibernian United Services Club; Chairman, Finance Committee - Irish Heart Foundation; Chairman, Belvedere Youth Club Concert Committee. Hobbies, tennis, golf, reading. Contact: Coyle Hamilton Group Ltd. 7/9 South Leinster Street, Dublin 2. Tel: 01 661 6211. Fax: 01 661 4369.

FEELY, Orla

FEELY, Orla; UNIVERSITY LECTURER; *b* 1965; *educ* Our Lady's School, Templeogue; National University of Ireland, BE, Electronics; University of California, Berkeley, MS, Ph.D., Electrical Engineering; *m* Philip Curran, Electronic Engineer; Lecturer, University College Dublin, 1992, Senior Lecturer, 1996 to date; Publications include numerous technical papers in books, journals and conferences; Member, Institution of Electrical and Electronic Engineers, Women in Technology and Science; recipient of numerous awards for teaching and research, including the U.C. Berkeley Sakrison Prize for Outstanding and Innovative Research. Contact: University College Dublin, Belfield, Dublin 4. Tel: 01 706 7777. Fax: 01 283 0921.

FEENEY, Angela

FEENEY, Angela; OPERA SINGER; *b* 1954; *educ* City of Belfast School of Music, with Douglas Armstrong; Dublin College of Music, with Veronica Dunne; Richard-Strauss-Conservatoire Munich with Ken Neate, Diploma Grade 1; Munich State Opera Studio, with Heinrich Bender; *m* Nikolaus Grüger; 1 *s;* Soloist Contract, Munich State Opera, 1982-89, roles include, Countessa, Fiordiligi, Gretel, Euridice, Echo; Guest Soloist: Hamburg, Frankfurt State Opera; Bamberger Symphoniker, Munich Symphony, Bavarian Radio Orchestra; Wexford Festival Opera - *Un Giorno di Regno*, 1983; DGOS, *Orfeo*, 1984; Cork Festival Opera - *Leonora - Il Travatore* (first live televised opera by RTE); Opera Northern Ireland - Butterfly - *Madam Butterfly*, 1984; Cork Opera Festival - Mimi - *La Boheme;* Berlin State Opera - Butterfly - *Madam Butterfly;* English National Opera - Guest soloist: Donna Elvira, Marie (*Bartered Bride*) Michaela, Nedda, Rusalka, 1985-88; London Arts Festival: Michaela, Nedda; DGOS, *Norma*, 1989; full CD recordings: C Orff's - *Peer Gynt* (Orfeo); d'Albert - *Tiefland* (RCA); Rossini's - *Stabet Mater*, successful concert / lieder singer in Germany, Switzerland, Holland, Belgium, UK, Ireland and USA; Artistic Director, West Belfast Classical Music Bursary; recipient, John McCormack Award, John Player Award, Munich Scholarship, Absa Award NI 1997, Absa Best Arts Group Award, 1999; Hobbies, swimming, photography, poetry, paintings. Contact: Josephspital Str. 6, 80331 Munich, Germany. Tel: 004989 260 4834.

FENNELLY, Teddy; MANAGING EDITOR LEINSTER EXPRESS NEWSPAPER GROUP; *b* 1943; *educ* C.B.S. Portlaoise; Member of Chartered Institute of Transport (London University); *m* Carmel Keogh; 4 *s* 4 *da*; Clerical/Administrative Officer, C.I.E., 1960-76; Sports Editor, *Leinster Express*, 1976-82; News Editor, *Leinster Express*, 1982-84; Managing Editor, Leinster Express Group, 1984 to date; author of *Fitz - and the Famous Flight* and *Laois Lives;* President, Portlaoise Chamber of Commerce and Trade; Vice-Chairman of Laois Heritage Society; Publisher of *The Land War in the Queen's Country 1889/92* and *Searching for a Place* by Bill Kelly. Hobbies, writing, Gaelic sport, golf, painting, local history. Contact: Leinster Express, Dublin Road, Portlaoise, Co. Louth. Tel: 0502 21666. Fax: 0502 20491.

FINAN, Mary; DEPUTY CHAIRMAN OGILVY AND MATHER GROUP (IRELAND); *b* 1944; *educ* St. Louis High School, Rathmines; University College Dublin, BA; *m* Geoffrey MacKechnie, Lecturer, Trinity College Dublin; 1 *da*; Public Relations Assistant, Kenny's Advertising, 1967-68; Public Relations Executive, Peter Owens Advertising 1967-68; Founding Partner Wilson Hartnell Public Relations, appointed Managing Director 1980 to date; Board member Ogilvy & Mather Group (Ireland) 1981, Deputy Chairman, 1999; Director, Gate Theatre, Canada LIfe (Ireland); Member, Council of the Economic and Social Research Institute (ESRI), Dublin Docklands Development Authority, Dublin International Sports Council; former President, Dublin Chamber of Commerce 1996-97; IBEC nominee on Commission on the Newspaper Industry. The elegant and approachable head of one of the most established PR agencies in the country, noted for her powerful presentation abilities; a quiet influence with some of the country's leading business moguls. Hobbies, running, reading, theatre and music. Contact: Wilson Hartnell PR Ltd., 14, Leeson Park, Dublin 6. Tel: 01 496 0244. Fax: 01 497 5163.

FINGLETON, Michael; MANAGING DIRECTOR IRISH NATIONWIDE BUILDING SOCIETY; *b* 1938; *educ* St. Nathy's College, Ballaghadereen; University College Dublin; Kings Inns; *m* Eileen McCarroll; 2*s* 2 *da;* worked as an Accountant; called to the Bar 1975; Paymaster General, Caritas and Concern Operations (Nigeria); joined ACEC as Management and Corporate Accountant 1971; Secretary, General Manager, Irish Industrial Benefits 1972 to date; changed Society's name to Irish Nationwide (benefitting from massive advertising campaign by similarly named society in UK); regarded as a networker *extraordinaire;* popular with his peers, considered one of the most astute observers of the Irish power scene. Hobby, golf. Contact: Irish Nationwide Building Society, Grand Parade, Dublin 6. Tel: 01 609 6000.

FENNELLY, Teddy

FINIS, Armando; MANAGING DIRECTOR ELECTROLUX GROUP (IRELAND) LTD.; *b* 1961; *educ* Universita L. Bucconi, Milan, MA Econ; INSEAD (France), AMP; *m* Geraldine Sampre; 1*s* 1 *da;* Marketing Manager, Electrolux Group, France, 1987; Divisional Manager, Group Manager and Group Marketing Director, 1992-94; Key Account Manager Electrolux White Goods Europe, 1996; Managing Director, Electrolux Group Ireland, 1998 to date; member, Alub, Paris, INSEAD Alumni Association. Hobbies, tennis, squash, golf, soccer, theatre and cinema. Contact: Electrolux Group Ireland, Long Mile Road, Dublin 12. Tel: 01 456 5222. Fax: 01 456 5097.

FINLAY GEOGHEGAN, Mary; SENIOR COUNSEL; *b* 1949; *educ* Sacred Heart Convent, Monkstown; Univeristy College Dublin, BA, Auditor, Literary and Historical Society 1970-71; Incorporated Law Society of Ireland, Solicitor; College of Europe, Bruges, Dip. European Law; King's Inns, Barrister-at-Law; *m* Mr Justice Geoghegan; 1 *s* 2 *da;* Solicitor, McCann Fitzgerald, 1973-79, Partner, 1975-79; called to the Bar, 1980; called to the Inner Bar, 1988; Bencher of Honorable Society of King's Inns 1996; Member of Board of Management of The Children's Hospital, Temple Street; member of Belmullet Golf Club and Fitzwilliam L.T.C.. Contact: Law Library, 145 -151 Church Street, Dublin 1. Tel: 01 817 4914. Fax: 01 817 4556.

FINAN, Mary

FINUCANE, Marian; BROADCASTER; *b* 1950; *educ* Scoil Chaitríona, Dublin; Dominicans, Dublin; College of Technology, Bolton Street; *m* John Clarke; 1 *s* 1 *da* (decd); worked in architectural practice before joining RTE 1974; Announcer, RTE, 1974-76; Presenter of numerous programmes on books, women's issues, social and political affairs, 1976-80; Editor, *Status,* 1980-81; freelance Broadcaster, 1981 to date; television presenter, *Consumer Choice* (RTE), *Crimeline* (RTE); Radio Presenter, *The Marian Finucane Show;* Director, Montrose Services Ltd., Montrose Productions Ltd.; recipient, Jacobs Award, 1980, Prix Italia, 1980 (for documentary on abortion), Radio Journalist of the Year Award, 1988; recognised as a thorough professional with a no nonsense approach; a seemingly relaxed presenter of one of the most popular current affairs/consumer programmes on radio; maintains a low personal profile. Hobbies, talking, reading, walking and horses. Contact: RTE, Donnybrook, Dublin 4. Tel: 208 3111.

FINUCANE, Marian

FITZGERALD, Frances, née Ryan; PUBLIC REPRESENTATIVE; *b* 1950; *educ* Sion Hill, Blackrock, Co. Dublin; University College Dublin; London School of Economics; (BSocSc, MSc); *m* Michael Fitzgerald; 3*s*; elected Fine Gael Deputy for Dublin South East 1992, re-elected 1997; spokesperson on Arts Culture & the Gaeltacht; represented Fine Gael on the All Party Oireachtas Committee on the Constitution and the National Economic and Social Forum Committee on State Sponsored Bodies and the Family Committee 1992-97; currently Spokesperson on Defence; member, Justice, Equality and Law Reform Committee; member, Fine Gael National Executive; former Chairperson of the Council for the Status of Women; member of the Second Commission on the Status of Women, 1990-93; member of the Forum for Peace and Reconciliation, 1995-96; Vice President of the Irish Council of the European Movement, 1991-93; Board member, Institute of European Affairs, 1993; served on the Board of the Employment Equality Agency and was Irish representative to the European Women's Lobby 1988-92; chairperson of the Women's Political Association between 1987 and 1989; well regarded within the Fine Gael party, seen as diligent and single minded. Hobbies, music, reading and walking. Contact; Dáil Eireann, Leinster House, Kildare Street, Dublin 2. Tel: 01 618 3771. Fax: 01 618 4511.

FITZGERALD, John; DUBLIN CITY MANAGER; *b* 1947; *educ* in Limerick; *widowed*; 4 children; Cork City Finance Officer; Finance Officer, Dublin Gas; Finance Officer, Dublin City Corporation; Assistant City and County Manager; when the new authorities were set up in the early nineties, creating Fingal, Dun Laoghaire/Rathdown and South Dublin County, was appointed to Dublin South County; Dublin City Manager, 1996 to date; regarded as a strong team worker who has transformed the Corporation into a pro-active organisation. Hobbies, tennis and walking. Contact: Dublin Corporation, Wood Quay, Dublin 8. Tel: 01 672 2222.

FITZGERALD, Mark

FITZGERALD, Mark; CHAIRMAN AND GROUP CHIEF EXECUTIVE SHERRY FITZGERALD GROUP; *b* 1957; *educ* Gonzaga College, Ranelagh, Dublin; College of Commerce Rathmines;

qualified as a member of The Irish Auctioneers & Valuers Institute, 1979; *m* Derval O' Higgins, solicitor; 1 *s* 4 *da*; elected Fellow of the IAVI, 1995; joined Fitzgerald and Partners, Auctioneers, 1975, Associate Director, 1981, Director, 1982, Founding Director, Sherry Fitzgerald, 1982; Managing Director, Sherry Fitzgerald, 1986; Chairman and Group Chief Executive, Sherry Fitzgerald Group, 1998 - the largest Property Advisory company in Ireland; regular contributor on property in the Irish media; Fellow Irish Auctioneers & Valuers Institute, member Stephens Green Club, Fitzwilliam Lawn Tennis Club; National Director of Elections for Fine Gael, 1997; former Chairman, B.I.M., 1996-97. Hobbies, family, politics, west of Ireland, walking. Contact: Sherry Fitzgerald Ltd., Merrion Row, Dublin 2. Tel: 01 661 6198. Fax: 01 661 9909.

FITZGERALD, Maurice; FINANCIAL ADVISOR, AUCTIONEER AND FOOTBALLER; *b* 1969; *educ* University College Cork, B.A. and HDip. in Ed.; *m* Sharon Moriarty; 1 *da*; Teacher, (Accounting, Economics and Mathematics), 1992-98; Financial Advisor and Auctioneer with Fitzgerald O'Connell Ltd., Cahirciveen, 1998-99; member, St. Mary's G.A.A. Club, Cahirciveen, Co. Kerry; awards include, All Ireland Medal in Football, Texaco Sportstar Awards, All Star Awards. Widely regarded as one of the finest footballers of his generation. Hobbies, boating, fishing and reading. Contact: Fitzgerald O'Connell Ltd., New Street, Cahirciveen, Co. Kerry. Tel. & Fax: 066 72085.

FITZGERALD, Susan

FITZGERALD, Susan; ACTRESS; *b* 1950; *educ* Evington Hall, Leicestershire; Trinity College Dublin, BA; *m* Michael Colgan, producer; 1*s* 2*da;* worked during the day with State Pathologist, Dr. John Harbison, and at night in the theatre; joined Edwards/MacLiammoir Company playing Lady Windermere in *Lady Windermere's Fan;* has played major roles in all Dublin theatres and toured with the Irish Theatre Company; theatre highlights include, *Educating Rita* (Gate), *Les Liaisons Dangereuses* (Gate), *A Doll's House* (Gate), *Present Laughter* (Gate), *Midsummer Nights Dream* (Abbey), *Hedda Gabler* (Abbey), *Seasons Greetings* (Gate), *The Heiress* (Gate), *Lady Windermere's Fan* (Gate and Spoleto Festival, Charleton, US), *Footfalls* (Gate and Lincoln Centre, New York) 1996, *Arcadia* (Gate); cinema credits include *Zardos, Portrait of the Artist, Serpent's Kiss, Sunburn, Angela's Ashes;* has worked extensively in radio and television in Ireland, UK and US, including *Fair City* (TV), *Monday at Nine* (radio); also various dramas and documentaries; nominated for Harvey Award for *Educating Rita*, nominated for *Irish Times* Award for *Lady Windermere's Fan,* 1998, Best Actress of the Year Award from *Sunday Independent*/Ka, 1998; a superb professional with a great ability to seize the comic moment. Hobbies, theatre, film, anthropology, alternative medicine. Contact: Lisa Richards Agency, 15 Lower Pembroke Street, Dublin 2. Tel: 01 662 4880.

FITZPATRICK, John W.

FITZMAURICE, Donald; SENIOR LECTURER IN CHEMISTRY, UNIVERSITY COLLEGE DUBLIN; CHIEF TECHNOLOGY OFFICER OF NANOMAT LTD.; *b* 1963; *educ* St. Paul's College, Raheny; University College Dublin, B.Sc (Hons., First), Ph.D.; Postdoctoral Fellow, University of California, Berkeley, 1988-90; Newman Scholar, University College Dublin, 1990-93; Visiting Scientist, Ecole Polytechnique Federal De Lausanne, 1990-90; Assistant Lecturer, University College Dublin, 1991-94, College Lecturer, 1994-98, Senior Lecturer, 1998 to date; CTO Nonomat Ltd., 1997 to date; member, Irish Council of Science Technology and Innovation; Chairman, National Technology Foresight (Pharmaceutical Panel); Chairman, National Science Education Benchmark Study; Awards include, Physics Scholarship, University College Dublin, 1982, Chemistry Scholarship, 1984, Newman Fellowship, 1991; Global Research Award, IBM, 1997; Research Award, Zeneca, 1998; publications include 70 papers, 3 book chapters and 3 patents. Hobbies, history and theory of cinema and visual arts. Contact: University College Dublin, Belfield, Dublin . Tel: 01 706 2441. Fax: 01 706 2127.

FITZPATRICK, John W.; CEO FITZPATRICK HOTEL GROUP NORTH AMERICA; *b* 1958; *educ* Blackrock College, Dublin; University of Las Vegas, *single;* Fitzpatrick Hotel Trainee; Shannon Shamrock - General Manager; Jointly operated Irish owned Hotels; Set up Fitzpatrick Hotels, North America, Currently CEO, Fitzpatrick Hotel Group, North America, comprising Fitzpatrick manhattan Hotel (Lexington Avenue), Fitzpatrick Grand Central Hotel (East 44th Street), Fitzpatrick Est 55th Hotel; Seen as an indefatigable networker; has achieved a high profile for Fitzpatrick Hotel Group in a city where competition is stiff. Hobbies, flying helecopter, planes, paramotor, golf, watersports. Contact: Fitzpatrick Manhattan Hotel, 687 Lexington Avenue, New , York, N.Y. 10022, U.S.A. Tel: 212 355 0100. Fax: 212 308 0711.

FITZPATRICK, Paul

FITZPATRICK, Paul; MANAGING DIRECTOR, EUROPE, FITZPATRICK HOTEL GROUP; *b* 1961; *educ* Blackrock College, Co. Dublin; UNLV, (USA); *single;* Managing Director, Fitzpatrick's Cork Hotel, 1987-90; Joint MD, Fitzpatrick Hotel Group, 1990-91, MD Europe, 1991 to date; the Fitzpatrick Hotel Group is a family owned company, recently restructured giving a substantial minority sharehold to a venture capital company, ACT, in order to expand; the company owns 5 hotels, 3 in Ireland - Fitzpatrick's Castle Hotel, Dublin, Fitzpatrick's Cork Hotel in Cork and Fitzpatrick's Bunratty Hotel, near Shannon, 2 in New York - Fitzpatrick's Manhattan Hotel &

Fitzpatrick's Grand Central Hotel; they are also contracted to manage a 150 bedroom hotel for British Airways, New York; subsidiary companies include GSA Agency for TWA, BWIA and Gulf Air and a seaside resort with 80 mobile homes; the three Irish hotels all have between 100-120 rooms, large convention facilities catering for up to 1000 people, extensive leisure complex (including 1 golf course), bars and restaurants. Hobbies, golf and Harley Davidsons. Contact: Fitzpatrick Hotel Group, 14 Windsor Terrace, Dun Laoghaire, Co. Dublin. Tel: 01 284 5656. Fax: 01 284 5655.

FITZPATRICK, Sean P.; CEO ANGLO IRISH BANK CORPORATION PLC; *b* 1948; *educ* Presentation College Bray; University College Dublin, BComm; Chartered Accountant; *m* Triona O'Toole, 2*s* 1 *da;* joined Anglo Irish Bank, 1978; Main Board in 1985, appointed CEO in 1986 to date; Fellow, Chartered Accountants in Ireland, Institute of Bankers, Institute of Taxation; member, Dublin Docklands Development Authority; member, Druids Glen Golf Club, Greystones Golf Club, Fitzwilliam LTC and Hibernian United Services Club. A personable man with the leadership qualities and imagination to take Anglo Irish Bank from a modest operation to a respected member of the banking community. Contact: Anglo Irish Bank, Stephen's Court, 18-21 St. Stephen's Green, Dublin 2. Tel: 01 676 0141. Fax: 661 8480.

FITZPATRICK, Sean P.

FLANNERY, Frank; CHIEF EXECUTIVE REHAB GROUP; *b* 1944; *educ* St. Clement's College Limerick; University College Galway, B.A., University College Dublin, M.B.A.; Irish Management Institute, Dip. Applied Finance; *m* Marguerite MacCurtin; President of Union of Students in Ireland, 1971-72; joined Rehab Group, 1973 as Executive Assistant to the General Manager, General Manager, Chief Executive in 1981 to date; The Group has developed from an organisation employing approx. 100 people with some 700 trainees, to its current position where it now spans Ireland, Scotland and England, employing a total of approx. 1,700. The Group comprises 27 companies with a turnover in excess of £70m. Member, RTE Authority 1990-1993; Chairman of Cablelink 1986-90; member of National Rehabilitation Board 1983-1997; member of St. Luke's and St. Anne's Hospitals Board 1995-1998; Founder: Rehab Lotteries and U.K. CHARITY Lotteries; Member, Killimordaly GAA, Loughrea Golf Club, Galway Bay Golf & Country Club, Fitzwilliam LTC, Irish Management Institute, Marketing Institute of Ireland, Hibernian United Services Club, Blackrock RFC and Luttrellstown GC. As Director of Local Elections for Fine Gael he is regarded as an excellent strategist, a highly influential figure on Party organisation. Hobbies, current affairs, politics, sport, especially Gaelic football, hurling and golf. Contact: Rehab Group, Roslyn Park, Sandymount, Dublin 4. Tel: 01 205 7200. Fax: 01 205 7211

FLAVIN, Jim; COMPANY DIRECTOR; *b* 1942; *educ* Blackrock College; University College Dublin, BComm, DPA; Chartered Accountancy, FCA; *m* Mary Ryan; 1 *s* 3 *da*; Head of Venture Capital, AIB 1971-76; Deputy Chairman/Chief Executive, DCC plc, which he founded in 1976; Recognised as the driving force behind the development of Ireland's largest and most successful industrial holding company which comprises four divisions, DCC SerCom, DCC Energy, DCC Foods and DCC Healthcare and is quoted on the Dublin and London stock exchanges; Director, Telecom Eireann plc, Fyffes plc; Member, Institute of Chartered Accountants. Clubs, RAC Club, Greystones Golf Club, Royal Irish Yacht Club. Contact: DCC House, Brewery Road, Stillorgan, Co. Dublin. Tel: 01 283 1011. Fax: 01 283 1017.

FLINN, Donal Patrick; CHAIRMAN AND DIRECTOR; *b* 1923; *educ* Christian Brothers College, Cork, University College Cork, B.Comm; *m* Heather Cole; 2 *s* 1 *da*; Joined Kevans & Sons Chartered Accountants, Partner Kevans & Sons, Founder, Chairman and Managing Partner Coopers & Lybrand; Former Chairman, Barclays Bank in Ireland, Irish Press plc.; Former Director, Canada Life Ireland, Abbey Life Ireland; Currently, Chairman, De La Rue Smurfit, Salomon Brothers Asset Management Ireland Ltd., Salomon Brothers Funds plc.; Director, Salomon Smith Barney Management Co. Ireland Ltd., Fitzwilton plc.; President, United States Chamber of Commerce, 1989-91. Hobbies, golf, tennis and fishing, Clubs, Partmarnock Golf Club, Fitzwilliam LTC, Royal St. George Yacht Club. Contact: PriceWaterhouseCooper, George's Quay, Dublin 2. Tel: 01 704 8500. Fax: 01 704 8600.

FLINN, William Hugo; GENERAL MANAGER - FINANCE - BANK OF IRELAND GROUP; *b* 1954; *educ* Gonzaga College, Dublin; Trinity College Dublin BA Econ.; Institute of Chartered Accountants, FCA.; *m* Jo Sheridan; 2*s* 5 *da*; joined Price Waterhouse, Dublin, 1979, Price Waterhouse, San José, California, 1981; various roles in finance, Measures Corp, California, 1983; Vice President, Finance, GPA Technologies (division of GPA), 1990; Senior Vice President, GE Capital Aviation Services (successor to GPA Group), 1993; General Manager - Finance - Bank of Ireland, 1998 to date; Director, Pacific Aerotec Inc, Seattle, Washington (specialists in aircraft window and electronic component repairs); Past President of various Toastmasters Clubs; member, Royal St. George Yacht Club, Charleville Golf Club, Fitzwilliam Lawn Tennis Club. Hobbies, golf, tennis, outdoor activities, bridge, politics, public affairs, public speaking. Contact: Bank of Ireland,

FLAVIN, Jim

Lower Baggot Street, Dublin 2. Tel: 01 604 3000.

FLINTER, Dan; CHIEF EXECUTIVE ENTERPRISE IRELAND; *b* 1951; *educ* Athy Christian Brothers School, Co. Kildare; University College Dublin MA Econ.; *married; three children*; Researcher in Planning Division, IDA, 1973, Senior Economist, Departmental Manager for Information Technology, Head of Planning, Director of Overseas Investment; Chief Executive, Forbairt, 1994-98; Chief Executive, Enterprise Ireland, 1998 to date. Hobbies, theatre and reading. Contact: Enterprise Ireland, Wilton Park House, Wilton Park, Dublin 2. Tel: 01 857 0000. Fax: 01 808 2020.

FLYNN, Martina

FLYNN, Martina; MANAGER, UNIVERSITY OF LIMERICK BUSINESS & TECHNICAL INFORMATION SERVICE; *b* 1962; *educ* St. Mary's Holy Faith Convent, Killester; University College Dublin, BA; Diploma, Library and Information Studies; *single;* Information Officer, Offshore Intelligence, Dublin, 1985-86; Trainee Library Assistant, British Museum (Natural History), London, 1987; Librarian, London, 1988; Senior Information Officer, John Brown Engineers & Constructors Ltd., London, 1988-90; currently Manager, University of Limerick Business and Technical Information Service (BTiS); has published papers in international business and academic journals; co-ordinator, MIDAS-NET IRELAND; member, Irish and U.K. Library Association. Hobbies, sailing, travel, art, archaeology, swimming, films. Contact: University of Limerick, Limerick. Tel: 061 202 700. Fax: 061 330 316.

FOGARTY, Stuart

FOGARTY, Stuart; MANAGING DIRECTOR AFA ADVERTISING; DIRECTOR CLUB INTERNET, MEDIANET; *b* 1961; *educ* St. Columba's, Rathfarnham; University College Dublin, B.Comm.; *m* Audrey Flanagan; previously Account Executive with AFA Advertising, currently Managing Director; Founder, ISP MediaNet/Club Internet; prime mover in Internet ad agency ICAN; President Institute of Advertising Practitioners, 1990-92; Chairman, Advertising Press Club, 1989; Council Member, Marketing Institute, 1993; Council Member, Publicity Club, 1990; Fellow, Institute of Advertising Practitioners, 1996; member, Institute of Creative Advertising and Design; Clubs, Suttonians RFC and Howth Yacht Club. Contact: AFA Advertising, 72 Haddington Road, Dublin 4. Tel: 01 668 1455. Fax: 01 668 1447.

FOTTRELL, Patrick Finbar; PRESIDENT NATIONAL UNIVERSITY OF IRELAND, GALWAY; *b* 1933; *educ* University College Cork, BSc., MSc.; University of Glasgow, Scotland, PhD; University College Galway, DSc.; *m* Esther Kennedy; *2s 2 da;* Senior Research Officer, Agricultural Institute (An Foras Taluntais), 1963-65; Lecturer, University College Galway, 1965-70, Associate Professor, 1970-76, Professor of Biochemistry, 1976-96, Registrar, Deputy President, 1986-92, President, National University of Ireland, Galway, 1996-2000; publications include 115 scientific papers published in international learned journals; two books, one on coeliac disease, one on HIV/AIDS; member, Royal Irish Academy (Vice President); awards include, Beit Memorial Fellowship (1960-63), Royal Dublin Society ASTRA Award for Applied Science and Technology (1982), EEC/GLAXCO Science Writers Award, (1983); other biographical listings include, *Who's Who in the World;* member, Oughterard Golf Club. Hobbies, music, reading and sport (soccer and golf). Contact: Office of the President, National University of Ireland, Galway. Tel: 091 524 411. Fax: 091 524 176.

FOX, Ian

FOX, Ian; CHIEF EXECUTIVE, INSTITUTE OF ADVERTISING PRACTITIONERS IN IRELAND, MUSIC CRITIC, BROADCASTER; *b* 1941; *educ* High School, Dublin, College of Commerce, Rathmines, Dip. Bus. Studies; *single*; Brand Manager, Unilever, 1967-70; Account Director, McConnells, Wilson Hartnell, O'Mearas, Cronins, Arks, Saatchi & Saatchi, 1970-93. Head of IAPI, the advertising industry's professional body, 1994 to date; Board Member, the European Association of Advertsing Agencies, Advertising Standards Authority for Ireland; Former Chairman, Marketing Society; Member, Arts Committee, R.D.S.; Council Member, Wexford Festival; Board Member, Guardian Dublin International Piano Competition; Governor, Royal Irish Academy of Music; Music Critic, *Sunday Tribune*, 1986 to date; RTE broadcaster, 1969 to date; music lecturer; editor, Wexford Festival history, *One Hundred Nights at the Opera*, founding editor, *Counterpoint* (magazine of the Music Association of Ireland), 1969; Awarded the International Nordring Prize for Joyce documentary *Bloomenlied*, 1981; A leading figure in Irish advertsing and a highly informed critic, recognised as a force in music in Ireland. Hobbies, music, gardening, cooking. Contact: The Institute of Advertising Practitioners in Ireland, 8, Upper Fitzwilliam Street, Dublin 2. Tel: 01 676 5991. Fax: 01 661 4589.

FOX, Robbie; PUBLICIAN AND RESTAURATEUR; *b* 1957; *educ* O'Connells C.B.S., N.C.R., Dublin; *m* Martina Meredith; 2 *da*; Left school and started as an apprentice bartender in The Towers Bar, Ballymun, 1973; Transferred to Hunters Bar and Restaurant, South Frederick Street, Dublin 2, Food & Beverage Manager, 1976; Opened The Pink Elephant Nightclub, 1978-86; Opened Judge Roy Beans, highly successful Tex Mex restaurant, 1986-88; Opened Tante Zoe's, first cajun / creole restaurant in Dublin, 1989 to date; Opened Lillies Bordello, Grafton Street, 1992-94; Moved to Renards Bar and Nightclub, one of Dublin's most prestigious night spots, 1995 to date; Member: Restaurant Owners Association, Licenced Vintners Association, Dublin Nightclub Owners Association, Powerscourt Golf Club. Hobbies, politics, business, sport, keeping fit. Contact: Renards, South Frederick Street, Dublin 2. Tel: 01 677 5876.

FREANEY, Eamonn Francis; CHARTERED ACCOUNANT; *b* 1961; *educ* Belvedere College, Dublin; University College Dublin, BComm; FCA; *m* Geraldine Ward; 2*s* 1*da*; joined company established by father, Oliver Freaney, Oliver M. Freaney & Co. Hobbies, golf and football. Contact: Oliver M. Freaney, 45 Northumberland Road, Dublin 4. Tel: 01 668 6644. Fax: 01 668 9755.

FREEHILL, Mary; PUBLIC REPRESENTATIVE, LORD MAYOR OF DUBLIN; *b* 1946; *educ* Convent of Mercy, Ballinmore, Institute of Education, Leeson Street, Dublin; *single;* joined National Rehabilitation Board 1973, currently Training Advisor; Vice Chairperson, Dublin Institute of Technology, has served on the EU's committee of the Regions; joined the Labour Party 1969; co-opted to the Council for the Pembroke Ward 1977; lost her seat 1985 and regained it 1991, represents the Rathmines Ward; elected Lord Mayor of Dublin, June 1999; former leader of the Labour Group and Chairperson of Cultural Committee, plays a leading role in Dublin Corporation's Equality, Cultural, Traffic and Planning Committees; regarded as a dedicated, tough minded socialist; a strong supporter of the disadvantaged. Hobbies, arts, reading, music and the Humbert and Merriman Summer Schools. Contact: Labour Party Headquarters, 17 Ely Place, Dublin 2. Tel: 01 661 2615.

FRENCH, Ian; CHARTERED SURVEYOR; *b* 1943; *educ* Wesley College, Dublin; Bolton Street College of Technology, RICS; *m* Rosemary Miley; 2 *da*; Assistant Surveyor, Lisney & Sons, 1964-87; Surveyor, Osborne King & Megran, 1967, Partner, 1970-87; Managing Director, Hamilton Osborne King 1987-95, Chairman, Hamilton Osborne King 1995 to date; Member, Society of Chartered Surveyors; Board member, The Kings Hospital School; Member, Institute of Arbitrators; Hobbies, sailing, golf, walking, skiing and gardening; Clubs, Royal St. George Yacht Club, Kildare Street and University Club, Carrickmines Golf Club. Contact: Hamilton Osborne King, Estate Agents, Auctioneers and Valuers, 32, Molesworth Street, Dublin 2. Tel: 01 618 1300. Fax: 01 676 7066.

FREYNE, Sean Vincent; PROFESSOR OF THEOLOGY TRINITY COLLEGE DUBLIN; *b* 1935; *educ* St. Jarlath's College, Tuam; St. Patrick's College, Maynooth (NUI, BA Ancient Classics, & Pontifical BD); Biblical Institute, Rome & Jerusalem: Licentiate in Scriptures DD, LSS; Jewish Institute, Tübingen, Germany, Post Doctoral Research; *m* Gail Grossman; 2*da;* Professor of Scripture, St. Patrick's College, Maynooth, 1969-75; Professor, Loyola University, New Orleans LA 1975-79; Professor, University of Queensland, Brisbane, Australia, 1979-80; Professor of Theology, Trinity College Dublin, Head of School of Hebrew, Biblical & Theological Studies, Head of Herzog Centre of Jewish and Near Eastern Religions & Culture, 1981 to date; Member, Editorial Board, *Concilium, an International Journal of Theology,* 1987 to date; Visiting Professor, Tulane University, New Orleans, Notre Dame University (Ind); Radio and TV programmes (BBC & RTE) on Bible, N. East, Theology; publications include, *Galilee from Alexander the Great to Hadrian, A Study of Second Temple Judaism* (1980, reprint 1998), *The World of the New Testament* (1981), *Galilee, Jesus and the Gospels, Literary Approaches and Historical Investigations* (1988), *The Twelve Disciples and Apostles, Galilee and Gospel* Collected Essays (1990); member, (past committee member), Society for the Study of the New Testament; member, European Association of Jewish Studies, American Society for Oriental Research, Irish Biblical Association (Past President), Irish Theological Association (Past Committee Member); awards include, Alexander von Humbold Stiftung Stipendiat (Research Fellow), 1969, Fellow Trinity College, 1982; member, Royal Irish Academy, 1986; Trustee, Chester Beatty Library and Gallery of Oriental Art 1984. Hobbies, all sport, especially Gaelic Games; holder of All Ireland Minor Medal (1953) as Captain of Mayo, theatre, hill walking and travel. Contact: Theology Department, Trinity College Dublin, Dublin 2. Tel: 01 608 1368.

FRIDAY, Gavin Fionàn Hanvey; COMPOSER, SINGER, SONGWRITER, PAINTER; *b* 1959; *educ* St. Kevin's College CBS Ballygal, Dublin; *m* Renée O'Reilly; founder, lead singer, Virgin Prunes; founder member, Avant Garde punk ensemble, 1978-85; currently solo performer, composer and painter; recordings include numerous albums with Virgin Prunes, including *If I Die, I Die,* other recordings *Each Man Kills the Thing He Loves* 1989, *Shag Tobacco,* 1995; film scores/soundtracks include, *In The Name of the Father,* 1994, *Angel Baby,* 1997, *The Boxer,* 1998; contributed to movie soundtracks in *Shortcuts, William Shakespeare, Romeo and Juliet;* solo Art Exhibition, Hendrick Gallery, Dublin, 1988; has been writing in collaboration with Maurice Seezer since 1986; member, I.M.R.O, Musicians Union (UK); recipient, Golden Globe nomination - Best Original Singer in Motion Picture, 1994; Ivor Novello Nomination - Best Song in Film, 1995; *Hotpress*

FRIDAY, Gavin

Award - best Irish Solo Performer, 1996; Australian Academy Awards - Best Song in Movie, 1997; recognised as an innovative catalyst, a post punk modernist and a strong influence on fellow musicians. Hobbies, "It's as on to my platform shoes". Contact: ALK Management, 7 Seapoint Terrace, Irishtown, Dublin 4. Tel: 01 667 7607. Fax: 01 667 7608.

FRIEL, Brian; PLAYWRIGHT; *b* 1929; educ St. Columb's College, Derry; St. Patrick's College, Maynooth, BA; St. Joseph's College, Belfast; *m* Anne Morrison; 1 *s* 4 *da;* School Teacher, Derry 1950-60; first plays broadcast on BBC Radio include *A Sort of Freedom* (1958), *A Doubtful Paradise* (1963); Plays for theatre in Ireland, UK and USA include: *The Enemy Within, The Blind Mice* (1963), *Philadelphia, Here I Come!* (1965), *Loves of Cass Maguire* (1967), *Lovers* (1968), *Crystal and Fox* (1968), *The Mundy Scheme* (1969), *The Gentle Island* (1989), *The Freedom of the City* (1973), *Volunteers* (1975), *Faith Healer* (1980), *Translations* (1981), *The Communication Cord* (1983), *Making History* (1988), *Aristocrats* (1968), *Dancing at Lughnasa* (1990), *Molly Sweeney* (1995), *Give Me Your Answer, Do!* (1997). Other publications include: *The Saucer of Larks* and *The Gold in the Sea* (short stories), editor of *The Last of the Name*; Co-founder, with Stephen Rea, Field Day Theatre Company (1980); member of Seanad Eireann 1987; Honorary Senior Fellow of University College Dublin, Member of American Academy of Arts and Letters, and Royal Society of Literature. One of the foremost playwrights in the English language. Hobby, fishing. Contact: Aosdána, 70 Merrion Square, Dublin 2. Tel: 01 661 1840. Fax: 01 676 1302.

FULLER, Ann, née Mahon; ADMINISTRATOR, GUARDIAN DUBLIN INTERNATIONAL PIANO COMPETITION *b* 1938 *educ* Convent of the Sacred Heart, Leeson Street, Dublin; Trinity College Dublin, MA; *m* Warren Fuller, US Diplomat (*decd.*); Cultural Officer, US Embassy (Dublin), 1965-70; Theatre Promoter, West End Theatre (UK), 1970-71; Editor, World Health Organisation, 1972-74; Co-Founder, with John O'Conor, Dublin International Piano Competition, 1987; Chairman, Cultural Relations Committee, Department of Foreign Affairs; Board Member, National Concert Hall, Ireland, - United States Commission for Educational Exchange, Opera Theatre Company, World Federation of International Music Competitions, Geneva; Governor, Royal Irish Academy of Music; Excellent administrative abilities, as demonstrated by running Dublin (Guardian) Piano Competition, have led to other major Board appointments; a considerable influence on the Arts, particularly music, in Ireland. Hobbies, reading, bridge, music, theatre, walking her dogs. Contact: Guardian International Piano Competition, Liffey House, Tara Street, Dublin 1. Tel: 01 677 3066. Fax: 01 671 1385

GAFFNEY, Lucy

GAFFNEY, Lucy; MANAGING DIRECTOR ESAT CLEAR; *b* 1960; *educ* Loreto Convent, Foxrock, Co. Dublin; College of Marketing & Design, Dublin; *m* Gerard Maguire; 2 *da*; started her career as a secretary in a recruitment agency; joined Bell Advertising as Accounts Director; joined Irish Press Group in mid 1980s as advertising and promotions manager; Marketing Director 98FM, 1989-1995; set up the Ideas Company, 1995; joined Esat Telecom as Marketing Director in 1997; Managing Director of Esat Clear, June 1998 to date; member, Marketing Institute of Ireland. Hobbies, children, cooking and reading. Contact: Esat Clear, Cardiff Lane, Dublin. Tel: 1800 212 321.

GAHAN, Irene H.; MANAGING DIRECTOR AND FOUNDER, THE INTERACTIVE AVENUE; *b* 1972; *educ* St. MacDara's College; University of Hertfordshire, University of Poitiers, France; Diploma in Journalism; *single*; Engineering Technician, Intel Ireland, 1993-96; Editor and Webmaster, RYA Media, 1996; Founder and Managing Director, The Interactive Avenue, Ireland's first Internet training company; Editor, *Go Direct*, Co-editor, *Wham, Deadline,* Assistant Editor, *Dot.ie,* contributing journalist, *IT, Business & Finance, IMJ*; Author, *Internet Marketing - Talking to the WWW*; Member: Irish Direct Marketing Association (IDMA), 1996; Committee for Irish Direct Marketing Association (IDMA) Brave New Media Conference with Telecom Eireann, 1996; Board Member: Irish Direct Marketing Association (IDMA), Irish Internet Association, Training Committee of Irish Internet Association; Awarded New Media Internet Marketing Award, IDMA Annual Awards, 1996; Speaker at Irish Internet Association, Law Society of Ireland, and various Chambers of Commerce and Enterprise Board meetings on Internet marketing and e-commerce. Hobbies, Formula 1 fanatic, travelling. Contact: The Interactive Avenue, 12-24, Herbert Lane, Dublin 2. Tel: 01 662 9929. Fax: 1800 334 567.

GAHAN, Irene H.

GALLAGHER, Anne Philomena Marie; MARKETING DIRECTOR, GALLAGHER BROTHERS (FISH MERCHANTS) LTD; *b* 1961; *educ* Ard Luis Convent, Bundoran; University College Galway, B.Comm, H.DipEd; Teachers Diploma Speech and Drama, London College of Music, LLCM; *single;* joined the accountancy department of the family fish business, Gallagher Bros.; Actively involved in the company's diversification into aquaculture; assisted in the formulation of the salmon farming company, Ocean Farms Ltd; currently Director of both Gallagher Brothers (Fish Merchants) Ltd. and Ocean Farms Ltd.; Board member, B.I.M. since 1998; represents Irish Salmon Growers Association on the Irish Marketing Committee for Salmon; Founder, Managing

Director, Print & Design Ltd; a hands on businesswoman with a commercial scuba diving qualification (HSE IV), which enables her to inspect the company's salmon farms; Founder, Artistic Director, Killybegs Dramatic Society. Hobbies, drama, water skiing, sailing, diving, travelling, fishing. Contact: Gallagher Bros. (Fish Merchants) Ltd., Killybegs, Co. Donegal. Tel: 073 31004. Fax: 073 31509.

GALLAGHER, Anne P.

GALLAGHER, Bernadette, "Bernie" née Doyle ; DIRECTOR JURYS HOTEL GROUP PLC.; *b* 1959; *educ* Our Lady's Convent, Rathnew, Co. Wicklow; Holy Child Convent, Killiney, Co. Dublin; University College Dublin, BA Econ Pol; *m* John Gallagher; 1*s* 2*da;* gained experience in the hotel business abroad during university holidays; joined family owned hotel group Doyle Hotels, founded by father, P.V. Doyle; worked in marketing, Marketing and Board Director, 1980; Doyle Hotel Group acquired by Jury Hotel Group for £185 million in 1999; Director, Jurys Hotel Group plc, 1999; Director, Bord Failte; Director, Celtic Utilities; member, Institute of Directors, former member, University College Dublin Council. Hobbies, art, horseriding, skiing and reading. Contact: Jurys Hotel Group, 146 Pembroke Road, Ballsbridge, Dublin 4. Tel: 01 607 0070.

GALLAGHER, Charles Hubert; CHAIRMAN, COMPANY DIRECTOR; *b* 1959; *educ* Jesus College, Cambridge; London Business School; *m* Patricia McCaffrey; 1 *s* 3 *da;* Appointed Director of Abbey plc in 1986; Deputy Chairman, 1988, Executive Chairman, 1993 to date; Abbey plc is a holiday company involved in residential housing and land development, property rental and trading, property investment and plant hire; A well respected businessman with a keen interest in politics; Clubs, St. Stephen's Green Club, Dublin. Contact: Abbey plc, Abbey House, 2, Southgate Road, Potters Bar, Hertfordshire EN6 5DU, England. Tel: 01707 651266. Fax: 01707 645920.

GALLAGHER, Conrad

GALLAGHER, Conrad; CHEF, RESTAURATEUR; *b* 1971; *educ* St. Eunan's College, Killybegs Catering College, City & Guilds Diploma, Restaurant Management Course, NYU; 1 *da*; Commis Chef, various local hotels, Donegal, 1986-88; Sous Chef, Renvyle House Hotel and New York, 1988-90; Sous Chef, Waldorf Astoria and Plaza Hotel, New York, 1990-93; Hotel de Paris under Alain Ducasse, 1993-94; Head Chef, Morels, 1995; opened Peacock Alley, Baggot Street, 1995; relocated to South William Street, 1996; opened Lloyds, 1997; opened Christopher's and relocated Peacock Alley to Fitzwilliam Hotel, 1998; Bagel Factory to open, 1999; Publications include: *New Irish Cooking*, October 1997, two more books planned; recipient of Award of Excellence from White House, prizes and awards for ice sculpting and junior competitions; Lloyds awarded Michelin 'Red M', 1999; Hard work, genius and a strong media approach are the ingredients of this chef/businessman's meteoric rise on the Irish catering scene. Hobbies, fishing, wine and art. Contact: Peacock Alley, 109, St. Stephen's Green, Dublin 2. Tel: 01 478 7015. Fax: 01 478 7025.

GALLAGHER, Dermot; SECOND SECRETARY-GENERAL DEPARTMENT OF FOREIGN AFFAIRS; *b* 1945; *educ* Presentation Brothers College, Carrick-on-Shannon, Co. Leitrim; University College Dublin, BA, MA; *married;* 1*s* 2 *da;* member of Irish Delegation to Annual General Assembly of the United Nations, New York, 1970-72; Third Secretary, San Francisco, 1971-73, First Secretary, Dublin, 1973, First Secretary, Press & Information, London, 1973-77, Counsellor, Dublin, 1977-80; Deputy Chef de Cabinet (on secondment) Commission of the European Communities, 1980-82; Counsellor, Dublin, 1983-85, Ambassador, Federal Republic of Nigeria, 1985-87, Assistant Secretary, Dublin, 1987-91, Ambassador, United States of America, 1991-97, Second Secretary-General, Department of Foreign Affairs, 1997 to date, with special responsibility for Anglo-Irish relations and the Northern Ireland peace process and negotiations; member, Kildare Street and University Club. Hobbies, all types of sport, especially football, hurling, rugby and tennis, reading, current affairs, theatre, travel and good dinner company and conversation. Contact: Department of Foreign Affairs, Iveagh House, St. Stephen's Green, Dublin 2. Tel: 01 408 2261. Fax: 01 475 7822.

GALLAGHER, Jackie; PUBLIC RELATIONS CONSULTANT / JOINT MANAGING DIRECTOR OF GALLAGHER-KELLY PUBLIC RELATIONS; *b* 1966; *educ* Cólaiste Phàdraig, Swinford, Co. Mayo; College of Journalism, Rathmines; National College of Industrial Relations; *m* Eileen Goold; 1 *da*; Business and Finance Reporter, *The Irish Times*, 1988-91, Industry and Employment Correspondent, 1991-94; Special Advisor to Leader of Fianna Fáil, Bertie Ahern, January 1995-June 1997, Special Advisor to Taoiseach, Bertie Ahern, June 1997-December 1998; Director Corporate Relations, Fleishman-Hillard Saunders, December, 1988-May 1999; Joint Managing Director, Gallagher-Kelly Public Relations, May 1999 to date; Joint Editor, *Taking the Long View - 70 Years of Fianna Fáil;* member, National Union of Journalists, Children's Millenium Fund Board. Contact: Gallagher-Kelly Public Relations, 31 Upper Merrion Street, Dublin 2. Tel: 01 618 2068.

GALVIN, Barry; CHIEF LEGAL OFFICER CRIMINAL ASSETS BUREAU / SOLICITOR; *b* 1946; *educ* in Cork; Kings Inns (awarded Brooke's Prize); called to the Bar, 1966; changed course and qualified as a solicitor; joined thriving, established family practice in Cork; appointed State Solicitor for Cork, 1983; appointed Chief Legal Officer, Criminal Assets Bureau, 1996; recognised

as a dedicated fighter, intellectual and relentless; a lawyer who hits criminals where it hurts - their profits. Contact: Criminal Assets Bureau, Dublin Metropolitan Area Headquarters, Harcourt Square, Dublin 2. Tel: 01 475 5555.

GALWAY, James, OBE; MUSICIAN; *b* 1939; *educ* St. Paul's School, Mountcellyer Secondary Modern School, Belfast; Royal College of Music, Guildhall School of Music, London; Paris Conservatory; *m dis;* 1*s* 2*da; m dis;* 1*s* 1 *da; m* Jeanne Cinnante; began career at Sadlers Wells Opera, then BBC Symphony Orchestra, London Symphony Orchestra, Royal Philharmonic (principal flute); appointed Principal Flute of Berlin Philharmonic 1969; in 1975 launched solo career; since then has toured extensively in the U.S.A. both in recital and with all major U.S. orchestras, also a regular visitor to Japan as well as all major European Festivals; recordings include over fifty best-selling RCA Victor Albums; has premiered specially commissioned works with leading European orchestras; appointed Principal Guest Conductor of the London Mozart Players 1999/2000; has played at both the White House and Buckingham Palace; recordings have been awarded numerous prizes including the Grand Prix du Disque; record awards from both *Billboard* and *Cash Box* magazines (U.S.) and platinum and gold albums; recipient of many honorary doctorates; recognised as a supreme interpreter of the classical flute repertoire and a consummate entertainer. Hobbies, music, walking, swimming, theatre, film, TV, chess, backgammon and conversation. Contact: IMG, Media House, 3 Burlington Lane, London, W4 2TH. Tel: 0044 181 233 5801. Fax: 0044 181 233 5849.

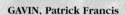

GAVIN, Patrick Francis

GAVIN, Patrick Francis, "Frankie"; MUSICIAN; *b* 1956; *educ* Franciscan Brothers Corrandulla, Co. Galway; *m* E Tracy Harris, fiction writer and musician; 2*s* 1 *da;* leader of De Dannan for 25 years (this year); recorded with the late Sir Yehudi Menuhin and Stephane Grappelli; more recently an album with Keith Richards entitled *Wingless Angels*; recorded on Voodoo Lounge with the Rolling Stones; performed for State visit of Prince Charles and on numerous other State occasions; members of De Dannan are, Alec Finn (bazouki), Brian McGrath (banjo and piano), Colm Murphy (bodhran), Andrew Murray (vocals); De Dannan embraces the roots of West of Ireland music combined with exciting contemporary arrangements; recordings include 10 band albums, 3 solo albums and 4 in progress; Patron, Irish Music (Traditional) School Galway; recipient, AIB Musician of the Year; Bank of Ireland Arts Award; a traditional fiddle player and an outstanding virtuoso, regarded as the finest in his field. Hobbies, gardening, fishing, hiking, collecting music and songs and meeting people with a sense of humour. Contact: Terri Connaughton. Tel: 01 496 8910.

GEOGHEGAN, The Hon. Mr. Justice Hugh; JUDGE OF THE HIGH COURT; *b* 1938; *educ* Clongowes Wood College, University College Dublin, King's Inns, B.C.L., LL.B; *m* Mary Finlay, S.C; 2 *da*; Called to the Bar, 1962; Practised in Midland Circuit and Dublin; Called to the Inner Bar, 1977; Called to the Bar of England and Northern Ireland; Former member of the Bar Council; Public Service Arbitration, 1982-92; Elected a Bencher of Kings Inns, 1992; Appointed Judge of the High Court, 1992; Member of Board of Governors, Clongowes Wood College; Member of the Council of the Royal Victoria Eye and Ear Hospital, Dublin. Hobbies, current affairs, travel, theatre, cinema and music; Clubs, Kildare Street and University Club, Fitzwilliam Lawn Tennis Club, Royal Dublin Society; Belmullet Golf Club. Contact: Four Courts, Morgan Place, Dublin 7. Tel: 01 872 5555.

GEOGHEGAN-QUINN, Màire; JOURNALIST, WRITER; *b* 1950; *educ* Convent of Mercy, Carna; Colàiste Mhuire, Tourmakeady; Carysfort Teacher Training College, Dublin; *m* John Quinn, Businessman; 2 *s;* Teacher, Scoil Bhride, Ranelagh, Dublin, 1970-73; Teacher, Scoil Caitriona, Renmore, 1973-75; elected Fianna Fáil Deputy for Galway West, 1975 to date; Parliamentary Secretary to Minister for Industry, Commerce and Energy, 1977-78; Minister of State at the same Department, with responsibility for Consumer Affairs, 1978-79; Minister for the Gaeltacht, 1979-81, becoming the first woman Deputy to reach Cabinet level since the foundation of the State; Minister of State at the Department of Education, with responsibility for Youth and Sport; Minister of State at the Department of the Taoiseach, with responsibility as Co-ordinator of government policy and EC Matters 1987-91; Minister For Tourism, Transport & Communications, 1992 and Minister for Justice 1993 and 1994; has served on Galway Borough Council and various local committees; former Chairperson, Joint Oireachtas Committee on Women's Rights; represented Ireland on EC Council of Budget Ministers and Council of Cultural Ministers. A highly competent ex-Minister, retired from politics in 1997; Now a columnist with *The Irish Times*; Broadcaster, Teilifis Na Gaeilge; Business Consultant and Non-Executive Director, Ryan Hotels plc, Aer Lingus plc.; Published first novel, *The Green Diamond*, 1996; A not always convincing voice, attempting to explain grass roots Fianna Fáil to *Irish Times* readers. Hobbies, reading, walking, theatre, music. Contact: The Irish Times, D'Olier Street, Dublin 2. Tel: 01 679 2022.

GIBNEY, Arthur; ARCHITECTURAL CONSULTANT, ARTIST; *b* 1932; *educ* National College of Art, Dublin; Institute of Technology, Dip. Arch.; Trinity College Dublin, PhD.; *m* Phyllis Burke, stained glass Artist; 1 *da*; Assistant to Michael Scott, 1958-61; Partner, Stephenson Gibney & Associates, 1961-75; Managing Partner, Arthur Gibney & Associates, 1975-98; currently Consultant with Arthur Gibney & Partners; designs include: IMI Headquarters, Sandyford, CTT Headquarters (Enterprise Ireland), Restoration Dr. Steeven's Hospital, Patrick Guilbaud's Restaurant; Fellow, Royal Institute of Architects of Ireland; member, former President, Society of Designers in Ireland; former President R.I.A.I.; awarded Triennial Gold Medal R.I.A.I. (I.M.I.) 1974-76; awarded Europa Nostra Award for Conservation (Dr. Steeven's Hospital), 1994; member, Board of National Gallery of Ireland; member, St. Stephen's Green Club. Hobbies, food and wine, travel, architectural history, the Arts generally. Contact: Arthur Gibney and Partners, 20 Harcourt Street, Dublin 2. Tel: 01 478 4300. Fax: 01 475 2092.

GILL, Michael

GILL, Michael; PUBLISHER; *b* 1940; *educ* Belvedere College; University College Dublin; *m* Anne Leonard, Psychotherapist and Counsellor; 3 *da*; worked in publishing in New York, London and Paris before returning to Dublin to become the fifth generation of the family to run the established publishing business; Editor, M.H. Gill & Son 1963-68; association formed with UK and international publishers, Macmillan 1967; Managing Director, Gill & Macmillan 1968 to date; past president, Irish Book Publishers Association; Irish Delegate, Federation of European Publishers; Director, Irish Copyright Licensing Agency; Director, Ireland Literature Exchange. A self effacing businessman; one of the most influential figures in Irish publishing. Hobbies, music, cycling, sailing, golf and reading; Club, Portmarnock Golf Club. Contact: Gill & Macmillan, Goldenbridge, Inchicore, Dublin 8. Tel: 01 453 1005. Fax: 01 454 1688.

GILLEN, Gerard

GILLEN, Gerard; ACADEMIC, ORGANIST; *b* 1942; *educ* St. James's Christian Brothers School, Dublin; University College Dublin, BMus, MA; Royal Conservatoire of Music, Antwerp, Pris d'Excellence; Oxford University, BLitt; *m* Patricia Nolan; 3 *s*; Lecturer in Music, University College Dublin, 1969-85; Professor, Head of Music Department, NUI, Maynooth, 1985 to date; Titular Organist, Pro-Cathedral, 1976 to date; Artistic Director, Dublin International Organ and Choral Festival, 1991 to date; an international organist, has performed extensively in Ireland, UK, Belgium, Germany, Scandinavia, Poland, US and Canada; has made numerous recordings; publications include contributions to international music journals, Editor of *Irish Music Studies*; conferred with Knighthood of St. Gregory, K.S.G. by Vatican, 1984; Visiting Fellow, Oxford, 1992; Member, Kildare Street & University Club, Royal Musical Association, Royal College of Organists. A powerhouse in re-establishing the popularity of the organ in the eighties and nineties, culminating in the arrival of the organ at the National Concert Hall, 1991. Hobbies, reading, theatre, walking and travel. Contact: National University of Ireland, Maynooth, Co. Kildare. Tel: 01 708 3768. Fax: 01 628 9432.

GILSENAN, Alan

GILSENAN, Alan; FILM-MAKER; *b* 1962; *educ* St. Conleths College, Dublin; Trinity College Dublin, BA - winner of the first A.J. Leventhal Scholarship; *single;* established Yellow Asylum Films, 1985; documentary work for BBC, ITV and RTE include *The Road to God Knows Where, Prophet Songs, Between Heaven and Woolworths, Stories from the Silence, Emerald Shoes* and *The Green Fields of France* (80th anniversary commemoration of the Irish who died in World War I), as well as the series *God Bless America* (with US writers including Gore Vidal, Neil Simon and Patricia Cornwall), *Home Movie Nights* and *The Irish Empire;* film drama includes Samuel Beckett's *Eh Joe* (Siobhan McKenna's final performance) and the experimental feature film *All Soul's Day;* theatre includes the premiere of Tom Murphy's *The Patriot Game,* Tennesee Williams' *Smallcraft Warnings* and Jean Genet's *The Balcony;* winner of two Jacobs' Awards and a European Film Award; former Chairman of Filmmakers Ireland; former Junior International Sprinter. Contact: Yellow Asylum Films, 1 Suffolk Street, Dublin 2. Tel : 01 679 0427.

GLEESON, Eileen

GLEESON, Eileen; MANAGING DIRECTOR, FINANCIAL AND CORPORATE COMMUNICATIONS LTD.; *b* 1960; *educ* Dominican College, Sion Hill; College of Commerce, Rathmines; *m* Gerry Hegarty, Army Officer; 1 *s;* Account Executive, Public Relations of Ireland Ltd., 1979-89; formed Financial and Corporate Communications Ltd., 1989, Managing Director to date; appointed Special Advisor to President McAleese, 1997; member, N.U.J., Network; former Director, numerous State bodies, former Chairperson, Public Relations Consultants Association; Vice Chairperson, UNICEF Irish National Committee, 1997 to date; company has been recipient of four awards for Excellence in Communications. One of the prime movers in the public relations arena, with strong political affiliations. Hobbies, current affairs, reading, relaxing with her family. Contact: Financial and Corporate Communications Ltd., 15, Clanwilliam Terrace, Dublin 2. Tel: 01 676 0168. Fax: 01 676 5241.

GLEESON, Peter Joseph Patrick; CHAIRMAN AND MANAGING DIRECTOR CASTLE HOSIERY CO. LTD. (CASTLE OF IRELAND), WILLIAM J. GLEESON & CO.; *b* 1946; *educ* Belvedere College Dublin; College of Textiles, Leicester; *m* Derville Hynes; 1 *s;* joined family business (estb. 1934) Castle Hosiery (Castle of Ireland) 1967; currently Chairman and Chief Executive; the Castle Brand

is one of Ireland's leading knitwear companies, exporting to over fifteen countries; Chairman, William J Gleeson & Co., 1980; Chairman, Gleeson Properties Development Co. Ltd., 1980; Main Board Director, Jefferson Smurfit Group plc, 1981; member, Milltown Golf Club, Fitzwilliam Lawn Tennis Club, Riverview Racquet & Fitness Club, All Ireland Polo Club, The Kildare Hotel and Country Club, Rosslare Golf Club and Old Belvedere Rugby Football Club. Hobbies, golf, tennis and travelling. Contact: Castle of Ireland, 2001 CityWest Business Campus, Naas Road, Dublin 2. Tel: 01 466 0363. Fax: 01 466 0375.

GLENNON, Patrick John; MANAGING DIRECTOR, GLENNON BROS TIMBER LTD.; *b* 1924; *educ* St. Michael's National School, Longford; Vocational School, Longford; *m* Patricia Campbell, Director; 3 *s* 3 *da*; Managing Director, Glennon Bros Timber Ltd., 1975 to date; President, HGTMA, 1976-80; Board member, Coillte Teo, 1989-98; Longford Association Dublin, Person of The Year Award, 1998; Advisor to Tim Severin on the timbers used in the Brendan Voyage; member of the Review Body involved in the setting up of a commercial body for the Forest and Wildlife Service. Hobbies, travel, shooting, and bridge; Clubs, County Longford Bridge Club, '67' Bridge Club. Contact: Glennon Bros., Kilnasavogue, Longford. Tel: 043 46223. Fax: 043 46262.

GLENNON, William, Augustine, 'Billy'; GROUP CHIEF EXECUTIVE VISION CONSULTING LTD.; *b* 1958; *educ* St. Michael's National School, Longford; St. Mel's College, Longford; Trinity College Dublin, B.A., B.A.I.; *separated;* joined Andersen Consulting in 1980; worked on technology implementation projects in Ireland, the UK and the Middle East; founded his own consulting business in 1988; merged with VISION Computing to create The VISION Group; Group Chief Executive, 1990 to date; member, Institute of Directors, Institute of Management Consultants, Irish Computer Society; the co-founder of this high-tech consultancy firm is noted as clear thinking and fast moving. Hobbies, jogging, Gaelic Football (all ball sports), skiing, hill walking, reading, Irish music and dance, travel. Contact: Vision Consulting Ltd., 4A Prince's Street South, Dublin 2. Tel: 01 677 1277. Fax: 01 677 1642.

GLIN, 29th Knight of, (The Black Knight), Desmond John Villiers FitzGerald; FINE ART SPECIALIST AND ACADEMIC, AUTHOR; *b* 1937; *educ* Stowe (UK); University of British Columbia, BA; Harvard University, MA; *m* Lulu (Louise) de la Falaise; (*m dis*); *m* Olda Anne Willes; 3 *da;* Assistant and Deputy Keeper, Furniture and Woodwork Department, Victoria and Albert Museum (London), 1965-75; Irish Agent for Christies, 1975 to date; President, Irish Georgian Society; Chairman and Director, Irish Georgian Foundation; Director, Great Houses, Castles and Gardens of Ireland; Trustee, Castletown Foundation; Director, Irish Architectural Archive, 1972 to date; Committee Member, Great Gardens of Ireland Restoration Programme, 1997 to date; member, Royal Institute of Architects of Ireland, Fellow, Society of Antiquaries; publications include numerous articles on Irish art and architecture for international journals, as well as: *Ireland Observed* (with Maurice Craig), *Lost Demenses* (with Edward Malins), *The Painters of Ireland* (with Anne Crookshank), *The Watercolours of Ireland* (with Anne Crookshank), contributor to *Vanishing Country Houses of Ireland.* A successful fine art specialist and international lecturer; the last of the high profile Anglo-Irish; he and his wife run Glin Castle as a notable historic house hotel; Clubs, Whites, Beefsteak, Kildare Street and University Club. Hobbies, art and history. Contact: Glin Castle, Glin, Co. Limerick. Tel: 068 34173. Fax: 068 34616.

GLENNON, Patrick John

GODSON, Rory; IRELAND EDITOR THE SUNDAY TIMES; *b* 1962; *educ* Gonzaga College, Dublin; Rockwell College, Cashel; Dublin Institute of Technology; *m* Hilary Hynes; 2*s;* Editor, *Dublin Tribune,* 1990-92; Business Editor, *Sunday Tribune,* 1992-94; Deputy Editor/News Editor, *Sunday Tribune,* 1994; *Sunday Independent,* 1995; Ireland Editor, *The Sunday Times,* Febuary 1996 to date; member, Delgany Golf Club; Lansdowne Football Club; HUSC; regarded as a top class newsman with high energy levels; the rising circulation of the paper in Ireland can be attributed to aggressive marketing tactics, keen news reporting and controversial columnists. Hobbies, news, history, golf, sailing, reading and horses. Contact: The Sunday Times, Huguenot House, 35 St. Stephen's Green, Dublin 2. Tel: 01 602 8800. Fax: 01 602 8816.

GOODMAN, Laurence 'Larry'; CHAIRMAN ANGLO IRISH BEEF PROCESSORS LTD.; *b* 1937; *educ* Marist College, Dundalk; *m* Kitty Brennan; 2*s*; a self-made Beef Baron with meat processing and exporting plants in the UK and Ireland; the company employs 3,600 and has an annual turnover of over £700 million; one of the most powerful and knowledgable figures in Irish agri-business. Contact: AIBP Ltd., St. Annes, Cloghran, Swords, Co. Dublin. Tel: 01 842 2411.

GORDON, Colin James

GORDON, Colin James; MANAGING DIRECTOR C&C (IRELAND) LTD.; *b* 1961; *educ* Christian Brother's College, Monkstown Park; Trinity College Dublin, BBS; University College Dublin, MBS; *m* Sue Bunworth; 1 *s* 3 *da;* Manager, Centre for Marketing Studies, UCD, 1983; Product Group Manager, Johnson & Johnson, (Ire) Ltd., 1984; Marketing Manager, John Player & Sons, 1986; Marketing Director, Showering (Ire) Ltd., 1989; Managing Director, C&C, (Wholesale) Ltd., 1994;

Managing Director, C&C (Ireland) Ltd., 1997; C&C is Ireland's leading soft drinks company; brands range from Club Orange, MiWadi, Pepsi and Volvic; Fellow, Marketing Institute of Ireland. Hobbies, tennis, music and golf. Contact: C&C (Ireland) Ltd., Kylemore Park West, Dublin 10. Tel: 01 626 6611. Fax: 01 626 2302.

GORDON, John Joseph; SENIOR COUNSEL; *b* 1951; *educ* CBS Tipperary; Mungret College, Limerick; University College Dublin, BCL; Kings Inns, Barrister-at-Law; called to the Bar, 1974; called to the Inner Bar, 1985; called to the Bar Middle Temple (London), 1986; called to the Bar New South Wales (Australia), 1993; member, RIAC Club, St. Stephen's Green Club. An extraordinary successful litigation lawyer; has one of the largest practices at the Bar. Hobbies, travel, opera and all things Italian. Contact: 2 Arran Square, Arran Quay, Dublin 7. Tel: 01 872 6544. Fax: 01 872 6524.

GORMAN, Jeremy "Jerry"; CHIEF EXECUTIVE IRISH ISPAT LTD.; *b* 1948; *educ* Queen Elizabeth Grammar School, Gainsborough; Salford University, BSc Mech Eng; *m* Heather Martin, 2 *da*; Flight Lieutenant, Royal Air Force, 1973-74; Misc. Engineering appointments, British Steel, 1974-84; Chief Engineer, British Steel Stainless, 1984-87; General Manager, Operations, British Steel Stainless; Director, Scunthorpe Works BS plc, 1989-91; Director, British Steel Stainless Ltd., 1991-92; Executive Vice President, Avesta Sheffield AB, 1992-97; Chief Executive, Irish Ispat Ltd., 1997 to date; Council member, Lincolnshire Iron and Steel Institute, (President, 1989-90); member, Cutlers Company of Hallamshire; awards include Royal Air Force Sword of Merit, 1973. Hobbies, model engineering, horology. Contact: Irish Ispat Ltd., Haulbowline, Cobh, Co. Cork. Tel: 021 378 011. Fax: 021 378 879.

GORRY, James; PICTURE RESTORER, FINE ART DEALER; *b* 1948; *educ* CUS, Leeson Street, Dublin; National College of Art; *m* Therese Butler, Director, Secretary, Gorry Gallery; 1 *s* 1 da; joined family art business, established 1885; Director, Gorry Gallery, Dublin, picture restorers and fine art dealers; the gallery specialises in Irish paintings of the 18th, 19th and 20th centuries, holding twice yearly exhibitions and some one man shows; member, Irish Professional Conservators' and Restorers' Association; Irish Antique Dealers Association; Confederation Internationale des Negociants en Oeuvrs d'Art, Friends of the National Collections of Ireland; Associate, British Picture Restorers Association. An influential figure in the Irish Art world, three generations of Irish Collectors have dealt with this distinguished gallery. Hobbies, blues music, sport. Contact: Gorry Gallery, 20 Molesworth Street, Dublin 2. Tel. & Fax: 01 679 5319.

GREENE, Judy; POTTER / MULTIPLE RETAILER; *b* 1952; *educ* L.S.U. College, Southampton, Teaching Dip in Art and Pottery; *m* Paul Fox; 2*da;* Teacher in Southampton, 1974; Art Teacher and Founder, Sewing Centre, Botswana, Africa, 1974-76; English Teacher, ceramics student, Berne, Switzerland, 1977; Teacher, Crawford School of Art, Cork, 1977-78; Founder/Manager, Cape Clear Pottery, 1978-82; Diploma in Clay, Denver, Colorado, 1981; Founder/Manager, Judy Greene Pottery, Galway, 1982 to date; has received commissions in clay for Galway Races; President, Galway Chamber of Commerce, 1998-99 (Deputy President, 1997/98); member, Network Galway, Crafts Potters Society; Recipient ACC/*Evening Press* Award 1994, winner Enterprising Women; featured in *Up and Running* RTE 1993, *Start Me Up*, RTE 1996, *The Last Resource,* RTE 1999, *Design in Ireland,* US Cable TV 1999. Hobbies, gardening, reading and swimming. Contact: Judy Greene, Pottery Workshop, 13 Cross Street, Galway. Tel: 091 561 753.

GREEVY, Bernadette; CLASSICAL SINGER; *b* 1940; *educ* Convent of the Holy Faith, Clontarf; *m* Peter Tattan (decd.); 1 *s*; International Professional Debut, Wigmore Hall, London, 1964; appears regularly with major orchestras in Europe, The Far East, Australia and New Zealand; has performed Opera and Recitals with conductors such as Sir John Barbirolli, Pierre Boulez, Sergiu Commissiona, Franz Paul Decker, Sir Charles Groves, Claudio Abbado, Simon Rattle and Esa-Pekka Salonen; recordings include: Elgar's *Sea Pictures* which won international acclaim, Berlioz's *Les Nuits D'Ete* and songs by Henri Duparc for Chandos, together with numerous other recordings; recipient, Harriet Cohen International Award for Outstanding Artistry, Dame Commander of the Holy Sepulchre, Order of Merit of the Order of Malta, Pro Ecclesia et Pontifice (conferred by the Holy See), Life Patron of the New Zealand Symphony Orchestra, AMB L'Argraiment de la Barcelona from University of Barcelona, Honorary Life Member Royal Dublin Society, Honorary Doctorates of Music, University College Dublin, (1983) and Trinity College Dublin (1988); Board Member, National Concert Hall. (1981-86, 1991-96); appointed first Artist in Residence of the D.I.T. Faculty of Applied Arts, 1996; Founder/Artistic Director of the Dublin Anna Livia International Opera Festival. Regarded as one of the world's finest mezzo sopranos; member, United Arts Club. Hobbies, reading, painting, cooking, walking dogs and gardening. Contact: Fax: 01 831 3131.

GREGORY, Tony

GREGORY, Tony; POLITICIAN; *b* 1947; *educ* St. Canice's School, Dublin; O'Connells Christian Brothers School, North Richmond Street; University College Dublin, BA, HDipEd; *single*;

Secondary School Teacher, Colaiste Eoin, Stillorgan, 1972-82; Independent member, Dublin City Council, 1979-81; Alderman, Dublin City Council, 1991 to date; elected Independent Deputy for Dublin Central, 1982 to date; A hard working constituency representative who inspires tremendous loyalty; regarded as a loner in Leinster House; a member of the Council of Europe which involves attendance at Committee meetings at European venues. Hobbies, swimming, films, outdoor pursuits. Contact: Dáil Eireann, Kildare Street, Dublin 2. Tel: 01 618 3488.

GUILBAUD, Patrick; RESTAURATEUR; *b* 1952; *educ* Le Vallous, France; *m* Sally Lloyd-Owen; 1 *s* 1 *da*; worked in family restaurant, Caen; Chef, British Embassy, Paris; Chef, Midland Hotel, Manchester; Proprietor, Patrick Guilbaud, Dublin, December 1981 to date; restaurant has recently moved premises, is now beside the Merrion Hotel and has been awarded a second Michelin Star; one Egon Ronay Star; numerous other awards, including the Bord Failte Ballygowan Supreme Award twice; restaurant listed in all the leading international guides; member, Euro Toque and Restaurant Association of Ireland. A cool professional, runs one of the most consistently fine restaurants in Ireland. Clubs, Sutton Golf Club, Donnybrook Tennis Club, Luttrellstown Golf Club, Hobbies, golf, tennis and cooking. Contact: Patrick Guilbaud Restaurant, Upper Merrion Street, Dublin 2. Tel: 01 676 4192. Fax: 01 661 0052.

GUINEY, Edward

GUINEY, Edward; FILM PRODUCER; *b* 1966; *educ* Gonzaga College; Trinity College Dublin, BBS; *single*; Producer, Strongbow Productions, Dublin, 1988-89; Development Manager/Producer, Windmill Lane Productions, Dublin, 1989-92; Managing Director and Producer, Temple Film and Television Productions, Dublin, 1992 to date; producer of various television programmes and feature films including *Ailsa* (1994), *Guiltrip* (1995), *Sweety Barrett* (1998); Chairman of Film Makers Ireland, 1997; Member of the Government Strategic Review of Irish Film Industry, 1999. Awards include Best Irish Short Film (1991), Best European Short Film (1991), Euskal Media Prize (1994), Kilkenny Cream of Irish Awards (1997). Representative of the young, talented and imaginative film makers of Ireland moving into the 21st Century. Hobbies, cinema, reading and travel. Contact: Temple Films, Shamrock Chambers, 1-2 Eustace Street, Dublin 2. Tel: 01 671 9313. Fax: 01 671 9323.

GUINNESS, Hon. Desmond W

GUINNESS, Hon. Desmond Walter; WRITER; *b* 1931; *educ* Gordonstoun, Christ Church, Oxford, MA; *m* HSH Princess Marie-Gabrielle Sophie Joti Elisabeth Albertine Almeria Von Ulrach; 1 *s* 1 *da*; (m dis.); *m* Penelope Cuthbertson; founded the Irish Georgian Society in 1958, for the preservation of eighteenth century architecture in Ireland, President 1958-91; publications include: *Irish Houses and Castles* (1971), *Mr. Jefferson, Architect* (1973), *Palladio, A Western Progress* (1976), *Georgian Dublin* (1979), *The White House* (1980), *Newport Restored* (1981), *Great Irish Houses & Castles* (with Jacqueline O'Brien, 1992), *Dublin - A Grand Tour* (with Jacqueline O'Brien, 1994); A frequent lecturer in the U.K., U.S., and Australia on Irish Georgian architecture. Member of the Guinness brewing family, son of Lord Moyne (poet and novelist) and Lady Mosley (one of the famous literary Mitford sisters); a knowledgeable writer and lecturer; a tireless fundraiser for the preservation of Georgian Ireland's architectural heritage; an urbane man who mixes in the international aristocracy, literary and pop music world. Clubs, Kildare Street and University Club, Chelsea Arts Club, London and the Irish Club, London. Contact: Irish Georgian Society, 74, Merrion Square, Dublin 2. Tel: 01 676 7053

GUIRY, Michael

GUIRY, (Ó GADHRA) Michael Dominic Richard; ACADEMIC AND MARINE BIOLOGIST; *b* 1949; *educ* Dominican College, Newbridge; University College Cork, B.Sc., M.Sc.; University of London, Ph.D, D.Sc.; *m* Gwendoline Mary Kilty; 1 *s*; 1 *da;* Research Fellow, Polytechnic of North London, U.K., 1972-75; Post Doctoral Fellow, Portsmouth Polytechnic, U.K., 1976-78; Lecturer, University College Galway, 1979-90; Visiting Research Fellow, University of Melbourne, Australia, 1987-88; James Professor in Pure & Applied Science, St. Francis Xavier University, Canada, 1989; Associate Professor, University College Galway, 1991-96; Professor of Botany, National University of Ireland, Galway, 1996 to date; Director, Martin Ryan Institute, National University of Ireland, Galway, 1997 to date; Publications include: Co-author, *Seaweed Resources in Europe - Uses and Potential* (1991) and over 150 scientific articles, books and reviews; Editor, *Phycologia*, Journal of the International Phycological Society, 1990-92; Member: Royal Irish Academy; President, International Phycological Society, 1996-97; Founder, Irish Seaweed Industry Organisation, 1994. Hobbies, seaweed, book collecting. Contact: National University of Ireland, Galway. Tel: 091 524 411 Fax: 091 525 700

GUNNE, Patrick Joseph Fintan; MANAGING DIRECTOR GUNNE COMMERCIAL, DIRECTOR

GUNNE PROPERTY CONSULTANTS; *b* 1972; *educ* Castleknock College; Dublin Institute of Technology, Dip. Property Econ.; Trinity College Dublin, BASc. in surveying; worked in the UK with Richard Ellis in commercial property, 1993-96; on untimely death of father, returned to Ireland to head up family firm; Managing Director, Gunne Commercial, Director, Gunne Property Consultants, 1996 to date; major recent Gunne transactions include Citibank Building IFSC, Mayor House IFSC, Sweepstake Centre, Ballsbridge and Liffey Valley Retail Park; member, Irish Auctioneers and Valuers Institute, Association of the Royal Institute of Chartered Surveyors, Association of the Society of Chartered Surveyors, Rotary Club of Dublin. Hobbies, horse riding, swimming, rugby. Contact: Gunne Commercial, 164 Shelbourne Road, Ballsbridge, Dublin . Tel: 01 618 5500. Fax: 01 668 9942.

HACKETT, Monica Mary, née McNabb; CHIEF EXECUTIVE HACKETT BOOKMAKERS; *b* 1942; *educ* Brigidine Convent, Tullow, Co. Carlow; Secretarial Course; *m* Cyril Hackett; 5*s* 1*da;* opened first betting shop in partnership with husband, Cyril; currently Chief Executive Hacketts Bookmakers, a chain of 42 shops employing 180 and with a turnover of £30 million; all the family are involved in the business and the Co. Kildare stud farm. Hobbies, travel, reading and gardening. Contact: Hackett Bookmakers, 79 Dame Street, Dublin 2. Tel: 01 677 5101. Fax: 01 677 7938.

HACKETT, Monica Mary

HALLIGAN, Brendan; NEWSPAPER EDITOR; *b* 1942; *educ* St. Aidan's Grammar School, Sutherland (UK); *m* Dorothy Maher; 3*s* 4*da;* Reporter with the Thomson Organisation, 1961-65; Reporter, *Daily Mail,* 1965-66; Sub Editor, *Sun* Newspapers, 1966-67; News Editor, *Limerick Leader and Chronicle*, 1967-70, Editor, 1970 to date; *The Limerick Leader and Chronicle* has a weekend circulation of thirty-three thousand in the South West. Hobbies, media, politics, sport, the outdoors and Guinness. Contact: Limerick Leader Ltd., O'Connell Street, Limerick. Tel: 061 315 233. Fax: 061 314 804.

HAMILTON, The Hon. Mr. Justice Liam; CHIEF JUSTICE; *b* 1928; *educ* Christian Brothers School, Mitchelstown; University College Dublin; Kings Inns (recipient of Brooke Scholarship); *m* Maeve Gibney; 3 children; called to the Bar, 1956; called to the Inner Bar, 1968; joined Labour Party 1958 and contested Local Election; had an extensive Bar practice, specialising in Trade Union affairs; President of Criminal Court for over a decade; appointed President of the High Court, 1995; presided over controversial inquiry into the Beef Industry, 1991; appointed Chief Justice, 1992 to date. A down to earth legal man, gregarious and well liked; Clubs, Milltown Golf Club (former Captain). Hobbies, golf and soccer. Contact: Four Courts, Morgan Place, Dublin. Tel: 01 872 5555.

HANLON, Andrew; DIRECTOR OF NEWS AND INFORMATION PROGRAMMES, TV3 TELEVISION NETWORK; *b* 1966; *educ* Presentation College Bray, Co. Wicklow; *m* Liz Allen, Crime Correspondent, *Sunday Independent;* 1 *s;* Journalist, RTE News (Radio) Dublin, 1986-89; Head of News, Editor, Classic Hits 98FM Dublin, 1989-97; Managing Director/Editor in Chief, Independent Network News, 1997-98; Director, News and Information Programming, TV3 Television Network, Ireland's independent TV network 1998 to date. Contact: TV3 Television Network Ltd., Westgate Business Park, Ballymount, Dublin 24. Tel: 01 419 3333. Fax: 01 419 3300.

HANLY, David; JOURNALIST; *b* 1944; *educ* Sexton Street Christian Brothers School, Limerick; *separated;* 2 *s* 1*da;* Junior Executive, Department of Industry & Commerce, 1962-63; Journalist, RTE, 1963-70; Publicity Officer, Bord Failte, 1970-76; Writer, 1975-81; Journalist/Presenter, *Morning Ireland* (radio), *Hanly's People* (RTE One), 1981 to date; recipient, Jacobs Award, 1985; Benson & Hedges Award, 1986; *Sunday Independent* - Irish Life Award, 1988; publications include *In Guilt and in Glory* (1979), a weekly column in the *Sunday Tribune.* A sharp, incisive writer and newsman; an entertaining, if somewhat daunting, radio interviewer. Hobbies, drinking and talking with friends. Contact: The Sunday Tribune, 15 Lower Baggot Street, Dublin 2. Tel: 01 661 5555. Fax: 01 661 5302.

HARAN, Paul Martin

HARAN, Paul Martin; SECRETARY GENERAL, DEPARTMENT OF ENTERPRISE, TRADE AND EMPLOYMENT; *b* 1957; *educ* Colaiste Choilm, Swords; Trinity College Dublin, BSc Computer Science, MSc Public Sector Analysis; *m* Anne Norton; 3*s* 1 *da;* joined Information Systems Division, Revenue Commissioners, 1975, Executive Officer, Systems Analyst; Policy Analyst, Department of Finance / Revenue Commissioners, 1985; Special Advisor to Des O'Malley, Minister for Industry and Commerce, 1989; Special Advisor, Chairman of the Revenue Commissioners, 1993; Chief Economist and Head of Corporate Services, Department of Enterprise and Employment, 1994, Secretary General, 1997; Board Member, Forfas and the Irish Management Institute; Council Member of the ESRI; member, Institute of Directors, the Statistical & Social Enquiry Society of Ireland; National Taxes Association. Hobbies, walking, reading, family sports activity, sports and music. Contact: Department of Enterprise, Trade and Employment, Frederick Building, Setanta Centre, South Frederick Street, Dublin 2. Tel: 01 661 4444.

HARDIMAN, Adrian; BARRISTER; *b* 1951; *educ* Belvedere College, Dublin; University College Dublin, BA; Kings Inns, BL (Auditor of the L&H and President of the Students Union); *m* Yvonne Murphy, Judge of the Circuit Court; 3*s*; called to the Bar 1974; called to the Inner Bar 1989; has an extensive practice dealing with administrative law, chancery, libel and some criminal work; frequent contributor to newspapers, journals and television programmes; Founder member, Progressive Democrats; a high profile lawyer, regarded as forceful and fearless in court; a keen historian, describes himself as an "historian *manqué*". Hobbies, reading, walking and visiting sites of historic interest. Contact: The Law Library, Blackhall Place, Dublin 7. Tel: 01 671 0711. Fax: 01 671 0704.

HAREN, Patrick; GROUP CHIEF EXECUTIVE VIRIDIAN GROUP PLC; *b* 1950; *educ* Queens University, Belfast; Research Fellow, CERN - European Centre for Nuclear Research, Geneva; worked with the ESB in Ireland, had board level responsibility for engineering consultancy in US and UK markets and for international financial services; active member, CIGRE, Paris; joined Northern Ireland Electricity plc 1992; became Group Chief Executive of Viridian Group plc following the company's restructuring 1998; was responsible for successfully steering Northern Ireland Electricity through privatisation; Chairman, Northern Ireland Growth Challenge; President, Northern Ireland Council for Voluntary Action; member, Northern Ireland Quality Centre. Contact: Viridian Group plc, 120 Malone Road, Belfast, BT9 5HT. Tel: 0801 232 689 262. Fax: 0801 232 689 266.

HARFORD, Joseph F

HARFORD, Joseph F; PRESIDENT AND CHIEF EXECUTIVE, YAMANOUCHI IRELAND CO. LTD.; *b* 1946; *educ* Mount St. Joseph, Roscrea; University College Dublin and Dublin Institute of Technology; *m* Sylvia Armstrong; 1 *s* 1 *da*; Process Manager, Bristol Myers Squibb, 1978-81; General Manager, Newport Pharmaceutical Ireland, 1981-86; President and CEO, Yamanouchi Ireland, 1986 to date; Chairman, Faulkner Packaging, 1998 to date; Past President, Federation of Irish Chemical Industries; Past Chairman of International Society of Pharmaceutical Engineers; Past Chairman of Chemical Society; Chairman of the Economic Social Research Institute, 1997 to date; Member, Board of Governors of Cistercian College, Mount St. Joseph, Roscrea; has published many papers on environmental, communication, management issues; Yamanouchi is Japan's third largest pharmaceutical company, with sales in excess of US $ 4 billion; an approachable hands on chief executive; the Irish face of the giant Yamanouchi Corporation. Hobbies, golf, gardening, music, art and drama. Contact: Yamanouchi Ireland Ltd., Damastown, Mulhuddart, Dublin 15. Tel: 01 803 0800. Fax: 01 803 0801.

HARNEY, Geraldine; JOURNALIST; *b* 1962; *educ* Newcastle NS; Colaiste Bríde Convent, Clondalkin; Sacred Heart Convent, Mount Anville; University College Dublin BA (Hons) History and Politics; *single;* worked for a Democratic Congressman, Washington (US), 1984-87; Freelance Journalist, 1987-89; Deputy Business Editor, *Irish Press,* 1989-95; joined Business News, RTE, 1995 to date; awards include, Business Journalist of the Year 1991, Gold Medal for Debating at UCD (L&H); seen as one of the few high profile journalists in the business world. Hobbies, reading (non fiction), GAA (especially the Dubs), travel, in warm climates, work and good food. Contact: RTE, Donnybrook, Dublin. Tel: 01 208 3111.

HARNEY, Mary

HARNEY, Mary; POLITICIAN; *b* 1953 *educ* Newcastle National School, Co. Dublin, Convent of Mercy, Inchicore; Colaiste Brid, Clondalkin; Trinity College Dublin, BA (first woman auditor, TCD History Society); *single;* joined the Fianna Fáil Party while a student; unsuccessful Dáil candidate, 1977; Taoiseach Jack Lynch's appointee to the Seanad, 1977-81; elected Deputy for Dublin South West, 1981 to date; member, Dublin County Council 1979-91; lost Fianna Fáil Whip for voting in favour of the Anglo-Irish Agreement, 1985; Co-founder (with Desmond O'Malley and Michael McDowell) of Progressive Democrats Party; following 1989 General Election the Progressive Democrats formed a coalition government with Fianna Fáil; Minister of State, Department of the Environment, 1989-92; Following the 1992 election, she returned to opposition, where she was her party's spokesperson on Enterprise and Employment. Following the 1997 Election, the Progressive Democrats formed a coalition government with Fianna Fáil; Appointed Tanaiste and Minister for Enterprise, Trade and Employment; the first woman to hold the position of Tanaiste; a committed politician, has shown courage and wise judgement over the years, extraordinary national popularity is not reflected in polls. Hobbies, travel, current affairs, swimming.

Contact: Department of Enterprise, Trade and Employment, Kildare Street, Dublin 2. Tel: 01 661 4444. Fax: 01 676 0431.

HARRINGTON, Jessica Jane, née Fowler; RACE HORSE TRAINER; *b* 1947; *educ* Hatherop Castle; *m* John Harrington; 1*s* 3 *da;* Three Event Rider, represented Ireland, 1966, 1967, 1979-86; obtained permit to train 1987, full licence, 1991; has won numerous races including, Galway Hurdle, Ladbrooke Hurdle, Murphy Hurdle (Cheltenham) 1997, Fighting Fit Hurdle (Newcastle) 1997, Grand Annual (Cheltenham) 1999; winners trained include, *Oh So Grumpy, Dance Beat, Space Trucker.* Hobbies, golf, gardening, travel, Three Day Eventing. Contact: Commonstown Stud, Moone, Co. Kildare. Tel: 0507 24153. Fax: 0507 24292.

HARRIS, Anne, née O'Sullivan; ASSISTANT EDITOR SUNDAY INDEPENDENT; *b* 1947; *educ* Ard Foyle, Blackrock Co. Cork; *m* Eoghan Harris, Screenwriter; 2 *da;* Journalist with *The Irish Press* (recipient Young Journalist of the Year award); freelance reporter with various journals including, *Hibernia;* joined Radio Telefis Eireann, Presenter, *Work and Money* (radio series), *Positively Healthy,* RTE One; Fashion Writer, *Irish Independent,* 1980-84; Editor, *Image,* 1984-85; Assistant Editor, *Sunday Independent,* 1985 to date; an experienced journalist, a determined and painstaking Editor; has established an unmistakable house style on the *Sunday Independent.* Hobbies, reading and politics. Contact: Sunday Independent, 90 Middle Abbey Street, Dublin 1. Tel: 01 705 5333.

HARRIS, Eoghan; JOURNALIST, SCREENWRITER; *b* 1943; *educ* Douglas National School; University College Cork, BA; *m* Ann O'Sullivan, Deputy Editor, *Sunday Independent;* 2 *da;* Producer, RTE, 1966-90; Theorist, Workers Party, 1966-90; Media Advisor, Mary Robinson Election Committee, 1990; Media Advisor, Fine Gael, 1990-91; recipient Jacobs Award, 1970, 1975; Silver Bear Award, (Berlin) for film documentary; Columnist *Sunday Times,* 1993 to date; publications include *Irish Industrial Revolution,* (1975), *The Necessity of Social Democracy* (1989); *Souper Sullivan* (play, 1985). Contact: Sunday Times, Huguenot House, 35 St. Stephen's Green Dublin 2. Tel: 01 602 8800. Fax: 01 602 8816.

HASTINGS, George William OBE; CHAIRMAN HASTINGS HOTEL GROUP; *b* 1928 *educ* Royal Belfast Institute; *m* Joy Hamilton; 1 *s* 3 *da*; Inherited family public house business; opened first hotel in Ballymena, 1964; the hotel empire now runs to seven hotels and two pub/restaurants; Hastings Hotels has a 50% interest in the prestigious Merrion Hotel, Dublin; Director, Queens University Business and Industrial Services, Landmark Ltd.; former directorships include Bank of Ireland (N.I.), Northern Ireland Tourist Board, former Chairman, Northern Ireland Venture Capital; an approachable and committed member of the Northern Ireland business and social community; Awarded O.B.E. for services to the community; recipient of Honorary Doctorate, D.Litt, University of Ulster, 1984; Hon. Fellow, Irish Hotel Catering Institute; Justice of the Peace; Paul Harris Fellow, International Rotary. Contact: Hastings Hotel Group Ltd., Midland Building, Whitla Street, Belfast BT15 1NH. Tel: 08 0232 745251. Fax: 08 0232 748152.

HAUGHEY, Edward

HAUGHEY, Edward; SENATOR, SEANAD EIREANN, COMPANY DIRECTOR; *b* 1944; *educ* Christian Brothers School, Dundalk; *m* Mary Gordon Young, Solicitor; 2 *s* 1 *da*; Founder, Norbrook Laboratories, 1968, Chairman and Managing Director since; Fellow, The Institute of Directors; Member, Reform Club, Belfast, Savage Club, London, Farmers Club, London; Featured in *Out On Their Own,* by Ivor Kenny; Awarded OBE for Services to Industry, 1986; Fellow of Irish Management Institute, 1987; Honorary Consul for Chile, 1988; Doctor of Business Administration - International Management Institute, 1992; Senator, Seanad Eireann, appointed by Albert Reynolds in 1994; re-appointed by Bertie Ahern in 1997; Fellow of the International Academy of Management, 1994; Gran Official Order of Bernardo O'Higgins (Chile), 1994; Doctor of Law, National University of Ireland, 1996; Fellow of the Royal College of Surgeons in Ireland, 1997; An immensely successful businessman with cross border interests and lifestyle. Contact: Norbrook Laboratories Ltd., Station Works, Newry, BT35 6JP, Northern Ireland. Tel: 0801 693 64435. Fax: 0801 693 69981.

HAYES, Freda, née Kelleher; CHIEF EXECUTIVE MEADOWS & BYRNE LTD.; *educ* Blarney Secondary School; Paris; *m* Colin Hayes; 1*s*; joined family firm, Chief Executive, Blarney Wooen Mills, 1966-88; left to form own company, Chief Executive of Meadows & Bryne, 1993 to date; Meadows & Bryne has four stores nationwide, Cork, Galway, Bunratty (Co. Clare), Dublin, also the Bunratty Village Mills Complex and Bunratty Castle Hotel; awards include, Businesswoman of the Year 1988 Veuve Clicquot; member, National Executive IBEC; Chairman, South Cork Enterprise Board; member, Cork Business Association, Small Firms Association, Michael Smurfit Graduate School of Business (UCD). Hobbies, reading, music, business and travel. Contact: Meadows & Bryne, 22 Academy Street, Cork. Tel: 021 344 100. Fax: 021 344 220.

HAYES, Liam Patrick; NEWSPAPER EDITOR/DIRECTOR; *b* 1962; *educ* St. Patrick's Classical School, Navan, Co. Meath; *m* Anne O'Boyle; 2*s* 1*da;* Journalist, *The Meath Chronicle,* Navan; Journalist and Sports Editor, *Sunday Press,* Editor/Co-founder, *Ireland on Sunday;* publications include *Out of our Skins* (biographical) and *Heroes;* awards include, Sports Journalist of the Year (1986), All-Ireland Football Final (winner, Meath, 1987 & 1988), All-Ireland Football Final Man of the Year (1987); a top class sportsman turned journalist; now edits Ireland's youngest national newspaper. Hobbies, reading, film, golf and running. Contact: Ireland on Sunday, 50 City Quay, Dublin 2. Tel: 01 671 8255.

HAYES, Margaret; SECRETARY GENERAL DEPARTMENT OF TOURISM, SPORT AND RECREATION; BA, HDip (Ed), Dip Adm. Science, CDip AF; *single;* joined Revenue Commissioners in 1976; Department of Health, 1978-86; Department of Tourism, Fisheries and Forestry, 1986-87; Department of Tourism, Transport and Communications, 1987-92; Tourism and Trade, 1992-97; Secretary General, Department of Tourism, Sport and Recreation, 1997 to date. Contact: Department of Tourism, Sport and Recreation, Kildare Street, Dublin 2. Tel: 01 662 1444. Fax: 01 661 1201.

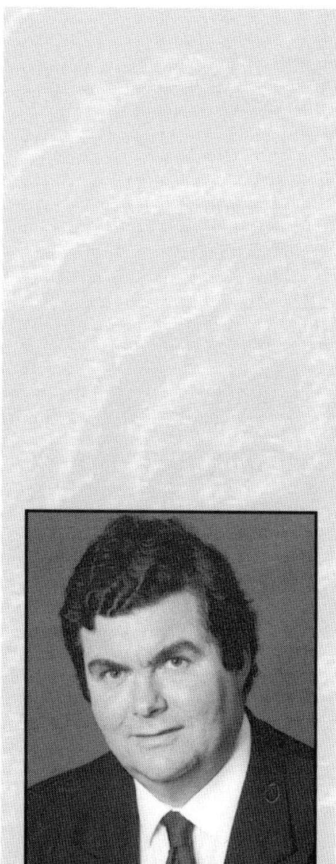

HEALY, Gerard P.

HEALY, Gerard Patrick Noel; CHIEF EXECUTIVE GUARDIAN PMPA GROUP; *b* 1952; *educ* Bedford School, England; Corpus Christi College, Cambridge University, MA; Open Business School, MBA; *m* Celine O'Neill; 2 *s;* Branch Manager, Guardian Royal Exchange Insurance, 1985-86, Senior Manager, 1986-90, Chief Executive, 1991 to date, Chairman, Guardian PMPA Insurance, 1991 to date; President, Irish Insurance Federation, 1994; Vice President European Insurance Association,(CEA) 1995; former President, Irish Croquet Association; Clubs, United Services Club, Carrickmines Croquet Club, K Club, Old Conna Golf Club. Hobbies, music and sport. Contact: Guardian PMPA Insurance Ltd., Wolfe Tone House, Wolfe Tone Street, Dublin 1. Tel: 01 872 9888. Fax: 01 872 9973.

HEALY, Liam

HEALY, Liam; CHIEF EXECUTIVE INDEPENDENT NEWSPAPERS PLC; *b 1929; educ* St. Nathy's College, Ballaghadereen, Co. Roscommon; *m* Eithne Corrigan; 1 *s* 2 *da*; Financial Controller, Independent Newspapers plc 1963, Finance Director, 1970, Managing Director (Ireland) 1978, Managing Director (International) 1981, Chief Executive Officer 1991 to date; member, Institute of Chartered Accountants. A quietly spoken man of influence, within the powerful Independent Group, and beyond; a hard headed businessman with a deceptively mild manner. Clubs, Royal St. George Yacht Club, United Services Club. Hobbies, music, theatre and walking. Contact: Independent Newspapers plc, Group Headquarters, 1-2 Upper Hatch Street, Dublin 2. Tel: 01 475 8432. Fax: 01 478 4933.

HEALY, Tom; CHIEF EXECUTIVE IRISH STOCK EXCHANGE; *b* 1950; *educ* St. Finian's School, Mullingar; Trinity College Dublin, BA (Mod); *m* Marie O'Grady; 1*s* 3 *da;* Civil Service, to 1975; various management positions, Industrial Development Authority, 1975-80; Head of Communications, Irish Export Board, 1980-87; General Manager, Irish Stock Exchange, 1987-95, Chief Executive, 1995 to date. Hobbies, reading, following rugby and Gaelic Football. Contact: Irish Stock Exchange, 28 Anglesea Street, Dublin 2. Tel: 01 617 4200. Fax: 01 667 6045.

HEANEY, Seamus; POET; *b* 1939; *educ* St. Columb's College, Derry; Queens University, Belfast, BA; *m* Marie Devlin; 3 *children*; Secondary School Teacher, 1962-63, Lecturer, St. Joseph's College of Education, Belfast, 1963-66; Lecturer in English, Queens University, Belfast, 1966-72; freelance Writer and Broadcaster before returning to teaching at Carysfort College, Dublin; frequent Visiting Lecturer in Europe and US; Professor of Poetry at Oxford, 1989-94; attached to Harvard University since 1982, currently Ralph Waldo Emerson Poet-in-Residence; member, Aosdána, Honorary Fellow of Royal Irish Academy; recipient of several honorary degrees; publications include, *Death of a Naturalist, A Lough Neagh Sequence, Door into the Dark, Land, Wintering Out, Sweeney Astray, The Haw Lantern, The Rattle Bag* (ed. with Ted Hughes), *Station Island, Seeing Things, The Government of the Tongue* (prose), *The Cure at Troy* (play), *The Spirit Level, Opened Ground*; won Nobel Prize in Literature 1995; regarded as the leading figure in the Irish literary renaissance of the late sixties and seventies; a quiet, warm, unaffected man whose humanity is reflected in his writings. Contact: Aosdána, 70 Merrion Square, Dublin 2. Tel: 01 661 1840. Fax: 01 676 1302.

HEASLIP, F.B. "Danno"; AUCTIONEER; *b* 1938; *educ* St. Joseph's College, Galway; Crescent College, Limerick; *m* Mary Murphy; 2*s* 2 *da*; Trainee, Norwich Union (UK), 1959-61; Principal in F.B.Heaslip Ltd., Estate Agents, Auctioneers and Valuers (Galway), 1961 to date; Fellow, The Irish Auctioneers and Valuers Institute; an innovative businessman who spearheaded the successful selling seminars by Irish Estate Agents in the UK; strong Progressive Democrat supporter; a rugby enthusiast who played with both London Irish and Galwegians. Hobbies, rugby, golf and racing. Club, Galwegians RFC (President 1991). Contact: Heaslips, Estate Agents, Auctioneers and

Valuers, 27 Woodquay, Galway. Tel: 091 565 261. Fax: 091 565 863.

HEAVEY, Aidan; CHIEF EXECUTIVE TULLOW OIL PLC.; *b* 1953; *educ* National School, Castlerea; Clongowes Wood College; University College Dublin, BComm; *m* Lorraine McCourt, Model/Actress; worked in several accountancy firms, 1974-84, before founding Tullow Oil; Chief Executive, Tullow Oil, 1984 to date, one of the few successful exploration companies based in Ireland; regarded internationally as having as exceptionally strong technical team; operates only outside of the country, mainly in Indian sub continent, Africa and Europe; member, Institute of Chartered Accountants. Hobbies, tennis and golf. Contact: Tullow Oil plc, Airfield House, Airfield Park, Donnybrook, Dublin . Tel: 01 260 2611. Fax: 01 260 2672.

HEDERMAN, Carmencita, née Cruess-Callaghan; COMPANY DIRECTOR; *b* 1939; *educ* Sacred Heart Convents, Dublin and Woldingham (UK); Trinity College Dublin, MA; Sorbonne University, Paris; scholarship to Institute Palladio, Venice; *m* William Hederman, Surgeon; 2 *s* 3 *da;* founder member, Upper Leeson Street Area Residents Association; Independent member, Dublin City Council, Alderman, 1974-99; former Dublin Corporation Committee member: Planning, General Purposes, Traffic, Protocol and Selection, Environmental; Lord Mayor of Dublin 1987-88; member, Seanad Eireann, 1989 -93; Life Governor, Royal Hospital, Donnybrook; Governor and member Executive Committee, National Maternity Hospital; Patron, War on Want; Honorary member An Oige, Trinity College Dublin Women Graduates Association; member of numerous cultural, environmental and political organisations; Board member, First Active plc; conferred with Honorary Doctorate in Law, Trinity College Dublin 1988, NUI 1988; recipient, People of the Year Award 1988, Spirit of Dublin Award 1988. Recognised as a remarkable, poll topping local politician; responsible for preserving many residential areas within Dublin city. Hobbies: gardening, riding and bridge. Contact: Fax: 01 660 5913.

HEDERMAN, Wendy E. A.; SOLICITOR; *b* 1967; *educ* Convent of the Sacred Heart, Mount Anville, Dublin; Trinity College Dublin, LLB; Université Libre de Bruxelles, Belgium, Masters in European Law; Law Society of Ireland, Solicitor; Certified Diploma in Accounting and Finance (C. Dip. A.F.) from the ACCA; *m* Brendan Cassidy, Psychiatrist; 1*s;* 1*da;* joined Mason Hayes & Curran Solicitors 1990, seconded to European Law Firm in Brussels 1993; appointed Senior Associate in Mason Hayes & Curran, 1998; specialises in information technology, telecommunications law, intellectual property, European Law, competition law and general commercial; Tutor in Intellectual Property and in European Law, Law Society of Ireland; publications include contributions to *Appointing Commercial Agents in Europe*, Irish Chapter, (Wiley 1993), *Intellectual Property Laws of Europe* Irish Chapter (1994), *Telecommunications Law in Ireland* (co-author) by Mason Hayes & Curran (1999); Chairman, Society of Young Solicitors, Ireland 1998-99; member EU and International Affairs Committee, Law Society of Ireland (former Vice Chairman); member, Society for Computers and Law; member, Licensing Executives Society, member, Association International des Jeunes Avocats, member, Network (the organisation for Women in Business). Hobbies, tennis, swimming, horseriding, skiing, Irish theatre, current affairs and spending time with family. Contact: Mason Hayes & Curran, 7 Fitzwilliam Square, Dublin 2. Tel: 01 661 1788.

HEFFERNAN, Margarert

HEFFERNAN, Margarert, née Dunne; MANAGING DIRECTOR DUNNES STORES; *b* 1942; *educ* Ursuline Convent, Blackrock, Co Cork; *m* Anthony Heffernan; 3*s* 1 *da;* joined growing family supermarket chain, Dunnes Stores, 1956, Director, 1964, Managing Director, 1993 to date; Dunnes Stores are the largest private Irish owned supermarket chain in the State and the largest employer with 5,000 employees in 65 stores and 20% of the market share; the chain extends to Northern Ireland and Spain; recognised as hard working, no-nonsense businesswoman and a tough negotiator; she is also involved in major charity fundraising and founded the *People in Need'* organisation (1989) which has raised over £10 million for smaller charities; awarded Lord Mayor's Millennium Award 1988. Hobby, racing. Contact: Dunnes Stores, 67 Stephen Street Upper, Dublin 8. Fax: 01 475 6450.

HEFFERNAN, Peter Brian; CHIEF EXECUTIVE MARINE INSTITUTE; *b* 1959; *educ* National University of Ireland, Galway, BSc., PhD.; Associate Professor, / Research Scientist, University of Georgia (USA), 1986-92; Manager, Martin Ryan Marine Science Institute, NUI, Galway, 1992-93; Chief Executive, Marine Institute, 1994 to date; has produced over thirty scientific articles in scientific journals. Hobbies, sports, especially soccer, Gaelic football, rugby, running, reading, travelling and fishing. Contact: Marine Institute, 80 Harcourt Street, Dublin 2. Tel: 01 478 0333. Fax: 01 478 4988.

HEGARTY, Adrian

HEGARTY, Adrian; GROUP MANAGING DIRECTOR FRIENDS FIRST HOLDINGS LTD.; *b* 1947; *educ* Institute of Bankers; University College Dublin, BComm; Fordham University, New York, MBA; Wharton, University of Pennsylvania, Advanced Management Program; *m* Anne Ellard; 2*s* 4 *da;* joined Bank of Ireland, 1967; Vice President, Corporate Banking, Bank of Ireland, New

York, USA, 1973-79; Chief Corporate Accounts Manager, Bank of Ireland, Dublin, 1979-83; Head of Marketing, Bank of Ireland, 1983-85, Regional Manager, Athlone, 1985-87, Director, Marketing and Branch Operations, Bank of Ireland Finance, Ltd., 1987-90; Managing Director, Premier Banking and Direct Insurance Services Ltd., 1990-96; Group Managing Director, Friends First Holdings Ltd., 1996 to date; Fellow, Institute of Bankers; member, Institute of Directors; member, St. Stephen's Green Club. Hobbies, horse racing, theatre, reading and cinema. Contact: Friends First, 29 Adelaide Road, Dublin 2. Tel: 01 661 0600. Fax: 01 661 6665.

HENEGHAN, Nigel David

HEMPHILL-MARTYN, Peter Patrick Fitzroy, 5th Baron Hemphill; FARMER, BLOODSTOCK BREEDER; *b* 1928; *educ* Glenstal Abbey; Downside (UK); Brasenose College, Oxford, MA (Hons) Jurisprudence; *married;* 1*s* 2 *da*; former Senior Steward, Turf Club; former Chairman, Galway Race Committee; former Senior Steward, National Hunt Steeplechase Committee; member, Galway Hunt - The Blazers (former MFH); decorations include Cross of Merit of the Order of Malta (1987). Hobbies, racing and country sports. Contact: Galway Blazers, Ballymore, Craughwell, Co. Galway. Tel. : 091 846 003.

HENEGHAN, Nigel David; PUBLIC RELATIONS CONSULTANT; *b* 1961; *educ* St. Michael's College, Ailesbury Road, Dublin; *m* Penny Alexander; 1 *da;* Dennehy Public Relations, (Dublin), 1980; Quest Public Relations, (Dublin), 1984; Welbeck Public Relations, (London), 1986; Director, Image Communications, Dubai, United Arab Emirates, 1988; Director, Heneghan Public Relations Consultants, 1990, Managing Director, 1998 to date; President, Public Relations Institute of Ireland, (1999 & 2000); member, International Public Relations Association, US-Ireland Chamber of Commerce; member, Royal Dublin Society, Portmarnock Golf Club. Brings a broad public relations experience to a strong father/son productive partnership. Hobbies, golf, football, travel and music. Contact: Heneghan Public Relations, 54 Pembroke Road, Dublin 4. Tel: 01 660 7395. Fax: 660 7588.

HENEGHAN, Patrick D.

HENEGHAN, Patrick David, 'Pat'; EXECUTIVE CHAIRMAN HENEGHAN PUBLIC RELATIONS; *b* 1936; *educ* St. Mary's College, Galway; St. Patrick's College, Maynooth; University College Galway; *m* Therese Woods; 3 *s* 3 *da;* P.J. Carroll & Co., 1958-1981; Director & Senior Partner, Public Relations of Ireland Ltd., 1981-90; Founder and current Executive Chairman of Heneghan Public Relations, 1990 to date; Fellow, Public Relations Institute of Ireland; Director, National Concert Hall; Director, Arthritic Foundation of Ireland. Clubs, Portmarnock Golf Club, Woodenbridge Golf Club. Trusted PR advisor to some of the country's leading, media shy businessmen; shrewd and unflappable, a leader in the field of crisis management. Hobbies, music, reading, travel and golf. Contact: Heneghan Public Relations Consultants, 54 Pembroke Road, Dublin 4. Tel: 01 660 7395. Fax: 01 660 7588.

HENNESSY, Charles; SOLICITOR; *b* 1931; *educ* Presentation Brothers College Cork; University College Cork, Hons MA; Incorporated Law Society; *m* Abbey Scott; Auditor, Solicitors Apprentices Debating Society, Gold Medal Oratory, 1952-53; played Munster schools rugby with U.C.C., Cork Constitution, Lansdowne and soccer with Western Rovers, Evergreen and U.C.D.; swam with Weavers Point S.C., U.C.C. S.C. and Sundays Well S.C.; joined J.W. O'Donovan, Solicitors, Senior Partner, 1988-98, currently consultant; Town Commissioner, 1973 to date; Chairman, Cork Opera House, 1989 to date; Chairman, Cork Film Festival; past Chairman Passage West Town Commissioners; past President Cobh and Harbour Chamber of Commerce; Board member, Film Institute of Ireland; former member, Arts Council; member, Cork Development Committee, Cork County Council and I.S.P.C.C.; Vice President Cork Constitution F.C.; Director, board, Opera South. A Corkonian with a deep commitment to his own place, a noted sportsman and patron of the Arts. Hobbies, theatre, the Arts, film and sport. Contact: J.W. O'Donovan, 53 South Mall, Cork. Tel: 021 275 352. Fax: 021 273 704.

HENRY, Patrick

HENRY, Patrick "Pat"; FITNESS CONSULTANT; *b* 1949; *educ* St. Lawrence O'Toole Christian Brothers School, Dublin; American Academy of Body Sculpture, MIHCA, AABS; *m* Marie Hickey, Managing Director, Cheese Products - Specialist Caterers; Lectures in Yoga, nutrition, health and fitness; runs Pat Henry Gym since 1985; contributed to newspapers and magazines; published *Holywood Legs* (Marine Press), 1998; consultant to *Live At Three* (television) 1997-98; has produced fitness video; film appearances include cameo roles in, *Braveheart, Michael Collins, Accelerator;* Director, Cheese Products; regarded as fitness guru to Dublin's top businessmen and women and visiting showbusiness personalities. Hobbies, walking, body surfing and weekend breaks. Contact: Pat Henry Fitness Centre, 14 Lower Pembroke Street, Dublin 2. Tel: 01 661 6195.

HERATY, Anne; CHIEF EXECUTIVE CPL SOLUTIONS; *b* 1960; *educ* Secondary School, Newtownforbes; University College Dublin, BA Econ; *m* Paul Carroll, Business Partner; 1*da;* Sales Executive with Xerox; joined Grafton Recruitment 1987-89; formed partnership with Keith

O'Malley in CPL 1989, eventually bought out the company, currently Chief Executive CPL Solutions; the company specialises in the information technology sector, one of the fastest growth areas in the state; the first woman Chief Executive of an Irish publicly quoted company; shuns the limelight preferring to maintain a hands-on approach with staff and candidates. Contact: CPL Solutions, 83 Merrion Square, Dublin 2. Tel: 01 614 6066.

HERBST, Michael Eamonn; MANAGING DIRECTOR HERBST GROUP; *b* 1941; *educ* Berlin; *m* Monica Kuhl (*m dis*); 1*s* 2*da;* *m* Wendy McCullough; 1*s* 1*da;* Founder, Managing Director Herbst Group, 1965 to date; the Group comprises Herbst Computer Systems and Software, Herbst Grain, Herbst Grain Peat and Energy, Warehousing; HT Farm Machinery; Founder/Owner Polo Wicklow, Ireland's only all weather polo grounds, polo school and polo horse training centre; committee member, Hurlingham Polo Association; President, All Ireland Polo Club; member, Farm Machinery Association, Chamber of Commerce (Wicklow), Irish Grain and Feed Association, plays an important part in Wicklow community and agri business life and on the international polo scene. Hobbies, polo and theatre. Contact: Herbst Group, Kilpoole Hill, Wicklow. Tel: 0404 67164.

HERBST, Michael E.

HESKIN, Edmond, Brigadier General; ARMY OFFICER - GENERAL OFFICER COMMANDING 2 EASTERN BRIGADE; *b* 1942; *educ* St. Colmans College, Fermoy; *m* Madeline Fitzpatrick; 1*s* 2 *da;* commissioned as an Officer, Defence Forces, 1962; appointed Captain, 1969, Commandant, 1977, Lt. Col., 1990, Colonel, 1994, Brigadier, 1997; studied at Command and General Staff Course, Fort Leavenworth, US, 1976; Military College, Co. Kildare, 1976; appointments held, Officer commanding 70 Infantry Bttln, UNIFIL; European Community (former Yugoslavia) 1996, UNIFIL (Lebanon) 1980, '88, '91; Served on Staff, UNIFIL Headquarters (Cyprus) 1964, 1968; currently Assistant Chief of Staff, General Officer Commanding 2 Eastern Brigade; member, Curragh Golf Club (former Captain). Hobbies, golf and general interest in all sports. Contact: Defence Forces Headquarters, Park Gate, Dublin 8. Tel: 01 804 2686. Fax; 01 677 9018.

HEWAT, Richard; CHIEF EXECUTIVE HEITON HOLDINGS PLC; *b* 1940; *educ* Aravon School, Bray, Co. Wicklow; Oundle, Northamptonshire; Trinity College Dublin; *married;* 1 *s* 1 *da;* qualified as a Chartered Accountant; joined established steel and timber business. Contact: Heiton Holdings plc, Ashfield, Naas Road, Clondalkin, Dublin 22. Tel: 01 403 4000. Fax: 01 459 3696.

HEWSON, Paul David, "Bono"; SINGER, SONGWRITER, GUITARIST; *b* 1960; *educ* Mount Temple Comprehensive School, Dublin; *m* Alison Stewart; 2*da*; lead vocalist with U2; members of the group are David "The Edge" Evans (guitars, piano, vocals), Larry Mullen Jnr (drums), Adam Clayton (bass); band formed in Dublin 1978; signed with Island Records 1980; consistent winners of *Hot Press* Readers Poll since 1980; U2 have toured throughout the world to critical and audience acclaim, topping international charts with single and album releases; albums include *Boy* (1980), *October* (1981), *War* (1983), *Unforgettable Fire* (1984), *The Joshua Tree* (1987), *Rattle and Hum* (1988), *Achtung Baby* (1991), *Zooropa* (1993); *The Joshua Tree* was the fastest selling album in record history; band have received various nominations for Grammy Awards; nominated "Best Band", *Rolling Stone* Magazine Readers Poll (US); have been described in *Time* magazine as "Rock's Hottest Ticket" (1987); frequent performers on radio and television, New Year's live show 1989 transmitted by BBC and RTE reached over 500 million; film *U2 Rattle and Hum* premiered worldwide 1988; have performed frequently for charities such as Live Aid (Wembley Stadium), Self Aid (Dublin), Amnesty International (UK); Dublin based Hewson and U2 are international stars. Contact: Principle Management Ltd., 30 Sir John Rogerson's Quay, Dublin 2. Tel: 01 677 7330.

HEWSON, Paul "Bono"

HICKEY, Brendan J.; CHAIRMAN, MANAGING DIRECTOR, DAVY HICKEY PROPERTIES; *b* 1952; *educ* C.B.S. Wexford; University College Dublin, B E(civil); *m* Claire ----; 1*s* 2*da;* Contractor, M.W.S. Board, Sydney, Australia, 1973-75; Bye Law Official, Dublin Co. Council, 1976-78; Consulting Engineer, Nicholas O'Dwyer, 1978-80; Director of Investment & Development, Rohan Group plc, 1980-90; Chairman, MD of Davy Hickey Properties, 1990 to date; property company set up in conjunction with J&E Davy Stockbrokers; developments include Citywest Business Campus, acted as Consultant/CEO, Sisk Properties Ltd., 1991-1994; member, Powerscourt Golf Club. Hobbies, music, sport and travel. Contact: Citywest, 27 Dawson Street, Dublin 2. Tel: 01 679 5222. Fax: 01 679 6377.

HICKEY, James J.; SOLICITOR; *b* 1953; *educ* Gonzaga College; Trinity College Dublin; *m* Fiona Macanna; 1*s* 1 *da;* qualified as a Solicitor, 1977; since 1992 a partner in Matheson Ormsby Prentice Solicitors in charge of the Entertainment Law Group, areas of practice include, film and television financing and production, copyright law and music; Chairman, Board of Directors, National Theatre Society Limited (Abbey and Peacock Theatres); Chairman, Broadcasting Subcommittee of Film Makers Ireland (film and TV producers representative organisation); Member, Board of Directors, Dublin Film Festival; member, Film Industry Review Group; Executive

HICKEY, Patrick

HILL, Noel;

HOEY, James Gerard

HOGAN, John

Producer of film and television documentaries including, *The Joy* for RTE; a legal eagle with a strong influence in the performing arts. Club, Kildare Street and University Club. Hobbies, theatre and cinema. Contact: Matheson Ormsby Prentice, 30 Herbert Street, Dublin 2. Tel: 01 619 9000. Fax: 01 619 9010.

HICKEY, Patrick; PROPERTY CONSULTANT/VALUER, PRESIDENT OLYMPIC COUNCIL OF IRELAND; *b* 1945; *educ* St. Vincent's School, Glasnevin; Certified Valuer; FLIA; *m* Sylviane Dufour-Bourreau, Company Director; 3*s* 1 *da;* Managing Director, Pat Hickey Financial Services, incorporating insurance, auctioneering and consultancy; Member, International Olympic Committee since 1995; Vice President of European Olympic Committee since 1997; President, Olympic Council of Ireland since 1989, responsible for directing the Council and it's twenty-eight member sports federation in selecting and entering teams for the Winter and Summer Olympics; awarded third degree Judo Black Belt by International Judo Federation, 1979; member, Life Insurance Association, Institute of Professional Auctioneers and Valuers. Hobbies, travelling, history, music and all sports. Club, Riverview Racquet and Fitness Club. Contact: Olympic Council of Ireland, 27 Mespil Road, Dublin . Tel: 01 668 0444. Fax: 01 668 0650.

HIGGINS, Anthony "Tony"; PHOTOGRAPHER; *b* 1939; *educ* National School, Celbridge; Technical College, Denmark Street, Dublin; *single;* trained as a carpenter, moved into photography 1962, worked in Con Conor's Studio, St. Stephen's Green; opened own studio 1967, regarded as one of Ireland's leading advertising and fashion photographers, work features in international magazines; recipient of numerous photographic awards; a low key professional, one of the country's leading photographic talents. Hobbies, carpentry and travel. Contact: The Studio, 33 Avenue Road, Dublin 8. Tel: 01 454 3513. Fax: 01 473 3114.

HIGGINS, John James; CORK CITY MANAGER AND TOWN CLERK; *b* 1936; *educ* North Monastry, Cork; Dip. Public Admin. (Gold Medal); *m* Philomena Coleman; 3*s* 3*da;* Clerical Officer, Cork County Council, 1955; Staff Officer, Clare County Council, 1965; County Accountant, Waterford County Council, 1972; County Secretary, Wicklow County Council, 1974; Assistant City Manager, Cork City, 1977; Limerick City Manager and Town Clerk, 1987; Cork City Manager and Town Clerk, 1995 to date. Hobbies, tennis, music. Contact: Cork City Hall, Cork. Tel: 021 966 222. Fax: 021 314 238.

HILL, Noel; MUSICIAN, WRITER, LECTURER, TEACHER; *b* 1958; *educ* St. Flannon's College, Ennis, Co. Clare; *separated;* 1 *s* 1*da;* Professional Musician, 1979-99; T.V. Researcher, RTE TV, 1980-81; Radio Presenter, RTE Radio, 1982; Music Producer/Record Producer, 1985-99; Programme Consultant, RTE TV, 1991-95; Teacher/Lecturer, various schools, colleges and institutes, 1979-99 such as Willie Clancy Summer School, na Piobairi Uilleann; Joe Mooney Summer School, Boston College, U.S.A.; Noel Hill School of Irish Concertina, Co. Clare, 1991-99; N.H. School of Concertina, USA, 1993-99; member, I.M.R.O.; M.C.P.S.; P.R.S.; Director, Foundation for the Preservation of the Irish Concertina Heritage; Regarded both nationally and internationally as Ireland's finest Concertina player; has performed worldwide; recordings include: *Noel Hill & Tony Linnane*, Tara 2006, (Album of the Year Award, 1979); *Noel Hill & Tony MacMahon*, CEF 114; (B.B.C. Radio Album of the Year 1985). Hobbies, sailing, swimming, painting, gardening, Gaelic games, motor sports. Contact: Musicwise Network, c/o Mill Lodge, Mill Lane, Shankill, Dublin. Fax: 01 282 3249.

HOEY, James Gerard; MANAGING DIRECTOR MASONITE IRELAND; *b* 1948; *educ* Christian Brother's, Dundalk; University College Dublin, BSc, PhD, MIE; *m* Marie Murray; 2 *s* 2 *da*; Production Chemist, Loctite Ireland Ltd., 1975-77; Technical Manager, GAF Ireland Ltd., 1977-80; Operations Manager, GAF Ireland Ltd., 1980-81; Operations Manager, C.R.Bard Ireland Ltd., 1981-83; Managing Director, Tarkett Ireland Ltd., 1983-96; Managing Director, Masonite Ireland, 1996 to present; Chairman, Westmeath Hospice Foundation, Past President, Rotary Club, Mullingar, Past Midland Regional President, IBEC North West Regional Executive; Chairman, Mullingar General Hospital; Awarded Most Enterprising Person of the Year Award by Mullingar Chamber of Commerce, 1993. Hobbies, fishing, photography, music and running. Contact: Masonite Ireland, Carrick-On-Shannon, Co. Leitrim. Tel: 078 59500. Fax: 078 59594.

HOGAN, John; MANAGING PARTNER ERNST & YOUNG; *b* 1940; *educ* University College Dublin, BComm; Institute of Chartered Accountants in Ireland, Fellow, 1964; *m* Bernadette Cullen; 1*s* 2 *da;* qualified as a Chartered Accountant with Reynolds McCarron & Co. 1964, Partner, 1966; appointed International Partner in KMG Reynolds McCarron, 1981; firm merged with Ernst & Whinney in 1987 and became Ernst & Young in 1989, elected Managing Partner, Ernst & Young 1994; member, K Club and Hermitage Golf Club. Hobby, golf. Contact: Ernst & Young, Block 1, Harcourt Centre, Harcourt Street, Dublin 2. Tel: 01 475 0555. Fax: 01 475 0599.

HOGAN, Michael Gerard "Mike"; PUBLISHER; *b* 1960; *educ* Knockbeg College, Carlow; St. Brigid's Vocational School, Athy; St. Mary's College, Castledermot; *m* Mari O'Leary, Public Relations Consultant; 2 *s;* Lighting Technician, RTE, 1979; Sales Representative, Sunshine Radio, 1980-82; General Manager, Radio Nova, 1982-86; General Manager, Q102, 1986-89; Chief Executive, FM 104, 1990-91; purchased *In Dublin* magazine, 1992; seen as a magazine mogul on the Irish publishing scene; now controls forty plus titles including, *Magill* (1998), *Dot.IE* (1996), *Medicine Weekly* (1997), *High Ball* (1998), *Boyzone* (1996); member, Riverview. Hobbies, family and friends. Contact: Hosoa Company, Camden Place, Dublin 2. Tel: 01 478 4322. Fax: 01 475 8139.

HOGAN, Michael

HOGAN, Thomas Francis "Frank"; COMPANY DIRECTOR; *b* 1945; *educ* Rockwell College; *m* Fran Nulty; 2*s*; worked for a time on family farm in Cashel, Co. Tipperary; started Frank Hogan Ltd, 1973, one of the largest motor businesses in the South West, authorised dealers for Mercedez Benz, Volkswagon, Audi and Mazda cars and commercial vehicles; Director, Hogan Oil; Director, Hogan Convenience Stores; Chairman, Garryowen Rugby Club (former inter-provincial player); member, Castletroy and Lahinch Golf Clubs. Hobbies, rugby and golf. Contact: Frank Hogan Ltd., Dublin Road, Limerick; Tel: 061 416 000. Fax: 061 416 043.

HOLLAND, Michael J.; MANAGING DIRECTOR, FITZWILLIAM HOTEL GROUP; *b* 1954; *educ* C.U.S., Leeson Street; *m* Carol Swift; 1 *s*; Managing Director, New City Investments, 1985-87; Director, Aviette - Acquired H. Williams Supermarket Group, 1987-89; Co-founder, Fitzwilliam Hotel Group, 1989; Acquired and re-developed Portmarnock Hotel and Golf Links, 1989; Acquired and re-developed Royal Dublin Hotel, 1989; Acquired and re-developed Metropole Hotel, Cork; Acquired Mespil Estate, Dublin, 1992; Developed Leeside Leisure Centre, Cork, 1992; Director, Irish Welcome Tours and Best Western Hotel, 1994; Developed Fitzwilliam Hotel, St. Stephen's Green, 1997; New City Estates opens London Office, 1998; Fitzwilliam Hotel opens, 1998; Member: Dublin Chamber of Commerce, Irish Property and Facility Managers Association, Dublin City Business Association, Royal St. George Yacht Club, National Yacht Clubs. Hobbies, sailing, reading and travel. Contact: Fitzwilliam Hotel Group, 66, Fitzwilliam Square, Dublin 2. Tel: 01 661 5422.

HOLLAND, Michael J.

HOLLAND, Ronald John; YACHT DESIGNER; *b* 1947; *m* Joanna Keltner; 4 *da*; Gained extensive sailing experience and worked as an apprentice boat builder, Auckland, New Zealand; Sailed to USA, 1967; Trained as Yacht Designer in California and Florida; Designed, built and raced the winner of the 1973 Quarter Tonne Cup in Cowes; Moved to Ireland, 1973; During the 70s and 80s designed many of the top international race boats; In the 80s, changed focus towards designing high performance, large, luxury yachts; Racing boats include: *Eygthenes, Shamrocks, Silver Apple, Big Apple, Swan 441s, Imp, Swan 39s, Morning Cloud, Regardless, Swan 371s, Swan 42s, Kialoa, Kiwi Magic* (America's Cup Challenger), *Lion New Zealand, NCB Ireland*; Large yachts include: *Whirlwind XII* (103 ft.), *Gleam* (109 ft.), *Sensation* (110 ft.), *Cyclos III* (110 ft.), *Royal Eagle II* (90 ft.), *Juliet* (141 ft.), *Shanakee* (108 ft.), *Thalia* (160 ft.), *Giobana* (118 ft.), *Charlatan* (110 ft.), *Affinity* (150 ft.); Books published include: *Splendour Under Sail* (1989). Awarded Showboats International Best Sailing Yacht for *Shanakee*, Monaco, 1992, Showboats International 'Best Sailing Yacht' for *Juliet*, Monaco, 1994, International Superboats Best Sailing Yacht for *Juliet*, Fort Lauderdale, 1994; Listed in *Who's Who in New Zealand.* Hobbies, sailing, music, reading, photography; Clubs, Royal New Zealand Yacht Squadron, New York Yacht Club, Kinsale Yacht Club. Contact: P.O. Box 23, Kinsale, Co. Cork. Tel: 021 774 866. Fax: 021 774 808.

HOLLAND, Ronald John

HOLOHAN, Renagh; JOURNALIST; *b* 1949; *educ* Pembroke School, Ballsbridge; University College Dublin, BA; Joined *The Irish Times*, Northern Editor, 1972-73; London Editor, 1974-76; Assistant News Editor, Dublin, 1977 to date; Quidnunc, *Irish Times,* 1992 to date; Publications include: *The Irish Chateaux - In Search of Descendants of The Wild Geese* (1989), *Ireland - An Illustrated Yearbook* (1991); Chair, Association of European Journalists (Irish Chapter), 1996 and 1997; A.T. Cross Woman Journalist Award, 1988, for coverage of the Gibraltar Inquests; Regarded as an experienced and versatile journalist, with an encyclopaedic knowledge of the political scene; one of the first women to achieve a senior position in the Irish print media. Contact: The Irish Times, D'Olier Street, Dublin 2. Tel: 01 679 2022.

HOOPER, Richard; COMPANY DIRECTOR; *b* 1936; *educ* Catholic University School, Dublin; University College Dublin, BE, MBA; *m* Kathleen Maxwell, Shop Owner; 4 *da*; Manager, Unidare 1958-66; Former Executive Director, The Investment Bank of Ireland; former Chairman, IBI Corporate Finance Ltd; Currently Chairman, Glencar Mining plc, National Toll Roads plc; Director, Irish Life and Permanent plc, Green Property plc, Jurys Hotel Group plc; a leading financial guru, much sought after adviser in merger and take-over situations. Hobby, sailing. Club, Royal St. George Yacht Club (Commodore). Contact: Glencar Mining plc, 26, Upper Mount Street, Dublin 2. Tel: 01 661 9974. Fax: 01 661 1205.

HORGAN, Conor; PHOTOGRAPHER, DIRECTOR; *b* 1962; *educ* Newpark Comprehensive School; University College Dublin, School of Film, Developing the Screenplay; worked as a puppeteer, a waiter, an illustrator, a pizza chef, a geo-electrical surveyor in northern Rif mountains in Morocco; since 1984 has worked as an Advertising / Fashion / Editorial Photographer with commissions from advertising agencies and magazines in Ireland and abroad, including *Vogue, Harpers & Queen, G.Q,* and *Conde Naste Traveller;* has directed pop videos and TV commercials since 1992; presents *Jazz FM* on Radio FM; clients include, ESB, TnaG, An Post, Hedex, Alone, TSB Bank, Andrews, Ritz, Heineken, Cerebral Palsy Institute, Satzenbrau, Telecom Eireann, AIB, Bord na Mona, Aero, Waterford Foods, Independent Newspapers and National Lottery Beneficiaries; exhibited photography, Conor Horgan - Portraits, The Gallery of Photography, recipient, Satzenbrau Fashion Oscar Photographer of the Year, 1989 and 1991; Craft Award for Photography, ICAD, 1992 and 1993; Craft Award for Direction, ICAD, 1993; Gold Award - Best Commercials, ICAD, 1994; Grand Prix Ireland and Silver Award - Best International Series, Kinsale International Advertising Festival, 1995; I.R.M.A. (Irish Recorded Music Awards) Video of the Year for O.T.T. Pop Video, 1997; member, National Union of Journalists - Dublin Freelance Branch, S.I.P.T.U. Film Directors Section, Board Member, Irish Film Institute, Director, Aids Aid Ltd., (an Irish Aids & HIV charity). Hobbies, music, reading, hanging around drinking coffee. Contact: 087 257 4621.

HORGAN, Cornelius George Mark "Con"; CHAIRMAN ABBEY TRAVEL GROUP / TOWER HOTEL GROUP; *b* 1940; *educ* University College Dublin, Dip Pub Adm.; *m* Allyson Ussher; 1*s* 5 *da*; Travel Industry Junior, Aer Lingus, 1958-62; District Sales Manager - Ireland, Iberia Airlines, 1962-68; Joint Managing Director, Ryan Hotels plc, 1968-78; Founder, Chief Executive & Chairman, Abbey Travel & Tower Hotel Groups, 1978 to date; member, Woodbrook Golf Club, The Royal Dublin Golf Club, Killarney Golf and Fishing Club, Faithlegg Golf Club (Honorary Life Member). Hobbies, golf and Grand Opera. Contact: Tower Hotel Group, 34 Lower Abbey Street, Dublin 1. Tel: 01 873 0199. Fax: 01 873 0194.

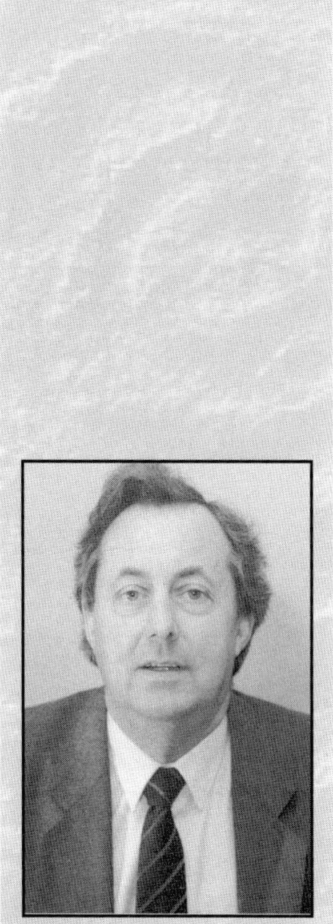
HORGAN, J. Noel

HORGAN, J. Noel; GENERAL MANAGER TIPPERARY CO-OPERATIVE CREAMERY LTD.; *b* 1938; *educ* Christian Brothers School, Callan, Co. Kilkenny; University College Cork, Food Science; *m* Jean Miles; 1*s* 1 *da;* Production Supervisor, Express Dairies, (UK), 1960-64; Nestle Scotland, 1964-66; Technical Marketing, Irish Dairy Board, London, 1966-69; Production Manager, Mitchelstown Creameries, 1969-74; General Manager, Tipperary Co-operative Creamery, 1974 to date. An ebulliant personality and astute business brain make him highly regarded in the dairy industry. Hobbies, golf and hunting. Contact: Tipperary Co-operative Creamery Ltd., Station Road, Tipperary. Tel: 062 33111. Fax: 062 51963.

HORN, Chris; CHAIRMAN AND CEO IONA TECHNOLOGIES PLC; *educ* Newpark, Blackrock; Trinity College Dublin, BA, BAI, PhD; *married;* 2*s* 2*da;* worked with European Commission, 1984; joined staff of TCD, 1985-93; Co-founder, IONA Technologies, 1991 to date; Chairman, Expert Group on Future Skills, (Forfas), 1998; member, Centre for Corporate Innovation, USA, 1999; member, Irish Software Association; IMI Council, 1999; board member Object Management Group, 1999; awards include, Europe's 500 Award, Edinburgh, 1999; *Business and Finance* - Company of the Year, 1999. Hobby, windsurfing. Contact: Iona Technologies plc, The Iona Building, Shelbourne Road, Dublin 4. Tel: 01 662 5255. Fax: 01 662 5244.

HOULIHAN, Michael P.; SOLICITOR & COMPANY DIRECTOR; *b* 1941; *educ* Ennis C.B.S.; Cistercian College, Roscrea; University College Dublin; Law Society of Ireland; *m* Joan Mulhern; 1 *s* 2 *da;* after qualifying as solicitor, returned to family practice, Houlihan McMahon, Ennis, 1963; currently running one of the largest legal practices in Munster; specialises in insurance, litigation and local authority legal work; frequently delivers papers on law office management, litigation and negligence topics; Founding Director, Rural ReSettlement Ireland Ltd.; member, Advisory Board, Ireland Funds; Former Director and Chairman, Shannon Free Airport Development Company Ltd. 1990-95; Former President, Law Society of Ireland, 1982-83, Co. Clare Law Association, Ennis Chamber of Commerce, Cistercian College Roscrea P.P.U., member, County Clare Law Association, Law Society of Ireland, International Bar Association, American Bar Association. Hobbies, music, opera, travel, art collections, community development. Contact: Houlihan McMahon, 9/10/11 Bindon Street, Ennis, Co. Clare. Tel: 065 682 8706. Fax: 065 682 1870.

HOULIHAN, Robert; CONDUCTOR; *b* 1952; *educ* Mount Street School; Licenciate, Trinity College London; *m* 2 stepsons; commenced musical studies in the Army School of Music, later the Municipal College of Music and Canford Summer School of Music (under George Hurst); awarded 2nd prize, Competition for Young Conductors, Besancon, France; Scholarship from Arts Council and French Government to study at European Centre for Musical Research in Metz and with Leon Barzin in Paris; awarded 3rd prize and special Public Prize, Hungarian Television International Conductor's Competition; Principal Conductor, State Philharmonic of Tirgu Mures, conductor with National Symphony Orchestra of Ireland, Irish National Youth Orchestra; frequent appearances with leading orchestras in France, Luxembourg, Holland, Switzerland, Spain, U.K. Hobbies, reading, walking, socialising. Contact: 22 bis Rue St. Marcel, 5700 Metz. France.

HOWARD, John

HOWARD, John; RESTAURATEUR; *b* 1949; *educ* National Schools, Ballyvaughan and Lisdoonvarna, Co. Clare; *m* Catherine Carroll, Director Le Coq Hardi; 1da; Trained in Switzerland, London and France; chef L'Ecu de France (London) and Kensington Palace (London) 1968-72; Head Chef, Whites Hotel, Wexford, 1972-77; Owner/Chef Le Coq Hardi, 1977 to date; Guest Chef, Hotel de Paris, Monte Carlo, for Dr. Michael Smurfit; Guest Chef, Waldorf Astoria, New York for dinner honouring Mr and Mrs Albert Reynolds; Organiser, All Irish Dinner at the White House for President and Mrs Clinton; numerous awards include: Award of Excellence 1992, '93, '94. '95; Graham's Port National Wine Award '91, '92, '93; Egon Ronay, Wine Cellar of the Year '88, '90, '91, '92, '93, '95; Ackerman Clover Award '94, '95, '96; Egon Ronay Star '94, '95, '96, '97; Irish Tourist Board Award of Excellence for 14 years; annual entries Good Food Guide and Michelin Guide, Egon Ronay Chef of the Year, 1997; Fellow, EWMCS, Hotel & Catering Institute of Ireland; member, Association Culinaire Francaise; Past President, Restaurant Association of Ireland; Founder Member, Euro Toques; runs one of the finest restaurants in the country; an enthusiastic bloodstock owner. Hobbies, fine wine and food, antiques and racing. Contact: Le Coq Hardi, 35 Pembroke Road, Dublin 4. Tel: 01 668 9070. Fax: 01 668 9887.

HOWLIN, Brendan; POLITICIAN; *b* 1956; *educ* Christian Brothers School, Wexford; St. Patrick's Teacher's Training College, Dublin; *single*; National School Teacher; failed candidate for Dáil seat 1982; Taoiseach's nominee to the Senate 1982-87; elected Fianna Fáil Deputy for Wexford 1984; Chief Whip, Labour Party 1987-93; Party spokesperson on Health and Youth Affairs 1989-93, on Health and Women's Rights 1987-89; Minister for Health 1993-94; Minister for the Environment 1994-97; currently spokesperson on Justice, Equality and Law Reform; elected Deputy Leader of Labour Party 1997; regarded as competent, hard working and cautious. Contact: Dáil Eireann, Leinster House, Kildare Street, Dublin 2. Tel: 01 618 3333.

HUGHES, Paddy; MANAGING DIRECTOR BORD NA MONA; *b* 1939; *educ* Pallaskenry Secondary College, Co. Limerick; Lausanne, Management Course at IMEDE; m Sadie O'Connor; 3s 1 da; joined Bord na Móna in 1959; served in a number of production and quality control areas, became Deputy Works Manager in Timahoe Sod Peat Works, 1974, General Works Manager, 1979-86, Group Manager responsible for the five milled peat works, 1986-88; appointed full-time Chairman of the Task Force on Company Re-Organisation which recommended the re-structuring which was implemented and which turned Bord na Móna into a decentralised divisionalised group, 1988; first Chief executive of the Peat Energy Division, 1989, overseeing a complete change both in the work systems and harvesting technology used in production operations, and the re-organisation and re-focusing of the Research and Development function, the creation and development of a number of small enterprises and introducing a comprehensive programme of Environmental Management; appointed Chief Operations Officer, 1994, appointed Managing Director, 1996; member, IMI, Institute of Directors; member of the Executive Board of the International Peat Society. Club, Tullamore Golf Club. Hobbies, golf, reading and a general interest in all sporting events. Contact: Bord na Móna plc, Main Street, Newbridge, Co. Kildare. Tel: 045 439 200. Fax: 045 439 291.

HUGHES, Paul

HUGHES, Paul; HOTELIER; *b* 1939; *educ* Marist Father, CUS, Leeson Street; St, Michael's Dublin; Christian Brothers School, Oaklands, Dublin; *m* June Cahill; 4 *s;* Hotel Trainee, Russell Hotel and hotels in Rome, Berne and Biarritz; Assistant Manager, Royal Hibernian Hotel and Moira Hotel, Dublin; Founder, Old Dublin Restaurant; Proprietor/Manager, Abbey Glen Castle, Clifden; Co-Founder (former Director), Connemara Golf Club; Chairman, Clifden West Connemara Airport plc; Director, Manor House Hotels Ltd.; President Clifden Chamber of Commerce 1995 & 1996; Chairman Clifden and West Connemara Tourism Council; member, Irish Hotels Federation, Restaurant Owners Association; Galway County Tourism Committee 1995 & 1995. A dynamic hotelier who has turned a luxury hotel overlooking Clifden into a mecca for movie moguls, including Peter O'Toole, Christopher Plummer, Woody Allen, Mia Farrow, Angela Lansbury, Gabriel Byrne and musicians such as Ronan Keating, the Carter Twins, Paul Harrington, the Saw Doctors and Sharon Shannon. Hobbies, work, golf and music. Clubs: Connemara Golf Club, Clifden Boat Club, Riverview Racquet and Fitness Club. Contact: Abbey Glen Castle Hotel, Clifden, Co Galway. Tel: 095 21201. Fax: 095 21797.

HUGHES, William Gerard 'Bill'; TV PRODUCER / DIRECTOR; *b* 1955; *educ* Knockbeg College, Carlow; University College Dublin, BA Phil. Lit.; Gold Medallist, London Academy of Music and Dramatic Art; joined RTE in 1983; became independent producer in 1985; produced / directed *MT – USA* with Vincent Hanley, 1985-87, *The Write Stuff*, ITV UK, 1988-90, *New Music From Ireland*, BBC UK, 1991, Book 94, RTE, Opening Nights, RTE, UTV, 1991-93; MC-USA 1992-94, Fair Share, RTE, 1996-97; also many magazine, arts and music programmes; documentary series, North of

HUMPHREYS, Daniel

HUNT, Fionnuala

HYLAND, Aine

HYNES, Jerome

Naples, South of Rome, 1995, *The Irish Tenors*, Network USA, 1999; other work includes documentary on coping with AIDS, *Fintan*, 1995, documentary on separation, What about the Children, 1998, *Gay life in Ireland The Love that dare not Speak its Name*, 1999, also five pop videos for Boyzone; member, Board of Directors of the Irish Hospice Foundation, member, Irish Film and Television Academy; awards include, The Irish Music Critics Award, for Production of the Year, 1990 and 1991, The Young Irelander Award RTE/Abbey 1973; nominated for the humanitarian award at the Bologna TV Festival for *Fintan*, the AIDS documentary; a regular guest critic and commentator on arts, entertainment, and food on TV, radio and print journalism. Contact: Radius, Television Productions Ltd., 37-39 Fitzwilliam Square, Dublin 2. Tel: 01 605 3777. Fax: 01 876 5181.

HUMPHREYS, Daniel Wyn; MANAGING DIRECTOR, SPRING GROVE SERVICES IRL; *b* 1949; *educ* Ffestiniog County School, North Wales; Kingsway College, London, Diploma in Sociology; *m* Iona ----; 4 *da*; Civil Service Commission, London, 1967-68; Personnel Assistant, Central Electricity Generating Board, Trawsfynydd Nuclear Power Station; Trainee Manager, Spring Grove Services, North Wales, 1970-74; Moved to Ireland to Poineer Workwear Rental, 1974; Currently Managing Director, Spring Grove Services Irl.; Works published include: *20th Century Poets* (1970s ed.); Member, I.M.I., Institute of Directors, Mensa, Association of Textile Renters (past President). Hobbies, participating in marathons, playing 5 a side soccer, rugby and travel. Contact: Spring Grove Services Irl, 160, Shelbourne Road, Dublin 4. Tel: 01 6680 655. Fax: 01 668 3478.

HUMPHRIES, Peter; PROFESSOR OF MEDICAL MOLECULAR GENETICS; *b* 1948; *educ* The King's School, Tynemouth, England; Trinity College Dublin, BA, PhD; *m* Marian Molloy; 1 *s*; Undertook research at the University of Strasbourg and the Beatson Institute for Cancer Research, Glasgow; Lecturer, Medical Genetics, Queen's University Belfast, 1979-83; Returned to Trinity College Dublin in 1983 as lecturer in Genetics; elected Fellow of TCD in 1988, and to Chair of Medical Genetics, 1992; Now runs the Wellcome Ocular Unit at TCD; The research interests of his team are directed towards the furtherment of knowledge of the cause of degenerative diseases of the eye and the development of therapies for such conditions; Author of over seventy scientific publications. His team localised the first two genes responsible for the cause of retinitis pigmentosa (RP), a disease causing severe visual handicap in at least 1.5 million people throughout the world; Member, The Royal Irish Academy, The Alcon Research Institute, The American Society of Human Genetics, The Association for Vision Research and Opthalmology; Founder Irish Member, The Human Gehome Organisation, President, Irish Society of Human Genetics; Fellow, Trinity College Dublin, 1988; Recipient, The Alcon Prize for Vision Research, 1993; Doctor of Science (Honoris Causa), University of Szeged, 1997; A low key academic of high international standing. Hobbies, angling, target shooting, hill walking. Contact: Department of Genetics, Trinity College, Dublin 8. Tel: 01 608 2108. Fax: 01 671 9394.

HUNT, Fionnuala; VIOLINIST, ARTISTIC & MUSIC DIRECTOR IRISH CHAMBER ORCHESTRA; *b* 1957; *educ* Ulster College of Music (with Jaroslav Vanacek); Royal College of Music, London; Hochschule fur Musik, Vienna, (with Wolfgang Schneiderhaun and Franz Samohyl); *single;* member, Vienna Chamber Orchestra, 1980-84; 1st Violin, Bavarian State Opera Orchestra, Munich, 1984-85; Co-leader, R.T.E. Symphony Orchestra, 1986-89; Leader & Artistic Director, Irish Chamber Orchestra, 1995 to date; Guest Leader, London Symphony Orchestra, Hallé Orchestra, Bournemouth Symphony Orchestra, Ulster Orchestra, B.B.C. Philharmonic Orchestra, B.B.C. Scottish Symphony Orchestra, Opera de Lyon, France, Orcestre de Cadaquez, Spain; member, Cultural Relations Committee; member, German Wine Academy; Honorary President, Dublin Youth Orchestra; recipient, The Spirit of Life Award, 1998. In addition to a fine solo career, her singleminded determination and strength play an important role in guiding the Irish Chamber Orchestra. Hobby, wine. Contact: John Owen, Owen and White Management, 39 Hillfield Avenue, London, N8 7DS. Tel: 0044 181 340 9571. Fax: 004 181 340 4056.

HYDE, Tim; BLOODSTOCK BREEDER; *b* 1941; *educ* Christian Brothers College, Cashel; *m* Patricia Roe; 1*s* 4 *da;* member of prominent Tipperary racing family, formerly leading National Hunt Rider; Owner/Manager, Camas Park Stud; the stud has bred numerous classic winners; Director, Doncaster Bloodstock Sales, Sean Barrett Bloodstock Insurance, Tipperary Racecourse; member, Irish National Hunt Steeplechase Committee, Turf Club; highly regarded in the bloodstock industry; one of the country's leading pinhookers. Hobbies, hunting, winter sports and golf Contact: Camas Park Stud, Cashel, Co. Tipperary. Tel: 062 61010. Fax: 062 61576.

HYLAND, Aine, née Donlon; PROFESSOR OF EDUCATION, UNIVERSITY COLLEGE CORK; *b* 1942; *educ* Convent of Mercy, Ballymahon, Co. Longford, 1953-59; University College Dublin, BA; Trinity College Dublin, H.Dip., M.Ed., PhD; *m* W.J. Hyland (*decd.*); 3 *da*; Executive Officer, Department of Education, 1959-64; Research Officer, International Labour Office, Geneva, 1964-65; Secondary School Teacher, 1969-73; Part time Tutor, Education Department, Trinity College Dublin, 1975-80; Senior Lecturer, Education and Admissions Officer, Carysfort College 1980-88;

Senior Lecturer in Education, University College Dublin, 1988-93; Professor of Education, University College Cork, 1993 to date; Publications include: *Irish Educational Documents*, Vols. 1-3 (editor), Author of over 40 articles and papers on education - history, policy, curriculum and assessment; Member, Educational Studies Association of Ireland, Irish Peace Institute, Conference on Pluralism in Education, Educate Together (Republic of Ireland); Patron of Northern Ireland Council for Integrated Education, Chairperson of Points Commission. Contact: University College Cork, Cork. Tel: 021 276 871.

HYNES, John

HYNES, Garry ARTISTIC DIRECTOR, DRUID THEATRE; *b* 1953; *educ* St. Louis Convent, Monaghan; Dominican College, Galway; University College Galway, BA; *single*; Artistic Director, Druid Theatre 1975-90; Freelance Director, Royal Shakespeare Company 1988-89; Artistic Director, Abbey Theatre, 1990-94; Artistic Director, Druid Theatre, Galway, 1994 to date; recipient of Director of the Year (1983 and 1985), *Time Out* London Award for Direction (1988); Received two L.L.D (Honoris Causa) both for service to the Irish Theatre, the first from the National Council for Educational Awards, the second from the National University of Ireland, Galway; First woman in the history of the Tonys to win a Best Director Award; Member, Arts Council of Ireland. A talented, innovative, and therefore controversial figure in Irish theatre. Hobbies, reading, food and poker. Contact: Druid Theatre Co., Chapel Lane, Galway. Tel: 091 568 660. Fax: 091 563 109.

HYNES, Jerome; CHIEF EXECUTIVE, WEXFORD OPERA FESTIVAL; *b* 1959; *educ* St. Ignatius College, Galway; University College Galway, BA, HDipEd, LLB; *m* Alma Quinn; 3 *s*; Administrator, Druid Theatre Company 1981-84; General Manager, Druid Theatre Company, 1984-88; Chief Executive, Wexford Festival Opera, 1988 to date; Member of the Board of Directors of: Druid Theatre Company, Galway, Watergate Theatre, Kilkenny, West Cork Chamber Festival; Wexford Chamber of Industry and Commerce; A hard working, tough negotiator, noted for success with sponsors. Hobbies, reading, theatre, opera, sports. Contact: Theatre Royal, High Street, Wexford. Tel: 053 22400. Fax: 053 24289

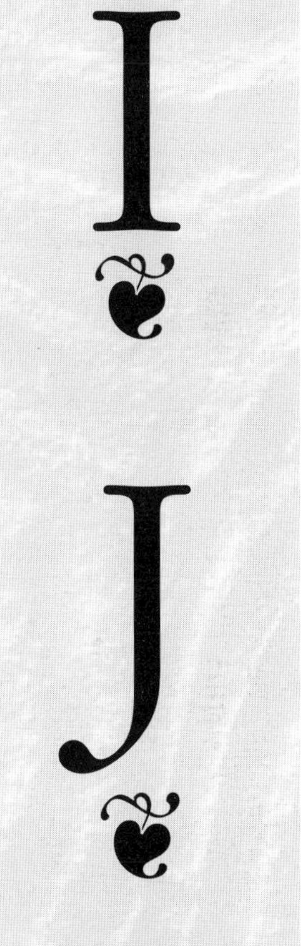

HYNES, John; CHIEF EXECUTIVE, AN POST; *b* 1945; *educ* BSc (Computer Science), MSc (Management); *married;* 1 *s* 3 *da;* currently Chief Executive, An Post; President, Irish Computer Society, Chairman, Crimestoppers. Contact: Postal Headquarters, G.P.O., O'Connell Street, Dublin 1. Tel: 01 705 7000.

IRVINE, Eddie; RACING DRIVER; *b* 1965 in Northern Ireland; *single;* began racing career in Irish FF 1600, 1983; first car was a Formula Ford 1600 Crossle 50 and first win was Brands Hatch FF Festival 1987; has raced at all the major international venues; wins and places include British FF 1600 Champion, winner of Brands Hatch Formula Ford Festival 1987, F3000/Eddie Jordan 3rd 1990, runner up F3000 in Japan, F1 Scuderia Ferrari Marlboro 4th 1998, winner Australian Grand Prix 1999; the Ferrrari Formula One driver "Irv the Swerve" is a slight, fun loving personality who enjoys the trappings of wealth - helicopter, yacht and a stable of motor bikes, but retains a North of Ireland practicality about finance. Hobbies, swimming, snowboarding, fishing, flying helicopters, playing guitar. Contact: The Coachhouse, Marlborough Lane, Donnybrook, Dublin 4. Tel: 01 496 7396.

IRWIN, Jonathan H.N.D.; CHIEF EXECUTIVE, DUBLIN INTERNATIONAL SPORTS COUNCIL; *b* 1941; *educ* Eton (UK); Trinity College Dublin; *m* The Hon. Mikaela Rawlinson; (*m. dis.*); 4 s; *m* Mary Ann O'Brien, Founder, Managing Director, Lily O'Brien Chocolates; 3 *s* (*2 s decd.*); 1 *da;* worked with B.B.A. Ireland, 1964-74; Managing Director, Goffs Bloodstock Sales Ltd., 1974-89; CEO, Phoenix Park Racecourse, 1984-90; Chairman, B.B.A. Ireland Ltd., 1990; Director, B.B.A. Ireland plc; currently Chief Executive Dublin International Sports Council; Director, Lily O'Brien's Chocolates; Chairman, Jack & Jill Children's Foundation; Director, International Racecourse Management; Member: Turf Club, recipient of Irish Thoroughbred Breeders Association (ITBA); Personality of the Year, 1990 and 1991; A charismatic man with an encyclopaedic knowledge of the Irish bloodstock industry. Contact: Dublin International Sports Council. TeL: 01 662 2855

JAGO, Tom; MANAGING DIRECTOR IRISH FERTILIZER INDUSTRIES LTD.; *b* 1934; *educ* Presentation College, Cobh; University College Cork, BE; *m* Ann Ginnity; Engineering Manager, NET, 1964-70; Engineering Manager, Irish Ropes Ltd., 1970-73; Managing Director, IIG Ltd., 1973-79; Divisional Chief Executive, Smurfit Group, 1979-84; Managing Director, NET, 1984-87; Managing Director, IFI Ltd., 1987 to date; recognised as an astute and articulate businessman. Hobbies, walking, reading, travel and music. Contact: Irish Fertilizer Industries Ltd., 2 Warrington Place, Dublin 2. Tel: 01 676 4081. Fax; 01 676 2318.

IRVINE, Eddie

JOHNSTON, Jennifer; WRITER; *b* 1930; *educ* Park House School, Dublin, Trinity College Dublin, FRSL; daughter of playwright Denis Johnston and actress/director Shelah Richards; *m* Ian Smyth (m dis); 2 *s* 2 *da*; *m* David Gilliland; publications include: *The Captain and Kings, The*

Gates, How Many Miles To Babylon (Yorkshire Post 'Book of the Year') *Shadows on our Skin* (runner up for Booker Prize), *The Old Jest, The Christmas Tree, The Railway Station Man, Fools Sanctuary, The Invisible Worm, The Illusionist*; Short plays, *Three Monologues, The Nightingale and not the Lark*; novels have been published in the U.S., France, Italy, Spain, Germany, Holland, Lithuania, Romania, Hungary and Russia; Member, Aosdána; a lyrical writer who describes poignantly the decline of the ascendancy in rural Ireland. Hobbies, cinema, theatre. Contact: Aosdána, 70 Merrion Square, Dublin 2. Tel: 01 661 1840. Fax: 01 676 1302.

JONES, Kenneth; ORGAN BUILDER; *b* 1936; *educ* Wesley College, Dublin; Trinity College Dublin, MA, BAI; *separated*; 2 *da*; Engineer with Nigerian Railways, 1957; formed organ building company, Nigeria, 1964; returned to Ireland, 1973; established Kenneth Jones Pipe Organs Ltd., Bray, Kenneth Jones & Associates; in the past 25 years, prestigious commissions completed include those for Christ Church Cathedral Dublin, the Cathedral of the Madeleine, Salt Lake City, USA, the National Concert Hall, Dublin, St. Peter's Church, Eaton Square, London, Trinity College, Melbourne University and Tewkesbury Abbey, England; recognised as a designer-craftsman of international repute; finest Irish organ builder this century, possibly of all time. Hobbies, country life, music, photography and house design. Contact: St. Paul's Church, Church Terrace, Bray, Co. Wicklow. Tel: 01 286 7662. Fax: 01 286 7664.

JORDAN, Edmund "Eddie"; FORMULA ONE TEAM OWNER; *b* 1948; *educ* St. Anne's, Milltown; Synge Street School; *m* Marie McCarthy; 2 *s* 2 *da;* switched career from banking to motor racing after a summer spent karting in Jersey; won major championships including three Formula Atlantic races, 1977, Irish Formula Atlantic, 1978, Formula Two Championship, 1978, '79, '80, British Formula Three Championship, 1982, '83, '84, '86; established Jordon Grand Prix, 1991, the team boasts one Grand Prix victory; membership of the Top Four teams in F1, and an impressive driver line up including Damon Hill; Jordon is the first Irishman to have achieved international prominence in this field; recognised as a lively companion, an astute negotiator who has broken new ground by securing investment from global equity investor, Warburg Pincus. Hobbies, music, skiing, boating and golf. Contact: Jordon Grand Prix, Silverstone, Northamptonshire, NN12 8TJ. Tel: 0044 1327 850 800. Fax: 0044 1327 850 866.

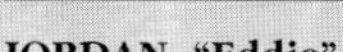
JORDAN, "Eddie"

JORDON, Neil; FILM MAKER, WRITER; *b* 1952; *educ* St. Paul's School Raheny; University College Dublin; *married; 2s 2 da;* recipient of Irish Arts Bursary 1976; *The Guardian* Fiction Prize 1977; publications include *Night in Tunisia and Other Stories, The Past, The Dream of a Beast, Sunrise with Sea Monster;* film credits include *The Company of Wolves,* (Director), *Angel* (Director and Screen Writer), *High Spirits* (Director), *Mona Lisa, We're No Angels* (Director), *The Miracle* (Director), *The Crying Game* (1992), *Interview with a Vampire* (1995), *Michael Collins* (1997), *The Butcher Boy* (1998), *In Dreams* (1999), *The End of the Affair* (1999); dark good looks and media unfriendly manner have led to him being described as "The Heathcliffe of the Film Industry". Contact: ICM Ltd, 76 Irishtown Road, Dublin 4. Tel: 01 667 6455.

JORGENSEN, Ib; ART GALLERY OWNER; *b* 1935; *educ* in Denmark; Morgan School, Castleknock, Co. Dublin; Grafton Academy of Dress Design; *m* Patricia Murray, Artist and Textile Designer); (*m. dis.*); 2 *da*; *m* Sonia Rogers, Bloodstock Breeder; worked with Nicholas O'Dwyer (Dublin) before opening own salon, 1956; designs for international clientele, theatre and airlines; Ireland's leading couturier, with an expanding market in the ready to wear (boutique) range; closed couture salon in 1996; opened Jorgensen Fine Art Gallery, 1990; dealing in Irish & European Art; an outspoken, urbane man, a leader in his field. Hobbies, gardening, theatre, the Arts and tennis. Contact: Jorgensen Fine Art, 29 Molesworth Street, Dublin 2. Tel: 01 661 9755. Fax: 01 661 9760.

JORGENSEN, Sonia, née Pilkington; BLOODSTOCK BREEDER; *b* 1937; *educ* Tudor Hall, Oxford; *m* Capt. Tim Rogers, M.C., Bloodstock Breeder (*decd.*); 2 *s*; *m* Ib Jorgensen, former Couturier, and now Owner/Director of Jorgensen Fine Art; Owner/Manager, Airlie Group of Studs, comprising Airlie, Simmonstown and Kilmacredock Studs; horses bred at these studs include: *Pitcairn, Glad Rags, Almaarad, Eurobird, Fair Of The Furze, Distant Relative, Chief Singer, White Muzzle, Vialli*; has horses in training in UK and Ireland; member, Turf Club; Director of Robert J. Goff; One of the major Bloodstock Breeders in the country. Hobbies, racing, visual arts, travel and gardening. Contact: Airlie Stud, Grangewilliam, Maynooth, Co.Kildare. Tel: 01 628 6336. Fax: 01 628 6674.

JORGENSEN, Ib

JOYCE, Brian; PROFESSIONAL COMPANY DIRECTOR; *b* 1940; *educ* St. Mary's College, Galway; University College Galway, BA, BComm. FCMA; *m* Peggy Glynn; 1*s* 1*da*; worked in RTE, 1967-69; joined the Irish Dairy Board, 1969, Managing Director, 1978-89, non Executive Director, 1989 to date; Chairman, C.I.E., Chairman, Educational Building Society, Mater Private Hospital, Norish plc and other companies; former President, Institute of Management Accountants, UCD Graduates Association; a highly respected figure in Irish agri-business. Hobbies, walking, reading and gardening. Contact: C.I.E., Heuston Station, Dublin 8. Tel: 01 677 1871. Fax: 01 703 2276.

KANE, Alfie; CHIEF EXECUTIVE EIRCOM; *b* 1934; B.Sc., D.M.S.; *married; 2da;* Chief Executive, British Telecom in Northern Ireland, 1984-88; a leading player in developing a unique application of the E.U. Star Programme; former Director of Operations, British Telecom's Worldwide Networks Division; Chief Executive and Board Director, Telecom Eireann, 1994 to date; Chairman, Eircell Ireland Ltd. and Cablelink Ireland Ltd.; Director, Irish Telecommunications Investment plc and Economic and Social Research Institute, Ireland; Fellow, I.E.I. and I.A.G. and I.E.E.; Council member, Dublin Chamber of Commerce (Chairman, Transport Committee); Council member, I.B.E.C. and I.M.I.; member, Board of Trustees, Dublin City University; President, Glencree Centre for Reconciliation. Contact: Eircom, St. Stephen's Green, Dublin 2. Tel: 01 671 4444.

KANE, Denis; CHIEF EXECUTIVE, DIRECTOR DRUIDS GLEN GOLF CLUB; *b* 1950; *educ* Christian Brothers School, Westland Row; Dublin College of Catering, Cathal Brugha Street; Westminster College, London, Degree in Hotel Admin.; Institute of Training and Development, Dip. Personnel Mgmt.; *m* Vicky Manning; 3*s* 1 *da;* Front Office Manager, Hotel Cecilia, Paris; Chef, Hotel Glion, Montreux, Switzerland; Food & Beverage Manager, Gleneagles Hotel, Scotland; General Manager, Kensington Close Hotel, London; Food & Beverage Manager, Edmonton Plaza, Alberta, Canada; Manager, Regional Advisory and Consultancy Services, CERT, 1980-90; General Manager, Hermitage Golf Club, 1990-92, Chief Executive and Director, Druids Glen Golf Club, 1992 to date; Druids Glen Golf Club was the venue for Murphys Irish Open, 1996, '97, '98, '99; member, Hotel and Catering Institute, Institute of Training and Development; former Chairman, Golfing Ireland, 1996-97; Director of Tourism Project & Research, DIT; clubs, Druids Glen GC, Kilmacud Crokes GAA. Hobbies, GAA sports (holder of All Ireland Minor Medal), golf and all other sports. Contact: Druids Glen Golf Club, Newtownmountkennedy, Co. Wicklow. Tel: 01 287 3600.

KANE, Alfie

KANE, Michael Francis; PRINTMAKER; *b* 1935; *educ* Local Schools, Co. Wicklow; National College of Art, Graphic Studio, Dublin; *m* Ruth Brandt (decd.); 1 *s* 1 *da; m* Shelley McNamara; First one man exhibition, 1960, Ritchie Hendricks Gallery, Dublin; Has held numerous solo exhibitions in Dublin, London and Zurich; Retrospective Exhibition, RHA Gallagher Gallery, Dublin, 1995; Where The Poet Has Been, Irish Museum of Modern Art, 1995; Member, Aosdána; Biographical books include: *Michael Kane, His Life And Art,* Henry Sharpe; *Modern Art in Ireland,* Dorothy Walker. Hobbies, reading, walking, swimming, cooking, eating, drinking, talking with friends. Contact: Aosdána, 70, Merrion Square, Dublin 1. Tel: 01 661 1840. Fax: 01 676 1302.

KANE, Denis

KAVANAGH, Commodore John Joseph; FLAG OFFICER COMMANDING NAVAL SERVICE; *b* 1941; *educ* Lieutenants Greenwich Course, UK; 1967; Naval Staff Course, 1974 Naval Command College Course 1981-82, US Naval War College, Newport, Rhode Island, USA; 7th Senior Officer's Course, Military College, Curragh, Ireland 1989; *m* Pauline Healy; 2 *da;* joined Naval Service as a Cadet in January 1959; Commissioned as an Ensign, 1961; has held various appointments both afloat and ashore including command of *Le Banba,* (Minesweeper) *Le Deirdre* (Offshore Patrol Vessel) and finally, commanding the *Le Eithne* (Helicopter Patrol Vessel) 1988-90; promotions include, Sub Lieutenant, 1963, Lieutenant, 1967, Lt. Commander, 1973, Commander, 1980, Captain, 1993, Commodore, 1993 and appointed Flag Officer Commanding Naval Service; Senior shore-based appointments held, Staff Officer Operations, Naval HQ, Dublin, Executive Officer, Naval Base, Commanding Officer, Naval Depot; Patron of the Naval Association; Honorary membership of Howth Yacht Club and Royal St. George Yacht Club; member, Ballina Golf Club; awarded Service Medal with Bar (1983). Hobbies, golf, bridge and gardening. Contact: Naval Services, Haulbowline, Cork. Tel: 021 811246.

KAVANAGH, Edward W.

KAVANAGH, Edward W.; MANAGING DIRECTOR, CHAIRMAN EDWARD KAVANAGH (MAYNOOTH); *b* 1949; *educ* Clongowes Wood College; Trinity College Dublin; joined Kildare based family business Edward Kavanagh (Animal Feed Millers, Property, Grain Merchants and Pig Farmers), 1971, Managing Director, 1989, Chairman, 1996 to date; former President, Irish Corn & Feed Association, 1982-83; Clubs, Fitzwilliam L.T.C., North Kildare Rugby Club, Lough Derg Yacht Club, Knockanally Golf Club, The K Club, Straffan. Hobbies, tennis, squash, rugby and golf. Contact: Edward Kavanagh (Maynooth), Manor Mills, Maynooth, Co. Kildare. Tel: 01 628 6161. Fax: 01 628 6635.

KAVANAGH, John; ACTOR; *b* 1946; *educ* Our Lady's National School, Milltown; Dundrum Technical School; Caffrey's College; *m* Anne McIvor; 1 *s* 2 *da;* a member of Ireland's National Theatre, The Abbey Theatre, for ten years; since leaving there in 1977 he has appeared in such musicals as *Pirates of Penzance, HMS Pinafore, Tom Foolery, Jacques Brel, Guys and Dolls, Les Miserables;* has appeared on Broadway on a number of occasions and received a Drama Desk nomination for his portrayal of Joxer in the Gate Theatre production of *Juno and the Paycock;* film

work includes: *Cal, Into the West, The Butcher Boy, Braveheart, Circle of Friends, Dancing at Lughnasa, Sweeney Todd, This is my Father;* television includes *Dr. Finlay, Bad Company, Ballroom of Romance, Sharpe, Shadow of a Gunman, Lovejoy, Children of the North, Vicious Circle;* recently at the Gate Theatre he played Mitch in *A Streetcar named Desire* and Astrov in Brian Friel's new version of *Uncle Vanya* for which he was given the Dublin Theatre Festival award; one of Ireland's leading character actors. Contact: Terri Hayden, The Agency, 47 Adelaide Road, Dublin 2.

KAVANAGH, John

KAVANAGH, Mark; PROPERTY DEVELOPER; *b* 1945; *educ* St. Gerard's School, Bray; Downside (UK); *m* Linda Hitzeman (*decd*); 1*s* 2 *da;* *m* Kathleen Shugrue; 2*s* 1 *da;* worked in various jobs including trainee surveyor with Jones Lang Wootton, 1967-69; General Manager, Screenprint Ltd., 1969-71; established Catering Ireland, 1971, restaurants included Captain America; Joint Managing Director, Hardwicke Ltd. (one of Ireland's largest privately owned property development companies), 1978-97; Chairman, 1997 to date; Chairman, Chief Executive, Hardwicke American Properties Inc. 1982 to date; Director, American Exploration Company, 1982 to date, (publicly quoted oil & gas company); Chairman, Custom House Docks Development Company Ltd., 1988 to date; Director of various private companies; member, Urban Land Institute (Washington DC), New York Real Estate Board; a polished and urbane businessman in the international mode. Hobbies, golf, skiing, shooting, tennis and travel. Contact: Hardwicke Ltd., 14 Wellington Road, Dublin 4. Tel: 01 668 3791. Fax: 01 668 0265.

KAVANAGH, Peter Edward; EDITOR DUNDALK DEMOCRAT; *b* 1934; *educ* St. Mary's College Dundalk; *m* Margaret Kelleher; 1*s* 1 *da;* worked as local correspondent for a number of media, including RTE and *TheIrish Times* mainly covering sport; joined *Dundalk Democrat* 1953, reporter, sub-editor, currently editor; founder member of local branch of N.U.J. (first Treasurer and former Chairman); member, Steering Committee on White Paper on Relationship between Government and Community and Voluntary organisations. Hobbies, soccer, chess, reading, gardening, debating and formerly amateur dramatics. Contact: Dundalk Democrat Ltd., 3 Earl Street, Dundalk. Tel: 042 34058. Fax: 042 31399.

KEAN, Gerald Ronan

KEAN, Gerald Ronan; SOLICITOR; *b* 1957; *educ* Colaiste Chriost Ri Cork; De La Salle, Wicklow; University College Dublin, BCL; Incorporated Law Society, Solicitor; *m* Clodagh Hopkins, B.A., Dip. LS.; 1 *d*; joined the firm of Michael Martin, Solicitors; set up own practice under the title of KEANS, specialising in acting on behalf of Artists in the entertainment world and sports personalities from the field of Golf, Soccer, Tennis, Snooker and Boxing; also acts on behalf of a number of major Financial Institutions based in the Republic of Ireland and multi-national Companies setting up operations in Ireland; author of a number of articles in the area of tax in the Entertainment Industry in Ireland and Artist exemption relief; part time Lecturer in the areas of Commercial and Company Law; member, Polo Club in Boca Raton, Elm Park Golf and Tennis Club (ex Committee), the K Club, (ex Committee), Wicklow Tennis Club (ex Committee); Riverview, Racquet Sports and Social Club, Fitzwilliam Lawn Tennis Club and Doral Golf Club in Miami; former member, Wicklow Golf Club and UCD Tennis Club; sits on the Practice and Procedure Committee of the Law Society; currently Honorary Chilean Consul in the Republic of Ireland; member, New York Bar. Hobbies, soccer, tennis golf and music. Contact: 2 Upper Pembroke Street, Dublin 2. Tel: 01 676 9955. Fax: 01 676 9975.

KERRY-KEANE, John

KEANE, Ann Therese 'Terry' née O'Donnell,; JOURNALIST; *b* 1939; *educ* Ursuline Convent, Wimbledon (U.K.); Poles, Hertfordshire (U.K.); Trinity College Dublin; *m* Ronan Keane, Supreme Court Judge; 1 *s* 3 *da;* Fashion Editor, *Irish Times* 1963-70; Fashion Editor, *Sunday Press* 1970-1989; Fashion Editor and Social Chronicler 'The Keane Edge', *Sunday Independent* 1989-99; columnist *The Sunday Times* 1999; publications include *Consuming Passions* (Recipe book) 1999; due to personal revelations on television and in print concerning herself and former Taoiseach Charles J. Haughey, is now a household name and one of the country's most widely read journalists. Hobbies, Irish Art, literature, travel. Contact: The Sunday Times, Hugenot House, 35 St. Stephens Green, Dublin 2. Tel: 01 602 8800.

KEANE, Frank A.; DIRECTOR, OWNER MOTOR IMPORT LTD; *b* 1933, *educ* Christian Brothers, Gorey, Wexford and C.B.C Monkstown; *m* Ursula Hinds; 2 *s* 1 *da*; Entered Motor Trade with Smithfield Motors Ltd., 1952, with P.R. Reilly, May 1953; joined Mount Merrion Motors, May 1962, Three Rock Garage, January 1966; Awarded the BMW Franchise and formed Motor Import Ltd., 1967; Expanded in 1974 with Pioneer Hi Fi products; Awarded the Mitsubishi Motor Cars and Trucks Franchise, 1984; combined companies under Frank Keane Holding banner; A keen rugby fan, former Motor Racing competitor, winner of the Sexton Trophy, 1963, supporter of opera in both Dublin and Wexford. Contact: Motor Import Ltd., John F. Kennedy Drive, Dublin 12. Tel: 01 450 8044.

KEANE, Gabriel Martin; GROUP MANAGING DIRECTOR WINDSOR MOTOR GROUP; *b* 1962; *educ* St. Jarlath's College, Tuam, Co. Galway; University College Galway, B.Comm. Hons; Chartered Accountant, FCA; *m* Rita O'Riordain; 2*s* 2 *da;* Trainee Accountant, Stokes Kennedy Crowley & Co., Dublin, 1982-86; Manager, Corporate Special Services, Touche Ross & Co., London, 1986-90; Group Treasurer, Goodman International, 1990-91; Financial Director, Dealer Services, Nissan Ireland, 1991-94; Group Managing Director, Windsor Motor Group, 1994 to date; member, Institute of Chartered Accountants in Ireland (FCA); Society of Irish Motor Industry (SIMA); Chairman, Dolphin House Task Force. Hobbies, walking, swimming. Contact: Windsor Motor Group, Belgard Road, Dublin 24. Tel: 01 451 6877. Fax: 01 462 6053.

KEANE, John Brendan; WRITER; *b* 1928; *educ* Listowel Boys School; St. Michael's College, Listowel; *m* Mary O'Connor, Publican; 3 *s* 1 *da*; publications include: *Sive, The Field* (made into a film and nominated for an Oscar, 1991), *Big Maggie, The Year of the Hiker, Letters Series, The Bodhran Makers, Durango* (a novel, made into a film, 1998) and many more; conferred with Doctorate of Literature, Trinity College Dublin 1977, Doctorate of Fine Arts, Marymount Manhattan College, recipient of *Sunday Independent* Award for Literature 1986, *Sunday Tribune* Award for Literature 1986, American-Irish Literary Award 1988, People of the Year Award 1990, Irish P.E.N. Inaugural Literary Award 1999. Honorary Life Membership of R.D.S. 1991; past President, Irish P.E.N.; member, Aosdána. A plain speaking man and a powerful portrayer of the emotional undercurrents in rural society; a driving force in the language movement of the 1960s. Hobbies, walking and cloud watching. Contact: Listowel, Co. Kerry.

KEANE, John Brendan

KEANE, John Edward KERRY; NEWSPAPER PUBLISHER AND PROPRIETOR; *b* 1938; *educ* Christian Brothers School, Kilkenny; C longowes Wood College; University College Dublin; Kings Inns; *m* Leonora Murray; 3 *da;* Editor and Managing Director, *The Kilkenny People* since 1960; Publisher, *Tipperary Star, The Nationalist* (Clonmel); Chancellor, Trustee of Irish Association of St. Lazarus (notable charity for the relief of leprosy). Board member, Royal Hibernian Gallery. A courteous man, prominent in both Kilkenny and Dublin social, commercial and cultural circles. Hobby, publishing newspapers; Clubs, Kildare Street and University Club. Contact: The Kilkenny People, High Street, Kilkenny. Tel: 056 21015. Fax: 056 21414.

KEANE, John Paul; CHIEF EXECUTIVE RESPONSE GROUP LTD.; *b* 1950; *educ* Terenure College, Dublin; University College Dublin, BComm; m Mary Mulhall; 1*s* 2*da*; Marketing Manager, O'Kennedy Brindley, 1970-74; Director, PHS (Ireland) Ltd., 1979 to date; Chief Executive, Response Group Ltd., a holding company controlling PHS and other companies, the largest sales and direct marketing group in the country; formerly Chairman, Irish Direct Marketing; Board member, Federation of European Direct Marketing; member, IMI; probably the hardest working and most successful man in his field; member, Lansdowne RFC, Fitzwilliam LTC. Hobbies, golf and all sport. Contact: Response Group Ltd., M50 Business Park, Ballymount, Dublin 12. Tel: 01 409 2700.

KEANE, Maurice

KEANE, Maurice; GROUP CHIEF, CHIEF EXECUTIVE, BANK OF IRELAND; *b* 1941; *educ* Good Counsel College, New Ross; University College Dublin, BComm, MEconSc; Harvard Business School, PhD; *m* Rosemary Ohle; 1 *s* 2 *da*; joined the National Bank, 1958, worked in various departments; Chief Corporate Accounts Manager, Corporate Division, Bank of Ireland, 1973; Manager, College Green, Dublin, 1975; General Manger, Financial Control, 1978; Divisional Managing Director, Bank of Ireland, 1983-87, Deputy Chief Executive, 1991, Group Chief Executive, Bank of Ireland Group, 1998 to date; Fellow, Institute of Bankers in Ireland, Former President, Irish Bankers Federation; recipient, Outstanding Alumunus Award, Michael Smurfit School of Business, 1998; Recognised as an astute and experienced banker, who has reached the top slot on merit. Hobby, skiing. Contact: Bank of Ireland Group, Lower Baggot Street, Dublin 2. Tel: 01 661 5933 Fax: 01 661 5675.

KEANE, The Hon. Mr. Justice Ronan; JUDGE OF THE SUPREME COURT; *b* 1932; *educ* Blackrock College, Dublin; University College Dublin; Kings Inns (winner of Brooke Scholarship); *m* Terry O'Donnell, Journalist; 1 *s* 2 *da*; called to the Bar, 1954; called to the Inner Bar, 1970; appointed Judge of the High Court, 1979; Head of the Stardust Inquiry, 1981; President of the Law Reform Commission, 1987-92; appointed to the Supreme Court, 1996; ran an extensive and broadly based practice before elevation to the Bench; publications include: *Law of Local Government in the Republic of Ireland, Walsh's Planning and Development Law* (second edition), *Company Law in the Republic of Ireland, Equity and the Laws of Trusts in the Republic of Ireland,* and numerous papers for legal journals. A gifted academic and highly regarded head of the Law Reform Commission; a highly articulate and literate man with a keen interest in the performing arts. Hobbies, reading, theatre and music. Contact: The Four Courts, Morgan Place, Dublin 7. Tel: 01 872 5555.

KEARNEY, Richard; ACADEMIC, AUTHOR; *b* 1954; *educ* Christian Brothers College, Cork; Glenstal Abbey; University College Dublin, BA; McGill University, Montreal, MA; University of Paris, PhD; *m* Anne Bernard, Architect, Translator; 2 *da*; Lecturer, University College Dublin 1981-89; Professor, Department of Philosophy, 1990 to date; Visiting Professor, Boston College, 1989 to date; University of Paris 1997; University of Nice 1999; publications include *Poetique du Possible, Dialogues, Modern Movements in European Philosophy, Transitions, Angel of Patrick's Hill* (poetry), *States of Mind, Postnationalist Ireland, Sam's Fall* (novel), *Walking at Sea Level* (novel); frequent broadcaster on Irish and French media; recipient of American Literary Association Award for 'Outstanding Academic Publication', London Independent Award 1989; member, Irish Film Centre, Higher Education Authority, Royal Irish Academy, Irish Philosophical Society. An exceptional and prolific academic with a strong media presence. Contact: Department of Philosophy, National University of Ireland, Donnybrook, Dublin 4. Tel: 01 269 3244. Fax: 01 269 3469

KEARNS, The Hon. Mr. Justice Nicholas James; JUDGE OF THE HIGH COURT; *b* 1946; *educ* St. Mary's College, Rathmines; University College Dublin; Kings Inns; *m* Eleanor Potter Cogan; 4*s*; called to the Bar, 1968; Diploma in European Law, 1970; called to the Inner Bar, 1982; Called to the English Bar, 1981; Junior Counsel in Bantry Inquiry, 1979; mixed legal practice included crime, personal injuries, defamation and probate; appointed to the High Court, 1998; set up AIDS Fund 1987; former Board Member of Research Council in Crumlin Children's Hospital; member, Blainroe Golf Club, Co. Wicklow, Castle Golf Club, Fitzwilliam Lawn Tennis Club. Hobbies, golf and reading. Contact: Four Courts, Morgan Place, Dublin 7. Tel: 01 872 5555.

KEARY, William 'Bill'; MANAGING DIRECTOR KEARY'S OF CORK; *b* 1954; *educ* C.U.S., Leeson St., Dublin; Technical College, Bolton Street, Dip Building Surveying; m Maureen Bellow; 1*s* 2*da*; worked for a time in family building firm; moved into motor business 1978; obtained Toyota franchise for Mallow, 1980, for Cork City, 1987; owner Kearys of Cork, main Toyota Dealers for Cork City and Mallow; director of various private companies; clubs, Waterville GC, Mallow GC. Hobbies, motor racing, golf. Contact: Kearys of Cork, Grange, Douglas, Cork. Tel: 021 361 800. Fax: 021 363 322.

KEATINGE, Richard Arthur Davis; INVESTMENT BANKER, MANAGING DIRECTOR IBI CORPORATE FINANCE; *b* 1947; *educ* Trinity College Dublin, B.A.; University College Dublin, MBA; *m* Athene ----; 2 *s* 1 *da;* Financial Journalist, Reuters Ltd., 1969-71; joined *The Irish Times*, 1971, Business Editor, 1975-78; joined Investment Bank of Ireland, 1978, London Office, 1982-84, Head of Group Strategy, 1984-86, Chief Executive (UK), 1986-90; Chairman, N.C.B. Corporate Finance, 1991-92; Director, Hardwicke Ltd., 1992-93; Managing Director, IBI Corporate Finance, 1993 to date; recipient, Sir Charles Harvey Award, 1978. Clubs, Kildare Street and University (member, Management Committee), Powerscourt Golf Club, Connemara Golf Club, Carrickmines Golf Club. Hobbies, fishing, golf and West of Ireland. Contact: IBI Corporate Finance Ltd., 26 Fitzwilliam Place, Dublin 2. Tel: 01 661 6633. Fax: 01 661 6821.

KEAVENEY, Mark

KEAVENEY, Mark; JOINT MANAGING DIRECTOR, PETER MARK; *b* 1940; *educ* Christian Brothers School, Kells; *single*; trained in hairdressing in Dublin; founded Peter Mark with brother, Peter; opened first salon in Dublin, 1960; Joint Managing Director (with Peter Keaveney), Peter Mark; there are now 65 hairdressing salons and three training academies operating throughout the thirty-two counties; nominated Meath Man of the Year, 1982, Best Dressed Man of the Year, 1983; President, Irish Hairdressing Federation, 1981-82. Hobbies, golf, swimming and tennis; Clubs, R.I.A.C., K Club, Riverview Racquet and Fitness Club. Contact: The Plaza, 15 Ely Place, Dublin 2. Tel: 01 661 4888. Fax: 01 661 3673.

KEENA, Colm Patrick; JOURNALIST; *b* 1960; *educ* Colaiste Mhuire, Parnell Square, Dublin; Trinity College Dublin, BA (mod); NIHE, Dip. Journalism; *m* Felicity Clear; 1 *da*; Irish Press Group, 1987-95; *The Irish Times*, 1995 to date; publications include *Biography of Gerry Adams*; awards include *Sunday Tribune*/Hennessy Award, 1993, Financial Journalist of the Year Award, Institute of Chartered Accountants, 1999; noted as a remarkable investigative political journalist; has now moved into the field of financial journalism. Contact: Irish Times, D'Olier Street, Dublin 2. Tel: 01 677 2022.

KELLEHER, Mary; LIBRARIAN; *educ* Convent of the Sacred Heart, Mount Anville, Dublin; Drishane Covent, Millstreet, Co. Cork; University College Dublin, BA; Trinity College Dublin, Dip. Information Studies; Institutio di Patalogia del Libro, Rome; *single*; joined Royal Dublin Society Library, Dublin 1963, Senior Assistant, Assistant Librarian, Librarian, Chief Librarian, 1987 to date; publications include various articles for in-house journal; member, Library Association of Ireland; Member of COLICO (Library Co-operation Committee); As head of one of the major libraries in the country, wields considerable influence in the world of books; inaugurated various exhibitions in the library; an innovator in her field. Hobbies, books, music and travel. Contact: R.D.S. Library,

Ballsbridge, Dublin 4. Tel: 01 668 0866.

KELLY, David; ACTOR; *b* 1929; *educ* C.B.S. Synge Street, Dublin; National College of Art and Design; Abbey Theatre School; *m* Laurie Morton, Actress; 1 *s* 1 *da*; Since 1952 has performed in the Dublin Theatres and the stages of Britain, Europe, Australia and the U.S.A.; also, hundreds of television and film roles; recent role in *Waking Ned*, co-starring Ian Bannen, a runaway success in the U.S.; Honoured with Chevalier Ordre Souverain et Militaire de la Milice du Saint Sepulcre, 1987; Helen Hayes Award for Excellence in the Theatre (nominee), 1990; Golden Satellite Award, Best Actor, Hollywood, 1998; Hollywood, American Screen Actors' Guild Awards, nominated Best Actor for film *Waking Ned*, 1999; Listed in *Who's Who in Film and Television* (UK). Hobby, painting. Contact: Agent, Ms. Joan Brown, 3 Earl Road, London SW14 7JH, England. Tel: 0044 181 87622

KELLY, David

KELLY, Declan; JOINT MANAGING DIRECTOR GALLAGHER & KELLY PUBLIC RELATIONS; *b* 1968; *educ* Nenagh C.B.S., Co. Tipperary; University College Galway, BA; Journalist, *Nenagh Guardian*, 1987-89; Journalist, *Tipperary Star*, 1989-91; Journalist, Examiner Group Publications, 1991-96; Director, Murray Consultants, Public Relations Ltd. 1996-98; Partner and Director of Corporate & Financial Communications, Fleishman-Hillard Saunders, 1998-99; Joint Managing Director, Gallagher & Kelly Public Relations, May 1999 to date; member, National Union of Journalists; awards include A.T. Cross Irish Business and Financial Journalist of the Year 1995. Hobbies, travel, reading and music. Contact: Gallagher & Kelly Public Relations, 31 Upper Merrion Street, Dublin 2. Tel: 01 618 2068.

KELLY, John; BROADCASTER, WRITER; *b* 1965; *educ* St. Michael's Grammar School, Enniskillen; Queens University Belfast, LLB, Institute of Professional Legal Studies, Belfast; *single*; Radio and Television producer and presenter who has worked for BBC (both network and regional), Channel 4 and UTV. Winner of UK Sony Award, 1991; Joined Radio Ireland (later Today FM) to produce/present *The Eclectic Ballroom* in 1997; moved to RTE in 1999 to present and produce *Mystery Train* on Radio One, and present *Later With John Kelly* on Network 2 Television; a regular contributor to various publications, columnist with *The Irish Times*; Publications include: *Grace Notes and Bad Thoughts* (Marino Books), *Cool About The Ankles* (Blackstaff Press); One of the most refreshing and innovative broadcasters on Irish radio. Contact: RTE, Donnybrook, Dublin 4. Tel: 01 208 3111.

KELLY, Kevin J.; BANKER; *b* 1941 *educ* Christian Brothers College, Cork; *m* Mary Keane-Stack; 1 *s* 2 *da*; qualified as an Accountant; worked as Audit Supervisor, responsible for multinational clients, with Price Waterhouse in Europe, 1966-69; Audit Manager, Coopers and Lybrand, London, 1969-71, Partner, Coopers & Lybrand, Dublin and Cork, 1972, Managing Partner, 1982-89; Group Chief Executive, Agra Group, 1989-91; Administrator, PMPA Insurance Company; Group Financial Director, A.I.B. Group, 1991-95; Managing Director, A.I.B. Bank, 1996 to date; Chairman, Cothu, Business Council for the Arts; Vice Chairman, IMI; Member, Fitzwilliam LTC, K Club, Killarney Golf Club; Hobbies golf, reading, music, photography. Contact: A.I.B. Bank, Bank Centre, Ballsbridge, Dublin 4. Tel: 01 660 0311.

KELLY, John

KELLY, Paul; MANAGING DIRECTOR BROWN THOMAS GROUP; *b* 1952; *educ* De La Salle College, Churchtown; *separated; 3s 2 da;* joined Brown Thomas Group, 1984, currently Managing Director; recognised as a retail expert, brings an aggressive buying and promotional approach to the Brown Thomas Group; has refocused the Group despite tremendous competition from the U.K. Hobbies, flying and Formula 1. Contact: Brown Thomas, Grafton Street, Dublin 2. Tel: 01 605 6666.

KELLY, The Hon, Mr. Justice Peter; HIGH COURT JUDGE; *b* 1950; *educ* O'Connells School, Dublin; University College Dublin; Kings Inns Dublin, (awarded Kings Inns Exhibition); *single;* Civil Servant, 1969-75; called to the Irish Bar, 1973; English Bar, 1981; N. Ireland Bar, 1983; Senior Counsel, 1986; Judge of the High Court, 1996; former member and Hon. Secretary and Hon.Treasurer of Bar Council; currently member of Council of Kings Inns; Chairman of Education Committee of Kings Inns; elected Member of Courts Service Board; member, Kildare Street & University Club Dublin. Hobbies, reading, music and travel. Contact: The Four Courts, Morgan Place, Dublin 7. Tel: 01 872 5555.

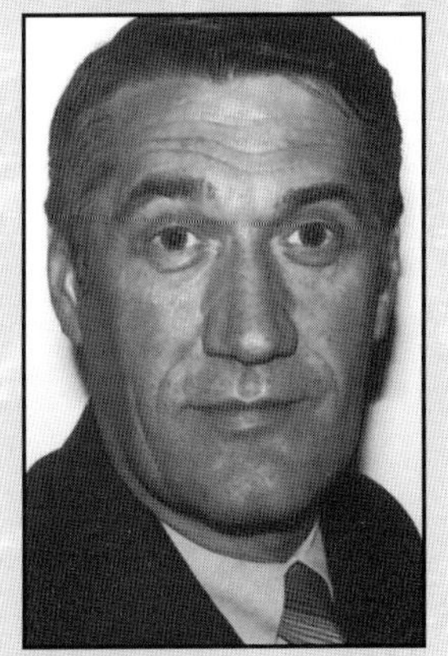
KELLY, Paul

KENNEDY, Brian; SINGER/WRITER; *b* 1966; *educ* St. Pauls School; *single;* released first solo album, *The Great War of Words*, 1990; collaborated with Mark E. Nevin, 1991, for the Sweetmouth album *Goodbye to Songtown*; joined Van Morrison's *Blues and Soul Revue* and contributed to live shows resulting in the double live album *A Night in San Fransisco*, 1994; contributed to 4 studio albums *No Prima Donna* (1994), *Days Like This* (1995), *The Healing Game* (1997), *Back on Top* (1999); duetted with Van Morrison in Belfast for President and Mrs Hilary Clinton, 1995;

released second solo album *A Better Man*, 1996 - number 1 in Irish Charts for a year; sang with Stevie Wonder at Ronnie Scotts, 1995, toured with Van Morrison, Bob Dylan and Joni Mitchell (America) 1998; toured with Van Morrison, James Brown and Ray Charles, 1997; toured with The Corrs, 1999; toured Australia/New Zealand with Donal Lunny, Ronnie Drew, Guinness Festival of Irish Music; other tours include Suzanne Vega, Jane Siberry; collaborated with Micheál Ó Suilleabhain for the platinum single *Lumen* (Eurovision interval performance); sang for President McAleese, 17 March 1998; contributed to *As I Roved Out* for Donal Lunny's *Common Ground* album; recorded *EIST* with Maire Breathnach, 1999; awards include, 2 IRMAs, 3 *Hot Press* Awards, Irish Entertainer of the Year. Hobbies, writing short stories, walking, running and reading. Contact: 19 Management Ltd., Unit 32 Ransome Dock, 35-37 Parkgate Road, London, SW11 4NP. Tel: 0044 171 738 1919. Fax: 0044 171 738 1819.

KENNEDY, Brian

KENNEDY, Caroline

KENNEDY, Caroline; MANAGING DIRECTOR KENNEDY PR & MARKETING LTD.; *b* 1964; *educ* Brigidine Convent Abbeyleix, Co. Laois; Dublin City University, BA Communications Studies; *single;* Database Designer, Cognotec Business Information Systems, 1984-85; Community TV Producer, University of Limerick, 1985-86; Student, European Orientation Programme, 1986-87; P.R. Manager, National Youth Council of Ireland, 1987-88; P.R. Manager, Co-Operation North, 1988-89; Producer, Century Radio, 1989-91; Founded, Kennedy PR & Marketing Ltd. 1991 to date; member, The Ireland-United States Council for Commerce & Industry; Board Director, Junior Dublin Film Festival; member, Irish Hospice Foundation Fundraising Committee. A dynamic young woman, unfazed by challenge. Hobbies, cinema, travel, retail industry. Contact: Kennedy PR, 38 Pembroke Road, Dublin 4. Tel: 01 667 0090. Fax: 01 667 1175.

KENNEDY, David; CHARTERED ACCOUNTANT, TAX PARTNER KPMG; *b* 1964; *educ* Tallaght Community College; University College Dublin, BComm; Diploma in Prof. Accountancy; *m* Anne Lee; *1 s 1da;* joined KPMG in 1986, working in tax department, became partner in 1995; leads KPMG ICE practice serving clients in the Information Communications and Entertainment sectors; member, KPMG's International ICE Committee and ECommerce Worldwide Tax Taskforce; member, Institute of Chartered Accountants, clubs, Thomas Dains GAA Club (Committee Member), Moate Golf Club, Ballinascorney Golf Club, St. Stephen's Green Club. Hobbies, all sports, in particular GAA and golf, supporter of Thomas Dains and Dublin Gaelic Football teams. Contact: KPMG 1 Stokes Place, St. Stephen's Green, Dublin 2. Tel: 01 410 1000. Fax: 01 412 1122.

KENNEDY, David

KENNEDY, David; COMPANY DIRECTOR; *b* 1938; *e duc* Terenure College; University College Dublin; Case Institute of Technology, Ohio; *m* Una Barry; *3 s 1 da*; joined Aer Lingus as Operations Research Analyst, 1962, Chief Executive, 1974-88; Currently Chairman, Drury Communications Ltd.; Director, CRH, Jurys Hotel Group, Lifetime Assurance Company, Bon Secours Health System, Drury Sports Management, Co-operation Ireland, Trans World Airlines Inc.; former President, International Air Transport Association; Life Fellow, Irish Management Institute; Fellow, Chartered Institute of Transport. Hobbies, golf, chess, reading, theatre; Clubs, Castle Golf Club, Fitzwilliam LTC. Contact: 46, Upper Mount Street, Dublin 2. Tel: 01 676 2463. Fax: 01 676 2489.

KENNEDY, Dennis

KENNEDY, Dennis; SAMUEL BECKETT PROFESSOR OF DRAMA AND THEATRE STUDIES, TRINITY COLLEGE DUBLIN; *b* 1940; *educ* University of San Francisco, BA; University of California, MA, PhD; *m* Ann Smyth-Tyrrell; *3 da*; Assistant and Associate Professor of English, Grand Valley State University, 1970-83; Professor of Theatre Arts, University of Pittsburgh, 1983-95; Samuel Beckett Professor of Drama and Theatre Studies, Trinity College Dublin, 1995 to date; Senior Fulbright Lecturer, University of Karachi, 1973; Visiting Associate Professor of English, University of Oregon, 1975-76; publications include numerous essays and books, *Granville Barker and The Dream of Theatre* (1985), *Plays by Harley Granville Barker* (1987), *Looking at Shakespeare* (1993), *Foreign Shakespeare* (1993); plays include *Internal Combustion, The Hypochondriac, Confessions of a Plumber;* member, International Federation for Theatre Research, American Society for Theatre Research (Executive Committee), International Shakespeare Association; recipient Freedley Award for Theatre History (1985 and 1993), Distinguished Research Award, University of Pittsburgh (1994), Distinguished Visiting Professor at University of Victoria (1994), McMaster University (1994), University of Wisconsin (1997); also listed in *Contemporary Authors, Dictionary of American Scholars, International Who's Who of Writers and Authors;* seen as somewhat of an oxymoron - a practical academic; capable of putting Trinity on the international drama map. Hobbies, wine, jazz, films, walking the springer spaniel. Contact: School of Drama, Trinity College, Dublin 2. Tel: 01 608 1239. Fax: 01 679 3488.

KENNEDY, Gary; GROUP FINANCIAL DIRECTOR AIB GROUP; *b* 1958; *educ* Armagh Grammar School; University of Lancaster, BA, Acct. & Fin. Control; m Annette Curley; 1*s* 1*da*; Audit Manager with Deloitte & Touche, 1978, Financial Manager, Northern Telecom (Ireland) Ltd.; moved to Northern Telecom Canada as Budgets and Forecasts Manager, Strategic Planning Manager,

Investment Analysis Manager, 1987; moved to Northern Telecom Europe, Regional Controller, Europe South, 1988, Financial Director, Northern Telecom (Ireland) Ltd., 1991; Vice President, Enterprise Networks Europe and Managing Director, Northern Telecom (Ireland) Ltd., 1992; joined A.I.B. Group as Group Financial Director, 1997 to date; Fellow of Institute of Chartered Accountants in Ireland; Fellow, Institute of Bankers. Hobbies, watching GAA, soccer and playing golf. Contact: AIB Bank Group, Bankcentre, Ballsbridge, Dublin 4. Tel: 01 660 0311.

KENNEDY, Geraldine

KENNEDY, Geraldine; JOURNALIST; *educ* Presentation Convent, Carrick-on-Suir; Convent of the Sacred Heart of Mary, Ferrybank, Co. Waterford; College of Commerce, Rathmines; *m* David Hegarty, Barrister; *2da;* worked as a junior reporter with *Cork Examiner*, Cork 1970-73; General Reporter, Deputy Industrial Correspondent and occasional Dáil Reporter with the *The Irish Times* 1973-80; Political Correspondent, *The Sunday Tribune* 1980-82, during this period was plunged into national prominence as one of the political correspondents who were victims of a telephone tapping scandal; Political Correspondent for *The Sunday Press* 1982-87; elected to the Dáil as Progressive Democrat Deputy for Dun Laoghaire 1987-89; following change of government returned to *The Irish Times*, contributed a Saturday Column, later Public Affairs Correspondent, Political Correspondent 1993, Political Editor 1999 to date; one of the most informed and respected political journalists in the country. Hobbies, food and family. Contact: The Irish Times, D'Olier Street, Dublin 2. Tel: 01 679 2022.

KENNEDY, Jerome Joseph; MANAGING PARTNER OF KPMG; *b* 1948; *educ* Salesian Secondary School, Pallaskenry, Co. Limerick; *m* Deirdre Lynch; *2da*; qualified as a Chartered Accountant with W. H. O'Donnell & Co. Limerick, 1971; joined Stokes Kennedy Crowley, 1972, became Partner, 1980, elected Managing Partner, 1995, re-elected Managing Partner, SKC now known as KPMG, 1998 to date; KPMG in Ireland is one of the major chartered accountancy and business advisory firms in the country, employing over 900 staff in Dublin, Cork, Galway and Belfast; Fellow, Institute of Chartered Accountants; member, various sporting clubs. Hobbies, horse riding, wind surfing, tennis and golf. Contact: KPMG, 1 Stokes Place, St. Stephen's Green, Dublin 2. Tel: 01 708 1000. Fax: 01 708 1127.

KENNEDY, Louise

KENNEDY, Louise; FASHION DESIGNER; *b* 1960; *educ* Brigidine Convent, Abbeyleix; Dominican School, Mount Merrion Avenue; College of Marketing and Design; Grafton Academy; *single*; started own fashion business, 1984; awarded *Late Late Show* /Ulster Bank Designer of the Year Award, 1989; designed, Aer Lingus Corporate Image, Ulster Bank Corporate Image, Louise Kennedy Crystal Collection for Tipperary Crystal; has large in-house space in Brown Thomas Dublin and new retail outlet, company headquarters and design studio in Merrion Square; clients include Enya, Meryl Streep, former Irish President Mary Robinson and current President Mary McAleese; features in *Debretts Elite 1000.* A gentle, elegant dynamo with an innate sense of good taste. Hobbies, travel, books, wine and art. Contact: 56 Merrion Square, Dublin 2. Tel: 01 662 0056. Fax: 662 0050.

KENNEDY, Patrick; GROUP DEVELOPMENT MANAGER GREENCORE GROUP PLC; *b* 1969; *educ* Gonzaga College, Dublin; University College Dublin, BComm (1st class Hon); ACA; *m* Jane Byrne; worked in Corporate Finance in KPMG, 1992-95; Consultant with McKinsey Management Consultants, London and Amsterdam, 1995-98; joined Greencore Group plc, 1998, currently Group Development Manager; seen as an emerging talent in the Irish commercial world. Hobbies, rugby, theatre, reading and marathon running. Contact: Greencore Group plc, Earlsfort Terrace, Dublin 2. Tel: 01 605 1000. Fax: 01 605 1100.

KENNEDY, Sr Stanislaus

KENNEDY, Sister Stanislaus; SISTER OF CHARITY, PRESIDENT OF FOCUS IRELAND; *b* 1939; *educ* Lispole Primary School; Dingle Secondary School; entered, Irish Sisters of Charity, 1958; University College Dublin, degree in Social Services; University of Manchester, Dip Social Work & Youth; Scholarship to Sweden (6 weeks); University College Dublin, MA (Social Policy); Trinity College Dublin, DDL; University College Dublin, Senior Research Fellow, 1983 to date; established and directed Kilkenny Social Services, 1964-85; Co-ordinator, European Rural Projects with Second EC Poverty Programme, 1985-89; Established and Directed, Focus Point, Dublin, a broadly based service for the homeless, 1985 to date; a frequent lecturer and contributor to journals nationally and internationally; books include *One Million Poor* and *Who Should Care,* 1981, *But Where Can I Go? Homeless Women in Dublin,* 1985, *Spiritual Journeys,* 1997, *Now is the Time,* 1998; Board member, Combat Poverty Agency, member, General Leadership Team of Irish Sisters of Charity; member, Council of State, 1997 to date; recipient, Person of the Year Award, (Kerry Association), 1981, Person of the Year, (Boston), 1986, Person of the Year Award (Dublin), 1994; Honorary Doctorate in Laws, TCD; Honorary Medalist (New York University), 1993; Honorary Life Member, National Federation of Youth Clubs. Regarded as a fearless champion of the poor. Hobbies, walking, theatre, music, poetry, writing and reading. Contact: Focus Ireland, 14A Eustace Street, Dublin 2. Tel: 01 671 2555.

KENNELLY, Brendan

KENNY, Barry

KENNY, Pat

KENNY, Thomas, "Tom"

KENNELLY, Brendan; PROFESSOR OF MODERN LITERATURE, TRINITY COLLEGE DUBLIN; *b* 1936; *educ* St. Ita's College, Tarbert, Co. Kerry; Trinity College Dublin, BA, MA; Leeds University, PhD; *m* Margaret Jane O'Brien; 1 *da*; Lecturer, Trinity College Dublin since 1963; Associate Professor of Modern Literature, 1969, Professor of Modern Literature since 1973; Guildersleeve Professor of Literature, Barnard College, New York, 1971, Swarthmac College, Pennsylvania, 1971-72; Recipient of numerous awards for poetry; publications include: forty books of poetry, *The Crooked Cross* (Alan Figgis), *The Florentines* (Alan Figgis); numerous plays, including: *Antigone* (Bloodaxe Books), 1996; *Blood Wedding* (Bloodaxe Books), 1996; various anthologies and criticisms; his work has been translated into Czech and Greek; a prolific writer of exceptional talent; a popular media performer and advertising personality; blends the arts and commerce with rare grace. Contact: School of English, Trinity College,Dublin. 2. Tel: 01 608 1161. Fax: 01 671 7114.

KENNY, Barry; CHIEF EXECUTIVE, IRISH MANAGEMENT INSTITUTE; *b* 1948; *educ* Newbridge College; University College Dublin, BE; Trinity College Dublin, MBA; *m* Bernice McDonnell; 3 *s*; Managing Director, Sight & Sound, 1971-76; PA Consulting Group, 1977-95; Appointed Chief Executive, PA Ireland and Partner, Global Consulting Practice; Chief Executive, Irish Management Institute, 1995 to date; Fellow, Institute of Management Consultants; President, 1993-94; Member: MBA Association, Marketing Institute, Member Kildare Street & University Club; Awarded Sir Charles Harvey Award, IMI, 1977, John Goode Prize, TCD, 1977. Hobbies, golf, fishing, shooting. Contact: Irish Management Institute, Sandyford Road, Dublin 6. Tel: 01 207 8400 Fax: 01 295 5150.

KENNY, Kevin Anthony Patrick; CHIEF EXECUTIVE FISHERS INTERNATIONAL PLC; *b* 1946; *educ* Beaumont College; Trinity College Dublin, B.A.; *m* Simone Judd; 3 *da*; Fund Manager, Allied Irish Investment Bank Ltd., 1970-72; Managing Director, Slater Walker Ireland Ltd., 1972-75; Managing Director, Harcourt Irish Holdings plc, 1975-83; Stockbroker, Simon & Coates, 1983-85; Managing Director, Tyndall & Co. Bankers, 1985-89; Managing Director, Tyndell Holdings plc, 1989-91; Chief Executive, Guinness & Mahon Bank Ltd., 1991-94; Chief Executive, Fishers International plc, 1994 to date; member, Kildare Street & University Club. Hobbies, shooting, tennis, travel, 18th century painting. Contact: Fishers International plc., 14 Upper Fitzwilliam Street, Dublin 2.

KENNY, Pat; BROADCASTER; *b* 1949; *educ* O'Connell Brothers School, Dublin; University College Dublin; Georgia Institute of Technology, USA; m Kathy Walshe; 2*da*; Lecturer, College of Technology, Bolton Street, 1970-72; joined RTE 1972 as Presenter/Reporter on radio and television; Presenter on current affairs programmes such as, *Public Account, Today Tonight*; currently presenter, *Today with Pat Kenny,* (radio) *Kenny Live* (television); has acted as co-producer, script writer, presenter on various documentary programmes; recipient of various media awards including, Glaxo Award for Scientific Broadcasting 1979, Jacobs Award 1982; runs own media company; a hard working, talented, high profile broadcaster, more profound than his handsome profile suggests; noted as an incisive and intelligent presenter of two top TAM rated shows; clubs, Fitzwilliam Lawn Tennis Club, Woodbrook Golf Club. Contact: RTE, Donnybrook, Dublin 4. Tel: 01 208 3111.

KENNY, Thomas, "Tom"; ART DEALER; *b* 1944; *educ* Scoil Fhursa; Colaiste Iognaid; University College Galway, BSc; *m* Maureen Shiel; 1 *s* 3 *da*; Joined the family business, worked in all aspects of bookselling - retailing, cataloging, exporting, publishing - antiquarian maps; since 1979 has concentrated on the visual arts side of the business, organising exhibitions, promoting and selling original work by Irish artists in Ireland and abroad; currently Chairman, Kenny's Bookshop and Art Galleries Ltd., Galway; publications include: *Webb* - a profile of the artist, Kenneth Webb, *Faces In a Bookshop* - Irish Literary Portraits; weekly newspaper column on Galway history and folklore. Member of the Irish Executive, the Ireland Fund. A man totally committed to his calling - to bring art to the people, particularly the people of Galway; the Kenny family run a cultural and social institution rather than just a shop. Hobbies, reading, theatre, Galway and good pub talk. Contact: Kennys Book Shops & Art Galleries Ltd., High Street, Galway. Tel: 091 562 739 Fax: 091 568 544.

KEOGH, Garrett; ACTOR / DIRECTOR; *b* 1953; *educ* O'Connell's CBS School, Dublin; Trinity College Dublin, BA Econ.Pol.; 2*da;* joined Abbey Theatre School and worked with Abbey Theatre 1973; acting highlights include *Juno and the Paycock* (Gate Theatre, Jerusalem and Broadway), *A Life* (Abbey Theatre, Old Vic Theatre, London), *Hedda Gabler* (Abbey Theatre, Playhouse Theatre, London), *The Risen People, Marat Sade, The Famine* (all at the Project Theatre), *The Good Thief* (Temple Bar), *Innocence* (Gate Theatre); as a Director of new Irish writers credits include *Rosie and Starwars* (Stewart Parker Award), *Talking to the Wall* by Gerard Mannix Flynn (Edinburgh Fringe Festival First Award), *Cell* by Paula Meehan in City Arts Centre; television credits include, *Fair City,* (RTE), *Murder in Eden* (BBC), *Troubles* (ITV); film credits include *The Bargain Shop, A Love Divided, Connemara;* Honorary Secretary, Theatrical Cavaliers Cricket Club. Hobbies, cricket, food, wine and walking. Contact: Teri Hayden, The Agency, 47 Adelaide Road,

Dublin 2. Tel: 01 661 8535.

KEOGH, Lainey; INTERNATIONAL KNITWEAR DESIGNER; *b* 1957; *educ* Loreto Convent, Balbriggan; Kevin St. College of Technology, Dip. Medical Sciences; worked in Medical Sciences until 1983; began to work with yarn, 1983; recognised for work by International Wool, 1987; Secretariat International Festival du Lin, 1989; British Fashion Council, 1994; Cable Ace Award Costume Design, 1995 for the film *Two Nudes Bathing* directed by John Boorman; developed fabrics for Dior Culture Studio, 1998; other awards include Prix de Coeur (France) 1998 and People of the Year Award, (Ireland), 1987. Hobbies, sky, walking and looking. Contact: 42 Dawson Street, Dublin 2. Tel: 01 679 3299. Fax: 01 679 4975.

KEOGH, Patrick James

KEOGH, Patrick James; CHIEF EXECUTIVE BORD IASCAIGH MHARA; *b* 1950; *educ* Knockbeg College, Carlow; Univeristy College Dublin, B Ag.Sc., MA (Econ.); *m* Siobhan Curtin; 3*s* 1 *da;* Research Assistant, ESRI, 1973-75; Economist, Pigs & Bacon Commission, 1975-78; Market Research Executive Bord Iascaigh Mhara (BIM) 1979-86, Divisional Manager, 1986-96, appointed Deputy Chief Executive, 1989, appointed Chief Executive 1997 to date; publications incude reports on the agriculture and fisheries sector; member, numerous professional bodies; recipient Walne Memorial Medal from the Shellfish Association of Great Britain, May 1998. Hobbies, cycling, walking and reading. Contact: BIM, PO Box 12, Crofton Road, Dun Laoghaire, Co. Dublin. Tel: 01 284 1544. Fax: 01 284 1134.

KERR, Brian

KERR, Brian; FOOTBALL COACH / TECHNICAL DIRECTOR F.A.I.; *b* 1953; *educ* St. Michael's C.B.S. Inchicore, Dublin; James's St. C.B.S.; College of Technology, Kevin Street Dublin; *m;* 4 *da;* Laboratory Technician, 1970-97, University College Dublin; Football: Manager, Crumlin Utd. 1968-78, Manager, Shamrock Rovers Youths, 1974-75; Manager, Shelbourne "B" 1978; Manager, St. Patrick's Athletic 1986-97; Manager, Ireland U16s, U18s, U20s 1997 to date; awards include, Irish Soccer Writer's Personality of the Year, 1996, Opel FAI Merit Award 1996, Philips Sports Manager of the Year, 1997, 1998, People of the Year Award, 1998, Texaco Soccer Award 1998/1999; a coach of unique talents who has given an international profile to Irish Youth Soccer. Hobbies, music and sport - all types. Contact: F.A.I. 80 Merrion Square, Dublin 2. Tel: 01 676 6864.

KERR, Virginia

KERR, Virginia; CLASSICAL SINGER; *b* 1954; *educ* Mt. Sackville Convent; Royal Irish Academy of Music; Guildhall School of Music and Drama (scholarship), Dip. in Teaching; *single*; early musical awards include, Player Wills Vocal Bursary 1974, Golden Voice of Ireland Competition 1981, Margaret Burke Sheridan Award 1996; recognised as one of the most distinguished sopranos of her generation; she is equally well known on the concert and oratorio platform as the operatic stage; she has had leading roles with Royal Opera House Covent Garden, Scottish Opera, Opera North, Opera Ireland, Leipzig Opera, Glyndebourne Festival Opera (and Proms) and many more as far afield as Singapore and Russia; premieres of 20th century music include Le Fanu's *Wild Man* and Victory's *Ultima Rerum;* holds masterclasses in Mexico, America and Russia and is a frequent radio and television performer. Hobbies, horse riding, sailing, racing, theatre and reading. Contact: c/o Peter Hall, Musichall, Vicarage Way, Ringmer, Sussex, BN8 5LA. Tel: 0044 1273 814 240.

KIBERD, Damien; NEWSPAPER EDITOR; *b* 1955; *educ* St. Paul's College, Sybil Hill, Raheny; Trinity College Dublin; *m* Terry Griffin, Journalist; 1 *da*; Financial Executive, ICC Ltd, 1977-79; Group Finance Editor, *Irish Press*, 1979-87; Finance Editor, *Sunday Tribune*, 1987-89; Editor, *Sunday Business Post,* 1989 to date; the only millionaire newspaper editor in the country, noted for intellectual vigour, republicanism and sometimes confrontational style. Contact: Sunday Business Post, 27 Merchants Quay, Dublin 8. Tel: 01 679 9777.

KIBERD, Declan Liam; PROFESSOR OF ANGLO IRISH LITERATURE AND DRAMA, UNIVERSITY COLLEGE DUBLIN; *b* 1951; *educ* St. Paul's College, Raheny, Dublin; Trinity College Dublin, BA (MOD), Oxford University, D.Phil Doctorate; *m* Elizabeth Moriarty; 1 *s* 2 *da*; Lecturer in English, University of Kent, Canterbury, 1976-77; Lecturer in Irish, Trinity College Dublin, 1977-79; Lecturer in English, University College Dublin, 1979-97; Professor of Anglo Irish Literature and Drama, University College Dublin, 1997 to date; Publications include: *Synge and The Irish Language* (1979); *Men and Feminism in Modern Literature* (1985); *Idir Dhà Chultùr* (1993); *Inventing Ireland* (1995); Member: Irish Manuscript Commission, Cultural Relations Committee, James Joyce International Foundation, Shaw Society (President), New Voices In Irish Criticism (Co-Sponsor); Awarded: Gold Medal for Moderatorship, Trinity College Dublin, 1973, Prendergast Scholarship, Oxford University, 1973-76, *Irish Times* Literature Award for Non-Fiction, 1997; Director, Yeats International Summer School, 1985-87; Presenter, *Exhibit A*, Arts Programme, RTE Television, 1984-86; Script Writer, *Samuel Beckett: Silence To Silence* Film, 1985. Hobbies, running, writing for newspapers. Contact: University College Dublin, Belfield, Dublin 4. Tel: 01 706 8348 Fax: 01 706

1174.

KIELTY, Patrick

KIELTY, Patrick, COMEDIAN, DIRECTOR, GREEN INC. PRODUCTIONS; *b* 1971; *educ* St. Patrick's Grammar, Downpatrick; Queen's University Belfast, B.A. (Hons.), Psychology; *single*; Host, Co-founder, Empire Comedy Club, Belfast, 1992-96, BBC Comic Relief, 1995, PK Tonight , BBC Belfast, 1995-96, Last Chance Lottery, Channel Four, 1997, BBC National Lottery Big Ticket, BBC1, 1998; Co-founded Green Inc. Productions, 1996, one of the fastest growing independent production companies in the British Isles; Productions include: Alan Tyler's *Big Night In* (Channel 4), *Stand Up For Sudan* (BBC), *Everything You Know Is Wrong* (ITV); sister company Salt Island Productions has produced two series of *Gas*, Channel 4; recently turned down the offer of becoming Gay Byrne's successor on *The Late Late Show*, a sign of his undoubted across the board appeal; hobbies, football, water-skiing. Contact: Green Inc. Productions, 47A Botanic Avenue, Belfast BT7 1JL, Northern Ireland. Tel: 0044 1232 573000 Fax: 0044 1232 579957.

KIERNAN, Buddy

KIERNAN, Buddy; FARMER, BUSINESSMAN; *b* 1931; *educ* Grammar School, New York; National School, Ballinamore; Newbridge College, Kildare; *m* Teresa Sweeney; *s* 4 *da*; Founder of Kiernan (Family) Group - Pig farm units on 2,000 acres in Counties Cavan, Longford, Westmeath, Sligo and Tipperary, producing 330,000 finished pigs annually (acknowledged to be the largest in Northern Europe); sole owner of HKM Milling Limited, a high technology animal feed mill, located in Granard, Co. Longford, with annual production in excess of 175,000 tons; Executive Director and 50% owner of Midland Radio Ltd. (incorporating Shannonside and Northern Sound); Former Chairman, Cavan County Council; Chairman, Fine Gael Trustees. Hobbies, politics and sport. Contact: Aughnakilmore, Kilnaleck, Co. Cavan. Tel: 049 36772.

KILCOYNE, The Rev. Colm; CATHOLIC PRIEST, COLUMNIST SUNDAY TRIBUNE; *b* 1934; *educ* St. Gerard's School, Castlebar; Maynooth College, B.A., BD. L.Ph; University College Galway, H.Dip; Ordained Catholic Priest, 1959; taught Glenamaddy Co-ed School, 1960-73; Curate, Achill, 1973-75; Director, Catholic Communications Centre, 1975-78; Director, Catholic Communications Ins., 1983-86; Parish Priest, Cong, 1996 to date; publications include *Just a Moment* Vol I, II, (Collections of *Sunday Press* Articles); *Twin Pulpits* (Co-editor); *The Splintered Heart* (Co-editor), Veritas Publications, *Celebrating the Sacraments;* awards include: Religious Journalist of the Year, 1995; Award from the Religious Press Association. Hobbies, reading, walking, Connemara. Contact: Cong, Co. Mayo. Tel. & Fax: 092 46030.

KILCULLEN, Justin M

KILCULLEN, Justin Michael; DIRECTOR TRÓCAIRE; *b* 1951; *educ* Oatlands, Mount Merrion; University College Dublin, BArch.; *m* Róisín O'Boyle; 2*s* 1 *da;* Architect, National Housing Corporation, Dar Es Salaam, Tanzania, (Design and Construction of low cost urban housing), 1976-78; Architect, N. Ireland Federation of Housing Associations, (Inner City housing renewal projects), 1978-79; UNHCR - Consultant on refugee camp design in SE Asia - Refugee camp construction for 500,000 refugees, 1979-80; Architect, Group Design Associates, Dun Laoghaire, 1980-81; Project Officer, Trócaire, 1981-88; Country Representative Trócaire/CIDSE, Laos, 1988-92; Director, Trócaire, 1993 to date; numerous architectural projects including an exhibition pavilion, Tanzania, private houses and educational buildings; President, CIDSE (Coopération Internationale pour le Developpement et la Solidarité) - the International Working Group of Catholic Development Agencies; National Delegate - EU-NGDO Liaison Committee, 1993-97; Member, Irish Aid Advisory Council, 1993-97; awards include, Photography - Photo of children in North Korea featured as one of the Pictures of the Year in both the *Times* and *Newsweek*, 1997. Hobbies, architecture, photography, cinema, theatre, tennis and jogging. Contact: Trócaire, 169 Booterstown Avenue, Blackrock, Co. Dublin. Tel: 01 288 5385. Fax: 01 288 3577.

KILLEEN, Michael; COUNTY MANAGER, LONGFORD; *b* 1940; *educ* Senten Street Christian Brothers School, Limerick; School of Commerce, Limerick, Dip Admin, Chartered Institute of Secretaries; *m* Eilis Slattery; 3 *s* 1 *da*; Town Clerk, Tullamore 1968-70; Accountant, Laois County Council 1970-71; Finance Officer, Midland Health Board 1971-74; Programme Manager, Western Health Board 1974-78; County Manager, Longford 1978 to date. Hobbies, jogging, fishing and boating. Contact: County Manager's Office, Great Water Street, Longford. Tel: 043 46231. Fax: 043 41233.

KILROY, Howard E.; GOVERNOR BANK OF IRELAND; *b* 1936; *educ* The High School Dublin; *m* Meriel McCullagh; 2*s* 3 *da;* articled to Kinnear & Company (Dublin); joined C.P.C., worked with them in Dublin, UK and Belgium; recruited by Smurfit Group, President and Chief Executive Officer until retirement in 1995; Governor, Bank of Ireland, 1991 to date; Board member, CRH, Smurfit Group Ltd.; nominated non Executive Director of the Year 1999; one of the country's leading businessmen with a strong aversion to personal publicity. Contact: Bank of Ireland, Lower Baggot Street, Dublin 2. Tel: 01 661 5933.

KILROY, Norman David; MANAGING DIRECTOR GRAFTON GROUP PLC; *b* 1939; *educ* High School, Dublin; *m* Dorothy Vaughan; *2s 2da;* Accountant, Financial Director, Managing Director, Nokia Ltd., 1963-1990; Managing Director, Grafton Group plc, 1990 to date; Fellow, Institute of Chartered Accountants; Board member, PEI Ltd., Carton Group, Banque Nationale de Paris, Erasmus Smith Trust/High School Dublin; President, Irish Management Institute, Hibernian Catch Club. Hobbies, golf, cricket and music. Contact: Unit 62, Stillorgan Industrial Park, Blackrock, Co. Dublin. Tel: 01 295 3377. Fax: 01 295 4470.

KILROY, Norman David

KITT, Proinsias Joseph; MANAGING PARTNER KITT NOONE & CO.; *b* 1959; *educ* St. Jarlath's College, Tuam. Co. Galway; National University of Ireland, Galway, BComm; Fellow, Institute of Chartered Accountants; *m* Anne McManus; *2s 1 da;* joined PriceWaterhouse Coopers (then Coopers & Lybrand), 1980-87; founded Kitt Noone & Co., Chartered Accountants with Terence Noone, 1987, currently Managing Partner; the company employs 30 people in offices in Dublin and Galway; composer *Seanachaí* type stories and songs; committee member, General Practice Committee of Chartered Accountants; member (past President), Past Pupils Union of St. Jarlath's College; member, Galway Football Supporters Club; member, numerous charitable organisations; for services to charity awarded Galway Person of the Year, 1999; former hurler and footballer for St. Jarlath's College and National University of Ireland, Galway; a leading personality in the commercial, sporting and community life in Galway. Hobbies, watching GAA games, golf, swimming and national politics. Contact: Kitt Noone & Co., Lock House, Dominick Street, Galway. Tel: 091 586 146. Fax: 091 586 161.

KNOWLES, Andrew Sheridan; FINANCIAL DIRECTOR / SECRETARY ARNOTTS PLC; *b* 1939; *educ* Mountjoy School (Mount Temple); College of Commerce, Rathmines; *m* Joan Mitchell; *2s 1 da;* Chief Accountant, Arnotts plc, 1968-90, Company Secretary, 1990-97, Financial Director/Secretary, 1997 to date; Secretary, Brinks Allied Ltd.; Secretary, Arnotts Staff Pension Fund; Fellow, Institute of Chartered Accountants in Ireland. Hobbies, sailing, rugby and golf. Contact: Arnotts plc, 12 Henry Street, Dublin 1. Tel: 01 805 0400.

LALLY, Michael Joseph "Mick"; ACTOR; *b* 1945; *educ* Trián Lár National School; St. Mary's College, Galway; University College Galway, BA, ATO, TTG; *m* Peige Ní Chonghaile; *2s 1da;* Teacher of Irish, Vocational Education System, 1969-75; Actor with Taibhdhearc na Gaillimhe before becoming a founder member of Druid Theatre Company 1975, credits with them include *Who's Afraid of Virginia Woolf, The Glass Menagerie, Treats, Playboy of the Western World* (Ireland and US), *Waiting for Godot, Wild Harvest;* moved to Dublin and has appeared in all major theatres; returned to Druid 1996 for their 21st birthday, appeared in *Loves of Cass Maguire* and *A Skull in Connemara* (part of the Leenane Trilogy), 1997 (Druid Theatre, Olympia Theatre, Royal Court Theatre London and a tour of Ireland), *The Dead School* with Macnas Galway (also toured); television credits include, *Glenroe, Tales from the Poorhouse* (in English and Irish); film credits include *The Year of the French, Fools of Fortune;* recipient Jacobs Award (1979), Entertainment Personality of the Year Award (1984-85); Rehabilitation Institute, Mayo Person of the Year (1985); Dublin Mayo People Association, Actor of the Festival (1989); Dublin Theatre Festival, various awards from provincial newspapers, P.A.T.S. Award (1991); Performing Artists Trust Society; recognised as one of the nicest men in the business; an actor whose truth and humanity show in his work. Hobbies, reading and listening to traditional music. Contact: Teri Hayden, The Agency, 47 Adelaide Road, Dublin 2. Tel: 01 661 8535.

LAPPIN, William "Arthur"; THEATRE AND FILM PRODUCER; *b* 1951; *educ* Clongowes Wood College; College of Surgeons - briefly; *m* Kathryn Lennon; *4s 1da;* worked with Bank of Ireland 1970-78; Drama and Dance Officer, The Arts Council 1978-85; Theatre and Film producer 1985 to date; ran theatre production company, Groundwork, with Ben Barnes 1986-94; currently Managing Director, Hells Kitchen, film production company; production credits include *My Left Foot* (Line Producer), *The Field* (Line Producer), *In the Name of the Father* (co-produced with Jim Sheridan), *Some Mothers Son* (co-produced with Jim Sheridan), *The Boxer* (co-produced with Jim Sheridan), *Agnes Brown* (co-produced with Jim Sheridan); former Chairperson National Training Committee (now Screen Training Ireland); Chairman, The Ark (children's cultural centre); member, Minister Sile de Valera's Think Tank on the film industry; member, Headfort Golf Club, Fitzwilliam LTC. Hobbies, family, golf and tennis. Contact: Hells Kitchen, 21 Mespil Road, Dublin . Tel: 01 667 5599.

LAVAN, The Hon. Mr. Justice Vivian H.; JUDGE OF THE HIGH COURT; *b* 1944; *educ* Terenure College, Dublin; University College Dublin; Kings Inns; *m* Una McCullough; *2s 2 da;* admitted to the Bar (Ireland), 1969, (England) 1975; co-founder of the Free Legal Advice Centres, 1969; Treasurer of the General Council of the Bar of Ireland, 1976-80; Member, Council of the Kings Inns, 1976-80; Director of the Legal Aid Board, 1979; Chairman of the Mining Board of Ireland, 1982; Honorary Member of the American Bar Association, 1983; Associate of the

Chartered Institute of Arbitrators, 1981; Government appointee on the Panel of Conciliators and on the Panel of Arbitrators maintained by the International Centre for Investment Disputes, Washington, DC, 1988; appointed a Judge of the High Court, 1989; appointed President of the Law Reform Commission 1998. Clubs, Fitzwilliam LTC, National Yacht Club. Contact: The Law Reform Commission, IPC House, 35-39 Shelbourne Road, Ballsbridge, Dublin 4. Tel: 01 637 7600. Fax: 01 637 7601.

LAVER, Michael John; PROFESSOR OF POLITICS, THE SENIOR LECTURER, TRINITY COLLEGE DUBLIN; *b* 1949; *educ* Essex University, BA (Hons), MA; Liverpool University, PhD; *m* Bríd O'Connor; 1 *s* 1 *da;* Lecturer in Politics, Queens University Belfast, 1972-73; Senior Lecturer in Politics, Liverpool University, 1973-83; Professor of Politics and Sociology, University College Galway, 1983-93; Professor of Politics, Trinity College Dublin, 1993 to date; Visiting Professor of Government, Harvard University, 1988-89; Visiting Professor of Politics, Duke University, 1994 to date; Has published fifteen books, including: *Making and Breaking Governments* (1996); *Private Desires, Political Action* (1998); *Playing Politics: The Nightmare Continues* (1998); Member: American Political Science Association, Political Studies Association of Ireland (Former President), Midwest Political Science Association, Constitution Review Group, Royal Irish Academy; Rockefeller Foundation, Scholar in Residence, Bellagio (1992). Hobbies, walking, gardening, travel. Contact: Trinity College Dublin, Dublin 2. Tel: 01 677 2941.

LAWLOR, Eamon

LAWLOR, Eamon; RADIO PRESENTER LYRIC FM; *b* 1951; *educ* Rockwell College; University College Dublin, BA, MA; *m* Maria Murray; 1*s*; joined RTE News, 1974, European Correspondent, 1979-89, Newscaster/Interviewer RTE TV News, 1989-96, Presenter/Interviewer, *Prime Time*, RTE TV, 1996-99; Presenter, Lyric FM, 1999 to date; Visiting Lecturer, International Academy of Broadcasting, Montreux. Hobbies, music, reading and walking. Contact: RTE, Donnybrook, Dublin 4. Tel: 01 208 3111.

LEAVY, Billy; FARMER; *b* 1933; *educ* Christian Brothers School, Mullingar; *m* Deirdre Flynn; 3*s* 4 *da;* inherited uncle's farm, has expanded over the years, now runs extensive acreage with tillage, mixed cattle and sheep; grows and mills own corn; Westmeath County Chairman of IFA. Hobbies, GAA supporter, reading and racing. Contact: Kilmore, Coralstown, Killucan, Mullingar, Co. Westmeath. Tel: 044 74172.

Le BROCQUY, Louis

Le BROCQUY, Louis; ARTIST; *b* 1916; *educ* St. Gerard's School, Bray; *m* Jean Stoney (*m dis*); 1 da; *m* Anne Madden (Simpson), Painter; 2 *s*; in 1938 left family business; self-taught artist, studied museum collections in London, Paris, Geneva, then exhibiting Prado Collection; Founder member, Irish Exhibition of Living Art, 1943; Visiting Tutor, Central School of Arts and Royal College of Art, London, 1947-58; recipient of Honorary LittD, Trinity College Dublin, 1962, Chevalier Legion d'Honneur, 1975, Honorary LLD, University College Dublin, 1988; Saoi Aosdána, 1993, Officier des Arts et des Lettres, 1998; Glen Dimplex Prize, Sustained Contribution to Arts, 1998; Honorary DPh., Dublin City University, 1999; Museum exhibitions include Venice Biennale (Premio Prealpino) 1956, Municipal Gallery; Dublin, 1966, 1978 and 1992, Ulster Museum, 1967 and 1987, Fondation Maeght, St. Paul, 1973, Musée d'Art Moderne, Paris, 1976, New York State Museum, 1980, Palais des Beaux Arts, Charleroi 1982, Festival Centre; Adelaide, National Gallery of Victoria, Museum of Contemporary Art, Brisbane, 1988, Musée Picasso, Antibes, 1989, Museum of Modern Art, Kamakura, Itami Museum of Modern Art, Osaka, City Museum of Contemporary Art, Hiroshima, 1991; Irish Museum of Modern Art, Dublin, 1996; Municipal Gallery of Art Ljubljana, 1998; An Irish artist with a high international profile. Contact: Taylor Galleries, 1 Kildare Street, Dublin 2. Tel: 01 676 6055.

LEE, George Damien; ECONOMICS EDITOR RTE; *b* 1962; *educ* Colaiste Enna, Ballyroan; University College Dublin, BA Econ; London School of Economics, MSc.; *m* Mary Kitson; 1*s* 1*da*; Lecturer in Economics, University College Galway, 1986-87; Economist, Central Bank, 1987-89; Treasury Economist, ESB, 1989-90; Economics Correspondent, *Sunday Business Post*, 1990-91; Senior Economist, RIADA Stockbrokers, 1991-92; Current Affairs Economist, RTE, 1992-95, Economics Correspondent, 1995-97, Economics Editor, 1997 to date; Published, *Breaking the Bank* – an account of the exposure of the NIB banking scandal; member, NUJ; awards include, Scholarship in Economics, UCD, 1983 & 1984; Post graduate Scholarship in Economics, ANCO, 1985; Roseberry Studentship from London School of Economics, 1985-86; Barrington Medal for Economics, Statistical and Social Inquiry Survey of Ireland, 1990; Journalist of the Year, 1998. A highly respected financial journalist with the ability to make complex financial issues understood by the ordinary viewer/listener. Contact: RTE, Donnybrook, Dublin 4. Tel: 01 208 3111.

LEE, Joseph; ACADEMIC; *b* 1942; *educ* Gormanston; University College Dublin, BA, MA; Institute of European History, Mainz; *m* Anne Mitchell; 1*s* 2 *da;* Fellow, Lecturer, Tutor, Peterhouse, Cambridge, 1968-74; Professor of Modern History/History, University College Cork since 1974; Dean of Arts, University College Cork, 1976-79; Visiting Mellon Professor, University of Pittsburgh, 1979-80; Vice President, University College Cork, 1982-85; Visiting Fellow, Austrian Academy, Vienna, 1987; Eisenhower Fellow, USA, 1989; Distinguished Visiting Professor of World Peace, University of Texas, Austin, 1989-90; Visiting Professor of Government, Colby College, 1991; Visiting Parnell Senior Fellow in Irish Studies, Magdalene College, Cambridge, 1992-3; Member, Seanad Eireann, 1993-97; Visiting Arbuthnott Fellow in Irish Studies, University of Edinburgh 1996; Visiting Glucksman Professor of Irish Studies, New York University, 1999; J.S. Donnelly Senior Prize, American Conference of Irish Studies, 1990; *Sunday Independent*-Irish Life Arts Award 1990, Aer Lingus-*Irish Times* Award for Literature (non-fiction) 1991; publications include *The Modernisation of Irish Society 1848-1918, Labour In German Industrialisation,* in *Cambridge Economic History of Europe, Ireland 1912-1985;* Columnist, *Sunday Tribune,* 1996 to date; Secretary, Irish Committee Historical Sciences, 1975-80; Chairman, Scholarship Exchange Board/Irish Fulbright Commission, 1980-95; President, Irish Association for European Studies, 1986-9. Member, Royal Irish Academy. noted as a gifted and imaginative teacher. Contact: National University of Ireland, Cork. Tel: 021 276 871. Fax: 021 271 568.

LEE, Lynda; OPERA SINGER; *b* 1964; *educ* Loreto Convent Wexford; Dublin College of Music, (with Dr. Veronica Dunne); Roles include: Dublin Grand Opera Society (Suzuki), 1993; Jonathan Miller's Dramatized *St. Matthew Passion,* (BBC), 1994; Karlsruhe Handelfestpicle (Agrippina) 1997-8; Halle Handelfestpiele (Xerxes), 1997-98; Oper Leipzig, on contract as Dramatic Soprano, 1998-2000; regular soloist with National Symphony Orchestra of Ireland and also a frequent oratorio performer in Ireland and throughout Europe. Several Feis Ceoil Awards, 1990-91; Represented Northern Ireland at Cardiff Singer of the World, 1993; Lombard & Ulster Vocal Winner, 1992; Finalist at the International Belvedere Competition. Hobbies, travel, reading and family. Contact: Tel: 0044 97 2161 3544.

LEE, Lynda

LENIHAN, Conor Patrick; POLITICIAN; *b* 1963; *educ* St. Brigid's National School; Belvedere College; University College Dublin, BA (Hons); Dublin City University, Post Grad. Dip. Journalism; INSEAD, Young Managers Programme; *m* Denise Russell; 1 *s*; Freelance Journalist, 1983-86; Economics Researcher, European Commission (London Office), 1986-87; Press Officer, Inner London Education Authority, 1987-90; Political Correspondent, Westminster for *Irish News,* 1987-90; Deputy Head of News, 98FM and IRN, 1990-95; Senior Executive Esat Digifone, 1995-97; elected Fianna Fail Deputy for Dublin South East, 1997 to date; Advisor, Esat Digifone and Torc Telecom; member, NUJ; former member, European Commission's Speakers Panel; former member, British Labour Party; Vice President, St. Kevins and St. Killians G.A.A. Club; son of former politician and statesman, Brian Lenihan and nephew of Minister Mary O'Rourke; seen as the next generation to carry the family colours to the Irish political arena. Hobbies, reading, soccer, football and sports in general, Irish art. Contact: Dail Eireann, Leinster House, Kildare Street, Dublin 2. Tel: 01 618 3333.

LENIHAN, Conor Patrick

LEONARD, Hugh; PLAYWRIGHT; *b* 1926; *educ* Presentation College, Dun Laoghaire; *m* Paula Jacquet; 1 *da*; worked in the offices of the Land Commission 1945-49; left to become a freelance writer; has written numerous scripts for television, Ireland and UK; contributor to various newspapers and magazines; weekly columnist with *Sunday Independent*; plays include *Da* (also a film), *A Life, Summer, Time Was, Pizzaz, Moving, Love in the Title, Magic, Fillums*; recipient Harvey Award, Writers Guild Award, Tony Award, Critic Circle Award, Outer Critics Award, Drama Desk Award - all for Best Play; has adapted for television the works of Destoyevsky, Wilkie Collins, Flaubert, Maupassant, Saki, O'Faolain, Maugham, O'Connor; has published two books of memoirs - *Home Before Night* and *Out After Dark* - and one novel, *Parnell and the Englishwoman;* conferred with Honorary Doctorate of Humane Letters, Rhode Island College, Honorary Doctorate of Literature, T.C.D; a writer of rare perception and humour, popular with the public. Hobbies, vintage films and France (canals and by-roads). Contact: Sunday Independent, 90 Middle Abbey Street, Dublin 1. Tel: 01 705 5333.

LEONHARD, Christian; MANAGING DIRECTOR BRAUN IRELAND; *b* 1957; *educ* Master Degree in Mechanical Engineering; Universities in Karlsruhe/Germany and Stuttgart/Germany; *m* Catherine Cottavoz; 2*s* 1 *da;* Chemical Industry, (R&D, Marketing), 1987-91; Managing Director, Silk Epil (subsidiary of Braun Germany); Managing Director, Braun Ireland, (Carlow), 1997 to date. Contact: Braun Ireland, Dublin Road, Carlow. Tel: 01 0503 76411. Fax: 0503 76401.

LEWIS, John Trevor; ACADEMIC; *b* 1932; *educ* Queens University of Belfast, BSc, PhD; *m* Maureen McEntee; 2*s* 2 *da;* Research Lecturer, Christ Church, Oxford 1956-59; Brasenose College, Oxford, Lecturer 1959-60, Tutorial Fellow 1960-72, Senior Dean 1963-65; Oxford University, Mathematical Institute, Junior Lecturer 1957-59, CUF Lecturer 1959-65, University Lecturer 1965-72; member, Institute for Advanced Study, Princeton 1969-70; Dublin Institute for Advanced Studies 1972 to date; Director, School of Theoretical Physics, 1975 to date; publications

LINEHAN, Fergus Daniel

LINEHAN, Rosaleen

LISTON, Jerry

LOMAX, Ian "Peter

include one hundred papers on mathematical physics in journals; member, Royal Irish Academy (Council 1985, 1989, 1997, Senior Vice President 1998-99); member, International Association of Mathematical Physics (Executive Committee 1982-88); conferred with PhD, Dublin Institute of Technology 1999, Honorary Professor, University of Wales, 1995, Honorary Professor, Trinity College Dublin, 1999. Hobbies, training on a Concept II ergometer. Contact: Dublin Institute for Advanced Studies, School of Theoretical Physics, 10 Burlington Road, Dublin . Tel: 01 614 0100. Fax: 01 668 0561.

LEWIS, Richard; DRESS DESIGNER; *b* 1945; *educ* Drimnagh Castle Dublin, Grafton Academy of Dress Design; *single;* freelance designer for various manufacturing companies; involved in every aspect of the fashion industry, manufacture, wholesale and couture; opened own business, 1977, took on business partner Jim Greeley, 1987; awarded Satzenbrau Fashion Oscar for Spring collection 1988 and for 'Outstanding Contribution to Fashion Industry', 1991; has designed for both stage and television and been associated with Eurovision Song Contest (dressing singer and producer); now designs exclusively for large private clientele; a small elfin like, immensely popular man who wears only black and white. Hobbies, decorating and collecting pictures. Contact: 72 South Frederick Street, Dublin 2. Tel: 01 679 7016.

LILLINGSTON, Alan; BLOODSTOCK BREEDER; *b* 1935; *educ* Eton College, Windsor, Trinity College Cambridge; *married; 2 s 2 da*; runs successful stud in Co. Limerick; principal winners include *One in a Million, Song of Ragtime, Babymacad, Piney Ridge, Deep Run, Gay Lemur, Sound Print, Tamarisk, Dr. Massini, Family Crest, Brave Music*; Member, Turf Club, INHS Committee, Bord Na gCoppal - Irish Horse Board; Awarded Team Gold Medal, European Championships, 3 Day Event, Germany, 1979; Rode winner of Champion Hurdle, Cheltenham, 1963; Steward, Turf Club, 1989-90; Senior Steward, INHS Committee, 1994-95; Irish Horse Authority, 1994-95. Hobby, golf. Contact: Tel: 063 98111. Fax: 063 98057.

LINEHAN, Fergus Daniel; DIRECTOR DUBLIN THEATRE FESTIVAL; *b* 1969; *educ* Gormanston College, University College Dublin, BA, English and Classics; *m* Catharine Loukes; 2 *s*; Director, Pigsback Theatre Company, 1989-91; General Manager, Tivoli Theatre, 1991-93; General Manager, Dublin Theatre Festival, 1993-96, Deputy Director, Dublin Theatre Festival, 1996-99, Director, Dublin Theatre Festival 2000. Highly regarded within the theatre community for his artistic judgement, singlemindedness and administrative ability. Hobbies, swimming, theatre, dance, music, reading, travel, Arsenal FC and his boys. Contact: Dublin Theatre Festival, 47 Nassau Street, Dublin 2. Tel: 01 677 8439. Fax: 01 679 7709.

LINEHAN, Rosaleen, née McMenamin; ACTRESS; *b* 1937; *educ* Loreto College, St. Stephen's Green; University College Dublin, B.Econ,; *m* Fergus Linehan, journalist, playwright and novelist; 3 *s* 1 *da;* worked in review with Des Keogh for a number of years; performance credits include, *A Long Days Journey into Night, Bailegaugaire* (Royal Court, London), *The Cripple of Innismaan* (Geffon Play-House, L.A), *Dancing at Lughnasa* (Dublin, London, Broadway), *Mother of All the Behans*, (Dublin, Edinburgh, Montreal, Broadway), *Happy Days* (Dublin, London, Broadway) and the Beckett Festival in the Barbican, 1999; films include, *The Butcher Boy, Hilo Country, Matchmaker, All About Adam*; has written the scores for twelve reviews and two musicals; member, Actors Equity Ireland and USA, Screen Actors Guild, USA. One of the most versatile and popular actresses in Ireland; a superb *comedienne*, equally at home in musical or dramatic roles. Contact: Aude Powell, Suite 8A, 169 Queensgate, London, SW7 5HE. Tel: 0044 171 581 3388.

LISTON, Jerry; CHIEF EXECUTIVE, UNITED DRUG PLC; *b* 1940; *educ* Gonzaga College, Dublin; University College Dublin, BA, MBA; King's Inns, Barrister at Law; *m* Noreen Wall; 3 *da*; Group Product Manager, P.J. Carroll & Co., 1962-68; Marketing Manager, W.R. Grace, 1968-70; General Manager Ireland, Warner Lambert, 1970-74; Chief Executive, United Drug plc., 1974 to date; Creative works include MBA Thesis, *Determination of Advertising Budgets*; Member: I.M.I. (Past President and Past Chairman), Marketing Society (Past Chairman), Clubs, Fitzwilliam LTC, Royal St. George YC, Connemara GC; Fellow of Marketing Institute, Life Fellow, Irish Management Institute. Hobbies, reading, golf and family. Contact: United Drug plc, United Drug House, Belgard Road, Dublin 24. Tel: 01 459 8877. Fax: 01 459 6893.

LOMAX, Ian "Peter"; MANAGING DIRECTOR DHL INTERNATIONAL (IRELAND) LTD.; *b* 1959; *educ* Arnold School, Blackpool, (U.K.); Demontfort University, (U.K), BA Econ (Hons); Cranfield Business School, (UK), MBA; *m* Deborah Payne; 1*s* 1 *da;* Graduate Trainee, Ford Motor Company, 1980-85; Product Manager, Norsk Hydro, 1985-87; Marketing Director, Business Development Director, Unipart Group, 1987-93; Commercial Director, Area Director - London & South East - DHL International (U.K.) Ltd, 1993-95; Managing Director, DHL International (Ireland) Ltd, 1998 to date; DHL Worldwide Express is the market leader in international air express with a network in 227 countries; Non-Executive Director, Vendcare Services, 1996-98; member, Institute of Directors, Irish Management Institute, Irish Association of International Express Carriers (Treasurer). Hobbies, family, golf, walking, music and travel. Contact: DHL International (Ireland) Ltd., Cargo Terminal 2, Dublin Airport. Tel: 1800 725 725. Fax: 01 844 4922.

LOONEY, Brian; EDITOR, THE EXAMINER; *b* 1959; *educ* Presentation Brothers College, Cork; single; Reporter with *Limerick Weekly Echo*, 1979-82; Reporter, *Irish Press*, 1982-85; Industrial Correspondent, *Irish Independent*, 1985-88; Editor, *The Kerryman*, 1988-94; Editor, *The Examiner*, 1994 to date; a newsman through and through, has broadened the title, given the paper a heavy news emphasis and embarked on a significant marketing campaign. Hobbies, work, work, work. Contact: The Examiner, PO Box 21, Academy Street, Cork. Tel: 021 272 722. Fax: 021 275 112.

LORTON, Harry

LORTON, Harry; CHIEF EXECUTIVE, TSB BANK, GROUP CHIEF EXECUTIVE DESIGNATE ACC/TSB BANKS; *b* 1951; *educ* Christian Brothers College, Cork; Trinity College, Dublin BBS 1975; Fellow: The Association of Chartered Certified Accountants, The Institute of Bankers; OPM Programme, Harvard Business School, 1990; *m* Mary Crowley; 1 *s* 1 *da*; Bank of Ireland, 1969-79; Financial Controller, Cork Savings Bank, 1979; Chief Executive, Cork & Limerick Savings Bank, 1991; Chief Executive, TSB Bank, 1992 to date; Former President: Irish Region Association of Chartered Certified Accountants, Institute of Bankers in Ireland; Member: Councils of IMI and FSIA, General Board of Administration of the European Savings Bank Group; Clubs, Fitzwilliam LTC, Sundays Well Boating and Tennis Club. Contact: Charlemont Place, Dublin 2. Tel: 01 418 4000. Fax: 01 418 4444.

LOUGHREY, John

LOUGHREY, John; SECRETARY GENERAL DEPARTMENT OF PUBLIC ENTERPRISE; *b* 1943; *educ* O'Connell Schools; Trinity College Dublin, BA, BComm, DPA; University College Dublin, MEcon.Sc.; Institute of Social Studies, The Hague, Post Graduate Diploma in Economic Planning; University of Dijon, Dip. French; *m* Eithne O'Riordan, Journalist/Author; 1*s* 2 *da;* served with Department of Finance, 1966-73; European Investment Bank, Luxembourg, 1974-78; Principal Officer, Department of Finance, 1979-86; Assistant Secretary, Department of Agriculture, 1987-88; Secretary, Department of Energy, 1988-92; Secretary, Department of Transport, Energy and Communications, 1993-97; Secretary General, Department of Public Enterprise, 1997 to date; Fellow, Institute of Transport of Ireland; Authority Member and Director, IDA, 1987-89; member, National Economic and Social Council (NESC), 1998 to date. Hobbies, hill walking, reading and cinema. Contact: Department of Public Enterprise, 44 Kildare Street, Dublin 2. Tel: 01 670 7444.

LOWERY, Martin D.

LOWERY, Martin D.; CHIEF EXECUTIVE, COILLTE TEO; *b* 1945; *educ* St. Joseph's College, Galway; University College Galway, BE, MEngSc; *m* Aileen Blighe; 1 *s* 3 *da;* Scientific Officer, Institute of Hydrology, UK 1968-69; Operations Research, Aer Lingus 1969-71; Executive Director, IDA 1971-89; Chief Executive, Coillte Teo, 1989 to date (the State Forestry Company, established 1988 - operations include: afforestation and reforestation, woodland industries, R&D and leisure areas). Member, Institute of Engineers of Ireland. With forestry as the largest single alternative to conventional agriculture, the role of Chief Executive of the Irish Forestry Board is a key one in Irish agribusiness; it is more than ably filled by Martin Lowery, who is coolly impressive and effective. Hobbies, fishing, theatre, gardening, family. Contact: Coillte, Leeson Lane, Dublin 2. Tel: 01 661 5666. Fax: 01 678 9527.

LUNDBERG, Gerald

LUNDBERG, Gerald "Gerry"; PUBLICIST; *b* 1945; *educ* O'Connell Christian Brothers School, Dublin, *single*; Advertising Clerk, *The Irish Times* 1963-64; worked at various jobs before becoming assistant to Brendan Smith, Dublin Theatre Festival 1974-84; Publicist: Most Dublin Theatres, *Riverdance - The Show*, Dublin Fringe Festival, films include: *My Left Foot, The Field, In the Name of the Father, Michael Collins, The Boxer, Dancing at Lughnasa, The Mammy,* restaurants, galleries (ROSC), most theatre organisations; member, National Union of Journalists, Public Relations Institute, Irish Actors Equity. Recognised as leading "show biz" publicist; a human dynamo whose success can be attributed to total commitment and boundless enthusiasm. Hobbies, work, travel, swimming and backgammon. Contact: Gerry Lundberg Public Relations, 27 Dawson Street, Dublin 2. Tel: 01 679 8476.

LYNCH, Anthony; EXECUTIVE CHAIRMAN & CHIEF EXECUTIVE PROTIM ABRASIVES LTD; *b* 1946; *educ* Rosary High School, Carrick-on-Shannon; Dublin Institute of Technology, Rathmines; *m* Ann Holland, former Secondary School Teacher; 2 *s* 2 *da;* Divisional General Manager, Denis Coakley & Co. Ltd. 1970-74; Director/General Manager, Castleragh Agencies Ltd 1974-77; Chief Executive, Camac Transport Ltd. 1977-80; Managing Director, Abrasives Ltd 1980-87; Executive Chairman, Fosroc Abrasives & Chemicals Ltd., 1987-92; Executive Chairman & Chief Executive, Protim Abrasives, 1992 to date; member, Marketing Institute of Ireland; Clubs, Knockanally Golf & Country Club, The K Club (Captain for the Year 2000); a businessman dedicated to customer service with a keen interest in Gaelic sports and golf. Contact: Protim Abrasives, Tolka Industrial

Park, Ballyboggan Road, Glasnevin, Dublin 11. Tel: 01 805 3966.

LYNCH, John; DIRECTOR GENERAL FÁS; *b* 1942; *educ* Drimnagh Castle Christian Brothers School; Kevin Street Technical School; Bolton Street Technical College, HNC (Mech Eng); University College Dublin, BComm, MBA; Trinity College Dublin, PhD; *single;* Managing Director, Pye Ireland Ltd., 1975-77; Director, Business Policy, CII, 1977-84; Chief Executive, Irish Productivity Centre, 1984-88; Chief Executive, Bord Gais, 1988-91; Director General, FÁS, 1991 to date; (FÁS is the training and employment authority employing over 2,000 in a network of sixty-six employment offices and training centres throughout the country); Visiting Professor of Business Policy, University of Maine and Boston College; publications include *Legal Aspects of Marketing;* founder member, The Irish Hospice Foundation; past President, Institute of Industrial Engineers (1988-90). FÁS, offering an important social service, is headed by a highly qualified and capable Chief Executive. Hobby, football. Contact: FÁS, 27-33 Upper Baggot Street, Dublin 4. Tel: 01 607 0500. Fax: 01 607 0600.

LYNCH, Philip

LYNCH, Philip; GROUP MANAGING DIRECTOR, IAWS GROUP PLC.; *b* 1946; *educ* Hamilton High School; Copswood College; Waterford RTC; *m* Eileen Crowley; 1 *s* 3 *da*; Former Executive with Odlum Group & R&H Hall; Group Managing Director IAWS, 1983 to date; IAWS is a major food and agri business group, with operations in Ireland, UK and France, and four major divisions - food, fertilisers, feed ingredients, proteins and oils; Doctor of Law (LLB) 1997; Chairman, Bord Bia - Irish Food Board, Dun Laoghaire Harbour Company; Director, FBD, Lithographic Universal, John Thompson & Sons Ltd; Member, Turf Club, Curragh Golf Club; An innovative, highly successful executive; has moved IAWS rapidly to the forefront of Irish agri-business; recently acquired Cuisine de France and is reported likely to continue growth rate. Hobbies, golf and other sports. Contact: IAWS Group plc., 151 Thomas Street, Dublin 8. Tel: 01 612 1200. Fax: 01 6121321.

LYONS, Anthony Henry Keith " Tony"; ARCHITECT; *b* 1942; *educ* Castleknock College; University College Dublin, BArch; Fellow, Royal Institute of Architects of Ireland; *m* Sandra Smith; 1 *s* 3 *da;* in practice with Henry J. Lyons & Partners Architects, 1967 to date; practice founded by grandfather Henry, succeeded by his son, Sam; one of the oldest and largest architectural practices in the country, with over 65 staff; practice has designed National Treasury Building, Percy Place Development, EPA Head office in Wexford, New Airport Extension, Pier C; Fellow, Royal Institute of Architects; awards include Winners Cup Medal, Senior Cup Team, Castleknock College, 1960; practice has received AAI Award, 1997, (special mention); RIAI Regional Awards, 1998; clubs, Portmarnock Golf Club (former Committee), Milltown Golf Club, Fitzwilliam LTC, Belvedere RFC. Hobbies, golf, rugby, reading, walking, wine and food, international affairs. Contact: Henry J. Lyons & Partners, 104 Lower Baggot Street, Dublin 2. Tel: 01 676 2691.

MacCANN, Kate; DIRECTOR OF SALES, MARKETING AND GOLF, MOUNT JULIET; *b* 1963; *educ* Mount Anville, Goatstown, Dublin; University College Dublin, B.Comm.; Institute of Chartered Accountancy, ACA; *single;* joined Price Waterhouse (now PriceWaterhouse Coopers), working in Audit Department, 1986-89, San Francisco Office, 1989-90, Corporate Finance, 1990-91; joined Mount Juliet, Director of Golf, 1991-94, Director of Sales and Marketing,1994-97, Director of Sales, Marketing and Golf, Mount Juliet, 1997 to date; International Golfer, played on Ladies Senior Team 1984, '85 and '86. Hobbies, travel and sports (particularly golf). Contact: Mount Juliet, Thomastown, Co. Kilkenny. Tel: 056 73000. Fax: 056 73009.

MacCANN, Peter Michael; GENERAL MANAGER MERRION HOTEL; *b* 1961; *educ* Clongowes Wood College; *m* Dorothy Whelan; 2*s*; trained in Hotel Management with Fitzpatrick's Hotels, Killiney and Shannon 1980-84; Trust House Forte (UK) 1984-90; Food and Beverage Manager, Conrad Hotel, Dublin 1990-94; General Manager, Sheen Falls Lodge, Kenmare 1994-96; General Manager, Merrion Hotel, Dublin 1996 to date; member, Academie de Champagne, Irish Hotel Federation, Fellow of the Irish Hotel and Catering Institute, RDS, Irish Georgian Society, Milltown GC, Headfort GC (Meath), Lansdowne RFC; a dedicated and experienced hotelier with exceptionally high standards. Hobbies, wine, golf and carpentry. Contact: The Merrion Hotel, 21-24 Upper Merrion Street, Dublin 2. Tel: 01 603 0600.

MacCANN, Peter Michael

MacCARTHY, James Martin Anthony "Jimmy"; SINGER/SONGWRITER; *b* 1953; *educ* Christian Brother's College, Cork; *single;* trainee trainer with Vincent O'Brien, 1968-70; apprentice Jockey with Billy O'Gorman, 1970-72; with Fergy Sutherland, 1973-74; Blarney Riding School, Joe O'Reilly, 1974-75; professional musician, 1975 to date; albums include: *The Song of the Singing Horseman* (Mulligan Records), 1990; *The Dreamer,* (Sony Records), 1994; *Warmer for the Spark* (Dara Records); compositions include *Ride On, No Frontiers, Katie, Bright Blue Rose,* and *Ancient Rain;* writer member, I.M.R.O., also Board of Directors; recipient, Smithwicks/*Hot Press* Song Writer of the Year, 1995. Hobbies, horse riding, health and holistic healing, Alexander Technique, I Ching. Contact: Pat Egan Management, Merchants Court, 24 Merchants Quay, Dublin 2. Tel: 01

679 8572.

MacCARTHY-MORROGH, Keith; DIRECTOR FINDLATER WINE MERCHANTS LTD.; *b* 1944; *educ* St. Gerards, Bray; Downside, UK; Trinity College Dublin; London Business School; *m* Rosemary Affleck-Graves; 2*s* 2 *da;* joined James J. Murphy (Brewers), 1969-70; Marketing Director, Gilbeys of Ireland, 1970-80; Deputy Chairman, R&A Bailey, 1980-93; Joint Managing Director, Findlaters Wine Merchants Ltd., 1993 to date; Fellow, Marketing Institute; Vice Chairman, Wine & Spirit Association; member, Royal St. George Yacht Club; other biographical listings include *Burkes Landed Gentry* (1957), *Burkes Irish Family Records* (1978). Hobby, sailing. Contact: Findlater Wine Merchants Ltd., Harcourt Street Vaults, Harcourt Street, Dublin 2. Tel: 01 475 1699. Fax: 01 475 2530.

MacCARTHY, James

MacCONGHAIL, Fiach; ARTISTIC DIRECTOR PROJECT ARTS CENTRE DUBLIN; *b* 1964; *educ* Colàiste Eoin, Stillorgan; Trinity College Dublin, BA (Mod) Politics and Sociology; *m* Bríd Ní Neachtain; 2*da;* worked as Executive Producer with Joe Dowling, Maurice Cassidy and Michael Colgan at the Gaiety Theatre, 1989; Assistant to Noel Pearson, Artistic Director, Abbey Theatre, 1989-91; Project Arts Centre, 1992 to date; Producer of two short films by Paul Mercier, *Before I Sleep* (1997) starring Brendan Gleeson, *Lipservice* (1998), starring Sean McGinley; both won prestigious awards and were shown on TV; member, National Theatre, (Abbey), Trycycle Theatre (London), Firestation Artists Studio, Brother Films; awards for films include Best Debut Film for *Before I Sleep,* Cork, 1998; Best Film Award Celtic Festival, *Lipservice,* 1999; a lively personality on the Art scene; some would see him as a future Minister of the Arts. Hobby, football, season ticket holder Queens Park Rangers. Contact: Project Arts Centre, 39 East Essex St. Temple Bar, Dublin 2. Tel: 01 679 6622.

MacDOUGALD, Suzanne

MacDOUGALD, Suzanne Mary; ART DEALER, ART GALLERY OWNER; *b* 1945; *educ* Alexandra College Dublin; *m* Kamraw Fazel; 1 *s*; (*m dis*); formerly leading Irish model and television hostess; opened Lad Lane Gallery, Dublin 1974-81; Managing Director, Solomon Gallery, Dublin since 1981; one of the leading contemporary art galleries in the city (also deals in 19th and 20th century Irish art); art consultant to corporate bodies; Chairperson, Contemporary Art Gallery Association. Hobbies, equestrian sports, gardening, interior design. Contact: Solomon Gallery, Powerscourt Townhouse Centre, Dublin 2. Tel: 01 679 4237.

MacGINTY, Colm; EDITOR SUNDAY WORLD; *b* 1951; *educ* Coole NS, Co. Westmeath; St. Mary's College Mullingar; Dublin Institute of Technology, Bolton Street; *m* Philippa Kidd; 1 *da;* Sub-editor, *Sunday Journal,* 1980-82; Sub-editor, *Evening Herald,* 1982-84; Features Editor, *Evening Herald,* 1984-89; Deputy Editor, *The Star,* 1989-92; Deputy Editor, *Sunday Independent,* 1992-94; Editor, *Sunday World,* 1994 to date. Hobbies, sports, Arts. Contact: Sunday World, 18 Rathfarnham Road, Dublin 16. Tel: 01 490 1980. Fax: 01 490 1838.

MacGONIGAL, Ciarán; MUSEUM DIRECTOR; *b* 1945; *educ* Catholic University School, Dublin; University College Dublin; University of Florence; National College of Art, Dublin; *single*; Lecturer, Municipal Gallery, Dublin, 1971-79; Director, Grafton Gallery, Dublin, 1983-92; Director, RHA Gallagher Gallery, 1992-98; Executive Director, Hunt Museum, Limerick, 1998 to date; Chairman, Art Advisory Committee, Dublin Corporation, 1980-87, 1988-91; Board member, National Gallery of Ireland, 1989 to date; member of the Arts Council, 1983-98; member of Stamp Design Committee - An Post, 1985 to date; member of Committee of EV+A, 1998 to date; Board member, Daghdhda Dance Company, University of Limerick, 1999 to date; contributor to lexicons and Art Journals and Art Critic with *Irish Independent* and *Irish Times;* member, Irish Art Critics Association; Irish Museums Association; Life member, Friends of the National Collections of Ireland. A networker *extraordinaire,* knowledgeable about every ripple in the Irish Art World. Hobbies, equestrian sports, tennis, fencing and gardening. Contact: Hunt Museum, Customs House, Rutland Street, Limerick. Tel: 061 312 833.

MACKEOWN, Hugh N.

MACKEOWN, Hugh N.; CHAIRMAN MUSGRAVE LTD.; *b* 1941; *educ* Radley College; Trinity College Dublin, BA; *m* Heather Thompson; 4 *s*; Director, (Distribution), Musgrave Ltd., 1967-71; Managing Director, 1971-96; Chairman, Musgrave Ltd. (a wholesale grocery company which ranks among the top twenty five companies in the State), 1996 to date; Fellow, Irish Management Institute. Hobbies, golf and sailing; Clubs, Cork Golf Club, Royal Cork Yacht Club, Portmarnock Golf Club. Contact: Musgrave Ltd., Group Head Office, Ballycurreen Airport Road, Cork. Tel: 021 963 700. Fax: 021 966 167

MacKERNAN, Padraic Nicholas; SECRETARY GENERAL DEPARTMENT OF FOREIGN AFFAIRS; *b* 1940; *educ* National University of Ireland, BA, MA; University of Paris; *m* Caitriona Gavin; 3*s*; Third Secretary, Department of Foreign Affairs, 1964; Vice Consul, Boston, 1965; Deputy Consul General, New York, 1968; Member Delegation of Ireland to the UN General Assembly,

1968-74; Counsellor Political Desk, Department of Foreign Affairs, Dublin, 1974; Assistant Secretary, Department of Foreign Affairs, 1980; Ambassador of Ireland to USA and Mexico, 1985-91; Permanent Representative of Ireland to EU, Brussels, 1991-95; Secretary General, Department of Foreign Affairs, 1995 to date. Contact: Secretary General's Office, Department of Foreign Affairs, St. Stephen's Green, Dublin 2. Tel: 01 478 0543. Fax: 01 478 5948.

MacLAUCHLAN, Julia; DIRECTOR EUROPEAN PRODUCT DEVELOPMENT CENTRE MICROSOFT; b 1956; educ University of New Brunswick, BA; University of Ottowa, BEd.; m Warren McKenzie; 1s; High School Teacher, 1979-84; Director of Educational Products, Wordware Publishing, (Texas), 1984-87; Editing Manager, Microsoft (USA), 1987-88, User Education Manager, Analysis Business Unit Microsoft (USA), 1988-89; User Education Manager, Office Business Unit Microsoft (USA), 1989-91; OE & International Manager, Workgroup Division Microsoft (USA), 1991-93; Product Unit Manager, Workgroup Division Microsoft (Ireland), 1993-95; Director, EPDC Microsoft, 1995 to date; creative works include, The Prentice-Hall Apprentice Series – 'WordStar; member, Institute of Directors, Canada Ireland Business Association. Hobbies, promoting opportunities for women in high tech, also, travel, sailing, skiing, and spending time with her son. Contact: Microsoft, South County Business Park, Leopardstown, Dublin 18. Tel: 01 706 6200.'

MacMENAMIN, Cecily Helena, née O'Brien; DIRECTOR BROWN THOMAS GROUP PLC; *b* 1941; *educ* Convent of the Holy Child, Killiney; Ling Physical Training College, Dublin; *m* Joseph MacMenamin, Developer; 2*da;* Sales Person and Stock Controller with Irene Gilbert, Dublin; Director, Donal Davies chain of fashion shops, UK and France, 1964-70; Fashion Buyer, Brown Thomas, 1970, Director and Designer Buyer, Brown Thomas Group plc, 1976 to date; fashion co-ordinator for Áras an Uachtaráin; recipient, Satzenbrau Buyer of the Year Award, 1991; member, UK Fashion Council; a fashion guru of discretion and style who dresses top Irish and international clients. Hobbies, cooking, gardening and reading. Contact: Brown Thomas Group plc, Grafton Street, Dublin 2. Tel: 01 605 6666.

MacSHARRY, Ray

MacSHARRY, Ray; COMPANY DIRECTOR, CHAIRMAN EIRCOM; *b* 1938; *educ* St. Vincents Ballicutranta and Marist Brothers National Schools; Summerhill College, Sligo; *m* Elaine Neilan; 3 *s*; 3 *da*; joined Sligo Junior Chamber of Commerce, 1966 (Past President); Member, Sligo County Council, Sligo Borough Council and Sligo Town Vocational Educational Committee, 1967-78; elected Fianna Fáil Dáil Deputy for Sligo-Leitrim, 1969-89; Minister of State, Department of Finance and Public Service, 1977-79; Minister for Agriculture, 1979-81; Tanaiste and Minister for Finance, 1982; Minister for Finance, 1987-88; Governor, European Investment Bank, 1982; MEP for Connaught/Ulster 1984-87; Member of the Commission of the European Communities with responsibility for Agriculture and Rural Development, 1989-93; recipient of *Business and Finance* Man of the Year; Marcora Prize (Italian), 1991; European of the Year, 1992; made Freeman of the Borough of Sligo, 1993; Awarded the Grand-Croix de l'Ordre de Leopold II by H.M. the King of the Belgians, 1993, an honorary doctorate by the National University of Ireland, 1994, an Honorary Doctorate of Economic Science by the University of Limerick, 1994; Elected Honorary President of the European Movement for 1998-99; Currently Chairman Bord Telecom Eireann, Director, Bank of Ireland Group plc, Jefferson Smurfit Group plc, Green Property plc and Ryanair. He is Chairman of London City Airport, Coillte Teoranta (The Irish Forestry Board) and the Irish Equine Centre. Contact: Beltra Consultants, 46 Upper Mount Street, Dublin 2. Tel: 01 676 2495. Fax: 01 676 2489.

MACKEY, Paul William; CHARTERED ACCOUNTANT; *b* 1941; *educ* Terenure College, Dublin; University College Dublin, BComm. *m* Lila Greene; 3*s* 1*da*; articled to Phillips Rooney & Co. (Dublin); joined family tyre distribution business, TAB Tyres & Batteries, 1965-70; established own practice, Mackay & Company, 1970, extended to Joy Mackay & Co., 1975-80; currently Mackay & Company are specialists in insolvency and company recovery; Board member, Telecom Eireann, National Credit Co. Ltd., Zoological Society and other private companies; Joint Hon. Treasurer and Trustee, Progressive Democrats; member, Fitzwilliam LTC, Hibernian United Services Club, Terenure College RFC, RDS. Hobbies, politics and sport. Contact: Gainsboro House, 24 Suffolk Street, Dublin 2. Tel: 01 671 7956. Fax: 01 671 3317.

MADDEN, Anne

MADDEN, Anne; ARTIST; of Irish and Anglo Chilean origin; *educ* Wychwood School Oxford; Chelsea School of Arts and Crafts, London; *m* Louis le Brocquy, Artist; 2 *s*; her work hangs in major international public and private collections, including Contemporary Art Society (London), Gulbenkian Foundation (Portugal), Arts Council (Ireland), Arts Council (UK), Hugh Lane Municipal Gallery of Modern Art (Dublin), Ulster Museum, J.H. Hirshhorn Foundation (Washington D.C.), Foundation Maeght (St. Paul, France), Musée d'Art Moderne de la Ville de Paris, Musée Picasso (Antibes); has exhibited with Leicester Galleries, London, the Dawson, Taylor and Kerlin Galleries (Dublin), Gimpel Weitzenhoffer Gallery (New York) 1970, Ulster Museum 1974, Gallery Maeght (Barcelona), Armstrong Gallery (New York), Galerie Jeanne Bucher (Paris), Foundation Maeght, 1983; New Arts Centre (London), 1970-90; major Retrospective at the RHA Gallagher Gallery

(Dublin) 1991; Galerie Maeght, Paris, 1996, *Imaginaire Irlandais*; Hugh Lane Municipal Gallery of Modern Art, Dublin, 1997; Butler Gallery, Kilkenny, 1998; Chateau de Carros 1998; Publications include: *Louis le Brocquy: Seeing His Way*, 1993. Contact: Taylor Galleries, 16 Kildare Street, Dublin 2. Tel: 01 676 6055.

MADDEN, Bernadette; PAINTER; *b* 1948; *educ* Maryfield College Dublin; National College of Art and Design, Diploma in Painting; set up own studio and gallery space in Dublin, 1969; graduated NCAD, Dublin, 1970; thirty-five solo exhibitions in Ireland, UK, USA and Australia, 1972-99; took part in group shows in Ireland, UK, USA and Australia, 1972-1999; Batik paintings in collections of Arts Council, Department of Defence, Office of Public Works, Ulster Museum, Aer Lingus, Shannon Airport, Guardian / PMPA Insurances, Anglo-Irish Bank, Coca-Cola, John Carroll University Ohio, Bank of Ireland, ESB, National Museum, Aer Rianta, All Hallows College; member Arts Club, RDS (member Arts Committee, 1995-97); Awards: Dept. of Education Scholarship to Paris, 1970; MacAuley Fellowship (Arts Council), 1976; Mont Kavanagh Award (nominated) 1980; Mont Kavanagh Award (Commended) 1983; Dublin Diocese Church Art Awards (commended), 1983; Board Member, NCAD, 1984-87, Crafts Council of Ireland, 1994-97; Member, Cultural Relations Committee, Department of Foreign Affairs, 1998 to present. Regarded as a leader in her field as an Art consultant / buyer for commercial companies. Plays an influential role in the Visual Arts in Ireland. Hobbies, reading, music, gardening. Contact: The Studio, Haddington Road, Dublin 4. Tel: 01 668 6874.

MADIGAN, Patrick 'Paddy'; PUBLICAN; *b* 1936; *educ* Belvedere College, Dublin; m Patricia Roberts; 2*s* 1*da*; joined family licensed Vintners business (established 1918); currently Managing Director, Madigan Group which controls the chain of Madigan and Mooney public houses and restaurants; Director, Le Coq Sportif (leisure wear from France); Council member, Licensed Vintners Association; former President, Leinster Branch IRFU and former President, Irish Rugby Football Union. A bluff genial businessman, a keen rugby supporter. Hobbies, tennis and golf. Contact: Madigan Group, 32 Merrion Road, Dublin 4. Tel: 01 660 4199.

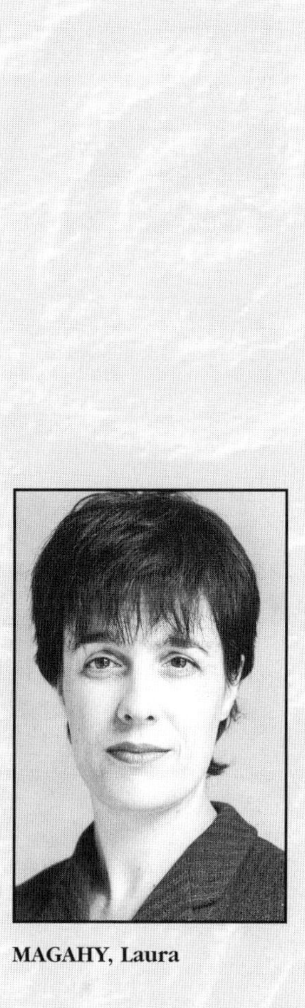

MAGAHY, Laura

MAGAHY, Laura; CHIEF EXECUTIVE TEMPLE BAR PROPERTIES LTD., *b* 1961; *educ* Regina Mundi College Cork; University College Cork, BA; Trinity College Dublin, MBA; *m* Ciaran Manning; 1*s* 1 *da;* Teacher, Berlin & Avignon, 1981-84; Founder Administrator, Graffiti Theatre Company, 1984-87; Financial Controller, Irish Film Institute, 1988-90; Producer, Ashling Films; Chief Executive, Irish Film Institute, 1990-93; Chief Executive, Temple Bar Properties, 1993 to date; was responsible for the rejuvenation of Temple Bar, a project in the Public/Private sector; Chairperson, Screen Training Ireland; Board member, Screen Commission, 1993-98, C.I.E., 1995-98, Dublin Chamber of Commerce; Honorary member, Royal Institute of Architects; Board member, Institute of Directors in Ireland. Regarded as a successful and singleminded property developer and administrator with a bright future, possibly in Europe. Hobbies, music, film, work. Contact: Temple Bar Properties, 18 Eustace Street, Dublin 2. Tel: 01 677 2255. Fax: 01 677 2525.

MAGAN, Michael James "Mike"; DAIRY FARMER; *b* 1953; *educ* Ballyleague Secondary School; Warrenstown Agricultural College, Hons Cert in Agriculture; *m* Mary Beirne; 3*s* 3 *da;* Owner/Manager, Dairy Farm, 1971 to date; involved in Consultancy work for the past ten years for various leading agricultural companies; regular contributor to *Irish Farmers Journal* and other farming publications; Past President, Irish Grassland Association, 1994; Executive Council member of Irish Friesian Breeders Council; Director, Board of Agri Aware; member, Dairy Advisory Committee of Irish Cattle Breeding Federation; member, National Dairy Committee; Board Member, Ardagh College, Longford; Past Chairman, European Dairy Farmers Irish Branch; Regional Award Winner of Irish Dairy Farmer of the Year, 1983, 1984; Best Breeder National Winner, 1994; Runner up in the Upjohn National Quality Milk Awards. Hobbies, sports, travel, speaking to farming groups. Contact: Tel: 043 41345. Fax: 043 46122.

MAGNIER, John; BLOODSTOCK BREEDER; *b* 1948; *educ* Glenstal Abbey, Co. Limerick; *m* Susan O'Brien, daughter of renowned trainer, Vincent O'Brien; 3*s* 2 *da;* comes from a racing background, nephew of trainer Clem Magnier; acquired first stud farm in the early 70s, now runs from base at Coolmore, one of the largest stallion stations operations worldwide with studs in the US (Ashford), Australia (Coolmore) and a move into China is on the cards; stallions standing at Coolmore (joint owner Vincent O'Brien) include, *Alzao, Be My Guest, Bigstone, Danehill, Desert King, Dr Devious, Entrepreneur, Fairy King, Grand Lodge, Lake Coniston, Night Shift, Peintre Celebre, Sadler's Wells, Tamarisk, Tale of the Cat;* the dominant force in thoroughbred breeding worldwide. Contact: Coolmore Stud Farm, Fethard, Co. Tipperary. Tel: 052 31298. Fax: 052 31382.

MAGUIRE, Conor J.; BARRISTER / CHAIRMAN BROADCASTING COMMISSION OF IRELAND; *b* 1946; *educ* National School, Claremorris; Clongowes Wood College, Co. Kildare; University

MAHER, Alice

MAHONY, John

MALONEY, Barry J

College Dublin, BCL; Kings Inns, BL; *m* Louisa MacAllister; 2 *s* 2 *da*; called to the Bar, 1971; Junior Counsel, Western Circuit; called to the Inner Bar, 1984 and to the Middle Temple (London); has a wide general practice; Chairman, Broadcasting Commission of Ireland (formerly Independent Radio Television Commission); member, Galway County Club. Hobbies, theatre, travel, cooking, wine and current affairs. Contact: The Law Library, PO Box 2424, Four Courts, Dublin 7. Tel: 01 872 0622. Fax: 01 872 0455.

MAHER, Alice; VISUAL ARTIST; *b* 1956; *educ* University of Limerick; Crawford College of Art; University of Ulster, MA Fine Arts; San Francisco Art Institute; *single*. Exhibitions include: 'Familiar' at Douglas Hyde Gallery, Dublin, 1995; 'Swimmers" at le Crédac; Paris, 1996; 'Coma Berenices' at Hugh Lane Municipal Gallery, Dublin, 1999. Represented Ireland at the Sao Paolo Biennale in 1994; nominated for Glen Dimplex award in 1996. Book covers include *Are you Somebody?* (Nuala O'Faolain) and *Greetings to our Friends in Brazil* (Paul Durcan); has also worked in collaboration with composer Trevor Knight on the performance of *The Sky Chair*, 1998. Member of Aosdána. Contact: Aosdána, 70 Merrion Square, Dublin 2. Tel: 01 661 1840. Fax: 01 676 1302.

MAHONY, Edmond; CHAIRMAN TATTERSALLS; *b* 1960; *educ* Headfort, Downside; *m* Fiona Watt; 1 *s* 1 *da*; Bloodstock Clerk, Tattersalls (U.K.), 1981-88; Director, Tattersalls (Ireland), 1988-93; Director Tattersalls (U.K.), 1989-93; Managing Director, Tattersalls (Ireland), 1991 to date; Chairman, Tattersalls (U.K.), 1993 to date; Chairman, Tattersalls (Ireland), 1999 to date. Hobby, hunting. Contact: Tattersalls Ltd., Terrace House, Newmarket, Suffolk. Tel: 01 638 665931. Fax: 01 638 660850.

MAHONY, John; CHAIRMAN EDELMAN IRELAND, MANAGING DIRECTOR EDELMAN U.K.; *b* 1962; *educ* Kilkenny Vocational School; Rathmines College of Commerce; Post graduate studies in Marketing, Television and Radio Broadcasting; *partner;* worked in Public Affairs, PR in Australia before returning to London where he specialised in corporate PR at Paragon Communications; joined John McMahon & Partners, became a director on the board of the merged McMahon Sheedy Communications; joined Edelman Public Relations as Managing Director, recently appointed Chairman, Edelman Ireland and Managing Director, Edelman U.K.; awards include commended in 1990 PR Week for Best Media Campaign and Best Use of Research in the U.K., Cothu Award, for the best sponsorship of a single Arts Project 1997, Edelman Dublin won Office of the Year, 1998. Hobbies, travel, current affairs, theatre, modern art, furniture and design. Contact: Edelman Public Relations, Huguenot House, 35-38 St. Stephen's Green, Dublin 2. Tel: 01 678 9333. Fax: 01 661 4408.

MALONE, John Christopher; SECRETARY GENERAL DEPARTMENT OF AGRICULTURE AND FOOD; *b* 1951; *educ* St. Flannan's College; University College Dublin, BA; *m* Mary Boyle; 2*s* 3 *da;* Principal Officer, 1984-88; Assistant Secretary, 1988-97; Secretary General, Department of Agriculture, 1997; member, Lansdowne RFC. Hobbies, sport and gardening. Contact: Agriculture House, Kildare Street, Dublin 2. Tel: 01 607 2184. Fax: 01 662 1739.

MALONE, Peter Gerard; MANAGING DIRECTOR JURYS HOTEL GROUP PLC; *b* 1944; *educ* St. Mary's College Dundalk; Shannon College of Hotel Management, Dip Hotel Mgmt; *m* Mary Brassil; 3 *da*; General Manager, Jurys Hotel Cork, 1979-88; General Manager Jurys Hotel Dublin, 1988-89; Managing Director Jurys Hotel Group plc 1989 to date; publications include six editions, Cork Chamber of Commerce magazine (1977); Fellow Irish Hotel and Catering Institute, Eisenhower Exchange Fellow (1989); Past President, Irish Hotels Federation; Member, Review Body on Higher Remuneration in the Public Sector, National Minimum Wage Committee; Director, Shannon College of Hotel Management, Hibernian Group plc, Irish Heart Foundation, Irish Brain Research Foundation. Hobbies, travel, all sports and walking. Contact: Jury's Hotel Group plc., 146 Pembroke Road, Dublin 4. Tel: 01 607 0070. Fax: 01 660 5728.

MALONEY, Barry J.; CHIEF EXECUTIVE ESAT DIGIFONE LTD.; *b* 1959; *educ* Newbridge College; University College Dublin, BA Econ and Politics; International Advanced Management Programme, IMD, Switzerland; *m* Aileen ----; 3 *da;* Graduate Trainee, Becton Dickinson Ireland, 1980-85; Administration and Logistics Manager, Digital Ireland, 1985-88; European Director, Software Business and Vice President, Components and Peripherals, Business Unit (both in Geneva, Switzerland); Corporate Vice President Channel Operations, Xerox (San Fransisco, USA), 1994-96; Chief Executive, Esat Digifone Ltd., 1996 to date; member, Institute of Directors; Phoenix Racing Club, Wanderers RFC, RDS, Westport Golf Club, Board of Junior Achievement, Hibernian Golf Club. Hobbies, rugby, soccer, golf, running and music. Contact: Esat Digifone, 70 Lower Baggot Street, Dublin 3. Tel: 01 609 5000. Fax: 01 609 5010.

MANAHAN, Anna Maria; ACTRESS; *educ* Convent of Mercy, Waterford; *widowed;* studied under Ria Mooney, Gaiety School of Acting; has worked with all major companies; highlights include *The Rose Tattoo, Bloomsday, Lovers* (also London & Broadway, Tony nomination), *The Plough and the Stars, Live Like Pigs, The Leenane Trilogy* (also London & Sydney), *The Loves of Cass Maguire, The Shaughran;* TV and films include: *The Riordains, Leave it to Mrs O'Brien, The Irish RM, The Bill, Lovejoy, Blind Justice, A Man of No Importance;* John B Keane wrote *Big Maggie* for her; Founder Member of Play Circle (Playwrights Work Shop), member, ADA (Association of Drama Adjudicators); Lecturer in Drama; recipient Tony Award, 1998; Tony Nomination, 1968; voted Best Actress, (Ireland) four times; Olivier Award Nomination, 1977; Eire Society of Boston Gold Medal, 1984. Regarded as Ireland's finest character actress. Hobbies, reading, music and cooking. Contact: Maureen McGlynn, First Call, 29-30 Dawson Street, Dublin 2. Tel: 01 679 8401.

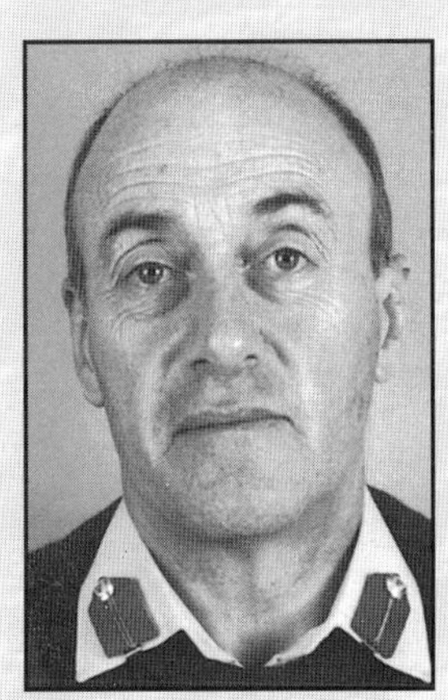
MANGAN, Colm Enri

MANGAN, Colm Enri; DEPUTY CHIEF OF STAFF (SUPPORT) DEFENCE FORCES; *b* 1941; *educ* Rockwell College; Cadet School; Defence Forces Command & Staff School; Fuhrungsakademie der Bundeswehr, Hamburg; *m*; 3*s;* Commissioned in the Defence Forces, 1961, Captain, 1968, Commandant, 1977, Lieutenant Colonel, 1989, Colonel, 1993, Brigadier General, 1995, Major General, 1998; served overseas in Cyprus, 1964 & 1968, Syria, 1972-74; Lebanon, 1985, 1990-91 and Yugoslavia, 1991-92; articles and reviews published in the *Irish Sword, An Cosantoir,* national newspapers and international defence and security publications; winner of the inaugural Seamus O'Kelly Award for a military paper in *An Cosantoir,* 1987; medals include, ECMM 1992, UN Peacekeeping 1990; UNIFIL 1985; Service Medal 1983; UNTSO, 1973; UNDOF, 1974; UNFICYP, 1964; member, Military History Society of Ireland, Royal United Services Institute, Newbridge Rugby Club and Curragh Golf Club. Hobbies, military history, drama, rugby and golf. Contact: Defence Forces Headquarters, Parkgate, Dublin 8. Tel: 01 804 2686. Fax: 01 677 9018.

MANGAN, Mary, née O'Neill; MD POSTGEM / IRELAND–ON–LINE; *b* 1959; *educ* in Kildare; University College Dublin, BSc.; *m* Philip Mangan; 1*da* has been employed in IT and Communications for the past seventeen years; Marketing Representative, IBM, 1984-87; Sales and Marketing Manager for Ireland, Hewlett Packard, 1987-91, where their major sales included, Dept. of Defence, Beaumont Hospital, Dept. of Education, also development of the re-seller channel for PC and peripheral products; Marketing Manager, ICL Ireland, 1991-96; Business Development Manager, AT&T in UK, 1996-98; Managing Director, PostGEM and Ireland-on-Line, 1998 to date; Board Director of both companies reporting directly to An Post Board; member, Blessington Sailing Club, Tulfarris Country Club. Hobbies, hillwalking, horseriding, sailing, beginners golf and all music. Contact: PostGEM, Alexander House, Earlsfort Plaza, Earlsfort Terrace, Dublin 2. Tel: 01 676 8744. Fax: 01 676 8727.

MANNING, Maurice; ACADEMIC, POLITICIAN; *b* 1943; *educ* De La Salle School, Bagnelstown; Rockwell College, Co. Tipperary; University College Dublin; University of Strathclyde; *m* Isabelle de Saint-Ouen (*m dis*); *m* Mary Hayes; 1*s;* Senior Lecturer in Politics, University College Dublin, 1966 to date; member, Governing Authority, University College Dublin, 1977 to date, member, Senate of NUI, 1982 to date; former Chairman, Irish Association of European Studies; lectures extensively in U.S. and France; Visiting Professor at University of Paris, 1978; member, Seanad Eireann Cultural and Educational Panel, 1981-82, 1989 to date; currently, Leader of Fine Gael in the Seanad and Front Bench Spokesman on Northern Ireland; publications include, *The Blue Shirts, Irish Political Parties, Betrayal* (novel) Blackwater Press, 1997, *James Dillon: A Life,* Wolfhound 1999; numerous articles for international journals; one of the best informed members of the Oireachtas, close to Party Leader; a charismatic communicator. Hobbies, golf and following all sports. Contact: Seanad Eireann, Leinster House, Kildare Street, Dublin 2. Tel: 01 1890 732 623.

MANSERGH, Martin; SPECIAL ADVISER TO THE TAOISEACH; *b* 1946; *educ* Kings School, Canterbury; Christchurch, Oxford, MA, DPhil; *m* Elizabeth Young, Antique Carpet Restorer; 1*s* 4 *da*; entered the Civil Service, 1974; Department of Foreign Affairs, 1974-81; Embassy in Bonn, 1975-77; Energy Section, Headquarters, 1978-80; Principal Officer, Department of the Taoiseach, January-June 1981, December 1981-March 1982; Special Adviser to Taoisigh Charles Haughey, Albert Reynolds and Bertie Ahern since 1982; member of Fianna Fáil Party since 1981; Head of Research, Fianna Fáil in opposition; publications include: *The Spirit of the Nation* (editor), *The Collected Speeches of Charles J. Haughey, 1957-86,* and a number of published articles on the peace process and Irish history. Co-Winner of the 1994 Tipperary Peace Prize with Fr. Alex Reid and Rev. Roy Magee. Member of long established Tipperary family, retains interest in family farm; father, Nicholas Mansergh was author of *The Irish Question.* A powerful political force. Member of Council of Alexandra College, Board of Cashel Bolton Library. Contact: Office of the Taoiseach, Government Buildings, Dublin 2. Tel: 01 662 4888

MARA, Patrick "PJ"; PUBLIC RELATIONS CONSULTANT; *b* 1942; *educ* Colaiste Mhuire, Dublin; *m* Breda Brogan; 1*s*; Proprietor, Beeline Clothing Company, sold subsequently to Penneys; member, National Executive of the Fianna Fail Party 1981-84, also Vice-Chairman, National Organisation Committee of Fianna Fail; member, Seanad Eireann 1982; Press Secretary of the Fianna Fail Party, Government Press Secretary 1987-92; Director of Elections 1997; Public Relations Consultant / Lobbyist 1992 to date; clients include Independent News and Media and Elan Corporation; an astute media manipulator, thoroughly at home in the corridors of power; recognised as a genial companion and a true survivor. Contact: 0862 592520.

MARREN, Paul Vincent; SOLICITOR; *b* 1961; *educ* Rockwell College; Trinity College Dublin, BA (Mod) History; College of Commerce, DLS; Law Society, Cert. Applied European Law; *m* Isabel Foley; 1*s* 1 *da*; qualified 1989; joined family law firm founded by father Enda Marren (1958); Assistant Solicitor, Martin E. Marren & Co., 1989-96; Senior Partner, 1996 to date; member, Law Society of Ireland, Dublin Solicitor's Bar Association, Society of Young Solicitors of Ireland, (Chairman 1995-96), European Young Bar Association (Secretary & Corporate Affairs 1996-99). Hobbies, reading, fishing, golf, tennis, hill walking and local history. Contact: 10 Northumberland Road, Dublin 4. Tel: 01 668 6266. Fax: 01 668 6351.

MARRY, Jack; PIG BREEDER, PRODUCER; *b* 1945; *educ* Mell Primary School; Warrenstown College; *m* Rosemary Gogarty, former SRN SCH HV; 3*s* 3*da;* established own major pig production company with sow units in counties Meath and Louth. Hobbies, shooting and fishing on 1,200 acres overlooking River Boyne. Contact: Little Grange, Drogheda, Co. Louth. Tel: 041 24678.

MARTIN, Geoffrey; NEWSPAPER EDITOR; *b* 1953; *educ* Ballymena Boys School; *m* Sue Vasey; 1 *s* 3 *da*; Reporter, *Ballymena Guardian*, 1973-76; Reporter and Sports Editor, *Newbury Weekly News*, 1976-79; Sports Editor, *Berks & Bucks Observer Group*, 1979-83; Editor, Windsor & Ascot Observer, 1983-85; Editor In Chief, Berks & Bucks Observer Group, 1985-90; Editor, *Belfast News Letter*, 1990 to date; Awarded UK Press Gazette Journalist of the Year, 1993; Newspaper Society Features Writer of the Year, 1993; Editor of four Newspaper of the Year award winning publications; A regular contributor to BBC Radio & Television, RTE and Worldwide independent television and radio. Hobbies, sport, music, current affairs: 20 handicap golfer, lifelong supporter of Chelsea F.C., Enthusiast of life and times of Bob Dylan; Travelling in Central and Southern America; Ancient Civilisations; Political Biographies. Contact: Belfast News Letter, 44-56, Boucher Crescent, Belfast BT12 6QY. Tel: 0801 232 680000. Fax: 0801 232 664412.

MARTIN, John; ARMY OFFICER; *b* 1942; *educ* De La Salle Secondary School, Ballyshannon; NIHE, Dublin, BA (Hons); *m* Monica McCrossan; 3*s* 1*da;* served Western Command; Instructor in Military College, 1970-79; Staff Officer, Defence Forces Headquarters, 1980-82; School Commandant, The Cadet School, 1990-93; Executive Officer, Curragh Command, 1994-95; Director, Information Technology, 1995-96; General Officer commanding Western Command, 1996; overseas service includes UNFICYP (Cyprus), 1964-65 and 1972; UNIFUL (Lebanon), 1979 and 1993; UNGOMAP (Afghanistan/Pakistan), 1988-89; Vice President, Kilcullen GFC; member, Military History Society of Ireland; member, Old Athlone Society; Fellow of The Salzberg Seminar. Hobbies, Gaelic football, painting, theatre and military history. Contact: 4W BDE HQ, Custume Barracks, Athlone, Co. Westmeath. Tel: 0902 92631. Fax: 0902 94296.

MARTIN, Micheál

MARTIN, Micheál; MINISTER FOR EDUCATION AND SCIENCE; *b* 1960; *educ* Colàiste Chríst Rí, Cork; University College Cork, BA, HDE, MA Pol. History; son of former boxer, Paddy Martin he is a full time public representative and former teacher; elected to Dáil Eireann for the Cork South-Central Constituency, 1989; Former Chairman, Oireachtas All Party Committee on the Irish Language; former member of Dáil Committee on Crime; member of the Dáil Committee on Finance and General Affairs; Minister for Education and Science, 1997 to date; elected to Cork Corporation in 1985 and was elected Alderman in 1991; Lord Mayor of Cork 1992-93; former Chairman of Cork Corporation's Art Committee, former Chairman, Cork Vocation Education Committee; former member, Board of the College of Commerce, Cork; former member, Governing Body, University College Cork; Governing Body, Regional Technical College Cork, National Sculpture Factory, Cork; Board of the Everyman Palace Theatre, Cork; Board of Cork Opera House; Board of Crawford Gallery, Cork; Board of Graffiti Theatre, Cork; Association of Secondary Teachers Ireland; former Chairman Ogra Fianna Fáil, member of Commission on the Aims and Structures of Fianna Fáil; member, Fianna Fáil National Executive since 1988; member, Nemo Rangers Hurling & Football Club, Cork; winner, *Cork Examiner* Political Speaker of the Year Award, 1987; seen as effortlessly successful in education, telegenic, personable and single-minded; a future Taoiseach perhaps. Contact: Department of Education and Science, Marlborough Street, Dublin 1. Tel: 01 873 4700. Fax: 01 878 6712.

MASON, Patrick Damien Stuart; ARTISTIC DIRECTOR ABBEY THEATRE; *b* 1951; *educ* Downside School; Central School of Speech and Drama; London University, Diploma of Dramatic

Art; Central School, Diploma of Speech and Drama; Voice Coach, Abbey Theatre, 1972-73; Fellow in Drama, Manchester University, 1973-74, Lecturer in Performance Studies, 1974-77; Resident Director, Abbey Theatre, 1977-80; Freelance Director, Theatre and Opera, Ireland, UK and USA, 1980-94; Artistic Director, Abbey Theatre, 1994-99; edited the *The Way to Keep Him* Arthur Murphy; published Policy Documents of National Theatre Society, *A High Ambition,* 1994, *A Real Theatre,* 1995, *The National Theatre,* 1996, *Art and Culture,* 1998; member, Cultural Relations Committee, Department of Foreign Affairs; member, Council of National Cultural Institutions; awards include Harvey's Theatre Awards, Best Director, 1985, 1986, 1988; Edinburgh Fringe First, 1986; Tony Awards, Best Director, 1992; Olivier Awards - Nominations, 1992, 1999. Hobbies include piano playing, gardening and hill walking. Contact: Abbey Theatre, 26 Lower Abbey Street, Dublin 1. Tel: 01 874 8741. Fax: 01 874 6507.

MASTERSON, Patrick; PRESIDENT OF THE EUROPEAN UNIVERSITY INSTITUTE; *b* 1936; *educ* Belvedere College Dublin, Castleknock College; University College Dublin, BA, MA; Travelling Studentship in Philosophy from the National University of Ireland; University of Louvain, PhD; *m* Frances Lenehan; 1 *s* 3 *da*; Joined full time staff of Department of Metaphysics, University College Dublin, 1963; Appointed Professor in the Faculties of Arts, Philosophy and Sociology, University College Dublin, 1972; Dean, Faculty of Philosophy and Sociology, University College Dublin, 1980-83; Registrar, University College Dublin, 1983-86; President, University College Dublin, 1986-93; Vice-Chancellor, National University of Ireland, 1987 and 1988; President of the European University Institute, Florence, 1994 to date; Publications include: *Atheism and Alienation: A Study of the Philosophical Sources of Contemporary Atheism,* Dublin 1971 (also London, Notre Dame, Kyoto); numerous articles in Philosophical collections and journals; Member: Royal Irish Academy, Lisbon Academy of Sciences, League of World Universities; Awarded Doctor Honoris Causa, University of Caen, Doctor Honoris Causa, Trinity College Dublin; Grande Oficial de Ordem de Mérito da República Portuguesa; Grande Ufficiale della Repubblica Italiana; Doctor Honoris Causa, New York University; An exceptional academic; an able administrator and cautious tactician; a gifted communicator who shines gently on the international academic stage; Hobbies, international affairs, reading, fishing, the company of friends. Contact: European University Institute, Badia Fiesole, Florence, Italy.

MAUGHAN, Gemma

MAUGHAN, Gemma Attilia, née Saccenda; DIRECTOR OF GOWAN GROUP AND SUBSIDIARY COMPANIES; *b* 1940; *educ* Graduated in Lausanne, Switzerland at the École Hotelière de la Societ Suisse des Hoteliérs; *m* Con Smith (*decd.*); 4 *da; m* Michael Maughan; Appointed Director of family controlled distribution group and joined main board of Gowan Group Ltd., 1977; Member R.I.A.C.; Awarded, Honour of Officier de L'Ordre National du Merite by President Mitterand of France, 1992. Hobbies, art, travel, gardening, walking. Contact: Gowan Group, 1 Herbert Avenue, Dublin 4. Tel: 01 260 1677. Fax: 01 260 1672.

MAUGHAN, Matthew Michael; CHAIRMAN, GOWAN GROUP LTD AND DIRECTOR SUBSIDIARY COMPANIES; *b* 1938; *educ* Clongowes Wood College, College of Commerce, Rathmines; *m* Gemma Smith; 4 *step da*; Domas Advertising, 1957-65; Acquired and managed Wilson Hartnell & Co. which became Ogilvy & Mather Group Ltd., 1965, currently President; Appointed Chairman of Gowan Group, Ltd., a family owned distribution company, and Director of all its subsidiaries, 1993 to date; Member, Publicity Club of Ireland, President,1993-96; Fellow, I.A.P.I.; Member, Marketing Institute; Fellow, Institute of Directors; Member, Cothu, I.M.I.; Clubs, Milltown Golf Club, Fitzwilliam Lawn Tennis Club, Royal Irish Yacht Club, R.I.A.C., R.D.S.; Awarded Ogilvy Eagle by Ogilvy & Mather Worldwide Board, 1988; Listed in *Who's Who International*; *Men of Achievement Annual,* 1990; *Success* 1983: *The People Who Run Ireland*; *Irish Management* 1990 - Management profile. Hobbies, art, antiques, gardening, golf, reading. Contact: Gowan Group, 1 Herbert Avenue. Tel: 01 260 1677. Fax: 01 260 1672.

McALEESE, Mary

McALEESE, Mary, née Leneghan; PRESIDENT OF IRELAND; *b* 1951; *educ* St. Dominic's High School, Falls Road, Belfast; The Queen's University Belfast, LLB (Hons); The Inn of Court of Northern Ireland; Trinity College Dublin, MA; The Institute of Linguists, Diploma in Spanish; *m* Martin McAleese; 1*s* 2*da;* Barrister-at-Law of the Inn of Court of Northern Ireland; Barrister-at-Law of the Honourable Society of King's Inns, Dublin; appointed Reid Professor of Criminal Law, Criminology and Penology in Trinity College Dublin, 1975-79 and 1981-87; joined RTE as current affairs journalist and presenter, 1979-81, continued as part-time presenter until 1985; Director of the Institute of Professional Legal Studies at the Queen's University of Belfast, 1987-97; Pro Vice Chancellor of the Queen's University of Belfast, 1994-97; elected President of Ireland, 1997; Member, Institute of Linguists (London), Fellow, Royal Society of Arts, LLD (Hon NUI, University of Nottingham, Victoria University of Technology, Aust., St. Mary's University, Halifax, Queen's University Belfast), Honorary Bencher (King's Inns), Honorary Fellow (Institute of Engineers of Ireland, TCD, Royal College of Surgeons, College of Anaesthetists, Liverpool John Moore's University); member, European Bar Association, International Bar Association (Northern Ireland

Rapporteur), Inns of Court Northern Ireland, King's Inns Dublin; recognised as having a distinguished legal mind, has brought a very different kind of energy and equally strong personality into what may have been regarded as a formal and more remote Presidency. Contact: Áras an Uachtaráin, The Phoenix Park, Dublin 8. Tel: 01 677 2815. Fax: 01 671 0529.

McALINDEN, Cormac

McALINDEN, Cormac Damien; EXECUTIVE CHAIRMAN THE LITHOGRAPHIC GROUP; *b* 1948; *educ* Franciscan College, Gormanston; University College Dublin, BA, B.Comm. Married to Geraldine Collins 2 *s* 1 *da;* Worked in Chemical Bank, New York; Wells Fargo Bank, San Francisco; returned to Ireland to run Lithographic Universal Limited, Bray, printing business; launched Lithoset Limited, Mac Publishing Limited, Core Director Marketing Limited. Currently Executive Chairman of The Lithographic Group. Hobbies; sailing, golf, rugby and socialising. Contact: The Lithographic Group, Bray Business Park, Bray, Co. Wicklow. Tel: 01 282 9001. Fax: 01 276 1893

McART, Patrick Francis; GROUP EDITOR DERRY JOURNAL NEWSPAPERS; *b* 1953; *educ* University of Ulster, MA Media, Culture & Society; Post Grad. Dip; *m* Rosemary McLaughlin; 3*s*; Journalist with *Derry People* and *Donegal News*, 1974-1980; Journalist, Sub Editor, RTE, 1980-81; Editor, *Derry Journal,* 1982-96, Group Editor, 1996 to date; Executive Editor *Irish Almanac & Yearbook of Facts,* 1996-99; ran London Marathon in 1989 and in the process helped to raise £35,000 for Foyle Hospice in Derry. Hobbies, travel, politics, reading and consuming pints of Guinness. Contact: Derry Journal, Buncrana Road, Derry. Tel: 080 1504 272 200. Fax: 080 1504 272 218.

McCANN, Carl Patrick

McBENNETT, Michael; FARMER, PROPERTY INTERESTS; *b* 1944; *educ* CBS Synge St.; Dominican College Newbridge; Warrenstown Agricultural College, National Agricultural Cert; *m* Mary Dunne; 2*s* 1 *da;* President, Irish Tillage & Land Use Society, 1984-85; Chairman, National Grain Committee, IFA, 1985-90; National Treasurer, IFA, 1990-94, Honorary Secretary/Returning Officer, IFA, 1994-97; Chairman, Cereals Committee, COPA/COGECA, Brussels, 1991-97; member, Cereals Advisory Committee of EU, 1985-97, EU Operational Committee for Dublin Region; Chairman, Newcastle-Lyons Rural Development Association; President, Irish Bioenergy Association (IeBA); Director, FBDT Trust Co.; Board member, National Farm IT Centre (Warrenstown); Board member, former Chairman, Agri Awareness Trust; Board member, PRO, Rural Dublin Leader Co. Hobbies, trying to keep fit, boating on the Shannon, shooting, skiing. Contact: Fax: 01 458 0154.

McCANN, David

McCAGUE, Sean; PRINCIPAL TEACHER, PRESIDENT ELECT GAA; *b* 1945; *educ* Secondary School, Ballybourney, Co. Cork; St. Patrick's College of Education, Drumcondra, Primary Teacher Graduate and Dip. Educational Management; m Bernie Connolly; 5da; Assistant Teacher, 1965-77, Principal Teacher, Scotstown, Co. Monaghan, 1977-81; Principal Teacher, Monaghan Town, 1981-99; Secretary, Chairman and Development Officer, Scotstown GAA Club; member, Ulster Council, Central Council GAA; Secretary Monaghan Co. Committee GAA; member, Management Committee GAA; Chairman, GAC, Games Development, Policy & Planning GAA; awards include, *Irish Press* Manager of the Month, April 1985, VEC Monaghan Person of the Year, 1996; Re-hab Monaghan Hall of Fame Winner, 1999; Elected President – elect GAA, 1999; Team Manager, Scotstown GAA Teams; Team Manager, Monaghan County teams for ten years. Hobbies, walking, fishing, shooting, Irish Cultural Events and all sports. Contact: Cumann Lúthchleas Gael, Páirc an Chrócaigh, Baile Atha Cliath 3. Tel: 01 836 3222. Fax: 01 836 6420.

McCANN, Carl Patrick; VICE CHAIRMAN FYFFES PLC; *b* 1953; *educ* St. Mary's College, Dundalk; St. Vincent's College, Castleknock; Trinity College Dublin, BBS; member, Institute of Chartered Accountants; *m* Marion Dempsey; 2*s;* joined Fyffes plc, 1980, an Irish multinational company founded/acquired by father, Neil; currently Vice Chairman, Fyffes plc; member, Fitzwilliam LTC, Donnybrook TC. Hobbies, tennis and running. Contact: Fyffes plc, 1 Beresford Street, Dublin 7. Tel: 01 809 5555.

McCANN, Neil

McCANN, David; CHIEF EXECUTIVE FYFFES PLC; *b* 1958; *educ* University College Dublin; Blackhall Place BCL, Solicitor; *m* Adrienne O'Connor; 3*s* 1 *da;* practiced in two solicitor's firms, Daniel O'Connell & Sons (Dundalk); partner, Ivor Fitzpatrick & Co. (Dublin); joined family firm Fyffes plc; is currently Chief Executive; member, Law Society of Ireland; member, Fitzwilliam L.T.C.. Hobbies, golf and tennis. Contact: Fyffes plc, 1 Beresford Street, Dublin 7. Tel: 01 809 5555.

McCANN, Neil; CHAIRMAN FYFFES PLC; *b* 1924; *educ* Marist College, Dundalk; Castleknock College Dublin; *m* Mary Hughes; 5*s* 1 *da;* Founder, Fruit Importers of Ireland, acquired Fyffes (U.K.), 1987, now Fyffes plc; formerly Chief Executive, currently Chairman, Fyffes plc; Fyffes is one of the few multi national Irish companies, the leading fresh produce company in Europe, sourcing fruit, vegetables and flowers from over sixty-five countries around the globe; clubs, Fitzwilliam LTC, Dundalk RFC. Hobbies, golf and tennis. Contact: Fyffes plc, 1 Beresford Street,

Dublin 7. Tel: 01 809 5555.

McCANN, Patrick Anthony "Pat"; CHIEF EXECUTIVE DESIGNATE JURY'S HOTEL GROUP PLC; *b* 1951; *educ* Coláiste Mhuire, Ballymote, Co. Sligo; University of North London, H. N. D Bus. Studies; *m* Ann Doyle; 1 *s* 2 *da;* held various positions from Trainee Manager to General Manager, Ryan Hotel Group plc, 1969-89; General Manager, Jury's Hotel, Ballsbridge, 1989-93, Group General Manager, Jury's Hotel Group plc, 1993-94, Operations Director, 1994-98, Chief Executive Designate, 1998 to date; member, Irish Hotel and Catering Institute; Marketing Institute of Ireland; Past President, Irish Hotels Federation. Hobbies, all sports, walking, reading and travel. Contact: Jury's Hotel Group plc, 146 Pembroke Road, Ballsbridge, Dublin 4. Tel: 01 607 0070. Fax: 01 660 5728.

McCARTHY, Brian; CHIEF EXECUTIVE OFFICER FEXCO FINANCIAL SERVICES CENTRE; *b* 1944; *educ* Presentation College, Cork; *m* Mary Nagle; 2*s* 3 *da*; AIB Bank, progressed to Assistant Manager Level, 1962-81; set up FEXCO, 1981; FEXCO is a financial services company employing over 500 in Ireland and administering Prize Bonds, Gulliver InfoRes Services, VAT refund scheme, Bureau de Change, Stockbroking, Western Union Agent, Multicurrency Card Management Services and Data Processing; member, Cork University Foundation; awards include Excellence in Marketing - Sean Lemass Award 1987. Hobbies, reading, classical music, boating and fishing. Contact: FEXCO Financial Services Centre, Iveragh Road, Killorglin, Co. Kerry. Tel: 066 976 1258. Fax: 066 976 2011.

McCARTHY, Justine Mary

McCARTHY, Justine Mary; JOURNALIST; *b* 1959; *educ* Ursuline Convent, Blackrock, Cork; College of Commerce, Rathmines, Diploma in Journalism; *m* Denis Murnaghan; 1 *s*; journalist *Commercial Transport* trade magazine, 1979-80; *Irish Business* magazine, 1980-81; *Aspect* magazine, 1981-82; freelance, 1982-84; joined *Irish Independent*, 1984 to date, currently Chief Features Writer and Assistant to the Editor; member, National Union of Journalists; recipient, AT Cross Woman Journalist Award, News Features Category, 1986; AT Cross Woman Journalist of the Year, 1988; AT Cross National Media Awards, Campaigning and Social Issues Category, 1991, contributor to international newspapers and journals including *Washington Post, The European, The Guardian* and *The Observer*. Combines hard news stories and superb writing style. Hobbies, news and crosswords. Contact: Irish Independent, 90 Middle Abbey Street, Dublin 1. Tel: 01 705 5333.

McCARTHY, Kate (Catherine) Mary, née O'Connell; GENERAL MANAGER CBT SYSTEMS WORLDWIDE DEVELOPMENT CENTRE; *educ* Pembroke School, Dublin; University College Dublin, BEng; Trinity College Dublin, Dip.Comp.Prog; Dublin City University, Masters in Computer Applications; *m* Dan McCarthy; 2*s* 1 *da;* Resident Engineer with Local Authority, 1985-86; Computer Operations with GTech Corp, 1987-88; joined CBT Systems as a Courseware Developer, 1989, Project Manager, Head of Product Development, currently General Manager of the development centre which employs 350 people; CBT Group is a publicly quoted company employing over 1,400 people worldwide, manufacturing IT training software for the web; member, Westwood Sports and Fitness Club. Hobbies, family, travelling, walking, swimming and socialising. Contact: CBT Systems, Beech Hill, Clonskeagh, Dublin 4. Tel: 01 283 0077. Fax: 01 283 0379.

McCARTHY, Mick

McCARTHY, Mick; FOOTBALL MANAGER REPUBLIC OF IRELAND; *b* 1959; *educ* Worsbrough High School; *m* Fiona Morgan; 1*s* 2*da;* made League debut for Barnsley 1977, made 272 appearances with them; moved to Manchester City 1983; made Republic of Ireland debut 1984; joined Celtic 1987, won Scottish League and Cup Winners Medal 1987 and 1988; joined Lyon (France) 1989; transferred to Millwall 1990; played in all of Ireland's World Cup Matches until defeat in Italy in 1990; Player / Manager, Millwall 1991; won last of Republic's 57 caps in 2-0 victory over Portugal; appointed Republic of Ireland Manager (to succeed Jack Charlton) 1995; re-appointed 1997; has made a more than commendable job in the demanding task of replacing Jack Charlton. Hobbies, golf and gardening. Contact: F.A.I. 80 Merrion Square, Dublin 2. Tel: 01 676 6864.

McCAUGHEY, Gerard Vincent; MANAGING DIRECTOR OF CENTURY HOMES; *b* 1962; *educ* Dundalk RTC, National Certificate in Business Studies; University College Dublin, B.Comm; University College Cork, Dip. in Corporate Direction; D.I.T., Certificate in Growth Management; *single*; Marketing Director, Century Homes, 1990-95; Managing Director, Century Homes, 1995 to date; Awards include: Finalist, Entrepreneur of the Year Award, 1998; Special Award for Entrepreneurial Achievement from Irish Management Institute; Shortlisted, Cecil King Young Manager of the Year Award; Participant in Export Japan Study Program; Participant in EU Trade Deregulation Talks with Japanese Government; Member, Marketing Institute of Ireland, Institute of Directors. A modest start in timber frame homes has led to an ever increasing home-building business. Hobbies, watersports, travelling, further learning. Contact: Century Homes, Tullgrimes,

Monaghan. Tel: 047 81270. Fax: 047 84397

McCLOSKEY, Malachy; CHAIRMAN BOYNE VALLEY GROUP; *educ* Christian Brothers School, Drogheda; ; St. Patrick's College, Armagh; *m* Ann Greene; *6s*; Founder and Managing Director, Boyne Valley Foods; Chairman, Boyne Valley Group, 1997 to date; Boyne Valley includes Boyne Valley Foods Ltd., Irish Cereals Ltd., Lifeforce Foods Ltd., Lakeshore Foods Ltd., Kileen Steel Wools Ltd., Irish Breeze Ltd., Boyne Valley are the largest importers and distributors of honey and olive oil (under the Don Carlos label) in the country; an innovative and successful businessman noted for original publicity campaigns which focus on the Irish National treasures; publisher of Peter Harbison's scholarly *High Crosses;* awarded Supreme Arts Award for *Treasures of the National Library*; awarded Special Recognition Award at the Jefferson Smurfit/Ernst & Young Entrepreneur of the Year Awards. Hobbies, trees, restoration, 17th century Ireland, long distance adventure holidays. Contact: Boyne Valley Foods Ltd., Plantin Road, Drogheda, Co. Louth. Tel: 041 70300. Fax: 041 70339.

McCLOSKEY, Phelim; CHAIRMAN, CHIEF EXECUTIVE MOSNEY IRISH HOLIDAYS PLC; *b* 1945; educ Marist College, Dundalk; Shannon College Hotel Management, Dip Hotel Mgmt; Movenpick Organisation, Geneva; m Betty McKevitt, Director, Mosney Irish holidays plc; 1*s* 2*da*; Food and Beverage Manager, Doyle Hotel Group, 1971-73; Catering Manager, Shelbourne Hotel, 1973-76; involved in business activities in Drogheda, including boutique, garage, nightclub and El Molino Hotel, Julianstown, 1973-87; acquired Mosney Holiday, Centre, Chairman/Chief Executive, Mosney Irish Holidays plc, 1982 to date; Director, various private companies; has instigated major re-development plans for the holiday camp, including the introduction of Funtropica, a £2.5million water playground. A workaholic with a hands on style of management. Hobbies, environment, nature and sports activities. Contact: Mosney Irish Holidays plc, Mosney, Co. Meath. Tel: 041 982 9200.

McCOLGAN, John

McCOLGAN, John; DIRECTOR, RIVERDANCE THE SHOW; *b* 1945; *educ* St. Joseph's School, Fairview; *married;* 3 *s* 1 *da;* turned down an acting scholarship to the Abbey Theatre to join R.T.E. as Vision Mixer; former Controller of Programmes, TV AM (London); former Head of Light Entertainment, R.T.E.; currently Director, Abhann (Riverdance The Show) with three companies touring worldwide; currently Director, Tyrone Productions; Chairman TodayFM; has produced and directed documentaries, including a tribute to Eamonn Kelly, *The Man from the Mountains,* a tribute to Maureen Potter, *Super Trouper;* produced/directed *Templewood* (drama series); played a key role in the development of *Riverdance The Show*, directed the video which is now best ever selling video in the world; recipient of Jacob's Television Award; *Riverdance The Show* has received numerous awards worldwide. Hobbies, walking, reading and music. Contact: Abhann Productions Ltd., 27 Lower Hatch Street, Dublin 2. Fax: 01 678 8006.

McCONNELL, David John; PROFESSOR OF GENETICS TRINITY COLLEGE DUBLIN; *b* 1944; *educ* Zion National School; Sandford Park School Dublin; Trinity College Dublin BA (Moderatorship) Genetics; California Institute of Technology, PhD Biochemistry; *m* Janet Overend; Lecturer, Trinity College Dublin, 1970-85, Associate Professor of Genetics, 1985-90, Professor of Genetics, 1990 to date; Vice Provost for Quatercentenary Affairs, 1991-92, Registrar, 1997-99; Research Fellow with Walter Gilbert (Nobel Laureate), Harvard University 1976-77; Visiting Professor, University of California (Davis), 1977; EMBO Fellow, University of Strasbourg, 1980; Board member, Tallaght Hospital Planning Board, 1983 to date; Council member, Zoological Society of Ireland, 1974 to date; Chairman, Irish National Centre for Bio-informatics, 1994 to date; Council member, Royal Irish Academy, 1997 to date, (Advisory Committee on Genetic Anthropology); Advisor, UN Industrial Development Organisation (Centre for Genetic Engineering and Biotechnology); former board member, Adelaide Hospital, Sandford Park School, Irish Council for Science, Technology and Innovation. Hobbies, gardening and windsurfing mostly in Kerry. Contact: Department of Genetics, Trinity College, Dublin 2. Tel: 01 679 5558.

McCOURT, Agnes

McCOURT, Agnes, née Quinn; FOUNDER DIRECTOR UNISLIM IRELAND LTD.; *b* 1943; *educ* Our Lady's School, Newry; Sedgley Park Teacher Training College, Manchester; Manchester University; *widowed;* 1*s* 2*da;* School Teacher, 1964-72; Founder of Unislim in 1972, is currently Director, Unislim Ireland Ltd.; Unislim is a weight reducing organisation with over 600 clubs and 50,000 members throughout the country; nominated Business Person of the Year 1987 (following the launch of Unislim Spritzer with Irish Distillers); as a personal contribution to the Omagh Bomb Victims' Fund bought, for a record price, a watercolour of Windsor Castle by Prince Charles, the painting hangs in the Newry Unislim offices. Hobbies, golf, bridge and reading. Contact: Unislim Ireland Ltd., 49 Lower Dorset Street, Dublin 1. Tel: 01 855 6111.

McCRACKEN, The Hon, Mr. Justice Brian Moore; JUDGE OF THE HIGH COURT; *b* 1934; *educ* The High School, Dublin; Trinity College Dublin, BA, LLB; Kings Inns, Barrister at Law; *married;* 1*s* 1 *da;* called to the Bar, 1957; called to the Inner Bar, 1975; had a substantial legal practice in chancery and commercial law; appointed a Judge of the High Court 1995; appointed

Chairman of the Tribunal of Payments to Politicians 1997; as a barrister specialised in intellectual property law; quiet, soft spoken, regarded as clear minded and sharp. Contact: Four Courts, Morgan Place, Dublin 7. Tel: 01 872 5555.

McCREEVY, Charles; MINISTER FOR FINANCE; *b* 1949; *educ* Christian Brothers School, Naas; Franciscan College Gormanstown; University College Dublin, BComm; *separated;* 7 children; Partner in Tynan Dillon & Company since 1974; elected Deputy for Kildare 1977; elected to Kildare County Council in 1979; Minister for Social Welfare, February 1992-January 1993, Minister for Tourism & Trade, January 1993 - December 1994, Frontbench Spokesperson on Finance, January 1995 - June 1997, Minister for Finance, June 1997 to date; represents a new, independent-minded, outspoken image of the Fianna Fáil party; unpredictability could be his strength; a keen intellect and high media profile; an enthusiastic follower of all sports, particularly horse racing and Gaelic games. Contact: Dept. of Finance, Upper Merrion Street, Dublin 2. Tel: 01 604 5636. Fax: 01 676 2285.

McCREEVY, Charles

McCULLOUGH Hugh; MANAGING DIRECTOR GLENCAR EXPLORATION PLC; *b* 1951; *educ* University College Dublin, BSc (Hons) Geology; Kings Inns, Barrister-at-Law; as a Consultant Geologist worked with Glencar in the 1970s; Managing Director, Glencar Explorations plc, 1982 to date; the Goldfinger of the Irish exploration industry, mining gold in the Wassa Mine, Ghana. Hobbies, sport, theatre and music. Contact: Glencar Explorations plc, 26 Upper Mount Street, Dublin 2. Tel: 01 661 9974. Fax: 01 661 1205.

McCULLOUGH, Denis John; SENIOR COUNSEL; *b* 1948; *educ* Ring College, Co. Waterford; De La Salle College, Churchtown; University College Dublin; BA; Kings Inns; *m* Ellie Kettle; *2s 1 da;* called to the Bar, 1971; called to the Inner Bar, 1985; called to the Bar, New South Wales, 1993; Elected to the Bar Council, 1998; Elected Bencher of the Honourable Society of Kings Inns, 1998; member, Kildare Street and University Club; Royal Irish Yacht Club; De La Salle Palmerstown RFC. Hobbies, reading, fishing, travel and drinking wine. Contact: Law Library, Four Courts, Dublin 7. Tel: 01 872 0622. Fax: 01 872 0455.

McDAID, James; POLITICIAN/DOCTOR; MINISTER OF TOURISM, SPORT AND RECREATION; *b* 1949; *educ* St. Eunan's College, Letterkenny; University College Galway, MB, BCH, BAO, MRCGP; qualified as a doctor and practices in Donegal; Surgical House Officer, Letterkenny General Hospital, 1974-79; Medical Officer to Donegal Senior Gaelic Athletic Association team 1983-87; Co-founder with Dr. Tom McGinley, Donegal Hospice, Chairman Donegal Hospice Movement since 1988; elected Fianna Fáil Dáil Deputy for Donegal North East 1989 to date; served on Committee on Women's Rights 1992, Committee of Public Accounts 1993; Spokesperson on North/South Developments 1995; Committee on Foreign Affairs/Northern Sub Committee 1995; Spokesperson for Equality and Law Reform 1996; Minister for Tourism, Sport and Recreation 1997 to date; a hard working, popular and elegant minister; a committed and fortunate follower of the bloodstock industry. Hobbies, all sports and horseracing. Contact: Department of Tourism, Sport and Recreation, Kildare Street, Dublin 2. Tel: 01 662 1444. Fax: 01 678 5906.

McDONALD, Frank; JOURNALIST; *b* 1950; *educ* Kelly's Private School, Cabra Road; St. Vincent's Christian Brothers School, Glasnevin; University College Dublin, BA; *single;* Editor, *Student,* University College Dublin, 1970-72; Deputy President, SRC, University College Dublin, 1970-71; New York Correspondent, *Irish Press,* 1972-73, Sub-Editor, *Irish Press,* 1973-77, Reporter, 1977-78; Reporter, *Irish Times,* 1979-85, Environment Correspondent, 1986 to date; recipient of Award for Outstanding Work in Irish Journalism (1979), Lord Mayor's Millennium Medal (1988), Chartered Institute of Transport Journalist of the Year, 1998; publications include *The Destruction of Dublin* (Gill & Macmillan, 1985), *Saving the City* (Tomar, 1989), *Ireland's Earthen Houses* (A&A Farmer, joint author, 1997), *The Ecological Footprint of Cities* (International Institute for Urban Environment, joint editor, 1998); member, National Union of Journalists; a knowledgeable and powerful lobbyist against the destruction of Dublin; seen by many as a champion of environmental preservation, a thorn in the side of some property speculators. Hobbies, food and drink, photography, architecture and visiting cities. Contact: The Irish Times, D'Olier Street, Dublin 2. Tel: 01 679 2022.

McDONNELL, Jane; MANAGING DIRECTOR, EDITORIAL DIRECTOR IMAGE PUBLICATIONS LTD.; *b* 1962; *educ* Notre Dame des Missions; Trinity College Dublin, BA Natural Sciences; *m* Donald Hickey; *2 s 1da;* Editorial Assistant, *Vogue* (UK), 1984-87; Features Co-ordinator, *W* (UK), 1987-88; Interiors Editor, *Riva* (UK), 1988-89; Editor, *Image* 1989-99 and Editor *Image Interiors,* 1992 to date; Managing Director and Group Editorial Director Image Publications Ltd. 1999 to date; Director, European Institute Women's Health, 1994-98; a deceptively youthful looking publishing dynamo who has made her mark on the Irish magazine media. Contact: Image Publications Ltd., 22 Crofton Road, Dun Laoghaire, Co. Dublin. Tel: 01 280 8415. Fax: 01 280 8309.

McDONNELL, Jane

McDONNELL, Michael J.

McDONNELL, Michael Joseph "Joe"; DIRECTOR TEGRAL HOLDINGS; *b* 1944; *educ* Patrician College, Ballyfin; University College Dublin, BComm, MEcon Sc; *m* Colette Knox; 1*s* 1 *da;* Chief Economist, CRH, 1967-77; Development Director, Van Neerbos BV, 1978-80; Marketing Manager, Tegral Group, 1980-85, Director, 1985 to date; President, Eternit Inc. (US); Chairman, Building Materials Federation (IBEC), 1999; Knight of Malta (KM); Knight of the Holy Sepulchre of Jerusalem (KCHS); member, Malahide Lions Club (former President), Island Golf Club, Malahide Lawn Tennis Club, Hibernian United Services Club. Hobbies, tennis, golf and reading. Contact: Tegral Building Products Ltd., 6 South Leinster Street, Dublin 2. Tel; 01 676 3974. Fax: 01 676 2820.

McDONNELL, Michael Patrick; GROUP CHIEF EXECUTIVE C.I.E.; *b* 1943; *educ* St. James' C.B.S.; MEcon Sc; BComm; DPA; FCIT; *m* Noreen Clarke; 2 *s* 1 *da*; Dublin Corporation City Manager's Department 1961-1967; Department of Finance 1967-87; Departments of Communications, Transport, Tourism 1987-1995; Chief Executive. C.I.E., 1995 to date. Contact: C.I.E. Head Office, Heuston Station Dublin 8. Tel: 01 677 1871. Fax: 01 670 3463.

McDONNELL, Niall

McDONNELL, Niall; CHIEF EXECUTIVE PANORAMA HOLIDAYS; *b* 1961; *educ* St. Fintan's High School, Sutton; Dublin Institute of Technology, Bolton Street; *m* Lisa ----; 2*s* 1*da;* held various positions with J.W.T. Holidays, including Sales Manager, 1989-95; Sales Manager, Thomson Holidays, 1995-96; joined Panorama Holidays as Sales Manager, 1997, currently Chief Executive; Board member, Panorama Holiday Group; Panorama, taken over recently by Airtours, have expansion plans in the Irish market. Hobby, golf. Contact: Panorama Holidays, 2nd Floor, 3 College Green, Dublin 2. Tel 01 670 7666. Fax: 01 670 7288.

McDONNELL, Sarah; EDITOR IMAGE MAGAZINE; *b* 1972; *educ* Notre Dame des Missions, Churchtown; Trinity College Dublin (Moderatorship); *married;* Freelance Journalist, 1994-95; joined Image Magazine, 1995, Editorial Assistant, Beauty Writer, 1995-96, Fashion and Beauty Editor, 1996-98; awards include, Highly Commended, Carter Award Young Style Journalist of the Year, 1998. Brings her own up to the minute style and knowledge to Ireland's leading glossie. Contact: Image, 22 Crofton Road, Dun Laoghaire, Co. Dublin. Tel: 01 280 8415. Fax: 01 280 8309.

McDONNELL, The Hon. Hector J; ARTIST/PAINTER; *b* 1947; *educ* Eton; Oxford; Munich and Vienna; *m dis;* 1*s* 1 *da;* the youngest son of the 13th Earl of Antrim; has exhibited widely, exhibitions include Bell Gallery (Belfast) 1975, Galarie Ariadne (Vienna) 1976, Lad Lane Gallery (Dublin), 1978, Sotheby Parke-Bernet (Munich) 1979, Mathild Enhote (Darmstadt) 1981, Solomon Gallery, Dublin 1982, Royal Ulster Academy, 1985, Fischer Fine Arts London, 1988; Galerie Valentian (Stuttgart) 1990, Galeria Yuguanzo (Madrid) 1995, Galerie Vielle du Temple (Paris) 1988-96, Galerie Netuschil (Darmstadt) 1995, Ireland House (New York) 1997, Solomon Gallery, 1999; publications include, *William Bloat* 1982, *Ould Orange Flute* 1983, *Night before Larry was Stretched* 1984, (all published by Blackstaff Press), also travel books of drawings and etchings published by Gshwendwr Blatter, *A Rwandan Journey* 1996 (Concern, Belfast); a popular artist whose work depicts a shrewd sense of the ordinary and commonplace. Hobbies, travel and skiing. Contact: The Solomon Gallery, Powerscourt Townhouse Centre, Dublin 2. Tel: 01 679 4237. Fax: 01 671 5262.

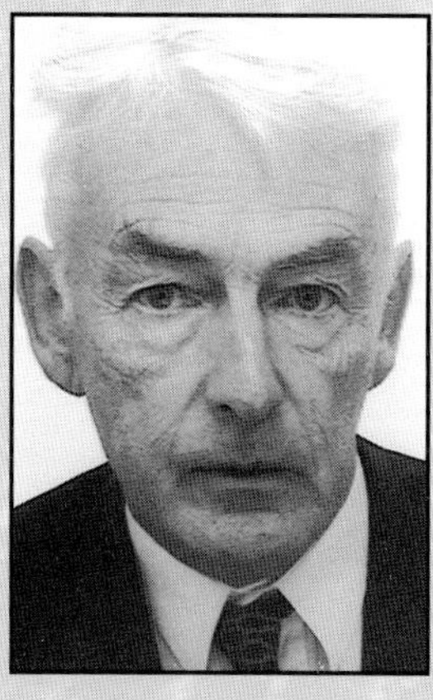
McDONOGH, Thomas

McDONOGH, Thomas; CHAIRMAN, CHIEF EXECUTIVE MCDONAGH GROUP OF COMPANIES; *b* 1935; *educ* St. Ignatius College, Galway; Clongowes Wood College; University College Dublin; *m* Patrizia Giachin; 1 *s;* Currently Chairman and Chief Executive, McDonogh Group of Companies, involved in fertilisers, animal feed stuffs, builders merchants, etc., among the top 200 companies in the State. A director of approximately twenty other companies, including Galway Harbour Company, and is active on many other local and national Bodies. McDonogh Group sponsor many events, including the second day of the Galway Summer Racing Festival. It also donates generously to the arts having given Druid Theatre their present home. Chairman, Galway Race Committee and a well known racehorse owner. Hobbies, walking, skiing, football, travel, reading and horseracing. Contact: McDonogh Group, Merchants Road, Galway. Tel: 091 566111 Fax: 091 567774.

McDOWELL, Michael; ATTORNEY GENERAL; *b* 1951; *educ* Pembroke School; Gonzaga College, Dublin; University College, Dublin; BA; Kings Inns, BL; *m* Niamh Brennan, Chartered Accountant, University Lecturer, 3 *s*; called to the Bar, 1974; called to the Inner Bar, 1987; Barrister in practice, 1974 to date; Co-founder, with Desmond O'Malley and Mary Harney, of the Progressive Democrats, 1985, Chairman of the Party and Spokesperson on Finance, 1985-97; elected Progressive Democrat deputy for Dublin South East, 1987-89, and 1992-97; Council member of Kings Inns, 1984 to date; appointed Attorney General, July 1999; A high profile law man with an astute legal brain; a relentless questioner of the capabilities and culpabilities of the power brokers.

Hobbies, running, reading and the company of friends; Clubs, Kildare Street and University Club. Contact: Office of the Attorney General, Government Buildings, Upper Merrion Street, Dublin 2; Tel. 01 661 6944. Fax. 01 676 1806.

McENIFF Sean; CHAIRMAN TYRCONNELL GROUP; *b* 1936; *educ* National School, Ardfarna, Bundoran; St. Macartan's College, Monaghan; *m* Eilis Diver; 6 *s* 2 *da*; worked in the family hotel on leaving school, (Bundoran); opened small restaurant and souvenir shop, 1959, opened 3 supermarkets, Bundoran, Ballyshannon & Monaghan, 1962; opened Amusement Arcade, sold supermarkets, 1972; purchased the Great Northern Hotel with his brother, Brian, 1977; sold share in Great Northern and purchased Mount Errigal, Letterkenny, 1984; set up All Ireland Holidays, bringing coach business to Ireland, 1990; built the Allingham (125 bed hotel), 1992; started Tyrconnell Holiday Homes & Blazing Saddles Complex, consisting of apartments, restaurants and Western Theme Bar, 1995; opened The Camden Court Hotel, Dublin (223 bedrooms and Leisure Centre), 1998; invested in McLoughlin Components, Ballyshannon after the closure of Donegal Rubber in the area, 1998; member, Bundoran U.D.C., 1960 to date; member, Donegal County Council, 1967 to date; Chairman, North West Health Board, 1997-98; former Chairman, VEC; elected to the Board of North West Tourism, 1977 to date, Chairman, 1986 to date; Director, Bord Failte, 1993-98; recipient, A.I.B. County Tourism Award, 1995; Donegal Person of the Year, 1996. An astute businessman deeply rooted in his own place; instrumental in developing Bundoran Waterworld and assisting local organisations with their various schemes and projects in the North West. Hobbies, golf, football and walking. Contact: Dinglei Coush, West End, Bundoran, Co. Donegal. Tel: 072 42277. Fax: 072 42278.

McENTEE, Barry; MANAGING DIRECTOR, MONAGHAN POULTRY PRODUCTS; *b* 1958; Trained as a mechanical engineer; *m* Joan Eakin; 2 *s*; Worked for an engineering company in Dublin, 1979-82; Joined Monaghan Poultry Products as Manager, 1982; Managing Director, 1993 to date. Hobbies, sailing and gardening. Contact: Monaghan Poultry Products Ltd., Gallinagh, Monaghan. Tel: 047 30200. Fax: 047 30252.

McEVADDY, Ulick; COMPANY DIRECTOR; *b* 1952; *educ* Garbally Park, Ballinasloe; *m* Mary Cranley; 1*s* *3da;* served with Irish Defence Forces, 1970-81; left the army to join brother Des in Omega Air, 1981; Omega Air are specialists in the aviation business in manufacturing and leasing with many international interests such as Sino Swearingen (W. Virginia) where executive jets are manufactured and the experimental programmes for aircraft tankards for aviation re-fuelling are conducted (San Antonio); member, Royal United Services Institute of Defence Studies; member, United Service Club, RDS; the two McEvaddy brothers are a major force in the Irish aviation scene. Hobbies, reading, horseriding and helicopter flying. Contact: Omega Air, San Antonio, Texas. Fax: 001 210 6678

McEVOY, Patrick; CHAIRMAN IRISH INTERCONTINENTAL BANK; *b* 1939; *educ* Belvedere College; University College Dublin, BComm; Harvard Business School, MBA; *m* Keyna McDwyer, Solicitor; 2*s;* Assistant General Manager - Corporate and Overseas, Bank of Ireland, 1971-73; Chief Executive, Irish Intercontinental Bank, 1973-94, Chairman, 1994 to date; Chairman, Kereskedelmi és Hittelbank R+ (Budapest); Clubs, Fitzwilliam LTC, Milltown GC and Courtown GC. Contact: Irish Intercontinental Bank, 91 Merrion Square, Dublin 2. Tel: 01 661 9744.

McGAHERN; John; WRITER; *b* 1934; *educ* St. Patrick's Training College, Dublin, NT; University College Dublin; *m* Madelaine Green; worked as a school teacher, 1955-64; Visiting Professor, US 1964-76; Arts Fellow, University of Newcastle, 1964-76; publications include: Novels: *The Barracks* (1963), *The Dark* (1965), *The Leavetaking* (1975), *The Pornographer* (1980), *Amongst Women* (1990); Short Stories: *Nightlines* (1970), *Getting Through* (1978), *High Ground* (1985), Collected Stories, (1993); Plays for Television: *Swallows* (1975), *The Rockingham Shoot* (1987); Play for radio, *Sinclair* (1971); Stage Play, *The Power of Darkness* (1991); recipient of AE Memorial Award 1962, Macaulay Fellowship 1964, Arts Council Award (1966, 1968, 1971, 1978), Society of Authors Travelling Fellowship 1975, American Irish Foundation Award (1985), *Amongst Women*, shortlisted for Booker Prize (1990) and won *Irish Times* Aer Lingus Literature Award and GPA Award, 1992; Chevalier de l'Ordre des Arts et des Lettres 1988; Prix Etrangere Ecureuil 1995; conferred with an Honorary Doctorate of Literature from Trinity College Dublin, 1991, University College Galway, 1993, Université de Poitiers, 1997; Recognised as one of the country's major literary figures; It has been said that no Irish writer since James Joyce has achieved greater mastery of both the short story and the novel form. Contact: Aosdana, 70 Merrion Square, Dublin 2. Tel: 01 661 1840. Fax: 01 676 1302.

McGANN, Gary

McGANN, Gary; CEO JEFFERSON SMURFIT GROUP PLC; *b* 1950; *educ* BA (1973), ACCA (1981), MScMgt (1987); *m* Moira O'Donoghue; *3da;* Auditor, Controller and Auditor General, 1968-76; Financial Controller, LM Ericsson Ltd., 1977-88; Financial Controller, Gilbeys, 1988-94,

Chief Executive, 1992-94; Group CEO, Aer Lingus Group plc, 1994-98; CEO, Jefferson Smurfit Group, 1998 to date; member, Athlone Golf Club, RIAC, Hibernian United Services Club, Fitzwilliam LTC and K Club; Chairman, Cardiac Surgical Foundation. Hobbies, golf, music and theatre. Contact: Jefferson Smurfit Group Ltd., Beech Hill, Dublin 4. Tel: 01 202 7000. Fax: 01 269 4481.

McGEOUGH, David James; SOLICITOR, DIRECTOR MATHESON ORMSBY PRENTICE; *b* 1965; *educ* St. Michael's College, Dublin; University College Dublin, BCL (magna cum laude); Incorporated Law Society of Ireland; *m* Emer Condon; *2s*; worked with a U.S. law firm, Los Angeles, 1987-88; joined Matheson Ormsby Prentice, 1988, Partner, 1991 (youngest ever); firm are specialists in corporate and financial law, adviser to leading international banks and institutions such as J.P. Morgan, Goldman Sachs, Lehman Brothers, Salomon Smith Barney, Templeton Worldwide Inc., Banco Santander, Zurich Insurance Group; has tutored law at UCD and spoken at numerous conferences, and contributed articles to various international publications on corporate finance and financial services matter, including those organised by the National Investment Company Service Association of America (NICSA), IBC, DFIA, etc.; member of the Department of An Taoiseach's International Banking and Treasury Sub-Group, the International Bar Association, the Law Society of Ireland, Association Internationale de Jeune Avocats, the IFSC Development Committee of the Financial Services Industry Association of Ireland, the Law Society's Financial Services Task Force; member, Fitzwilliam Lawn Tennis Club, Powerscourt Golf Club and Milltown Golf Club. Hobbies, football, skiing, music and people, engaging literature. Contact: Matheson Ormsby Prentice, 30 Herbert Street, Dublin 2. Tel: 01 619 9000. Fax: 01 619 9010.

McGETTIGAN, Eoin Patrick; CHIEF EXECUTIVE MUSGRAVE, SUPERVALU, CENTRA; *b* 1960; *educ* St. Benilda's DLS, Kilmacud, University of Strathclyde, MBA; Chartered Institute of Management Accountants; *m* Breeda O'Shea; 2 *da;* Trainee, Coopers & Lybrand, 1979-81; Accountant, BWG, 1981-85; Financial Controller, Irish Sewing Ltd., 1985-87; Operations Director, McDaniels, (subsidiary James Crean),1987-90; Group Financial Controller, Musgrave, 1990-93; Finance Director, Musgrace Supervalu Centra, 1993-96; Chief Executive, Musgrave, Supervalu, Centra, 1996 to date; member Sundays Well, Kinsale Golf Club; Fellow of Chartered Institute of Management Accountants. Hobbies, tennis, golf, guitar, chess. Contact: Supervalu Central Distribution Ltd., Tramore Road, Cork. Tel: 021 803 000; Fax: 021 313 621.

McGETTIGAN, Eoin P.

McGINLEY, John; COUNTY MANAGER, NORTH TIPPERARY; *b* 1934; *educ* Christian Brothers School, Drogheda; Rathmines College of Commerce, ACIS; Institute of Public Administration, DipSoc Studies and Local Admin; *m* Mairead Ruttledge; 4 *da*; Clerk with Bord Iascaigh Mhara, 1952-59; Court Clerk, Department of Justice, 1959-60; Town Clerk, Cavan, 1960-62; Borough Accountant, Sligo Corporation, 1962-65; Town Clerk, Ballina, 1965-70; Town Clerk, Drogheda, 1970-75; County Secretary, Clare 1975-78; County Manager, North Tipperary, 1978 to date; Member: Geographical Society of Ireland, Statistical & Social Inquiry Society of Ireland; Commandant FCA Veterans, 1991. Hobbies, boating, travel and painting. Contact: The Courthouse, Nenagh, Co. Tipperary.

McGINLEY, John

McGINLEY, Paul; PROFESSIONAL GOLFER; *b* 1966; *educ* Certificate, Retail Marketing; Diploma, Retail Marketing; Degree, International Business; *m* Ally ----; 1 *da;* Irish Amateur Champion, 1989; Walker Cup, 1991; turned Professional, Sept. 1991; European Under 25 Champion (Professional), 1991; Austrian Open Champion, 1996; Oki Pro Am, 1998; World Cup Winner, 1998 (with P. Harrington); member, Professional Golfers Association (Ireland) since 1991; member, European Tour since 1991. Hobbies, Formula One (motor racing), music, dogs, basically all sports. Contact: I.S.M., Colshaw Hall, Stocks Lane, Knutsford, Cheshire, WA16 8TW. Tel: 0044 1565 722 755.

McGOLDRICK, Patrick Joseph, "P.J."; CHAIRMAN, CHIEF EXECUTIVE, TRANSAER INTERNATIONAL AIRLINES; *b* 1940; *educ* Marist Brothers, Sligo; Sligo Regional College; *m* Jeanette Brady; 2 *s*; served in the Irish Air Corps; joined TransMeridian Air Cargo as pilot and training captain, rising to Managing Director; Launched Heavy Lift Cargo Airlines, 1980; Deputy Chairman and Chief Executive and Board Director, Cunard, 1984; Launched TransAer International Airlines, Chairman and Chief Executive, 1991 to date; TransAer are the largest independent charter in Europe; Fellow, Institute of Directors, Institute of Managers. Hobbies, sailing, flying, reading, flying, boats, music, aviation history. Contact: TransAer, TransAer House, Dublin Airport, Dublin. Tel: 01 808 0800. Fax: 01 808 0801.

McGONAGLE; Declan George; DIRECTOR IRISH MUSEUM OF MODERN ART; *b* 1952; *educ* St. Columb's College, Derry; College of Art, Belfast, BA Hons Fine Art, HDip (Painting); *m* Moira Carlin, Teacher; *2s;* Lecturer in Fine Art, Letterkenny RTC 1976; Orchard Gallery Organiser, Derry City Council, 1978-84; Exhibitions Director, ICA London, 1984-86; Visual Arts Director, Derry City

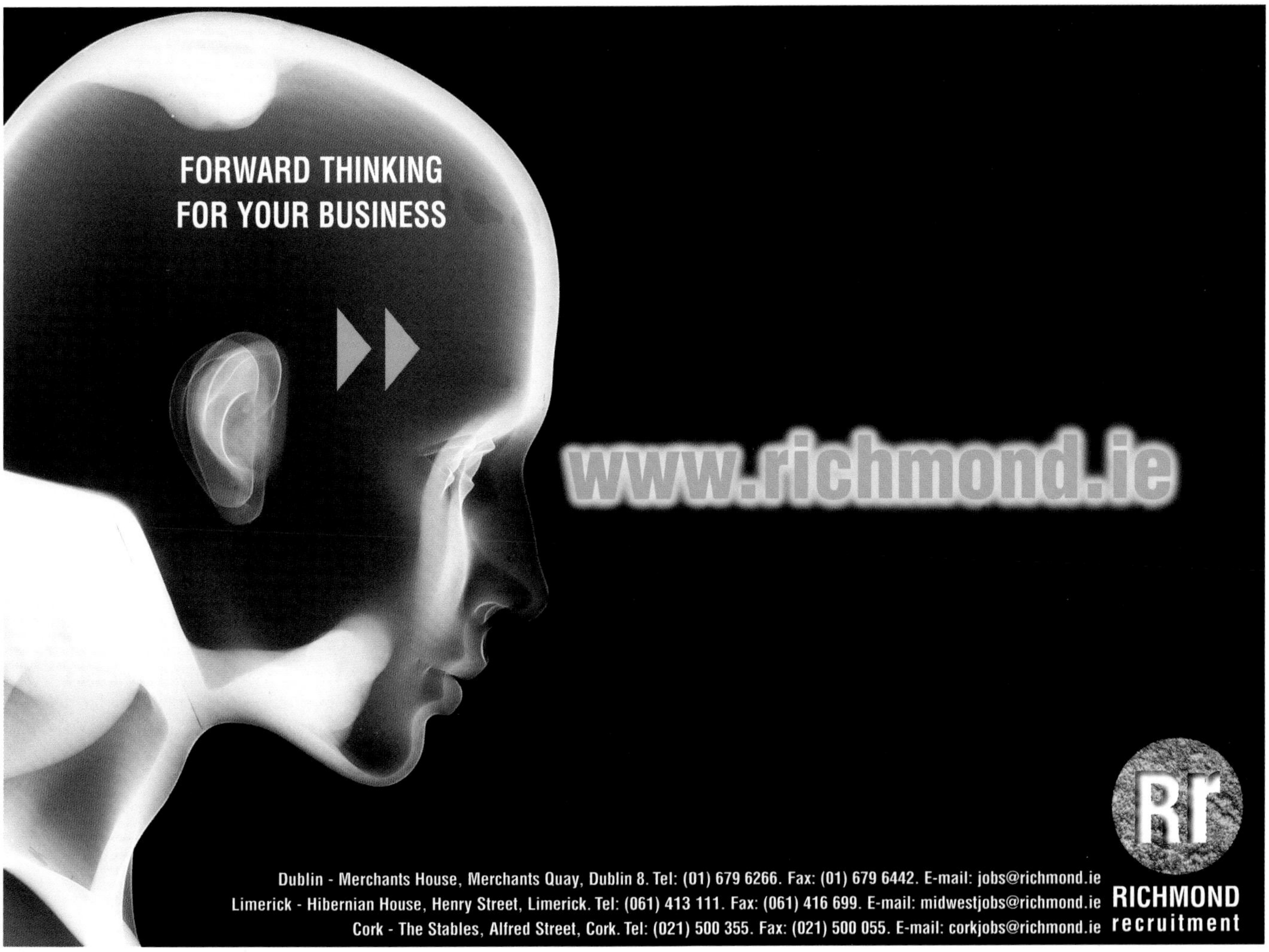

McGORAN, Kevin

McGOVERN, Barry Kevin

McGOVERN, Gerry

Council, 1986-90; Director, Irish Museum of Modern Art, 1990 to date; recipient of *Sunday Tribune* Visual Arts Award 1987, Distinguished Graduates Award, New University of Ulster 1999; publications include articles and texts in *Artscribe* (London), *Art Monthly* (London), *Alba* (Edinburgh), *Circa* (Belfast). A growing figure in the powerful politics of the European Art world. Hobbies, painting and literature. Contact: Irish Museum of Modern Art, Royal Hospital Kilmainham, Dublin 8. Tel: 01 612 990.

McGORAN, Kevin Columba; CHAIRMAN FITZWILTON PLC, CHAIRMAN WATERFORD CRYSTAL LTD; *b* 1935; *educ* Belvedere College, Dublin; University College Dublin, BComm; Irish Management Institute, Dip. Bus. Mgmt.; *m* Betty O'Donoghue; 2 *s* 3 *da*; Finance Controller, de Beers (Shannon), 1963-68; Finance Controller, Gaeltarra Eireann (Ireland), 1968-71; Deputy Managing Director, Avery International, 1971-77; Director of Finance and Development (Europe), 1977-79; Chief Financial Officer, Jefferson Smurfit Group, 1979-83; Chairman and co-founder, Kevin McGoran & Associates, CFI Ltd. (Corporate Finance and Investment Advisors) 1983-88; Deputy Chairman, Chief Executive, Fitzwilton plc 1988-99; Executive Chairman Fitzwilton plc 1999 to date; Chairman, Waterford Crystal Ltd., 1998 to date; Fellow, Institute of Chartered Accountants in Ireland; member Fitzwilliam L.T.C., Old Belvedere RFC, Portmarnock Hotel & Golf Links. Hobbies, golf, tennis, rugby, music and reading. Contact: Fitzwilton plc, 1-2 Upper Hatch St, Dublin 2. Tel: 01 475 5411. Fax: 01 475 5415.

McGORNAN, Pat; CHIEF EXECUTIVE DESIGNATE OF HIBERNIAN GROUP; *educ* Queen's University Belfast, degree in Mathematics; Strathclyde University, Glasgow, MSc in Op. Research; *m* Eileen ----; joined Bank of Ireland 1969; Director, Bank of Ireland Group Treasury; Managing Director, Hibernian Investment Managers 1996; Chief Executive Designate, Hibernian Group, June 1999; member of the Committee of Management of the Irish Pension Fund Property Unit Trust; Associate, Institute of Actuaries. Hobbies, watching sports, golf, walking and travel. Contact: Hibernian Group plc, Haddington Road, Dublin 4. Tel: 01 607 8000. Fax: 01 660 8730.

McGOVERN, Barry Kevin; ACTOR; *b* 1948; *educ* St. Michael's College Dublin; Castleknock College; University College Dublin, BA; Abbey School of Acting; *m* Medb Ruane, writer/journalist; 1*s* 1*da* 1 *stepson;* toured Gaeltacht with Abbey Theatre 1969; joined RTE Players 1971-74; worked extensively with Irish Theatre Company 1975-77 and 1982 in a number of leading roles in numerous productions including, *As You Like It, Thieves Carnival, Waiting for Godot;* worked with Abbey Theatre Company 1978-81, in numerous roles including Fr. Jack in the original production of *Dancing at Lughnasa;* has gained international acclaim for his work in Beckett - Lucky in *Estragon,* Vladamir in *Waiting for Godot,* Clov in *Endgame,* Willie in *Happy Days,* Krapp in *Krapps Last Tape;* directed *All That Fall* for RTE Radio; Artistic Director, Opera Theatre Company 1989-90; written music for a number of productions; TV work includes major roles in *Dear Sarah, The Treaty, A Vertical Man;* films include *Joe Versus the Volcano, Far and Away, Braveheart, The General;* recipient, Harvey's Best Actor Award 1985 (*I'll Go On), Sunday Independent*/Irish Life Award 1991, International Radio Festival of New York Gold Medal (for Beckett) 1989; awarded honorary doctorate Ltt.D. Trinity College Dublin 1998; biographical details in *Who's Who in Contemporary World Theatre* 1999; member, Arts Council 1984-88; member, Theatre Cavaliers Cricket Club. Hobbies, music, rugby, football and walking. Contact: Teri Hayden, The Agency, 47 Adelaide Road, Dublin 2. Tel: 01 661 8535.

McGOVERN, Gerry; CHIEF EXECUTIVE OFFICER NUA / LOCAL IRELAND; *b* 1962; *educ* St. Mel's College, Longford; Trinity College Dublin, Bsc; *m* Maighread Medbh; 2 *s*; Writer and Journalist, 1984-94; CEO Nua and Local Ireland, 1995-1998; writings include *Smuggle Donnelly* (RTE Radio Play), 1989; *I am Ireland* (RTE Radio Play), 1991; *The Caring Economy: Internet Business Principles,* (Blackhall Publishing), 1999. Regarded as one of Ireland's leading experts in Internet technology. Contact: Nua Internet Consultancy, Westland Court, Dublin 2. Tel: 01 676 8996.

McGOWAN, Paul Patrick; JOINT MANAGING DIRECTOR DOLMEN BUTLER BRISCOE; *b* 1963; *educ* Blackrock College; University College Dublin, BComm; qualified as Chartered Accountant in 1991; *m* Gwen McNulty; Trainee Chartered Accountant, P. Griffin & Co., 1984-89; Lending Executive, Merchant Banking, ICC Bank plc, 1989-90; Director, Private Clients, NCB Stockbrokers, 1990-94; Joint Managing Director, Dolmen Securities Ltd, Joint Managing Director, Dolmen Butler Briscoe, Director, Dolmen Corporate Finance, 1995 to date; member, Institute of Chartered Accountants in Ireland; member, National Yacht Club, Dun Laoghaire, member, Barnardo's Fund Raising Board. Hobbies, sailing, reading and cinema. Contact: Dolmen Butler Briscoe, 3 College Green, Dublin 2. Tel: 01 633 3800.

McGUCKIAN, Alistair; CHIEF EXECUTIVE MASSTOCK (IRELAND) LTD.; *b* 1936; *educ* St. McNissi's, Co. Antrim; Greenmount Agricultural College, National Dip Agr.; *m* Margery

O'Donoghue; 2*s* 2 *da;* Founder/Chairman, Masstock (Ireland) Ltd. 1970 to date; Masstock specialise in the development of unused third world resources by investment and training, mainly in USA, Middle East and Central Africa; recipient, Honorary Doctorate of Laws (NUI), 1988; Honorary Doctorate, Agricultural Science (Queen's University Belfast), 1988; Fellow, Royal Agricultural Societies and British Royal Agricultural Society; member, Powerscourt Golf Club, Fitzwilliam LTC; composer of musical composition *A Terrible Beauty.* Recognised as a pioneer in worldwide agriculture. Hobbies, piano, music and golf. Contact: Masstock (Ireland) Ltd. Crescent Hall, Mount Street Crescent, Dublin 2. Tel: 01 662 8555.

McGUCKIAN, John Brendan; CHAIRMAN ULSTER TELEVISION; *b* 1939; *educ* St. McNissis College, Garrontower, Queen's University of Belfast, BSc.; *m* Carmel McGowan; 2*s* 2*da*; Chairman, Cloughmills Mfg Co. 1967; Ulster TV plc 1991; Director, Munster & Leinster Bank, 1972; Allied Irish Bank plc, 1976 to date; Harbour GP Ltd., 1978 to date; Aer Lingus plc, 1979-84; Unidare plc, 1987 to date; Irish Continental Group plc, 1988 to date; member, Derry Development Committee, 1968-71, Laganside Corporation, 1988-92; Chairman, International Fund for Ireland, 1990-93; Northern Ireland Industrial Development Board, 1991 to date; Pro Chancellor, Queen's University, Belfast, 1990 to date; Chairman, Tedcastle Ltd., 1996 to date. Contact: U.T.V. Havelock House, Ormeau Road, Belfast, BT7 1EB. Tel: 0801 232 3281 22.

McGUCKIAN, Mary; FILM MAKER; *b* 1963; *educ* St. Gerard's School, Bray; Trinity College Dublin, BAI (Mech Eng); *m* John Lynch; Actor, Playwright, Film maker, 1987 to date; films include, *Words Upon the Window Pane,* (Producer, Writer, Director), *This is the Sea* (Producer, Writer, Director), *Best* (Producer, Writer, Director). Contact: Best Films (IOM) Ltd., Goldcrest, Flat 10, 36-44 Brewer Street, London W1R 3HP. Tel: 0044 171 437 7972. Fax: 0044 171 468 1004.

McGUINNESS, The Hon. Mrs. Justice Catherine; JUDGE OF THE HIGH COURT; *b* 1934; *educ* Dunmurry PE School; Alexandra College and School; Trinity College Dublin, BA (Mod), MA; Kings Inns, BL; *m* Proinsias MacAonghusa, Journalist, Broadcaster, Writer; 2 *s* 1 *da*; Teacher, freelance writer 1957-61; Parliamentary Officer, Labour Party 1961-67; member, Adoption Board 1970-77; Barrister-at-Law 1977-89; Senior Counsel 1989-94; Judge of the Circuit Court, 1994-96; Judge of the High Court, 1996 to date; D. Litt. (honoris causa), University of Ulster, 1998; member, Seanad Eireann, 1979-87; Chairperson: National School Service Board, 1973-82, Board of National College of Art and Design, 1987-93, Employment Equality Agency 1988-93; member: Council of State 1988-91, Inner Bar of Ireland, Family Lawyers' Association (ex Chairperson), Voluntary Health Insurance Board 1975-79, National Economic and Social Council 1982-83, General Synod of the Church of Ireland, Second Commission on the Status of Women; Chairperson: Kilkenny Incest Inquiry, 1993, Forum for Peace and Reconciliation, 1994 to date; Fellow, International Academy of Matrimonial Lawyers. Much admired for her fine intellect and fearless chairmanship of the Forum for Peace and Reconciliation. Hobby, choral singing (President, Culwick Choral Society). Contact: Four Courts, Morgan Place, Dublin 7. Tel: 01 872 5555.

McGUINNESS, Paul

McGUINNESS, Frank; LECTURER/PLAYWRIGHT; *b* 1953; *educ* University College Dublin, BA. M.Phil.; Lecturer in English, Coleraine University, 1977-79; Lecturer, Maynooth University, 1983-97; Lecturer in English, University College Dublin, 1997 to date; plays include *The Factory Girls, Observe the Sons of Ulster Marching Towards the Somme, Baglady, Innocence, Carthaginians, Mary and Lizzie, The Bread Man, Someone Who'll Watch Over Me, The Bird Sanctuary, Mutabilitie, Dolly West's Kitchen; Booterstown* (poems); awards include, Rooney Prize (1985), *Evening Standard* Award (1986), Harveys Award (1986), Irish American Literary Prize (1992), Writers Guild Award (1993), New York Critics Award (1993), Tony Award: Best Revival (1997), Officier des Artes et Lettres (1996). Hobbies, walking. Contact: University College Dublin, Belfield, Dublin 4. Tel: 01 706 7777.

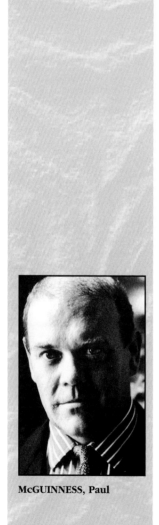

McGUINNESS, Paul; MANAGER U2; *b* 1951; *educ* Clongowes Wood College; Trinity College Dublin; *m* Kathy Gilfillan, writer; 1 *s* 1 *da*; worked in the film industry; Producer/Assistant Director of Television Commercials; Manager of internationally famous Irish rock group U2 since 1978. Founder, Principle Management, McGuinness Whelan Music; Shareholder T.V.3, Ardmore Film Studios; Director, Leisure Corporation; Recipient Honorary Doctorate LlD. University College Dublin 1998; member, The Arts Council, Taoiseach's Millennium Committee 1998. A worldwide reputation together with Irish government appointments equal a force to be reckoned with in the Irish Arts and entertainment arena; Clubs, St. Stephen's Green Club, Groucho Club, London. Contact: Principle Management Ltd.. 30 Sir John Rogerson's Quay, Dublin 2. Tel: 01 677 7330.

McGUIRE, Cyril Patrick; CO-FOUNDER, PRESIDENT, TRINTECH TECHNOLOGIES; *b* 1960; *educ* Presentation College Bray; University College Dublin, BComm, MBS; *single* ; Investment Manager, Industrial Credit Corporation, responsible for investment opportunities, appraisals and the IT corporate sector, 1981-86; Co-founder and President, Trintech Technologies, 1986 to date;

THE INSIDERS GUIDE TO EUROPE

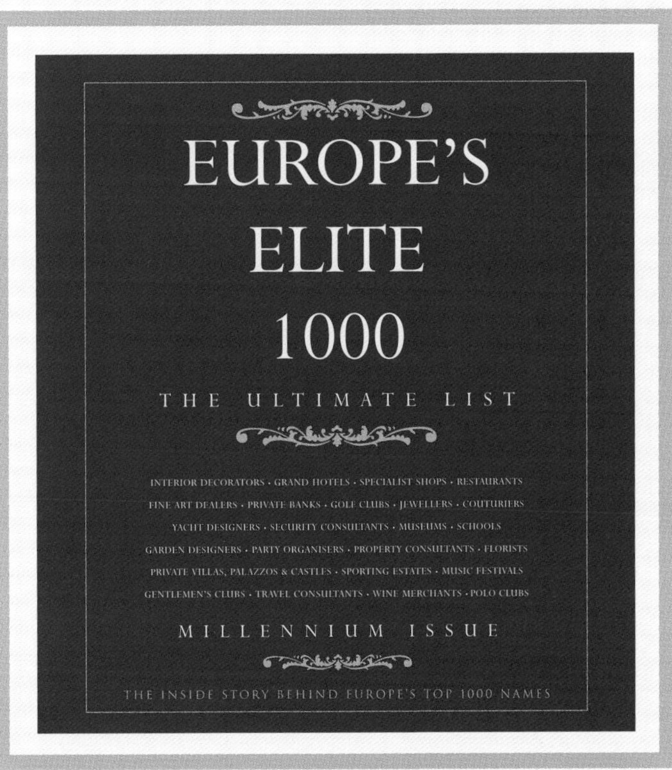

Acclaimed internationally – a spectacular directory of the best of the best in Europe listing a broad range of luxury goods and services. This stunning publication will appeal to sophisticated travellers to Europe – a must for any library or coffee table.

To order the most beautiful book in the world:

Tel: +1-212-633 6488 Fax: +1-212-633 2869

Cadogan Publications

27 West 24th Street, New York, NY 10010, U.S.A

email: nycdublin@aol.com

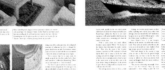

area of responsibilities within this company includes financial, marketing, legal and human resources as well as corporate affairs and worldwide strategic planning; in 1988 was responsible for securing US $20 million investment from U.S. and European banks, largest private investment in Irish IT company in corporate history; member, Government Trade Advisory Forum; speaker at numerous international eCommerce industry events and investment banking conferences; awards include, Up and Running Award for Technical Innovation (1991), European Design Prize (1996), ISA Marketing Achievement Award (1977), Business Person of the Month (December 1998); member, Marketing Institute of Ireland, MII, Irish Software Association. Hobbies, reading, current affairs, sport and theatre. Contact: Trintech Technologies, Trintech House, South County Business Park, Dublin 18. Tel: 01 207 4000. Fax: 01 207 4005.

McHUGH, Anna May

McHUGH, Anna May, née Brennan; MANAGING DIRECTOR NATIONAL PLOUGHING ASSOCIATION OF IRELAND LTD.; *b* 1934; *educ* St. Patrick's National School, Ballylinan; St. Brigid's School, Athy; *m* John McHugh; 1*s* 1 *da;* appointed Secretary, National Ploughing Association of Ireland, 1956, Managing Director since 1973; runs the largest and most successful agricultural show in the country; represents Ireland on World Ploughing Board, affiliated in 31 countries; adjudicator at international competitions; nominated Laois Person of the Year 1990; People of the Year Award 1998; Honorary member, RDS; member, National Ploughing Association, Laois Ploughing Association, Laois for Investment, Laois Enterprise Board, Laois Strategic Policy Committee, Diocesan Finance Committee, Ballylinan ICA, Ballylinan Community Council; President, Kildare Agricultural Show; Board member, Leader Board (Agricultural Section); a well known and respected figure in Irish agriculture; a committed worker at community as well as national level. Hobbies, drama, gardening, organising events. Contact: INPA, Fallaghmore, Athy, Co. Kildare. Tel: 0507 25125. Fax: 0507 25172.

McHUGH, Kevin; FISHERMAN, HOTEL PROPRIETOR; *b* 1947; *educ* National School, Castlebar. *m* Vera Ryan; 3 *s* 1 *da;* served apprenticeship with BIM; qualified at skipper level and worked on various trawlers before investing in own fishing fleet; Chief Executive, Atlantic Dawn Ltd.; the company owns one factory fishing vessel *Veronica* (300ft and 4,000 tons) and has a new similar type vessel due for delivery next year; also proprietor, Cope House Hotel, Killybegs and the Bayview Hotel, Killybegs (a forty bedroom luxury hotel and leisure centre); member, Killybegs Fisherman's Organisation. A self made success story in the fishing industry; a hard working businessman who has invested extensively in the fishing, leisure and tourism industries. Contact: Atlantic Dawn Ltd., Elmwood Terrace, Killybegs, Co. Donegal. Tel: 073 31644. Fax: 073 31646.

McINERNEY, Marcus James; OFFICIAL OF THE EUROPEAN COMMISSION BRUSSELS; *b* 1937; *educ* Crescent College, Limerick; University College Galway; University College Dublin; BAcSc; University of Uppsala, Sweden, Diploma in International Affairs; Kansas State University, USA, MEcon; Georgetown University, Robert Kennedy Fellowship, Study of U.S. Government, United States Department of State; *m* Joan Griffin; 2*s* 1 *da;* Agricultural Advisor in Cabinet of Dr. P. Hillery, Vice-President of the Commission, 1973-74; Principal Administrator in DG VI/A, responsible for agricultural trade relations with United States, Canada, Australia and New Zealand, 1975-78; Principal Administrator in DG VI/G/3, analysis of agri-industry and administration of EEC Reg. 355/77, 1979-83; Head of Unit XX/B/2, Control of EAGGF, Guidance and Guarantee, of Fisheries, 1983-86; Head of Unit XX/B, Control of EAGGF Guidance Section, of Fisheries-structures, of PEDIP and of IMPs and co-ordination of control of structural funds, 1986-99; Acting Director, Structural Funds Directorate DG XX/B, 1999 to date; member, St. Stephen's Green Club, Royal Irish Yacht Club, RDS Dublin, Chateau St. Anne Brussels, Iniscealtra Sailing Club, Co. Clare. Hobbies, sailing, fishing, agriculture and travel. Contact: Directorate General XX, Rue de la Loi, B-1049, Brussels.

McKENNA, John Gerard

McKENNA, David Patrick; MANAGING DIRECTOR MARLBOROUGH INTERNATIONAL PLC; *b* 1961; *m* Liz Carroll; 1*s* 1*da*; prior to 1986 worked in plumbing and heating contracting sector in Ireland and overseas; managed subcontracting business in London, installing sprinkler systems, 1986-88; Managing Director, Worldwide Recruitment Ltd., Dublin, 1989-92; Managing Director, Marlborough International plc, (Ireland's largest recruitment company), 1992 to date; Board member, Enterprise Ireland; member IOD Golf Club; awards include, *Sunday Tribune*/National Irish Bank Young Business Achiever of the Year Award, 1997, runner up, Ernst and Young Entrepreneur of the Year Award 1998. Hobbies, avid Manchester United supporter and golf. Contact: Marlborough International, Marlborough House, 11-13 Tara Street, Dublin 2. Tel: 01 617 3800. Fax: 01 677 7546.

McKENNA, John Gerard; WRITER; *b* 1959; *educ* St. Patrick's College, Belfast; University College Dublin, BCL; King's Inns, Barrister at law, 1982; *m* Sally Deverell, co-publisher and co-presenter with husband John; Practiced at the Bar, 1982-89; Freelance Food Writer, Journalist, Publisher; *Irish Times* columnist since 1989; Co-presenter/writer, *McKenna's Ireland*, RTE Television, 1995-

96; contributor to international newspapers and magazines; Publications include: *The Bridgestone Guides*, 1989 to date; *How To Run A Restaurant, McKenna's Ireland*; Chairman, West Cork Chamber Music Festival; Recipient, André Simon Memorial Award, 1992; Glenfiddich Regional Writer of the Year, 1993; Glenfiddich Radio Programme of the Year, 1994; Glenfiddich Restaurant Writer of the Year, 1995; A food writer with an encyclopaedic knowledge of produce and places; regarded as one of the country's foremost food experts, but a rather bland restaurant critic; Hobby, music. Contact: The Irish Times, D'Olier Street, Dublin 2. Tel: 01 679 2022.

McKENNA, Patricia; MEMBER OF THE EUROPEAN PARLIAMENT; *b* 1957; *educ* Regional Technical College, Letterkenny; Limerick School of Art & Design; National College of Art & Design; Dip. Fine Art, Teaching Dip. in Art & Design; *m* Martin Gillen; 1 *s;* Art Teacher, St. Mary's School, Rathmines; elected Member of the European Parliament, 1994-99 and 1999-2005; an artist who has sold a number of paintings 1982-85, including works to the US Ambassador to Ireland; publications include *Amsterdam Treaty - The Road to an Undemocratic and Military Superstate* 1998 and contributions to a number of political opinions and commentaries; President, Anti-Vivisection Society; Trustee, Irish African Asian Conservation Trust; Patron, Outhouse Gay & Lesbian Trust; Patron, Samhain; a major force within the Green Party, seen as energetic, hard working and courageous to the point of combatitive. Hobbies, art and design. Contact: 43 Molesworth Street, Dublin 2. Tel: 01 661 6833. Fax: 01 676 3969.

McKENNA, Thomas Patrick "TP"; ACTOR, DIRECTOR; *b* 1929; *educ* Mullagh National School, St. Patrick's College, Cavan; *m* May White; 4 *s* 1 *da*; worked six years in banking; Became a member of the Abbey Theatre Company, 1955; Spent eight years in the company; Made Honorary Life Member of Company in 1966; Made first appearance in London's West End in *'Stephen D.'* at St. Martin's Theatre in 1963; Joined Nottingham Playhouse Co., 1968-69; Member, Royal Shakespearean Company, 1971-72 season, and again in 1976; Member, Royal National Theatre Company, 1991; Appeared in Gate Theatre Productions, Dublin in 1987, 1993, 1994, 1997, 1998; Appeared in thirty-seven Feature Films for the cinema, and in over one hundred television dramas. Made numerous radio dramas and gave poetry readings for the BBC. Hobbies, music and sport. Contact: Joy Jameson Ltd., 19 The Plaza, 535, Kings Road, London SW10 0SZ, England.

McKENNA-LAWLOR, Susan, née McKenna; ACADEMIC; *educ* Sacred Heart Convent, Leeson Street, Dublin; University College Dublin, BSc, MSc, PhD; University of Michigan, USA; Dublin Institute of Advanced Studies, Post Graduate Scholarship; *m* Michael Lawlor, Animal Nutritionist with Foras Talantais; Research Assistant, Dunsink Observatory, and University of Michigan; Junior Lecturer, Lecturer, Professor, Department of Experimental Physics, Maynooth College, 1986 to date; Managing Director, Space Technology Ireland Ltd., 1987; awarded Tsiolkovsky Gold Medal by the Federation of Cosmonauties 1987, People of the Year Award 1986, Honorary Citizen of San Jose, California 1991, Woman of the Year, London; publications include over fifty papers in scientific journals and three books; Principal Investigator/Co-Investigator to eleven space experiments, including Halley's Comet, Irish stamp commemorated experimental work; Fellow of Royal Astronomical Society, International Astronautical Federation. Hobbies, mountain climbing and opera. Contact: Dept. of Experimental Physics, National University of Ireland, Maynooth, Co. Kildare. Tel: 01 628 5222. Fax: 01 628 9063.

McKEON, Clare

McKEON, Clare; BROADCASTER; *b* 1961; *educ* Alexandra College, Dublin; Dublin City University, BA Communications; California State University, Sacramento, M.A. Communications; *m* Eamonn McLoughlin; 1*s;* Reporter with B.B.C. Dublin; Talk Show Host, Century Radio; Talk Show Host, 98FM Radio; Talk Show Host, FM104; Co-presenter *Sweet Talk*, R.T.E. Television, 1994-95, *Movable Feast*, 1995-98, currently Presenter, *Later with Clare McKeon*, RTE Television; publications include articles for newspapers and magazines, *The Emotional Cook* (O'Brien Press); Founder/proprietor, Bliss, Beauty and Massage, Sandycove; widely regarded as Ireland's answer to Oprah Winfrey - only better looking. Hobbies, eating, planes, trains and automobiles. Contact: R.T.E., Donnybrook, Dublin 4. Tel: 01 208 3111.

McKEON, Eamonn

McKEON, Eamonn; CHIEF EXECUTIVE, GREAT SOUTHERN HOTELS, CHAIRMAN OF CERT; *b* 1947; *educ* Summerhill College, Sligo; College of Commerce, Marketing Diploma; *m* Carol O'Connor; 1 *s*; 2 *da*; Joined Bord Failte; Sales Executive, Great Southern Hotels; Executive Vice President, CIE Tours, New York, 1976-82; Chief Executive, Great Southern Hotels, 1982 to date; Member: Institute of Directors, Ireland United States Council, Dun Laoghaire Golf Club; Former President, Irish Hotels Federation, 1992-93; Chairman, I.T.I.C., Irish Tourist Industry Confederation, 1994-95. Hobbies, golf, reading and music. Contact: Great Southern Hotels, 6 Charlemont Terrace, Crofton Road, Dun Laoghaire, Co. Dublin. Tel: 01 280 8581. Fax: 01 230 1374.

McKINNEY, Craig; CHAIRMAN, MANAGING DIRECTOR WOODCHESTER INVESTMENTS; *b* 1948; *educ* Coatbridge Secondary School, Lanarkshire (Scotland); Herriot Watt University,

Edinburgh (briefly); *m* Joan Ann Chasney; (*m dis*); 1 *s* 3 *da;* Sales Manager, Hamilton Leasing Ltd. (U.K.), 1970, Scottish Regional Manager, 1972; Managing Director, (Ireland) Ltd., 1975; Director Hamilton Leasing (Scotland) Ltd, 1976; founded Woodchester Investments Ltd. as 50% shareholder and Managing Director, 1977, Chairman, Managing Director, Woodchester Investments plc, 1982 - 1997; Chairman, GE Capital Woodchester, 1997 to date; Director of some fifty-one companies; Joint Master, South County Hunt; member, All Ireland Polo Club. A canny Scotsman who can identify business opportunities; both fearless and a realist; said to be a loyal friend; works hard and plays hard. Contact: Woodchester House, Golden Lane, Dublin 8. Tel: 01 478 0000. Fax: 01 402 1849.

McLOUGHLIN, Kieran

McMANUS, Padraig

McLOUGHLIN, Kieran Francis; DIRECTOR THE IRELAND FUNDS; *b* 1966; *educ* Blackrock College; Trinity College, BA (Pol. & Econ.); ACCA, C.Dip; *single* ; Development Director, Dublin Chamber of Commerce, 1988-96; Director, Environmental Inventory Ltd., 1993-96; Director, Schools Business Partnership Ltd., 1992-96; Projects Director, Dublin International Sports Council, 1994-96; Member, Consultative Panel, Dublin Transportation Initiative, 1994-97; Director, Ireland, The Ireland Funds, 1996 to date, Member Ireland Funds' Executive Committee, 1996 to date, Ireland Funds' Finance Committee, 1996 to date, Ireland Funds' Marketing Group, 1996 to date, Ireland Funds Advisory Committee, 1996 to date, Peace, Culture, Education and Community Development Working Parties; associations include member, Chartered Certified Accountants, 1995; Executive Committee, The Jack & Jill Foundation, 1997; Committee Member, Dalkey Players, (1995-97). Hobbies, travel - as exotic as possible, drama - to attend and to act, modern Irish history and current affairs, wine, all sports - as a spectator. Contact: The Ireland Funds, Oscar Wilde House, 1 Merrion Square, Dublin 2. Tel: 01 662 7878. Fax: 01 662 7879.

McMANUS, J.P.; BLOODSTOCK BREEDER / GAMBLER; *b* 1957; *educ* Roxboro National School; Sexton Street Christian Brother's School, Limerick; *m* Noreen ----; 3 children; started gambling at the age of nine; joined father's Plant Hire business on leaving school; left to set up bookmaker establishment, 1971; eventually moved out of bookie business into gambling; first major betting coup backing the local Limerick hurling team in the 1975 interprovincial, subsequently adopted their colours as racing colours; nicknamed "Sundance Kid" by UK broadsheet; winning horses include *Cill Dara* 1975-77, *Jack of Trumps, Laura's Beau, Mister Donovan* 1982, *Bit of a Skite* 1985, *Danny Connors* 1991, *Blitzkrieg, Le Coudray, Shannon Gale, Istabraq*; a noted fund raiser for Limerick charities; a competitive Backgammon player; Director, Sandy Lane Hotel, Barbados; a popular man on the international racing scene and within his own community; recognised as having an amazing financial brain. Contact: Martinstown Stud, Killmalock, Co. Limerick.

McMANUS, Liz; POLITICIAN; *b* 1947 (Montreal); *educ* Holy Child Convent, Killiney; University College Dublin, BArch; *m* John McManus; 3*s* 1*da*; daughter of the late Dr. Tim O'Driscoll, one of the States most prominent public servants, former Ambassador and Head of Board Fáilte; practised as an architect, Derry, Galway, Dublin, Wicklow, 1969-73; Homemaker, 1973-92; Writer / Columnist, 1981 to date; elected Democratic Left, now Labour, Dáil Deputy for Wicklow, 1992 to date; Minister for Housing and Urban Renewal (Rainbow Coalition, 1992-97); Spokesperson on Agriculture and Food, Equality and Law Reform, Health, 1993 to date; publications include, *Act of Subversion* (novel); nominated for Aer Lingus/*Irish Times* Award, short stories received Irish P.E.N. Award, 1984, Hennessy Award and Listowel Award, 1989; Chairperson of Taskforce on the Needs of the Travelling Community, 1992-94; member, NUJ; seen by some Dáil colleagues as a Patrician amongst Plebs; a serious, high-minded and dedicated Deputy. Hobbies, writing, reading and hill walking. Contact: Dáil Eireann, Leinster House, Kildare Street, Dublin 2. Tel: 01 618 3333.

McMANUS, Padraig; MANAGING DIRECTOR ESB INTERNATIONAL; *b* 1951; *educ* Naas CBS Secondary School; University College Dublin, BE (Elec); *m* Marie Coughlan; 1*s* 1 *da;* Professional Engineer, ESB 1973-80; Regional Engineer, Riyadh, Saudia Arabia, 1981-83; Senior Engineer, ESBI Jubail Project, Saudi Arabia, 1984-86, Project Manager, ESBI Ghana Project, 1987-94; General Manager, HR & Training, ESB, 1994-97, Managing Director, ESB International, 1998 to date; published case study on the implementation of energy projects in developing countries sponsored by the World Bank; Fellow, Institute of Engineers of Ireland; Council member, Irish Management Consultants of Ireland. Hobbies, GAA, golf and cycling. Contact: ESB International Ltd., 18 St. Stephen's Green, Dublin 2. Tel: 01 703 8000.

McNUTT, Patrick Anthony; CHAIRPERSON COMPETITION AUTHORITY, DUBLIN; *b* 1957; *educ* University College Dublin, BA; Oxford University, MPhil; University of Ulster, DPhil; *m* Maeve Doherty; Research Assistant, ESRI Dublin, 1978-80; Lecturer in Economics, University College Galway, 1982-94; Professor of Political Economy, University of Ulster, Belfast, 1994-96; Chairperson, Competition Authority, Dublin, 1996 to date; books include, *The Economics of Public Choice* (1996), publisher: Edward Elgar Publishing, UK; Executive Board member, European Public Choice Society; Research Associate, Department of Political Science, TCD, member,

McQUAID, Patrick

American Economics Association, The Literati Club, Royal Economics Society. Hobbies, jazz, cooking, Matisse, Chagalle and (overseas) travel, occasional golf and gardening. Contact: Parnell House, Parnell Square, Dublin 1. Tel: 01 804 5400.

McQUAID, Patrick David; SPORTS PROMOTOR; *b* 1949; *educ* Strawberry Hill London, Degree in Physical Education; *separated; 3s* 1 *da;* P.E. Teacher, Greenhills College, Ballinteer Community School, 1973-84; Sports Promotor 1984 to date; promotional work includes Race Director Nissan International Classic, 1985-92, Race Director Kelloggs Tour of Britain, 1986-93, Race Director Protour, 1998,'99, Race Director Tour of the Phillipines, 1996-98, Tour de France in Ireland, 1998, Race Director Tour of Langkawi, Malaysia, 1996-99; President, Irish Cycling Federation, 1996-99; member, Management Committee, Union Cycliste Internationale; President, Road Commission, UCI. Hobbies, sport, travel and music. Contact: Sport for Television, 12 Prince of Wales Terrace, Bray, Co. Wicklow. Tel: 01 286 4451.

McSWINEY, Veronica; CLASSICAL PIANIST; *b* 1940; *educ* Loreto College, St. Stephen's Green, Dublin; College of Music; Mozarteum, Salzburg; studied privately with Ilona Kabos (London); *m* Michael O'Dea *(decd)*; 1*s* 2 *da*; *m* Christopher Sample, Captain with Merchant Navy; Dublin debut aged sixteen; admired by Sir Robert and Lady Mayer, she subsequently appeared with the London Symphony Orchestra, Festival Hall, London; has toured extensively and played with all the major orchestras in Germany, Holland, USSR and U.S. (with Bernadette Greevey); a sought after soloist, chamber musician and international adjudicator; former Director of Music, Irish National Opera; on returning to Ireland from U.K. has joined the staff at the Royal Irish Academy of Music and formed Oirfia Piano Trio with Geraldine O'Grady (violin) and David James (cello); a much admired musician, noted for her generous approach to young artists. Hobbies, gardening and animals, particularly two golden retrievers and four Persian cats. Contact: Stephannie Williams, 12 Central Chambers, Wood Street, Stratford-on-Avon, CV37 6JQ.

McVEY, Eoin; JOURNALIST; *b* 1951; *educ* Gonzaga College; Castleknock College; *m* Kathryn O'Kelly; 1 s 2*da*; Accountant with Coopers and Lybrand, Dublin 1973-78; Business Reporter, *The Irish Times* 1978-85, Assistant Editor 1985-89, Managing Editor 1989 to date; Director of Irish Times Ltd., 1997 to date. A top class financial journalist who has moved from the business pages to an influential management position but maintains a low key profile. Contact: The Irish Times, 10-16 D'Olier Street, Dublin 2. Tel: 01 679 2022. Fax: 01 671 9407.

MEADE, Noel; RACE-HORSE TRAINER; *b* 1951; *educ* St. Pat's, Navan; *partner* Gillian O'Brien; obtained Trainer's Licence in 1975; started training on home farm with a couple of horses; has trained 1,600 winners both on the flat and over jumps; a highly respected figure within the racing community; currently leading National Hunt trainer in Ireland. Hobby, a committed Meath Football fan. Tel: 046 54197. Fax: 046 54459.

MEAGHER, Joe; MANAGING DIRECTOR IARNRÓD EIREANN; *b* 1951; *educ* St. Kieran College, Kilkenny; University College Dublin, BEng (Civil); Leeds University, MSc (Transportation Engineering); Lausanne, Senior Management Diploma; *m* Mary McGettigan; 1*s* 3 *da*; Operating Manager, Dublin Bus, 1980-83; Manager, Road Passenger Planning, CIE, 1983-87; Manager, Business Development, Bus Eireann, 1987-93; General Manager, Transportation, Iarnród Eireann, 1994-97; Chief Executive, Iarnród Eireann, 1997-99; Managing Director, Iarnród Eireann, 1999 to date; Fellow, Institute of Engineers; member, Chartered Institute of Transport, Marketing Institute. Hobby, plays some golf. Contact: Head Office, Connolly Station, Dublin 1. Tel: 01 703 2608. Fax: 01 703 2466.

MEAGHER, John; ARCHITECT; *b* 1947; *educ* Pembroke School, Dublin; St. Michael's College; Blackrock College; School of Architecture, Dublin Institute of Technology, Dip Arch; Helsinki University of Technology; School of Architecture, Otaniemi, Finland; *single;* Studio Master, University College Dublin 1975-83; worked in Germany and the US before setting up practice with Shane de Blacam in Dublin - de Blacam and Meagher Architects, 1976; some of the projects of the practice of de Blacam and Meagher are: The Dining Hall, Atrium and The Samuel Beckett Centre for Performing Arts (Trinity College Dublin); The Michael Smurfit Graduate School of Business (University College Dublin); new Library, IT and Catering School at Cork Institute of Technology; School of Art, Galway - Mayo Institute of Technology, Galway; Chapel of Reconciliation, Knock, Co. Mayo; Restoration of Lyons House and Demesne, Co. Kildare; Headquarters for Esat Telecom, Dublin; invited Lecturer at the School of Art (Glasgow), Edinburgh University, Architectural Association of Ireland, North London Polytechnic, University of London, Portsmouth Polytechnic, Designs on Europe Symposium, Humberside Polytechnic, Arts Council of Northern Ireland, Belfast RIBA; President, Architectural Association of Ireland 1977-80; member, Art Advisory Board Hugh Lane Municipal Gallery of Modern Art 1983-90; ROSC committee member 1975-83; Trustee, Dublin Graphic Studio 1989-92; Board member, Irish Museum of Modern

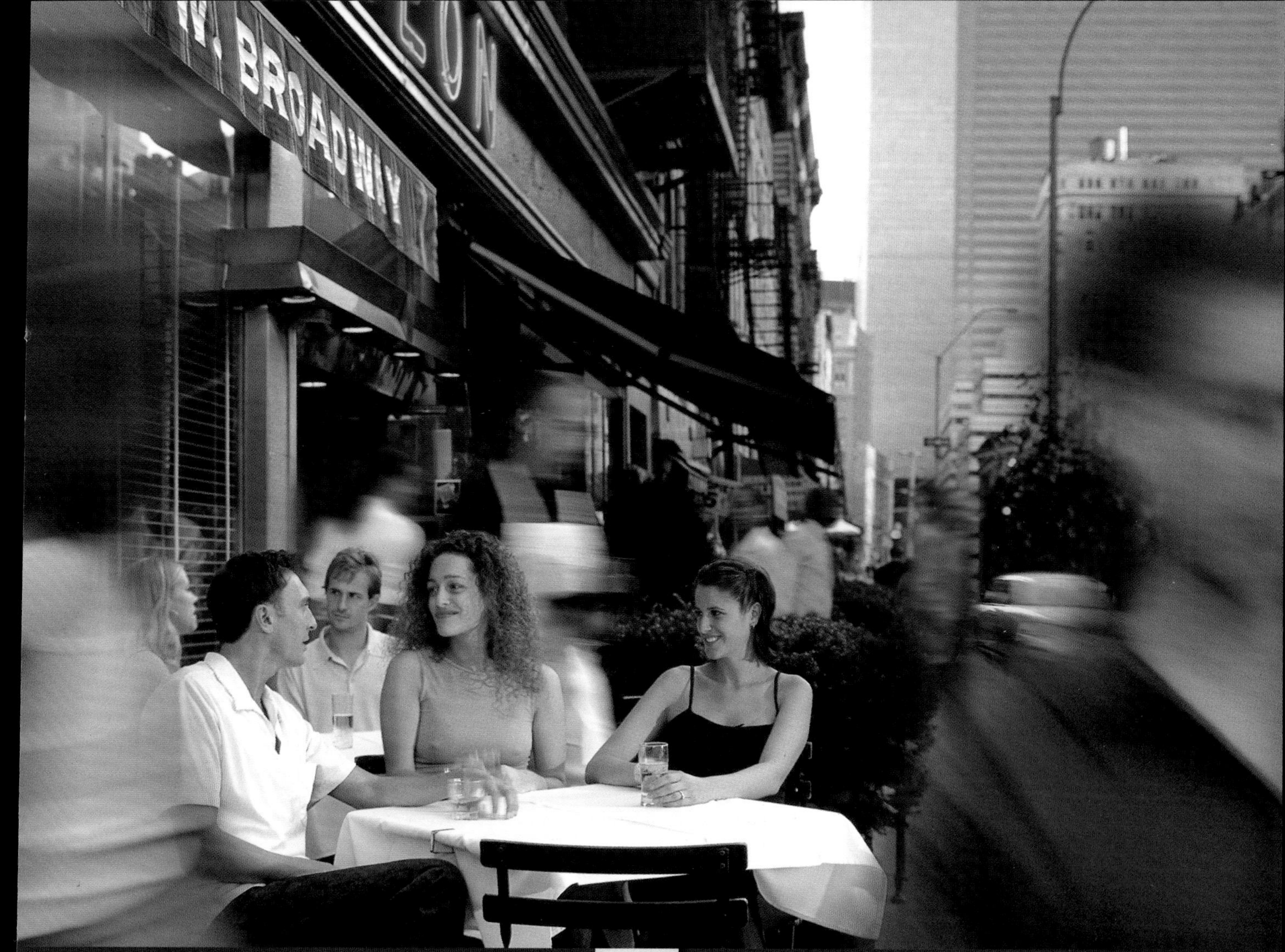
W. BROADWAY

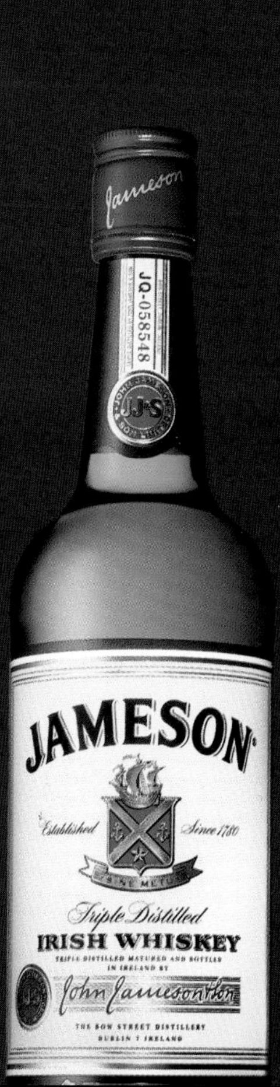
JAMESON
Established
Since 1780
Triple Distilled
IRISH WHISKEY

Art at Royal Hospital Kilmainham 1989-95, Board member, Black Church Print Studio, Dublin, 1995 to date; *Irish Arts Review*, editorial board 1986 to date; MRIAI, MSDI, FRIAI; a strong influence in both architecture and design in Ireland, a well informed and lively companion. Contact: de Blacam and Meagher, 29 Raglan Road, Dublin 4. Tel.: 01 668 1555. Fax: 01 668 1075.

MEAGHER, John; BUSINESSMAN; *b* 1938; *educ* Willow Park School; Blackrock College; *separated;* 1 *s* 2 *da;* worked with International Surveys Ltd. (Toronto), 1957-63; Founder, Proprietary Shareholder, Irish Marketing Surveys Group (including Irish Marketing Surveys Ltd., Lansdowne Market Research Ltd., Ulster Marketing Surveys, Ltd. Belfast) 1963 to date; Director, Independent Newspapers plc, 1982 to date, Deputy Chairman, 1984 to date, Chief Executive, 1985-90; Director, Friends Provident Insurance Company Ltd.; Fellow, The Marketing Institute of Ireland, former Chairman, Marketing Research Society of Ireland and Marketing Society of Ireland; Governor, National Maternity Hospital; Director, Arcon plc, Tribune Newspapers; publications include numerous papers on marketing and market research; a significant player on a strong corporate team; widely regarded as an expert in the marketing field; a witty after dinner speaker. Clubs, Kildare Street and University, Fitzwilliam L.T.C., Royal St. George Yacht Club. Contact: Irish Marketing Surveys Ltd., 19-21 Upper Pembroke Street, Dublin 2. Tel: 01 676 1196.

MEALY, Alphonsus, "Fonsie"; MANAGING DIRECTOR MEALYS, FINE ART AUCTIONEERS; *b 1949; educ* Castlecomer National School; Rockwell College; *m* Eileen O'Malley; 1 *s* 3 *da*; started as porter in family auctioneering firm, 1968, Manager, 1975-81, Mealys, Fine Art & Rare Book Auctioneering Specialists, Managing Director 1981 to date, A major Irish Auction House conducting important sales, both in their galleries and house sales; specialists in sale of rare and Antiquarian books; Lectures on Fine Art and Rare Books; contributor to television programmes and journals; property valuer; Member of Fine Art Committee Irish Auctioneers Valuers Institute; member of General Purposes Committee, Royal Dublin Society; Fellow of Irish Auctioneers and Valuers Institute F.I.A.V.I; Past President Kilkenny Rotary Club. Hobbies, badminton, squash, walking, acting, book collecting, charity work and local history. Contact: George Mealy & Sons, Chatsworth Street, Castlecomer, Co. Kilkenny. Tel: 056 41229. Fax: 056 41627.

MELLON, Niall J.; FINANCIAL BROKER, HOTELIER; *b* 1967; *educ* Colaiste Éanna, CBS, Rathfarnham; *single;* set up Mellon Financial Services 1989; built and opened the Charleville Hotel (£12 million) in 1998; owner of Marley Grange Hotel, currently being developed into an Irish music venue (£8 million); the Mellon Group is a fast expanding business empire currently employing 200; President, I.M.A.F. (Irish Mortgage Advisor Federation). Hobbies, horse-breeding, art collection, Irish music and fundraising for charity. Contact: Niall J. Mellon, Ardee Court, Ardee Road, Rathmines, Dublin 6. Tel: 01 460 4333. Fax: 01 496 8379.

MELLY, Seàn J.

MELLY, Seàn J.; CHIEF EXECUTIVE, MCI WORLDCOM, ENTREPRENEUR & PRIVATE INVESTOR; *b* 1964; *educ* St. Clonkeen College, Foxrock, Co. Dublin; Trinity College Dublin, BBS (Hons), 1985; University College Dublin, MBS (Finance), 1986; *m* Heidi Haerschko; 3 *da*; Citicorp/Harvard Institute for Global Finance, 1988; joined Citicorp Investment Bank, London and New York, 1986-89; Vice President, Corporate Finance, First City, London, 1989-90; Board Director, Corporate Development, R&J Emmet plc, New York, 1990-92; Founder, Telatlantic Telecommunications, New York, 1993; Founder, TCL Telecom, Dublin, 1994; TCL Telecom acquired by Worldcom, 1997; Currently Chief Executive, MCI Worldcom; Member, Institute of Directors, American Chamber of Commerce in Ireland, Securities Exchange of Great Britain and Ireland; Clubs: Kildare Street & University Club. Hobbies, travel, gym and reading. Contact: World Com, Embassy House, Ballsbridge, Dublin 4. Tel: 01 679 0404. Fax: 01 670 8222.

MILLER, Eric; PROFESSIONAL RUGBY PLAYER; *b* 1975; *educ* Wesley College, Dublin; Waterford RTC; Shefield Hallam University; *single;* played for one season with Old Wesley RFC, 1994-95; moved to Leicester Tigers, 1995-98; currently with Terenure College and Ulster, 1998-2000; selected for Lions Tour, 1997 (youngest ever forward); capped for Ireland 14 times; represented Provincial and National Schools and Colleges and under 21 XVs; member, Professional Rugby Players Association (UK); awarded Young Leinster Player of the Year 1995, Player of the Year 1997. Hobbies, reading, golf and watching television. Contact: John Baker, 47 Upper Leeson Street, Dublin 4. Tel: 01 660 3033.

MILLER, Liam Francis

MILLER, Liam Francis; MANAGING DIRECTOR, ORGANISATION AND DEVELOPMENT, RTE; *b* 1949; *educ* Scoil Lorcain, Sandymount, Dublin; High School; *m* Britt Hällzon; 2 *da*; Assistant Cameraman, Aengus Films, 1968-69; worked on sound TV RTE, 1969, Director, RTE, 1977, Producer, 1980, Controller, Production and Resources TV, 1990-93, Director, Television Programmes, 1993-97, Managing Director, Organisation & Development, 1997 to date; production works include *Twice Shy* (TV film); *The Lilac Bus, Dear Sarah* (Associate Producer) *Brides of Christ, The Treaty* (film drama) and Executive Producer of 1993 and 1988 Eurovision Song

BERRY BROS & RUDD

Established in the XVII Century

Extraordinary wines from an extraordinary wine merchant

4 Harry Street, Dublin 2 Tel: (01) 677-3444

Contests; Director, Dublin Film Festival, Tara Television; Governor, Banff International TV Festival. Hobbies, cycling and flying (licensed pilot). Contact: R.T.E., Donnybrook, Dublin . Tel: 01 208 2538. Fax: 208 2082.

MILLS, Kingston H.G.; DEAN OF SCIENCE NATIONAL UNIVERSITY OF IRELAND, MAYNOOTH; *b* 1955; *educ* Wilson's Hospital Secondary School, Multyfarnham, Co. Westmeath; Trinity College Dublin, BA (Mod), Biochemistry (Hons), PhD, Immunology; *m* Dr Marina Lynch; 1*s* 1 *da;* Post Doctoral Research Fellow, Department of Haematology, University College, London, 1981-83; Scientific Staff, Division of Immunology, National Institute for Medical Research, Mill Hill, London, 1983-87; Scientist/Senior Scientist, Division of Immunobiology, National Institute for Biological Standards and Control, South Mimms, (UK), 1987-92; Lecturer, Department of Biology, St. Patrick's College Maynooth, 1993-95; Senior Lecturer, National University of Ireland, Maynooth, 1995-98, Dean of the Faculty of Science, 1997, Associate Professor, 1999; elected to Fellowship of the Royal Society for Medicine of Ireland; elected to Membership of the Institute of Biology of Ireland; invited to join Editorial Board of European Federation of Microbiology Societies; selected to present the 39th Annual Graves Lecture of the Royal Academy of Medicine in Ireland; member, Irish Society for Immunology, Institute of Biology Ireland, British Society for Immunology, Society for General Microbiology, Biochemical Society, International Society for Mucasal Immunology, Irish Research Scientists Association; member of over twenty professional bodies; a leading Irish scientist with a growing international reputation. Hobbies, running, cycling, organic vegetable gardening, wine and opera. Contact: National University of Maynooth, Maynooth, Co. Kildare. Tel: 01 708 3838.

MILTON, James; PUBLIC RELATIONS CONSULTANT; *b* 1945; *educ* St. Michael's and St. James's Christian Brothers Schools, Dublin; College of Technology, Kevin Street; *m* Carmel Barron; 4 *children;* Journalist with *Business and Finance* 1964-70, Editor 1970-73; Founding Director, with Joseph Murray, Murray Consultants Ltd., one of the major public relations companies in the country; member Public Relations Institute and Marketing Institute of Ireland. An urbane, handsome man with a polished, professional approach. Hobbies, walking, boating and gliding. Contact: Murray Consultants, 35 Upper Mount Street, Dublin 2. Tel: 01 661 4666. Fax: 01 661 1936.

MITCHELL, James "Jim"; POLITICIAN; *b* 1946; *educ* St. Michael's Christian Brothers School, Inchicore; St. James' Christian Brothers School; Emmet Road Vocational School; College of Commerce, Rathmines; Trinity College Dublin, Dip Systems Analysis; *m* Patricia Kenny; 2*s* 3*da;* Computer Executive, Guinness Group; joined Fine Gael Party 1976; City Councillor, Dublin Corporation, 1974-81, 1991-94; Alderman, 1979-81; Lord Mayor of Dublin, 1976-77; elected Fine Gael Deputy for Dublin Ballyfermot, 1977, following constituency boundary changes for Dublin West, 1981-92, Dublin Central, 1992 to date; Minister for Justice, 1981-82; Minister for Transport, 1982-84; Minister for Posts and Telegraphs, 1982-84; Minister for Communications, 1990-91; Minister for the Environment, 1991-93; Chairman, Parliamentary Committee of Public Accounts, 1993-95, 1997 to date; Front Bench Spokesman on Institutional and Public Service Reforms, 1999; has held various EU and Parliamentary positions; an independent minded and outspoken politician, noted as an excellent campaigner. Contact: Dáil Eireann, Leinster House, Kildare Street, Dublin 2. Tel: 01 618 3730.

MITCHELL, Thomas

MITCHELL, James; FILM PRODUCER; *b* 1948; *educ* Bishops Stortford College; Cambridge University, MA; *m* Jane Hickie; qualified as a Barrister; member of Lincoln's Inn, London; moved into the film world, Partner, Margulies & Company 1971-78; Chief Executive, Little Bird, 1981 to date; Executive Producer of films, television drama and documentaries including *The Disappearance, The Irish R.M., Troubles, December Bride, Into the West, A Man of No Importance, The Hanging Gale, The Writing on the Wall, All for Love, Undressed, Waiting for Harvey, My Mother's Courage, Ordinary Decent Criminal.* Contact: Little Bird, 13 Merrion Square, Dublin 2. Tel: 01 661 4245. Fax: 01 662 4647.

MIZZONI, Aine Maria

MITCHELL, Thomas; PROVOST TRINITY COLLEGE; *b* 1939; *educ* University College Galway, BA, MA; Cornell University, Ithaca, New York, PhD., University of Dublin, Litt. D; *m* Lynn Hunter, Biologist; 3 *s* 1 *da;* Lecturer, University College Cork, 1967-68; Associate Professor, Swarthmore College, 1968, Professor of Classics, 1978-79; Professor of Latin, Trinity College Dublin, 1979-91, Provost, 1991 to date; Fellow, Trinity College, 1980; member, Royal Irish Academy, 1986, Senior Vice-President, 1989; appointed to Cornell Visiting Professorship for Distinguished Scholars by Swarthmore College, 1986; awards include: Honorary LL.D, by National University of Ireland, 1992; Honorary doctorate of Humane Letters by Swarthmore College, 1992; Honorary LL.D. by Queen's University Belfast, 1992; Honorary Fellowship of the Royal College of Physicians of Ireland, 1992; named Mayo Person of the Year, 1993; awarded Honorary Fellowship of the Royal College of Surgeons of Ireland, 1993; elected Member of the American Philosophical Society, 1996; Honorary Doctorate of Humane Letters by Lynn University, 1998; Honorary PhD. by Charles

University, Prague, 1998; Honorary Doctorate of Humane Letters by the State University of New York, 1998; publications include: *Cicero: The Ascending Years, Cicero: The Senior Statesman, Cicero: Verrines II I.* Hobbies, theatre, gardening and reading. Contact: Trinity College, Dublin 2. Tel: 01 677 2941.

MIZZONI, Aine Maria, née Wynn; CHIEF EXECUTIVE E-SMART.; *b* 1961; *educ* St. Louis Convent, Rathmines; Certified Public Accountant, Dip. Computer Systems Analysis and Design (IMI); *m* Gerry Mizzoni, Restaurateur; 4 *da;* Assistant Accountant, Coughlan Moore Ltd., 1979-81; joined Sedgwick Dineen Group Ltd. as Assistant Financial Accountant, 1981, Associate Director, 1987, Director/Financial Controller, 1989, Group Operations Director, 1991, Chief Operating Officer, 1997 to Oct 1999; Chief Executive E-Smart Oct, 1999, member, Institute of Directors, Institute of Certified Public Accountants; Council member, Dublin Chamber of Commerce; a hands-on insurance executive who puts people first. Hobbies, reading, painting, listening to music, family holidays. Contact: Sedgwick Dineen Group, 25 Adelaide Road, Dublin 2. Tel: 01 604 8100.

MOLONEY, Alan James; FILM AND TELEVISION PRODUCER; *b* 1966; *educ* Gonzaga College; Castleknock College; *m* Mari Kennedy; Researcher, Line Producer, Emdee Productions, 1986-92; Managing Director, Parallel Film Productions, 1993 to date; Film Credits include: Co-Producer, *Last of the High Kings*, Feature Film; Producer, *A Love Divided*, Feature Film; Executive Producer, *Amongst Women, Falling for a Dancer, D.D.U,* televison series; Executive Committee Member, Film Makers Ireland; Member, Fitzwilliam Lawn Tennis Club; Seen as a confident, fortright film maker, who has had heady number of recent successes. Hobbies, skiing, films and reading. Contact: Parallel Film Productions Ltd., 14-15 Sir John Rogerson's Quay, Dublin 2. Tel: 01 671 8555. Fax: 01 6718 242.

MOLONEY, Maurice

MOLONEY, Maurice; CORK COUNTY MANAGER; *b* 1943; *educ* Ballyduff, Co. Waterford; Mount Melleray College; University College Cork, BA, MA; *m* Mary Lane; 1*s;* 1 *da;* Clerical Officer, Waterford County Council; Staff Officer, Administration Officer, Assistant Town Clerk, Assistant City Manager, Cork Corporation; City Manager & Town Clerk, Cork Corporation, (temporary); City Manager & Town Clerk, Limerick; currently, County Manager, Cork. Contact: County Hall, Carrigrohane Road, Cork. Tel: 021 276 891. Fax: 021 276 321.

MOLONEY, Paddy; MUSICIAN; *b* 1938; *educ* Scoil Mhuire; St. Joseph's School, Fairview; *m* Rita O'Reilly; 2*s* 1 *da;* formed traditional music group The Chieftains 1961, comprising Martin Fay, Sean Keane, Derek Bell, Kevin Cunniffe, Matt Molloy; the group has toured extensively world wide; they have released thirty-five albums, received twenty-six Grammy nominations and won six; also received numerous other music awards; recipient of Honorary Doctorate, D. Mus., Trinity College. Hobbies, gardening, tree planing and eating out. Contact: MCMA, The Factory Studies, 35A Barrow Street, Dublin 4. Tel: 01 667 4171. Fax: 01 667 3920.

MOLONY, Ronan

MOLONEY, Thomas; BLOODSTOCK BREEDER; *b* 1938; *educ* Christian Brothers School, Kilkenny; *m* Ann Maher; 3 *s* 2 *da;* breeds international class showjumping horses on family farm, also runs equestrian centre; horses bred from the famous *Highland Flight* stallion include *Black and Amber Flight, Carrolls Flight, Oak Flight, Highland Serpent, Super Flight, Valentine Flight* (silver medal winner), *Top Flight, Speedy Flight* (bronze medal winner, European Championships); member, Irish Showjumping Association; a knowledgeable and highly regarded bloodstock breeder and the father of some international class riders; entire family involved in equestrian empire. Contact: Top Flight Equestrian Centre, Warrington Stud, Warrington, Kilkenny. Tel: 056 22682.

MOLONY, Ronan; SOLICITOR; *b* 1959; *educ* Blackrock College; University College Dublin, Incorporated Law Society; B.C.L., A.I.T.I.; *m* Christine Lavelle; 2 *s;* 1 *da;* Apprentice Solicitor, McCann FitzGerald, 1980; Solicitor, 1983; Partner, 1984; Chairman, 1997 to date; McCann FitzGerald are one of the larger practices in the State with ninety lawyers and offices in London, Brussels and New York; Member: Incorporated Law Society of Ireland, Associate Institute of Taxation in Ireland; Director, Commerzbank Europe (Ireland), Caterpillar International Bank plc and Bank of Montreal; member, Royal St. George Yacht Club and Royal Irish Yacht Club; Hobbies, sailing, skiing. Contact: McCann FitzGerald, 2 Harbourmaster Place, Custom House Dock, Dublin 1. Tel: 01 829 0000. Fax: 01 8290010.

MONAGHAN, Philip

MONAGHAN, Philip; CHAIRMAN, CHIEF EXECUTIVE, MONARCH PROPERTIES, LTD.; *b* 1928; *educ* Knockbridge National School; Dundalk Technical School, All Ireland Bronze Medal; *m* Mary Connor; 4 *s* 2 *da;* worked in agriculture, 1942-44; Apprentice Fitter/Turner, Corry & Walls, 1944-49; Fitter/Turner, Gypsum Industries, 1949-50; Trades Teacher, Dundalk Technical School, 1949-58; Technical Manager, McCann Fruit (FII/Fyffes), 1950-66; Chairman, Chief Executive, Monarch Properties Ltd., 1966 to date; regarded as one of the foremost property developers in the country and a generous sponsor of cultural events; clubs, Dundalk G.C., Luttrellstown G.C.

Hobbies, cars and car racing, rotary and fixed wing flying. Contact: Monarch Properties Ltd., Somerton, Castleknock, Dublin 15. Tel: 01 820 5600. Fax: 820 5653.

MOONEY, Carmel

MOONEY, Carmel, née Delaney; ARTIST; *b* 1936; *educ* Ursuline Convent, Thurles; University College Dublin, Diploma in History of Painting; National College of Art & Design, Diploma in Painting; *m* Robert Mooney; 2 *s* 1 *da*; Has been a full time artist since university; has mounted numerous exhibitions both in Ireland and abroad, including nine solo exhibitions in Dublin, London and Hong Kong; Selected exhibitions: Dublin, Tokyo, New York; Member: Contemporary Irish Arts Society, Hon. Life Member, United Arts Club; Recipient of Arts Grants including Arts Council Travel Grant, Cultural relations Committee Department of Foreign Affairs; Works hang in private and public collections in Ireland, UK, US, Hong Kong, Taiwan, Europe and Canada. Hobbies: reading, music, art history. Contact: Fax: 01 611 5200.

MOONEY, Martin; ARTIST; *b* 1960; *educ* University of Ulster; Brighton Polytechnic College of Art and Design, BA Fine Art; University College, London, The Slade School of Fine Art, (Post Graduate); *m* Trudie Crowhurst; 2*da;* part-time tutor, Brighton College of Art, 1986-87; emigrated to Spain in 1987 and exhibited with the Galleria Minerva d'Art in Barcelona; returned to Ireland in 1994 and currently lives and works in Co. Donegal; exhibitions include, Stowells Trophy Exhibition, Royal Academy, London, 1983; *The Mail on Sunday* Young Masters'Exhibition, 1985; Royal Hibernian Academy, Dublin, 1991-94; Cabinet Paintings Theo Waddington Fine Art, London, Everard Read Gallery, Johannesburg, South Africa, 1995; Miami International Art Fair, Florida, USA, 1998 and 1999; Waterman Fine Art, London, 1993 to date; Mitchell Gallery, Toronto, 1994; Solomon Gallery, Dublin, 1992 to date; works in many public collections such as Ulster Museum, Belfast, British Government Art Collection, Harvard University, USA, AIB Bank and Jefferson Smurfit Group plc; private collections include Dr & Mrs AJF O' Reilly, Dr Michael Smurfit, Mrs Norma Smurfit, The Rt Hon Christopher Patten, Dr Derek Hill and Mr Bruce Cairnduff; Mooney has also undertaken many important commissions, the largest being ten panels for the entrance staircase at the Hotel Merrion, Dublin and a special commission for Waterford Wedgwood plc; awards include, Emily Lucy Boyce Travel Scholarship, Brighton Faculty of Art, 1983; Richard Ford Award, The Royal Academy, London, 1985; George Campbell Memorial Grant, Arts Council of Ireland, Arts Council of Northern Ireland and the Spanish Cultural Institute, Dublin, 1987. Hobbies, travel and walking. Contact: Solomon Gallery, Powerscourt Town House Centre, Dublin 2. Tel: 01 679 4237. Fax: 01 671 5262.

MOONEY, Michael; BOATBUILDER; *educ* Killybegs National School; *m* Philomena Doherty; 2*s* 2*da*; started up own boat building company in Killybegs over thirty years ago; dedication to work and affinity with boats have made Mooney Boats one of the most successful boatbuilding and refurbishment operations both on a national and international level. Hobby, travel. Contact: Mooney Boats, Killybegs, Co. Donegal. Tel: 073 31152.

MORAN, Joseph "Joe"; CHIEF EXECUTIVE IRISH WIRE PRODUCTS (IWP) PLC; *b* 1935; *educ* Rockwell College, Co. Tipperary; University College Cork, BSc; *m* Marie Hogan; 1*s* 3*da;* Proprietor, F&T Buckley (Fireplace Manufacturers) 1964, with controlling interest in R&J Dwyer (Hardware Merchants), Meldrums, Sligo, and Cork Iron Hardware Company; formed Moran Group 1973, subsequently acquired UK company; Executive Chairman, Irish Wire Products (IWP), 1990 to date; Chairman, IFG, Deputy Chairman, Flogas. Hobbies, bridge and golf. Contact 19 Fitzwilliam Square, Dublin 2. Tel: 01 661 1954 Fax: 01 661 1957.

MORAN, Mark Patrick; CHIEF EXECUTIVE, MATER PRIVATE HOSPITAL; *b* 1962; *educ* University College Dublin, B.E; Erasmus University, Rotterdam, M.B.A; *m* Mary O'Connell; 1 *s* 1 *da*; Production Engineer, Smithkline Beecham, Cork, 1985-88; Engineering Manager, Millipore Corporation, Cork, 1988-90; Finance Director, Centocor Corporation, Leiden, Holland, 1992-95; Managing Director, Meridian Vat Reclaim, Dublin, 1995-97; Chief Executive, Mater Private Hospital, 1997 to date. Hobbies, bridge, golf and football; Clubs, Regent Bridge Club, Bankers' Bridge Club, St. Margaret's Golf Club. Contact: Mater Private Hospital, Eccles Street, Dublin 7. Tel: 01 838 4444.

MORIARTY, The Hon. Mr. Justice Michael "Mossie"; JUDGE OF THE HIGH COURT; *b* 1946; *educ* Blackrock College; University College Dublin; Kings Inns; *m* Mary Irvine SC; 1*s* 2 *da;* called to the Bar, 1968; called to the Inner Bar, 1982; appointed Chairman of the Employment Appeals Tribunal, 1986; appointed Circuit Court Judge, 1987; appointed to the High Court, 1996; Chairman, Moriarty Tribunal, established to investigate payments to politicians, Mr. Charles Haughey and Mr. Michael Lowry, 1998; was a junior prosecuting counsel in the Mountbatten case, also counsel for the Kerry Babies Tribunal; Senior Counsel for the Attorney General in the Dominic McGlinchey extradition case; member, Fitzwilliam LTC, Pembroke Cricket Club (President); regarded by all as a fairminded, thoughtful and compassionate judge; extremely polite and equally determined. Hobbies, cricket, music and books. Contact: Four Courts, Morgan Place, Dublin 7. Tel: 01 872 5555.

MORRICE, Gordon William; MANAGING DIRECTOR CABLE & WIRELESS IRELAND LTD.; *b* 1941; *educ* Institute of Bankers; *married*; 1*da*; Sales Manager, N England Telephone Rentals plc, 1984-88, Regional Sales Manager, Scotland Telephone Rentals plc, 1988-90; Regional Sales Manager, North & Scotland, Mercury Communications Ltd., 1990-94, Customer Director, North, Midlands, Scotland & N Ireland, 1994-96; Customer Director, Cable & Wireless plc, 1996-98; Managing Director, Cable & Wireless Ireland, 1998 to date. Hobbies, golf and rugby union. Contact: Cable & Wireless Ltd., 1 Airton Road, Tallaght, Dublin 24. Tel: 01 404 9333. Fax: 01 404 0428.

MORRIS, The Hon. Mr. Justice Frederick, PRESIDENT OF THE HIGH COURT; *b* 1929; *educ* Glenstal Abbey, University College Dublin, Kings Inns, Middle Temple, London; *m* Valerie Farrell; 2 *da*; called to the Bar, 1952; called to the English Bar, 1969; called to the Inner Bar, 1973; appointed Judge of the High Court, 1990; appointed President of the High Court, 1998; served on Bar Council for ten years and on the High Court Rules Committeee for seventeen years; Member of the Personal Injuries Compensation Tribunal for ten years; awarded Freedom of City of Waterford, 1963; Elected Honorary Bencher of Middle Temple, London, 1999. A popular member of the judiciary, noted for his strong administrative abilities. Hobbies, sailing, golf and tennis; Clubs, Royal Irish Yacht Club, Milltown G.C., Blainroe Golf Club, U.C.D. Rugby Football Club. Contact: The Four Courts, Morgan Place, Dublin 7. Tel: 01 872 5555.

MORRIS, Frederick

MORRIS, Melanie Rose Josephine; EDITOR AND PUBLISHER; *b* 1966; *educ* Our Lady's School, Rathnew, Co. Wicklow; University College Dublin, B.Comm.; *single;* PR Account Manager, (Fashion & Retail), Lynne Franks, 1987-90; Account Director, Freud Communications, 1990-92; Producer with Voodoo Films (Youth TV Programmes), 1992-93; Established Wardon Publishing, Published *dSide* Magazine, 1993 to date. Awards: Brownie of the Year, 1977; Dublin Winner, Irish Permanent Young Business Woman of the Year, 1997. A young woman with the energy and imagination to take on the established publishing world - and win. Hobbies, film, contemporary art, architecture, travel, youth culture, fashion, collects Sesame Street muppets. Contact: dSide, The Factory, 35a Barrow St. Dublin 4. Tel: 01 668 4966. Fax: 01 668 4859.

MORRIS, Melanie Rose

MORRISON, Conall; THEATRE DIRECTOR; *b* 1966; *educ* St. Patrick's College, Armagh; Liverpool Polytechnic, BA Drama; *single;* productions include *The Conquest of the South Pole, Measure for Measure, Emma, Macbeth* and *The Marlboro Man* for the Lyric Theatre, Belfast; *Juno and the Paycock, Dancing at Lughnasa* for the Abbey Theatre, Dublin; *In a Little World* and *As the Beast Sleeps* (by Gary Mitchell); *Twenty Grand* (by Declan Hughes) and *The Colleen Bawn* (by Dion Boucicault); also adaptation and direction of *Tarry Flynn* by Patrick Kavanagh; as an author, plays professionally produced include *Green, Orange and Pink; Hard to Believe; Rough Justice; Tarry Flynn* (adapted from Patrick Kavanagh); awards include, *Sunday Independent*/Ford Cars Spirit of Life Award 1997 and *Irish Times*/ESB Theatre Award, Best Director, and Best Production for *Tarry Flynn* 1998. Hobbies, reading, theatre, music and walking. Contact: Abbey Theatre, 26 Lower Abbey Street, Dublin 1. Tel: 01 874 8741.

MORTELL, Mark Charles Philip; MANAGING DIRECTOR DIMENSION ADVERTISING AND MARKETING; *b* 1961; *educ* Blackrock College; Presentation College, Bray; Dublin City University B.B.S.; *m* Aisling Skelly; 2 *da;* Brand Manager, Guinness Ireland, 1984-87; Marketing Manager, MARS Ireland, 1987-89; Marketing Director, Ballygowan Spring Water Co. Ltd., 1989-93; Marketing Director, Bank of Ireland, Lifetime, 1993-97; Managing Director, McConnells Marketing Communications Ltd., Managing Director, Dimension Advertising & Marketing, 1997 to date; member, Marketing Institute of Ireland, Public Relations Institute of Ireland, Marketing Society, Bective Rangers Football Club, Fitzwilliam Lawn Tennis Club, Newcastle Lions Riding Club; member, Bray Urban District Council, 1983-85, Wicklow County Council, 1985-89, appointed to National Youth Policy Committee, 1982; Chairman, OTMI, 1995-97; Chairman, Bord Failte, 1997 to present. A fast moving executive, functions equally skilfully at State or commercial level. Hobbies, public affairs, theatre, reading fiction, horse-riding, rugby, tennis, golf. Contact: Dimension, 70 Upper Leeson Street, Dublin 4. Tel: 01 667 3222. Fax: 01 667 3077.

MOYLAN, Patricia "Pat"; OWNER/ARTISTIC DIRECTOR, ANDREWS LANE THEATRE; *b* 1952; *educ* Presentation Convent, Portlaoise; *m* Hugh McCusker, actor; worked in insurance and moved into theatre via publishing; Co-owner, with Mike Hogan, Irish Theatre Publications, publishers of programmes such as *Riverdance* worldwide and theatre related material; Manager, Andrews Lane Theatre, 1989-98, owner, 1998 to date; film productions include *The Breakfast* (written and directed by Peter Sheridan), 1998, *Borstal Boy* (written by Peter Sheridan); Director, Double Joint Productions (Belfast), Co-producer, *Women on the Verge of HRT,* currently touring U.K. Hobby, knitting. Contact: Andrews Lane Theatre, St. Andrews Lane, Dublin 2. Tel: 01 679 5720.

MULCAHY, John; PUBLISHER; *b* 1932 (Perth, Australia); *educ* Clongowes Wood College, Co. Kildare; Trinity College Dublin; *m* Nuala O'Farrell; 6*s* 2*da;* worked in the investment and financial area in Canada, contributor to *Montreal Financial Times*; Director, Smith Holdings Ltd., 1960-67; Editor/Publisher, *Hibernia*, a fortnightly current affairs magazine, 1968-80; Editor, *Sunday Tribune*, 1980-81; Publisher, *Phoenix* magazine, 1983 to date; member, National Union of Journalists; regarded with some wariness by members of the financial, political and media world due to the sometimes unwelcome publicity in Ireland's leading satirical magazine; a pragmatic man, mildly surprised by the notoriety. Hobbies, reading, walking. Contact: Phoenix Magazine, 44 Lower Baggot Street, Dublin 2. Tel: 01 661 1062. Fax: 01 662 4532.

MULCAHY, John F; DIRECTOR JONES LANG LASALLE; *b* 1949; *educ* Oatlands College, Mount Merrion; DIT, Environmental Economics; *m* Margaret Clandillon; 3 *s* 1 *da;* joined Jones Lang Wootton, 1970, Salaried Partner, 1974, Property Partner, 1976; International Managing Director, Jones Lang LaSalle, 1999; as manager of one of the largest commercial surveyors and property companies in the State has been associated with major developments such as Temple Bar, East Point and CityWest, adviser to the Consortium awarded the contract for development of the International Financial Services Centre (Dublin); elected member, Royal Institution of Chartered Surveyors, 1972, elected Fellow, 1978; former Chairman of the General Practice Division of Society of Chartered Surveyors in Ireland and of the Asset Valuation Standards Committee (Ireland, UK and Europe); member, Fitzwilliam LTC, Stephen's Green Club. Hobbies, running and golf. Contact: Jones Lang LaSalle, 10-11 Molesworth Street, Dublin 2. Tel: 01 679 4622. Fax: 01 679 5147.

MULCAHY, Nicholas; PUBLISHER; *b* 1958; *educ* St. Conleth's College; Trinity College Dublin, BA (Mod); *m* Ann O'Neill; 2*s*; 2*da;* Reporter, *Sunday Tribune*, 1980-82; Deputy Editor, *Phoenix* Magazine, 1983-89; News Editor, *Sunday Business Post*; 1989-97; Editor, *Business Plus* Magazine, 1998 to date; two unpublished (unpublishable) novels. Hobbies, hill-walking, supporting Chelsea FC, reading magazines. Contact: Business Plus, 88 Ranelagh Road, Dublin 6. Tel: 01 496 0666. Fax: 01 496 2456.

MULCAHY, Thomas P; CHIEF EXECUTIVE ALLIED IRISH BANKS PLC; *b* 1941; *educ* CBS Carrick-on-Suir; St. Kieran's College, Kilkenny; University College Dublin, BComm; *m* June Clampett; 2 *da*; joined National Bank 1958; joined A.I.B. Investment Bank 1972, launched A.I.B. Merchant Banking subsidiary, London 1973, General Manager, London until 1980, Banking Director, A.I.B., Merchant Bank 1980-85; appointed to bank's top management team as Group General Manager, Corporate and International, 1985-89; Head of A.I.B. Capital Markets 1989; appointed to main board 1990; Chief Executive, Allied Irish Banks plc 1994 to date; Fellow, Institute of Chartered Accountants in Ireland and the Institute of Bankers in Ireland (former President); member, Killiney Golf Club. Hobby, golf. Contact: Allied Irish Banks plc, Bankcentre, PO Box 452, Ballsbridge, Dublin 4. Tel: 01 660 0311.

MULDOON, Paul; POET; *b* 1951; *educ* local school, The Moy; Queens University, Belfast; *m* Jean Hanff Korelitz, Writer; worked as a radio and television producer with the BBC for thirteen years; taught at Columbia, Berkeley and Massachusetts Universities (US); currently teaching at Princeton (US); elected Professor of Poetry, Oxford University 1999; publications include *New Weather* (1973), *Mules* (1977), *Why Brownie Left* (1980), *Quoff* (1983), *Meeting the British* (1987), *Madoc: A Mystery* (1990), *The Annals of Chile* (1994), was awarded the T. S. Eliot Prize, *New Selected Poems 1964-94* (1996), was awarded *Irish Times* Literary Prize; *Hay* (1989); member, Aosdána; probably the foremost figure in the second wave of Ulster poets; elected unopposed to the most prestigious position in the English Academy - Professor of Poetry at Oxford, Seamus Heaney held the position 1989-9. Contact: Aosdána, 70 Merrion Square, Dublin 2. Tel: 01 676 1302.

MULHOLLAND, Joe; MANAGING DIRECTOR TELEVISION, RTE; *b* 1940; *educ* Finn College, Ballybofey; Del La Salle Training College, HDipEd; University of Nancy (France), Doctorat ès Lettres; University of London, BA; Universities of Caen and Barcelona; *m* Annie Vuillemin, Teacher; 2*s* 1*da*; English Teacher, Lycée St. Joseph, 1964-69; Producer/Director, RTE, 1970-80, Head of Current Affairs, 1980-86, Controller, TV Productions, 1986-90, Director of News, RTE, 1990, currently MD Television; recipient of three Jacobs Awards for television documentaries, Neptune Prize at Riga Film Festival; contributor to French newspapers and journals, Co-Editor, MacGill Summer School publication; Director, MacGill Summer School, 1980 to date. A sartorially elegant and powerful figure within Irish broadcasting. Hobbies, reading, theatre, cinema, walking, swimming and sailing. Contact: RTE, Donnybrook, Dublin 4. Tel: 01 208 3111. Fax: 208 3080.

MULLIN, Brendan; STOCKBROKER; *b* 1963; *educ* Blackrock College; Trinity College Dublin, BA Mod Law; Oxford University, MSc(Mgt); *m* Sharon McGrath; 1 *s* 1 *da*; worked in Corporate Finance, AIB (UK) 1988-89; moved to Davy Stockbrokers 1989 to 1996; joined Goodbody Stockbrokers 1996 to date; International Rugby Player 1985 to 1995, capped for Ireland fifty-five times. Recognised as one of the country's finest sportsmen. Hobbies, rugby union, tennis and interested in art. Contact: Goodbody Stockbrokers, 122 Pembroke Road, Dublin 4. Tel: 01 667 0400. Fax: 01 667 0230.

MULLINS, William Peter; RACEHORSE TRAINER; *b* 1956; *educ* Cistercian College, Roscrea; *m* Jacqueline Mary Longton; 1 *s*; Assistant Trainer to Jim Bolger 1982; Assistant Trainer to father, Patrick Mullins 1984-87; Obtained Trainers' Licence, 1988; has trained five Cheltenham winners to date, among them, *Tourist Attraction* 1995, *Whither or Which* 1996, *Florida Pearl*, (also won Hennessy Cognac Gold Cup, Leopardstown 1999), *Alexander Banquet* 1998, also rider of three Cheltenham winners and foxhunters and *Atha Cliath* at Aintree 1983; nominated Champion Amateur Rider in Ireland six times; Chairman, Irish Racehorse Trainers Association 1997-99; member, Mount Juliet Golf Club. Hobby, golf. Contact: Closutton, Muine Beag, Co. Carlow. Tel: 0503 21786.

MULRENNAN, Frank; JOURNALIST; *b* 1960; *educ* FCJ Secondary School, Bunclody, Co. Wexford; Kildalton College, Kilkenny; University College Dublin, BAgEcon; *m* Teresa Carragher; 3 *da;* Trainee Accountant, KPMG, 1982-83; Producer/Presenter, Radio Agriculture, RTE, 1983-85; Press Relations Manager, Irish Farmers Association, 1985-87; Agricultural Editor, *Irish Independent*, 1987-96; Business Editor & Associate Editor, *Irish Independent*, 1996 to date; former Chairman, Guild of Agricultural Journalists; KPMG Association; Business Journalists Association; awards include Gold Medal Public Speaking (LAMDA); a newspaper man moving steadily up the editorial ladder thanks to his imagination and leadership skills. Hobbies, golf, own farm and watching sports. Contact: Independent Newspapers, 90 Middle Abbey Street, Dublin 1. Tel: 01 873 1333. Fax: 01 873 1787.

MULRYAN, Sean Martin; COMPANY CHAIRMAN; *b* 1954; *educ* Roscommon Secondary School; ANCO, Galway; *m* Bernadine ______; 3 *s* 2 *da;* served apprenticeship in stonemasonry; mortgaged first home to move into house building; Ballymore Homes are now the largest housebuilders in the State; Founder, Chairman, Ballymore Properties Ltd., 1981 to date; purchased land in Blackrock, 1986, with Michael Bailey, built Merrion Park Developments; other housebuilding developments include Tallaght, Swords and Rathfarnham; main shareholder in Galway Bay Golf and Country Club; major developer of London Docklands and Westminster, estimated at £850million; plans are for a move into the Orient; a quiet, low key family man; recognised for his energy and attention to detail, both in the boardroom and on site; a passionate follower of Bloodstock and Stud Owner; member, K Club and Rathsallagh Golf Club. Hobbies, horse racing and breeding, art, golf and travel. Contact: Ballymore Properties, 35-38 St. Stephen's Green, Dublin 2. Tel: 01 662 2300. Fax: 01 662 2302.

MULRYAN, Sean

MULVIHILL, Liam; DIRECTOR GENERAL GAA; *b* 1946; *educ* St. Mel's College, Longford; St. Patrick's College, Drumcondra, NT; University College Dublin, BA; St. Patrick's College, Maynooth, HDipEd; *m* Máire Ni Shiochrú; 2*s* 1*da*; Primary Teacher, Department of Education, 1966-71; Schools Inspector, Department of Education 1971-79; Director General, GAA 1979 to date; as head of the largest sporting body in the State, is responsible for maintaining the traditional values of the GAA while dealing with the commercial aspects of sport in the nineties. Contact: Cumann Lúthchleas Gael, Páirc an Chrócaigh, Baile Atha Cliath 3. Tel: 01 836 3222. Fax: 01 836 6420.

MURFI, Mikel

MURFI, Mikel; ACTOR, DIRECTOR; *b* 1965; *educ* Summerhill College, Sligo; University College Dublin, B.A.; Ecole Jacques Lecoq, Paris; 1988-90 and 1995-96; *partner* Eithne Hand; worked in RTE with Gerard Stembridge, *Nothing to It*; returned to Ecole Jacques Lecoq, Paris, obtained Pedeagogical Degree, only 40 worldwide with this qualification; worked with Passion Machine, Pigsback, Rough Magic, The Abbey, Druid; founded Barabbas.... The Company 1993; performances with them include *The Whiteheaded Boy* (Andrews Lane and American Tour 1999); Films include *The Butcher Boy, The Commitments, Words upon a Window Pane, Guiltrip, Love and Rage;* has directed *Diamonds in the Soil* and Theatre Fest (Macras) 1998, *Come Down from the Mountain, Out the Back Door* and numerous other plays for Barabbas.....The Company. Hobbies, Microlights, Gyrocopters, Permaculture. Contact: The Lisa Richards Agency, 15 Lower Pembroke Street, Dublin 2. Tel: 01 662 4880. Fax: 01 662 4884.

MURLESS, Charles Richard Stuart "Charlie"; CHIEF EXECUTIVE PUNCHESTOWN RACECOURSE AND EQUESTRIAN CENTRE; *b* 1959; *educ* Headford School, Meath; Cheltenham College, (UK); *m* Rhona Blake; 1*s* 1*da;* Marketing Manager Goffs Bloodstock Sales, 1990-94; travelled extensively to US and Australia; Director, International Racecourse Management Ltd.

MURPHY, Andrew

MURPHY, Denis

(responsible for introducing Sunday racing in UK), 1990-94; Chief Executive, Blackhall Racing Ltd. holding company for Punchestown Racecourse and Equestrian Centre; awards won by Punchestown include, Best Racecourse 1996 and 1997, awarded by Irish Racehorse Owners Association; voted Racecourse Merit Award, 1998 by Racing Club of Ireland; £15m recent refurbishment programme on racecourse has made it a worldwide leader in its field; son of Anglo Irish racing family; an entertaining companion and a dedicated racecourse manager. Hobbies, sleeping and having lunch. Contact: Punchestown Racecourse, Naas, Co. Kildare. Tel: 045 897 704.

MURPHY, Andrew, Eugene; OPERA SINGER; *b* 1959; *educ* Trained for six years under Dr. Veronica Dunne; hired by the Bavarian State Opera before his studies were finished; *(m. dis)*; 1 *da*; Bavarian State Opera Studio, 1987-89; Wiener Kammeroper, Vienna, 1989-92; Municipal Theatre, Ulm, Germany, 1992-95; Solo Bass Baritone at the State Opera, Saarbrücken, Germany 1995 to date; Guest appearances in Ireland, Italy, Austria, Japan, Korea, Poland and China. Hobbies, golf, travel, Irish Literature. Contact: State Opera, Saarbrücken, Germany.

MURPHY, Denis; CHAIRMAN, MANAGING DIRECTOR ST. PATRICK'S WOOLLEN MILLS LTD; *b* 1933; *educ* Glenstal Abbey, Limerick; Leeds University; *m* Anne Upton; 1 *s* 1 *da*; joined established family textile firm 1956, currently Chairman and Managing Director, St. Patrick's Woollen Mills Ltd., Cork; Chairman, Swansea Cork Ferries; Vice Chairman, Cork Racecourse Ltd.; Past President, Cork Chamber of Commerce, Chambers of Commerce of Ireland; past Chairman, Cork Harbour Commissioners; member of Cork commercial establishment with strong political ties, suffered a brief change of political direction, but has returned to Fianna Fáil fold. Hobbies, hunting (Master, United Hunt) and shooting (Chairman, Cork Game). Contact: St. Patrick's Woollen Mills Ltd., Douglas, Co. Cork. Tel: 021 894 851. Fax: 021 894 852.

MURPHY, Fachtna; DETECTIVE CHIEF SUPERINTENDENT, HEAD OF CRIMINAL ASSETS BUREAU; *b* 1949; *educ* in Cork; joined An Garda Siochana, 1967; served in various posts before being appointed Head of the Fraud Squad, 1991; established Money Laundering Unit, 1995; appointed Head of Criminal Assets Bureau, 1996; recognised as hardworking, cautious, clever and ambitious; the Criminal Assets Bureau (CAB) and its legislation are at the cutting edge worldwide of anti drug law enforcement; The British Home Office White Paper is based mainly on CAB, its legislation and implementation. Contact: Criminal Assets Bureau, Dublin Metropolitan Area Headquarters, Harcourt Square, Dublin 2. Tel: 01 475 5555.

MURPHY, The Hon, Mr. Justice Francis; JUDGE OF THE SUPREME COURT; *b* 1932; *educ* St. Mary's College, Rathmines; University College Dublin; Kings Inns; *m* Mary Bacon; 1*s* 1 *da;* called to the Bar, 1953; called to the Inner Bar, 1969; maintained a top Bar practice specialising in Company Law and Taxation; former Chairman of the Bar Council; appointed to the High Court, 1982; appointed to the Supreme Court, 1996 to date; highly regarded for his concise, common sense approach. Hobby, golf. Contact: Four Courts, Morgan Place, Dublin 7. Tel: 01 872 5555.

MURPHY, James "Jim"; CHIEF EXECUTIVE GOLDEN VALE PLC; *b* 1946; *educ* in Dublin; *m* Maura -----; 3 *children;* joined Grand Metropolitan in the early 70s until 1992; member, management buy-out group purchasing The Cheese Company from Grand Metropolitan, 1992 (bought for £96 million, sold to Waterford Foods for £125 million, 1995); Senior Manager, Express Foods and the Cheese Company; Chief Executive, Golden Vale plc, 1996 to date; Golden Vale are one of the country's largest milk processors, employing over 2,000 and with a turnover in excess of £565 million; recognised as a tough, low key manager, more than capable of healing inward rifts and moving towards expansion. Contact: Golden Vale, Charleville, Co. Cork. Tel: 063 81501. Fax: 063 89900

MURPHY, John Joseph; COMPANY DIRECTOR; *b* 1952; *educ* Ard Scoil Phobal, Bantry, Co. Cork; *m* Maria Hegarty; 4*s*; opened Monica John, Bantry, Co. Cork, 1977, opened Monica John, Cork, 1980, opened Monica John, Dublin, 1981; founded Fastnet Mussels Ltd. Incorporated, 1984; Fastnet Mussels Ltd. supply prestige markets throughout Europe and UK with their patented frozen mussel products including Belgo chain of restaurants; company awarded, West Cork Enterprise Board Company of the Year 1996; member, Bantry Harbour Board. Hobbies, seafaring activities, skiing, water and snow. Contact: Fastnet Mussels Ltd., Gearhies, Bantry, Co. Cork. Tel: 027 61276. Fax: 027 61264.

MURPHY, Liam A.; VICE PRESIDENT EUROPEAN MANUFACTURING LOCTITE IRELAND LTD.; *b* 1955; *educ* Trinity College Dublin, BA (Mod); University College Dublin, DipChem.Eng., M.Ind Eng.; *m* Veronica Murphy; 2 da; Industrial Chemist, Donnelly Mirrors Ltd., 1976-79; Process Engineer, Loctite Ireland Ltd., 1979-82; Chemical Plant Manager, 1982-87; Plant Manager, 1987-95; Director of Operations, 1995-96; General Manager, 1996-97; Vice President, Manufacturing Europe, Loctite Ireland Ltd., 1997 to date; Awarded Robert H. Kreeble Enterprise Award, 1989.

Hobbies, Photography, Music, Motor Caravaning. Contact: Loctite (Ireland) Ltd., Whitestown, Tallaght, Dublin 24. Tel: 01 451 9466. Fax: 01 451 9414.

MURPHY, Martin; MANAGING DIRECTOR R&H HALL; *b* 1949; *educ* Mt. St. Alphonsos, Limerick; CBS, New Ross; University College Dublin; IMI, Management Diploma (1992); *m* Tess Carroll; 1*s* 1 *da;* Director, Unigrain, Dublin, 1973-89; Trading Director, Unigrain International, 1989-91; Trading Director, R&H Hall, 1991-96; Managing Director, R&H Hall Ltd, 1996 to date; member, Rotary International, Irish Grain and Feed Association. Hobbies, walking, travel and sport. Contact: R&H Hall Ltd, 151 Thomas Street, Dublin 8. Tel: 01 612 1234.

MURPHY, Michael, "Mike"; BROADCASTER; *b* 1941; *educ* St. Louis National School, Rathmines; Terenure College; *m* Eileen Dixon; *(separated)* 1 *s* 3 *da*; Partner, Ann Walsh; Apprentice Draper, Crowe Wilson, 1959-61 (describes responsible position as "counting socks"); Junior Clerk, Castrol Ireland Ltd., 1961-62; Freelance Actor, 1961-64; Radio Announcer, RTE, 1965-70; Broadcaster, Programme Presenter, RTE, 1970 to date; Director, Harcourt Developments Ltd., and Park West Business Park; recipient of Jacobs Awards for *Morning Call* (1978); *Live Mike* (1981), *Murphy's America* (1983), *Murphy's Australia* (1987); Business Person of the Month, *Irish Press,* February 1990; Director, Irish Museum of Modern Art; Published memoirs, *Mike and Me,* 1977; One of the best known faces and voices in Irish broadcasting; has become a pundit on all aspects of art in Ireland. Hobbies, golf, arts and tennis; Clubs, Royal Dublin Golf Club. Contact: Harcourt Developments, Harcourt House, 18-19 Harcourt Street, Dublin 2. Tel: 01 475 3928. Fax: 01 475 3943.

MURPHY, Michael; FARMER; *b* 1948; *educ* Christian Brothers School, Cork; Warrenstown Agricultural College; University College Cork, MBA; *m* Geraldine O'Brien; 2*s* 2*da;* worked for many years in England, US and in the Norwegian Merchant Navy; entered farming 1970, trained with Farm Apprenticeship Board for three years, qualified Farm Manager 1973; has been involved in dairy farming 1973 to date; recipient of Charles Harvey Award; periodic columnist for *Farmers Journal*; member, Irish Grassland and Animal Production Association, Blackwater Discussion Group. Regarded as one of the major dairy farmers in the country, his own philosophy on successful farming is 'high output at reasonable cost'. Hobbies, travelling, all sports, current affairs and reading. Clubs, All Christians Rugby Club, Cork.

MURPHY, Patrick; MALTSTER, CHAIRMAN, SOCIETY OF IRISH MALTSTERS; *b* 1939; *educ* St. Joseph's Christian Brothers School, New Ross; Trinity College Dublin, BA, BComm, DPA, MBA; College of Commerce, Rathmines, Cert. Institute of Bankers in Ireland; *m* Antoinette Cummins, Director, Jorgensen Fine Art; 3 *s* 1 *da*; Junior Executive, Central Bank of Ireland, 1956-59; joined Brewing Management team, Guinness Ltd. (Dublin), 1959-68; Brewer, Production Manager, Guinness (Malaysia), 1969-70; Brewery Manager, Guinness (Ghana), 1971-73; Managing Director, Irish Malt Exports Ltd., 1973-90; Managing Director, Minch Norton Ltd., 1989-91; Chairman, Society of Irish Malsters, 1989 to date; Sales and Marketing Director, Minch Malt Ltd., 1998 to date; President, European Sales Maltsters Association (EUROMALT), 1990-91; Chairman, National Review Committee on Ports, 1990-92; recipient, Sir Charles Harvey Management Award (IMI, 1965), Lord Mayor's Millennium Award for Outstanding Achievement, 1988; Chairman, Rosc, 1981 to date; member, World Arts Forum Geneva, 1990; Chairman, AM & Associates, 1990 to date; Member, International Council, Museum of Modern Art (New York), 1994 to date; Chairman, Contemporary Irish Art Society, 1992 to date; Trustee, National Self Portrait Collection, 1991 to date; Member, Institute of Brewers (London); recipient, Royal Hibernian Academy Gold Medal, 1999; publications include articles in international journals, *Murphy Report on Ports and Harbours* (1992), contributor to *Tony O'Malley* (1995), Biography, *Patrick J. Twohy* (2000), *Book of Reminiscences* (1999); has worked tirelessly for the exhibition and appreciation of modern art in Ireland; a collector of international note. Hobbies, modern art and shooting; Clubs, Kildare Street and University Club, R.D.S. Contact: Minch Malt Ltd., Athy, Co. Kildare. Tel: 0507 40300. Fax: 0507 31046.

MURPHY, Paul

MURPHY, Rory

MURPHY, Paul; MANAGING DIRECTOR, AGRA TRADING; *b* 1963; *educ* Templeogue College, Dublin, University College Dublin, B.Comm; *m* Sinead Lennon; 2 *da;* Joined Agra Trading, 1985; Trading Director, 1992; Trading Director/General Manager, 1995; Managing Director, 1997 to date; Agra Trading is part of the Kepak Group, one of the leading meat processing companies in Europe; Member: St. Mary's College RFC, Powerscourt Golf Club. Hobbies, golf, rugby, travel. Contact: Agra Trading, Temple House, Temple Road, Blackrock, Co. Dublin. Tel: 01 283 2411.

MURPHY, Rory; HOTEL DIRECTOR; *b* 1939; *educ* Garbally College; Shannon College of Hotel Management, Diploma in Hotel Management, FIHCI; *m* Patricia O'Higgins; 2 *s;* worked in the prestigious St. Gotthard's Hotel in Zurich before taking up position as Manager of The Great Southern Hotel, Parknasilla 1965-68; Manager, The Great Southern Hotel, Galway, 1968-73;

General Manager, Ashford Castle 1973-84; appointed Managing Director of Ashford Castle Hotel and Dromoland Castle Hotel in 1984 to date; awards include: Egon Ronay's Top Six Hotel Managers in Great Britain and Ireland 1989; member of the Board of Shannon College of Hotel Management since 1972; Fellow, Hotel and Catering Institute. A consummate hotelier, has left a sense of style with hoteliers trained under him; noted for his sartorial elegance, winner of Best Dressed Award 1991. Hobbies, boating and golf; Clubs, Portmarnock, Galway Bay & Galway Salthill. Contact: Ashford Castle Hotel, Cong, Co. Mayo. Tel: 092 46003. Fax: 092 46260.

MURPHY, Thomas "Tom"; PLAYWRIGHT; *b* 1935; *educ* Christian Brothers School, Tuam, Co. Galway; Vocational Teachers Training College, Ringsend; *m* Mary Hippisley; 3 *children;* worked as an Apprentice Welder and Fitter prior to obtaining Teachers Diploma; taught for a period in secondary schools in Ireland; has pursued full-time writing career since 1962; Director, Abbey Theatre 1972-83; numerous plays include *A Crucial Week in the Life of a Grocer's Assistant, The Morning after Optimism, The Sanctuary Lamp, The Gigli Concert, Too late for Logic, The Patriot Game, She Stoops To Folly, The Wake; The Seduction of Morality* (a novel); his works have been performed and broadcast widely in Europe and the US; recipient of various awards; D. Litt (honoris causa), Trinity College Dublin; member, Irish Academy of Letters, Aosdána. One of Ireland's most important playwrights; has been described as a "hyper-realist" whose work encapsulates small town Irish life with all its absurdities. Hobbies, music and gardening. Contact: Aosdána, 70 Merrion Square, Dublin 2. Tel: 01 661 1840. Fax: 01 676 1302.

MURPHY, William

MURPHY, William M. "Billy"; MANAGING DIRECTOR, DRURY COMMUNICATIONS LTD.; *b* 1959; *educ* Rockwell College; University College Dublin, B,.Comm, HDMP; *m* Kathryn Connolly; 1 s 1 *da*; Public Relations Consultant, Murray Consultants Ltd., 1982-85; Public Relations Consultant, Pembroke PR Ltd., 1985-88; Co-founder, Drury Communications Ltd., (now Ireland's leading corporate communications consultancy), 1988; Director, Drury Communications Ltd., Drury Sports Management Ltd., 1988-98; Managing Director, Drury Communications Ltd., Director, Drury Communications Hungary and Drury Communications (Northern Ireland) Ltd.; Vice President, University College Dublin, R.F.C., Member, Seapoint, Blainroe Golf Clubs, Fundraising Committee of Co-operation Ireland, Rockwell Past Pupils Union, Phoenix Racing Club Horse Racing Syndicate ; Awarded various junior rugby trophies. Hobbies, sports, especially rugby, soccer, hurling, golf, horse racing, painting abstract oils (not yet exhibited), classical and rock music, Italian food and wine, the media, especially newspapers. Contact: Drury Communications, 1 Richview Office Park, Clonskeagh, Dublin 14. Tel: 01 260 5000. Fax: 01 260 5066.

MURRAY, Niamh

MURRAY, Niamh; LYRIC SOPRANO; *b* 1967 (Nigeria); *educ* B.Ed. Carysfort College Dublin; Associate of London College of Music; RIAM; Licentiate Speech and Drama, Leinster School of Music, where she studied under Dr. Veronica Dunne; Royal Northern College of Music, Manchester; International studies with Brigitte Fassbaender, Ugo Benelli and Thomas Helmsley; Italian government scholarship facilitated further study with Maestro Carlo Bergonzi in Sienna; *single;* most frequently requested artiste to appear at the National Concert Hall; performed extensively in opera, operetta, oratorio and stage musical; grand opera appearances include Turandot, *Orfeo;* opera roles include Marguerite *(Faust)*, Micaela *(Carmen)*; highly regarded throughout the world, appearing to great critical acclaim including BBC's *Songs of Praise* production in 1997; guest soloist at the televised Pioneer Centenary Mass in 1999; leading lady in Jurys Irish Cabaret; regular guest presenter on Lyric FM; recipient John Count McCormack and Margaret Burke Sheridan gold medals; recordings include *A Fairer Paradise, When Irish Eyes Are Smiling* and *Wedding memories from Ireland.* A multi-talented lady with a warm and charismatic personality. Contact: Agent, Anne Boylan, 4, St. Catherine's Park, Glenageary, Co. Dublin. Tel: 01 280 5982.

MURRIN, Joseph

MURRAY, Peter; CURATOR CRAWFORD MUNICIPAL ART GALLERY; *b* 1956; *educ* St. Paul's College, Raheny; University College Dublin, BA; Trinity College Dublin, MLitt; *m* Sarah Iremonger, Artist; 1*s*; Lecturer in Art History, National College of Art and Design, 1981-84; Lecturer, Crawford College of Art and Design, 1982-84; Curator, Crawford Municipal Art Gallery, 1984 to date; member, Association of Irish Art Historians, College Art Association, AAM, IMA, FNCI, member, Cultural Relations Committee of Department of Foreign Affairs. Hobbies, painting, drawing and restoring old buildings. Contact: Crawford Municipal Art Gallery, Emmet Place, Cork. Tel: 021 273 377.

MURRAY, The Hon Mr. Justice John; JUDGE OF THE EUROPEAN COURT OF JUSTICE; *b* 1943; *educ* Crescent College, Limerick; Rockwell College, Co. Tipperary; University College Dublin; King's Inns; *m* Gabrielle Walsh, daughter of Mr. Justice Brian Walsh; *2 children*; called to the Bar 1967; called to the Inner Bar, 1981; Attorney General, August-December 1981, 1987-91; appointed Judge of the European Court of Justice, 1991; recipient, Doctor of Laws, (Honoris Causa), University of Limerick, 1993; since 1997 Professor of Law, invité, Université de Louvain; he is the fourth Irish member of the Court, the supreme judicial body in EC Law; as a lawyer, had a large practice in both Dublin and Western Circuit; was a highly respected Attorney General; said to possess a cool and concise legal brain and a good sense of humour. Contact: Court of Justice of the European Communities, Palais de la Cour de Justice, Luxembourg, L 2925 Tel: 0035 2 43031.

MURRIN, Joseph "Joey"; CHIEF EXECUTIVE, KILLYBEGS FISHERMEN'S ORGANISATION; *b* 1937; *educ* Niall Mor National School, Killybegs; *m* Elizabeth Fagan; 3 *s* 2 *da*; a fisherman for over 20 years; former Chairman, Irish Fishermen's Organisation; former Chairman, Bord Iascaigh Mhara, 1984-89; Chief Executive, Killybegs Fishermen's Organisation, 1979 to date; Director, Marine Institute; Director Gundry Ireland Ltd. (net manufactures and ships chandlers); a frequent speaker at fishing symposia at home and abroad; former soccer referee and member, Irish Soccer Referees' Society. Recognised as "Mr. Fish" of the North West; an able spokesman for the Donegal fishing industry. Hobbies, golf, soccer and watching hurling. Contact: Killybegs Fishermen's Association, Bruach na Mara, Killybegs, Co. Donegal. Tel: 073 31089. Fax: 073 31577.

MURTAGH, Laurence

MURTAGH, Laurence Michael "Larry"; MANAGING DIRECTOR N.E.C. SEMICONDUCTORS IRELAND, LTD.; *b* 1943; *educ* C.B.S. Dundalk; University College Galway, BSc; *m* Helen O'Connell; 2 *s* 1 *da;* QC Manager, Bird Eye Foods, Eastbourne, Sussex, 1967-71; Manager (QC/Eng) ECCO, Dundalk, 1981-85, (large USA semiconductor); Production Director, NEC, 1985-1990, Managing Director, 1990 to date; Semiconductors Ireland are one of the largest and most diversified semiconductor companies in the world; Chairman, TIDE (South Meath Community Development Company); member, IMI Council, 1999. Hobbies, Community Development, golf. Contact: NEC Semiconductors Ireland Ltd., Ballivor, Co. Meath. Tel: 0405 67100. Fax: 0405 67101.

MYERS, Kevin; JOURNALIST; *b* 1947; *educ* Ratcliffe College, Leicestershire (UK); University College Dublin, BA; *m* Rachel Nolan; Reporter in Belfast for Radio Telefis Eireann, *The Observer* and BBC, 1971-78; freelance Journalist, 1978-80; joined *The Irish Times*, 1980, Editor, *Irishman's Diary* 1981 to date; Writer, Presenter, *The Law Courts,* winner of Jacobs Award for Documentary, 1980; Presenter, *Challenging Times,* university quiz programme for RTE Television, 1991 to date; occasional Presenter, *The Last Word,* Today FM Radio; recipient of Benson & Hedges Journalist of the Year Award for war reports from Beirut 1982, Hickson Travel Writer of the Year Award 1982; an entertaining, controversial and unpredictable columnist; one of his strengths lies in his disregard for political correctness. Hobbies, military history, travel, pubs and racing. Contact: The Irish Times, D'Olier Street, Dublin 2. Tel: 01 679 2022.

MYERSCOUGH, Philip; MANAGING DIRECTOR, GOFFS BLOODSTOCK SALES; *b* 1948; *educ* Castle Park; St. Columba's College; Trinity College Dublin; *m* Jane O'Brien (daughter of Vincent O'Brien), Stud Farm Manager, 2 *s* 2 *da*; trained as a Bloodstock Auctioneer, joined Goffs (Bloodstock Auctioneers) 1972, Marketing Director, 1975-80; set up (with Jane Myerscough) Ballysheehan Stud, 1981-90, Set up Baroda Stud in 1998; Jane Myerscough is now Stud Farm Manager; returned to Goffs as Managing Director, 1991 to date; the Myerscough Family has been closely connected with Goffs for three generations, majority shareholders in the company from 1923 until 1975; Former Director, Coyle Hamilton Group, Ltd.; Director, Headfort School; Chairman, The Curragh Racecourse Committee; Member, The Turf Club, Kildare Street and University Club, K Club, Portmarnock Golf Club. Hobbies, golf, skiing and bridge. Contact: Goffs Bloodstock Sales Ltd., Kildare Paddocks, Kill, Co. Kildare. Tel: 045 877 211. Fax: 045 877 119.

NASH, Richard

NASH, Richard; CHAIRMAN, CHIEF EXECUTIVE, RICHARD NASH & COMPANY LTD.; *b* 1943; *educ* Castleknock College, Dublin and Fordham University, BSc; *m* Vicki Sheehan; 2 *s* 1 *da*; joined long established family bottling company as Sales Manager in 1966; appointed Chairman and Chief Executive in 1972; Co-founder of Ballygowan Spring Water Company Ltd., bottling the water from a natural spring within the company's Newcastle premises; sold to Cantrell & Cochrane, 1993; Director, Carbonated Beverage Institute, Washington D.C. A person of standing within the Limerick business community, intends moving into the European market with Nash's sophisticated soft drinks and mineral water; a keen golfer who enjoys travel and family skiing holidays. Contact: Nash's Mineral Waters Ltd., The Square, Newcastle West, Co. Limerick. Tel: 069 62022.

NATHAN, Regina

NATHAN, Regina; OPERA SINGER; *b* 1960; *educ* St. Patrick's College Maynooth, BA and Higher Diploma in Education; Trinity College London, Post Graduate Diploma in Singing; attended The National Opera Studio, London; *m* Joseph Lynch; has sung in the major European Opera Houses, New York's Carnegie Hall and special guest at the opening concert of the 1998 Commonwealth Games in Kuala Lumpar; roles include Susanna/*Marriage of Figaro,* Mimi/*La Boheme,* Violetta/*La Traviata,* Adina/*L'Elisir d'Amore,* Gilda/*Rigalotto,* Sophie/*Der Rosenkavalier* and Susanna/*Susanna* by Floyd; she also sings oratoria, symphonic works and is in much demand as a recitalist throughout Europe; recently recorded a series of Britten songs with Malcolm

Martineau for Hyperion Records, Mahler's *Symphony No 8* with Edo de Waart (BMG), Rachmaninov's *The Bells* and *Vocalise* with Djong Victorim Yu Carlton Classics, *Faith of Our Fathers* (Enigma Records); was the subject of a TV documentary (RTE), 1993; awards include Outstanding New Entertainer, 1991 (National Entertainment Awards), Irish Life/*Sunday Independent* Music Award, 1991; a singer of great charm with a richly golden voice. Hobby, reading. Contact: 19 Millington Road, Burnt Oak, Edgeware, Middlesex HA8 OPL, England. Tel: 0044 181 9310 811.

NAUGHTON, Martin; CHAIRMAN, GLEN DIMPLEX; *b* 1939; *educ* De La Salle, Dundalk; Southhampton College of Technology, HNC (Mechanical & Production Engineering); *m* Carmel McCarthy, Chairman, Board of Governors and Guardians, National Gallery of Ireland, Board Member, immediate Past Chairman, Co-operation Ireland; 2 *s* 1 *da*; Student Apprentice, Hawker Siddley Aircraft 1957-61; Work Study Engineer, SPS (Shannon) 1961; Chief Work Study Engineer, AET (Dunleer), 1961-65; Services Manager, Callins (Shannon), 1965-67; Works Manager, AET (Dunleer), 1967-73; Founder, Managing Director, Glen Electric 1973, company was built into the Glen Dimplex Group; Chairman, Glen Dimplex Group; the purchase of Westcan (Canada), Siemens Heating and Chromalox (Canada), the Muller Group in France makes Glen Dimplex the major player in the North American heating market, and the world's largest manufacturers of electrical heating appliances, with 17 manufacturing companies, employing 6000 people with annual sales of £600 million. Although one of the most successful businessmen in the State, has retained a down to earth approach and a quiet, and effective charm; conferred with Honorary Doctorate of Laws, University College Dublin, 1991, Trinity College Dublin, 1995, Queen's University Belfast, 1998, Notre Dame U.S.A, 1998; Member of the Council of State. Hobby, relaxing with family. Contact: Glen Dimplex, Ardee Road, Dundalk, Co. Louth. Tel: 041 51700. Fax: 041 51807.

NEARY, Peter; ACADEMIC; *b* 1950; *educ* Christian Brothers Schools, Dundalk and Drogheda; Clongowes Wood College; University College Dublin, BA,.MA; University of Oxford, BPhil, DPhil; *m* Frances Ruane (*m dis*); 2 *s*; *m* Mairéad Hanrahan; 1*da;* Research Assistant, Economic and Social Research Institute Dublin, 1970-72; Junior Lecturer, Trinity College Dublin, 1972-74; Heyworth Research Fellow, Nuffield College, Oxford, 1976-78; Lecturer, Trinity College Dublin, 1978-80; Professor of Political Economy, University College Dublin, 1980 to date; Head of Department of Economics, 1983-86, 1989-92; Research Associate, London School of Economics, 1993 to date; Visiting Professor: Princeton 1980, Berkeley 1982, Queen's University (Kingston) 1986-88, University of Ulster at Jordanstown 1992-93; Current or former Council Member: Econometric Society, Economic and Social Studies, European Economic Association, Irish Economic Association, (President, 1990-92), Royal Economic Society; member, Academia Europaea, Royal Irish Academy; publications include over seventy professional papers, mainly international economics; other biographical listings: M. Blaug (ed.), *Who's Who in Economics: A Biographical Dictionary of Major Economists 1700-1995,* Third Edition, Aldershot: Edward Elgar, 1999. A world class economist, a highly regarded contributor at international economic fora. Hobbies, reading, cinema, music and travel. Contact: Department of Economics, University College Dublin, Donnybrook, Dublin . Tel: 01 706 8334. Fax: 01 283 0068.

NÍ DHOMHNAILL, Nuala; POET; *b* 1952; *educ* St. Mary's School, St. Helens, Lancashire; Scoil Caitlíona Naofa, Ventry; Laurel Hill Convent, Limerick; University College Cork BA, HDipEd; *m* Dogan Leflef, Poet; 1*s* 3 *da;* Teacher at various schools in Ireland and Middle East Technical University, Ankara (Turkey) 1972-80; Tutor in Irish, Maynooth College 1985-88; Leader of Creative Irish Workshop, Irish Department 1986-88; has run extensive seminars and workshops throughout Ireland; frequent broadcaster on Irish, UK and American radio and television; also guest lecturer in Belgium, Austria, France, US, Canada and the UK; publications include An *Dealg Droighin* (1981), *Féar Suaithinseach* (1984), *Feis, Phaorah's Daughter* (1990), *The Astrakhan Cloak* (1992), *Cead Aighnis, Selected Poems;* awards include Arts Council Literary Bursary 1979 and 1981, Duais Sheain Ui Riordain of the Oireachtas 1981, 1984 and 1990, Gradam An Oireachtais 1984, Duais Filiochta (Arts Council) 1985 and 1988, Irish American O'Shaugnesssy Award 1988, Irish American Foundation Award 1991; awarded honorary doctorate DPhil. Dublin City University 1995; member, Aosdána, Poetry Ireland, The Irish Writers Union. Hobbies, reading, swimming, sean-nós singing and walking. Contact: Aosdána, 70 Merrion Square, Dublin 2. Tel: 01 661 1840. Fax: 01 676 1302.

NOLAN, Edwin James

NOLAN, Edwin James; CHAIRMAN, MANAGING DIRECTOR HENRY FORD & SONS LTD; *b* 1940; *educ* Presentation Brothers College, Cork; Diploma in Marketing from Dukes University, U.S.A., Marketing Institute of Ireland; *m* Cintra Caverley; 3 *s* 1 *da*; joined Henry Ford & Son Ltd. on leaving school, 1958, has worked his way up through the ranks; Tractor Sales Manager, 1977, General Sales Manager, 1986, Chairman and Managing Director, 1987 to date; the Ford Company in Ireland employs over 2,000 in service and distribution, have fifty-eight dealers throughout the country and a turnover in the region of £270 million. Recognised as a plain speaking and decisive manager, a good team leader. Hobbies, gardening and sailing. Contact: Henry Ford & Sons Ltd., Elm Court, Boreenmanna Road, Cork. Tel: 021 329 277. Fax: 021 962 634.

NOLAN, Frances Catherine "Fran" née Duff; MANAGING DIRECTOR REGINE LTD; *b* 1950; *educ* Sisters of Charity, Walkinstown; *m* Roger Dell (*m dis*); 1*s*; *m* George Nolan (*m dis*); 1*s* 1 *da*; worked in retail clothing trade with Frends and Richard Lewis; established own company Regine Ltd. 1973, manufacturers of high fashion women's clothing with a strong export market, operate in-house shops in the Brown Thomas Group and Arnotts; *Late Late Show* Award Winner; member, National Yacht Club. Hobbies, sailing and golf. Contact: Regine Ltd., 13-14 Dame Street, Dublin 2. Tel: 01 679 8122.

NOLAN, Vincent;

NOLAN, Vincent; CHAIRMAN H.J. NOLAN LTD.; *b* 1923; *educ* St. Malachy's College, Belfast; *m* Yvonne Callaghan; 5 *s;* joined H.J. Nolan (Dublin) Ltd. on leaving school; expanded and developed fish business which had been established by Belfast based father in 1935; 3rd generation son, George, is now Managing Director; Chairman, H.J. Nolan (Dublin) Ltd., one of the largest fish businesses in Ireland, involved in catching, processing, importing and exporting fish worldwide; with emphasis on smoked salmon. An established figure in the low profile fishing industry; a gregarious and talented piano player. Hobbies, golf and music; Clubs, Portmarnock GC, (Vice President), Stephen's Green Club, Milltown GC. Contact: H.J. Nolan, Corporation Fish Market, Dublin 7. Tel: 01 872 6377. Fax: 01 868 0260.

NOONAN, Thomas J.; CHIEF EXECUTIVE, THE MAXOL GROUP; *b* 1951; *e duc* Terenure College Dublin, College of Commerce, Rathmines, Diploma in Business Studies; *m* Mary ---- 2 *s*; Industrial Relations Executive, Federated Union of Employers (now IBEC), 1973-80; joined Maxol Group, held various positions in the company; Group Chief Executive, 1996 to date; Former President of the Society of the Irish Motor Industry; Chairman of the Irish Petroleum Industry Association; Government nominee on the Social Welfare Tribunal and on the Motor Insurance Advisory Board; member of the Transportation Strategic Policy Committee of Fingal County Council; Member: IBEC/CBI Northern Ireland Joint Business Council, Dublin Regional Committee of IBEC, Steering Committee of Plato North Dublin, Marketing Institute. Hobbies, a keen rugby fan, and a golf enthusiast. Contact: Maxol Ltd., 3, Custom House Plaza, International Financial Services Centre, Dublin 1. Tel: 01 607 6800. Fax: 01 607 6850.

NORRIS, David; UNIVERSITY LECTURER, SENATOR; *b* 1944; *educ* St. Andrew's College, Dublin; High School, Dublin; Trinity College Dublin, BA (First Class Moderatorship); *single*; Senior Lecturer in English Literature, Trinity College Dublin, 1968 to date; elected to Seanad Eireann, 1987, re-elected 1989 to date; first Foundation Scholar in English Literature and Language, Trinity College Dublin, 1965; Gold Medal Philosophical Society, TCD, 1967; Diplome D'Honneur, Centre for the Study of Sexual Minorities (Paris); nominated for European Human Rights Prize, 1989; Gold Medal, Brazilian Academy of Letters, 1997; publications include many articles and contributions in books and journals on literary and sociological subjects; Irish Editor, Proceedings of James Joyce Centenary Symposium; frequent international radio and television broadcaster; Irish Trustee, International Joyce Foundation; Chairman, James Joyce Cultural Centre, North Great George's Street Preservation Society; member, Board of the AIDS Foundation. An eloquent and fearless fighter for human rights, best known for his action in the Irish Courts, and subsequently in the Court of Human Rights, to have the laws against homosexual acts between consenting adults declared unconstitutional and in breach of the Convention of Human Rights; recognised as an important and informed speaker in the Upper House; a witty academic, the world authority on James Joyce. Hobbies, jogging (completed Dublin Marathons 1988, '89, and '91), weight training and gardening; clubs, Kildare Street and University Club, Royal Dublin Society, Royal Zoological Society. Contact: Seanad Éireann, Leinster House, Kildare Street, Dublin 2. Tel: 01 678 9911.

NOTEN, Jules; CHAIRMAN VAN DEN BERGH FOODS Ltd.; *b* 1960; *educ* Catholic University of Louvain; Flemish Business School of Economics (VLEKHO); University of Bruges; Degree in Commercial & Financial Services; *m* Daniele Leufkens; 2*s* 2 *da;* Management Trainee, Organisation Analyst, Unilever 1985; Sales Manager, IGLO-OLA, Belgium, 1987, Logistics Director, 1988, Sales and Distribution Director, 1990; Senior Sales Member Foods Executive, Unilever (Europe & N. America), 1992; Managing Director, Mora Snacks Benelux (Belgium & Netherlands); Company Chairman Van Den Bergh Foods, 1999 to date. Hobbies, travel, reading, golf and skiing. Contact: Van den Berg Foods Ltd., Whitehall Road, Rathfarnham, Dublin 14. Tel: 01 298 4344.

NUGENT, Barbara

NOWLAN, David; THEATRE CRITIC, MANAGING EDITOR, THE IRISH TIMES; *b* 1936; *educ* The High School, Dublin; St. Columba's College, Rathfarnham, Dublin; Trinity College Dublin, BA, MB, BCh, BAO; *m* Nora Gray, Sociologist, Community Welfare Officer with the Eastern Health Board; 3 *da*; worked with Meath Hospital and Dr. Steeven's Hospital, Dublin; joined British National Health Service; Government Medical Officer, Hospital Service, Jamaica; Physician,

Southampton, Long Island, USA; joined *The Irish Times* as Medical Correspondent 1969; succeeded Seamus Kelly as Theatre Critic, *The Irish Times* 1976 to date; Managing Editor, *The Irish Times* 1989 to date; member: Family Planning Association, Board Member of the European Journalism Centre in Maastricht. A fair minded and ethical journalist; regarded as the most influential theatre critic in Ireland. Enjoys boating on the Shannon and Erne; member, Inland Waterways Association of Ireland. Contact: Irish Times, 11-15 D'Olier Street, Dublin 2. Tel: 01 679 2022. Fax: 01 679 0067.

NUGENT, Barbara, née Ryle; CHIEF EXECUTIVE SUNDAY BUSINESS POST; *educ* Mount Sackville Convent, Co. Dublin; Miss Merediths, Pembroke Road; College of Catering, Cathal Brugha Street, Dublin; University College Dublin; *m* Edward Nugent; 3*s*; taught English and Mathematics at Willow Park Junior School, Dublin; joined *Image* magazine as Advertising Manager and Promotions Editor 1979-82; Advertising Manager, *The Sunday Tribune* 1982-92; Chief Executive *Sunday Business Post*, 1992 to date; Board member, Stephen's Green Publications; Chairman, Board of the National Museum of Ireland; the charming and dynamic doyenne of newspaper advertising; from a solid early grounding in advertising from Kevin Kelly in *Image* magazine she has emerged as a potent force in the success of the *Sunday Business Post.* Contact: Sunday Business Post, 27 Merchant's Quay, Dublin 8. Tel: 01 679 9777. Fax: 01 679 6496.

O'BEIRNE, Patrick Gerard

O'BEIRNE, John; RESTAURATEUR; *b* 1936; *educ* Ard Scania, Rathfarnham; *m* Marie Coleman; 3*s* 4*da;* worked for a time in the milk business and the motor industry; commodity trader, London, 1971-73; returned to Ireland, formed partnership with Ken Bates to purchase Dobbins Restaurant, subsequently bought out partner, Chief Executive, Dobbins Restaurant and Dobbins Outdoor Catering (catering for all major government hospitality) 1974 to date; Owner, Chief Executive, Becketts Hotel and Restaurant, Leixlip; recently opened a wine market on Web site; a convivial host whose restaurant is regarded among the business community as Dublin's answer to New York's 21 Club; member, Irish Restaurant Association, Hotel Federation; member, Rathfarnham Golf Club. Hobbies, golf, wine, cigars and travel. Contact: Dobbins Wine Bistro Ltd., 15 Stephen's Lane, Dublin 2. Tel: 01 676 4679.

O'BEIRNE, Patrick Gerard; GENERAL MANAGER AVID TECHNOLOGY INTERNATIONAL BV; *b* 1960; *educ* CBS, Kells, Co. Meath; University College Dublin, BA, HDip in Educ.; Institute of Public Administration, Dip in Management and Administration; *m* Brenda Kirwan; 2 *s* 1 *da;* Customer Services Manager, Apple Computer Ltd., 1985-93; Director European Services, Avid Technology, 1993-96, General Manager, Avid Technology, 1996 to date; Avid Technology is a multi national high tech company manufacturing and distributing throughout Europe from Dublin base; Avid was recipient of Academy Award for scientific and technical contribution to motion picture industry, 1999; member, Institute of Directors; Irish Management Institute. Hobbies, cinema, reading, food and wine. Contact: Avid Technology, 22 Butterfield Drive, Rathfarnham, Dublin 14. Tel: 01 493 3643.

O'BRIEN, Aidan P.

O'BRIC, Ruan; CHIEF EXECUTIVE ÚDARÁS NA GAELTACHTA; *b* 1943; *educ* St. Joseph's Christian Brothers School, Marino; University College Dublin, BSc, MBA; *m* Patricia Walsh; 2 *s* 1 *da*; Chief Executive, Plastic Packaging Ltd., and Iona Print Company (part of the Smurfit Group); Deputy Chief Executive, Údarás na Gaeltachta 1980, Chief Executive 1984 to date. Contact: Údarás na Gaeltachta, Ardoifig na Forbacha, Gallimh. Tel: 091 503 100.

O'BRIEN, Aidan Patrick; RACEHORSE TRAINER; *b* 1969; *m* Ann Marie Crowley; 2*s* 2 *da;* obtained trainer's licence, 1993; National Hunt Champion Trainer, 1994,'95, '96, '97/'98 season; Champion Flat Trainer, 1997; First Winner as Trainer, *Wandering Thoughts* (Tralee) 1993; First Pattern Winner, *Dancing Sunset* (Royal Whip Stakes), 1994; First Group 1 Winner, *Desert King* (National Stakes), 1996; First Classic Winner, *Classic Park* (Irish 1,000 Guineas), 1997; First Royal Ascot Winner, *Harbour Master* (Coventry Stakes) 1997; other notable winners, *Shatoush* (Epsom Oaks), 1998, *King of Kings* (2,000 Guineas), 1997, *Desert King* (Irish Derby & Irish 2,000 Guineas), 1997, *Istabraq* (Champion Hurdle), 1999; awarded Goffs Irish Racing Personality of the Year, 1997; recognised as the most dynamic trainer in the country at present, following in the footsteps of his namesake Vincent O'Brien (no relation) to international prominence. Contact: Baldoyle Stables, Cashel, Co. Tipperary. Tel: 062 62615.

O'BRIEN, Denis

O'BRIEN, Denis; CHAIRMAN AND CHIEF EXECUTIVE ESAT TELECOM GROUP; *b* 1958; *educ* High School, Rathgar; University College Dublin; Boston College (US), MBA; *m* Catherine Walsh; joined GPA as Personal Assistant to Tony Ryan; currently Chairman and CEO Communicorp Group, controlling 98FM Dublin, the Czech Republic and Poland; Chairman, CEO Esat Telecom Group; Chairman Organising Committee Special Olympics 2003; probably the most enterprising entrepreneur of his generation. Contact: ESAT Telecom, The Malt House, Grand Canal Quay, Dublin 2. Tel: 01 609 5000. Fax: 01 609 5010.

O'BRIEN, Helen; VICE PRESIDENT CORPORATE EVENTS JEFFERSON SMURFIT GROUP PLC; *b* 1949; *educ* Mercy Convent, Doon, Co. Limerick; Mercy Convent, Kilmallock, Co. Limerick; High School of Commerce, Limerick, Strategic Management, Financial Management, Philosophy, Communications; *single*; joined Smurfit Cartons in 1979; worked in the Smurfit Print and Publishing Division, Smurfit Distributing Division and The Jefferson Smurfit Group HQ, 1985 to date; currently Vice President Corporate Events, Jefferson Smurfit Group; member, Institute of Travel Managers; Director, Rutland Centre; Trustee of the Jack & Jill Foundation; recipient, Jefferson Smurfit Group Worldwide Person of the Year 1989; member, Links Golfing Society & Committee member, member, K Club, Riverview Racquet & Fitness Club. Hobbies, golf, tennis, theatre, cinema, reading and socialising. Contact: Jefferson Smurfit Group plc, Beech Hill, Clonskeagh, Dublin . Tel: 01 207 7000. Fax: 01 269 6162.

O'BRIEN, Helen

O'BRIEN, Mary Ann; COMPANY DIRECTOR; *b* 1960; *educ* Loreto Abbey, Rathfarnham; Ursuline College, Waterford; University Grenoble and Sorbonne (France); *m* Jonathan Irwin; 1*s* 1*da* (2*s* decd); Marketing Manager, Phoenix Park Racecourse, 1981-90; Managing Director & Founder of Lily O'Brien's Chocolates, 1991 to date; Lily O'Brien's export over 60% of ever increasing output, major clients include Marks & Spencer's; clubs, hates all clubs. Hobbies, family, gardening, travel, wine and people. Contact: Lily O'Brien Chocolates Ltd., Monread Road, Naas, Co. Kildare. Tel: 045 894 270.

O'BRIEN, Michael; PUBLISHER; *b* 1941; *educ* St. Mary's National School, Crumlin, Clogher Road Vocational School; National College of Art; College of Commerce, Rathmines; *m* Valerie Price; 3 s; (m dis); partner Eileen O'Driscoll, Physiotherapist; 1 s; 1 *step s;* 1 *step da*; Graphic Designer/Sales, Taylor Signs, 1961-67; Graphic Director, E&T O'Brien, 1967-73; Artist 1973-74; Director/Founder, Irish Book Sales, 1980-86; Director/Founder, The O'Brien Press, 1974 to date; The O'Brien Press awards include Books Ireland Publishers' Award, 1976 and '78; Irish Book Design Award, 1978 and '81 (Silver Medal), 1984 (Bronze Medal); 1988 (Silver Medal), 1990 (Silver Medal); Reading Association of Ireland, 1987 and 1989 (Special Merit Award); Bisto Award of the Decade, 1990; awards for children's books include Bisto Book of the Year awards, 1996, 1997, 1998; International Reading Association Award, 1991; Recent publications include *The Mammy* by Brendan O'Carroll (made into a movie); *The General* by Paul Williams (made into a movie by John Boorman), *Between the Mountains and the Sea* by Peter Pearson, *Under the Hawthorn Tree* by Marita Conlon McKenna, *Sisters, No Way!* by Siobhán Parkinson; Trustee, Irish Children's Books Trust; Founding Member, Children's Books Ireland and first President (1998) of IBBY Ireland - Ireland Section of International Board on Books for Young People. A man who seriously loves books and runs a small and influential general publishing house with a special flair for children's books; has expanded into export market, which now accounts for one third of turnover. Hobbies, sailing, portrait painting; Clubs, Bray Sailing Club, National Yacht Club. Contact: The O'Brien Press Ltd., 20 Victoria Road, Dublin 6. Tel: 01 492 3333 Fax: 01 492 2777.

O'BRIEN, Rory; FARMER, HOTELIER; *b* 1954; *educ* Mitchelstown Secondary School; *m* Monica Sheehan; 2*s* 3*da;* started off in pig breeding, now runs large pig breeding unit with wife, Rory and Monica O'Brien Pig Enterprise; Owner, Clonmel Arms Hotel; Owner, construction company, Ardsa Ltd.; Owner, Killicane Feeds Ltd.; Chairman, Industrial Committee I.F.A.. Hobbies, hunting and racing. Contact: Killicane, Mitchelstown, Co. Cork. Tel: 025 851167.

O'BRIEN, Vincent; RACEHORSE TRAINER, BLOODSTOCK BREEDER; *b* 1917; *educ* Mungret College, Limerick; *m* Jacqueline Wittenoom; 2 s 3 *da*; Amateur Jockey, First win, 1940; obtained Trainers Licence 1943; has trained winners of such races as Grand National (three successive), Cheltenham Gold Cup (four), Champion Hurdle (three successive), Epsom Derby (six), Epsom Oaks (two), St. Leger (three), 2,000 Guineas (four), 1,000 Guineas, Prix de L'Arc de Triomphe (three), King George VI and Queen Elizabeth Stakes (three); Ascot Gold Cup, Eclipse Stakes (five), Champion Stakes (two), Benson & Hedges Gold Cup (two), Irish Derby (six), Irish Oaks (four), Irish St. Leger (nine), Irish 2,000 Guineas (five), Irish 1,000 Guineas (three), Washington D.C. International, Breeders Cup Mile, Prix du Jockey Club, Dewhurst Stakes (seven), Chevely Park Stakes (three), Observer Gold Cup; awarded Honorary Doctorate in Law (NUI), Hon DSC (University of Ulster) 1995. A quietly spoken man; a legendary figure in racing throughout the world; favourite racetrack is The Curragh. Hobbies, fishing and golf. Contact: Ballydoyle House, Cashel, Co. Tipperary. Fax: 062 612 601

O'BYRNE, Bernard John

O'BYRNE, Bernard John; CHIEF EXECUTIVE, FOOTBALL ASSOCIATION OF IRELAND; *b* 1954; *educ* St. Michael's C.B.S., Inchicore; James' Street, C.B.S.; College of Commerce, Rathmines, H.Dip Business Studies; *m* Tina Costigan; 1 *da*; Trainee Management Accountant, Coca Cola Ireland, 1974-77; Management Accountant, Nestlé Ireland, 1977-79; Treasury Desk Manager, CRH plc., 1979-96; Chief Executive, FAI, 1996 to date; Life Vice President, Athlete Union League; Former President,

O'BYRNE, Robert

O'CALLAGHAN, David

O'CLERY, Conor

O'CONNELL, Maurice

F.A.I. Junior Council, Leinster F.A., former Treasurer, F.A.I.; Hobbies, politics, reading, golf, snooker. Contact: The Football Association of Ireland, 80, Merrion Square, Dublin 2. Tel: 01 676 6864. Fax: 01 661 0931.

O'BYRNE, Robert; JOURNALIST; *b* 1959; *educ* Gonzaga College Dublin; Trinity College Dublin; *single*; Curator, Damer House and Roscrea Heritage Centre, 1983-84; Mid-West Regional Arts Officer, 1984-86; Director, The Music Network, 1986-91; Journalist, *The Irish Times,* 1991 to date; currently Fashion and Fine Art Correspondent; has created a sense of liveliness and style in the fashion pages in *The Irish Times*; an inveterate party goer with an international network. Hobbies, reading and sleeping. Contact: The Irish Times, 10-16 D'Olier Street, Dublin 2. Tel: 01 679 2022. Fax: 677 9181.

O'CALLAGHAN, David; SECRETARY GENERAL, DEPARTMENT OF DEFENCE; *b* 1946; *educ* Patrician Academy, Mallow, University College Dublin; *m* Mary Delamere; 1 s 2 *da;* Career Civil Servant, 1964; Revenue Commissioners, 1964-93; Assistant Secretary, Department of Defence 1993-95; Secretary General, 1995. Hobbies, reading, theatre and family. Contact: Department of Defence, Parkgate, Infirmary Road, Dublin 7. Tel: 01 804 2000 Fax: 01 670 3399.

O'CALLAGHAN, Noel; MANAGING DIRECTOR O'CALLAGHAN HOTEL GROUP; *b* 1949; *educ* Cistercian College, Roscrea; qualified as an accountant; *m* Miriam Ronan; 3 *da*; Started in hotel business with Mont Clare Hotel, Dublin, re-opened hotel following extensive refurbishment 1990; acquired former Plymouth Brethren gospel hall, Merrion Hall, renovated it and opened it as Davenport Hotel 1993; acquired Whites Hotel, Gibralter 1996, refurbished and renamed it, opened as The Elliot 1998; opened Alexander Hotel, Dublin 1996; fourth Dublin property St. Stephen's Hotel, St Stephen's Green opened 1999; Global Partner, Inter-Continental Hotels; a hands-on executive with a meticulous eye for detail; a passionate follower of the bloodstock industry. Hobby, horseracing. Contact: O'Callaghan Hotel Group, 16-20 South Cumberland Street, Dublin 2. Tel: 01 607 3900. Fax: 01 661 5663.

O'CALLAGHAN, Owen; MANAGING DIRECTOR O'CALLAGHAN PROPERTIES LTD; *b* 1940 *educ* Presentation Brothers College, Cork; Farranferris College, Cork; *m* Shelagh Harrington 1 s 2 *da;* Quantity Surveyor, O'Connell & Harly, Cork 1959-67; left to form own property company, Managing Director, Chairman, O'Callaghan (Properties) Ltd., 1967 to date; company specialises in retail developments, mainly in urban renewal areas throughout Ireland, such as Golden Island Shopping Centre, Athlone, Carlow Shopping Centre, Liffey Valley Shopping Centre, Co. Dublin; Fellow, Architects and Surveyors Institute; former Board member, Bord Gais Eireann (BGE); member, Showjumping Association of Ireland; Hobbies, horses, football. Contact: Owen O'Callaghan Properties Ltd., 21-24 Lavitt's Quay, Cork. Tel: 021 275 008 Fax: 021 275 626.

O'CEALLAIGH, Dáithí; ASSISTANT SECRETARY DEPARTMENT OF FOREIGN AFFAIRS; *b* 1945; *educ* Christian Brother's School, Dun Laoghaire; University College Dublin, BA; *m* Antoinette Reilly; 1*s* 1 *da;* School Teacher, Dublin, Zambia, 1966-73; joined Department of Foreign Affairs, 1973; Embassy Moscow, 1975; Embassy London, 1977; Department of Foreign Affairs, 1982; Anglo Irish Secretariat, 1985; Consul General, New York, 1987; Ambassador to Finland, 1993; Assistant Secretary, Department of Foreign Affairs, 1998 to date. Hobbies, ornithology, reading, jazz. Contact: Department of Foreign Affairs, 80 St. Stephen's Green, Dublin 2. Tel: 01 478 0822.

O'CLERY, Conor; JOURNALIST; *b* 1940; *educ* Queen's University Belfast, B.A; *m; 2 s 4 da*; joined *The Irish Times* in 1972; Northern Editor, 1973-76, London Editor, 1976-79, Assistant Editor, 1979-82, News Editor, 1982-86, Moscow Correspondent, 1987-91, Washington Correspondent, 1991-1996, Asia Correspondent, 1996 to date; publications include: *Phrases Make History Here* , 1986; *Melting Snow, an Irishman in Moscow,* 1991; *America, A Place Called Hope,* 1993; *The Greening of the White House,* 1996; *Irish Political Quotations in the 20th Century,* 1999; Journalist of the Year, 1987; regarded as Ireland's leading foreign correspondant; an intrepid pioneer who has reported from some of the world's least accomodating venues. Contact: The Irish Times, D'Olier Street, Dublin 1. Tel: 01 679 2022.

O'CONNELL, Maurice; GOVERNOR, CENTRAL BANK OF IRELAND; *b* 1936 *educ* St. Michael's College, Listowel; St. Brendan's College, Killarney; St. Patrick's College, Maynooth; University College, Dublin; holds a post graduate degree in Ancient Classics; *m* Marjorie Tracey, 2 *s* 2 *da*; Worked for a number of years as a second level teacher both in Ireland and overseas; Joined the Department of Finance, 1962; worked in all areas of the Department; also worked in both the Department of the Public Service and the Department of Economic Planning and Development; A former Director of the European Investment Bank and Irish Telecommunications Investments; Former Member, the Monetary Committee of the European Community; Governor of the Central Bank of Ireland, 1994 to date. Contact: Central Bank of Ireland, PO Box 559, Dame Street, Dublin

2. Tel: 01 671 6666. Fax: 01 671 6561.

O'CONNELL, Owen; SOLICITOR; *b* 1955; *educ* Presentation College, Glasthule, Dublin; University College Dublin; *m* Denise Toher; 3 *s;* joined William Fry Solicitors 1979, Partner since 1985, Managing Partner since 1998; specialist in commercial and corporate law. Hobbies, cooking and travel. Contact: William Fry Solicitors, Fitzwilton House, Fitzwilton Place, Dublin 2. Tel: 01 639 5000 Fax: 01 639 5333.

O'CONNELL; John J; ARCHITECT; *b* 1949; *educ* Clongowes Wood College, Co. Kildare; College of Technology, Bolton Street, Dip.Arch.; *single;* established own practice, 1978, and has been involved in a number of restoration projects including College of St. Columba, Rathfarnham, the design and erection of a new Choir Gallery, 1989; The William Walton Foundation, Ishia, Italy, 1992; University College Cork, The North Wing, 1994; The Wallace Collection, Manchester Square, London, the restoration of the late 19th century French revival interiors, 1994-96; The Royal Irish Academy, Dawson Street, Dublin, 1996; publications include, measured drawings published in Dr. Maurice Craig's book, *Classic Irish Houses of the Middle Size;* drawings showing the reconstruction of Waterford Courthouse by James Gandon published in Dr. McParland's Biography, *James Gandon Vitruvius Hibernicus,* 1976; wrote the Conservation Guidelines in connection with Interior Decoration and Finishes for Department of The Environment, 1996; Member, Royal Institute of Architects of Ireland (1977), Fellow, Royal Institute of Architects (1993), Member, Accessions Committee of the Irish Architectural Archive; Member, Kildare Street and University Club, Dublin; awards include Silver Medal for Architectural Conservation, 1989; one of the most sensitive restoration architects in these islands. Hobbies, collects 18th and 19th century wallpaper samples. Contact: 14 North Great Georges Street, Dublin 1. Tel: 01 874 7154. Fax: 01 872 7834.

O'CONNOR, Christy; GOLF PROFESSIONAL, COURSE DESIGNER; *b* 1948; *educ* St. Patrick's, Galway; St. Enda's College, Galway; *m* Ann O'Boyle; 2*s* (*1 decd*) 1*da*; one of Ireland's leading professionals; winner of Ryder Cup 1975 and 89, World Cup (5), Dunhill Cup (2), Hennessy Cup, Philip Morris International Tournament, Zambian Open, Carrolls Irish Open, Sumrie Better-Ball (2), Kenyan Open, Jersey Open, Irish Match Play Championship (3), Irish Dunlop; recipient of Texaco Award, Galway Person of the Year Award, Tooting Bec 1985 (for lowest round in British Open by British and Irish player); Course Designer of numerous golf clubs including Galway Bay Golf and Country Club, City West Golf Club, Glasson Golf Club, Rathsallagh Golf Club. Hobbies, fishing and shooting. Contact: Galway Bay Golf and Country Club, Renville, Oranmore, Co. Galway. Tel: 091 790 500.

O'CONNOR, John; MANAGING DIRECTOR FOLENS AND BLACKWATER PRESS; *b* 1948; *educ* Presentation College, Birr, Co. Offaly; University College Dublin, B.Comm.; *m* Laserina McCool; 2*s*; Teacher for many years before joining Folens Publishers as Marketing Director, promoted to Managing Director; extensive lecturing and promotional experience nationwide; author of books on Accounting and Business; titles published by Blackwater Press include *Thanks a Million Big Fella, Dear John* (both by Sam Smith); Blackwater Press have had eight top sellers in eight consecutive years; Honorary member, Dublin Branch of BSTAI, former President of Association. Hobbies, sporting and socialising. Contact: Folens Publishers, 8 Broomhill Business Park, Dublin 24. Tel: 01 451 5311. Fax: 01 451 5306.

O'CONNOR, Joyce née Fitzpatrick; PRESIDENT NATIONAL COLLEGE OF IRELAND, RANELAGH; *b* 1947; *educ* University College Dublin, BSoc Sc, MSoc Sc, PhD; Harvard University, Inst. for Educational Management - Programme for University Presidents & Senior Administrators; *m* Pat O'Connor; 1*s* 1 *da;* Research Fellow, Dept. of Psychiatry, University College Dublin 1968-70; Lecturer (part-time), Milltown Park Institute of Theology and Philosophy 1968-72; Senior Research Fellow, University College Dublin 1971-76; Lecturer, Director of Social Research Centre, Senior Lecturer in College of Humanities at University of Limerick 1974-87 and Associate Professor 1986; Visiting Professor, University of Calgary 1986; Adjunct Association Professor, Worcester Polytechnic Institute (U.S.A) 1986; Head of Dept. of Languages & Applied Social Studies, University of Limerick 1987-90; appointed first lay President of National College of Ireland (formerly NCIR); has held numerous positions in national and international semi-state, private and voluntary bodies; member, Dublin Chamber of Commerce; Chairperson, National Accreditation Committee, National Vocational Awards; Board member, ICS Building Society; member, Labour Relations Commission; publications include books, videos, papers on social behaviour; recipient Award of Honour from International Council on Alcohol Addiction, Eisenhower Fellowship, N.I.H.E. Excellence in Research Award, Bronze Medal at Film & TV Festival (NY); University of London Dent Memorial Lecture. Hobbies, walking, reading, sport and travel. Contact: National College of Ireland, Sandford Road, Ranelagh, Dublin 6. Tel: 01 406 0501. Fax: 01 497 2200.

O'CONNOR, Michael Denis; MANAGING DIRECTOR CAPPOQUIN CHICKENS; *b* 1930; *educ* Mount Mellery, Co. Waterford; *m* Mary Cahill; 5*s* 2 *da;* Managing Director, Cappoquin Chickens, 1966 to date; member of Waterford All Ireland Senior Hurling Team 1959; member of Railway Cup Hurling Munster Victorious Team 1957; member of 1948 victorious Waterford All Ireland Minor Hurling Team; member, Dungarvan Golf Club. Hobby, joint owner, *Feather Gale,* winner of Irish Grand National. Contact: Cappoquin Chickens, Lefanta, Cappoquin, Co. Waterford. Tel: 058 54402. Fax: 058 54668.

O'CONNOR, Pat; FILM DIRECTOR; *b* 1943; *educ* Christian Brothers School, Limerick; Christian Brothers College, Cork; UCLA California; Ryerson Institute, Toronto; *m* Mary Elizabeth Mastrantonio, Actress; 2 *children;* joined RTE as Producer/Director 1970-81, working mainly in current affairs and features; film credits include *Cal* (Irish Arts Best Film Award), 1984; *A Month in the Country* (Irish Arts Award and NY Film Festival Award), 1987; *Stars and Bars,* 1988; *The January Man,* 1989; *Fools of Fortune* (Grand Prix at Barcelona Film Festival), 1990; *Zelda, 1993; Circle of Friends,* 1994, *Inventing the Abbots,* 1996, *Dancing at Lughnasa,* 1997, television credits include *Force of Duty, Ballroom of Romance* (British Academy Award), *Night in Tunisia, One of Ourselves,* regarded as an independent minded, dedicated and highly talented director. Contact: ICM, Oxford House, 76 Oxford Street, London, W1N OAX, UK. Tel: 0044 171 635 6868. Fax: 0044 171 323 0101.

O'CONNOR, Patrick

O'CONNOR, Patrick; SOLICITOR, CORONER, NOTARY PUBLIC; *b* 1952; *educ* National School, Swinford; Glenstal Abbey, Co. Limerick; University College Dublin, BCL (Hons), University College Galway, LL.B (Hons); *m* Gillian Flannery; 3 *s;* 1 *da*; Admitted to the Roll of Solicitors in Ireland, 1974; Northern Ireland, 1994; England and Wales, 1995; Joined established family firm, P. O'Connor & Son, Swinford, Co. Mayo; Appointed a Notary Public for the County of Mayo, 1977, and subsequently for the counties of Sligo, Roscommon and Galway; Deputy Coroner, Mayo East, 1979; Appointed Coroner, 1989; Publications include: *Handbook for Coroners in the Republic of Ireland,* 1997; *The Royal O'Connors of Connaught,* 1997; *The O'Connors of Swinford, County Mayo,* 1998; Member: Hibernian United Services Club, Irish Club, (London), Royal Irish Automobile Club, Royal Zoological Society, Law Society of Ireland, Glenstal Old Boys Society, Management Committee of the O'Dwyer Cheshire Home; Chairman, Board of Management of St. Louis Community School, Kiltimagh; Board of Management, Scoil Mhuire and Padraig, Swinford, HOPE House - Addiction Treatment Centre, Foxford Resources Limited, I.R.D. Kiltimagh Limited; Awarded Irish Quality Association, National Services Award, 1995-96, Excellence Ireland Award, Small Service Companies, 1999; Law Director, Law Society of Ireland, Director, International Bar Association; listed in *Martindale-Hubbell International Law Directory, Russell Law List.* Hobbies, rugby (acts as I.R.F.U. under age coach), tennis, sailing, soccer, Gaelic football, fishing, walking, reading, "The Law". Contact: P. O'Connor & Son, Swinford, Co. Mayo. Tel: 094 51333 Fax: 094 51833.

O'CONOR, Hugh; ACTOR; *b* 1975; *educ* Gonzaga College, Dublin; Trinity College, Dublin; graduated with a First in Theatre and Drama Studies; awarded a Fulbright Scholarship to New York University to study film making; started in film aged eight; films include *Lamb* with Liam Neesan, *Da, My Left Foot* (and was acknowledged as co-winner of the Best Actor at the Oscar awards ceremony by Daniel Day-Lewis; other films include, *The Three Musketeers, The Boy from Mercury, The Young Poisoner's Handbook.* Currently continuing to take acting roles and studying film directing. Contact: Sue Latimer, William Morris Agency, (U.K.) Ltd., 1 Stratton Street, London W1X 6HB, England. Tel: 171 355 8500.

O'CONOR, John; CONCERT PIANIST, DIRECTOR ROYAL IRISH ACADEMY OF MUSIC; *b* 1947; *educ* Belvedere College; University College Dublin, BMus; Hochschule Fur Musik, Vienna, Konzert Diplom; *m* Mary Murphy, Sex Therapist; 2 *s*; Professor of Piano, Royal Irish Academy of Music, 1976, Director, 1994 to date; Co-founder and Artistic Director, Guardian Dublin International Piano Competition; as a concert pianist, he has played with such world renowned orchestras as The Vienna Symphony, Czech Philharmonic, Royal Philharmonic, L'Orchestre National de France, NHK Orchestra of Tokyo and the Symphonies of Cleveland, San Francisco, Detroit, Montreal and Washington D.C.; recordings include *Complete Piano Concertos* (Claddagh), *Field Nocturnes and Sonatas* (Telarc), *Complete Beethoven Sonatas, Mozart Concertos* with the Scottish Chamber Orchestra, and *Chamber Music* with the Cleveland Quartet; recipient of First Prize International Beethoven Piano Competition Vienna (1973), First Prize Bosendorfer Competition, Vienna (1975); conferred with Honorary Doctorate of Music NUI (1985); Officier de l'Ordre des Arts et des Lettres (France), Ehrenkreuz fur Wissenschaft und Kunst (Austria) as well as others from Italy and Poland; a frequent broadcaster, has presented own music series on RTE TV and radio. Could be termed the major force in music in Ireland; remains an internationally sought after performing artist; increasingly in demand abroad as a jury member and teacher; a shrewd handler of people with the vision, energy and tact to bring his plans for music to fruition.

Hobbies, bridge, theatre and seeing friends. Contact: Royal Irish Academy of Music, 36, Westland Row, Dublin 2 . Tel: 01 676 4412. Fax: 01 662 2798

Ó DÁLAIGH, Tony; ARTS ADMINISTRATOR; *b* 1933; *educ* Patrician Academy, Mallow; *m* Margaret O'Callaghan; 2 *s* 2 *da*; Private Secretary, Minister for Education, 1965-70; Manager, Damer Theatre, 1963-65; Co-founder and Manager, Irish National Opera, 1964-85; Assistant Principal, Department of Education (Youth and Sport) 1970-74; General Administrator, Irish Theatre Company, 1974-78; Head of Youth Section, Departments of Education and Labour, 1978-86; Director, Royal Hospital Kilmainham 1986-90; Director, Dublin Theatre Festival, 1990-99; Gate Theatre Board Member. A man knowledgeable in the politics of the arts in Ireland. Hobbies, classical music, *The Guardian* crossword, counting and making lists. Contact: Dublin Theatre Festival, 47, Nassau Street, Dublin 2. Tel: 01 671 2860. Fax: 01 679 7709.

O'DONNELL, Daniel; ENTERTAINER; *b* 1961; *educ* Belcruit National School: Rosses Community School; *single*; has been in the entertainment business since leaving school in 1980; one of the country's most popular and successful entertainers with eighteen top selling albums and eleven videos to his credit; recipient of numerous awards. A singer with a large and devoted following; a hard working professional with a squeaky clean, upright image. Hobby, golf. Contact: Ritz Productions, 5-6 Lombard Street, Dublin 2. Tel: 01 677 9046.

O'DONNELL, Elizabeth "Liz"; MINISTER OF STATE AT THE DEPARTMENT OF FOREIGN AFFAIRS; *b* 1956; *educ* Salesian College, Limerick; Law School, Trinity College Dublin; *m* Michael Carson; 1*s* 1 *da;* worked in theatre management with Noel Pearson; Executive Administrator, McCann Fitzgerald Solicitors; elected to City Council for Progressive Democrats, 1991; elected to Dáil Eireann, 1992; Spokesperson on Justice and Chief Party Whip, 1993-97; following the General Election, negotiated the Programme for Coalition Government; appointed Minister of State at the Department of Foreign Affairs with responsibility for Overseas Development Assistance, July 1997; one of the Government Negotiators in the Multi Party Negotiations at Stormont, culminating in the Good Friday Agreement, 1998; probably the most attractive deputy in Leinster House, certainly one of the most single-minded and politically astute. Hobbies, theatre, painting and all forms of Art and Design. Contact: Department of Foreign Affairs, 80 St. Stephen's Green, Dublin 2. Tel: 01 478 0822. Fax: 01 478 4780.

O'DONNELL, "Liz"

O'DONOGHUE, Donal; GALWAY COUNTY MANAGER; *b* 1942; *educ* Diploma in Public Administration (I.P.A.), 1970; married; 1 *s* 1 *da*; Town Clerk, Listowel U.D.C., 1964-67; Staff Officer, Limerick Corporation, 1967-70; Urban Accountant, Tralee, U.D.C., 1970-1973; County Accountant, Roscommon County Council, 1974-79; Finance Officer, Limerick Corporation, 1979-87; Galway Assistant City and County Manager, 1988-92; Meath County Manager, 1993-1994; Galway County Manager, 1994 to date; Member: County and City Managers Association, National Economic and Social Forum. Hobbies, golf, walking. Contact: County Council, Liosban Industrial Estate, Tuam Road, Galway. Tel: 091 509 000 Fax: 091 509 010

O'DONOGHUE, Donal

O'DONOGHUE, Hughie; ARTIST; *b* 1953; *educ* Manchester and Goldsmiths College, London, MA; *m* Clare Reynolds; 2*s* 1 *da;* taught for a time before becoming a full time artist; one man exhibitions worldwide include: Rubicon Gallery (Dublin), Pfefferle Gallery (Munich), Purdy Hicks Gallery (London), Galerie Helmut Pabst (Frankfurt), Haus der Kurst (Munich), 1997, Irish Musuem of Modern Art and R.H.A. Gallery (Dublin), 1998; group exhibitions include: Walker Gallery (Liverpool), University of California Art Museum, Grey Art Gallery (New York), Barbican Art Gallery (London), 1998, Yale Centre (New Haven), 1999, Museum of Fine Art (Boston), 1999; hangs in numerous public collections, including: Arts Council of Great Britain, Fitzwilliam Museum (Cambridge), Irish Museum of Modern Art and Hugh Lane Gallery (Dublin), The National Gallery (London); a world class artist renowned for memorable series of vast paintings *Episodes from the Passion* painted on a renaissance scale; charcoal drawings on same subject are equally impressive. Hobbies, music, film and theatre. Contact: Agent: Purdy Hicks Gallery, 65 Hopton Street, Bankside, London, SE1 9G2. Tel: 0044 171 401 9229.

O'DONOGHUE, John; MINISTER FOR JUSTICE, EQUALITY AND LAW REFORM; SOLICITOR; *b* 1956; *educ* Christian Brothers Primary and Secondary School, Caherciveen, Co. Kerry; University College, Cork, BCL, LLB; Incorporated Law Society of Ireland, Solicitor; *m* Kate Murphy; 2*s* 1*da*; member, Kerry County Council and other Boards 1985-91; elected Fianna Fáil Deputy for Kerry South 1987; member, Oireachtas Joint Committee on Secondary Legislation of European Communities 1989-91; Minister of State at the Department of Finance, with responsibility for the Office of Public Works 1991-92; Special Dáil Committee on Judicial Separation, Child Care, Foreign Adoptions, Solicitors' Bill, British–Irish Parliamentary Body 1993; currently Minister for Justice, Equality and Law Reform; member, St. Mary's GAA Club, Caherciveen, Caherciveen Social Services Committee. Hobbies, English literature, history, Gaelic Games and horse racing. Contact: Office of the Minister of Justice, Equality and Law Reform, 72-76 St. Stephen's Green, Dublin 2. Tel: 01 602 8202.

O'DONOGHUE, Maurice; HOTELIER; *b* 1938; *educ* St. Brendan's Seminary, Killarney; Blackrock College, Dublin; College of Pharmacy; qualified 1964; *m* Margaret O'Sullivan; 4*s* 3 *da;* joined family pharmaceutical company, Killarney; purchased Gleneagles, a large private residence, now Gleneagles Hotel and Country Club, 1958; Gleneagles is a noted Events venue, one of the largest in the South West; owner, Scotts Hotel, Killarney, Destination Killarney Ltd., Torc Travel, Killarney and Killarney Lake Tours; Chairman, Killarney Race Company; member (past Chairman) Killarney U.D.C.; Council member, Irish Transport Museum; member (past Captain), Killarney Golf and Fishing Club; Director, Bord Fáilte; a highly successful businessman with a deep commitment to Killarney and Kerry tourism. Hobbies, vintage cars, golf, Irish language, Gleneagles Concert Band. Contact: Gleneagles Hotel, Killarney, Co. Kerry. Tel: 064 34063. Fax: 064 32646.

O'DONOGHUE, Redmond; CHIEF EXECUTIVE OFFICER WATERFORD CRYSTAL; *b* 1943; *educ* Waterpark College, Waterford; University College Dublin, B.Comm.; Harvard Business School, AMP; *m* Anthea Goodbody; 1*s* 1*da;* Harringtons and Goodlass Wall Ltd. Cork, 1964-68; Ford Motor Company, Ireland, UK and Spain, 1968-85; Sales and Marketing Director, Waterford Crystal, 1985-95; on secondment as Chief Executive Officer, Waterford Wedgwood Inc, USA, 1990; Chief Operating Officer, Waterford Crystal, 1995-96, Chief Executive Officer, 1996 to date; member, Marketing Institute of Ireland (Chairman, 1996-97); member, Waterford Chamber of Commerce, (President, 1999-2000); Fellow, Marketing Institute of Ireland (May 1999); member of boards of Waterford Wedgwood plc, Waterford Wedgwood UK plc, Waterford Wedgwood Inc., Waterford Crystal, Stuart Crystal, Edward Flahavan & Sons Ltd., Waterford Regional Airport plc, Waterford Tourism Ltd. (Chairman), Waterford Chamber of Commerce. Hobbies, tennis and golf. Contact: Kilbarry, Co. Waterford. Tel: 051 373311. Fax: 051 378539.

O'DONOVAN, Patricia; TRADE UNION OFFICIAL; *b* 1953; *educ* University College Cork, BCL, LLB; Kings Inns, BL; Harvard University, LLM; *single* called to the Bar, 1975; joined Irish Congress of Trade Unions as Information Officer, 1977, Deputy Legislative Officer, 1980, Assistant General Secretary, 1988, Deputy General Secretary, 1998 to date; has overall responsibility for economic and social policy, also European and international affairs; represents the Irish Congress of Trade Unions on the following national and international bodies: National Economic and Social Council (NESC); member of the Governing Body of the International Labour Organisation (ILO), elected Vice-Chairperson, June 1999; Economic Committee and Social Policy Committee of the European Trade Union Confederation (ETUC); Euro Changeover Board of Ireland (ECBI); former member of the Council of State; a highly influential trade unionist; noted as single minded and dedicated. Contact: Irish Congress of Trade Unions, 31-32 Parnell Square, Dublin 1. Tel: 01 889 7777. Fax: 01 660 9027.

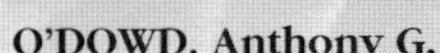
O'DOWD, Anthony G.

O'DOWD, Anthony George; EXECUTIVE VICE PRESIDENT, COREL CORPORATION OF IRELAND; *b* 1966; *educ* O'Connells C.B.S. Schools; Trinity College Dublin, B.Sc; *m* Noreen McGrath; 1 *s* 1 *da*; Joined Lotus Development Corporation, Principal Development Engineer, 1988-92; Senior Technology Manager, Symantec Corporation, 1992-95; Executive Vice President & General Manager, Corel Corporation Ltd., 1995 to date; Chairman Fit Ltd.; Director, Junior Achievement Ireland; Member, Irish Computer Society; Runs a highly successful outlet with a small number of employees and sales in excess of £280 million. Hobbies, golf, tennis, digital music recording. Contact: Corel Corporation Ltd., Europa House, 3rd Floor, Harcourt Street, Dublin 2. Tel: 01 478 2855. Fax: 01 478 5962.

Ó'DUINN, Proinnsias; CONDUCTOR; *b* 1941; *educ* Christian Brothers School, Marino; College of Commerce, Rathmines; Royal Irish Academy of Music; College of Music; private tuition with Pierre Monteux and Leopold Stokowski; (*m dis*) 1*s* 1 *da; m* Joan Merrigan; Principal Conductor, Iceland Symphony Orchestra, 1963-64; Principal Conductor and Music Director, Orquestra Sifonica Nacional del Ecuador, 1965-89; Permanent Principal Conductor, RTE Concert Orchestra since 1978; Music Director, Our Lady's Choral Society since 1979; Guest Conductor with engagements in various concert, opera, ballet and oratorio; Fellowship, Irish Arts Council, 1962; recipient, Jacobs Award for radio and television, 1975; creative works include various symphonic and chamber music compositions, *Stuff and Nonsense* (musical), composed soundtrack of *Strumpet City* TV series. Recognised as one of Ireland's senior conductors, has helped shape the RTE Concert Orchestra. Hobbies, gardening and DIY. Contact: R.T.E., Donnybrook, Dublin 4. Tel: 01 208 3111.

O'DWYER, Conor; JOCKEY; *b* 1966; *educ* Wexford C.B.S.; *m* Audrey Cross; 1 *s* 1 *da;* Professional N.H. Jockey, first ride *Davy's Hall* Roscommon, Sept. 1982; first winner was *Gayfield* in Limerick, 28/12/82; approx. 350 winners ridden to date, Ireland and England; currently stable jockey to A.L.T. Moore; currently in 4th place in Irish Jockeys Table and has finished 2nd for the past three seasons; prizes include, Cheltenham Gold Cup, 1996 on *Imperial Call*, Hennessy Gold Cup, 1996 on *Imperial Call*, Ladbroke Hurdle twice, on *Redundant Pal*, 1990 and *Graphic Equalizer*, 1998, Midlands Grand National on *Lauras Beau*, 1992, 4 Year Old Champion Hurdle on *Grimes*, 1997. Hobbies, golf, sea fishing and rallying. Contact: Ballysax, The Curragh, Co. Kildare. Tel: 045 441 352.

O'FAOLAIN, Nuala Aine Brigid; WRITER; *b* 1942; *educ* University College Dublin, MA; Oxon, B.Phil; *single;* Lecturer, University College Dublin; Television and Radio Producer, BBC / The Open University; Television Producer, RTE; Lecturer in Media Studies, DCU; Columnist, *The Irish Times;* publications include *Are You Somebody?* Memoir & Selected Journalism (1996), *My Everything Always* - A Romance (in preparation). Contact: The Irish Times, D'Olier Street, Dublin 2. Tel: 01 679 2022.

O'GRADY, Edward; RACEHORSE TRAINER; *b* 1940; *educ* Blackrock College; University College Dublin; *m* Judith Mullins; 1*s* 2*da;* son of the late Willie O'Grady, renowned jockey and trainer; attained Trainers License, 1972; trained winners of such races as, fifteen at Cheltenham Festival, Whitbread Gold Cup, Leopardstown Chase (twice), Galway Plate (3 times), Galway Hurdle, Irish Grand National; Vice Chairman, Irish Racehorse Trainers Association; member, Management Committee, Kildare Street and University Club; Secretary, Tipperary Foxhounds. Hobby, foxhunting. Contact: Kildare Street and University Club, 17 St. Stephen's Green, Dublin 2. Tel: 01 676 2975.

O'HALLORAN, James Michael; FINE ART AUCTIONEER & VALUER; *b* 1958; *educ* Blackrock College; College of Commerce Rathmines; University College Dublin, BA; Trinity College Dublin, Diploma in Art History; *m* Helen Long; 1 *s* 2 *da;* joined James Adam & Sons as Salesroom Assistant, 1981; qualified as a member of Irish Auctioneers and Valuers Institute, 1986; made Associate Director, James Adam & Sons, 1987, Director, 1993, Managing Director, 1997; Fellow, Irish Auctioneers & Valuers Institute (IAVI), Chairman, Fine Art Committee of the IAVI, member, National Council, IAVI, Education Committee of IAVI; awarded the IAVI Institute Prize for a Fine Art Study / Thesis, 1986; Presenter and Irish Art Expert in RTE series for television *Treasure Ireland* 1993; main contributor to BBC TV Programme on the life and work of Paul Henry; Lecturer on Irish Art at IAVI Fine Art Lecture Series. Hobbies, cross country (mountain) cycling, travel, Irish painting, food and gardening. Contact: James Adam & Sons, 26 St. Stephen's Green, Dublin 2. Tel: 01 676 3885.

O'HANLON, Ardal

O'HANLON, Ardal; ACTOR, COMEDIAN; b 1966; educ Blackrock College, Dublin; Dublin City University; *single;* Co-founded the first comedy club in Dublin, The Comedy Cellar, after leaving college; Moved to London, 1994, winning the Hackney Empire New Act of the Year; played Father Dougal in three series of the internationally successful sitcom *Father Ted*, winning a British Comedy Award for Best Newcomer, 1995, with Best Actor nominations in 1996, 1997 and 1998, and a BAFTA Award nomination in 1999; his debut novel, *The Talk of the Town* has been a best seller since its publication in May 1998; film appearances include *The Butcher Boy, Flying Saucer Rock'n'Roll;* currently writing his second novel and appearing in the ITV drama series *Big Bad World* and the BBC sitcom *My Hero*; hobbies, football, literature, cinema. Contact: Dawn Sedgwick, Dawn Sedgwick Management, 3 Goodwins Court, London, WC2N 4LL, England. Tel: 0044 171 240 0404 Fax: 0044 171 240 0415.

O'HANLON, Noel; CHAIRMAN AER RIANTA; *b* 1940; *educ* St. Mels College, Longford; *m* Finnuala Murtagh; eight children; worked with Fords Detroit before setting up N. O'Hanlon (Ireland) Ltd; Chairman, Aer Rianta, 1994 to date; Chairman Aer Rianta International; Chairman, VHI; Deputy Chairman, Birmingham Airport; Director, ARI/Nat West Ventures; a strong Fianna Fail supporter and an astute businessman; a flying enthusiast with a pilot's licence. Contact: Aer Rianta, Head Office, Dublin Airport. Tel: 01 814 1111. Fax: 01 844 5113.

O'HARA, Ken

O'HARA, Ken; CHIEF EXECUTIVE E.S.B; *b* 1939; *educ* Good Counsel College, New Ross; University College Dublin, B.E. Electrical Engineering; University College Galway, M.I.E; *single;* joined ESB 1961, consultancy assignment Bahrain 1976-77; District Engineer 1977-79; District Manager 1979-85; Regional Manager 1985-87, Director, Customer Operations, 1987-93, Managing Director Power Generation 1993-97; Chief Executive Electricity Supply Board 1997 to date; Fellow, Institute of Engineers of Ireland; member, Tramore and Elm Park Golf Clubs; Graduate of the year 1998 (U.C.G.). Hobbies, golf, walking. Contact: E.S.B., Lower Fitzwilliam Street, Dublin 2. Tel: 01 676 5831. Fax: 01 676 0727.

Ó'HÉEALAITHE, Tadhg; SECRETARY GENERAL THE DEPARTMENT OF ARTS, HERITAGE,

O'HERLIHY, William, "Bill

O'HUIGINN, Padraig

GAELTACHT AND THE ISLANDS; *b* 1948; *educ* Clondrohid, Macroom, Co.Cork; University College Dublin, Dip Pub Admin, BComm, MEconSc; *m* Mai O'Brien; 1*s* 2 *da;* Clerical Officer, ESB, 1965-70; Executive Officer, Office of Revenue Commissioners, 1970-71; Executive Officer, Department of an Taoiseach, 1971; Administrative Officer, Department of the Gaeltacht, 1971-75, Assistant Principal,1975-81, Principal, 1981-87, Assistant Secretary, 1987-91, Secretary, 1991-93; Secretary, Department of Arts, Culture and the Gaeltacht, 1993-97; Secretary General, Department of Arts, Heritage, Gaeltacht and the Islands, 1997 to date. Hobbies, reading, cycling and theatre. Contact: Dept. of Arts, Heritage, Gaeltacht and the Islands, 43-49 Mespil Road, Dublin . Tel: 01 667 0788. Fax: 01 667 0827.

O'HERLIHY, William, "Bill"; PUBLIC RELATIONS EXECUTIVE, TELEVISION PRESENTER; *b* 1938; *educ* St. Finbarr's College, Cork; *m* Hilary Patterson; 2 *da*; Journalist, *Cork Examiner*, occasional Broadcaster with RTE, Cork Correspondent for *Newsbeat*; joined *Seven Days* current affairs programme; moved to RTE Sport 1972, Presenter of major sports events, including the Olympic Games, World Cup and Rugby World Cup; established Public Relations of Ireland Ltd. 1973 and Mediawise (producing TV programmes, corporate videos and media training) 1989, Bill O'Herlihy Strategic Training 1992; Producer/Presenter, *The Distant Drums*, interview series for RTE; involved in development of environmental series, *What On Earth Are We Doing*; recipient of Jacobs Award, 1990. Member: Public Relations Consultants Association, Public Relations Institute; a Corkman with an apparently natural flair for media presentation; a genial PR executive with a renowned capacity for hard work. Hobbies, golf and all sports. Clubs, Hibernian United Services, Foxrock GC, Elm Park GC, Royal Dublin Society. Contact: O'Herlihy Communications Group, 40 Eastmoreland Lane, Dublin 4. Tel: 01 660 2744. Fax: 01 660 2745.

O'HUIGINN, Padraig; SPECIAL ADVISOR TO DR. JAMES McDAID, T.D.; *b* 1924; *educ* St. Finbarr's College, Cork; University of Edinburgh, M.Sc (Economic and Social Planning); *m* Patricia Ní Lideadha; 3*s* 1 *da;* has had a distinguished career as a national and international Civil Servant; was Secretary-General, Department of the Taoiseach, 1982-93; held, for ten years, senior posts in the United Nations in Geneva and New York and in the EU Council of Ministers in Brussels; as Secretary-General of the Department of the Taoiseach, was the Chief Government negotiator of the social partnership programmes which laid the foundations for the remarkable growth of the Irish economy and employment from 1987; Chairman of the National Economic and Social Council, which provided the blueprints for economic recovery; Chairman of the Committee which established and developed the highly successful International Financial Services Centre; since retired from Civil Service, has accepted directorships in private sector including, Esat Telecom, Irish subsidiaries of the Bank of Bermuda and Serco Services Ireland Ltd. (the Irish branch of the largest participant in public/private partnerships in Britain); has been Chairman (and is still a Director) of Bord Fáilte; Special Advisor to Dr. James McDaid, T.D., Minister for Tourism, Sport and Recreation, 1997 to date; one of the four Directors of the Millennium Theatre Company which has taken over the lease of the Ambassador-Rotunda Theatre; Trustee of the Worth Library, the Iveagh Trust and the Irish Recorded Music Association Trust (established to help young musicians); Fellow, Irish Management Institute; Honorary Fellow, Institution of the Engineers of Ireland; Honorary Member, Royal Institute of Architects of Ireland and Honorary Life Member, Ballybunion Golf Club. Contact: Department of Tourism, Sport & Recreation, Kildare Street, Dublin 2. Tel: 01 662 1444.

O'KEEFFE, Paddy; CHAIRMAN FARMERS JOURNAL; *b* 1923; *educ* CBS Fermoy; Athenry Agric. College; Albert Agric. College, Dip Agr 1942; University College Dublin, B Ag Sc, 1946; Agriculture Adviser Co. Louth, 1946-47; Farm Development Officer Portrame, Grangegorman Hospitals 1947-1951; Editor *Farmers Journal*, 1951-88; Chief Executive *Farmers Journal* 1988-93; Chairman *Farmers Journal* 1993 to date; Chairman FBD Insurances, Irish Farm Centre, Equine Research Institute, Limerick University, Blackwater Salmon Development. Agricultural Institute; former President Irish Grassland Association. Honorary Life Member Royal Dublin Society, 1988; Honorary LL.D NUI, 1990; Bastow Memorial Award, Irish Meat Association 1987. An expert on who's who and what's what in Irish Agribusiness; a highly respected figure in the Irish farming and agribusiness community. Hobbies, farming and dairy farm development. Contact: Irish Farmers Journal, Irish Farm Centre, Bluebell, Dublin 12. Tel: 01 450 1166. Fax: 01 452 0876

O'KELLY, Patricia Florence; BLOODSTOCK BREEDER, COMPANY DIRECTOR; *b* 1931; *educ* University of London; *single;* Runs Kilcarn Stud founded by father, Major E. O'Kelly, in 1943; Kilcarn Stud headed the list of breeders in England and Ireland in 1966; bred the winners of major classics; winners include: *Salsabil* (Prix Marcel Boussac, 1,000 Guineas, Oaks, Irish Derby, Prix Vermeille), *Marju* (St. James Palace Stakes, Craven Stakes, Second Derby '91), *Dance Royale* (Prix de Psyche) *Poliuto* (Italian 2,000 Guineas), *Flame of Athens* (Railway Stakes), *Second Empire* (Grand Criterium and Prix de Chenes), *Ringwood Pearl* (Desmond Stakes); winning breeder, Irish Derby 1990, I.T.B.A. Awards 1990, Meath Region I.T.B.A. Awards 1989, '90, '91, '93, All Ireland

Leading 2yr Old, 1997; member, Irish Thoroughbred Breeders Association; Director, Irish National Stud; member, Kildare Street and University Club. Considered one of the leading thoroughbred breeders worldwide. Hobbies, gardening and skiing. Contact: 046 22622.

O'LEARY, Jane, née Strong; COMPOSER, MUSICIAN; *b* 1946; *educ* Vassar College, BA; Princeton University M.F.A. PhD; *m* Patrick O'Leary; 1*s* 1*da;* Lecturer in music, Swarthmore College, Pennsylvania, 1971-72; College of Music, Dublin, 1974-77; National University of Ireland, Galway, 1972-74, 1978-83 (extra-mural studies), Arts Administration Diploma Tutor, 1994 to date; Artistic Director and Pianist of Concorde, contemporary music ensemble, since 1976; musical compositions include, *Islands of Discovery, Distant Voices, Into the Wordless, Mystic Play of Shadows:* string quartet movement, *Piano Trio, Silenzio della Terra, A Silver Thread,* Duo for Violin and Cello, Duo for Alto Flute and Guitar, *From the Crest of a Green Wave* and *Dream Songs;* member of Aosdana since 1981; member of Arts Council of Ireland, 1988 to date; Chair of Contemporary Music Centre, 1989-97; Board of Directors, National Concert Hall, 1986-96; member, Cultural Relations Committee, Department of Foreign Affairs, 1990-95; member, Toscaireacht, Aosdana, 1991-96; founding member, Music for Galway, (PRO, 1981-83, Chair, 1984-92, Programme Director, 1992 to date); Board of International League of Women Composers, 1986-94; member, Galway Steinway Trust; member, IMRO; awards include, Marten Toonder Award, 1994; selected for representation at ISCM World Music Days, 1998; represented at International Rostrum of Composers, 1988, 1994; Guest Composer at *Donne in Musica* Festival, Fiuggi, Italy, 1996, 1998; Vienna Modern Masters Recording Award, Special Commendation, 1992; Guest Composer with Voices of Change, Dallas, Texas, 1992; 8th International Competition for Women Composers, Mannheim, Distinction, 1985; W.K. Rose Fellowship in Creative Arts, 1978; music recorded on CD with Capstone & Black Box Labels. Contact: Aosdana, 70 Merrion Square, Dublin 2. Tel: 01 661 1840.

O'LEARY, Margaret, née Shore; COMPANY DIRECTOR AND SECRETARY CRANE HIRE LTD.; *b* 1945; *educ* SCJ Bunclody, Co. Wexford; St. Mary's College, Mountmellick, Co. Laois; RGN; various courses in accounting, navigation, interior design, photography etc.; *m* Thomas O'Leary *(decd);* 1*s* 2 *da;* built up business, Crane Hire Ltd. with late husband Thomas, has been running the highly successful male dominated company 1992 to date; Crane Hire houses the largest cranes in the biggest company in Ireland; member, Association of Irish Racehorse Owners, Riverview Health and Fitness Club. Hobbies, riding, horse racing, cycling, walking, interior design and photography. Contact: Crane Hire Ltd., Kylemore Park North, Dublin 10. Tel: 01 626 8426. Fax: 01 626 8061.

O'LEARY, Michael; CHIEF EXECUTIVE RYANAIR; *b* 1961; *educ* Clongowes Wood College; Trinity College, Dublin BBS; *single*; worked in Stokes Kennedy Crowley, now KPMG, dealing in tax; moved into property, buying and selling some newsagents; joined Ryanair as Chief Operations Officer, 1991, Chief Executive 1993 to date; would see Ryanair as 'the people's airline' and many would agree with him; a tough, sometimes aggressive, negotiator, runs a highly successful operation. Hobbies, avoiding the media, sport and reading. Contact: Ryanair, Head Office, Dublin Airport. Tel: 01 844 4400.

O'LEARY, Olivia; JOURNALIST; *b* 1949; *educ* St. Leo's Convent of Mercy, Carlow; University College, Dublin, BA; *m* Paul Tansey, Economic Consultant; 1 *da;* Reporter, *Nationalist and Leinster Times* (Carlow) 1969-72; Reporter, RTE, 1972-78; Reporter, (widely read Parliamentary Sketchwriter), *Irish Times* 1978-84; Presenter, BBC *Newsnight* 1985-86; Presenter, *Today Tonight, Questions and Answers* (1986-88), *First Tuesday,* Yorkshire TV; recipient of three Jacobs Awards - for radio 1974, television 1982, 1987; Presenter, BBC Radio 4 *Between Ourselves* 1998-99; Co-author, *Mary Robinson - The Authorised Biography,* published 1998 (Hodder and Stoughton); Recognised as one of the finest current affairs journalists/presenters in Ireland, also has a high profile in the UK; an intelligent, sometimes tough, professional; off screen a relaxed, amusing companion. Hobbies, Borris, Co. Carlow and tennis. Contact: Agent, Declan O'Hanlon, Farrell, Grant, Sparks, Molyneux House, Bride Street, Dublin 8. Tel: 01 418 2022.

O'MAHONY, Eddie

O'MAHONY, Eddie; MANAGING DIRECTOR PETER OWENS LTD.; *educ* Rockwell College Co. Tipperary; University College Dublin, BA, MBA,; *m* Bernie D'Arcy; 5 *s;* Production Manager, Peter Owens Ltd., 1972, Account Executive, 1978, Account Director, 1982, Director Client Services, 1983, Managing Director, 1992 to date; Council member and past Chairman, Publicity Club of Ireland; member, Dublin Chamber of Commerce, Bray & District Chamber of Commerce, Marketing Institute of Ireland, Marketing Society; awarded Fellowship of Institute of Advertising Practitioners in Ireland; recipient, Bray Endeavours Award, presented by Bray & District Chamber of Commerce. Hobbies, fishing, reading biographies, walking and swimming. Contact: Peter Owens Ltd., 38 Fitzwilliam Place, Dublin 2. Tel: 01 676 1191. Fax: 01 676 1042.

O'MAHONY, Liam; CHIEF EXECUTIVE DESIGNATE, CRH PLC; *b* 1947; *educ* University College Cork, BEng.; Trinity College Dublin, M.B.A.; Kings Inns, BL, (awarded Brooke Scholarship); *married;* 2*s*; worked as a civil engineer in design and project management; joined CRH as Development Manager, 1971; held managerial positions in CRH in Ireland and US; member, CRH Board, 1992; Chief Executive, Oldcastle Inc (US) 1994; Chief Executive Designate CRH plc, 1999; CRH is a global building materials group employing 30,000 in 950 locations mainly in Europe and North America; it is the largest industrial company on the Irish Stock Exchange with 90% of its business outside Ireland. Contact: CRH plc, Belgard Castle, Dublin 22. Tel: 01 404 1000.

O'MALLEY, Desmond

O'MALLEY, Desmond; POLITICIAN; *b* 1939; *educ* Crescent College, Limerick; University College Dublin, BCL (Civil Law); Incorporated Law Society, Solicitor; *m* Patricia McAleer; 2*s* 4 *da;* joined established family legal practice in Limerick; elected Fianna Fail Deputy for Limerick East 1968; Parliamentary Secretary to the Taoiseach (Jack Lynch), to the Minister for Defence and Government Chief Whip 1969-70; Minister for Justice 1970-73; Opposition Spokesperson for Health 1973-75; Opposition Spokesperson for Industry and Commerce 1975-77; Minister for Industry, Commerce and Energy 1977-80; Minister for Industry Commerce and Tourism 1980-81; Minister, Trade, Commerce and Tourism March-October 1982; expelled from Fianna Fail Party 1984, founded Progressive Democrat Party 1985, Leader, Progressive Democrats 1985-93; following the 1989 general election the Progressive Democrats formed a coalition government with Fianna Fail; Minister for Industry and Commerce (coalition government) 1989-92; re-elected to Dáil in 1997 for the eleventh time; now Progressive Democrats Whip and Chairman of the Joint Oireachtas Committee on Foreign Affairs; recognised as one of the most able and astute politicians in government; a uniquely courageous, sometimes uncomfortable colleague. Hobbies, golf, poetry readings and fishing. Contact: Dáil Eireann, Leinster House, Dublin 2. Tel.: 01 618 3000.

O'MALLEY, Raymond; FARMER; *b* 1951; *educ* de la Salle Brothers, Ardee; Trinity College; *m* Máire Campbell; 1*s* 2*da*:; commenced farming on family farm after Trinity, has extended farm considerably, currently one of the leading pedigree beef producers in the State with pedigree herd of Simmental cattle; awards include RDS Supreme Champion, Inter Breed Champion and all major awards obtainable for cattle; member, IFA currently National Livestock Chairman; elected President Standing Group on Beef and Veal (Brussels); member, Bord Bia, Irish Cattle Breeders Association; currently member, Ministerial Task Force on Beef; one of the country's foremost authorities on beef production; an astute farmer and businessman with a deep commitment to the industry and a valued promoter of Irish beef and cattle abroad. Hobbies, film, theatre, food and wine. Contact: Millockston, Ardee, Co. Louth. Tel.: 041 53963.

O'MALLEY, Tony; ARTIST; *b* 1913; *m* Jane Harris, Artist; started painting, 1947; moved to St. Ives, Cornwall for a time; worked during winter in the Bahamas and Lanzarote; has had group and mixed exhibitions in Ireland, UK, Germany and Belgium since 1951, and one man exhibitions in numerous galleries, including Sail Loft Gallery (St. Ives), Arts Council of Northern Ireland, Taylor Galleries (Dublin), Festival Gallery (Bath), Caldwell Gallery (Dublin and Belfast), Arts Council of Ireland, Castlefield Gallery (Manchester); awarded retrospective exhibitions in Ulster Museum, Belfast, 1984, Douglas Hyde Gallery (Dublin), 1984, Crawford Institute (Cork), 1984, Nordjyllands Kunst Museum, (Denmark), 1999, in conjunction with Jack B. Yeats at Gl. Holtegaard (Copenhagen); his work hangs in major private and public collections in England, Canada, Ireland, USA, Switzerland, Australia, Japan, Bahamas, Denmark, Sweden and Germany. Subject of a biography, *Tony O'Malley*, edited by Brian Lynch, Scholar Press, 1996; Awarded Douglas Hyde Gold Medal (Arts Council of Ireland) 1981, Guardian Art Critics Award for Painting (Tom Hilton) 1989, Irish American Cultural Award (for painting) 1989; Honorary member, Royal Hibernian Academy, 1989; Member Newlyn Society of Artists, Penwith Society of Artists; Elected *Saoí* by members of Aosdana; Conferred with Honorary Doctorate by Trinity College Dublin 1994. A quiet, determined figure in the art world; enjoys a major reputation outside Ireland; his own country is only recently coming to terms with his importance. Contact: Taylor Galleries, 16 Kildare Street, Dublin 2. Tel: 01 676 6055.

O'MARA WALSH, Eileen; MANAGING DIRECTOR O'MARA TRAVEL COMPANY; *b* 1941; *educ* Laurel Hill, Limerick; Muckross Park, Dublin; Institut Catholique, Paris; *single;* 1 *s* ; Hotel Trainee, Grosvenor House Hotel, London, 1959-61; Secretary, French Embassy / Alliance Francaise, 1962-66; Travel Advisor, BFE (Paris), 1967-69; Manager, Usit Travel Group, 1969-77; established own travel group, O'Mara Travel, 1978 to date; General Sales Agent, Club Mediterranee, 1978 to date. Founder, Chair Irish Tourist Industry Confederation, 1983-85; former Director, Aer Lingus plc, 1985-89; Director Medieval Trust/Dublinia, 1988 to date; Director Great Southern Hotels (Chairwoman, 1984-91); Chairwoman, Heritage Island Ltd., 1992 to date; Chairwoman, Forbairt, 1993-98; Director OTMI (Overseas Tourism Marketing Initiative) 1994 to date; Director, ERDF Management Board (Shannon), 1996 to date; Chairwoman, Opera Ireland, 1998 to date; Director, Millennium Festivals Ltd., 1998 to date; Incoming Chairwoman ITIC (Irish Tourist Industry Confederation), 1999-2001; Member, Dublin Chamber of Commerce, Institute of

Directors. Hobbies, 1 dog, 2 cats, visual arts, opera, theatre, film buff, nineteenth century English novelists, country pursuits (not strenuous), politics and current affairs. Contact: O'Mara Travel, 37 Main Street, Donnybrook, Dublin 4. Tel: 01 269 6944. Fax: 01 269 6705.

O'NEILL, Marc; FASHION DESIGNER; *b* 1970; *educ* St. Columba's College, Rathfarnham; National College of Art and Design; de Montfort University, Leicester (U.K.); *single;* after college was commissioned to design collections for A-Wear (part of Brown Thomas Group); set up own label, 1995; since then has been designing collections for the Brown Thomas Group, private clients (including U2, The Corrs), uniforms for hotels, restaurants and banks; currently exporting label abroad to prestigious stores including Barneys and Saks (New York); exhibits at London Fashion Week; designs have featured in *Vogue*, (U.K. and Italy), *Elle, Hello, 1-D, The Observer, The Evening Standard, W, Oyster, Drapers Record, The Telegraph, Harper Queen,* and on international television networks; awards include, Irish Fashion Graduate of the Year, 1992, N.C.A.D. Fashion Graduate of the Year, 1992, Smirnoff Young Designer, 1992; biographical appearances in the young section *Who's Who 1991, Fabric and Form - Irish Fashion since 1950* (Elizabeth McCrum); a talented designer and a social and style catalyst for the fashionable and active young professionals. Hobbies, photography, fashion history and contemporary Irish Art. Contact: M.A. International, 6-7 Newmarket Square, Dublin 8. Tel: 01 454 4361.

O'NEILL, Tony; SPORTS ADMINISTRATOR / DOCTOR; *b* 1946; *decd 1999, educ* De La Salle, Churchtown; University College Dublin, MB, BCL, BAO, BSc (Pharm); *single;* Intern, Casualty Officer, SHO Drug Treatment Centre, Jervis Street Hospital; Staff, Department of Physiology and Department Pharmacology, University College Dublin; Medical Director, O'Neills Sports Injuries Clinic; General Secretary, FAI; Director of Sport, University College Dublin. Member, UCD Association Football Club, (General Manager), UEFA European Championship Organising Committee and Bureau, UEFA Media Committee. Recognised as the outstanding figure in Irish sporting administration. Contact: University College Dublin, Sports Centre, Belfield, Dublin 4. Tel: 01 706 2183. Fax: 01 269 8099.

O'REGAN, Frank; GENERAL MANAGER BAUSCH & LOMB IRELAND; *b* 1959; *educ* CBS Youghal, Cork; University College Cork, BE (Civil Engineering), Dip Mech Eng; INSEAD, Fontainebleau, France, MBA; *m* Nena ______; 4 *da;* joined Simon Eurolift, 1981, Product Development Leader, 1983-87; Operations with United Technologies (OTIS), UK 1989-90; General Manager, Glen Moulinex, Thurles, 1990-98; created first European base for Lake Region (Medical Device Manufacturer), New Ross, 1994-98; General Manager, Bausch and Lomb, 1998 to date; Bausch and Lomb are creators of the original software contact lens; world leaders in medical eye care; member, Institute of Engineers of Ireland (Chartered Engineer), INSEAD Alumni Association; Director, Waterford Chamber of Commerce (Chairman, Arts & Culture Committee). Hobbies, current affairs, sailing, tennis and music. Contact: Bausch & Lomb Ireland, Industrial Park, Old Kilmeadon Road, Waterford. Tel: 051 355001.

O'REILLY, Anthony "Tony"

O'REILLY, Anthony John Francis "Tony" ; CHAIRMAN, Independent Newspapers, PLC, Waterford Wedgewood PLC, H.J. Heinz Company and Matheson Ormsby Prentice; *b* 1936; *educ* Belvedere College; University College Dublin; Incorporated Law Society of Ireland; University of Bradford, PhD (Agri Marketing); *m* Susan Cameron' *(m dis);* 3 *s* 3 *da; m* Chryssanthie Goulandris, Bloodstock Breeder; Industrial Consultant, Weston Evans (UK) 1958-60; Executive, Suttons Ltd, Cork 1960-62; General Manager, Bord Bainne 1962-66; Managing Director, Irish Sugar Company and Erin Foods 1966-69; Managing Director, H.J. Heinz Company (UK) 1969 and progressed through the organisation to become, the Chief Executive Officer of the Heinz Corporation, (1979 to 1998). Doctorates from the following institutions: Wheeling College (US), Rollins College (US), Trinity College (Dublin), Indiana State University (US), Allegheny College (US), Boston College (US), De Paul University (US), University College Dublin, Queens University (Belfast), Carnegie Mellon University (US), Westminster College (US), Rhodes University (South Africa); recipient, Medal of the American-Irish Historical Society, Life Fellow, Irish Management Institute, Honorary Officer in the Order of Australia; Council Member of Rockefeller University, New York, Pro-chancellor of Trinity College (Dublin). Founder and worldwide Chairman of the Ireland Funds which operates in 12 countries and has raised over US$100 million for projects promoting peace, culture, community, and education across the island of Ireland-North and South. A fine student and an outstanding sportsman (29 Irish Rugby Caps and 10 Lions Tests); a cosmopolitan businessman with an international network of top level contacts; noted for amazing personal charisma, deal making ability and philanthropy. He has endowed the O'Reilly Foundation and funded the institute for Communications and Technology in Trinity College (Dublin), The O'Reilly Hall, University College (Dublin), the Barrington-O'Reilly Pavilion at the Institute of Public Administration (Dublin) and the O'Reilly Theater', Pittsburgh, Pennsylvania. Hobbies, reading and tennis. Contact: Independent Newspapers plc, 1 Upper Hatch Street, Dublin 2. Tel: 01 475 8432.

O'REILLY, Emily; *b* 1957; *educ* University College Dublin, BA; Trinity College Dublin,

H.Dip.Ed.; *m* Stephen Ryan; 1 *s* 3 *da*; Reporter, *Sunday Tribune*, 1981-84 ; Reporter, *Today Tonight*, 1984-86; Northern Ireland Correspondent, *Sunday Tribune*, 1986-87; Political Correspondent, *Irish Press*, 1989-94; Political Editor, *Sunday Business Post*, 1994-99; Editor, *Magill*, 1999 ; Publications include *Candidate*, 1991 (Attic Press), *Masterminds of the Right*, 1992 (Attic Press), *Veronica Guerin, Life and Death of a Crime Reporter*, 1998 (Vintage); Awarded: Womans Journalist of the year, 1986; Journalist of the Year, 1994; Nieman Fellowship at Harvard University, 1987-88; Probably one of the sharpest minds in her generation of journalists; an attractive, sometimes abrasive, always competent, investigative journalist; displays more writing style than most hard copy writers. Hobby, childminding. Contact: Independent Newspapers, 90 Middle Abbey Street, Dublin 1. Tel: 01 705 5333 Fax: 01 872 0304

O'REILLY, Gavin

O'REILLY, Gavin; MANAGING DIRECTOR INDEPENDENT NEWSPAPERS (IRELAND); *b* 1968; *educ* Clongowes Wood College, Co. Kildare; Georgetown University Business School (US); *m* Alison Doody, Actress; *2da;* Business Development Manager, Doyle Dale Burnbach, 1985-87; Institutional Sales Executive, First Pacific Securities, 1988-89; Managing Director, Independent Directories, 1993-96; Director of Production Operations, Independent Newspapers (Ireland) 1996-97, Deputy Managing Director, Independent Newspapers (Ireland) 1997-98, Managing Director, Independent Newspapers (Ireland) 1999 to date; involved in charity fund raising for The Hole in the Wall Gang at Barretstown Castle, The Ireland Fund and The O'Reilly Foundation; the boss's son is known as 'Baby Doc'; has a natural hands-on approach and is popular with fellow workers. Contact: Independent Newspapers plc, 1 Upper Hatch Street, Dublin 2. Tel: 01 475 8432.

O'REILLY, Oliver Stephen

O'REILLY, Michael; CHAIRMAN WINDSOR MOTORS; *b* 1937; *educ* St. Patrick's College, Cavan *m* Rita Caulfiend; *2s* 1 *da;* worked in the finance section of Buckley's Motors (now defunct); founder, former Chief Executive, now Chairman, Windsor Motors Ltd.; Windsor Motors are the largest Nissan dealers in the county and one of the major motor retailers; sons, Merlin and Patrick are now involved in running the company; member, SIMI. Hobby, work. Contact: Windsor Motors Ltd., South Circular Road, Dublin 8. Tel: 01 454 0800.

O'REILLY, Oliver Stephen; CHIEF EXECUTIVE R.J. GOFF & CO. PLC; *b* 1948; *educ* St. Patrick's College, Cavan; University College Dublin, BA HDip, C Dip AF (CACA), Diploma in Co. Direction, 1997, Institute of Directors, London, UK; *m* Marie Mooney; 1*s* 2*da*; Brand Manager, Beechams Ireland and UK, 1973-78; Sales and Marketing Manager, RTV Rentals Ltd., 1978-80; Marketing Manager, Bristol Myers Ireland, 1980-85; Sales & Marketing Manager, Coal Distributors Ltd., 1985-89; Managing Director, Maguire & Paterson Ltd. (Swedish Match), 1989-94; Managing Director, Swedish Match UK, 1994-99; CEO, R.J. Goff & Co. plc., 1999 to date; Chairman, UNICOS (Europe), 1992-94; UNICOS is an association of European distributors involved in F.M.C.G.; Member: Marketing Institute of Ireland, Institute of Directors, UK; Hobbies, fishing, hunting, gardening, current affairs and the application of management theory. Contact: R.J. Goff & Co. plc., Kildare Paddocks, Kill, Co. Kildare. Tel: 045 877211. 1 Fax: 045 877119.

O'REILLY, Patrick; CHIEF EXECUTIVE EBS BUILDING SOCIETY; *b* 1941; *educ* St. Patrick's College, Cavan; University College Dublin, BComm, MEconSc; *m* Angela O'Reilly; 1 *s* 3 *da;* Executive with Ulster Bank, 1960-66; Company Secretary, Irish Merchants Ltd., 1966-71; General Manager (Banking), Industrial Credit Corporation, 1971-86; Chief Executive, EBS Building Society, 1987 to date. Hobbies, golf and jogging. Contact: EBS Building Society, 30/34 Westmoreland Street, Dublin 2. Tel: 01 677 5599. Fax: 01 671 8496.

O'RIORDAIN, Dolores; SINGER/SONGWRITER; *b* 1972; *educ* Laurel Hill Convent, Limerick; *m* Don Burton; 1*s;* joined the Cranberries Saw Us as a vocalist, 1990; previous experience was in local church; band now known as The Cranberries, comprises, Fergal Lawler (drums), Noel Hogan (guitar/songwriter), Mike Hogan (bass guitar); first gig was in Cruises Hotel in Limerick; shortly after they moved to London; after a slow start and a signing with Island Records they left for a U.S. Tour; released first album, *Everybody Else is Doing It, So Why Can't We*, 1993, *Linger* from the album was the first big breakthrough, climbing to No. 8 in the U.S. charts; released, *To The Faithful Departed*, 1996; released *Bury the Hatchet*, 1999; to date have sold over 35 million albums, making them, together with U2, the most successful Irish rock band of all time, with a captivating lead singer, small but with both attitude and talent. Contact: Lindsay Holmes, L.H.P., The Rise, 6 Cullenswood Park, Ranelagh, Dublin 6. Tel: 01 497 0313.

O'ROURKE, Liam A; MANAGING DIRECTOR CHIVERS IRELAND / CHAIRMAN ORCHARD PRINT; *b* 1953; *educ* Newbridge College, Co. Kildare; University College Cork, BA Psychology & Economics; *m* Norma Gaffney; 3 *da;* Federated Union of Employers, 1979-82; Personnel Officer, HB/Birds Eye, 1982-85; Sales & Marketing, Birds Eye/Walls (UK), 1985-89; Marketing Director, HB/Birds Eye, 1989-92; ; Sales and Distribution Director, van den Berg Foods, 1992-95; Langnese Germany, Marketing Director & International Brands Director, Unilever, 1995-97; Marketing Director, Chivers Ireland, 1997-98; Managing Director, 1998 to date; member, Irish

Marketing Institute; member, Riverview Club, Royal St. George Yacht Club, Athy Golf Club. Hobbies, rugby, sailing and reading. Contact: Chivers Ireland Ltd, Coolock Drive, Coolock, Dublin 5. Tel: 01 848 4044. Fax: 01 848 4053.

O'ROURKE, Mary, née Lenihan; POLITICIAN; *b* 1937; *educ* St. Peter's Convent, Athlone; Loreto Convent, Bray; University College Dublin; St. Patrick's College, Maynooth; *m* Enda O'Rourke, Businessman; 2 *s;* former secondary school teacher; member, Athlone Urban District Council, 1974-87; Board of Management of Athlone Regional Technical College, 1974-79; Westmeath Vocational Educational Committee, 1979-87, (Chairperson 1985-87); Athlone and District Soroptimist Council, Athlone Chamber of Commerce; member of Seanad Eireann, April 1982-August 1982; elected Fianna Fail Deputy for Longford Westmeath 1982; Opposition Spokesperson for Education; Minister for Education 1987-89; reappointed 1989-91; Minister for Health, November 1991-February 1992; Minister for Trade and Marketing, February 1992-January 1993; Minister for Labour Affairs, January 1993-December 1994; Deputy Leader of Fianna Fail, Frontbench Spokesperson on Enterprise and Employment, January 1995-June 1997; Minister for Public Enterprise, June 1997 to date. The Lenihan family has a long record of service to the State; father, Patrick Lenihan, was Deputy for Longford / Westmeath, brother, Brian, served as Tanaiste; a consummate politician, hard working, tough, media friendly and always well on top of her brief. Hobbies, reading and walking. Contact: Dail Eireann, Leinster House, Dublin 2. Tel: 01 618 3000.

O'ROURKE, Mary

ORREN, Michael, John; HEAD OF DEPARTMENT OF OCEANOGRAPHY NATIONAL UNIVERSITY OF IRELAND, GALWAY; *b* 1940; *educ* University of Capetown M.Sc (Chemistry), PhD (Geochemistry); *m* Ann; 2 children; Sea Fisheries Research Institute, Cape Town, 1960-65; Geochemistry Research Unit, University of Capetown, 1965-74; National Research Institute for Oceanology, Stellenbosch, South Africa, 1974-80; Woods Hole Oceanographic Institution, U.S.A. 1975-76; Associate Professor, University of Capetown, 1980-87; Professor and Head of Department of Oceanography, National University of Galway (the only such department in Ireland), 1987 to date; has published over 75 scientific papers; Board member, National Marine Institute of Ireland, 1992 to date; Founding member, Irish National Committee for the International Geosphere/Biosphere Programme; Irish delegate to numerous prestigious international bodies; Fellow, Royal Society of Chemistry, U.K; member, American Association for Advancement of Science; Founding member, Irish National Museum Institute; President, Rotary Club of Galway. Hobbies, Swimming, walking. Contact: Department of Oceanography, National University of Ireland, Galway. Tel: 091 524411. Fax: 091 525700.

OSBORNE, James R.

OSBORNE, James Reginald; CONSULTANT; *b* 1949; *educ* Campbell College, Belfast; Trinity College Dublin, BA Mod,; *m* Heather ----; 1*s* 1 *da;* Solicitor, A&L Goodbody Solicitors, 1973-94 (opened NY office), Managing Partner, 1982-94; Consultant to A&L Goodbody and director of numerous public and private companies, 1994 to date; Chairman, Blackstar Com; Director, Golden Vale, Ryanair, Transcom, Webstet, Slendertone, Punchestown Racecoures; member, Royal Irish Yacht Club, Fitzwilliam Lawn Tennis Club, Institute of Directors, Law Society of Ireland. An urbane lawyer, highly versed in commercial law, who took an early retirement and is now seen as a tough boardroom negotiator. Hobbies, National Hunt Racing, sailing, golf and squash. Contact: 1 Earlsfort Centre, Hatch Street, Dublin 2. Tel: 01 661 3311.

O'SHEA, John

O'SHEA, John; DIRECTOR GOAL; *b* 1944; *educ* CBS Schools, Charleville, Westport, O'Connells, Monkstown; University College Dublin; *m* Judy Gallagher; 2 *s* 2 da; Salesman for coal and oil company, 1962-1967; Sports journalist with Irish Press Group, 1967-94; founded GOAL, third world relief and development agency, 1977; full time director, GOAL, 1994 to date; publications include *The Book of the Dubs;* recipient, Dublin (Under 21) Gaelic football medal, Schools Basketball International, Former Inter Provincial Tennis Player, Ballygowan Outstanding Achievement Award, 1988, Publicity Club of Ireland Communications Award, 1990, MIR Award, 1992, Citizen of the Year - Dun Laoghaire, 1992, People of the Year, 1987 and 1992, Association of Tennis Professionals - Humanitarian of the Year, 1993, *Late Late Show* Tribute, 1995, Texaco Outstanding Achievement Award, 1995; Current Veteran Tennis International, former interprovincial tennis player; member, Honorary Life Member, Sandycove LTC, Blackrock Rugby Club and Westport Golf Club, member, Monkstown Tennis Club, Fitzwilliam Tennis Club and Woodbrook Golf Club. Recognised as a man of singleminded determination. Hobbies, practically all sporting activities, currently playing golf and tennis competitively, Tip rugby; played soccer, Gaelic, rugby, basketball, racketball and was a middle distance runner in youth. Contact: GOAL, 9 Northumberland Avenue, Dun Laoghaire, Co. Dublin. Tel: 01 280 9779.

Ó'SUÍLLEABHÁIN, Mícheál; MUSICIAN; *b* 1950; *educ* University College Cork, B.Mus., MA, L.T.C.L; Queens University Belfast, Ph.D.; *m* Noírín Ní Riain; 2*s*; Assistant Lecturer, University College Cork, Music Department, 1975, College Lecturer, 1978; Visiting Professor, Boston College (U.S.), 1990-91; Senior Lecturer, University College Cork, 1991, Acting Head, 1992; Professor of

Music, University of Limerick, 1994 to date; discography includes - Mícheal Ó'Suílleabháin, solo performances on piano, harpiscord, clavicord, pedal organ and Moog synthesiser (Gael Linn 1976, re-released 1992) *Cry of the Mountains* (Gael Linn 1981); *The Dolphins Way* (Venture Virgin 1987), *Casadh/Turning* (Venture Virgin 1990), *A River of Sound*, *Lumen, Between Worlds* (Virgin 1995), *Becoming* (Virgin 1998); publications include *Buntings Ancient Music of Ireland* (with Dr. Donal O'Sullivan), *The Bodhrán* and numerous articles in journals; Chairman, Irish traditional Music Archive; Founder/Chairman, Clare Music Education Centre; member, Board of Directors, Irish chamber Orchestra, Daghdha Dance Company, University Concert Hall, Limerick; established Irish Traditional Music and Dance Archive (UCC, University of Limerick and Boston College); Presented/Scripted, T.V. series *A River of Sound: The Changing Course of Irish Music* BBC; an enlightened performer and composer whose vision and imagination have created a unique academic institution in the Irish World Music Centre. Contact: Irish World Music Centre, University of Limerick, Limerick. Tel: 061 202 590. Fax: 061 202 589.

O'SULLIVAN, Chantal

O'SULLIVAN, Chantal Francoise; ANTIQUE DEALER; *b* 1961; *educ* The High School, Rathgar; Leinster Secretarial College, Rathmines; *single*; travelled and lived in Sydney Australia, 1979-81; waitress/barwork etc.; Operations Manageress, Nock & Kirby, Sydney; Shop Manager, Cooke Antiques, 1981-91; Owner/founder, O'Sullivan Antiques, Francis Street, 1991; opened O'Sullivan Antiques Inc. New York, 1996, O'Sullivan Antiques Kenmare, 1997; the only Irish Antique shop with a U.S. branch and two national branches; member, American Antique Dealers Association; Irish Antique Dealers Association; Patron, Glucksman House (U.S.), Guggenheim Museum, (N.Y.); Junior Interprovincial and international Golf, 1975-76; member, Irish-US Council, Milltown Golf Club. Hobbies, golf, music and history. Contact: O'Sullivan Antiques, 3 Francis Street, Dublin 8. Tel: 01 454 1143.

O'SULLIVAN, David; EUROPEAN CIVIL SERVANT; *b* 1953; *educ* St. Mary's College, Rathmines; Trinity College Dublin, M.A. Econ.; College of Europe, Bruges, Diploma in European Studies; *m* Agnes O'Hare; 1 *s* 1 *da*; joined Department of Foreign Affairs, 1976-79; Directorate General for External Relations, DGI, European Commission, Brussels, 1979-81; First Secretary (Economic and Commercial), Delegation of the Commission in Japan, 1981-85; Member of the Cabinet of Commissioner Peter Sutherland responsible for Social Affairs and Relations with the European Parliament, 1985-89; Head of Unit, Task Force for Human Resources, Education, Youth and Training (now DG XXII) responsible for the COMETT and TEMPUS programmes, and co-ordination of training and assistance to Central and Eastern Europe, 1989-92; Member - and from December 1994 - Deputy Head of Cabinet to Commissioner Padraig Flynn responsible for employment policy, the social dialogue and labour law, 1993-96; Director DG V/B - responsible for the policy co-ordination, the European Social Fund, 1996-98; Director DG V/B - responsible for the management of resources, 1998-99; Director-General DGXXIII (Education, Training and Youth), May 1999, appointed Chef de Cabinet to Commissioner Romano Prodi. A noted linguist, now he holds the key post in the Brussels hierarchy; son of former Chief of Staff, Gerry O'Sullivan. Hobbies, tennis, cinema, music. Contact: European Commission, rue de la Loi, 1049, Brussels, Belgium. Fax: 00322 285 7397.

O'SULLIVAN, Joe; CHIEF EXECUTIVE DRINAGH CO-OPERATIVE LTD.; *b* 1955; *educ* Castletownbere Secondary School; University College Cork, BSc.; *m* Áine Harrington; 1*s* 3*da*; Factory Manager, Tipperary Co-operative, 1982-90; Chief Executive, Drinagh Co-operative Ltd., 1990 to date; member, Bord Bía, Carberry Milk Products, West Cork Leader Co-operative, Irish Co-operative Society (Limerick); member, Skibbereen Golf Club. Hobbies, golf, gardening and reading. Contact: Drinagh Co-operative Ltd., Drinagh, Dunmanway, Co. Cork. Tel: 028 30116. Fax: 028 30266

O'SULLIVAN, John Roger; RESTAURATEUR / COMPANY DIRECTOR; *b* 1943; *educ* Glenstal Abbey Nieves Lydon; 1*s* 1 *da;* held various management positions with Connacht Laundry Group, Taylor Catering (U.K.), Lydon House, Galway; owner Galleon Restaurant since 1987; Director, Renvyle House Hotel, Co. Galway; Director, Galway Chamber of Commerce and Industry; former Council Member, Galway Oyster Festival; Clubs, Galway County Club, Galway Bay Sailing Club. Hobbies, sailing and travel. Contact: 210 Upper Salthill, Galway. Tel: 091 522 963.

O'SULLIVAN, Morgan; FILM PRODUCER; *b* 1945; *educ* Presentation College, Bray; joined R.T.E. as a camera presenter; moved on to Producer, radio and television; in mid 60s worked in Australian broadcasting with ABC and commercial broadcaster, Channel 3; returned R.T.E. as Presenter, 1970; brought M.T.M. Enterprises to Ireland, put together consortium (led by M.T.M.) to take over Ardmore Studios, Bray 1986-90; Director World 2000 Entertainments Ltd., Executive Producer of numerous films, including *Angela's Ashes, Animal Farm, Mystic Knights, Moll Flanders, Braveheart, The Nephew;* Chairman, Irish Film and Television Academy; member, Irish

Film Board, Filmakers of Ireland; an enthusiastic and knowledgeable executive with celluloid in his blood; recipient Jacobs Award. Hobby, golf. Contact: Ardmore Studios, Bray, Co. Wicklow. Tel: 01 286 2971. Fax: 01 286 6810.

O'SULLIVAN, The Hon. Mr Justice Philip John Roger; HIGH COURT JUDGE; *b* 1940; *educ* Crescent College Limerick; Glenstal Abbey; National University of Ireland, Cork and Dublin; St. Bennet's Hall, Oxford; Kings Inns; BA, Barrister, SC; *m* Heidi Roseneck; 2*s*; various teaching posts including tutorial teaching in English Department, University College Dublin; Leader Writer *Irish Independent*; practised as a Barrister 1969-97; High Court Judge 1997 to date; publications include *A Source Book of Irish Planning Law* (co-author) (1984), *Irish Planning and Acquisition Law* (1978). Hobby, organic gardening. Contact: Four Courts, Morgan Place, Dublin 7. Tel.: 01 872 5555.

O'SULLIVAN, Sean; CHIEF EXECUTIVE CORK CO-OP MARTS LTD.; *b* 1962; *educ* Mill Street Community School; University of Limerick, Bachelor of Business Studies; ACMA; *m* Mary O'Neill; 3*s;* Financial Accountant, Ballyclough Co-op Creamery Ltd., 1986-90; Group Management Accountant, Dairygold Co-Op Society Ltd., 1990-91; Finance Manager, Logitech Ireland Ltd., 1991-94; Financial Controller, Cork Co-Op Marts Ltd., 1995-96, Chief Executive, 1996 to date. Contact; Cork Co-Operative Marts Ltd., Cork Farm Centre, Wilton, Cork. Tel: 021 545733. Fax: 021 545325.

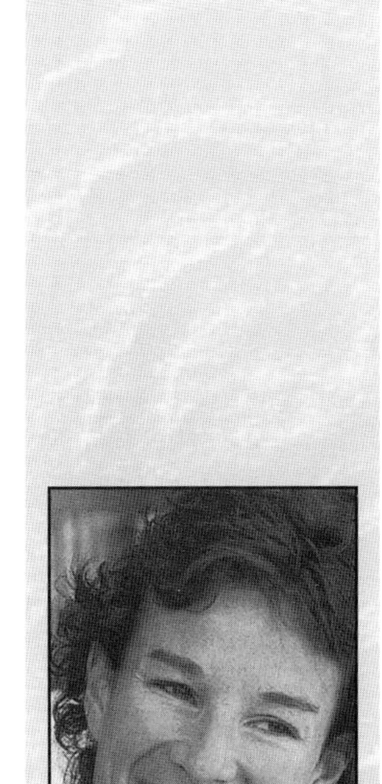

O'SULLIVAN, Sonia

O'SULLIVAN, Sonia; ATHLETE; *b* 1969; *educ* St. Mary's Convent, Cobh; Cobh Vocational School; Villanova University, U.S.A., Accountancy; *1 da.*; her performance highlights include, World Cross Country 8k & 4k Champion; European 5,000m and 10,000m; World Cup 5,000m and World Best 2 miles, 1998; among numerous previous wins were, 1st in 500m 1993, World 2,000m Record, European 3000m Record and 3,000m Champion; *Track & Field News* World Ranking, 1st 3000m and 5000m 1994; World 5,000m Champion; *Track & Field News* World Ranking, 1st 1500m, 1st 3000m, 1st 5,000, Athlete of the Year, 1995; World Cross Country, 8k & 4k Champion; European 5,000m and 10,000m Champion; World Cup 5,000m winner; World Best 2 miles (9:19.56 1998); a world class athlete who has represented her country with distinction both on and off the Track. Hobbies, reading and music. Contact: KIM, 201 High Street, Hampton Hill, Middlesex, TW12 1NL. Tel: 0044 181 941 9732.

O'SULLIVAN, Thaddeus Patrick; FILM DIRECTOR; *educ* Westland Row C.B.S.; College of Commerce, Rathmines; Ealing School of Art, London, Dip. A.D.; Royal College of Art, London, MA (RCA); *married;* 1 *s;* worked as director of photography; made short and experimental films throughout the 70s and 80s; work as a Director includes, *December Bride, Nothing Personal* and *Ordinary Decent Criminal;* member, Directors Guild of America, British Film Institute (Production Board), European Film Academy; recipient of many awards including European Film Academy Award, *December Bride,* 1990. Contact: ICM, Oxford House, 76 Oxford Street, London, WIN, OAX. Tel: 0044 171 636 6565.

O'TOOLE, Annrai

O'TOOLE, Annrai; CHIEF TECHNICAL OFFICER IONA TECHNOLOGIES; *b* 1965; *educ* St. Joseph's CBS, Fairview; Trinity College Dublin, BA, BAI, MSc; *single*, 1 *s;* Research Assistant and Lecturer, Trinity College Dublin; Chief Technical Officer, IONA Technologies; IONA is regarded as world leader in making software work together; creative works include ORBIX (IONA's core product); Known to his fellow students in TCD as "the smiler compiler"; a visionary who saw a niche within a niche in the software industry; Hobbies, the fine things in life. Contact: IONA Technologies plc, IONA Building, Shelbourne Road, Dublin 4. Tel: 01 662 5255. Fax: 01 662 5244.

O'TOOLE, Joe; SENATOR, GENERAL SECRETARY INTO; *b* 1947; *educ* Christian Brothers School, Dingle, Co. Kerry; St. Patrick's College of Education, NT; University College Dublin, BA; St. Patrick's College, Maynooth, HDipEd; *m* Joan Lynam, Teacher; 2 *s* 3 *da*; Principal Teacher, Rochestown Primary School, Co. Dublin 1974-87; member of Seanad Eireann, 1987 to date; Executive Committee, Irish Congress of Trade Unions, 1991 to date; General Secretary, Irish National Teachers Organisation, 1990 to date; publications include a number of textbooks and articles on education; member of national and international bodies co-ordinating education and trade unionism. A committed Trade Unionist with a thorough understanding of the media. Hobbies, walking, reading, music and working. Contact: INTO, 35, Parnell Square, Dublin 1. Tel: 01 872 2533. Fax: 01 872 2462.

O'TOOLE, Paraic J. A.; GENERAL MANAGER CAMBRIDGE TECHNOLGY PARTNERS (IRL); *b* 1962; *educ* St. Gerald's School, Castlebar; Trinity College Dublin; *m* Susan Collier; 1*s* 1*da*; joined the Civil Service, executive and higher executive positions in Government offices 1980-89; Senior Manager, Vision Consulting 1989-90; Head of Corporate Development, Head of Marketing and Head of IT, Lifetime Assurance (Bank of Ireland) 1990-93; Partner and Co-founder Picus (strategy firm) 1993-

96; joined Cambridge Technology Partners 1996, Head of Marketing Consulting in Western Europe, currently General Manager Ireland, with responsibility for Europe; member, Advisory Board of US-Ireland Alliance; member, Castlebar Golf Club; Captain 11th Cavalry Squadron (FCA). Hobbies, golf (badly but enthusiastically), skiing, sailing and fine wines. Contact: Cambridge Technology Partners, 118 Lower Baggot Street, Dublin 2. Tel: 01 607 9000. Fax: 01 607 9001.

OWEN, Nora, née O'Mahony; POLITICIAN; *b* 1945; *educ* Dominican Convent, Wicklow; University College Dublin, BSc., Dip. Microbiology; *m* Brian Owen; 3 *s;* worked as a chemist in industry; member, Dublin County Council, 1979-94; elected Fine Gael Deputy for Dublin North, 1981-87 and 1989 to date; Chairperson, Oireachtas Joint Committee on Development Co-operation, 1982-87; Spokesperson on Overseas Development, 1982-87, on Health, 1992-93, on Foreign Affairs, 1993-94; appointed Deputy Leader, Fine Gael, 1993 to date; Minister for Justice, 1994-97; Opposition Spokesperson on Enterprise, Trade and Employment, 1997 to date; member, Executive of Trocaire, 1987-89, Volunteer in Rwanda with Concern, 1994; member of an Irish political dynasty, grandniece of Michael Collins and sister of Mary Banotti MEP. Hobbies, reading, card playing and dinner with friends. Contact: Dail Eireann, Leinster House, Dublin 2. Tel: 01 618 3333.

OXX, John; RACEHORSE TRAINER; *b* 1950; *educ* Clongowes Wood College; University College Dublin, MUB, MRCVS; *m* Catriona O' Sullivan; 1 *s* 2 *da*; Assistant trainer to father, John Oxx Snr.; obtained Trainers Licence 1979; Trainer number of of Group 1 winners, in Ireland, U.K., U.S., France and Italy; most successful horses include *Ridgewood Pearl* and *Timarida*; has won such classics as: Irish St. Leger 1987 and 1989, Irish 1000 Guineas, 1995; Irish Oaks, 1997 and 1998; Leading Trainer, 1995; Texaco Sportstar of the Year Award for Racing 1995; Bisquit Cognac & Independent Newspapers Racing Award 1995; a softly spoken, intellectual, racing man, trainer for many top international owners; Hobby, reading. Contact: Creeve, Curraghbeg, Co. Kildare. Tel: 045 521 310.

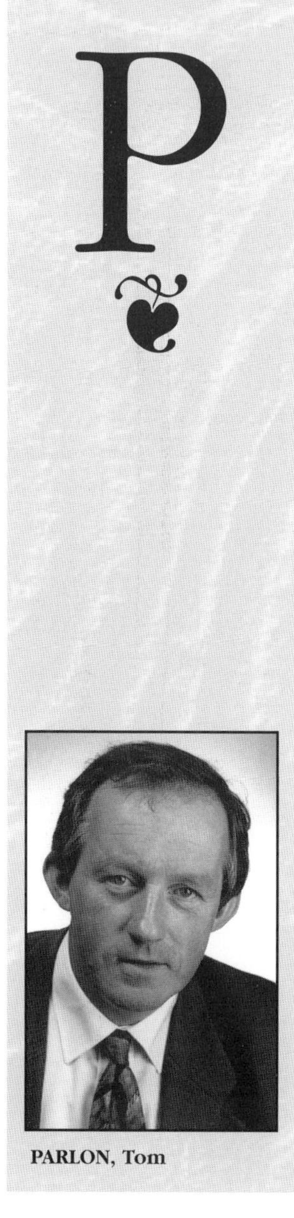
PARLON, Tom

PALMER, David Erroll Prior; CHAIRMAN INDEPENDENT NEWSPAPERS (IRELAND); *b* 1941; *educ* Christ Church Oxford, MA; *m* Elizabeth Young, novelist; 2*s* 1 *da;* joined *Financial Times*, 1964, New York Correspondent, 1967-70, Management Editor, 1970-72, News Editor, 1972-77; Launch Editor, Frankfurt Edition, 1977-79, Foreign Editor, 1979-81, Deputy Editor, 1981-83, General Manager & Production Director, 1983-89, Deputy Chief Executive, 1989-90, Group Chief Executive, 1990-93; joined Independent Newspapers (Ireland) Ltd. as Managing Director, Chairman, Independent Newspapers (Ireland) Ltd. 1999 to date; author, *The Atlantic Challenge*, 1977; Director & Council Member, Irish Management Institute; Council Member, Dublin Chamber of Commerce; member, Fitzwilliam LTC, Royal St. George Yacht Club, Royal Yacht Squadron; 3rd in Class, 7th Overall, *Observer* Singlehanded Transatlantic Race (1976). Recognised as newspaper man with strong editorial experience and a proven record in the implementation of a high tech programme. Hobbies, sailing and skiing. Contact: Independent Newspapers (Ireland), 1 Upper Hatch Street, Dublin 2. Tel: 01 475 8432.

PARKER, Lynne Elizabeth; THEATRE DIRECTOR; *b* 1961; *educ* Strathearn Grammar, Belfast; Trinity College Dublin, BA; Co-founder and Artistic Director, Rough Magic Theatre Company, 1984 to date; work for Rough Magic includes *Top Girls, Decadence, The Country Wife, Nightshade, Serious Money, Aunt Dan and Lemon, The Tempest, Lady Windermere's Fan, Digging for Fire, Love and a Bottle, I Can't Get Started, New Morning, Danti Dan, Down onto Blue, The Dogs, Hidden Charges, Halloween Night, The Way of the World, Pentecost, Northern Star, The School for Scandal and The Whisperers;* other theatre credits include, *Bernarda Alba* (Charabanc), *Shadow of a Gunman* (Gate), *The Clearing* (The Bush), *Doctors Dilemma* (Abbey), *Playboy of the Western World* (Almeida), *Silver Tassie* (Almeida), *Playhouse Creatures* (Old Vic), *The Importance of Being Earnest* (West Yorkshire Playhouse), *Love Me?!* (*The Car Show* - The Corn Exchange); awards include, Harveys Theatre Award 1988, *Time Out* Award 1992, Bank of Ireland/Arts Show, Dublin Theatre Festival - Best Irish Production 1995. Contact: Rough Magic Ltd., 5/6 South Great George's Street, Dublin 2. Tel: 01 671 9278. Fax: 01 671 9301.

PARKHILL, Kenneth; BLOODSTOCK BREEDER; *b* 1953; *educ* Newtown School, Waterford; University College Dublin, Veterinary Surgeon; *m* Lulu ----; 2*s*; took over successful Boyne Bank Stud from father Marshall Parkhill in 1995; concentrates on thoroughbred horses whereas stud had previously kept half bred horses also; principal winners include *Corbiere, Mole Board, Morley Street, Deep Dawn, Granville Again, Sound of Islay*. Contact: Boyne Bank Stud, Trim, Co. Meath. Tel: 046 31442.

PARLON, Tom; IFA PRESIDENT; *b* 1953; *educ* Roscrea CBS; Gurteen Agricultural College; *m* Martha Loughnane; 2*s* 3*da;* actively involved in Macra since 1970s; former Chairman Coolderry IFA Branch and Offaly IFA Chairman; National IFA Sheep Committee Chairman, 1986-90; IFA

Deputy President, 1991-94, National Treasurer, 1994-98, President, 1999 to date; Board member, Bord Bia, FBD plc; member, Partnership 2000, IFAP (International Federation of Agricultural Producers), Copa Presidium - European Association of Farmers Unions; awards include Stephen Cullinane Scholarship, studied in New Zealand for one year, Offaly Person of the Year, 1998; considered to be a very capable leader; one of the new breed of realists in today's agri business world. Hobbies, active member and supporter of county and branch GAA, a keen supporter of both hurling and football, active member of Offaly Supporters' Club in 1990s. Contact; The Irish Farmers Association, Irish Farm Centre, Bluebell, Dublin 12. Tel: 01 450 1931. Fax: 450 9811.

PARSONS, Anna Juliet "Julie" ; WRITER; *b* 1951; *educ* The Hall School, Monkstown; University College Dublin, BSoc.Sci., MSoc.Sci.; *m* John Caden; 1*da;* Radio Producer, RTE, 1984-1990, TV Producer, 1990-97; Writer, 1997 to date; author of *Mary, Mary*, (Town House & Country House) 1998, the novel has been published in fifteen countries and the film rights sold to Paul McGuinness for a six figure sum; *The Courtship Gift*, (Town House & Country House) 1999; member, Crime Writers' Association. Hobbies, family, garden, food & drink, sailing, gossip and story telling. Contact: Town House and Country House, Trinity House, Charleston Road, Ranelagh, Dublin 6. Tel: 01 497 2399. Fax: 498 0927.

PARSONS, Anna Juliet

PATTERSON, Brian; CHIEF EXECUTIVE OFFICER WEDGWOOD; *b* 1944; *educ* Newtown School, Waterford; St. Andrew's College, Dublin; University College Dublin, BA; *m* Jennifer Beaven; 2*s;* head of Management Services, A. Guinness Son & Co., 1972-76, Personnel Manager, 1976-79, Distribution Manager, 1979-81, Personnel Director, 1981-82; Director General, Irish Management Institute, 1982-87; Director of Corporate & Management Development, Waterford Wedgwood plc, 1987-88, Assistant Chief Executive, Waterford Crystal, 1988-92, Chief Operating Officer, 1992-1995; Chief Executive Officer, Wedgwood, 1995 to date; member, Institute of Personnel and Development, (Fellow), Irish Management Institute (Fellow), British Institute of Management (Fellow), Irish Institute of Industrial Engineers (Past President); Eisenhower Exchange Fellowship 1983; member of the boards of Waterford Wedgwood plc, Waterford Wedgwood UK plc, Waterford Crystal, Rosenthal AG; Chairman of the National Competitiveness Council for Ireland, Council Member, Irish Management Institute, former Chairman, Advisory group for Stoke-On-Trent Common Purpose, Trustee of the New Victoria Theatre and Staffordshire University. Hobbies, music, history and art. Contact: Waterford Wedgwood UK Ltd., Barlaston, Stoke-on-Trent, ST12 9ES, England. Tel: 0044 1782 204 141.

PATTON, Barbara

PATTON, Barbara; MARKETING MANAGER, IRISH PERMANENT; b 1960 educ Holy Faith Convent, Clontarf; College of Marketing & Design, Dublin; Smurfit School of Business, UCD; Graduateship, Marketing Institute (Student of the year 1986); Awarded Sir Charles Harvey Award (MBS, UCD 1992), *m* Adrian Robinson; *1s;* Guinness Group Sales (Ireland) Ltd. 1978-1987, Showerings (Ireland) Ltd. 1987-89, AIB Capital Markets 1989-92, Irish Permanent plc 1992-to date, Awarded Fellowship of Marketing Institute in 1997, elected Chairman of The Marketing Institute 1999/2000 - first woman to hold this position since inception of Institute in 1962, Contact: Irish Permanent, 56-59 St. Stephen's Green, Dublin 2. Tel: 01 661 5577 Fax: 01 661 5828

PAUL, John T; MANAGING DIRECTOR JOHN PAUL AND COMPANY; *b* 1937; *educ* High School, Dublin; Trinity College Dublin, BA, BAI; *m* Jean E. Blyth; 2 *s* 2 *da*; Site Engineer, John Laing Construction 1958-63; Site Agent, John Paul & Company 1963-75; Contracts Director, John Paul Construction 1975-85; Managing Director, John Paul & Company, 1985 to date; President, Master Builders Association, 1990-91; Fellow, Institute of Engineers of Ireland, 1980; Clubs, Fitzwilliam LTC, Kildare Street and University Club. Contact: John Paul Construction Ltd., Dundrum Business Park, Dundrum Road, Dublin 14. Tel: 01 298 3044. Fax: 01 298 1710.

PEARCE, Colman; ORCHESTRAL CONDUCTOR; *b* 1938; *educ* Christian Brothers School, Synge Street, Dublin; University College Dublin, BMus, LTCL; Musik Akademie, Vienna; divorced; 1*da*; Music Scriptwriter, RTE 1961, Acting Assistant, Director of Music 1962, Orchestral Conductor 1965-77; Co-Principal Conductor, RTE Symphony Orchestra 1978-80, Principal Conductor 1981-83; Principal Conductor and Musical Director, Mississippi Symphony Orchestra 1987-99; creative works include *Robinson the Cat* premiered in Jackson (Miss.) 1998, also choral and orchestral pieces; recordings include works by Boydell, Stanford, Buckley, Wilson, Dean, Corcoran, Bodley; publications include *Music in Ireland* (BBC publication); a conductor with a notable reputation at home and abroad, especially on the US circuit. Hobbies, reading, arts in general, collecting paintings, movies and theatre.

PEARSON, Noel; THEATRE IMPRESSARIO, FILM PRODUCER; *educ* Belcamp College, Malahide; *separated*; 2 *children*; Cost Accountant, Cloride Ltd.; moved full-time into the entertainment business managing The Dubliners for fourteen years on major international and international tours; has been nominated three times for Tony Awards winning two, for *Dancing at Lughnasa* (1991-92) and

An Inspector Calls (1993-94); other award winning Broadway productions include *Someone To Watch Over Me* and *Translations*; Chairman, The Abbey Theatre 1988-91; Producer with Ferndale Films, My Left Foot was awarded two Oscars in 1990, *The Field* was nominated for an Oscar in 1991; other films include *Frankie Starlight, Gold in the Streets* and most recently a film version of Brian Friel's Dancing at Lughnasa; theatre productions 1999-2000 will include a new production of Sean O'Casey's *Juno and the Paycock* in Dublin and on Broadway. A documentary on Dubliner Luke Kelly will be completed in the summer of 1999. Future films include Lulu (based on the life of Louise Brooks) and *A Fall to Grace* – the story of Samuel Beckett; a street-wise, dynamic talent; seen by many as the Napoleon of the Irish entertainment industry. Contact: Ferndale Films, 61 Merrion Square, Dublin 2. Tel: 01 676 8890. Fax: 01 676 8874.

PETERS, Liam; MANAGING DIRECTOR, JOHN PLAYER & SONS; *b* 1954; *educ* St. Joseph's College, Cahir, Co. Tipperary; University College Dublin, BComm, MBA; Fellow of Chartered Institute of Management Accountants; *m* Sally McManus; 2 *da*; Accountancy Trainee, Gaffney McKeon & Co. Chartered Accountants, 1977-81; Finance Director, Michael Grant Opelcentre, 1981-85; Regional Manager, BWG Foods, 1986-91; Commercial Manager, John Player & Sons, 1991-96, Sales and Marketing Director, 1996-98, Managing Director, 1998 to date; Clubs, Riverview Fitness Club, Wicklow Golf Club. Hobbies, an avid reader, golf, a bad tennis player. Contact: John Player & Sons, 286 South Circular Road, Dublin 8. Tel: 01 453 7900. Fax: 01 454 6351.

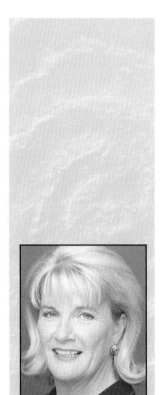

PHELAN, Angela A

PHELAN, Angela A., née Jones; JOURNALIST; *b* 1946; *educ* St. Angela's College, Cork; University College Cork; Stanford University, California; *m* Tom Phelan; 2 *s* 1 *da*; Freelance Journalist, *Sunday Tribune*, and *Sunday Press*; Features Writer and Social Diarist, *Irish Independent*, 1984 to date; Features Writer, Social Diarist; Contributor, *Image, Social & Personal*; Occasional Television Broadcaster, RTE and Channel 21, New York; Publications include: *To Mayo and Back: A Biography of Brian Lenihan*; Member: Irish Chamber of Commerce, U.S.A., Irish US Council, Sky Club, New York City; A hard working, widely read columnist; noted for worldwide network of contacts, particularly in the U.S. Hobbies, theatre, opera, movies, travel, reading, racing and 'thrifting' in New York. Contact: The Irish Independent, 90 Middle Abbey Street, Dublin 1. Tel: 01 705 5333.

POTTER, Maureen; ENTERTAINER; *b* 1925; *educ* St. Mary's, Fairview, Dublin; *m* Jack O'Leary, Retired Army Officer; 2*s*; stage debut, St. Theresa's Hall, Clarendon Street, aged seven; professional stage career began with Jimmy O'Dea in pantomime, 1935, one of the most famous partnerships in the Irish theatre; has played in almost half a century of Irish pantomime; also has many straight theatre and television credits including a memorable Maisie Madigan in the Gate Theatre production of *Juno and the Paycock*, 1986; other productions include, *School for Scandal, Tartuffe* (Gate Theatre), *Arsenic and Old Lace* (Gaiety Theatre); Grand Marshall, St. Patrick's Day Parade (Dublin) 1999; played extensively in Cabaret at Clontarf Castle; recipient, Harvey's Award, National Entertainment Award, People of the Year Award, Honorary Doctorate of Letters from Trinity College Dublin 1988; awarded Freedom of the City of Dublin 1984; publications include *The Theatre Cat* (children's story); a consummate professional, a quintessential Dubliner, probably the best loved entertainer in the country. Hobbies, reading and watching sport on television.

POTTERTON, Homan; EDITOR IRISH ARTS REVIEW; *b* 1946; *educ* Kilkenny College; Trinity College Dublin, BA, MA; Edinburgh University, Dip. Hist. of Art; FSA; *single;* Cataloguer, National Gallery of Ireland, 1971-73; Assistant Keeper, National Gallery, London, 1974-80; Director, National Gallery of Ireland, 1980-88; Board member, GPA Dublin International Piano Competition, 1987-92; HRHA, 1982; Editor, *Irish Arts Review*, 1993 to date; publications include *Irish Art and Architecture* (co-author), *Venetian Seventeenth Century Painting, Irish Church Monuments: 1570-1880, A Guide to the National Gallery* (German, French, Italian, Japanese editions), *The National Gallery London, Reynolds and Gainsborough: Themes and Painters in the National Gallery, Pageant and Panorama: The Elegant World of Canaletto, Introduction to the National Gallery of Ireland, National Gallery of Ireland 50 pictures* (co-author), *Dutch 17th and 18th Century Paintings in the National Gallery of Ireland,* also frequent contributor to international art journals and magazines; an innovative, informed and lively editor, produces an erudite and interesting Arts Review. Hobby, France. Contact: Irish Arts Review, State Apartments, Dublin Castle, Dublin 2. Tel: 01 679 3503.

PRATT, Maurice

PRATT, Hilary, née Kirwan; JOINT OWNER AND DIRECTOR AVOCA HANDWEAVERS LTD.; *b* 1938; *educ* St. Leonard's School, St. Andrews, Fife, Scotland; Trinity College Dublin, B.A. (Hist); *m* Donald Pratt, co-founder / owner Avoca Handweavers; 3 *s* 2 *da*; Secondary School Teacher, 1960-73; Co-founder / owner / manager, Avoca Handweavers - Ireland's premier craft design and retail company with six shops and restaurants in Ireland, Kilmacanogue (Co. Wicklow), Powerscourt (Enniskerry), Avoca Mill (Avoca), Bunratty (Co. Clare), Letterfrack (Co. Galway), Molls Gap (Co. Kerry), one shop in Canada and another in U.S.A. 1974 to date; Founder member and past Chair, Women's Political Association; Board Member, European Women's Foundation; Founder Member and presently Trustee of the Dalkey School Project; Board Member, Dublin Rape Crisis Centre; past Board member, Kilkenny Design Workshops, National College of Art & Design, Craft Council of Ireland. Hobbies, hill walking, reading historical biography, running political workshops for women in Eastern Europe. Contact: Avoca Handweavers, Kilmacanogue, Bray, Co. Wicklow. Tel: 01 286 7466. Fax: 01 286 2367.

PRATT, Maurice Alan; MANAGING DIRECTOR TESCO IRELAND; *b* 1955; *educ* St. Benildas College, Kilmacud, Co. Dublin; College of Commerce, Rathmines, Marketing Diploma; *m* Pauline Farrell; 5*s*; Technild Communications Ltd. 1972-73; Media Executive, Hunter Advertising Ltd., 1973-74; Media Manager, Account Director, Des O'Meara and Partners, 1974-82; Marketing Manager, Power Supermarkets, 1982-87, Marketing Director, 1987, Managing Director, 1996; Managing Director, Tesco Ireland Ltd., 1997 to date; member, Marketing Institute, Irish Management Institute, Institute of Directors, Riverview Racquet and Fitness Club, (President, 1993-98), Foxrock Golf Club; Board member, Irish Heart Foundation. Hobbies, tennis, cycling, golf, soccer and travel. Contact: Tesco, Gresham House, Marine Road, Dun Laoghaire, Co. Dublin. Tel: 01 280 8441.

PRENDERGAST, Peter; DIRECTOR, EC FOOD AND VETERINARY OFFICE; *b* 1939; *educ* Clongowes Wood College; University College Dublin, B Comm; *m* Madeleine Lyons; 1 *s* 2 *da*; Marketing Executive with the Irish Sugar Company and Unilever; unsuccessful Fine Gael Dáil candidate in two elections, turned down a nomination to the Seanad 1981; appointed General Secretary, Fine Gael Party 1977; Special Advisor to the Minister of Finance 1981; Government Press Secretary 1982-87, his tough marketing approach for ultra conservative Party paid dividends; appointed EC Official, Director Consumer Policy Service 1987-97; Appointed Director of the EC Food and Veterinary Office, 1997 to date. Hobbies, golf and horse racing. Contact: Food and Veterinary Office, Trident House, Rockhill, Blackrock, Co. Dublin. Tel: 01 206 4711. Fax: 01 206 4704.

PRESTON, Caroline Mary, née Orr; SOLICITOR; b 1955; educ Secondary School education in England, studied History and Political Science in Trinity College Dublin, awarded Joint Honours Degree in 1977, Law Society of Ireland, qualified solicitor 1981; m Punch; 1s 1da; joined A & L Goodbody in 1981, joined the Partnership in 1986, appointed Head of Litigation 1997, specialised practice in Commercial Litigation; Governor of St. Patrick's Hospital, member of the Foundation Irish Chapter of the International Woman's Forum, Joint Master of the Westmeath Foxhounds; appointed Charities Solicitor to the Attorney General 1994; regarded as one of the brightest and toughest lawyers in the Goodbody stable. Hobbies, fishing, wide open spaces and adventurous travel. Contact: A&L Goodbody, 1 Earlsfort Centre, Hatch Street, Dublin 2. Tel: 01 661 3311. Fax: 01 661 3278.

PRONE, Terry

PRONE, Terry; MANAGING DIRECTOR CARR COMMUNICATIONS; *b* 1949; *educ* 2nd level; *m* Tom Savage; 1*s*; selected as Ireland's Outstanding Teenager in 1969 by *Seventeen* Magazine (US) having been a regular broadcaster and newspaper writer from mid-teens; Scholarship to Abbey Theatre School of Acting at 16 - member of Abbey Company at 20; published *Write and Get Paid for It* in the early 1970s; other publications include 9 non-fiction, 4 fiction including *The Scattering of Mrs Blake* (novel, published by Marion Boyars, London 1985), *Blood Brothers, Soul Sisters* (short story collection, Poolbeg 1994), *Racing the Moon* (novel, Marino Books 1998), *Skywriting* (Marino Books 1999); recipient Francis McManus Award. Hobbies eating and reading. Contact: Carr Communications Ltd., The Communications Centre, Booterstown Avenue, Blackrock, Co. Dublin. Tel: 01 278 5000. Fax: 01 278 5001.

PROUD, Malcolm Patrick

PROUD, Malcolm Patrick; MUSICIAN; *b* 1952; *educ* Taney School, Dundrum; St. Andrew's College; Trinity College Dublin, BMus; awarded a Danish government scholarship, Copenhagen Conservatory of Music; Sweelinck Conservatory, Amsterdam (Teacher, Gustav Leonhardt), Dip Harpsichord; *m* Susan Carolan, Chairperson of Butler Gallery, Kilkenny and Music Director of Kilkenny Arts Week; 2 *s* 1 *d*; Teacher, College of Music, Dublin, 1973-79; Harpsichord Teacher, Royal Irish Academy of Music, 1985-86; Lecturer, Waterford Institute of Technology, 1982 to date; Organist and Choirmaster, St. Canice's Cathedral, Kilkenny, 1985 to date; recordings include: solo harpischord music on Claddagh, Bach's *Fifth Brandenburg Concerto* with Orchestra of the Age of Enlightenment on Virgin, Bach violin and harpischord sonatas on MAYA and others on Hyperion, Meridian, EMI, CRD and most recently on Centaur with American gambist John Dornenburg; member, Orchestra of the Age of Enlightenment, Chandos Baroque Players, Trio Virtuoso, Proud-Homburger Duo, Christ Church Baroque. An acclaimed soloist and continuo player, he has toured Europe and North America playing recitals at venues such as Stanford and Harvard Universities and the Wigmore Hall, London. Hobbies, hill walking, bird-watching, poetry and the visual arts. Contact: Music Department, Waterford Institute of Technology, College St. Campus, Waterford.

Tel: 051 302263.

PURCELL, Deirdre;

PURCELL, Deirdre; WRITER; *b* 1945; *educ* Scoil Mhuire, Marlborough Street, Dublin; Gortnor Abbey, Crossmolina, Co. Mayo; Loyola University, Chicago (1 year diploma in theatre); *m* Kevin Healy; 2*s;* Civil Service Commission, 1962-63; Aer Lingus, 1963-65; Actress with Abbey Theatre, 1965-68; Radio Continuity, Newsreader, News Journalist, with RTE, 1974-83; Journalist, *Sunday Tribune*, 1983-90; Novelist, 1990-97; Screenwriter/novelist, 1997 to date; publications include 6 novels, screenplay for *Falling for a Dancer*, contributions to various short story and feature compendiums, charity publications etc.; Ghostwriter to Gay Byrne for his autobiography *The Time of My Life;* Author, with Pat Langan (photographer) of *The Dark Hunter* about the Ethiopian Famine; also *On Lough Derg* with Liam Blake (photographer); Board member, Abbey Theatre, 1991 to date; Council member, Financial Institutions' Ombudsman, 1998 to date; member, National Millennium Committee, 1999; awards include, AT Cross Woman Journalist of the Year 1984, Benson and Hedges Journalist of the Year 1987, Shortlisted Orange Prize for Fiction (*Love Like Hate Adore)* 1998; one of Ireland's best selling novelists whose dramatic works adapt well to the small screen. Hobbies, theatre, music, art and media. Contact: Townhouse, Trinity House, Charleston Road, Ranelagh, Dublin 6. Tel: 01 497 2399.

PURCELL, Gerard

PURCELL, Gerard; MANAGING DIRECTOR PURCELL BROS. LTD.; *b* 1964 *educ* St. Michael's College, Ballsbridge; Villanova University (U.S.A.); Richmond University London, BA Econ; *single;* worked with Hong Kong Trading Company, 1987-88; Tokyo, importing Irish fish, 1988-91; exporting Japanese cars, 1988-91; Managing Director, Purcell Bros. Ltd., 1992 to date. Purcell Brothers are one of the largest lifestock exporters in the industry. Hobbies, golf, wine and art. Contact: Purcell Bros. Ltd., The Mews, 10 Pembroke Place, Dublin 2. Tel: 01 662 4966. Fax: 01 661 1717.

QUIGLEY, Dermot B; CHAIRMAN OF REVENUE COMMISSIONERS; *b* 1942; *educ* CBS Westland Row; University College Dublin, BA, Dip. Pub. Admin.; International Monetary Fund Washington D.C., Dip. Financial Analysis and Policy; *married;* 4*s* 2 *da;* appointed to Administrative Office in Department of Finance, 1965; Assistant Principal and Principal Officer in various sections dealing with domestic, EC and international financial affairs; worked on Ireland's entry to EMS in 1979; Assistant Secretary for Borrowing and Debt Management in 1985 and Director of Irish Telecommunications Investments Ltd.; Assistant Secretary in charge of Budgetary and Taxation matters in Department of Finance, 1988-90; promoted to Revenue Commissioner 1990; is one of the three members of the Board of Revenue Commissioners; appointed Chairman of the Revenue Commissioners, 1998; member, EU Tax Policy Group (Monti Group). Hobbies, music and athletics. Contact: Revenue Commission, Chairman's Office, Dublin Castle, Dublin 2. Tel: 01 679 2777.

QUINN, David Anthony; JOURNALIST; *b* 1963; *educ* St. Pauls College, Raheny; Dublin City University, Bachelor of Business Studies; *m* Rachael Bermingham; Corporate Superannuation Consultant, MLC Life, Brisbane, Australia, 1988-93; Department Administrator, Investor Relations, AIB, Dublin, 1993-94; Columnist, *Sunday Business Post* 1994-97; Columnist, *Sunday Times* 1997 to date; Editor, *Irish Catholic,* 1996 to date; A frequent contributor to radio and television programmes; Member, National Union of Journalists; Comes from a strong journalistic background, third generation of family in the profession, grand father P.J. Quinn was political correspondent, *Irish Independent,* father, Brian Quinn was editor, *Evening Herald..* Club, Clontarf Lawn Tennis Club. Hobby, tennis. Contact: 55 Lower Gardiner Street, Dublin 1. Tel: 01 855 5619. Fax: 01 836 4805.

QUINN, Feargal

QUINN, Feargal; CHIEF EXECUTIVE SUPERQUINN, SENATOR; *educ* Newbridge College, Co. Kildare; University College Dublin, BComm; *m* Denise Prendergast; 3 *s* 2 *da;* worked in family owned Red Island Holiday Camp, Skerries; opened first supermarket in Dundalk, 1960; Chief Executive, Superquinn, now a chain of 17 shops employing over 3,000; Senator, 1993 to date; former Chairman, Irish Management Institute; Chairman, An Post; President, Irish Quality Association; Chairman, Finance Committee, Archdiocese; Governor, Dublin Skin & Cancer Hospital since 1972; Chairman, Steering Committee, Leaving Cert. Applied, National Council for Curriculum Assessment; Board member, Food Marketing Institute (USA) and Chairman, CIES - The Food Business Forum (France); has published *Crowning the Customer* (1990); awarded Honorary Doctor of Laws, NCEA (1987), Honorary Doctor of Laws, TCD (1988), Papal Knighthood (1994); his innovative hands on management style has produced a legion of loyal customers. Hobbies, horse riding, golf and fishing. Contact: Superquinn, PO Box 99, Sutton Cross, Sutton, Dublin 13. Tel: 01 832 5700. Fax: 01 832 6544.

QUINN, Frank; PUBLISHER; *b* 1957; *educ* Belvedere College; Trinity College Dublin; *m* Laura Cooney; 1 *s* 3 *da;* worked in trade and specialist press (*Checkout, Success* magazine) before joining *Sunday Tribune* as Deputy Advertising Manager; set up own business in 1985, launching

ComputerScope in 1985 as Ireland's first controlled-circulation magazine for IT professionals; launch *PC Live!* 1996; Launched recruitment website *JobFinder* (www.jobfinder.ie) in 1997; in 1998 agreed deal with *International Data Group*, world's largest publisher of IT media, to export JobFinder concept by translating and hosting recruitment websites in Dublin for IDG magazines worldwide; Founded Irish Internet Association, 1997; awarded Business Website of the Year for recruitment website *JobFinder*, 1998, *Deadline* magazine Outstanding Achievement Award for market leadership of *ComputerScope* and *PC Live!* magazines. Hobbies, family, playing the guitar and music generally, skiing enthusiast, lover of cars and gadgets. Contact: ComputerScope Ltd., Prospect House, Prospect Road, Dublin 9. Tel: 01 830 3455.

QUINN, Frank

QUINN, Lochlann; CHAIRMAN AIB; DEPUTY CHAIRMAN GLEN DIMPLEX; *b* 1940; *educ* Blackrock College, Dublin; University College Dublin, BComm.; *married;* 6 children; qualified as an Accountant, partner with Arthur Andersen (Dublin); joined Martin Naughton in Glen Dimplex in the seventies, currently shareholder and Deputy Chairman; Board member, Allied Irish Banks since 1995, Chairman, 1997 to date; Director, Irish Museum of Modern Art; Board member, Michael Smurfit Graduate Business School; director, Merrion Hotel (Dublin) and Patrick Guilbaud Restaurant. Hobbies, cars, art, wine and golf. Contact: Allied Irish Bank, Bankcentre, Ballsbridge, Dublin 4. Tel: 01 660 0311.

QUINN, Patricia; DIRECTOR OF THE ARTS COUNCIL; *b* 1959; *educ* Loreto College, North Great George's Street; Mount Temple Comprehensive; Trinity College Dublin, BA; MBA, IMI; *partner* John Banville, author; *2da;* worked in rare book conservation at Trinity College Dublin and Cambridge University; Specialist Officer, responsible for music and opera development, The Arts Council, 1984-92; Cultural Director, Temple Bar Properties, 1992-96; Director, Arts Council, 1996 to date; as the head of the Arts Council wields great power in the public arts sector; seen as an efficient and formidable leader for the 3rd millennium. Hobbies, reading and playing music (viol and piano). Contact: The Arts Council, 70 Merrion Square, Dublin 2. Tel: 01 618 0200. Fax: 01 676 1302.

QUINN, Ruairi

QUINN, Ruairi; LABOUR PARTY LEADER; *b* 1946; *educ* Blackrock College, Dublin; University College Dublin, BArch; Athens School of Ekistics, DipEkistics; *m* Nicola Underwood; *(m dis)*; 1 *s* 1 *da*; *m* Elizabeth Allman; 1 s; Junior Architect, Campbell Conroy Hickey, 1969-70; Assistant Design Architect, Dublin Corporation; Partner, Burke Kennedy Doyle and Partners, 1974-82; formerly Principal in Ruairi Quin and Associates, Architectural and Planning Consultants; elected to Dublin Corporation, 1974, 1977 and 1991; member, Seanad Eireann, 1976-77; elected Labour Deputy for Dublin South East, 1977 to date; Minister for State at the Department of the Environment, 1982-83; Minister for Labour and the Public Service, 1983-87; Deputy Leader of the Labour Party, 1990-97; Chairman, Campaign Committee and Director of Elections for Mary Robinson's Presidential Campaign, 1990; Director, Local Elections, Dublin, 1990; Minister for Enterprise and Employment, 1993-94; Minister for Finance, 1994-97; Leader of the Labour Party, 1997 to date; Vice President of the Party of European Socialists, 1999 to date; member, Royal Institute of Architects of Ireland, Irish Planning Institute, Royal Institute of British Architects; publications include numerous articles on housing, urban design, planning and environmental issues. Regarded as a technocrat attentive to detail; an excellent constituency politician; considered a passionate man, a promising national leader and perhaps a Taoiseach for the twenty first century. Hobbies, politics, reading, cycling, sketching, cooking and walking. Contact: Dáil Eireann, Leinster House, Kildare Street, Dublin 2. Tel: 01 618 3434. Fax: 01 618 4153.

QUINN, Sean

QUINN, Sean; CHAIRMAN AND MANAGING DIRECTOR QUINN GROUP LTD.; *b* 1946; *educ* Garvery National School; *m* Patricia Quinn; 1 *s* 4 *da;* worked on the family farm on leaving school; moved into agricultural contracting; formed his first company in 1973 - washing sand and selling it to local builders and farmers; expanded into the manufacture of various products for the construction industry; made a huge breakthrough in 1989 when he successfully completed a major new cement manufacturing plant; opened a £75m container glass manufacturing plant in Derrylin in 1998 and is currently building another cement plant at Ballyconnell, Co. Cavan. Owns eleven of the top public houses in Dublin; also the Iveagh Fitness Club; and seven hotels (including Slieve Russell Hotel Golf & Country Club in Ballyconnell; Buswells Hotel in Dublin and the Holiday Inn, Cambridge, England). Opened Quinn Direct general insurance company in 1996, intends to expand into the Life Assurance business in the near future. An astute, dynamic and hardworking entrepreneur who now employs over 2,000 people. Hobbies, business and GAA. Contact: Quinn Group Ltd., Derrylin, Co. Fermanagh. Tel: 0801 3657 48866. Fax: 0801 3657 48894.

QUINN, Shaun

QUINN, Shaun; CHIEF EXECUTIVE C.E.R.T; *b* 1962; *educ* Royal and Prior, Raphoe, Co. Donegal; University College Dublin, B Agr. Sc., MBA; *m* Mary Norris; 1*s*; Director, Market Planning & Development, CBF - Irish Meat Board, 1992-94; Strategic Planning Director, Bord Bia,

1994-96; Head of Marketing, 1996-98; Chief Executive, CERT, 1998 to date. CERT is the national body responsible for co-ordinating the education, recruitment and training of personnel for the Irish tourism industry; member, Marketing Institute of Ireland, Sutton Lawn Tennis Club, Hollywood Lakes Golf Club. Hobbies, golf, tennis, outdoor pursuits. Contact: CERT House, Amien Street, Dublin 1. Tel: 01 855 6555. Fax: 855 6821.

QUIRKE, The Hon, Mr. Justice John Michael Thornton; JUDGE OF THE HIGH COURT; *b* 1944; *educ* Willow Park School, Blackrock College, Trinity College Dublin; Kings Inns; *m* Mary Cruise; 3 *s* 1 *da*; Called to the Bar, 1974; Called to the Bar, Middle Temple (England), 1981; Called to Inner Bar, 1984; appointed Judge of the High Court, 1997; Regarded as an expert in personal injury cases when at the Bar; a keen sportsman, a rugby international, 1962-68; Captain, Blackrock R.F.C. 1969; Captain, Blainroe Golf Club, 1991, currently trustee. Contact: Four Courts, Morgan Place, Dublin 7. Tel: 01 872 5555.

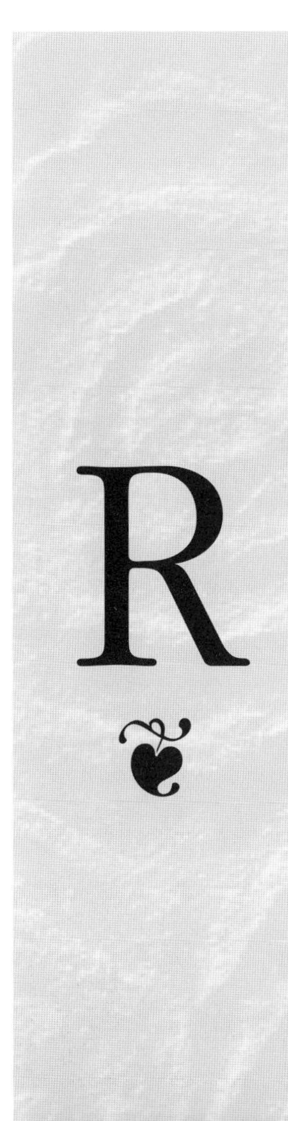

RABBITTE, Patrick; POLITICIAN; *b* 1949; *educ* St. Colman's College; University College Galway, BA, LLB, HDipEd; *m* Derry McDermott; 3 *da;* President, University College Galway Students Union, 1970-71; President, Union of Students in Ireland, 1972-74; Union Official, ITGWU, 1974-80; National Secretary, ITGWU, 1980-89; elected Workers Party Deputy for Dublin South West, 1989; Minister for Commerce, Science and Technology, 1994-97; following amalgamation of Democratic Left and Labour Party, appointed Labour spokesperson, Enterprise, Trade and Employment, 1999 to date; Non-Executive Director, USIT Ltd., 1972 to date; member, Governing Body, University College Galway, 1972-75; Publications include: *What's Mined Is Ours, Bertie's Bill - An Analysis of 1990 Industrial Relations Act.* A poll topper in Dublin South West, a highly professional and effective performer. Recognized as the wittiest speaker in the house and popular with the media. Hobbies, reading, music and drinking a pint - preferably not simultaneously. Contact: Dáil Eireann, Leinster House, Kildare Street, Dublin 2. Tel: 1890 337889.

RAFTER, Gary; MANAGING DIRECTOR BRYAN S. RYAN LTD.; *b* 1948; *m* Gena -----; 2*da;* spent 13 years with Xerox 1970-83, holding positions including Training Manager & Sales Manager, General Manager, Computer Staff Recruitment, 1983-1984; Managing Director, Bryan S. Ryan Ltd., 1984 to date. Hobbies, golf. Contact: Bryan S. Ryan, Main Road, Tallaght, Dublin 24. Tel: 01 452 4499. Fax: 01 452 4845.

RAPPLE, Colm; JOURNALIST; *b* 1940; *educ* St. Joseph's School, Marino; University College Dublin, BA, MBA; *m* Nuala O'Toole-King; 1 *s* 1 *da;* spent six years in the Merchant Navy with Cunard Lines, 1958-64; Sub-editor, Business Page Reporter, 1969; Business Correspondent, Group Business Editor, *Irish Independent,* 1971-85; Business Editor, Irish Press Newspapers, 1985 -95; Since 1995, Freelance Journalist, Columnist, *Sunday Business Post*, Presenter, *Money Talks*, RTE Radio 1, Columnist, *Examiner.* Publications include: *Family Finance* (annual), *Start Your Own Business, Living with the Recession, Your Guide to Pensions.* A widely read and respected financial journalist. Hobbies, reading, theatre and running a small holding in Mayo. Contact: Sunday Business Post, 27, Merchants Quay, Dublin 8. Tel: 01 679 9777. Fax: 01 679 6496

REDMOND, Mary P

REDMOND, Mary Patricia Martina; SOLICITOR, COMPANY DIRECTOR; *b* 1950; *educ* University College Dublin, BCL; Solicitor, Incorporated Law Society of Ireland; Cambridge University PhD; *m* Patrick Ussher, former Fellow T.C.D.; 1 *s* 3 *step-daughters*; Assistant Lecturer, Law Faculty U.C.D, 1973-80; Fellow, Churchill College, Cambridge, 1980-81; Fellow, Christ's College Cambridge, 1981-85; set up solicitor's practice Dublin, specialising in employment law, 1985; Director, Bank of Ireland Group, 1994 to date; Director, Jefferson Smurfit Group, 1997 to date; Director, Campbell Bewley Group, 1998 to date; Director, Barretstown Gang Camp Fund, 1998 to date; member, Labour Relations Commission, 1995 to date; set up Irish Hospice Foundation, 1985, Director, 1985-96, Patron, 1997 to date; member, R.S.A.; Fellow, Institute of Directors; Club, Kildare Street and University; awards include: Tutorial Scholarship (1970), Winter Williams Commonwealth Studentship in Law, Oxford, (1972), British Council Research Grant, (1978), Person of the Year, 1996; Publications include: *Dismissal Law,* 1982, *Dismissal Law,* 1999; one of the most outstanding women in Irish professional, commercial and community life, an indefatigable worker for the Hospice Foundation. Hobbies, painting, the simpler side of country life, the voluntary sector. Contact: 36 Wellington Road, Dublin 4. Tel: 01 668 0248. Fax: 01 660 7752.

REED, Leslie Philip; CHIEF EXECUTIVE OF CRAFTS COUNCIL OF IRELAND; *b* 1950; *educ* Dartford Grammar School (UK); Loughborough College of Art & Design (UK), BA; *m* Inga White; 3*s*; Lecturer, Head of the Ceramics Department, Crawford College of Art & Design, 1977-89; Director of Training, Crafts Council of Ireland, 1989-96; Chief Executive, Crafts Council of Ireland, 1996 to date; works extensively in ceramic design; Chairman, Kilkenny School Project Association. Hobbies, gardening and stone carving Contact: Crafts Council of Ireland, Castle Yard, Kilkenny.

Tel: 056 61804. Fax: 056 63754.

REGAN, Gerard "Gerry"; NEWSPAPER EDITOR - THE STAR; *b* 1949; *educ* Tralee CBS; *m* Sheila Moriarty; 2 *s* 1 *da;* Reporter, *Tuam Herald, Leinster Express,* 1978; News Reporter, *Irish Independent,* Subsequently Assistant Editor, Features Editor, News Analysis Editor, Night Editor, Deputy Editor, *Irish Independent,* 1995; Editor, *The Star,* 1995 to date; *The Star* is currently the leading newspaper for the under 35s. Hobbies, reading, music, travel, walking and the Media. Contact: The Star Newspaper, 62A Terenure Road, Dublin 6W. Tel: 01 490 1228. Fax: 01 490 2193.

REID, Ronan Paul; JOINT MANAGING DIRECTOR DOLMEN, BUTLER, BRISCOE; *b* 1965; *educ* Rockwell College, University College Dublin, B.Comm.; *m* Karen O'Gorman; 2 *s*; joined Investment Bank of Ireland, 1986; worked with Riada Stockbrokers, 1988. Managing Director, WPMC, 1989; Futures Director, NCB, 1992; Joint Managing Director, Dolmen, Butler, Briscoe, 1994 to date; clubs, Riverview Racquet and Fitness; Carrickmines LTC, Rockwell Past Pupils; Hobbies, tennis, represented Ireland World Games, represented Leinster Senior Team, Captain Carrickmines 1st Team, Class I Division, 1990, '95, '98. Contact: Dolmen Butler Briscoe, 3 College Green, Dublin 1. Tel: 01 677 7348.

REIHILL, Ann; née McCoy; PUBLISHER; *b* 1936; *educ* Loreto Convent, Balbriggan; University College Dublin; *m* Patrick Dillon-Malone (*decd.*); 2 s, *(1 decd.),* 1 *da; m* John Reihill; 3 step s *3 step da*; Research Assistant, *The Sunday Times*; Assistant Editor, *Times Guide to Travel* 1972-74; Editor, *Image* 1976-80; currently Group Director of Image and Publisher of *Irish Arts Review*; Governor and Guardian, National Gallery of Ireland, 1985-90; Director, Hugh Lane Municipal Gallery of Modern Art, 1988 to date. Hobbies, tennis, golf, reading and travel. Contact: Image Publications, 22 Crofton Road, Dun Laoghaire, Co. Dublin. Tel: 01 280 8415.

REYNOLDS, John; CLUB OWNER; *b* 1966; *educ* Castleknock College; Trinity College Dublin, BBS; *single;* managed Ministry of Sound Club (London); opened POD (Dublin), 1993, creating the first large scale, sophisticated night spot in the city; Co-manager, with Louis Walsh, Boyzone; opened The Chocolate Bar, adjoining POD and Red Box, a performance space; Director, The Home Clubs, designed by Ron McCullach, in Sydney (Australia), New York and London; a disciplined, shrewd and ambitious businessman with a great deal of charm, responsible for changing the Dublin nightclub scene. Hobbies, music, interior design and football. Contact: POD, Harcourt Street, Dublin 2. Tel: 01 478 0166.

REYNOLDS, Philip

REYNOLDS, Philip; MANAGING DIRECTOR C&D FOODS; *b* 1964; *educ* Cistercian College Roscrea; IMI Sandyford; *m* Anne Farrell; 2 *s* 1 *da;* joined family pet food manufacturing company, C&D Foods Ltd., 1982, Production Controller, 1984-86, Sales Manager, 1986-88, Marketing Director, 1988-90, Managing Director, 1990 to date; C&D Foods Ltd. is the largest pet food manufacturers in the State with a turnover of approx. £30 million; member, Lions Club, Mullingar, Mullingar Golf Club, Showjumping Association of Ireland. Hobbies, horses and golf. Contact: C&D Foods Ltd., Edgworthstown, Co. Longford. Tel: 043 71067. Fax: 043 71388.

RIGNEY, Patrick James "Pat"; JOINT MANAGING DIRECTOR BORU VODKA; *b* 1961; *educ* Sandford Park School, Dublin; Trinity College Dublin, BComm; *m* Denise Kelly; 1*s* *2da;* Marketing Assistant, Gilbeys of Ireland 1982-84; Brand Manager, Gilbeys of Ireland 1984-86; Export Development Manager, Cantrell and Cochrane 1986-90; Director, Baileys 1990-98; formed Roaring Water Bay Spirits with David Phelan 1998; the company are currently involved in the manufacture of Boru Vodka with more brands to follow; the handcrafted vodka, a recent arrival on the vodka market has already reached the No. 1 slot; the company has received various awards including Glen Dimplex Award for Design 1998; voted Best New Vodka US 1999; member, Woodenbridge Golf Club, Royal Irish Yacht Club, Sportsco. Hobbies, family, friends, golf and squash. Contact: Roaring Water Bay Spirits, 4 Herbert Place, Dublin 2. Tel.; 01 662 9200.

ROBINSON, Mary, née Bourke; UNITED NATIONS HIGH COMMISSIONER FOR HUMAN RIGHTS AND CHANCELLOR OF DUBLIN UNIVERSITY; *b* 1944; *educ* Sacred Heart Convent, Mount Anville, Dublin; Trinity College Dublin, BA, MA, LLB; King's Inns, Barrister-at-Law; Harvard University, fellowship 1967; LLM 1968; *m* Nicholas Robinson; 2 *s* 1 *da;* Reid Professor, Trinity College Dublin, 1969-75; Lecturer in Law, Trinity College Dublin, 1975-90; member of Seanad Eireann, 1969-89; member of English Bar (Middle Temple), 1973-90; Senior Counsel, 1980-90; Founder, with others, Irish Centre for European Law, 1988; Labour Party member Dublin City Council, 1979-83; member of Advisory Committee of Interights, London, 1984-90; member, International Committee of Jurists, Geneva, 1987-90; member of various Oireachtas committees including EC Secondary Legislation, Social Affairs, Legal Affairs, Marital Breakdown; President of CHERISH, 1973-90; President of Ireland, 1990-97; publications include articles on Family Law,

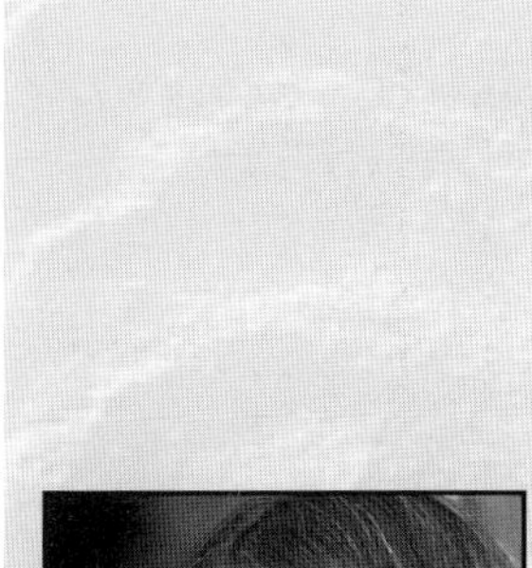

Constitutional issues and Human Rights for numerous journals.; Doctor of Laws by Diploma, Oxford; Doctor of Laws (honoris causa): National University of Ireland, Cambridge, Brown, Liverpool, Dublin, Montpellier, St. Andrew's, Colombia, National University of Wales, Poznan, Toronto, Fordham, Queen's University of Belfast, London, Harvard; Doctor of Public Service (honoris causa): Northeastern University; Diplome de Doctorat en Sciences Humaines (honoris causa): Université de Rennes; Honorary Bencher King's Inns, Dublin and Middle Temple, London; Honorary Professor of Law, University of Manchester; Honorary Fellow: Trinity College Dublin, Hertford College Oxford; European Media Prize; Global Leadership Award; International Human Rights Award; International League of Human Special Humanitarian Award, CARE, Washington; Collar of Hussein Bin Ali, Hashmite Kingdom of Jordan. An outstanding President of Ireland, setting new standards at home and abroad; retaining high standards in her current international post. Contact: Fax: 0041 22 917 9012.

ROCHA, John

ROCHA, John; DESIGNER; *b* 1953; *educ* St. Luke's College, Hong Kong; State Registered Psychiatric Nurse, Banstead Hospital; Croydon College of Art & Design, Dip.Fashion Design; *m* Odette Gleeson; 1*s* 2*da;* studied design in London; opened the first of his own shops in Ireland in 1995; in 1987 he moved to Italy to work under licence to Reflections Milan, one of the then leading licensing houses in Europe, producing collections including Dries van Noten and Martine Sitbon; continued to produce his own collections while further developing and perfecting his tailoring and cutting techniques; returning to Dublin in 1989, he continued to expand and promote the John Rocha Collections and to develop his customer base, showing twice yearly in London; launched menswear collection in 1993; company produces over one hundred thousand garments a year, the John Rocha collections for men and women are now stocked by over 300 stores worldwide; launched contemporary crystal range with Waterford Glass, 1997; opened London Store (Sloane Avenue), 1998, stocking mainline collection, Rocha Jeans, crystal and home accessories; designed Virgin Atlantic uniform, 1999; has moved into interior design with work on Morrison Hotel, Dublin 1999; awarded British Designer of the Year, 1994; Honorary Doctor, University of Ulster 1994; Club, The Groucho Club (London); a multi faceted designer with an international reputation; has a warm, unspoilt personality. Hobbies, fly fishing, football and travel. Contact: John Rocha Head Office, 27-29 Lower Rathmines Road, Dublin 6. Tel: 01 496 9300. Fax: 01 496 9313.

ROCHE, Adrienne "Adi"; EXECUTIVE DIRECTOR CHERNOBYL CHILDREN'S PROJECT; *b* 1955; *educ* Presentation Convent, Clonmel; Dominican College, Eccles Street, Dublin; *m* Seán Dunne; worked for Aer Lingus, 1975-83; took voluntary redundancy to work full-time as a volunteer for the Irish Campaign for Nuclear Disarmament (ICND), 1983; represented Ireland on 'The Great Peace Journey' travelling to over ten European countries; initiated, and is now Executive Director of Chernobyl Children's Project 1990; the project aims to help children suffering from the radioactive fall-out which followed the Chernobyl Reactor Explosion in 1986, through a comprehensive aid and development programme; author, *Children of Chernobyl* - Adi's account of the 1986 disaster and its aftermath; TV Documentaries include *Black Wind, White Land - Living with Chernobyl* - the effects of Chernobyl on the people of Belarus, Russia and the Ukraine, *Chernobyl Legacy* for BBC/RTE, *Deaths Dream Kingdom;* member, Board of Directors of the International Peace Bureau (IPB) in Geneva; Government Appointee to the Board of the Radiological Protection Institute of Ireland; recipient, European Woman Laureate Award (1994), Irish Person of the Year (1994), European of the Year (1996), Frantsysk Skrayna Order, Belarus National Honour (1998), Liquidators Medal in Belarus in recognition of work there (1998); Presidential Candidate (1997); has worked extensively with the United Nations in highlighting humanitarian issues. Hobbies, politics, environmental issues, reading, music, set-dancing, walking and singing. Contact: Chernobyl Children's Project, 2 Camden Place, Camden Quay, Cork. Tel: 021 506 411. Fax: 021 551 544.

ROCHE, Donal Aidan

ROCHE, Donal Aidan; MANAGING PARTNER, MATHESON ORMSBY PRENTICE SOLICITORS; *b* 1953; *educ* Blackrock College; Trinity College Dublin, MA TCD Legal Science, Incorporated Law Society; *m* Mary O'Flynn; 1 *s* 3 *da*; Joined the practice of Gerrard Scallan & O'Brien, 1977-83; Moved to Arthur Cox, 1983-85; Partner, Matheson Ormsby Prentice, 1985-96; Managing partner, Matheson Ormsby Prentice, 1996 to date; Member, Incorporated Law Society, International Bar Association, St. Stephen's Green Club, Royal St. George Yacht Club, Killiney Golf Club, Glen of the Downs Golf Club. Hobbies, reading, fishing, golf. Contact: Matheson Ormsby Prentice, 30 Herbert Street, Dublin 2. Tel: 01 619 9000. Fax: 01 619 9010.

ROCHE, Michael F.

ROCHE, Michael F; NEWSPAPER EXECUTIVE; *b* 1955; *educ* Terenure College, Dublin; *m;* 2 *s* 1 *da*; Financial Journalist 1977-86; Managing Director, Drogheda Independent Company Ltd. 1987-89; Managing Director, People Newspapers Ltd., 1989-98; Managing Editor, Independent Newspapers, 1998 to date. Former journalist who now has a pivotal role in cutting the Independent's escalating costs; a single minded newspaper manager, not without charm; Clubs, Grange Golf Club, Lahinch Golf Club, Rosslare Golf Club, Terenure College RFC. Contact: Independent Newspapers (Ireland) Ltd., 90 Middle Abbey Street, Dublin 1. Tel: 01 705 5333. Fax:

01 872 0304.

ROHAN, Kenneth C.; PROPERTY DEVELOPER; *b* 1944; *educ* St. Gerard's School, Bray, Castleknock College; *m* Brenda MacManus; 2 *s* 1 *da;* Managing Director, Rohan Group plc (a company specialising in industrial and commercial development and construction) until its sale in 1987 to a UK plc; Re-acquired the company, 1992 and is currently Chairman and Chief Executive of Rohan Holdings Ltd.; a cool headed businessman who enjoys a cultured lifestyle. Hobbies, horse racing, shooting, golf and collecting Irish Art. Contact: Rohan Holdings Ltd., 5 Mount Street Crescent, Dublin 2. Tel: 01 662 4455. Fax: 01 676 5404.

RONAN, John

RONAN, John; PROPERTY DEVELOPER; *b* 1953; *educ* Castleknock College; Chartered Accountant, (F.C.A.); *m* Mary Tilson; 2*s* 1 *da;* has been involved in property development for the past twenty-five years; formed Treasury Holdings Ltd. with partner, Richard Barret in the late eighties; developments include Treasury Building, Grand Canal Street, A.I.B. Investment House, Percy Place, Connaught House, Herbert Street, the controversial development on College Street and Westmoreland Street for Westin Hotels; involved in the development of the the Conference Centre and ancillary developments at Spencer Dock, the largest single urban development ever proposed in Ireland (6 million sq. feet); also significant shareholders in the latest Government franchise for alternative energy, wind farms; widely considered to have a natural instinct for the development business; a gregarious mixer with a good deal of charm. Hobbies, hunting, cycling and football. Contact: Treasury Holdings Ltd., Treasury Building, Lower Grand Canal Street, Dublin 2. Tel: 01 661 3207. Fax: 01 661 2258.

ROONEY, Francis Joseph "Fran"; CHIEF EXECUTIVE BALTIMORE TECHNOLOGIES; *b* 1956; *educ* qualified as a Chartered Accountant and holds a number of qualifications in Information Technology; *m* Mary ----; 1*s* 2 *da;* worked in Irish Government Sector and Post Office; National Irish Bank; Meridian International; Quay Financial Software; Investment and Underwriting Limited; Chief Executive, Baltimore Technologies, appointed Chief Executive Officer, Baltimore Technologies Worldwide 1999; member, Irish Computer Society; Institute of Chartered Accountants; Irish Software Association; elected to the Board, Key Recovery Alliance; awards include 1998 Irish Software Association Company of the Year; Europe's largest independent internet security firm. Hobbies, golf, swimming, reading, rugby and football. Contact: Baltimore Technologies, Ltd., I.F.S.C., Custom House Quay, Dublin 1. Tel: 01 605 4399.

ROONEY, Raymond John; MANAGING DIRECTOR ROONEY AUCTIONEERS LTD / ROONEY INSURANCES LTD; *b* 1939; *educ* St. Ignatius College, Galway; Mungret College, Limerick; *m* Helen O'Sullivan; 3*s*; joined Insurance Corporation of Ireland, 1957, Inspector, 1960; Founded Insurance Brokerage of Rooney Insurances, 1962; Founded Rooney Auctioneers Ltd. (separate company), 1966; Associate, Chartered Insurance Institute (ACII); Associate, Institute of Arbitrators (A.Inst.Arb.); Fellow, Irish Auctioneers and Valuers Institute (FIAVI); Norwegian Consulate for West of Ireland; Chairman, West of Ireland Cardiology Foundation; Deputy Senior Steward, Irish Turf Club; Member, Irish National Hunt & Steeplechase; Director, Galway Boston Ventures Ltd.; Director, Chairman, Galway Development Board; Member, Galway Harbour Board Ltd. Hobbies, fishing, tennis (international player on senior team), racing and golf. Contact: Rooney Auctioneers Ltd., Victoria House, Eyre Square, Galway. Tel: 091 567 391. Fax: 091 567 394.

ROSNEY, Bride

ROSNEY, Bride; EXECUTIVE DIRECTOR BILL O'HERLIHY COMMUNICATIONS; *b* 1949; *educ* Dominican College, Eccles Street, Dublin; University College Dublin, BSc., HDipEd; Trinity College Dublin, DipCmpEd, MSc; *single;* Teacher, Dominican Convent, Ballyfermot, 1971-75; Research Officer, Curriculum Development Unit, Trinity College Dublin, 1975-79; Teacher, Portmarnock Community School, 1979-82; Vice-Principal, 1982-86 and Principal, Rosmini Community School, 1986-90; Special Advisor to Mary Robinson, President of Ireland 1990-97; Principal Advisor to Mary Robinson, UN High Commissioner for Human Rights, 1997-98; Executive Director, Bill O'Herlihy Communications, 1999; Editor of various science materials for schools; member, Institute of Biology, RIA's Committee for Teaching of Biology (former Chairperson); former National Officer, An Taisce; former Executive Member and Branch Chairperson, TUI. Her professional skill and formidable intelligence were the hallmark of the Robinson presidency. Hobbies, reading, travel, theatre and the media. Contact: Bill O'Herlihy Communications Group, 40 Eastmoreland Lane, Dublin 4. Tel: 01 660 2744. Fax: 01 660 2745.

ROSS, Shane Peter Nathaniel; SENATOR, JOURNALIST, COMPANY DIRECTOR; *b* 1949; *educ* Rugby School (U.K.); Trinity College Dublin, BA; *m* Ruth Buchanan, broadcaster / journalist; Partner with Dillon & Waldron Stockbrokers 1980-85, Chairman, 1985-89; elected senator for Trinity College 1981, 1982, 1983, 1987, 1989, 1993, 1997 to date; Business Editor, *Sunday Independent*, 1995 to date; member, Wicklow County Council 1991 to date; Chairman, Kleinwort Benson Privatisation Investment Trust plc, 1994-96; Chairman Warrants & Value Investment Trust

plc, 1998 to date; Director, ING Barings New Russia Fund, 1997 to date; clubs, Kildare Street and University Club. Contact: Sunday Independent, 90 Middle Abbey Street, Dublin 1. Tel: 01 705 5333.

ROSSE 7th EARL OF, Brendan Parsons; Hon FIEI; *b* 1936; *educ* Aiglon College; Grenoble University; Christchurch Oxford, MA; *m* Alison Cooke-Hurle; 2 *s* 1 *da;* formerly 2nd Lt Irish Guards; Principal Officer, United Nations Development Programme from 1963: first UNV Field Director, Iran 1970-75, Disaster Relief Co-ordinator, Bangladesh, 1975-78, Algeria 1978-80 etc.; inheritance of the Earldom and of the Birr Castle Estate, cut short UN career and occasioned return to Ireland; appointed a member of the Government's Advisory Council on Development Co-operation, and Director, APSO (Agency for Personal Service Overseas) 1981-89; subsequently founded Birr Scientific and Heritage Foundation as vehicle for the restoration of the great Rosse Telescope (the world's largest in the last century) and the establishment of Ireland's Historic Science Centre, now open at Birr; has initiated and contributed to numerous exhibitions and publications highlighting the scientific achievements of Irishmen and women; a keen member of the IDS (International Dendrology Society); both fervently nationalist and internationalist, his exhibitions and lecture tours here and particularly overseas have started to change the rather fixed out-dated image which those like the British and Americans have often had of the Irish, and hence make him an unusual force, to find in a scion of the old Ascendency. Contact: Birr Castle, Birr, Co. Offaly. Tel: 0509 20023. Fax: 0509 20425.

RUANE, Frances, née Virzi; LECTURER IN HISTORY OF ART & DESIGN NCAD; *educ* Queens College of the City University of New York, BA; The Pennsylvania State University, MA Fine Arts, PhD, Art Ed.; *m* James J. Ruane; *2s*; Education Officer, National Gallery of Ireland, Merrion Square, Dublin 2, 1974-77; Art Critic, *The Evening Press*, 1977-80; Art Advisor, AIB Group, Bankcentre, Ballsbridge, Dublin 4, 1980 to date; Art Critic, Presenter, RTE television programme on *ROSC 1981*, 1981; RTE television weekly Arts programme, *Exhibit A,* 1984-86; Art Critic, *The Irish Times,* 1990-92; Presenter, RTE television programme, *Beyond the Hall Door,* 1996; Lecturer in History of Art & Design, National College of Art & Design, Thomas Street, Dublin 8, 1977 to date; Chairperson, Crafts Council of Ireland; has written and lectured extensively in the area of Irish Art, as well as organising several major touring exhibitions; publications include *The Delighted Eye* (Arts Councils, Dublin & Belfast, 1980), *Modern Irish Landscape Painting* (recent Irish Art Slide Series, Arts Councils, Dublin & Belfast, 1981), *Patrick Collins* (Arts Councils, Dublin & Belfast, 1982), *Six Artists from Ireland* (Department of Foreign Affairs, 1983), *The Allied Irish Bank Collection* (The Douglas Hyde Gallery, 1986), 'Personal Inscapes' in *Tony O'Malley,* (Scolar Press, 1996), *AIB Art* (AIB Group, 1996), *Art into Art* (National Gallery of Ireland, 1998); Board member, Cothu, 1995 to date; Board member, The Douglas Hyde Gallery, 1983-93. Contact: National College of Art & Design, 100 Thomas Street, Dublin 2. Tel: 01 671 1377.

RUANE, Frances

RUANE, Frances Philomena; HEAD OF DEPARTMENT OF ECONOMICS, TRINITY COLLEGE DUBLIN; *b* 1951; *educ* Univeristy College Dublin, BA, MA; Nuffield College, Oxford, B.Phil (Oxon), D.Phil (Oxon); *m* Peter Neary, (*m dis*); 2 *s; partner* James Slevin; Planning Officer with IDA Dublin, 1971-73; Research Economist, Central Bank of Ireland, 1973-74; Lecturer, Trinity College Dublin, 1977-86, Lecturer and Fellow, 1985-91; Burser 1991-95, Associate Professor and Fellow 1991 to date; Head, Department of Economics, Trinity College Dublin 1997 to date; visiting Consultant World Bank, Washington 1978 and 1980; visiting Associate Professor, Queens University, Kingston, Ontario; other posts held: Economics Editor, *Economic and Social Review,* Research Director, Foundation for Fiscal Studies, President Elect, Irish Economics Association, Board member, National Board for Science & Technology, Director, Irish National Theatre Soc., Authority Member, I.D.A., Board member Forfás, sits on numerous public sector Boards; Chairperson, National Statistics Board; member, Foundation for Fiscal Studies, Economic and Social Studies and other international Economic Bodies; Publications include papers in national and international journals. Hobbies, reading, walking, theatre. Contact: Department of Economics, Trinity College, Dublin 2. Tel: 01 608 1027. Fax: 01 677 2503.

RYALL, Christine

RYALL, Christine, née Roesler; REPRESENTATIVE FOR PHILLIPS INTERNATIONAL; *b* 1945; *educ* Germany; Royal Society of Arts and College of Commerce Bristol; Sorbonne, Paris; Institute of Languages Stuttgart, Germany; *m* Patrick Ryall, Chief Executive ELOPAK Ltd; Correspondent for Foreign Economic Affairs, Berlin 1962; Sales & Marketing British Airways, Berlin & Northern Ireland, 1968; representative for Phillips International Fine Art Auctioneers in Ireland 1986 to date; member of Committee of the Friends of St. Patrick's Hospital; reputation for efficiency, discretion and customer care. Hobbies, cooking, tennis, wine tasting and reading. Contact: Phillips Auctioneers & Valuers, The Old Rectory, Timolin, Moone, Athy, Co. Kildare. Tel: 0507 24130. Fax: 0507 24280.

RYAN, Eoin; POLITICIAN; *b* 1953; *educ* Willow Park; St. Mary's College; Rathmines College of Commerce; Kildalton Horticultural College; *m* Sheila McKeever; 1*s* 2 *da;* started commercial career as proprietor of health foods shops and restaurant; later involved in European consultancy work; member, Dublin Corporation, 1989 to date; Taoiseach's nominee to Senate, 1989-92; elected Fianna Fail deputy for Dublin South East, 1992 to date; currently Chairperson of Joint Committee on Justice, Equality and Women's Rights; a third generation politician, father Eoin served as Vice-President of Fianna Fail and in the Seanad, grandfather James served as Minister; represents, for many, the old party values. Hobbies, walking, swimming and music. Contact: Dáil Eireann, Leinster House, Kildare Street, Dublin 2. Tel: 01 618 3333.

RYAN, Gerry

RYAN, Gerry; RADIO/TELEVISION PRESENTER; *b* 1956; *educ* St. Paul's School, Raheny; Trinity College Dublin; Incorporated Law Society; *m* Morah Brennan; 2*s* 2 *da;* Solicitor's Apprentice, Malone and Potter Solicitors, Dublin; joined RTE 1979, hosting mini chat show for Radio 2, moved gradually into presenting late night music show; started the *Gerry Ryan Show,* morning chat show, 1988 to date; Presenter of the popular television shows, *Secrets* and *School Around the Corner;* recipient of Jacobs Award for the *Gerry Ryan Show* radio 1991; *Sunday Independent*/Irish Life Radio Arts Award 1989; a reflective and talented television personality; on air, an exuberant and forceful presenter who has captured a large segment of the younger listening public; an influential force on the Irish airwaves. Hobbies, reading, cinema, television and helicopter flying. Contact: RTE, Donnybrook, Dublin 4. Tel: 208 3111.

RYAN, John Paul Denis; JOURNALIST, PUBLISHER; *b* 1968; *educ* C.B.C. Monkstown; Harlow College, Middlesex, Cert. in Journalism & Law; *single;* Reporter with *Hornsey Journal,* 1989, freelance Journalist, Bosnia, Rwanda, 1993; Features, *Sunday Independent,* 1994; Editor, *In Dublin,* 1996; *Irish Independent,* 1997; Managing Editor, *Magill,* 1997; Editor, "Culture", *Sunday Times* 1998-99; Publisher, *VIP,* 1999 to date; Presenter, *Sunday Supplement* Today FM, 1997-98; debonair journalist turned publisher with his finger on the pulse of the popular zeitgeist. Hobbies, swimming and skiing. Contact; The Sunday Times, Huguenot House, 35 St. Stephen's Green, Dublin 2. Tel: 01 602 8800. Fax: 01 602 8816.

RYAN, Liam

RYAN, The Rev, Liam; PROFESSOR OF SOCIOLOGY NUI MAYNOOTH; *b* 1936; *educ* Maynooth College, NUI, B.A.; Pontifical University, Maynooth College, D.D.; St. Louis University, Missouri, USA, M.A., PhD.; (Dissertation on The Irish In London); Ordained priest for the Archdiocese of Cashel, 1960; Lecturer in Theology, St. Louis University, USA, 1962-64; Lecturer in Sociology, University College Cork, 1964-69; Professor of Sociology, Maynooth College (now NUI Maynooth), 1969 to present; Vice-president, Maynooth College, 1974-77; publications include: *Irish Values and Attitudes,* with Michael Fogarty and J. J. Lee, 1984; *Counselling the Adolescent in a Changing Ireland,* 1992; regular contributor to radio & T.V. on social, cultural and religious issues; member of the Higher Education Authority, 1975-85; Whitaker Commission on Prison Reform, 1984-85; National Council for Educational Awards; Captain Limerick Senior Hurling Team, Munster Champions, 1955; President, Bodenstown Golf Club, 1983-89; External Examiner, North London University, 1993-98; Irish representative on the International Social Survey Programme (ISSP). Hobbies, golf and sport generally, hill-walking, theatre-goer. Contact: National University of Ireland, Maynooth, Co. Kildare. Tel: 01 708 3688. Fax: 01 708 3528.

RYAN, Richard; DIPLOMAT; *b* 1946; *educ* University College Dublin, BA, MA; *m* Heeun Hyun; 3 *s;* Visiting Professor of Poetry, College of St. Thomas, St. Paul, Minnesota, 1970-71; Lecture programmes and seminars on Anglo-Irish literature at Universities and Colleges in 38 American States, 1970-73; Lecturer, English Department, University College Dublin, 1972-73; Diplomatic postings include Third Secretary, Department of Foreign Affairs, 1973; Third Secretary, Embassy, Tokyo, 1974; First Secretary, Embassy, Tokyo, 1975; First Secretary, Headquarters, 1977; First Secretary, Permanent Representation of Ireland to the European Commission, Brussels, 1980; member of Cabinet, Commission of the European Communities, Brussels, 1982; Counsellor, Embassy, London, 1983; Minister-Counsellor, Embassy, London, 1988; Ambassador to the Republic of Korea,1989; Ambassador to Spain with concurrent accreditation to Algeria, Andorra and Tunisia 1994; Ambassador / Permanent Representative of Ireland to the United Nations, New York, 1998 to date; publications include, *Ledges,* 1970, *Ravenswood,* 1973 (Dolmen Press, Dublin, Oxford University Press, London); awards and honours include, May Morton Memorial Prize for Poetry, 1968, *Irish Times* Award for Poetry, 1969, EUROTIR Large Calibre Rifle Champion, 1982, Decoration of the Home Government of Greenland, 1983, Kwanghwamun Order of Diplomatic Merit (Republic of Korea), 1993, Seok-Ho-Jeong Award of the Korean Archery Association, 1993, Order of Merit Cross, Federación Madrilena de Tiro Olimpico Spain, 1998; Clubs, Kildare Street and University Club, Dublin, Royal Irish Yacht Club, Dublin, Garrick Club, London and Half Moon Swimming Club, Dublin Bay. Hobbies, literature, art, music, wine, swimming, shooting and archery. Contact: Permanent Mission of Ireland to the United Nations, 1 Dag Hammarskjöld Plaza, 885 Second Avenue (19th floor), New York 10017, New York, USA.

RYAN, Thomas; ARTIST; *b* 1929; *educ* Christian Brothers School, Limerick; School of Art, Limerick; National College of Art and Design, Dublin; *m* Mary Joyce; 4*s* 2 *da;* an established artist whose work hangs in major collections; Designer of one pound coin and Millennium fifty pence; President, Royal Hibernian Academy of Arts, 1982-92; Honorary member, Royal Academy (London) and Royal Scottish Academy (Edinburgh); former Governor, National Gallery of Ireland; President, United Arts Club; President, Limerick Art Society; Associate, National College of Art & Design; Board member, Stamp Design Committee (An Post); Founder member, Union of European Academies for Fine Art; Knight Hositaller Order of St. Lazarus of Jerusalem; Knight Commander of the Equestrian Order of the Holy Sepulchre of Jerusalem; Council member, British School at Rome; recipient, Hon Dr. Lit. University of Limerick; member, Arts Club. Hobbies, collecting medals of Irish interest. Contact: RHA, 15 Ely Place, Dublin 2. Tel: 01 873 3666.

RYAN, Thomas Anthony "Tony"; CHAIRMAN IRELANDIA INVESTMENTS AND TIPPERARY CRYSTAL; DIRECTOR OF RYANAIR; *b* 1936; *educ* Christian Brothers School, Thurles, Co. Tipperary; 3*s;* held senior management positions with Aer Lingus in Ireland and US; founded GPA Group plc, 1975 which later translated initial $50,000 investment into $4billion, but was affected by a bungled IPO in 1992; today the company trades as AerFi plc; created the Ryanair Group in 1985, which today has a $1billion plus market capitalisation and is Europe's largest low cost airline; conferred with Honorary Doctorates by Trinity College, NUI and Limerick Universities; a businessman of courage and incredible entrepreneurial skills; noted for ability to pick outstanding executives and the best boardroom expertise available. Hobbies, farming and horsebreeding. Contact: 9 Merrion Square, Dublin 2. Tel: 01 661 2843.

RYAN, Tom; CHIEF EXECUTIVE RYAN INTERNATIONAL CORPORATION; *b* 1967; *educ* St. Joseph's College, Newport, Co. Tipperary; *single;* joined Bill O'Herlihy Public Relations, 1990-92; set up own lobbying and public relations company, Tom Ryan 1992; formed Ryan International Corporation 1993 with the Irish residential and commercial property arm of the corporation; moved into helicopter manufacturing and leasing with Frazcer Group Aviation (US) 1994; manufacturer and distributor, Ryans Irish Cream Liqueur 1995; software manufacturing operation opened in Paris, 1996; an entrepreneur with flair and vision, a man continuously on the move. Hobbies, sailing, motor boat racing, water skiing. Contact: Ryan International Corporation, 44 Northumberland Road, Ballsbridge, Dublin 4. Tel: 01 668 8244. Fax: 01 668 6769.

RYDER, Michael; MANAGING DIRECTOR EASON AND SON LTD.; *b* 1943; *educ* Trinity College Dublin, BA; *married;* 2*s;* 1 *da;* started in Eason, 1973, Managing Director, 1995 to date; Eason are the principal distributors of the written word in Ireland and the largest booksellers with shops throughout N. Ireland and the Republic; in 1999 they took over the well established Fred Hanna's bookshop in Nassau Street (Dublin) which will be their sole books only shop; former Chairman, Dublin City Centre Business Association, 1995-1998. Hobbies, rowing and Donegal. Contact: Eason & Sons Ltd., 80 Middle Abbey Street, Dublin 1. Tel: 01 873 3811. Fax: 01 873 3545.

SAUNDERS, John

SAUNDERS, John; PUBLIC RELATIONS CONSULTANT; *b* 1958; *educ* Belvedere College; *m* Jean O'Brien, Company Director; 1*s* 2 *da;* former RTE Radio and TV Sports Presenter; Managing Director, Pembroke Public Relations, 1981-90; Managing Director, Fleishman-Hillard Saunders, 1990 to date; the youthful looking head of Fleishman-Hillard Saunders, Ireland's largest corporate communications company with offices in Belfast and Dublin; the company has been awarded six PRCA awards in the past two years; member, Public Relations Institute of Ireland, Institute of Directors, Marketing Society; Clubs, Old Belvedere RFC, Fitzwilliam Lawn Tennis Club, Luttrelstown Golf Club. Hobbies, music, reading and tennis. Contact: Fleishman-Hillard Saunders, 15 Fitzwilliam Quay, Dublin 4. Tel: 01 618 8444. Fax: 01 660 2244.

SCALLON, Rosemary D.

SCALLON, Rosemary Dana née Brown; MEMBER OF THE EUROPEAN PARLIAMENT; *b* 1951; *educ* Thornhill Convent, Derry; *m* Damien Scallon; 2*s* 2 *da;* won the Eurovision Song Contest Singing *All Kinds of Everything* 1970 (No. 1 throughout Europe); international career incudes numerous recordings, television series and a film, *The Flight of the Doves;* accompanied husband / manager Damien to the US 1991; broadcasting career in the U.S. includes *Say Yes* on EWTN, the Catholic Cable Network with 30 million viewers worldwide; wrote and sang *We are One Body* for Papal visit to Denver 1993; recipient, the Rotary Harris Award 1995; Irish Presidential Candidate 1997, made political history as first ever nominee of County Councils; elected Member of the European Parliament for Connacht-Ulster 1999; a practising Catholic who espouses family values, strongly anti abortion; homely charisma has immense appeal for the conservative voter; a force to be reckoned with. Hobbies, embroidery, knitting and reading. Contact: European Parliament Offices, 43 Molesworth Street, Dublin 2. Tel: 01 605 7900. Fax: 01 605 7999.

SCALLY, Seamus; GROUP MANAGING DIRECTOR MUSGRAVE GROUP; *b* 1943; *educ* Carmelite

College, Moate, Co. Westmeath; *m* Carmel O'Neill; 2 *s* 2 *da;* Trainee Manager/ Manager, Five Star Supermarket, 1961-67; joined Musgrave Group, 1967, held various positions within the company, appointed Operations Director, Musgrave SuperValu-Centra, 1985; Chairman, Musgrave SuperValu-Centra, 1987 to date; voted *Checkout* magazine Person of the Year, 1988 and 1997; member, Marketing Institute of Ireland. The top man in the largest grocery wholesale group in the country (Musgraves' turnover in region of £1.2billion on an annualised basis); recognised as a down to earth Westmeath man who speaks the language of the retailer; highly regarded within the trade. Hobbies, golf, tennis and GAA. Contact: Musgrave Group, Head Office, Airport Road, Cork. Tel: 021 963 700.

SCALLY, Seamus

SCANLAN, Patricia; WRITER; *b* 1956; *educ* St. Pappins NS and Our Lady of Victories, GNS; Dominican College, Eccles Street; *single;* worked in Dublin Public Libraries from 1975-92; was first published in 1990; left DPL 1992; has been a full time writer since; novels include *City Girl, Apt. 3B, City Woman, Foreign Affairs, Promises Promises, Mirror Mirror, City Lives;* deeply involved in adult literacy, has published one literacy novel *Second Chance,* two more to follow; an extraordinarily prolific, successful and unassuming writer with over 2.5 million sales worldwide; a publisher's dream. Contact: Poolbeg Press Ltd., 123 Baldoyle Industrial Estate, Dublin 13. Tel: 01 832 1477. Fax: 01 832 1430.

SCANLON, Mark Fergal

SCANLON, Mark Fergal; AMATEUR CYCLIST; *b* 1980; *educ* Summerhill College, Sligo; *single*; An exceptional young sportsman, World Junior Road Racing Champion; In January 1999 signed a one year contract with the Dutch Rabobank Team; Awarded: Irish Cycling Federation, Sports Star of the Year, 1998; Texaco Sports Star of the Year, 1998; Sports Star of the Year - Ulster Bank & *Sligo Weekender;* Junior Road Race Champion, 1998; Junior Tour of Ireland, 1998; Het Volk Junior Classic, Belgium, 1998; World Junior Road Race Champion, 1998; Hobbies, TV, reading sports books and magazines, cinema. Contact: Irish Cycling Federation, 619 North Circular Road, Dublin 1. Tel: 01 855 1522.

SCOTT, Andrew James Patrick; ACTOR; *b* 1976; *educ* Ardtona House School, Churchtown, Dublin; Gonzaga College, Dublin; Trinity College, Samuel Beckett Centre (one year); *single*; stage appearances include: *Six Characters in search of an Author,* (Abbey Theatre), 1996; *A Woman of No Importance* (Abbey Theatre), 1996; *The Marriage of Figaro* (Abbey Theatre), 1996; *The Secret Fall of Constance Wilde* (Abbey Theatre), 1997; *The Lonesome West* (Druid), 1998; *Long Days Journey into Night* (Gate Theatre), 1998; film work includes: *Korea,* 1994; *The Budgie,* 1996; *Miracle at Midnight,* 1997; *Saving Private Ryan,* 1997; *Sweety Barrett,* 1998; Awards: nominated Best Actor, 1996, *Sunday Tribune,* Review of the Year; Actor of the Year, 1998; *Sunday Independent* Spirit of Life Arts Awards, 1999; nominated Best Supporting Actor - *Long Days Journey into Night*; *Irish Times* / ESB Theatre Awards, 1999. Hobbies, painting (received Bewleys national £5,000 bursary for the Arts, 1994 for a large watercolour entitled 'Grieving'), cinema, reading, writing, tennis and theatre. Contact: Lisa Richards Agency, 15 Lower Pembroke Street, Dublin 2. Tel: 01 662 4880.

SCOTT, Michael; PRODUCER, DIRECTOR AND COMPOSER; *b* 1956; *educ* Monkstown Park School, Dublin; University College Dublin, BA; former theatre director, Project Arts Centre; Programme Director, Dublin Theatre Festival; Director, Tivoli Theatre and RHA Downstairs; currently Artistic Director, SFX City Theatre; productions include *Bent, Torchlight and Laser Beams* (collaborated with Christopher Nolan), *The Woman in Black, The Wizard of Oz* and *Aspects of Love;* has written several productions including *Those Three Days* and his own adaptation of *Dracula*; composed the music for *Songs of Leaving* (for Siamse Tire); received particular acclaim for his original score *The Cuchulain Cycle* and two operas, *Purgatory* and *The Dreaming of the Bones,* both by W.B. Yeats; has worked with Wexford Festival Opera and directed several musicals; director and co-founder, Leinster Opera Studio with David Wray and Dr. Veronica Dunne; theatre productions have been seen in Ireland, England, Wales, Scotland, France, Germany, Iceland and the United States; *The Chuchulain Cycle* and *Purgatory* will tour America in 2000 and 2001. Contact: The Machine, 24 Upper Sherrard Street, Dublin 1. Fax: 01 874 5179.

SCOTT, Niall John Ultan; ARCHITECT; *b* 1940; *educ* Gonzaga College, Dublin; College of Technology, Bolton Street, Dip Arch; *m* Monica Edminson; 1 *stepson* 1 *stepdaughter;* joined Michael Scott & Partners, 1964, Associate, 1974; Director, Scott Tallon Walker Architects, 1976; Managing Director, Scott Tallon Walker Architects, UK, 1984; returned to Scott Tallon Walker Architects, Dublin with continued responsibility for managing London practice; designs include, Goffs Sales Complex, 1972, Marks & Spencer, Dublin, 1976, Chancery for Spanish Embassy, 1978, Dublin Port & Docks Port HQ, 1982, Light Source London, 1983, Sealark HQ, Barking, 1986 Leisure Development, Turkey, 1987, Fyffes HQ Offices, Basingstoke, 1988, Vangen Facility, Worcester, 1989, Church, Chelmsford, 1990, Winery, Morocco, 1990, Apartment Block, London Docklands, 1991, Office Development, Curzon Street, W1, 1992, Commercial Development, Croydon, 1993,

Vice-Chancellor House, University of Surrey, 1994; Fellow, Royal Institute of Architects of Ireland (FRIAI), Member, Royal Institute of British Architects (RIBA); awards include, Highly Commended RIAI Gold Medal, 1974-76 (Goffs); British Steel Colorcoat Building award, 1998 (commercial & warehousing, Basingstoke); RIAI Regional Awards 1998 (apartment building, Isle of Dogs); Civic Guildford Heritage Award 1996 (Vice Chancellor's Residence, University of Surrey); Civic Trust Award 1983, (Marks & Spencer plc, Belfast); member, Annabel's Club, London, Chelsea Arts Club, London. Contact: Scott Tallon Walker, 19 Merrion Square, Dublin 2. Tel: 01 676 0621. Fax: 01 661 3300.

SCOTT, Patrick

SCOTT, Patrick; PAINTER; *b* 1921; *educ* Monkstown Park; St. Columba's College, Rathfarnham; University College Dublin, BArch; *single;* Partner, in charge of projects, Michael Scott & Partners (Architects) 1945-60; gave up architecture in favour of full-time painting, 1960; his works have been exhibited worldwide and are in many public and private collections, including the Hugh Lane Municipal Gallery of Modern Art, Dublin, Hirschorn Gallery, Washington, Ulster Museum, Belfast, Museum of Modern Art, New York, and IMMA, Dublin; has had many tapestry commissions from among others, the Bank of Ireland, Bord Failte, Central Bank of Ireland, the European Parliament, Strasbourg, and St. Paul's School London; solo exhibitions include: White Stag Gallery, Dublin, (1944), XXX Biennale, Venice (1960), Dawson Gallery, Dublin (1961-77), Hamilton Galleries, London (1964), New Gallery, Belfast (1965), Oxford Gallery, Oxford (1978), Taylor Galleries, Dublin (1980, 1984, 1986, 1991, 1994), Annely Juda Fine Art, London (1980), Butler Gallery, Kilkenny Castle (1980), Douglas Hyde Gallery, Dublin (1981), Stirling Gallery, Scotland (1982), Parnham House, Dorset (1984); Retrospective Exhibition, Douglas Hyde Gallery, Dublin, BP Gallery, Brussels, (1990); Honorary Member, RIAI; Honorary Associate, NCAD; Honorary, RHA; member, Aosdána; Hon LLD, National University, Director, KDW; Governor, National Gallery, 1975-85. Hobby, enjoying life. Contact: Taylor Galleries, 16 Kildare Street, Dublin 2. Tel: 01 676 6055.

SCOTT-GALL, Ian Harold; CHIEF EXECUTIVE SILVERMINES PLC; *b* 1949; *educ* Stowe School; Manchester University, BSc (Hons); *m* Catherine Jane ----; 2*s*; joined Touche Ross, 1971-74; Finance Manager, Burmah Oil plc, 1974-84; Group Managing Director, Blick plc, 1984-98; Chief Executive, Silvermines plc, 1999 to date; member, Institute of Chartered Accountants - FCA; member, RSA, Institute of Directors. Hobbies, photography, travel and country pursuits. Contact: Silvermines Group plc, Gloucester Crescent, Wigston, Leicester LE18 4YN. Tel: 0044 116 222 2111. Fax: 0044 116 278 7545.

SHAW, Helen

SHAW, Helen; DIRECTOR OF RADIO, RTE; *b* 1962; *educ* Holy Faith, Glasnevin; University College Dublin, BA (Hons) MA (First Class); Higher Diploma. Journalism, DCU; *single*; Staff reporter, *Irish Times*, 1985-88; Producer, RTE, 1988-95; Head of Radio New & Current Affairs, Northern Ireland, 1996-97; RTE, Director of Radio, 1997 to date; Awarded Journalist of the Year (Features) for series in *Magill*, 1985; Journalist in Europe Scholarship, Paris, 1990-91; Young Europeans Essay Scholarship, Japan, 1993; Gold Sony Radio Awards, for coverage of Drumcree, 1997; Worked as an observer in South African Elections for 2 months, 1994. Hobbies, reading, creative writing, cinema, theatre, current affairs, world politics, friends and family. Contact: RTE, Donnybrook, Dublin 4. Tel: 01 208 3111. Fax: 01 208 3080.

SHEANE, Paul; CHIEF EXECUTIVE SHANNON DEVELOPMENT; *b* 1952; *educ* Wesley College, Dublin; Trinity College Dublin, BA, BAI (Mech. Eng); National University of Ireland, Galway, MBA; *m* Heather Plunkett; 2 *da;* Courtaulds Northern Weaving Division, (UK) 1973-75; Roan Consolidated Mines (Zambia) 1975-77; Howard Humphreys Consulting Engineers (Nairobi, Kenya) 1977-80; joined Shannon Free Airport Development Co. Ltd. 1980, Chief Executive 1992 to date; publications include numerous papers and presentations related to regional economic development; Chartered Engineer and Fellow, Institution of Engineers of Ireland (C Eng, FIEI); Chairman, National Technological Park, Limerick; Trustee, Bunratty Castle Ownership Trust. Hobbies, dinghy sailing, hill walking, opera and classical music. Contact: Shannon Development, Shannon, Co. Clare. Tel: 061 361 555. Fax: 061 361 903.

SHEEHAN, Garrett; SOLICITOR; *b* 1947; *educ* Gonzaga College; University College Dublin, BCL, LLB; Incorporated Law Society of Ireland, Solicitor; *m* Helen Spillane, Psychoanalyst; Assistant Solicitor, Guinan & Sheehan 1970-72; Principal, Garrett Sheehan & Company, 1972 to date. Contact: Garrett Sheehan & Co., 32 Francis Street, Dublin 8. Tel: 01 453 3477. Fax: 01 453 3528.

SHERIDAN, Jim; FILM DIRECTOR / SCRIPT WRITER; *b* 1949; *educ* St. Laurence O'Toole National School, Dublin; O'Connell Christian Brothers School, Dublin; University College Dublin, BA; *m* Frances Roe; 3 *da*; joined a bank for a short while, moved into the theatre as Assistant to Lelia Doolan, then Artistic Director of the Abbey Theatre; directed and wrote plays for the

Peacock; Artistic Director and Chairman of the Project 1976-80; ran The Children's T Company productions; Artistic Director The Irish Arts Centre (New York) 1981; collaborated with Noel Pearson 1987, directing the Oscar winning films, *My Left Foot* and *The Field;* script writer *Into The West* (Miramax); wrote, directed, co-produced (with Arthur Lappin) *In The Name of the Father;* co-scriptwriter (with Terry George) and co-producer (with Arthur Lappin) *Some Mother's Son* , directed by Terry George; scriptwriter, director and co-producer (with Arthur Lappin) *The Boxer;* co-producer (with Arthur Lappin) *Agnes Brown* directed by and starring Angelica Huston; recognised as an actor's director; a talented "Dub" with an international reputation. Hobbies, swimming and soccer. Contact: Hells Kitchen, 21 Mespil Road, Dublin 4. Tel: 01 667 5599.

SHERIDAN, Noel; DIRECTOR NATIONAL COLLEGE OF ART AND DESIGN; *b* 1936; *educ* Trinity College Dublin, DPA, BA, BComm; Columbia University, New York, MFA; *m* Liz Murphy; 1*s* 4 *da;* Painter (self-employed) 1960-75; Director, Experimental Art Foundation (EAF), Adelaide, South Australia, 1975-80; Director, National College of Art and Design, Dublin, 1980-89; Director, Perth Institute of Contemporary Art, Western Australia, 1989-93; Director, National College of Art and Design, Dublin, 1994 to date; member, AOSDANA, National Council for Education Awards (NCEA Ireland), AICA (Association Internationale des Critiques d'Art); recipient, J.B. McCauley Grant, Irish Arts Council, 1959, Represented Ireland, UNIESCO Convention of Young Painters, Paris, 1962, Carroll Prize for Painting, Living Art, Dublin, 1965 and 1969, Bevroot/Eckmeyer Scholarship, Columbia University, 1965-67, Emeritus Fellow, Australia Council, Australian Government, 1993; noted as an excellent administrator. Contact: National College of Art and Design, 100 Thomas Street, Dublin 8. Tel: 01 636 4260. Fax: 01 636 4267.

SHIELDS, Laurence Kyran; SOLICITOR; *b* 1950; *educ* St. Michael's College; Clongowes Wood College; University College Dublin, B.C.L. (Hons); Law Society of Ireland, *m* Helen Hackett; 1*s* 1*da;* Solicitor; Lecturer and Examiner, Company Law and Partnership, Law Society of Ireland, 1973-78; Lecturer, Institute of Public Administration, 1972 and 1973; Solicitor in private practice, 1972 to date; currently Senior Partner, L.K. Shields Solicitors, Company Director; President, Law Society of Ireland, 1997-98; President, Dublin Solicitors Bar Association, 1983-84; Associate, Institute of Taxation in Ireland; Fellow, Chartered Institute of Arbitrators; Council Member, International Bar Association; member, Fitzwilliam Lawn Tennis Club and K Club; awards include 2nd place B.C.L. Degree, UCD; awarded Special Certificate for Proficiency in 2nd and 3rd Law Examinations, Law Society of Ireland; Auditor, Solicitors Apprentices Debating Society of Ireland, 1971-72; member, UCD Faculty of Law Development Council; member, Disciplinary Scheme Appeal Board of Society of Actuaries in Ireland; member, Court Services Transitional Board. Hobbies, golf, swimming. Contact: L.K. Shields, 39-40 Upper Mount Street, Dublin 2. Tel: 01 661 0866. Fax: 01 661 0883.

SHIPSEY, Tom

SHIPSEY, Tom; CHIEF EXECUTIVE NATIONAL WHOLESALE; *b* 1960; *educ* St. Vincent's College, Castleknock; University College Dublin, BAgrSci (Hons); *m* Deirdre O' Doherty; 1*da*; Farm Manager, Waterford, 1984-89; Operations Manager, Monaghan Mushrooms, 1989-91; Commercial Manager, National Wholesale, Dublin, 1991-93; Group Manager, Keencost, Dublin, 1993-96; Chief Executive, National Wholesale, Dublin, 1996 to date; Rotary Foundation Scholar, University of Illinois, USA, 1983-84; Past Auditor, Agricultural Society, University College Dublin; member, Strandhill Golf Club, Sligo. Hobbies, football, golf, art and walking. Contact: National Wholesale, 12 Dundrum Business Park, Dublin 14. Tel: 01 296 6000. Fax: 01 296 6002.

SILKE, Raymond

SILKE, Raymond; BUSINESS DEVELOPMENT MANAGER IRISH NATIONWIDE AND GAA PLAYER; *b* 1970; *educ* St. Jarlath's College, Tuam; University of Limerick, BBusSt., Graduate Diploma in Education; *m* Sonia Nic Lochlainn; Teacher, (Business Studies, Maths and Accounting) CBS Roscommon Town, Roscommon, 1993-95; Teacher, (Accountancy and Business Studies), St. Gerard's College, Castlebar, 1995-96; Youth Projects Development Co-ordinator, City of Galway Vocational Education Committee, responsibilities included co-ordination & development of projects with particular emphasis on disadvantaged youth, early school leavers within the catchment area of Galway City, 1997-99; joined Irish Nationwide Building Society, as Business Development Manager for Galway Branch, 1999; played Sigerson & Collingwood football with University of Limerick, 1988-93; won five County Championships with Corofin since 1991; two Connacht Inter County & three Connacht Club Medals; Captain of All Ireland Winning Football Team, Galway, 1998, Captain of first Connacht team to win All Ireland Club Football Championship, 1998, with Corofin Football Club. Hobbies, all sport including soccer, golf, hurling, reading, movies and theatre, most activities that are 'a bit of craic'. Contact: Irish Nationwide Building Society, 11 Eyre Square, Galway. Tel: 091 566 177.

SIMPSON, David; CHARTERED ACCOUNTANT; *b* 1955; *educ* Synge Street Christian Brothers School; University College Dublin, BComm; *m* Catherine Martin; 2 *s* 1 *da*; Audit Senior, Stokes Kennedy Crowley, 1975-81, Founding Partner, BDO Simpson Xavier Chartered Accountants, 1982 to date; Managing Partner, 1987-93; Institute of Chartered Accountants in Ireland, Deputy President, 1999; Chairman Membership Services Directorate, 1998-99; Chairman, Finance & Resources Directorate, 1994-98; Chairman, Practice Review Committee, 1992-94. A former League of Ireland and Irish University International Soccer Player, 1974-75; Member, Skerries Golf Club; Honorary Treasurer, CYMS Terenure. Hobbies, soccer, golf and rugby. Contact: BDO Simpson Xavier, Merchants Quay, Dublin 8. Tel: 01 617 0100. Fax: 01 617 0111.

SINNOTT, Charles John

SINNOTT, Charles John; HOTELIER, COMPANY DIRECTOR; *b* 1947; *educ* Christian Brothers College, Cork; Terenure College, Dublin; *m* Bridget Nolan; 3 *s*; Trainee Manager, Gresham Hotel Dublin, 1966-70; Palace Hotel, Madrid, 1970-71; Deputy Manager, Talbot Hotel, Wexford, 1970-72; Deputy General Manager, Gresham Hotel Dublin, 1972-74, General Manager, Gresham Hotel Dublin, 1974-76; Managing Director, Trusthouse Forte (Irl.) Ltd., 1976-80; Proprietor, Connemara Gateway Hotel, 1980 to date, Connemara Coast Hotel, 1986 to date, Brooks Hotel in Dublin, 1997 to date; Chairman, Galvia Hospital Holdings, 1992 to date; Member of the Hibernian United Services Club, Fellow of the Irish Hotel and Catering Institute, Member of the Galway Chamber of Commerce and Industry, of the Irish Hotels Federation. Former Chairman and Director of the Western Regional Tourism Organisation, 1984-90; Former Director of Bord Failte, 1985-89; Former Chairman of Oughterard Tourist Association, 1989-93; Former Chairman of the Friends of the Galway Mentally Handicapped Association; Recipient of the UDT Endeavour Award for Tourism, 1983; Past Pupil of the Year, Terenure College, 1991; Seen as a proven hotelier in the process of creating a hotel chain. Hobbies, politics, walking and cars. Contact: Connemara Gateway Hotel, Oughterard, Co. Galway. Tel: 091 552 328.

SMIDDY, Alf

SMIDDY, Alf; MANAGING DIRECTOR, BEAMISH & CRAWFORD PLC; *b* 1962; *educ* Coláiste Iognáid Rís, Cork; University College Cork, B.Comm; Diploma in Corporate Direction; *m* Josephine, "Jo" McAuliffe; 2 *s* 1 *da*; Joined Price Waterhouse, 1983; qualified as Chartered Accountant, 1987; Joined Beamish & Crawford plc., 1988 as Financial Controller; Financial Director, Company Secretary, 1990; General Manager, 1992; Managing Director, 1995 to date; Fellow of the Institute of Chartered Accountants; Awarded Cork Business Person of the Year, 1997. Hobbies, swimming, horses and horse riding, sport, travel and leisure, entertainment. Contact: Beamish and Crawford Ltd., South Main Street, Cork. Tel: 021 276841. Fax: 021 272210

SMITH, Sheamus; OFFICIAL FILM CENSOR; *b* 1936; *educ* Monkstown Park Dun Laoghaire; University of British Columbia, Canada; New York Institute of Photography; *separated;* 1 *da;* Lighting Cameraman, RTE, 1961-63, Producer/Director, 1963-70, Editor, Current Affairs, 1970-75; Managing Director, National Film Studios of Ireland, 1975-82; freelance Producer/Director, 1982-85; Official Government Film and Video Censor, 1986 to date; recipient Golden Ear, Berlin Festival of Agricultural Films, 1968; film credits (as Producer/Director) include Peter Ustinov's *People, The Distant Drum* (Director); member, British Academy Film and Television Arts; Director, Elstree Ireland Ltd. A man committed to the celluloid art, both as film maker and censor; has top contacts worldwide in the industry; member, Elm Park Golf Club. Hobbies, golf, cooking and photography. Contact: Film Censor's Office, 16 Harcourt Terrace, Dublin 2. Tel: 01 676 1985. Fax: 01 676 1898.

SMURFIT, Michael; CHAIRMAN, CHIEF EXECUTIVE JEFFERSON SMURFIT GROUP PLC; *b* 1936; *educ* St. Mary's College, Rathmines; Clongowes Wood College; Management Training Continental Can Corp, USA; *m* Norma Treisman; (m dis); 2 *s* 2 *da*; *m* Birgitta Beimark; *(m dis)*; 2*s;* joined Jefferson Smurfit and Sons Ltd., 1955, corrugated box manufacturing business founded by father, Jefferson Smurfit; left the company in Dublin 1961, to form Jefferson Smurfit Packaging Ltd. (Lancashire); rejoined Jefferson Smurfit Group and appointed Director 1964, Joint Managing Director 1966, Deputy Chairman 1969, Chairman and Chief Executive, Jefferson Smurfit Group plc 1977 to date; Non Executive Chairman and Director, Smurfit Stone Container Corporation; Director: Jefferson Smurfit Trust Ltd., John Jefferson Smurfit Foundation, SIBV/MS Holdings Incorporated, Beach Hill Life and Pensions Ltd.; Fellow, International Academy of Management; conferred with Honorary Doctorate of Laws, Trinity College Dublin, NUI, University of Scranton, Pennsylvania; recipient of numerous honours and decorations, national and international; former Chairman, The Racing Board (1985-90); Honorary Irish Consul Monaco. Turned a successful family business into an internationally quoted company, ranked in the world's top nine hundred companies by *International Business Week*; a handsome, fast moving man, equally at home in boardroom, racecourse or golf course; said to be intolerant of incompetence and unquestionably loyal to old friends. Hobbies, golf, tennis, horse riding and skiing. Clubs include Monte Carlo Golf Club, Royal Dublin Golf Club, Woodbrook Golf Club (Honorary member), Walton Heath Golf Club (U.K.), Turnberry Isle Golf Club (U.S.) and K Club. Contact: Smurfit Group, Beech Hill, Dublin . Tel: 01 202 7000.

SMURFIT, Michael

SMURFIT, Norma, née Treisman; PRESIDENT IRISH YOUTH FOUNDATION; *b* 1939; *educ* in

London; *m* Michael Smurfit (*m dis*); 2*s* 2 *da*; President Irish Youth Foundation (fund raising body for national youth projects); Council member, Arthritis Foundation; Council member, Gaisce / President's Award (world wide youth achievement award); Chairperson First Step (job creation programme for start up entrepreneurs); Chairperson Famine Commemoration Fund, Children's Millennium Fund; Advisory Board Member, Ireland Fund; Board member, National History Museum Development Fund (London); Director, Smurfit Foundation; recognised as a dedicated worker for youth projects. Hobbies, cinema, theatre, television and collecting Irish art. Contact: Jefferson House, Eglinton Road, Dublin 4. Tel.: 01 260 0988.

SMYTH, John Joseph

SMYTH, John Joseph; GROUP MANAGING DIRECTOR FIRST ACTIVE PLC; *b* 1949; *educ* Blackrock College, Co. Dublin; Fellow, Chartered Institute of Bankers; Fellow, Chartered Institute of Secretaries and Administrators; *m* Jeanne Havelin; 4 *s;* Apprentice Auctioneer, St. Andrews Auctioneers, Dublin, 1968-69; Junior Negotiator, Albert Estate Agency, Dublin, 1969-70; Junior Negotiator, Morrisseys Auctioneers, Dublin; joined First National Building Society 1972; converted to First Active plc and floated on Dublin and London Stock Exchanges, 1998; Lending Officer, 1972-74, Assistant Branch Manager, Phibsborough, 1974-75, Network Relief Branch Manager, 1975-76, Personnel Manager, 1976-88, General Manager, Development, 1989-91, Group Operations Director, Secretary, 1991-93, Group Managing Director, 1993 to date; contributed to business publications; Fellow, Irish Auctioneers and Valuers Association - FIAVI; Fellow, Irish Institute of Bankers; President, Republic of Ireland Region - Institute of Chartered Secretaries and Administrators, 1994-95; Vice President - European Mortgage Federation, 1996; President, Blackrock College Union, 1995-96; Council member, Institute of Directors in Ireland; Irish Mortgage and Savings Association; Clubs, Blackrock College R.F.C., Foxrock Golf Club, Oughterard Golf Club, St. Stephen's Green Club. Hobbies, sport - rugby, golf, Gaelic games, soccer etc., music - jazz, sixties popular music, classical, reading - biographies, history, collecting historical letters, autographs, travel - Ireland and abroad. Contact: First Active plc, Skehan House, Booterstown, Co. Dublin. Tel: 01 283 1801. Fax: 283 4734.

SMYTH, Samuel 'Sam'; JOURNALIST / WRITER / BROADCASTER; *b* 1945; *educ* Technical High School, Belfast; *m* Janet Martin (*m dis*); 1*s* 1*da*; *m* Faela Watson; 1*da*; worked for a time as messenger boy; apprentice electrician; show business impressario bringing U.K. and U.S. acts for all Ireland Tours; Showbusiness Columnist, *City Week*, Belfast; Manager, Romanos Group Entertainment Centre, 1967-71; Director of Entertainment, City of Belfast 1972; Reporter, *Spotlight Magazine*, 1972; Reporter, *Sunday World*, 1973-87; Leader Writer/Features Editor, *Star*, 1987-88; joined Sunday Independent, 1988; moved to *Irish Independent*, 1995 to date; Columnist, *Sunday Tribune*, 1997 to date; Presenter, *Sunday Supplement*, (Today FM), 1998 to date; publications include, *Dear John*, co-writer with Michael Nugent, 1994; *Thanks a Million Big Fella*, 1997 both topped best seller lists in Ireland; awarded, Journalist of the Year Award, 1991 (Greencore story), 1997 (Lowry/Haughey story), In Dublin Journalist's Journalist Award 1997; widely regarded as one of the finest investigative journalists in the country. Hobby, walking. Contact: Irish Independent, 90 Middle Abbey Street, Dublin 1. Tel: 01 705 5333.

SOMERS, Jimmy

SOMERS, Jimmy; GENERAL PRESIDENT OF S.I.P.T.U.; *b* 1939; *educ* C.B.S. North Brunswick Street, Dublin; College of Industrial Relations, Diploma in Trade Union Studies; *m* Alice McGrath; 2*s* 1 *da;* commenced employment as a full-time Trade Union Official with the then Irish Transport & General Workers' Union, served in a number of Branches in Dublin and Galway, as well as the Union's Head Office, 1960; became Branch Secretary of the ITGWU's Civil Aviation Branch, 1972; National Industrial Group Secretary with responsibility for the Food, Drink, Tobacco and Hotel, Catering and Tourism sectors, 1983; following establishment of SIPTU, which was formed by the amalgamation of the Irish Transport & General Workers' Union and the Federated Workers' Union of Ireland appointed as Assistant National Executive Officer, dealing mainly with industrial affairs within the Private Sector, 1990; elected SIPTU Vice President, 1994; elected SIPTU General President, 1997; member, Congress team which meets quarterly with the Government and Employers to review the Partnership Programme, member, Labour Relations Commission, Convention Bureau of Ireland, National Economic and Social Council and various European and International Trade Union Committees, board member of Bord Fáilte, 1998 to date, member of the Labour Party, former Labour Party member of Dublin City Council and Dáil candidate for Dublin North Central. Hobbies, sport, politics, walking, swimming, reading, gardening. Contact: SIPTU, Liberty Hall, Dublin 1. Tel: 01 874 9731. Fax: 01 874 9368.

SOMERS, Michael; CHIEF EXECUTIVE NATIONAL TREASURY MANAGEMENT AGENCY; *educ* St. Mary's, Rathmines; University College Dublin, BComm., MA, PhD Econ.; joined Foras Tionscàil 1960-63; Department of Finance, 1963-68; Central Bank, 1968-70; Assistant Secretary, Department of Finance, 1985-87; appointed Secretary, National Debt Management, 1987-90; Chief Executive National Treasury Management Agency, 1990 to date; member, Audit Committee of European Investment Bank; Director, Stock Exchange; Director, UCD Foundation; Council member, Dublin

Chamber of Commerce; Council member, Financial Services Investment Authority; regarded as the mandarin of State finance; one of the most professional borrowers in the Western World; a finance mandarin who has little time for the slower pace of Government Departments. Contact: National Treasury Management Agency, Treasury Building, Grand Canal Street, Dublin 2. Tel: 01 676 2266. Fax: 01 676 6661.

SOUTER, Betty Pamela "Camille", née Holmes; PAINTER; *b* 1929; *educ* Glengara Park School, Dun Laoghaire; Guys Hospital (London), S.R.N.; *m* Gordon Souter (*m dis*); *m* Frank Morris *(decd)*; 1*s* 4 *da;* a self taught artist, held first solo exhibition 1956; exhibited with Living Art, Independent Artists, Municipal Gallery, Twelve Irish Painters (New York), Ulster Museum, Royal Hibernian Academy, Oireachtas, Dawson Gallery, Festival International de la Peinture (Haute de Cagnes, France), Monaco, Project Art Centre, The Delighted Eye London/Dublin, Douglas Hyde Gallery, Taylor Gallery; hangs in private collections and in Hugh Lane Gallery, Ulster Museum, Crawford Municipal Gallery, The Arts Council; Awards include Italian Government Scholarship, Landscape Prize at Oireachtas (twice), Gainey Award, Grand Prix International d'Art Contemporain de Monte Carlo; Claremorris National Art Competition, Eva (Limerick); awarded Doctorate of Laws (NUI) 1986, O'Malley Art Award 1998, member, Aosdána, Irish Meteorological Society, R.N.L.I. Shoreline; Club, United Arts Club; regarded as the painter's painter. Hobbies, the Earth, all its natural and man made uses - the changes and consequent results, meteorology, geology and medicine. Contact: The Taylor Galleries, 16 Kildare Street, Dublin 2. Tel: 01 676 6055.

SPARKS, Brian P

SPARKS, Brian P.; MANAGING DIRECTOR, McCANN ERICKSON; *b* 1953; *educ* Terenure College, University College Dublin; *m* Rosmund Sandys; 3 *s;* Marketing Manager, Guinness Ireland, 1980-88; Marketing Director, Guinness, Africa, Malaysia, London, 1988-96; Managing Director, McCann Erickson, 1996 to date. Hobbies, Keeping fit, rugby, golf; Clubs, Lansdowne Rugby Club, Blainroe Golf Club, Elm Park Golf Club. Contact: McCann-Erickson Dublin, Hambleden House, 19-26 Lower Pembroke Street, Dublin 2. Tel: 01 676 6366. Fax: 01 676 7077.

SPARKS, Gregory Gerard; PARTNER FARRELL GRANT SPARKS; *b* 1951; *educ* Chanel College, Coolock; University College Dublin, BComm; Institute of Chartered Accountants; *m* Catherine Hayes; 1*s* 3 *da;* worked in industry, 1977-82; established practice 1982; seconded to Tanaiste's Office as Programme Manager for Dick Spring, 1993-97; member, Institute of Chartered Accountants; member, St. Annes Golf Club. Hobbies, family and reading. Contact: Farrell-Grant-Sparks, Molyneux House, Bride Street, Dublin 8. Tel: 01 418 2000. Fax: 01 418 2050.

SPENCE, Susan, née Coffey; CO-FOUNDER AND DIRECTOR SOFTCO GROUP; *b* 1960; *educ* Loreto Abbey, Dalkey; Diploma Computer Programming; *m* Nigel Spence; 2*s*; held management positions with Hewlett Packard, McDonnell Douglas and Philips BV, 1981-90; Co-founded SoftCo with Jim Coffey 1990, currently Director, SoftCo Ireland, SoftCo UK, SoftCo America Inc and eCom Ireland; member, Institute of Project Managers of Ireland, Irish Computer Society, Irish Management Institute; awarded Veuve Clicquot Business Woman of the Year 1999; Chamber of Commerce - Company of the Year 1994; member, Hermes Hockey Club. Hobbies, hockey (represented Leinster and Ireland in the 1980s), all sports, literature and politics. Contact: SoftCo Ltd., South County Business Park, Leopardstown, Dublin 18. Tel: 01 294 2420. Fax: 01 294 2442.

SPRING, Richard "Dick

SPRING, Richard "Dick"; POLITICIAN; *b* 1950; *educ* Mount St. Joseph's, Roscrea; Trinity College Dublin, BA; Kings Inns, BL; *m* Kristi Hutcheson; 2*s* 1 *da;* practiced briefly at the Bar; elected to Kerry County Council, Tralee Urban Council and Fenit Harbour Commission, 1979; elected Labour Dail Deputy for Kerry North, 1981; Leader of the Labour Party 1982-1997; served as Deputy Prime Minister in three Coalition Governments, 1982-87, 1993-94, 1994-97; he also held ministerial office in Justice, Energy, Environment and Foreign Affairs; involved in Anglo-Irish developments over the past fifteen years, including the negotiation of the Anglo-Irish Agreement of 1985 and the Downing Street Declaration of 1993; co-chaired the British-Irish Intergovernmental Conference in 1993-97; as Foreign Minister he represented Ireland at the General Council of the EU, Chairman 1996; Fellow, Salzburg Seminar; Associate Fellow, Kennedy School of Government, Harvard; International Counsel to the Washington/Boston law firm Mintz, Levin, Cohen, Ferris, Glovsky and Popeo; Director, Fexco (Killorglin), Sifco (Cork); a noted sportsman, played intercounty football and hurling with Kerry and won three caps with Irish Rugby Team; although a backbencher, remains a powerful force within his party; a politician of stature on the national and international stage. Contact: Dail Eireann, Leinster House, Kildare Street, Dublin 2. Tel: 01 618 3333.

STACK, The Rev. Thomas; CLERIC, PARISH PRIEST, MILLTOWN; *b* 1933; *educ* Crescent College, Limerick; University College Dublin; Harvard University, US; ordained as a priest of the Dublin Archdiocese, 1958; has worked in both pastoral and journalistic fields; frequent media spokesper-

son; occasional scriptwriter/presenter/researcher, Radharc Films; weekly columnist, *The Irish Catholic*, contributor to numerous newspapers and journals. A noted raconteur and communicator, represents for many a contemporary presence of the Dublin archdiocese. Hobby, reading. Contact: The Irish Catholic, 55 Lower Gardiner Street, Dublin 1. Tel: 01 855 5619. Fax: 01 836 4805.

STAINES, Michael; SOLICITOR; *b* 1953; *educ* Sandymount High School; University College Dublin, BCL; Solicitor, LLM; University of Amsterdam, Dip Eur. Integration; *m* Doirbhile Flanagan; 4 *s;* joined the office of John J. O'Hare & Co., 1976-85; opened own firm, 1985, Michael A. Staines; recognised as one of the most prominent criminal lawyers in the country; member, Law Society, Kilmacud Crokes, Chairman, Wexford Centre Project, member, Adventure Sports Project. Hobbies, sport (particularly football & running), mountain walking, music and French. Contact: Michael A . Staines, 25 Phoenix Street, Dublin 7. Tel: 01 873 1366. Fax: 01 872 6239.

STANFORD, Alan; ACTOR; *b* 1949; *educ* Cowes, Isle of Wight; Guildhall School of Music and Drama, London; *m* Sharon Harris; 2 *s*; Has nearly thirty years experience as a leading actor and director in the Irish Theatre working with most of the major companies; Director of Theatre at the Project Arts Centre for four years, directing and appearing in many productions, his most notable performance being de Sade in *Marat/Sade*; Best known for his work at the Gate Theatre, Dublin over the past twenty years, roles include Salieri in *Amadeus*, Astrov in *Uncle Vanya*, Higgins in *Pygmalion*, Valmont in *Les Liaisons Dangereuses*, Rochester in *Jane Eyre*, Victor in *Private Lives* and many roles by Alan Ayckbourn and Oscar Wilde, his performance as Herod in Oscar Wilde's *Salome* has been acclaimed internationally, during the Beckett Festival he performed as Pozzo in *Waiting for Godot* and as Hamm in *Endgame*, performances he repeated to considerable critical acclaim at the Lincoln Center in New York; As director, his work includes; *Hamlet, Othello, Macbeth, Pride and Prejudice, The Picture of Dorian Gray*, which he co-adapted, *Great Expectations, A Tale of Two Cities, The Collection*, staring Harold Pinter, *Lady Windermere's Fan, The Weeping of Angels, Cyrano de Bergerac*; Film and television work includes *Educating Rita, The Irish R.M., The Treaty, Moll Flanders* and *Animal Farm*; Former Vice President, Irish Actors Equity, member Amnesty International; granted Irish citizenship, 1990; Member C.R.C., Department of Foreign Affairs. An extremely popular actor of great versatility; has a strong sense of national and community involvment; active member of the Progressive Democrats. Hobbies, reading, writing, gardening and drinking claret. Contact: Agent, First Call Management, 29-30 Dame Street, Dublin 2. Tel: 01 679 8401.

STAPLETON, David F; CHIEF OF STAFF OF THE DEFENCE FORCES; *b* 1937; *educ* CBS Clonmel; Graduate of Staff College in Camberley, U.K.; *m* Maureen Dillon; 1*s* 3 *da;* Commissioned in the Defence Forces, 1957; held a series of Appointments in the Supply and Transport Corps and served as an Instructor in the Command and Staff School, Military College; first President of the Representative Association of Commissioned Officers in 1990-92; served as OC 6 Brigade; became Director of the Supply and Transport Corps in 1991; promoted Brigadier Gen, Jan.'1995 and Major General, Feb. 1995; served as Quartermaster General; Force Commander, UNDOF in the Golon Heights, 1998; appointed Chief of State, 1998 to date. Contact: Chief of Staff, Parkgate, Dublin 8. Tel: 01 837 9911.

STEPHENS, Stewart; MANAGING DIRECTOR GULLIVER INFORES SERVICES LTD.; *b* 1962; *educ* Ashton School, Cork; University College Dublin, BAgSc., MAgSc; UNE Armidale, (Australia) PhD Genetics; *m* Dr Joan Cleary; 1*s* 1 *da;* joined FEXCO (Foreign Exchange Company) in Killorglin, Co. Kerry, Managing Director, Gulliver InfoRes Services Ltd., 1997 to date. Hobbies, reading and fishing. Contact: Gulliver InfoRes Services Ltd., Killorglin, Co. Kerry. Tel: 066 92200.

STEPHENSON, Samuel, "Sam"; ARCHITECT; *b* 1933; *educ* Belvedere College Dublin, College of Technology, Bolton Street; FRIAI, MSIA; *m* Bernadette Flood; 2 *s* 2 *da;* (*m dis*); *m* Caroline Sweetman; 2 *s;* founding Partner Stephenson Gibney and Associates; currently operates practice, Sam Stephenson & Company in London and Dublin; projects completed include the Central Bank (Dublin), ESB Offices and Bord na Mona offices (Dublin), Civic Offices; member and exhibitor, RHA, an architect who had a considerable, sometimes controversial, influence on the skyline of Dublin, a cultured and charismatic man. Hobbies, painting and cooking. Contact: Fax: 01 624 6233.

STEWART, Ercus; SENIOR COUNSEL/BARRISTER; *b* 1949; *educ* Colaiste Mhuire, Dublin; University College Dublin; King's Inns, BL; *m* Ria Stassen, Secondary School Teacher; 2*s* 2 *da;* called to the Bar 1970; called to the Inner Bar 1982; called to the Bar, Northern Ireland (1976), England and Wales (1982); New South Wales (1991); practice in international and domestic commercial arbitration and litigation; Lecturer in Law to: Kings Inns, University College Dublin; Fellow, Chartered Institute of Arbitrators (London); Honorary member: Institute of Occupational

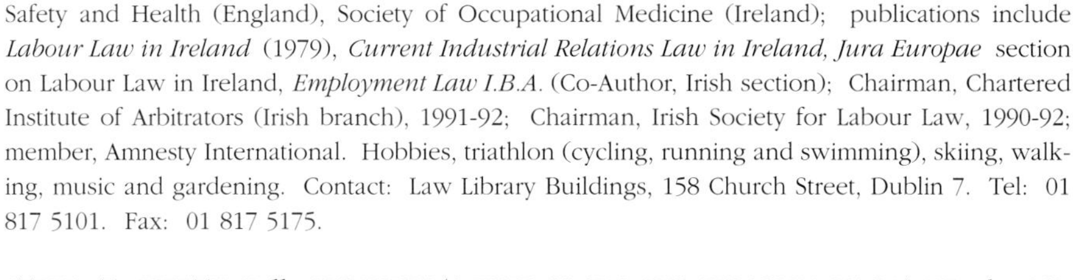

Safety and Health (England), Society of Occupational Medicine (Ireland); publications include *Labour Law in Ireland* (1979), *Current Industrial Relations Law in Ireland, Jura Europae* section on Labour Law in Ireland, *Employment Law I.B.A.* (Co-Author, Irish section); Chairman, Chartered Institute of Arbitrators (Irish branch), 1991-92; Chairman, Irish Society for Labour Law, 1990-92; member, Amnesty International. Hobbies, triathlon (cycling, running and swimming), skiing, walking, music and gardening. Contact: Law Library Buildings, 158 Church Street, Dublin 7. Tel: 01 817 5101. Fax: 01 817 5175.

STEWART LIBERTY, Nell; PUBLISHER/OWNER SOCIAL AND PERSONAL MAGAZINE; *b* 1953; *educ* Derry High School; Oxford College of Further Education; *m* Joe Beattie; trained in China Restoration with Desiree Short (Dublin); worked in the Collectibles Department, Sothebys (London); freelance journalist, contributed to *The Mail on Sunday, Hello, The Sunday Express* (UK) as well as Irish newspapers and magazines; Managing Editor, Irish Tatler Publications, 1986-93; purchased the title *Social & Personal* from the estate of the late Sir Robert Maxwell; great grand niece of Sir Arthur Liberty, founder of Liberty in Regent Street, (London); member, Coollattin Golf Club, Shillelagh and District Foxhounds. Hobbies, golf and gardening. Contact: Social and Personal, The Yellow House, Coollattin, Shillelagh, Co. Wicklow. Tel: 055 29403. Fax: 055 29441.

STOKES, Niall; PUBLISHER; *b* 1951; *educ* Synge Street Christian Brothers School; University College Dublin, BA; *m* Maureen Sheehy, Company Director; 2*s*; started work as a freelance Journalist with *The Irish Times* and *Irish Independent;* Founder, *Book Out,* Dublin based magazine 1972-73; Editor, *Scene* magazine 1976-77; Founder / Publisher, *Hot Press* (Ireland's top selling popular music magazine) 1977 to date; recipient of Irish Family Planning Association (IFPA) Award for Awareness of Sexuality; publications include *The U2 File* (1985), *U2 - Three Chords and the Truth* (1990); Guitarist with Brothers who have released an album, *Torch* (1991); member, NUJ; a dynamic editor who has broadened the magazine's influence by focusing the attention of international record companies and the media on Irish music makers; notable also for controversial interviews with such luminaries as Mary Robinson, Charles Haughey and Gay Byrne. Hobbies, music, reading and soccer. Contact: Hot Press, 13 Trinity Street, Dublin 2. Tel: 01 679 5077.

SULLIVAN, Edmond F; SECRETARY-GENERAL, DEPT OF SOCIAL, COMMUNITY AND FAMILY AFFAIRS; *b* 1952; *educ* St. Aidan's CBS, Whitehall; Institute of Public Administration, Dip AdminSc.; Trinity College Dublin, B.Sc.; Dublin City University, Dip Info.Tech.; *m* Frances Twomey; 1*s* 2 *da;* Executive Officer, Dept. of Social Welfare, 1970; Higher Executive Officer, Dept. of Public Service, Management Services Unit, 1976; Assistant Principal, Dept. of Social Welfare, 1980; IT & Policy Divisions, 1986; Assistant Secretary, Social Welfare Services, 1990, Director-General, (DSW), 1995; Secretary-General, Department of Social, Community and Family Affairs, 1997 to date; Council Member, Economic and Social Research Institute (ESRI); member (Chairman, Ireland Section), European Institute of Social Security (EISS). Hobbies, reading and sport. Contact: Department of Social, Community and Family Affairs, Store Street, Dublin 1. Tel: 01 874 3905.

SUTHERLAND, Peter

SUTHERLAND, Peter CHAIRMAN & MANAGING DIRECTOR GOLDMAN SACHS INTERNATIONAL; *b* 1946; *educ* Gonzaga College; University College Dublin; King's Inns; *m* Maruja Cabria Valcarcel; 2*s* 1 *da*; called to the Bar 1969; called to the Inner Bar 1980; called to the English Bar (Middle Temple); called to the New York Bar. Admitted to practice before the Supreme Court of the United States. Attorney General of Ireland (1981-84); EC Commissioner responsible for Competition Policy (1985-89); Chairman, Allied Irish Banks, 1989-93; Chairman and Managing Director Goldman Sachs International, 1995 to date; non Executive Co-Chairman of BP Amoco plc (1998 to date) former Chairman of the British Petroleum Company plc. Board member: ABB Asea Brown Boveri Ltd.; Investor AB; Telefonaktiebolaget LM Ericsson. He is Chairman of the Overseas Development Council (Washington) and an Advisory Board member of Allianz. Recipient of nine honorary doctorates from universities in Europe and America; awarded an honorary fellowship of the London Business School in recognition of his contribution to business and trade (1997); the first commissioner to be awarded the Gold Medal of the European Parliament (1988); other awards include the first European Law Prize (Paris 1988); The Grand Cross of Civil Merit (Spain 1989); the Grand Cross of King Leopold II (Belgium 1989); the New Zealand Commemorative Medal (1990); Chevalier de la Legion d'Honneur (France 1993); Commandeur du Wissam (Morocco 1994); the Order of Rio Branco (Brazil 1996) and the Grand Cross of the Order of Infante Dom Henrique (Portugal 1998); Honorary Consul for Uruguay in Ireland; awarded the Robert Schuman Medal for work for European integration; the Irish People of the Year Award (1989); the Consumer for World Trade Annual Award (1994); the David Rockefeller International Leadership Award (1998); Publications include the book *Premier Janvier 1993 ce qui va Changer en Europe* (1989) and numerous articles in law journals. Chaired the Committee that reported to the EEC Commission on the functioning of the Internal Market after 1992 (the Sutherland Report). An astute businessman with unique international networking skills and an impeccable sense of timing. Clubs, Lansdowne FC (former Captain), UCD RFC (former Captain), Fitzwilliam LTC, Hibernian United Services Club, Royal Irish Yacht Club and Milltown Golf Club. Hobbies, rugby, tennis and reading. Contact: Goldman Sachs International, Peterborough Court, 133 Fleet Street, London EC 4A 2BB. Tel: 0044 171 774 1000. Fax: 0044 171 774 4477.

SWAN, Charles Francis Thomas; TRAINER, JOCKEY; *b* 1968; *educ* Wilson's Hospital School, Headford, Co. Meath; *m* Tina Daly; entered into family tradition of trainer and jockey; rode 59 flat winners including six listed and one group race; major National Hunt wins include: Irish Champion Hurdle, 1991, 1998, 1999, Grand National 1993, Smurfit Champion Hurdle (Cheltenham) 1998; nominated Champion Jockey nine times, holds N.H. record for 150 winners in a season; attained trainers licence, 1998; recipient, Texaco Sport Star of the Year, 1992, Ballygowan Sport Award, 1993; has been the subject of an authorised biography by Michael Clower, *Champion Charlie*; Hobbies, golf, water skiing, tennis, rugby. Contact: The Cobs, Modreeny, Cloughjordan, Co. Tipperary. Tel/Fax: 0505 42410.

SWEENEY, Brody; MANAGING DIRECTOR O'BRIEN'S IRISH SANDWICH BARS; *b* 1961; *educ* DCU Business Course; *m* Lulu -----; 3*s* 1 *da;* worked in Pronto Print Irish franchise, built it up to sixteen outlets; opened O'Brien's Irish Sandwich Bars 1988; ICI bought 20% of company for £1m in 1999; O'Brien's chain has a combined turnover, including franchises, of £8m; as well as Ireland there are outlets in Germany, the UK and US; an entrepreneur who has hit on a winner. Contact: O'Brien's Irish Sandwich Bars, 24 South William Street, Dublin 2. Tel: 01 671 5176.

SWEENEY, Eric; COMPOSER; *b* 1948; *educ* St. Patrick's Cathedral Grammar School; Trinity College Dublin, Conservatorio di Santa Cecilia Rome; Ulster University; Mus.B, MA, DPhil, LRAM, LRSM, Dip Rome Conservatoire; *married* ; 1 *s* 2 *da;* Lectured at College of Music Dublin and Trinity College; Choral Director in RTE, 1980-82; Currently Head of Music, Waterford Institute of Technology and organist/choirmaster of Christ Church Cathedral, Waterford; member, Aosdána, The Arts Council (1989-93); Visiting Scholar in Composition at University of Illinois 1998; Composer in Residence, Newport Festival Rhode Island, 1995 and Young European Strings 1996; Compositions include: *The Blackberry Blossom, The Windhover,* Sonata (for piano), *Deirdre,* 2 symphonies, *Dance, Music, Circles,* Concerto for saxophone, Concertino for trumpet (for orchestra), *Mandala Suite, Strings in the Earth and Air,* String quartet, *Combra* (for strings), *The Bright Seraphim, Adventus, Movement* (for organ), *Missa Brevis, The Moon Cradle, Memorials, Deise Dei* (for voices) *Pulsation, Refrains, Babylon, "Its the rhythm that counts",* Quatrain, Watermusic, Drive (for multiple keyboards) Duo, *Acclamations, Dance Clarion Air* (for wind); has received commissions from: Royal Philharmonic Orchestra, European Music for Youth, Newport Festival Rhode Island, USA, Abbey Theatre, Festivall International de Musique Universitaire, Belfort, France, GPA International Piano Competition, RTE, Kilkenny Arts Week, Cork International Choral Festival, Municipalité de Saint Herblain, France, Festival in Great Irish Houses. Chairman, Symphony Club of Waterford, member, Aosdána. Hobbies, gardening, walking, food and wine, languages. Contact: Waterford Institute of Technology, Waterford. Tel: 051 302000. Fax: 051 378292.

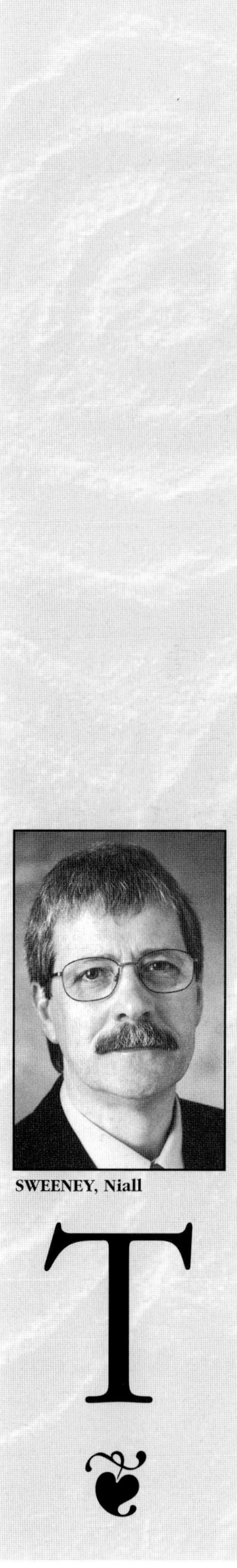

SWEENEY, Niall

SWEENEY, Niall; OFFALY COUNTY MANAGER; *b* 1948; *educ* St. Columba's CBS, Tullamore, Co. Offaly; University College Dublin, Civil Engineering (Hons); *m* Dolores Hughes; 3*s* 2 *da;* Consulting Engineer, based in Dublin, 1971-73; Executive Engineer, Offaly County Council, 1973-81, Senior Executive Engineer, Laois County Council, 1981-86; Senior Executive Engineer, Offaly County Council, 1986-90; County Engineer, Clare County Council, 1990-97; County Manager, Offaly County Council, 1997 to date; Chartered Member and Fellow, Institution of Engineers of Ireland; awards include, Gold Medal, Leaving Certificate and University Scholarship. Hobbies, walking, golf, reading, painting and photography. Contact: Offaly County Council, Courthouse, Tullamore, Co. Offaly. Tel: 0506 21419. Fax: 0506 41160.

T

TALLON, Ronald; ARCHITECT; *b* 1927; *educ* Colaiste Mhuire, Dublin; University College Dublin, BArch; *m* Nora Vize; 1 *s* 4 *da*; Architect with the Board of Works prior to joining Michael Scott's practice; Senior Partner in Scott Tallon Walker Architects 1958 to date, Chairman 1975 to date; Design projects include: Carrolls Building (Dundalk), Genetics, Pharmacy and Computers Building, (Trinity College Dublin), School of Engineering Aula Maxima and Biotechnology Buildings (University College Dublin), Masterplanning for Galway University and Dublin Institute of Technology, New Civic Offices Dublin; recipient of Triennial Gold Medal of RIAI - twice - for RTE Buildings, Donnybrook, 1964 and GEC Factory, Dundalk, 1970, RIAI Medal for Housing, 1980; awarded Papal Knighthood 1980; conferred with an Honorary Doctorate of Laws, NUI, 1990; Director, Gate Theatre; FRIAI, RIBA. Regarded as Ireland's most distinguished architect. Hobby, has commissioned many works of art for private and public collections. Contact: Scott Tallon Walker Architects, 19 Merrion Square, Dublin 2. Tel: 01 676 0621. Fax: 01 661 3300.

TANSEY, Paul; ECONOMIC CONSULTANT; *b* 1949; *educ* Blackrock College; Trinity College

Dublin, BA (Mod); London School of Economics - Research; Trinity College Dublin, MBA (First Class); *m* Olivia O'Leary; 1 *da;* Sub-Editor, Business Reporter, Economics Correspondent, Assistant Editor, *The Irish Times*, 1973-83; Deputy Editor and Economics Columnist, *The Sunday Tribune*, 1983-95; Managing Partner, Tansey, Webster Associates (Economic Consultants, Dublin) 1986 to date; Adjunct Professor of Economics, University of Limerick, 1997 to date; Labour Market Expert - Ireland European Social Fund, 1997 to date; books include *Ireland At Work - Economic Growth and the Labour Market 1987-97* (Oak Tree Press, 1998), *Making the Irish Labour Market Work* (Gill and Macmillan); recipient, Sir Charles Harvey Award/Irish Management Institute (1988), A.T. Cross Journalism Award Commentator of the Year (1993); member, Irish Economics Association, Carlow Farmers' Hunt, Monkstown Lawn Tennis Club. Hobbies, showjumping *Glenbrook King* and *Sorrento Lad* on the National Amateur Circuit - with diminishing success. Contact: 10 Pembroke Mews, Dublin 4.

TATTON, Oliver; CHIEF EXECUTIVE VOLUNTARY HEALTH INSURANCE BOARD; *b* 1964; *educ*; CBS, Cashel; University College Dublin, B Ch Eng.; University of South Africa, Industrial Psychology; Insead, France, MBA; *m* Beatriz de sa Ferreira Villanova; 1 *s* 2 *da*; Assistant Managing Director, John Somers Estanhos Ltd., Brazil, 1988; Product & Production Manager, Heraus Holding GmbH, 1989-90, Sales & Marketing Manager / International Subsidiaries Director, 1992, General Manager, (Hanau, Germany), 1993-1996; Chief Executive, Irish Trade Board; Non-executive Member of the Board of Forfas, 1996-98; Acting Chief Executive, Voluntary Health Insurance Board, 1998 to date. Contact: VHI House, Lower Abbey Street, Dublin 1. Tel: 01 872 4499. Fax: 01 874 1950.

TAYLOR, David; ARMY OFFICER; *b* 1942; *educ* St. Ignatius College, Galway; The Military College; *m* Margaret Quinn; 2 *s* 1 *da*; Cadet 1961, 2 Lieut. 1962, Lieut. 1964, Captain 1969, Comdt. 1977, Lieut.-Col. 1990, Col. 1994, Brig.-Gen. 1996, present appointment, G.O.C. 1st Southern Brigade; awards include, U.N. Peacekeeping Medals, UNFICYP 1967, UNTSO 1973, UNDOF 1974, UNIFIL 1980, 1989; member, Cork Golf Club, Galway Golf Club. Hobbies, personal fitness, sport, music and travel. Contact: Collins Barracks, Cork. Tel: 021 397 577.

TAYLOR, John; ART DEALER; *b* 1948; *educ* De La Salle Brothers; *m* Mary Preece, Dept. of an Taoiseach; 2 *s* 1 *da;* Manager, Dawson Gallery, 1964-78 (working with Leo Smith); Director, (with brother, Patrick), Taylor Galleries, Dublin, 1978 to date; the Gallery represents many leading Irish and international artists, including Louis le Brocquy, Brian Bourke, Patrick Scott, Camille Souter and Tony O'Malley; member, Irish Contemporary Art Galleries Association; an established Gallery representing the various strands of Irish Art. Contact: Taylor Galleries, 16 Kildare Street, Dublin 2. Tel: 01 676 6055.

TEAHON, Patrick

TEAHON, Patrick, "Paddy"; SECRETARY GENERAL, DEPARTMENT OF THE TAOISEACH; *b* 1945; *educ* St. Brendan's College, Killarney; University College Dublin; Institute of Social Studies, Netherlands; Trinity College Dublin/Irish Management Institute; Fellow of Irish Management Institute; *m* Mary Morrissey; 1 *s* 2 *da*; entered the Civil Service, 1962; served in Departments of Posts and Telegraphs, Finance, Economic Planning and Development and Department of the Taoiseach. Secretary General, Department of the Taoiseach, 1993 to date; A Kerryman with significant involvement in Irish Social Partnership, the Northern Peace Process, the International Financial Services Centre and Irish Public Service Reform. Contact: Government Buildings, Dublin 2. Tel: 01 662 4888.

TEELING, John James; EXECUTIVE CHAIRMAN, COOLEY DISTILLERY PLC AND OTHER COMPANIES; *b* 1946; *educ* St. Joseph's Christian Brothers School, Fairview; University College Dublin, BComm, MEconSc; Wharton School, University of Pennsylvania, MBA; Harvard Business School, Boston, DBA; *m* Deirdre Shaw, Guidance Counsellor; 2 *s* 1 *da*; Lecturer, University College Dublin, 1968-88; Managing Director, Seafield Group plc, 1979-81 Chairman, Countyglen plc, 1983-93; Executive Chairman, Cooley Distillery plc, 1987 to date; Founder Chairman, Pan Andean Resources plc, 1987 to date, African Gold plc, 1987 to date, Irish Marine Oil plc, 1995 to date, Petrel Resources, plc, 1997 to date. Publications include: *Modern Irish Business, Business Organisation, Financial Management* (co-author). A former academic with exceptional entrepreneurial flair; a supporter of individual enterprise over monopolies. Clubs, Clontarf Rugby Club, Clontarf Cricket Club, Royal Dublin Golf Club. Contact: Cooley Distillery plc, Cooley, Co. Louth. Tel: 042 937 6102. Fax: 042 937 6484.

TEMPLE LANG, John; DIRECTOR, DIRECTORATE C GENERAL IV, COMPETITION AUTHORITY, BRUSSELS; *b* 1936; *educ* Trinity College Dublin, BA, LLB, MA, LLD; Foundation Scholar (1956), Julian Prize Winner (1958), first place, Solicitors Exams; Hague Academy of Law; *m* Gillian Hussey; *(m dis); m* Lean Hyland; 2 *s* 1 *da;* Solicitor, Whitney, Moore and Keller, Dublin 1958-61; Second Parliamentary Counsel, Attorney-General's Office (Ghana) 1961; Bigelow Teaching

Fellow, University of Chicago Law School 1961-62; Research Attorney, American Bar Foundation (Chicago) 1962-64; Special Advisor, Department of Finance 1964-68; Solicitor, Partner, McCann FitzGerald Roche & Dudley 1968-74; Legal Adviser, Competition Équipe, Commission of the European Communities 1974-84; Legal Advisor, Équipe for External Relations 1984-88; called to the Bar 1986; Director, Directorate C General IV Competition, Commission of the European Communities, Brussels and Visiting Lecturer in European Community Law, Trinity College Dublin 1988 to date; member, Incorporated Law Society of Ireland, Irish Society for European Law, International Council for Environmental Law, International Law Association, Royal Society for the Protection of Birds; Joint Secretary, Congress Standing Committee on Applied Ornithology; former Council member, British Trust for Ornithology, An Taisce, the National Trust for Ireland; former Chairman, Irish Wildbird Conservancy; publications include *The Common Market and Common Law: Legal Aspects for Foreign Investment and Economic Integration in the European Community, with Ireland as a Prototype*, and more than one hundred articles on law for national and international journals. Contact: Council of the European Union, General Secretariat, Rue de la Loi 175, 1048 Brussels. Tel: 00 322 285 6111.

THORNTON, Kevin; RESTAURATEUR, CHEF; *b* 1958; *educ* RTC Galway, DIT Cathal Brugha Street and Teachers Training Course at DIT, Cathal Brugha St.; *m* Muriel O'Connor; 1*s;* Lecturer, Cathal Brugha Street DIT; worked for a year under Paul Bocuse, Lyon, France; gained experience in Canada, France, Switzerland and London; opened Wine Epergne Restaurant, Rathmines, 1990-92; opened Thornton's Restaurant, 1995 to date; Publications include: Food Stylist for Georgina Campbell's *Food for All Seasons,* Contributor, Four Seasons Hotel Group, *Low Calorie Cookbook;* member, Eurotogues (Irish Branch); awarded: 1 Michelin Star, 1996, 1997, 1998, 1999; 1 Star *Egon Ronay Guide*, 1996, 1997; 2 Stars *Tipperary Water Guide*, 1999; Chef of the Year - Egon Ronay, 1996; Restaurant of the Year - Egon Ronay, 1997; Gilbeys Gold Medal Award, 1996; 1 Star *Bridgestone Food Guide*, 1996, 1997, 1998, 1999; Best Newcomer - *British Good Food Guide*, 1996; Chef of the Year, Tipperary Water, 1999; *AA Guide* - 3 Rosettes, 1999. A chef of international standard, runs one of the finest restaurants in the country. Hobbies, photography, horse-riding, scuba diving, theatre, mountain walking, mushroom picking (in season). Contact: Thorntons Restaurant, 1 Portobello Road, Dublin 8. Tel: 01 454 9067. Fax: 01 453 2947.

THORNTON, Kevin

TIERNAN, Tommy; ACTOR, COMEDIAN, WRITER; b 1969; educ St. Patrick's Classical School, Navan; Garbally College, Ballinasloe; *single*; trained as an actor at Bull Alley Theatre, Galway, subsequently appeared in theatre productions including *Shadow of a Gunman* and the film *Angela Mooney Dies Again*; turned to comedy, winning the Channel 4 *So You Think You're Funny?* Award, 1996; has toured Ireland and the UK extensively; had his own stand up special on Channel 4, 1998; co-starred in the films *The Matchmaker* and *About Adam*; won The Perrier Award and The British Comedy Award For Best Stand Up, 1998; currently starring in *Fantasies*, part of the Love in the 21st Century drama series on Channel 4, and in the title lead of Ed Hewitt in the Channel 4 comedy series, *Hewitt;* plans to publish his debut, as yet, untitled novel in May 2000; hobbies, modern fiction, Americana, coffee. Contact: Dawn Sedgwick, Dawn Sedgwick Management, 3 Goodwins Court, London WC2N 4LL, England. Tel: 0044 171 2400404 Fax: 0044 171 2400415.

TIERNAN, Tommy

TIERNEY, Donal Thomas; CHIEF EXECUTIVE OFFICER FUISZ INTERNATIONAL LTD.; *b* 1965; *educ* Blackrock College; University College Dublin, BA Econ., MBA; *m* Sarah Murphy; 1*s* 1 *da;* worked with Prudential Bache Capital Funding, New York, 1986-88; Cross Vetpharm Group, 1989-92; Cross Group, 1992-97; Fuisz International Ltd., 1997 to date; the company acquired Clonmel Healthcare from the Cross Group; member, Fitzwilliam LTC, Powerscourt GC. Hobbies, golf and squash. Contact: Fuisz International Ltd., 26 Windsor Place, Dublin 2. Tel: 01 676 0984.

TIMMINS, William Godfrey "Billy"; FULL TIME PUBLIC REPRESENTATIVE; *b* 1959; *educ* Patrician College, Ballyfin, Co. Laois; University College Galway, BA (Econ. & Legal Sc.); Diploma, Public Relations, Marketing and Advertising; *m* Madeleine F. Hyland; 1 *s* 2*da;* Army Officer, served with An Chead Cath 1 Infantry Battalion (Galway), the 28 Infantry Battalion (Donegal) and the 30 Infantry Battalion (Kilkenny), served with United Nations in Lebanon and Cyprus, 1979-97; elected Fine Gael Deputy for Wicklow, 1997 to date; Fine Gael Spokesperson on Peacekeeping & Humanitarian Aid, member, Joint Oireachtas Committee on Tourism & Sport, member, National Economic and Social Forum; member, West Wicklow Historical Society; member, Baltinglass GAA Club; recipient, Sportsman of the Year, Ballyfin College, 1977; *Irish Times* Debating Competition Finalist, 1978; Leinster & All Ireland Club Football Medal, 1990; one of the most impressive of the new breed of Fine Gael deputies; widely respected, expected to go far. Hobbies, reading, hill-walking, all sports, fishing and water colouring. Contact: Dáil Eireann, Dublin 2. Tel: 0508 81016.

TINNEY, Hugh

TINNEY, Hugh; CONCERT PIANIST; *b* 1958; *educ* Gonzaga College; Trinity College Dublin; *single*; member of well known musical family; teachers included Mabel Swainson and Louis Kentner, (London); winner of RTE Musicians of the Future, 1976; Pozzoli Competition, Seregno,

Italy (first place), 1983; Santander Competition, Spain (first place), 1984; Leeds Competition, UK (prizewinner) 1987; recordings include concerto, solo, chamber and song repertory; returned to live in Dublin after (nearly) twenty years in London, 1996; joined piano faculty R.I.A.M.. Recognised as a man of penetrating intellect, also a sportsman of note; internationally acclaimed pianist. Hobbies, tennis, mathematics, computers, cinema and reading novels. Contact: Royal Irish Academy of Music, 36 Westland Row, Dublin 2. Tel: 01 676 4412.

TOHILL, Anthony; CIVIL ENGINEER, G.A.A. PLAYER; *b* 1971; *educ* St. Patrick's College, Maghera, Co. Derry; Queen's University Belfast, B.Eng (civil), M.Sc (civil); *m* Sinead; awarded sports scholarship to Melbourne to play Australian Rules, 1990-91; plays with Michael Davitt Club Swatragh, 1987 to date; represented Derry as a Minor, 1989; Senior, 1991 to date, currently Captain; represented Ulster, 1992 to date (Captain 1996); played for Ireland, International Rules Series, against Australia 1998; played soccer for Park F.C. 1995; obtained two week Trial with Manchester United; awards include, All Ireland Minor, 1989; All Ireland Colleges (Horgan Cup) 1989; All Ireland Universities 1993; National League Winners, 1992, '95, '96; Ulster Senior Football Winners 1993, '98; All Ireland Senior Football Winners 1993; 5 Interprovincial Championships 1992, '93, '94, '95, '98; 3 All Stars 1992, '93, '95; member, Institute of Engineers of Ireland. Hobbies, soccer, golf and cricket. Contact: Gerry Donnelly, The Gables, Randalstown, Co. Antrim.

TÓIBÍN, Colm; JOURNALIST/AUTHOR; *b* 1955; *educ* Christian Brother's School, Enniscorthy; St. Peter's College, Wexford; University College Dublin, BA; *single;* worked as a teacher in Barcelona and with the English Department, University College Dublin; Features Editor, *In Dublin* magazine, 1981-82; Editor, *Magill*, 1982-85; contributed to *Sunday Independent* (Dublin) and London *Review of Books*; publications include: *Walking Along the Border, The South* (shortlisted for Whitbread Award (London)), *Homage to Barcelona, The Trial of the Generals: Selected Journalism, The Heather Blazing* (1992), *The Sign of the Cross* (1994), *The Story of the Night* (1996), *The Blackwater LIghtship* (1999); recipient, Bank of Ireland/Arts Show Award (Dublin), *Irish Times* /Aer Lingus Literary Award, 1991, E.M.Forster Prize from American Academy of Arts and Letters (1995). The ascerbic wit and pithy comments of the journalist are still there, but there is an increasing air of gravitas about the author. Contact: c/o A.P. Watt, 20 John Street, London WC1. Tel: 0044 171 405 6774.

TONER, Tom; COMPANY DIRECTOR; *b* 1932; *educ* St. Joseph's Academy, Kildare; University College Dublin, BComm, MEconSc, MBA; *m* Audre Isdell *(decd)*; 3 *s* 1 *da;* worked in various positions with CIE 1954-68; Executive Director, Allied Irish Investment Bank, 1968-72; Chief Executive, BWG Ltd., 1972-84; Executive Director, Irish Distillers Group, 1984-86; Chairman, Arnotts plc, Irish Ferries, Tullow Oil, Forfas, Council member, NESC; former President, FIE and member, Executive Committee, CII, IMI; member, Royal St. George Yacht Club. Highly regarded for analytical financial skills; an impressive company chairman and board member. Hobbies, gardening, travel and reading. Contact: Arnott plc, PO Box 406, Dublin 1. Tel: 01 872 1111. Fax: 01 872 1403.

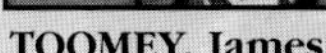

TOOMEY, James

TOOMEY, James Francis "Jim"; ARCHITECT; *b* 1945; *educ* Christian Brothers Limerick; University College Dublin, B.Arch; *m* Colleen Curtis; 3 *da*; gained work experience in the UK; Joined Kelly & Barry (Cork) 1973-75; Development Director, Power Corporation, 1975-94; opened own practice, 1994 to date; designs include Powerscourt Townhouse Centre Re-development, Powerscourt House, Enniskerry, St. Stephen's Green Shopping Centre, Jervis Street Shopping Centre, Investment Bank of Ireland, Leeson Street Bridge, re-development of Punchestown Racecourse; member, Royal Institute of Architects of Ireland, Royal Institute of British Architects; member, Donnybrook Tennis Club; recipient of An Taisce Architectural Award, 1981; a genial Limerick man with taste and talent. Hobbies, tennis and sailing. Contact: James Toomey Architects, Powerscourt Townhouse Centre, Dublin 2. Tel: 01 679 7522.

TRAVERS, John

TRAVERS, John; CHIEF EXECUTIVE FORFÁS; *b* 1939; *educ* Coláiste Chríost Rí, Cork; University College Cork, B.A.; post-graduate, DIT Dublin, Town Planning; University College Dublin, MBA; University of Pennsylvania, Masters in Economic and Regional Planning; *m* Mary O'Dwyer; 1*s* 4 *da;* Town Planner, Department of Local Government, 1967-78; Former IDA Manager, 1970s; Principal Officer, Department of Finance and Department of Taoiseach, 1979-88; Chief Economic Advisor, Department of Industry & Commerce, 1988-1994; Consultant, World Bank and U.N. projects, 1985 to date; Chief Executive Forfás, 1994 to date; Member, Board of Forfás, Management Board of Department of Enterprise, Trade and Employment, Board of the Michael Smurfit Graduate School of Business (UCD), National Competitiveness Council which reports to Taoiseach, Irish Council for Science, Technology & Innovation (National Science Council), Government Strategy Committee on Telecommunications, 1988; member, Government Strategy on the Information Society, Government Trade Advisory Forum; Executive responsibility for Industrial Policy Review Group Report (Culliton Report 1992) and Vice-Chairman of

Implementation Group. Significant role in Government policy formulation and implementation over the past 20 years. Hobbies, Gaelic Games, athletics, hill walking, boating, reading and theatre. Contact: Forfás, Wilton Park House, Wilton Place, Dublin 2. Tel: 01 607 3000. Fax: 01 607 3099.

TREACY, Blaise

TREACY, Blaise; COUNTY MANAGER WICKLOW; *b* 1935; *educ* St. Joseph's Academy, Kildare; Institute of Public Administration, Dip Admin.; *m* Imelda Laverty; 4*s* 1 *da;* Town Clerk, Carlow UDC, 1966-73; Town Clerk, Dundalk UDC, 1973-74; County Secretary, Kerry County Council, 1974-78; Assistant County Manager, Clare Co. Council, 1978-82; Wicklow County Manager, 1984 to date; Chairman, Wicklow County Development Team, East Coast Radio, Wicklow County Enterprise Board, Wicklow Enterprise Park; Director of Area Development Management Ltd., Director and Founder member, Wicklow County Tourism, Ltd.; member, Wicklow Rural Partnership; member, City and County Managers Association, ICMA, Institute of Wastes Management. Hobbies, golf and horse racing. Clubs, Delgany GC, Leopardstown. Contact: Wicklow County Council, Wicklow. Tel: 0402 20100. Fax: 0402 67792.

TREVOR, William; WRITER; *b* 1928; *educ* St. Columba's College Dublin; Trinity College Dublin; *m* Jane Ryan; 2 *children;* author of novels and plays; television plays include *The Mark 2 Wife, O Fat White Woman, The General's Day, Secret Orchard;* radio plays include, *Beyond the Pale,* (Giles Cooper Award 1989), *Autumn Sunshine* (Giles Cooper Award 1982); plays include, *Going Home* (1972), *A Night with Mrs da Tanka* (1972), *Scenes from an Album* (1981); books include, *The Old Boys* (Hawthornden Prize 1964), *Ballroom of Romance* (1972, adapted for BBC TV), *Angels at the Ritz* (1975, RSL Award), *The Children of Dynmouth* (1976 Whitbread Prize), *Fools of Fortune* (1983 Whitbread Prize, adapted for film), *Nights at the Alexandra* (1987), *Excursions in the Real World* (1993), *Ireland Selected Short Stories* (1995), *Felicia's Journey* (1975); recipient of numerous awards including, Allied Irish Banks Award for Literature (1976), decorated Comdr. Order Brit. Empire (1977); member, Irish Academy of Letters.

TUOMEY, John David

TUOMEY, John David; ARCHITECT; *b* 1954; *educ* National University of Ireland, B.Arch.; *m* Sheila O'Donnell; 2*s*; James Stirling and Partners, London, 1976-80; Office of Public Works, Dublin, 1981-87; O'Donnell & Tuomey, 1988 to date; member of Group 91 Architects for Temple Bar Framework Plan, 1991-97; Studio Lecturer, School of Architecture, UCD; Visiting Critic, Princeton and Harvard School of Design, USA; External Examiner, Cambridge, AA and VEL Schools of Architecture, UK; architectural design of public projects include: Irish Pavilion The Netherlands, IMMA, Irish Film Centre, Gallery of Photography, National Photography Centre, Blackwood Golf Centre, Connemara West Centre and Zuidport Delft (The Netherlands); President, Architectural Association of Ireland, 1992-93; Fellow, Royal Institute of Architects of Ireland, 1994; awards include: AAI Downes Medals, 1988, 1990, 1992, 1997, 1999; AAI Awards, 1987, 1997, 1999; RIAI Awards, 1993, 1995; finalist for Palladio prize, 1993 and Miers van der Rohe Award, 1997, 1999. Hobbies, cinema, reading, travel, archaeology and architecture. Contact: O'Donnell and Tuomey, 20a Camden Row, Dublin 8. Tel: 01 475 2500.

VIZE, John A; ASSISTANT CHIEF OF STAFF (SUPPORT) AND DIRECTOR OF LOGISTICS - DEFENCE FORCES; *b* 1942; *educ* St. Joseph's De La Salle College, Wicklow; Military College; School of Infantry - Warminster, UK; Command and Staff College, Curragh; *m* Maureen O'Flynn; 3*s* 3 *da;* commissioned into Infantry Corps, 1962; Posted to General Training Depot, 1962-68; Staff Officer HQ Curragh Training Camp, 1969-73; Company Commander, 27 Infantry Battalion, 1977-78; Company Commander, 5 Infantry Battalion, 1978-79; School Commandant - Infantry Weapons School, 1988; Officer Commanding Army Apprentice School, 1992; Command Adjutant - Curragh Command, 1994; School Commandant - United Nations Training School, Ireland, 1995; Executive Officer and Second in Command, Curragh Command, 1997; Assistant Chief of Staff (Support) and Director of Logistics, 1998 to date; Overseas service incudes, Platoon Commander, (Cyprus), 1965; Second in Command (Cyprus), 1970; Battalion Operations Officer (Lebanon), 1979-80; Second in Command (Lebanon), 1989-90; Operations Officer and Chief Military Observer (Cambodia), 1992; awards include, United Nations Medals for Cyprus (UNFICYP), Lebanon (UNIFIL) and Cambodia (UNAMIL and UNTAC); National Peacekeeping Medal; Service Medal with Bar; Chairman and Secretary, Blessington Art Club, 1984 to date; Captain, Curragh Golf Club, 1991, Vice-President, Curragh Golf Club, 1996-98. Hobbies, golf (8 handicap), painting, pistol and rifle shooting, sailing, guitar and ukulele. Contact: Defence Forces Headquarters, Parkgate, Dublin 8. Tel: 01 804 2607.

WADDELL, Robert, "Bob" J.; CHIEF EXECUTIVE GOWAN GROUP; *b* 1938; *educ* Blackrock College, Rosses Commercial College; McGill University, Canada, DipRetailMgmt; *m* Claire Phillips; 2 *s*, 3 *da*; Bank of Ireland, 1957-59; Assistant General Manager, Zellers Montreal, 1959-63; Managing Director, Smith Group Company, 1963-85; Chief Executive, Gowan Group, Chairman of over 20 Gowan Group subsidiary companies, 1985 to date; The Gowan Group is ranked 109th out of the top 1000 companies; Fellow, Marketing institute of Ireland; member, Institute of Directors, Irish Management Institute, Dublin Chamber of Commerce, France Ireland Chamber of Commerce, Blackrock College Union. An executive who practises team management, a family man with a strong role in community activities. Hobbies, veteran car enthusiast, home supporter of Shamrock Rovers and Manchester United, a much travelled supporter of the Irish soccer team, enjoys music, theatre, art and reading. Contact: Gowan Group, 1 Herbert Avenue, Dublin 4. Tel: 01 260 1677. Fax: 01 260 1672.

WALKER, Dorothy, née Cole, ART HISTORIAN AND CRITIC; *b* 1929; *educ* Dominican Convent, Wicklow; Ecole de Louvre, Paris; *m* Robin Walker *(decd.)*; 3 *s;* 2 *da*; Free-lance art critic, RTE, 1964-67; *Hibernia*, 1967-77; Contributing Editor, *Studio International*; contributer to numerous Irish and international art publications world-wide. Lecturer on Irish and international 20th century art universities, and art schools world-wide. Numerous essays translated into German, French, Spanish, Italian and Japanese. Currently art critic, *Sunday Times* (Irish edition). Publications include *Louis le Brocquy* (Ward River Press, Dublin 1991); *Michael Scott architect in (casual) conversation with Dorothy Walker* (Gandon Editions, Cork 1995); *Modern Art in Ireland* (Lilliput Press, Dublin, 1997). President, Irish Section of the International Association of Art Critics, AICA; Former Vice-President of the world body, 1979-81; founding member of the Board of the International Center for Advanced Studies in Art, New York University, 1981; founding member of ROSC, 1967; founding member of the Board of the Irish Museum of Modern Art, 1989; member of the Board of the Gallery of Photography. Hobbies, travel and cooking. Contact: Fax: 01 668 2773.

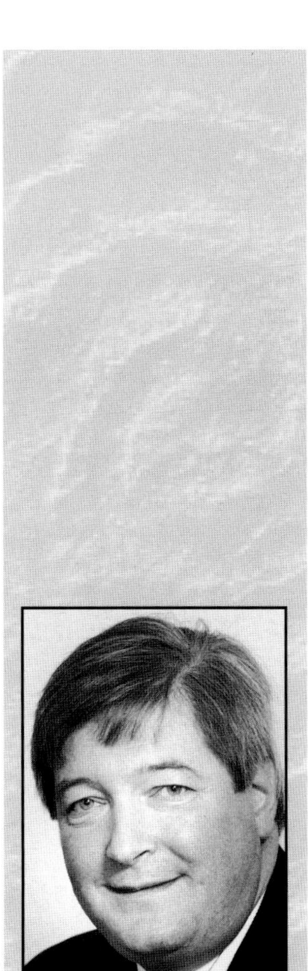

WALL, Christopher

WALL, Christopher Joseph, "Chris"; BUSINESS CONSULTANT *b* 1942; *educ* St. Vincents, Glasnevin; College of Technology, Bolton St.; National College of Ireland; member, Irish Institute of Purchasing and Materials Management; *m* Myra O'Shea; 1 *s* 3 *da*; Credit Controller & Chief Clerk, Booth Poole & Co. Dublin, 1962-1968; Supply Services Manager, Wellcome Ireland Ltd., 1968-95; Production/Distribution Manager, Glaxo Wellcome Ltd., 1995-98; Business Consultant, 1999 to date; Life Vice President, Dublin City Harriers; Chairman, Dublin Athletics Board, 1979-87; International Secretary, Bord Luthchleas na hEireann, 1987 to date; Chairman, Fianna Fáil Dublin Central Comhair, 1989 to date; National Executive member, Fianna Fáil, 1990 to date; Finance Committee Member, Fianna Fáil, 1990 to date. Award: National 880 yards champion, 1959; Manager, Track & Field Team Seoul Olympics, 1988; Manager World Championships Tokyo,1991, Gotenburg, 1995; Delegation Head, IAAF Congress, 1987, 1989, 1991, 1993, 1995, 1997; Governor, Dublin Institute of Technology, 1985-89; Director, Irish Goods Council, 1987-91; Director ACC Bank, 1992-1996; Director, Aer Lingus, 1998 to present, Director, Intranets, 1999; Director Eco-Parks Europe, 1999. Hobbies, sports, politics. Contact: Cabracote, 188 New Cabra Road, Dublin 7. Tel: 01 838 9967.

WALL, Niall James; CHIEF EXECUTIVE TIPPERARY CRYSTAL DESIGNS LTD; *b* 1962; *educ* Castleknock College; College of Marketing and Design; *m* Fiona Laverty; established Ferndale Quail Ltd. in partnership with Fennella Steele 1986-94, sold out interest to Silverhill Foods; Director, Lites Marketing (sales & marketing services company), 1994-97; Chief Executive, Tipperary Crystal Designs Ltd., 1997 to date; an innovative manager for this successful Irish company with a strong export market; only Irish crystal company to supply Tiffanys (Sybil Connolly's designs); launched Louise Kennedy designed crystal collection on the market 1999; member, Fitzwilliam Lawn Tennis Club. Hobbies, sport, reading and theatre. Contact: Tipperary Crystal Designs Ltd., Carrick-on-Suir, Co. Tipperary. Tel: 051 64118.

WALLACE, Patrick; DIRECTOR NATIONAL MUSEUM OF IRELAND; *b* 1948; *educ* University College Galway, BA, PhD; *m* Siobhan Cuffe, Printmaker/Architect; Archaeologist with National Museum of Ireland, 1971-88, responsible for direction of Wood Quay Excavations, 1974-81; Director, National Museum of Ireland, 1988 to date; Fellow, Society of Antiquaries (London); member, Royal Society of Antiquaries of Ireland (Hon. General Secretary 1983-89); Board Member, Shannon Heritage; publications include numerous papers on Viking Age Archaeology and two volume study *The Architecture of Viking Dublin;* conceived and designed Irish Life's Viking Adventure (1988); oversaw the move of part of the National Museum's collections to Collins Barracks site, Phase 1 of which opened in 1997; currently involved with Phase 2 of the development of the Museum's exhibitions at Collins Barracks as well as the move to the Museum's regional branch at Castlebar, Co. Mayo; the Museum is constantly growing; the profile of its four branches (Kildare Street - archaeology; Collins Barracks - decorative Arts and Social History; Merrion Street - National History and Castlebar - Folklife) has also been raised in recent years; a regular contributor to radio and television programmes at home and abroad, presented his own series *Legacy,* on the archaeology of Ireland, RTE 1, 1999; presented an Irish Language version (*Oidhreacht)* of the same series on TnaG. Hobbies, film, Gaelic Games, walking and most recently the refurbishment of his and his wife's 16th century Gaelic Tower, Co. Clare. Contact: National

Museum of Ireland, Kildare Street, Dublin 2. Tel: 01 677 7444. Fax: 01 676 6116.

WALPOLE, Robert; FILM PRODUCER; *b* 1965; *educ* St. Kevins CBS, Greystones; Presentation College, Bray; Trinity College Dublin, BA (Hons); *partner,* Sarah Power; established Treasure Films with director, Paddy Breathnach, 1992; produced 90 minute documentary *The Road to America,* 1993 which became the best-selling Irish produced sell through film ever; produced *The Long Way Home, WRH* a six part series for RTE and *The Charlton Years,* 1995; first feature film *I Went Down* premiered at Cannes Film Festival, 1997 and won four awards at the San Sebastian Film Festival Sept. 1997; on domestic release *I Went Down* went straight to number one at the Irish Box Office and was selected for the World Cinema Section at The Sundance Film Festival, 1998 and premiered in New York, 1998; produced *Southpaw,* 1997-98, premiered at Galway Film Fleadh July 1998, general release, 1999 and England, 1999; *Saltwater,* a feature film (adapted and directed by Conor McPherson) from his screenplay *This Lime Tree Bower;* member, Filmmakers Ireland, Screen Training Ireland; awards include Special Jury Prize, Cork Film Festival 1991 for *A Stone of the Heart;* Best New Director, San Sebastian Film Festival 1997, Silver Sea Shell Jury Prize, San Sebastian Film Festival 1997, Silver Disc Award, Bogota International Film Festival, 1998, Special Award, American Independent Film Festival, 1998 for *I Went Down;* the successful Walpole/Breathnach partnership make them the leading lights of the new generation of Irish film makers. Contact: Treasure Films, Shamrock Chambers, 1-2 Eustace Street, Dublin 2. Tel: 01 670 9609. Fax: 01 670 9612.

WALSH, Brendan; UNIVERSITY PROFESSOR; *b* 1940; *educ* Gonzaga College Dublin; University College Dublin, BEconSc (Hons); University of Tennessee, MEconSc; Boston College, PhD; *m* Patricia Noonan; 3 children; Assistant Professor, Tufts University (Mass), 1966-69; worked at Economic and Social Research Institute 1969-80; Professor of the National Economics of Ireland and Applied Economics, University College Dublin 1980 to date; member, National Planning Board, Royal Irish Academy; Council member, Statistical and Social Inquiry Society of Ireland, Economic and Social Studies; served on numerous consultancy Boards nationally and internationally; publications include, *Ireland in the European Monetary System: The Effects of a Change in Exchange Rate Mechanism, The Macroeconomy of Ireland* (4th ed. 1998 with A. Leddin); contributor to numerous national and international journals including, *Understanding Ireland's Economic Growth* (ed. Frank Barry 1999); an economist well respected in government circles. Contact: University College Dublin, Belfield, Donnybrook, Dublin 4. Tel: 01 706 7777.

WALSH, Caroline; LITERARY EDITOR, IRISH TIMES; *b* 1952; *educ* University College Dublin, MA; *m* James Ryan; 1 *s* 1 *da*; Reporter, *Irish Times,* 1974-83; Features Writer, 1983-86; Assistant Features Editor, 1987-91; Features Editor, 1992-97; Assistant Editor, Regional News, 1998-99; Literary Editor, 1999; Author of *The Home of Irish Writers* (1982, Anvil Books); Editor of *Modern Irish Stories from The Irish Times* (1985, Irish Times), *Virgins and Hyacinths,* new Irish fiction by women writers (1993 Attic Press). Contact: The Irish Times, D'Olier Street, Dublin 2. Tel: 01 679 2022.

WALSH, David

WALSH, David; CHIEF EXECUTIVE JOE WALSH TOURS LTD.; *b* 1968; *educ* Gonzaga College, Dublin; College of Marketing & Design, Advanced Diploma in Marketing and Administration; Graduateship of Marketing Institute of Ireland; *single*; Bank of Ireland Group, 1990-92; Chief Executive, Joe Walsh Tours Ltd., 1992 to date; joined family travel company founded by his late father, Joe Walsh; Joe Walsh Tours is Ireland's largest privately owned travel company; member, Irish Travel Agents Association; member, Riverview Tennis Club. Hobbies, travelling and sport. Contact: 8 Lower Baggot Street, Dublin 2. Tel: 01 678 9555.

WALSH, Joe; POLITICIAN; *b* 1943; *educ* St. Finbarr's College, Farranferris, Cork; University College Cork; *m* Marie Donegan; 3*s* 2 *da*; formerly Dairy Manager; member, Cork County Council 1974-91; member, Cork County Committee of Agriculture 1974-88; Chairman, Cork County Committee of Agriculture 1976-77, 1985-86; elected Fianna Fáil Deputy for Cork South West, 1977-81 and 1982 to date; member, Cork County Vocational Education Committee 1979-91; member, Seanad Eireann, August 1981-February 1982; Minister of State at Department of Agriculture and Food from March 1987-92; Minister for Agriculture and Food 1992; re-appointed Minister for Agriculture, Food and Forestry 1993-94; re-appointed Minister for Agriculture, Food and Forestry 1997 and, due to change of Ministerial titles and responsibilities, renamed Minister for Agriculture and Food from July 1997 to date. Contact: Department of Agriculture and Food, Agriculture House, Kildare Street, Dublin 2. Tel.: 01 607 2000.

WALSH, Kieran Joseph; MANAGING DIRECTOR, EDITOR, MUNSTER EXPRESS; *b* 1957; *educ* Waterpark College, Waterford, London South Bank, BA Business Studies; Marketing Institute, Dip.; College of Commerce Rathmines, Dip. Legal Studies, London College of Printing, Dip. Post Grad.;*m* Roswitha Hertrich; Market Researcher, Harrison Printers, London, 1977-78; Financial

Journalist, *Business & Finance*, Dublin, 1980-81; Business Editor, *Sunday Journal*, Dublin, 1981-82; Monday Money, *Irish Press*, Dublin, 1982-83; Advertising Manager and News Editor, *Munster Express*, Waterford, 1985-88, Managing Director and Editor, *Munster Express*, 1993 to date; publications include numerous newspaper articles; member, Irish Management Institute - South East, Marketing Institute, Provincial Newspaper Association - IRL, IMPA, Tramore Golf Club, Tramore Tennis Club; initiated newspaper web site, 1996, and achieved Doras 5 Star Award with Ireland-On-Line for firm; appears in International *Who's Who of Professionals*, Ivor Kenny book on Newspapers. Hobbies, theatre, film, music, internet, reading, current affairs, travel, golf, tennis, spectator skiing, rugby, soccer and hurling. Contact: The Munster Express, 1-3 Hanover Street, Waterford. Tel: 051 872 141. Fax: 051 873 452.

WALSH, Michael, "Louis" Vincent; POP BAND MANAGER / IMPRESARIO; *b* 1956; *educ* St. Nathy's College, Ballaghadereen; St. Patrick's College, Swinford; *single* ; worked with Tommy Hayden in Dublin, managing artists such as Johnny Logan and Linda Martin; started Boyzone 1994, has brought the band into one of the leading groups worldwide; in 1999 launched a new band called Westlife; awarded I.R.M.A. music industry award 1997. A media wise impresario; a pop promotor of vision and a tough negotiator. Hobbies, music, movies, travel, Irish culture - music and art. Contact: c/o Carol Hanna, 57 Meadow Bank, Bushy Park Road, Dublin 6. Tel: 01 490 9339.

WALSH, Patrick; CHIEF EXECUTIVE WALSH MUSHROOMS LTD; *b* 1940; *educ* Castleknock College; *m* Deirdre McDonnell, Proprietor Health and Beauty centre; 3*s* 1 *da;* Manager, Top Quality Products Ltd, 1970-79; Owner / Chief Executive, Walsh Mushrooms Ltd. 1979 to date, one of the major mushroom producers in the country, supplying the home market and principal suppliers to the major UK multiples; recipient of Trading House Licence (1990), International Standard ISO 9000 (1991). Hobby, hunting. Contact: Walsh Mushrooms Ltd., Creagh, Gorey, Co. Wexford. Tel: 055 21182.

WALSH, Most Rev. William "Willie"; BISHOP OF KILLALOE; *b* 1935; *educ* Corville National School, Roscrea; St. Flannan's College, Ennis; St. Patrick's College, Maynooth; Irish College, Rome; ordained in Rome 1959; completed Canon Law studies, Lateran University, Rome; taught at Coláiste Einde, Galway; joined the staff at St. Flannan's College, Ennis, 1963; appointed Curate at Ennis Cathedral, Administrator, 1990; involved with ACCORD since its foundation in Killaloe; ordained Bishop of Killaloe, 1994; a straight talking prelate who has shown courage and compassion in his open-minded approach to pastoral issues. Hobbies, all sports, coaches hurling teams at college, club and county level. Contact: Killaloe Diocesan Office, Westbourne, Ennis, Co. Clare. Tel: 065 28638. Fax: 065 42538.

WALSHE, Charles Andrew

WALSHE, Charles Andrew; MANAGING DIRECTOR, KRAFT JACOBS SUCHARD IRELAND LTD.; *b* 1942; *educ* St. Jarlath's College; University College Dublin, BComm; *m* Patricia Marrinan; 2 *s* 1 *da*; Sales Manager (Farley Food Products), Glaxco Laboratories, 1973-77; Sales Manager, Alfred Bird & Sons, 1977-83, Sales Director 1983-86, Managing Director, 1986-89; Managing Director, Kraft Jacobs Suchard Ireland, 1989 to date; recipient of Diploma in Marketing, Marketing Management Certificate (IMI); Member, Policy Committee, IBEC. Hobbies, tennis, squash and reading; Club, Riverview Racquet and Health Club. Contact: Kraft Jacobs Suchard Ireland Ltd., 47 Pembroke Road, Dublin 4. Tel: 01 605 2600. Fax: 01 605 2626.

WARD, James J; VICE-PRESIDENT NATIONAL UNIVERSITY OF IRELAND GALWAY; *b* 1946; *educ* De La Salle College, Wicklow; University College Dublin, BComm., MEcon Sc.; The George Washington University, Washington DC, Dr. Bus. Admin.; *m* Jeanie Cullivan; 2*da*; Assistant Professor, California State University, Hayward, (CA), 1971-73; Lecturer & Dean of Commerce, University College Galway, 1973-79; Trade Promotion Advisor, International Trade Centre, (Geneva), 1979-80; Professor of Marketing, University College Galway, 1980-99; Vice-President, National University of Ireland, Galway, 1999 to date; books include *The European Approach to US Markets* (Praeger, New York), *Export Marketing Management* (ITC, Geneva), *Export Marketing Research* (ITC Geneva), *Cases in Marketing Management,* (Marketing Institute, Dublin); also contributed various articles and monographs for marketing journals; Fellow, Marketing Institute of Ireland; member, European Marketing Academy; awards include Friendly Sons of St. Patrick, Fellowship for Doctoral Study, 1996; Doctoral Dissertation Award, Academy of International Business, 1972. Hobbies, golf and tennis. Contact: National University of Ireland, Galway. Tel: 091 524 411.

WARD, Michael; PLANT MANAGER BOSE IRELAND; *b* 1960; *educ* Trinity College Dublin, BA, BAI,; University College Galway, MBA; *m* Francesca Counihan; Engineer, Engineering Management Materials, Northern Telecom, Galway, 1983-91; Engineering Plant Manager, Bose Corporation, 1991 to date. Hobbies, cycling, running, reading, internet. Contact: Bose

Corporation, Carrickmacross, Co. Monaghan. Tel: 042 61988. Fax: 042 61998.

WEAIRE, Denis Lawrence; ERASMUS SMITH PROFESSOR OF NATURAL AND EXPERIMENTAL PHILOSOPHY; *b* 1942; *educ* Belfast Royal Academy; Cambridge University, BA, PhD Physics; *m* Colette O'Regan; 1*s*; Fellow, Clare College, Cambridge, 1967-69; Professorships, Yale University, 1970-74, Heriot-Watt University, 1974-80, University College Dublin, 1980-84, Trinity College Dublin, 1984 to date, (Erasmus Smith Professor of Natural and Experimental Philosophy); Dean of Science, 1989-92; Director, Magnetic Solutions Ltd., 1994 to date; Editor-in-Chief, *J Physics: Condensed Matter,* 1994-97; publications include *The Physics of Foams* (with S. Hutzler) 1999, *The Pursuit of Perfect Packing* (with T. Aste) 1999; member, Institute of Physics, American Physical Society, Royal Institution; Larmor Lecturer, QUB, 1998; President of the European Physical Society, 1997-99; member, Royal Irish Academy, 1987, Academia Europaea, 1998; Fellow, Royal Society, 1999; member, University and Kildare Street Club; an academic with an international reputation; the only Fellow of the Royal Society in Ireland. Hobbies, history of science and theatre. Contact: Trinity College Dublin, Dublin 2. Tel: 01 677 2941.

WEAIRE, Denis Lawrence

WEJCHERT, Andrzej; ARCHITECT; *b* 1937; *educ* Faculty of Architecture, Warsaw Polytechnic, Poland, SARP, FRIAI, RIBA; *m* Danuta Kornaus, Architect, MgrEngArch, SARP, FRIAI, also an architect from Warsaw and a full partner in the practice; 1*s* 1 *da;* the Dublin based practice of A & W Wejchert was formed as a result of winning the International Architectural Competition for the UCD campus; for the Administration Building at Belfield, awarded the Triennial Gold Medal 1971-73, Irish Concrete Society's Award 1979 for the Water Tower; other awards include: Aillwee Caves access building, The Environment Award 1979; An Taisce Commendation and the Europa Nostra Award 1980, Mont Kavanagh Award for Industrial Units at Clonshaugh 1982, *Sunday Independent* Award for the AnCo Training Centre at Loughlinstown 1983, also the Plan Building of the Year Awards in 1980, 1984, 1987, 1992, 1996, RIAI Regional Award for Naas General Hospital 1990 and for the Office Building at Lower Mount Street in 1992; conferred with Honorary Degree of Doctor of Laws, NUI, 1997; the Wejcherts partnership is expanding rapidly with technological parks as far afield as Turkey and with office buildings in Warsaw, Poland; commercial architecture is represented by Irish Life Beresford Court Offices, The Blanchardstown Centre and Smithfield Village; other projects include Naas General Hospital and James Connolly Memorial Hospital in Blanchardstown; University College Cork and University of Limerick; currently, Performance Arts Centre for Dublin City University; their strength lies in dedication to detail in user and environment friendly constructions. Mutual hobbies, gardening and travel. Contact: A & D Wejchert, 23 Lower Baggot Street, Dublin 2. Tel: 01 661 0321. Fax: 01 661 0203.

WEJCHERT, Andrzej

WELCH, Thomas, Niall; MANAGING PARTNER WELCH & CO. CHARTERED ACCOUNTANTS; *b* 1944; *educ* Christian Brothers College, Cork; University College Cork, B.Comm, Chartered Accountant; *m* Eileen O'Brien; 1 *s* 2 *da;* Joined Touche Ross & Co., Partner, 1971-89; Formed Welch & Co., Managing Partner, 1989 to date; Chairman, Nitrigin Eirean Teo, 1987 to date; Chairman, Irish Fertiliser Industries Ltd., 1993 to date; Director, Irish Ispat Ltd., 1996 to date; Director, Freefoam Plastics, 1996 to date; Chairman, Marlborough International plc., 1997 to date; Member: Institute of Directors, Institute of Chartered Accountants, Cork Golf Club - former Captain, Cork Arts Society. Hobbies, golf, rugby, tennis. Contact: Welch & Co., 6 South Bank, Crosses Green, Cork. Tel: 021 319 844. Fax: 021 319 711.

WELCH, Thomas, Niall

WELD, Dermot K.; RACE HORSE TRAINER; *b* 1948; *educ* Newbridge College; University College Dublin, Veterinary Surgeon; *m* Mary Nugent; 2 *s*; 3 times Champion Amateur Rider; Obtained Trainers Licence, 1972; Leading Trainer of Winners, 17 times; Champion Trainer, 9 times; the only trainer in Europe to win an American Triple Crown Race, the only non-Australian trainer to win The Melbourne Cup; Director: Irish National Stud, Irish Horseracing Authority (IHA); Awarded two Texaco Awards, Irish Sports Star of the Year, 1993; Australian Sports Star of the Year, 1993; Follows family tradition, regarded as one of the country's leading trainers. Hobbies, tennis and golf, Club, K Club. Contact: Rosewell House, Curragh, Co. Kildare. Tel: 045 441 273. Fax: 045 441 119.

WELSFORD, Michael Paul; CHAIRMAN OGILVY AND MATHER GROUP IRELAND; *b* 1949; *educ* University of Natal, South Africa, BEcon; *m* Margaret Jean ----; 2*s* Area Manager, Edgars Stores, Johannesburg, 1970-72; Brand Manager, Ciba-Geigy, Johannesburg, 1973-74; Brand Manager, Alcan Aluminium, Johannesburg, 1975-76; New Products Manager, Wilkinson Sword, Johannesburg, 1976-79; Managing Director, Ogilvy and Mather, South Africa and Africa, 1979-98; Chairman, Ogilvy and Mather Group Ireland and Managing Director, Ogilvy and Mather, Africa, 1999 to date. Hobby, golf. Contact: Ogilvy and Mather, 8-9 Appian Way, Dublin 6. Tel: 01 660 9300. Fax: 01 660 5363.

WENT, David; CHIEF EXECUTIVE, IRISH LIFE & PERMANENT PLC; *b* 1947; *educ* High School

WENT, David

WHELAN, Bill

WHELEHAN, Harold

Dublin, Trinity College Dublin, BA(Mod), LLB; King's Inn, Barrister at Law, Brooke Scholar, 1970; *m* Mary Milligan; 1 *s* 1 *da*; Joined Citibank NA (Dublin), 1970; General Manager, Citibank, Jeddah, 1975-76; Director Banking, Ulster Investment Bank, 1976-87, Chief Executive, 1982; Deputy Chief Executive, Belfast, 1987; Chief Executive, 1988-94; Coutts & Co., London, 1994-97; Chief Executive, Irish Life plc., 1998; Chief Executive, Irish Life & Permanent plc., 1999 to date; Member, Royal North of Ireland Yacht Club, Fitzwilliam LTC, Sandycove Tennis Club, Killiney Golf Club, Kildare Street and University Club; Fellow, Institute of Bankers, President: Irish Bankers Federation, 1991, Institute of Bankers, 1993; Chairman, Northern Ireland Bankers Association, 1989-91; A hard -working and gregarious executive; regarded as a formidable boardroom presence. Hobbies, tennis, reading. Contact: Irish Life plc., Irish Life Centre, Lower Abbey Street, Dublin 1. Tel: 01 704 2000. Fax: 01 704 1900

WHELAN, Bill; COMPOSER; *b* 1950; *educ* Crescent College, Limerick; University College Dublin,BCL; Kings Inns; *m* Denise ------; 2 *s* 2 *da;* film scores include *Bloomfield;* joined Planxty, 1979; Record Producer for folk artists such as Andy Irvine, Patrick Street, Stockton's Wing, Davy Spillane; wrote first major orchestral suite commemorating the film music of Sean O'Riada, 1987; composed music for such films as *Lamb, At the Cinema Palace, Some Mother's Son, Dancing at Lughnasa*; specially commissioned orchestral work, *The Seville Suite* performed at Seville 1992, *The Spirit of Mayo* performed at National Concert Hall Dublin, 1993; *Riverdance* was composed for the interval of the Eurovision Song Contest 1994, topped the Irish charts for 18 weeks also a Top Ten hit in the UK; *Riverdance, Music from the Show* blends Russian/Spanish/Irish folk music and has topped charts worldwide; awards include Grammy Award 1997, People of the Year 1999; Honorary Doctorate of Philosophy, DIT 1999; a major Irish composer with a worldwide reputation. Hobbies, boating, fishing, walking and travel. Contact: Aislinn Meehan, McGuinness/Whelan, 30-32 Sir John Rogerson's Quay, Dublin 2. Tel: 01 677 7330. Fax: 01 677 7276.

WHELAN, Ruth Elizabeth; PROFESSOR OF FRENCH NATIONAL UNIVERSITY OF IRELAND, MAYNOOTH; *b* 1956; *educ* Trinity College Dublin, BA, HDipEd; University of Paris Nanterre; Trinity College Dublin, PhD; recipient of numerous scholarships and international research awards; instructor in English, Ecole Supérieure de la Statistique et des Affairs Economiques, Paris 1983-84; Lecturer in French, Trinity College Dublin, 1984-96; member, Editorial Board of the *Correspondence de Pierre Bayle* (Oxford), 1988 to date; Fellow, Trinity College Dublin, 1990-97; Senior Lecturer in French, Trinity College Dublin, 1996-97; member, Editorial Board *Encyclopedia of the Enlightenment* (Oxford University Press, New York); Professor of French, National University of Ireland, Maynooth, 1997 to date; has published numerous papers in academic journals, also *The Anatomy of Superstition: a study of the historical theory and practice of Pierre Bayle, Ancient Bestsellers* (with Muriel McCarthy), *And then there were Twelve* (with Muriel McCarthy), *Correspondence de Pierre Bayle.* Hobbies, hill walking, swimming, work-out, roller blading, DIY, music, theatre, cinema, detective fiction and reading. Contact: National University of Ireland, Maynooth, Co. Kildare. Tel: 01 628 5222. Fax: 01 628 9397

WHELEHAN, Harold, "Harry"; BARRISTER; *b* 1944; *educ* St. Mary's Christian Brothers School, Mullingar; Glenstal Abbey; University College Dublin, B.C.L.; King's Inns, Auditor, Law Society, 1965; Salzburg, 1965; *m* Joyce Boland, Solicitor; 4 *s*; 2 *da*; Called to the Bar, 1966, English Bar, 1970; Senior Counsel, 1980; Bar of New South Wales, 1993; Appointed Attorney General, 1991-94, during which time there were such controversial and divisive issues as Abortion, The X Case, The Beef Tribunal, Cabinet confidentiality; The Attorney General's judgement was endorsed by the Supreme Court, but criticised in the media and the Dáil; Appointed President of the High Court 1994, resigned shortly after due to internal political upheavel; returned to general practice at the Bar; an unpretentious and experienced lawyer, popular among all branches of the profession; represents the Irish Bar on the Council of the Bars and Law Societies of the E.U.; Member, Irish Centre for European Law, Irish Cruising Club, Hibernian United Service Club, Royal Alfred Yacht Club. Hobbies, yachting and country pursuits. Contact: The Law Library Building, 158-159 Church Street, Dublin 7. Tel: 01 804 5102. Fax: 01 804 5139.

WHITAKER, Thomas Kenneth; FORMER CHANCELLOR, NATIONAL UNIVERSITY OF IRELAND; *b* 1916; *educ* Christian Brothers School, Drogheda; London University (External Student), MSc (Econ); *m* Nora Fogarty; 5 *s* 1 *da*; entered the Civil Service, Secretary of the Department of Finance, 1956-69; Governor, Central Bank of Ireland, 1969-76; Director, Guinness Board of Directors, 1976-84; Director, Bank of Ireland, 1976-85; President, Economic and Social Research Institute, 1970-85; Chairman of Council, Dublin Institute for Advanced Studies, 1980-95; Chancellor, National University of Ireland, 1976-96; recipient of the following Honorary Degrees: DEconSc (NUI), LLD (University of Dublin, Queens University), DSc (University of Ulster), Ph.D, DCU; Member, The Royal Irish Academy (President 1985-87); Hon. Life Member, Royal Dublin Society; Hon. Fellow of the Institute of Engineers and of the Royal College of Surgeons in Ireland;

Commandeur de la Légion d'Honneur; publications include: *Financing by Credit Creation* (main contributor), *Economic Development, Interests,* and papers in journals and newspapers; chaired Inquiry into Penal system, 1985, Common Fisheries Policy Review 1991, Review of Constitution 1995-96. Recognised as a major contributor to the economic and social life of the State; a highly respected, non pompous man; a noted angler, also enjoys music. Contact: c/o Royal College of Surgeons, 123 St. Stephen's Green, Dublin 2. Tel: 01 402 2100. Fax: 01 402 2345.

WHITE Mary Margaret, née Casey; MANAGING DIRECTOR/MARKETING LIR CHOCOLATES LTD.; *b* 1944 in Dundalk; *educ* Holy Family Convent, Newbridge; College of Technology, Bolton Street, Dip Arch Tech.; University College Dublin, BA; *m* Padraic White; 1 *da;* Architectural Technologist with Office of Public Works; worked in Architects Department, Aer Rianta; Architectural Technologist, National Building Agency 1974-86; co-founder with Connie Doody, Lir Chocolates Ltd. 1986, joint Managing Director/Marketing 1986 to date; Lir Chocolates are one of Ireland's leading luxury brands exporting 30% of production; creators of Bailey's Handmade Chocolates with Tesco accredition 1998; Inspirational Irish Women chocolates exclusive to Superquinn; Chairwoman, Presidents Award/Gaisce; Council member, Dublin Chamber of Commerce; Board member, Bord Bia; Council member, Institute of Sales; Dublin Women's Representative on National Executive of Fianna Fáil 1993-98; during Peace Process became involved with the Dublin Fianna Fáil women working towards developing relationships with Nationalist and Unionist women in Northern Ireland. Hobbies, politics, political biographies. Contact: Lir Chocolates Ltd., East Wall Road, Dublin 3. Tel: 01 874 0365. Fax: 01 874 9341.

WHITE, Padraic; COMPANY DIRECTOR; *b* 1942; *educ* De la Salle College, Ballyshannon; University College Dublin BComm (Hons); *m* Mary Casey; 1 *da;* Civil Service, Executive Officer, Department of Defence, 1960-64; Administrative Officer, Department of Health, 1964-70; held various positions in Industrial Development Authority, 1970-90; appointed Managing Director, IDA, 1980-90; entered private sector, 1990; Chairman, Northside Partnership, 1991 to date; Opinion Writer, in the *Irish Independent,* business section; Chairman, Cable Management Ireland Ltd. (CMI), (third largest cable TV company in Republic), Flexicom Ltd., (pioneering Irish company in software for multi-currency credit card transactions), Schoepp Velours of Ireland Ltd., Wexford, Arigna Fuels Ltd., Roscommon, (leading Irish producer of smokeless fuels), Gaoithe Saor Teoranta, Roscommon (wind energy company); member, Executive Committee of the Economic & Social Research Institute of Ireland, Board of Trustees of the Eisenhower Exchange Fellowships Inc., USA; appointed by Minister Mary O'Rourke, as Chairman of the Dublin Light Rail Advisory & Action Group, 1998; appointed by Minister Michael Woods, Chairman of the National Strategy Review Group on the Common Fisheries Policy; in 1999, was appointed by the Minister of Finance to the Board supervising the merger and flotation of TSB & ACC Banks; Director, Dresdner Bank Ireland, Dresdner Investment Management Services Ltd., London Life and General Re-Insurance Co Ltd., Novell Software Ireland Ltd, Coyle Hamilton Insurance Ltd., RS Group, Hanover Quay. Hobby, keeping fit. Contact: Padraic A. White, 36 Lower Baggot Street, Dublin 2. Tel: 01 662 0806. Fax: 01 676 6097.

WHITE, Peter S; DIRECTOR PROPERTY INVESTMENT COMPANIES; *b* 1940 Glasgow, Scotland; *educ* Gordonstoun School (Scotland); Sandford Park School, Dublin; Trinity College Dublin, MA; *m* Alicia Fitzsimons; 3 *s;* Estate Agent with Gilbert Leon White 1969-80; Director, Dublin Land Securities (commercial and residential property investment company) 1980 to date; established and ran award winning restaurant Whites on the Green 1985-1989; Governor Sandford Park School; Director of various private companies in Ireland and U.K.; member, Irish Auctioneers and Valuers Institute. A noted collector of fine wines; a genial host and Francophile, a highly successful, low key businessman. Hobbies, good food, fine wine and tennis; Club, Fitzwilliam LTC, RIAC. Contact: Dublin Land Securities Ltd., 16 Wellington Road, Dublin 4. Tel: 01 668 3516.

WHITE, Peter

WHITTAKER, Peter Anthony; PROFESSOR OF BIOLOGY; *b* 1939; *educ* St. Mary's College Blackburn; Liverpool University, B.Sc.; Leicester University, PhD.; *m* Lynne Bowering; 2 *s* (one decd) 2*da;* Lecturer, Botany Department, Hull University, 1964-1968; Lecturer, School of Botany, Sussex University, 1968-78, Sub-Dean of Biology, 1973-76; Professor of Biology, Head of Biology Department, St. Patrick's College, Maynooth, 1978-97, N.U.I. Maynooth, 1997 to date; Co-ordinator, EU-Jordan Science Research Co-operation Programme, 1993-97; member, Zoological Society of Ireland (Vice President, 1992-96); Institute of Biology of Ireland, (President, 1992-95); Royal Irish Academy, National Committee for Biology, (Chairman, 1996 to date); International Union of Biological Sciences (member of Executive Committee, 1997 to date); member, European Commission Group of Advisors on Ethics in Science, 1998 to date; awarded, Fellowship of Institute of Biology (UK), 1981; Fellowship of Institute of Biology of Ireland, 1997; awarded Title-European Biologist, 1998, also awarded several Research Grants from Eolas, Forbairt, HRB and EU; other listings include, *Who's Who in the World,* (1993-94); *Who's Who in Science and Engineering,* (1994-95). Hobbies, walking, photography, classical music and bioethics. Contact: National University of Ireland, Maynooth, Co. KIldare. Tel: 01 708 3842. Fax: 01 708 3845.

WOOD, Keith

WILLIAMS, Paul Noel; JOURNALIST/AUTHOR; *b* 1964; *educ* Carrigallen Vocational School, Leitrim; School of Journalism, Rathmines; Post Grad. Dip Criminological Studies, DIT College, Rathmines, 1990-92; *partner* Anne Sweeney; 1*s* 1 *da;* Junior Reporter, *Leitrim Observer,* 1984-85; Senior Reporter, *Longford News,* 1985-87; Senior Crime Correspondent, *Sunday World,* 1987 to date; publications include, *The General, Godfather of Crime,* 1995 (adapted for film directed by John Boorman), *Secret Love,* 1995, the story of Fr. Michael Cleary's secret life, *Gangland,* 1998; *The General, Godfather of Crime* was numbered as 55 in Easons Top 100 Books of All Time, *The General* and *Gangland,* best selling true crime books in Ireland; recipient, Print Journalist of the Year Award 1995, Campaigning Journalist of the Year Award 1996, voted top Journalist of the Year by all national journalists; the finest crime correspondent in Ireland, exposes crime weekly in the *Sunday World..* Hobbies, keeping fit, adventure training, movies, socialising, also involved in cinematic and television projects. Contact: Sunday World, Sunday Newspapers Ltd., PO Box 641, Newspaper House, 18 Rathfarnham Road, Dublin 6. Tel: 01 490 1980. Fax: 01 490 1838.

WOOD, Keith Gerard Mallinson; PROFESSIONAL RUGBY PLAYER; *b* 1972; *educ* St. Munchen's College, Limerick; University of Limerick; *single*; Sponsorship Executive, Irish Permanent, 1991-96; Professional Rugby Player with Harlequins R.F.C. (UK), 1996 to date; capped for Ireland 23 times; 2 caps for British and Irish Lions; formerly with Garryowen F.C.; awarded: Sport Celebrity Award, 1997, Texaco Sport Star, 1998. Regarded as the finest hooker in world rugby at present. Hobbies, golf and reading. Contact: Harlequins F.C., The Stoop Memorial Ground, Langborne Drive, Twickenham, England. Tel: 0044 181 410 6000.

WOODWORTH, Judith

WOODWORTH, Judith; CONCERT PROMOTER/ARTISTIC DIRECTOR; *b* 1951; *educ* Alexandra College, Dublin; Trinity College Dublin, BA; Royal Irish Academy of Music, awarded various scholarships and prizes for piano and solo singing; *single*; Artists' Manager, Harrison Parrott, London, 1978-86; Artistic Director, GPA Music in Great Irish Houses, 1982 to date; Concert Promoter, Celebrity Concert series, National Concert Hall - presenting international artists such as Nigel Kennedy, Anne Sophia Multer, Kyung-wha Chung, Alfred Brendel, 1988 to date; Director, National Concert Hall, 1993 to date; Chairman, Council of National Cultural Institutions; Committee Member, Association of Chief Executives of State Agencies; Council Member, Alexandra College, Dublin; a cool, effective manager, has developed and raised standards in the National Concert Hall. Hobbies, gardening, music (classical and opera), art, travel, photography, reading and hill walking. Contact: The National Concert Hall, Earlsfort Terrace, Dublin 2. Tel: 01 475 1666. Fax: 01 478 3797.

WRIGHT, Finbar

WRIGHT, Finbar; SINGER/SONGWRITER; *b* 1959; *educ* Farranferris College, Cork; University of Palencia, Spain; Maynooth College; University College Cork; *m* Angela Desmond, Marketing Consultant; 1 *s* 1 *da*; Presenter *Music of the Night* series on RTE Television; five albums released with Sony Music, currently recording album number six; career highlights include: performing for President Clinton at State Dinner at Dublin Castle, 1995; performing with Montserrat Caballé, Point Theatre, 1993; own songs include *The Girl in Love with Depardieu, Black Wind, Freedom, Sometimes*; awards include Best Male Artist, IRMA 1993 and 1994. Hobbies, gardening, horse-riding, antiques and reading. Contact: Matty Fox, Derryneel, Ballinalee, Co. Longford. Tel: 043 23165.

WRIGHT, Patrick J.; PRESIDENT & CHIEF OPERATIONS OFFICER, JEFFERSON SMURFIT GROUP; *b* 1941; *educ* O'Connells Christian Brothers School, Dublin; *m* Carol Lambert; *5 children;* various management positions, B&I, 1959-71; Operations & Marketing Executive, Managing Director, Odeon (Ireland) 1971-75; Personal Assistant to Michael Smurfit, 1976; Managing Director, Smurfit Corrugated & Allied Packaging Division; Managing Director, Smurfit Ireland & UK, currently President & Chief Operations Officer, Jefferson Smurfit Group; Past Chairman, Bord Iascaigh Mhara; Past President, Confederation of Irish Industry; Trustee IBEC, Director, Aer Lingus, Fellow of The National College of Ireland, The Irish Management Institute and The Marketing Institute; Chairman of the Educational Trust of Dublin City University; recognised as a tough, straight talking executive; the ideal company man, hard working and loyal. Hobbies, golf, GAA, soccer and all sports. Contact: Smurfit Group, Beech Hill, Clonskeagh, Dublin 4. Tel: 01 202 7000.

WRIGHT, Patrick J

YOUNG, Ian; MANAGING DIRECTOR IRISH INTERNATIONAL GROUP; *b* 1958; *educ* Wesley College; The High School; Trinity College Dublin; *separated;* 1 *s* 2 *da;* worked in advertising companies (Adsell, Hunters); spent 7 years in RHM Foods; Managing Director, Des O'Meara & Partners, 1988-92 (inaugural agency of the year, 1991); Group Managing Director, Killeen Investments (Toyota, Lexus, Mount Juliet etc.), 1992-94; acquired Shareholding in Irish International, 1994, currently Managing Director; the agency has been awarded The Agency of the Year title twice; 3 times Managing Director of Agency of the Year (1991, 1995, 1997); member, Marketing Institute, MMI, RDS, K Club and Powerscourt Golf Club; Hobbies, family, music and sport. Contact: Irish International Group, 17 Gilford Road, Sandymount, Dublin 4. Tel: 01 260 2000. Fax: 01 260 2111.

THE 200 RISING STARS

SPONSORED BY ESAT TELECOM

Esat
TELECOM

THE 200 RISING STARS

As we begin a new Millennium, Ireland is on the cusp of the Information Age. How we live, work and interact in the global village of tomorrow is as much reliant on how willing we are to embrace change as it is on change itself. There are huge changes taking place in Ireland and being driven by young,energetic people who are willing to take risks, seize opportunities and see a vision through to completion.

Behind every success story there is perseverance and hard work. The economic success story that Ireland has become should be credited to the many people who have strived to not only make things work but make things better. As a company that has both created and encouraged change, Esat Telecom has led the way in revolutionising Ireland's telecommunications market, bringing choice to consumers through future proofed technology.

For these reasons, we are very proud to be associated with Ireland's Who's Who, specifically the young decision-makers of tomorrow. In this section, some of Ireland's rising talents are profiled. These individuals are the torchbearers of the future and their expertise will help maintain Ireland's position as the 'Jewel in the Crown' of Europe. Like stars, these individuals are the shifting constants that will ensure a bright future for everyone in Ireland.

Denis O'Brien
Chairman
Esat Telecom Group plc

Esat
TELECOM

ALLEN, Rachel; née O'Neill; COOK, COOKERY TEACHER; *b* 1971 *educ* Alexandra College, Dublin; Certificate Cooking Course, Ballymaloe Cookery School; *m* Isaac Allen; Cook, Ballymaloe House, 1990-91; Assistant, Ballymaloe Cookery School, 1991-93, Teacher, 1995 to date; hobbies, travelling, skiing, eating out. Contact: Ballymaloe Cookery School, Shanagarry, Co. Cork. Tel: 021 646 785 Fax: 021 646 909.

ALLEN, Rachel

ASHMORE, Sean; CHIEF EXECUTIVE, EAST COAST RADIO; *b* 1970; *educ* Synge Street Dublin, St. MacDara's Community College, Templeogue; Ballyfermot Senior College, Cert. Presentation & Broadcasting Skills; Institute of Advertising Practitioners in Ireland, Dip., Advertising; *single;* Production Manager, Horizon Radio, 1990; Production Manager, East Coast Radio, 1992-93, Station Engineer, 1993-94, Station Manager, 1994, Joint Chief Executive, 1994-98, Chief Executive, 1998 to date; Director, Chairman Independent Network News, 1997 to date; Member, Future of Bray Committee; a quietly confident broadcasting executive; hobbies, cinema, hill walking; Contact: East Coast Radio, 9, Prince of Wales Terrace, Bray Co. Wicklow. Tel: 01 286 6414.

ASHMORE, Sean

BALLAGH, Rachel; ARTIST; *b* 1968; *educ* Sandymount High School, Dublin; Ballyfermot Senior College, Art Design and Media Studies; National College of Art and Design, Degree, Fine Art; *single;* Exhibitions include: National Portrait Awards, Arnotts, 1994, Group Show, Gallery and Edition, Caoc, Berlin, Germany, 1995, Broadstrokes, The Arts Council, 1996, Signals, Festival of Women's Photography, The Gallery of Photography, 1996, Flock, Temple Bar Gallery, 1997; Members Show, Temple Bar Gallery, 1997; On Site Group Show, Temple Bar Gallery, 1998; Ramus Group Show, Botanical Gardens, 1998; The Birds, Project Arts Centre, 1998, Kosovo Project, Meeting House Square, Dublin, 1999; Collections include: The Gordon Lambert Collection, Microsoft Ireland Permanent Art Collection, various private collections; Awards include: Materials Grant, The Arts Council, 1998, Shortlisted for the PSI, 1998, Arts Council Travel Award, 1999; hobbies, travelling, cinema, flamenco dancing; Contact: Temple Bar Gallery and Studios, Temple Bar, Dublin 2. Tel: 01 671 0073.

BANOTTI, Tania; DIRECTOR, FILMMAKERS IRELAND; *b* 1969; *educ* Mount Sackville, St. Columba's; Trinity College Dublin, BA; Dublin City University, MA, Film and Television; *single;* Programme Officer, G.L.O.B.E., Washington DC, U.S.A., 1991; Account Director, Herbison Public Affairs, Brussels, Belgium, 1992-96; Co-ordinator, UNESCO, Gaza Strip, Palestine, 1996-98; Director, Filmmakers Ireland, 1998 to date; The daughter of Mary Banotti, has a proven track record as a lobbyist; currently applying her skills to the Irish film industry; hobbies, diving, cinema; Contact: The Studio Building, Meeting House Square, Temple Bar, Dublin 2. Tel: 01-6713525.

BANOTTI, Tania

BEGLEY, David; ARTIST; *b* 1972; *educ* Graphic Design, National College of Art and Design; Freelance Illustrator, *Hot Press, dSide, Dublin Event Guide, U Magazine,* 1995; solo exhibitions: David and Goliath, Ormond Multimedia Centre, Dublin, 1996, We Could Be Golden, Eamon Dorans Gallery, 1998, The Last Supper, Toscas, 1999; Commissions include James Joyce Room, Bewleys, Grafton Street, Dublin, 1998, *Hot Press* Hall of Fame, 1999; A multi talented artist, who has also worked on Ireland's most popular music and culture magazines; hobbies, writing, film, music. Contact: 087 272 1100.

BIRDTHISTLE, Elizabeth Marian; SALES MANAGER, GULLIVER INFORES; *b* 1969; *educ* Kylemore Abbey, Co. Galway; Trinity College Dublin, BA, MA; *single;* Marketing Manager, Funderland, Dublin, Cork, Belfast, 1993-95; National Youth Education Officer, Progressive Democrats, 1995-97; Sales Manager, Gulliver Infores, 1997 to date; Member, Toastmasters International, National Geographic Society, Operatic Society, Druid Theatre, Galway, Limerick Sub Aqua Club; recognised as a one woman sales force; hobbies, cooking, travel, scuba diving, cetaceanics. Contact: Fexco Centre, Killorglin, Co. Kerry. Tel: 066 921 12.

BIRDTHISTLE, Elizabeth

BOLGER, Jillian; EDITOR, FOOD & WINE MAGAZINE; *b* 1973; *educ* Notre Dame des Missions, Dublin; University College Cork; BA German, Geography; *single*, Lived in Germany for 18 months; Travelled extensively in Asia & North America; Began freelance writing at 25; Joined Food & Wine Magazine as Features Editor, Jan 1999, Editor *Food & Wine* Magazine August 1999 to date. Hobbies; cooking, mountain biking, travel, Formula 1, art; Contact: Food & Wine Magazine, 1-3 Dungar Terrace, Dun Laoghaire, Co Dublin, Tel: 01 2300322.

BOLGER, Jillian

BRADFIELD, Dawn

BRENNAN, Rory;

BOWE, Laura Maria Lucia; SET DRESSER; *b* 1969; *educ* St. Gerard's School, Bray; University College Dublin, BA; Chelsea College of Art HND (Design); North London University BA (Hons) Design; *single;* worked as 'Girl Friday' on *My Left Foot*; formed her own company as Freelance Set Dresser and Props Buyer; film work includes *A Man Of No Importance, Frankie Starlight,* a brief spell on *Divine Rapture,* the movie that never happened, *Sweety Barrett, Nora* - The James Joyce Story; television credits include *The Ambassador* BBC, *Amongst Women* BBC; hobbies, cooking, horseriding, socialising; Contact: 36 St. Alban's Road, Dublin 8.

BRADFIELD, Dawn; ACTOR; *b* 1970; *educ* Convent of Mercy, Macroom, Cork; College of Commerce, Cork, Dip. Business Studies; Gaiety School of Acting; *single;* Freelance Actor, 1992 to date; worked with TEAM, 1992-93; appearances include: *Sive, Danti Dan,* Project Arts Centre Dublin, London; *The Broken Jug, The Duty Master, The Importance of Being Earnest, She Stoops to Folly, Translations,* Abbey Theatre; *The Singular Life of Albert Knobbs,* Druid Theatre, Galway; *The Lonesome West,* Dublin, Galway, London, Sydney, New York, nominated for Best Supporting Actress, Tony Awards, 1999; *Elton John's Glasses, Yard,* London; screen appearances include *The Run of the Country, Dancing at Lughnasa, Sweety Barrett, Brood, The Life of Reilly, Bent Out of Shape, Father Ted, Making the Cut;* awarded *The Irish Times* Best Supporting Actress Award for *The Lonesome West,* 1998; predominantly a stage actress, interested in originating new roles; hobby, writing; Contact: Teri Hayden, The Agency, 47 Adelaide Road, Dublin 2. Tel: 01 661 8535. Fax: 01 676 0052.

BRANGAN, Pamela; MODEL; *b* 1974; *educ* Our Lady's School, Claremont, Rathnew; University College Dublin, BA, Philosophy, Greek and Roman Civilisation; *m* St. John Walshe; modelling while in college, started with Smirnoff Student Fashion Shows; moved to New York, joined Pauline Model Agency; has worked extensively in New York, Paris, Milan, Tokyo, London; television commercials include: Revlon, with Cindy Crawford, Oil Of Ulay; has appeared in *Marie Claire, Elle, Vogue, Donna, Image Magazine, i-D,* among others; has worked with Mario Testino, Patrick De Marchelier, Perry Ogden; a highly successful Irish model who has become a face on the international fashion scene; hobbies, tennis, swimming, working out. Contact: Morgan the Agency, 13, Herbert Place, Dublin 2. Tel: 01 661 4572.

BRENNAN, Rory; SENIOR CONSULTANT, MARK MITCHELL RECRUITMENT; *b* 1966; *educ* Cabinteely Community School, Dublin; Rathmines College of Commerce, Certificate, Business Studies; *single;* Co-founded Clean Life International, 1986; joined Professional Placement Group as Trainee Consultant, 1987, Senior Consultant, 1988-89; travelled to Australia, worked in Bureau Executive as Consultant, Sydney, 1989-90; Senior Consultant, Harrison Willis plc., Reading, U.K., 1991-92; Senior Consultant, Sales & Marketing Division, PPG Advantage, Divisional Manager PPG Advantage, 1996; currently Senior Consultant, Mark Mitchell Recruitment, 1999; responsible for executive search and recruitment campaigns for food, drink and marketing service groups; clients include: Irish Distillers, Coca Cola, Gilbeys, Murphy's Brewery, Mars Inc.; hobbies, Formula 1, horse racing; Contact: Mark Mitchell Recruitment, 8 Ontario Terrace, Dublin 6. Tel: 01 475 2609 Fax: 01 475 4225

BROWNE, Trevor; PROPRIETOR, DISH RESTAURANT; *b* 1971; *educ* Gonzaga College; *single;* 1 s; has worked in the restaurant business for six years; started off waiting tables; set up Dish Restaurant, in Temple Bar, Dublin, 1997; Dish has gained a reputation for its modern international cuisine and casual yet elegant ambience; hobby, spending time with his son; Contact: Dish Restaurant, 2, Crowe Street, Dublin 2. Tel: 01 671 1248.

BUCKLEY, John; 3D DESIGNER; *b* 1970; *educ* C.B.S., Ballinteer, Dublin; National College of Art and Design, Degree, Fine Art, History of Art; *single;* Trainer, Arthouse Multimedia Centre for the Arts, 1995; Web Designer, Daily Planet Communications, Paris, France, 1997; Freelance Web Designer, 1997-98; 3D Artist, The Yard, 1998 to date; hobbies, music, clubbing; Contact: The Yard, Sheriff Street, Dublin 1. Tel: 01 855 3545.

BURKE, Jarlath; DIRECTOR OF LEGAL AND REGULATORY AFFAIRS, ESAT TELECOM; *b* 1972; *educ* St. Joseph's, Foxford, Co. Mayo; University College Dublin, BCL, MA, European

Law; *single;* joined Esat Telecom straight after completing college; has been employed in the position of Director of Legal and Regulatory Affairs since, with a special focus on the application of competition rules to the State sector; responsible for all regulatory and competition affairs in Esat Telecom, including relations with the European Commission; was a member of the legal team which negotiated the Esat Digifone Mobile Licence; member, The International Bar Association; hobbies, politics, reading, walking, football. Contact: Esat Telecom, Malt House, Grand Canal Quay, Dublin 2. Tel: 01 661 6010 Fax: 01 602 6285.

BURKE-KENNEDY, Wendy; VIDEO EDITOR;*b* 1973; *educ* Loretto Abbey, Dalkey; University College Dublin, BA; *single;* Assistant Editor, The Yard, 1997-99; Freelance Assistant Editor, Dreamchaser Productions, 1999 to date; one of the leading lights in digital video editing in Ireland; hobby, water skiing. Contact: Printed Light, 41, Victoria Street, Portobello, Dublin 6.

BURTON, Karl; ARCHITECT, SCOTT TALLON WALKER ARCHITECTS; *b* 1969; *educ* Portmarnock Community School, Dublin; Oxford Brooks University, Oxford, U.K.; DIT Bolton Street, BA (Hons.), Architecture; *single;* Architect, Gilroy MacMahon Architects, 1996-97; Architect, Scott Tallon Walker, 1997 to date; has worked on The Woodchester European Service Centre, 1996-97, Food Science Building, University College Dublin, 1998-99; although working mainly in the public arena has also been commissioned to work on a number of private dwellings; Scott Tallon Walker are one of the biggest architectural companies in Ireland; hobby, golf; Contact: Scott Tallon Walker Architects, 19, Merrion Square, Dublin 2. Tel: 01 676 0621.

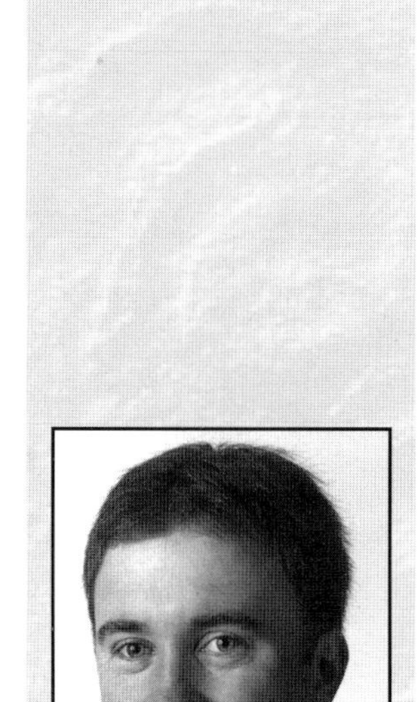

BUTLER, Sean

BUTLER, John, DOCUMENTARY MAKER; *b* 1972 *educ* Blackrock College, Dublin; University College Dublin, BA, MA, Film; Producer, *TV.com,* technology magazine programme, syndicated in the U.S.A., 1995-98; Producer, Director, *The Million Dollar Deal,* RTE, 1999; Contact: Doubledown Productions, 15a, Arbour Hill, Stoneybatter, Dublin 7. Tel: 087 286 1226.

BUTLER, Sean; POLITICIAN; *b* 1972; *educ* St. Kieran's College, Kilkenny; Carlow Institute of Technology, BBS Degree in Services Marketing (Hons); Graduate, Marketing Institute of Ireland, MMII; worked as Sales Executive, Duggan Steel, Kilkenny and Business Manager, Students Union Waterford Institute of Technology; joined the Labour Party, 1990; member, Labour Youth, The Ballycallan Branch, former member, Party General Council; Contact: Dáil Eireann, Kildare Street, Dublin 2. Tel: 01 618 3333.

CALLAGHAN, Justin; INTERNATIONAL CASH MANAGER, DELTA INTERNATIONAL FINANCE; *b* 1972; *educ* St. Paul's Raheny; St. Michael's; University College Dublin, BA, Psychology, NBS; AIB Capital Markets, 1995-98; International Cash Manager, Delta International Finance, 1998 to date; the friendly, personable face of international money management; hobbies, soccer, music. Contact; c/o Delta International, West Block, IFSC, Dublin 1. Tel: 01 829 0288.

CAMPBELL, Conor; QUANTITATIVE TRADER, CREDIT SUISSE; *b* 1972; *educ* St Columba's College, Dublin; Clare College, Cambridge, England BA Classics, MA Theoretical Linguistics; *single;* worked for BZW in Equity Derivatives,1996; Credit Suisse bought out BZW 1998, began trading on the cash and futures markets last year; a member of an elite band of young, dynamic traders; hobby, playing pool; Contact: Credit Suisse, 5 North Colonade, Canary Wharf, London, E14 4QJ, England.

CANTWELL, Alan

CANTWELL, Alan; TV3 NEWS ANCHOR; *b* 1969; *educ* Christian Brothers, Clonkeen Road, Dublin; *single;* Presenter, Promoter, Capitol Radio, 1985-89; Presenter, Head of Music, Clare FM, 1989-92; Broadcast Journalist, Classic Hits 98FM, 1992-93; Head of News & Current Affairs Programming, Clare FM, 1993-97; News Editor, Independent Network News, Dublin, 1997-98; TV3 News Anchor, 1998 to date; hobbies, swimming, mountain walking, current affairs; Contact: TV3, Unit 5, Westgate Business Park, Ballymount Industrial Estate, Dublin 24. Tel: 01 419 3333.

CARNEY, John; DIRECTOR, WRITER; *b* 1972 *educ* De La Salle, Churchtown; *single;* origi-

nally a musician, playing with The Frames, has been working in film production since 1995; made first feature film, *November Afternoon*, 1997, voted Best Feature Film by *The Irish Times*, 1997, followed by *Just in Time*, voted Best Television Film of the Year, *The Irish Times*; 1998; his third film, *Park*, was premiered at the Dublin Film Festival, 1999, the first Irish film to be shot entirely on digital video; currently writing, directing and developing a sitcom, *Bachelor's Walk*, in conjunction with Temple Films and developing a musical feature film, *The Tender Trap* with Ed Guiney; an award winning young writer and director, whose films tackle the social taboos in Irish society. Contact: Temple Films, 1, Eustace Street, Dublin 2. Tel: 01 671 9313.

CARROLL, Jim; EDITOR, TELECOM INTERNET NEW MEDIA PUBLISHING; *b* 1969 *educ* Doon C.B.S., Doon, Co. Limerick; *single;* Freelance Journalist, *DropOut, Hot Press, Evening Herald, Irish Independent, Irish Times, Sounds, Dublin Event Guide, NME, Sunday Tribune, Melody Maker, i-D, dSide, Muzik, PC Live!* 1988 to date; DJ, Club Promoter, *Wild, DropOut,* 1992-95; Founder, Misinformation Music PR Agency, 1989-95, A&R Consultant, WEA, Go! Discs, Rondor Music, Dedicated, 1990-95; Co-founder, Lakota Records,1995; Press Officer, London Records, 1996-97; Editor, *Muse*, 1997 to date; Editor, *Doras Movies*, 1998 to date; Broadcaster, Anna Livia FM, 1999 to date; Editor in Chief, Telecom Internet New Media Publishing Division, 1999 to date; Ireland's most prolific music journalist, now bringing Telecom Eireann into The Information Age with a wide range of electronic publications; hobbies, travel, relaxing, DJing, drinking coffee; Contact: E-mail: fierce@tinet.ie.

CASEY, Patrick, "Paddy"

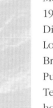

CASEY, Patrick, "Paddy"; MUSICIAN; *b* 1975; *single;* began busking in Dublin and Galway, before working with Elliot Smith, Blondie, Otis Redding III, David Gray and Tracey Chapman; has performed in Ireland and the UK, recently releasing his debut album, *Amen (So Be It)* on Sony; has been "tipped for great things" and described as "Dublin's singer-song-writer prodigy"; hobby, shirtmaking; Contact: Principle Management, Sir John Rogerson's Quay, Dublin 2. Tel: 01-6777330.

CHEESEBOROUGH, Susan; MAKE UP ARTIST, FASHION STYLIST; *b* 1972 *educ* Loretto Convent, Killarney; Mallow College of Fashion Design and Tailoring; *single;* Manager, The Body Wise Shop, 1990; Trainee Make Up Artist, Make Up Forever, 1991-92; Fashion Editor, *Irish Weddings and New Homes*, 1996; Teacher, Anne Weekes Beauty School, Dublin, 1996-97; Make Up Artist, *Head To Toe*, Network 2, 1994-97; Personal Make Up Artist, Mary Banotti, Presidential Campaign, 1998; Make Up Artist for Boyzone, Sinéad O' Connor, The Corrs, 1993 to date; Private Make Up and Fashion Consultant, 1993 to date; Adjudicator, Society of Applied Cosmetology Competition, 1996-97; Freelance Make Up Artist, *Image Magazine, dSide, U Magazine, Himself Magazine, IT Magazine, Social & Personal,* 1993 to date; the make up artist for politicians and pop stars alike, her work has graced the pages of Ireland's most stylish publications; hobbies, reading, art; Contact: First Option, 40, Dame Street, Dublin 2. Tel: 01 6705233.

CITRON, Lana; AUTHOR, SCRIPT WRITER; *b* 1969; *educ* The High School Rathgar; Trinity College Dublin, BA, History; Radio work includes: comedy scripting, *Sarah Parnell Show,* Viva Radio, 1995, *Now & Forever*, BBC Radio 4 Short Story, 1997; published work includes: *Lapdog Days,* 1996, *Sucker,* 1998, *The Kiss Hoarder,* 1998, *The Craic Run,* 1999, *The Scoreboard,* 1999, *100% Love & Eternal Optimist,* 1999; film work includes: *I Was The Cigarette Girl,* commissioned by BBC Northern Ireland, 1999; work has been feted as "the emergence of a brave new prose stylist"; Contact: Jonny Geller, Curtis Brown, Haymarket House, 28-29, Haymarket, London, SW1Y 4SP, England. Tel: 0044-171-3966600 Fax: 0044 171 3960110.

CLARKE, Robert; ARTIST; *b* 1973; *educ* Royal and Prior Comprehensive, Donegal; National College of Art and Design, Degree in Fine Art, (First Class Hons.); *single;* solo exhibitions include: Solo Exhibition, Hallward Gallery, 1996, Athanor, Hallward Gallery, 1998, New Works, Hallward Gallery, 2000; numerous group exhibitions, The Hallward Gallery, 1996 to date; collections include: Irish Society of Contemporary Art, KPMG, Butler Gallery, various private collections; Manager, Nude, the newly opened healthy fast food restaurant in Dublin; plans to study MA in Fine Art, Slade School of Art, London; an abstract landscape painter concerned primarily with organic textures; hobby, music. Contact: Hallward Gallery, Merrion

Square, Dublin 2. Tel: 01 662 1482.

CLEARY, Catherine; JOURNALIST; *b* 1970; *educ* Dominican Convent, Wicklow; DIT Rathmines, Dip. Advertising Copywriting; University of Kent, Cantebury, England, BA; Dublin City University, MA Journalism; *single;* Freelance Reporter, *The Irish Times,* 1994-96, Staff Reporter, 1996-98, Drugs and Crime Correspondent, 1998-99; Security Correspondent, *The Sunday Tribune,* 1999 to date; a hard hitting crime journalist; Contact: The Sunday Tribune, 15, Lower Baggot Street, Dublin 2. Tel: 01 661 5555.

COFFEY, Eoin; MARKETING MANAGER, INTEROUTE IRELAND; *b* 1970 *educ* St. Paul's Raheny, Trinity College Dublin, BA; *single;* Music Promoter, 1994-96; Managing Director, Cappawhite Communications, Australia, 1996-98; currently Marketing Manager, Interoute Ireland, Europe's most innovative telecommunications company; hobbies, scuba diving, reading. Contact: Interoute Ireland, 19-26 Pembroke Street, Dublin 2. Tel: 01-6617360.

COLEMAN, Naimee; SINGER;*b* 1976; *educ* Loreto College, St. Stephen's Green, Dublin; *single;* signed to EMI Records, 1995; Singer, The Wilde Oscars, 1993-94; released debut album *Silver Wrists,* 1996; currently working on a second album which should propel her onto an international forum; hobbies, cinema, painting, drama. Contact: Simon Watson, Sidewinder Management. Tel: 0044 127 324 9700.

COLEMAN, Naimee

COLLINS, John; JOURNALIST; *b* 1972; *educ* Presentation College, Carlow; University College Dublin, BA, English, Philosophy, DIT Aungier Street, Post Graduate Diploma, Public Relations; *m* Sandra Whitney; Account Executive, Edelman Public Relations, 1994-95; Freelance Journalist, *Hot Press, Muzik, Mixmag, i-D, dSide, The Event Guide, Business Plus, Irish Independent, The Web Magazine, Muse,* 1994 to date; Co-promoter, UFO night, 1994-97; Editor, *PC Live!* 1996 to date; Presenter, *TechTV,* RTE, 1998; Regular Contributor, *The Gerry Ryan Show,* 2FM, *Future Tense,* Radio 1, 1999; hobbies, Volkswagen Beetles, working out, music; Contact: Prospect House, 1, Prospect Road, Glasnevin, Dublin 9. Tel: 01 830 3455.

COMYN, Annabel; THEATRE DIRECTOR; *b* 1973; *educ* Holy Child Convent, Killiney; Trinity College Dublin; Goldsmith College, London; *single;* currently Associate Director, *The Weir,* for the Royal Court; has directed *B22, Party People* (Young Writers Festival 1998), *Rough Road to Survival; The Lament for Arthur Cleary* (Brockley Jack), *The Rock Station* (Finberough); *The Real Inspector Hound, Black Comedy* as resident director; member, National Theatre Studio Directors Forum; described in *Time Out* as "a dynamic new director"; hobby, kite flying. Contact: The Royal Court Theatre. Tel: 0044 171 565 5050.

COMYN, Annabel

CONNELLY, Sharon, MARKETING MANAGER, HOT PRESS MAGAZINE; *b* 1970; *educ* St. Mary's College, Ballygar, Galway; Trinity College Dublin, B.Sc. Management; single; Graduate Investment Banker, Boston, U.S.A, 1994; Advertising Executive, Smurfit Publications, 1995-97; Marketing Manager, *Hot Press* Magazine, 1997 to date; responsible for bringing *Hot Press* to a new generation of music lovers; hobbies, live music, cinema, millinery. Contact: Hot Press Magazine, 13, Trinity Street, Dublin 2.

CONNOLLY, John, WRITER; *b* 1968; *educ* Synge Street, CBS, Trinity College Dublin, BA, English; Dublin City University, MA Journalism; *single;* worked as a clerical Officer with Dublin Corporation, before attending University; Freelance Journalist, *The Irish Times, Sunday Press,* for a short time; First novel, *Every Dead Thing,* published, 1999; has finished writing second novel, *Requiem for the Damned,* to be published at the end of 1999; both works are detective crime thrillers, set in the US; one of the first Irish writers to receive a big advance for his debut novel; hobbies, reading, cinema, physical fitness, travel; Contact: Darley Anderson, Estelle House, 11, Eustace Road, London SW6 1JB, England.

CONNELLY, Sharon

CONNOLLY, Mark Andrew; OPERATIONS DIRECTOR, FINIVIA HOLDINGS LTD; *b* 1969; *educ* St. Columba's College, Rathfarnham, Diploma, Marketing; *m* Phyllida Lawson; obtained commercial pilot's licence, 1991; Pilot with RST, freight carriers, Africa, 1991-93; Operations Manager, Finivia Holdings Ltd., 1993-95, Operations Director, 1995 to date; Finivia are involved in the manufacture, sale and leasing of aircraft in the U.K., Ireland and

worldwide; Director, Cirrus, Aviation Consultants; hobbies, flying, golf, horses (former competitor in Punchestown Three Day Event). Contact: Finivia Holdings Ltd., 39, King Henry's Reach, Manbrae Road, London W6 9RH, England.

CONNOR, Feargal; DIRECTOR, EYE-LEVEL LTD.; *b* 1969 *educ* Marian College, Dublin; College of Marketing and Design, Mountjoy Square, Dublin; *single;* Sales Representative, Coca Cola Bottlers, 1991, Space Manager, 1992-93; Trade Marketing Manager, Green Isle Foods, 1994-95, Brand Manager, 1995-97; Co-Founded Eye Level Ltd., with Damian Byrne, 1997, Director, 1997 to date; Eye Level is Ireland's most innovative trade research and merchandising strategy company; hobbies, reading, sports, playing the guitar; Contact: Eye Level Ltd., Wentworth Mews, 19-20 Hogan Place, Dublin 2. Tel: 01 662 7245.

COVENEY, Rory; WRITER; *b* 1974; *educ* Clongowes Wood College; National University of Ireland, Cork, BA, Hist.; Michael Smurfit Graduate School of Business, Dip. Bus. Studies; in between Cork University and The Michael Smurfit Graduate School took a year out, working as Maintenance Manager at the Sydney Opera House, Australia, 1995; set out in an around the world fund raising sail in aid of The Chernobyl Children's Project, 1998; has been commissioned to write about the voyage, *Voyage of Hope* (Mercier Press), 1999; member, Royal Cork Yacht Club; hobbies, photography, travel, reading, politics, Irish history. Contact: 6a, Anglesea Street, Cork. Tel: 021 31300.

COX, Maurice Anthony; MANAGEMENT CONSULTANT; *b* 1968; *educ* Headfort School, Kells; St. Columba's College, Rathfarnham; Trinity College Dublin, MB, BcH, BAO, BA Mod.; Cambridge University, M.Phil.; *single;* Intern in Meath and Adelaide Hospitals; Senior House Officer, Meath and Adelaide Hospitals, 1995-97; Registrar Orthopaedics, St. Vincent's Hospital, 1997-98; Consultant, McKinsey & Co., international management consultants, 1998 to date; a young man with remarkable qualifications who chose a complete career change; a star player on the rugby and commercial arenas; member, R.A.C., Riverview Fitness Club, Hawks Club (Cambridge), Old Wesley RFC; played rugby for Trinity College, Irish Universities, Cambridge (Blue), Old Wesley; hobbies, sailing, water-skiing, debating. Contact: McKinsey & Co., 80 Harcourt Street, Dublin 2. Tel: 01 478 5500.

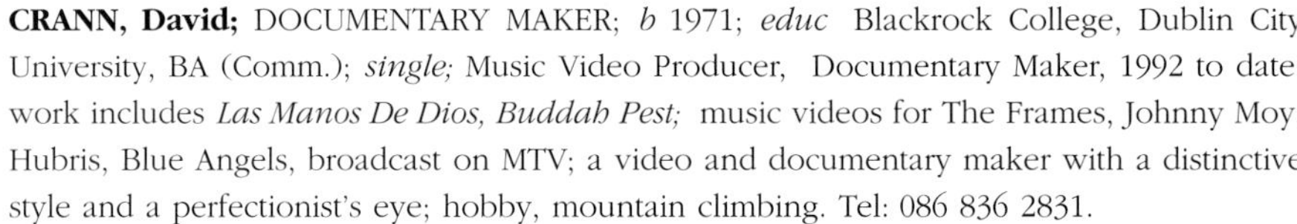

CRANN, David; DOCUMENTARY MAKER; *b* 1971; *educ* Blackrock College, Dublin City University, BA (Comm.); *single;* Music Video Producer, Documentary Maker, 1992 to date; work includes *Las Manos De Dios, Buddah Pest;* music videos for The Frames, Johnny Moy, Hubris, Blue Angels, broadcast on MTV; a video and documentary maker with a distinctive style and a perfectionist's eye; hobby, mountain climbing. Tel: 086 836 2831.

CURRAN, Doreen

CURRAN, Doreen; SINGER; *b* 1974; *educ* Thornhill College, Derry; DIT, College of Music, B.Mus. (First Class Hons.); currently studying under Anne Marie O'Sullivan; performances include: *Orfeo*, The Opera Theatre Company, Dublin, *Dido and Aeneas,* The Irish National Concert Hall, Dublin, touring to London and Derry, Recital of Lieder , The National Concert Hall, Dublin, Paris, *Beethoven's Ninth Symphony,* The National Concert Hall, *Frauenliebe und Leben,* Galway, *La Fiamma, Carmen,* The Wexford Festival, excerpts from operas including: *Der Rosencavalier, Carmen, Orfeo, Hansel and Gretel, Cosi Fan Tutte, The Rake's Progress* ; sang as a soloist in The National Concert Hall in *St. Matthew's Passion, St. John's Passion,* Haydn *Stabetmater,* Mozart's *Requiem,* Handel's *Messiah, Saint-Saens Christmas Oratorio,* Schubert's *Mass in A Flat, Schubert's Mass in C* , and Charpentier's *Mass*; has won numerous awards, including RTE Young Irish Singer of the Future, 1998; hobbies, reading, keeping fit, cinema, socialising; Contact: School of Vocal, Operatic and Drama Studies, DIT Rathmines, Dublin 6. Tel: 01 402 3471 Fax: 01 402 3470.

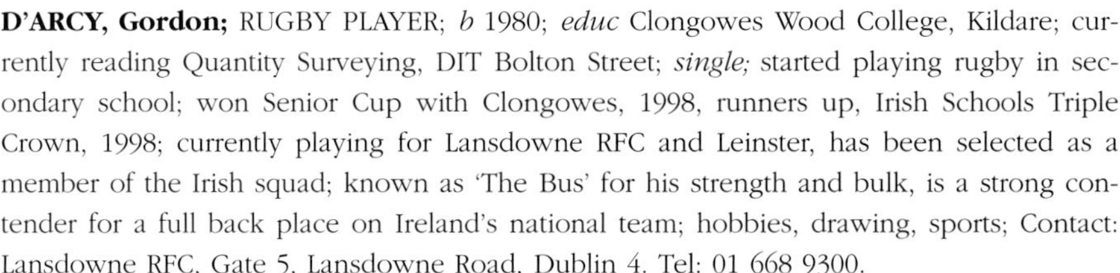

D'ARCY, Gordon; RUGBY PLAYER; *b* 1980; *educ* Clongowes Wood College, Kildare; currently reading Quantity Surveying, DIT Bolton Street; *single;* started playing rugby in secondary school; won Senior Cup with Clongowes, 1998, runners up, Irish Schools Triple Crown, 1998; currently playing for Lansdowne RFC and Leinster, has been selected as a member of the Irish squad; known as 'The Bus' for his strength and bulk, is a strong contender for a full back place on Ireland's national team; hobbies, drawing, sports; Contact: Lansdowne RFC, Gate 5, Lansdowne Road, Dublin 4. Tel: 01 668 9300.

DAVIS, Paul; MUSIC PROMOTER; *b* 1971; *educ* Belvedere College, Dublin; University College Dublin, BA History, Ancient Civilisation; *single;* Entertainments Officer, Students Union, University College Dublin, 1993-94; Events Manager, The Furnace, 1994-95; Promotions Manager, The Ormond Multimedia Centre, 1995-96; co-founded Influx Records and Productions, the most successful independent music promoters in Ireland; hobbies, reading, travelling. Contact: Influx Records and Productions, 3, Princes Court, Princes Street South, Dublin 2. Tel: 01 670 3771.

DEEGAN, Michael, "Mike"; DIRECTOR, ONLINE ALPSTREET; *b* 1974; *educ* St. Michael's College, Dublin; read History of Art, Italian and Politics, University College Dublin; *single;* trained as a programmer and networker with Siemens Nixdorf, 1994; one of the first employees of Ireland Online, now Ireland's biggest Internet Service Provider, 1995-96; founded Alpstreet, providing strategic consultancy development and management services for domestic and international clients; involved in the Internet industry since the start, Alpstreet are seen as leaders in their field; hobbies, BMX bike riding, golf; Contact: 15, Adelaide Street, Dun Laoghaire Co. Dublin. Tel: 01 260 0001

DELANEY, Gary; ARTIST, MULTIMEDIA DESIGNER; *b* 1970; *educ* Coláiste Eoin, University College Dublin, BA; Dun Laoghaire College of Art and Design, Diploma, Production Design; *single;* Assistant Designer, Bruno Schwengl, 1997; Multimedia Designer, Riverdeep, 1997 to date; Solo Exhibitions include: Blue Cathedral, Christchurch, 1992; Group Exhibitions include; Banquet Exhibition, RHA Gallery, 1992; *Oireachtas,* RHA Gallery, 1996; Oireachtas, Guinness Hop Store, 1997; currently returning to the visual art medium; hobbies, film, running; Contact: Riverdeep, 8th Floor, Apollo House, Tara Street, Dublin 2. Tel: 01 670 7570.

DENNEHY, Donnacha

DENNEHY, Donnacha; COMPOSER, LECTURER; *b* 1970; *educ* Templeogue College, Dublin; Trinity College Dublin, BA Music (Hons); University of Illinois, U.S.A., M.Mus; IRCAM Stage, D'Informatique Musicale, Paris, France; *single;* Lecturer, Music and Music Technology, Trinity College Dublin; composing music since an early age, compositions include: *Pluck, Stroke and Hammer,* written for Van Brugh String Quartet and pianist Hugh Tinney 1997, *Junk Box Fraud,* written for Amplified Ensemble, 1997, *Metropolis Mutabilis,* written for own group, The Crash Ensemble, 1996, *Traces of a Revolutionary Song,* commissioned by Music Network for the Celebration of 200th Anniversary of The 1798 Irish Rebellion; *Swerve,* premiered at The Saarbrucken 20th Century Music Festival, Germany, 1998; has completed an as yet untitled piece for The European Broadcasting Union for the Celebration of the Millennium; hobby, theatre; Contact: School of Music, 5, Trinity College, Dublin 2.

DEVINE, Alan

DEVINE, Alan; ACTOR; *b* 1970; *educ* Blackrock College, Dublin; Trinity College Dublin, BA, Philosophy, Sociology; *single*; while in college appeared on *Nighthawks,* RTE and working in the Focus Theatre, Dublin; has since worked in film, theatre and television, most notably as Ray O'Driscoll in *Glenroe,* RTE,1997-98; has worked with Second Age, The Machine, Focus Theatre, Barnstorm, Storytellers theatre companies, 1992 to date; films include: various short films, *Miracle at Midnight,* alongside Mia Farrow, Sam Waterston, Justin Whailon, 1997; has recently completed filming *Nora,* a film about James Joyce and Nora Barnacle, alongside Ewan MacGregor; hobbies, playing football, cooking, horse racing. Contact: Teri Hayden, The Agency, 47 Adelaide Road, Dublin 2. Tel: 01 661 8535 Fax: 01 676 0052.

DOLAN, Patrick, "Pat"

DOLAN, Patrick, "Pat"; MANAGING DIRECTOR, DIRECTOR OF FOOTBALL, ST. PATRICK'S ATHLETIC FC; *b* 1968; *educ* King Edward VI Grammar School, Chelmsford, U.K.; *single;* Professional Footballer, Arsenal FC, 1983-87, Walsall FC, 1987-89, Galway United FC, 1989-90, Shamrock Rovers FC, 1990-91, St. Patrick's Athletic, 1991-94; Chief Executive, St. Patrick's Athletic, 1993-97, Team Manager, 1997-98, Director of Football and Managing Director, 1998 to date; captained the first Irish team to qualify for a major championship, Liam Tuohy's Ireland Youth Team at the European Championships in the USSR; the youngest ever manager of National League Champions, is seen as the main motivator behind the current revival of Irish professional football; hobbies, golf, youth projects in West Dublin. Contact: St. Patrick's Athletic, Richmond Park, Emmet Road, Inchicore, Dublin 8. Tel: 01 454 6332 Fax: 01 454 6211.

DOYLE, Keith

DOYLE, Keith; SOCCER PLAYER, ST. PATRICK'S ATHLETIC; *b* 1979; *educ* Coláiste Cholm, Swords; Dublin City University, currently reading Accounting and Finance; *single;* a football fanatic since childhood, has played with Swords Celtic, Belvedere Football Club and St. Patrick's Athletic since1998; hobbies, golf, cinema, socialising; Contact: St. Patrick's Athletic, Richmond Park, Emmet Road, Dublin 8. Tel: 01 454 6332 Fax: 01 454 6211.

DOYLE, Marc; DIGITAL DESIGNER; *b* 1972 *educ* Marian College, Trinity College Dublin, BA, MSc; *single;* Digital Designer, 44k, DV4, 1998 to date; Music Video Director, 1997 to date; work has been featured on RTE and MTV; has exhibited work at Arthouse, Dublin, 1997; hobbies, football, reading, cinema, music. Contact: 44k, 30 East Essex Street, Dublin 2. Tel: 01 670 3344.

DUNNE, Dermot; ACCORDIONIST; *b* 1975; *educ* St. Benildus' College, Kilmacud, Dublin; Ballinteer Community School, Dublin; University College Dublin, Degree in Actuarial and Financial Studies; currently studying Accordion and Symphonic and Operatic Conducting at The Tchaikovsky Conservatory, Kiev, Ukraine; *single;* winner, RTE Musician of The Future, 1996; winner of numerous international accordion competitions in France, Italy and Ireland; has performed extensively in Ireland, France, Ukraine, Germany; has played with The Co-Opera Ireland, National Symphony Orchestra, Concert Orchestra, National Youth Orchestra; hobbies, travelling, reading; Contact: The Tchaikovsky Conservatory, Kiev, Ukraine.

DUNNE, Paul; DIRECTOR, 44k, DV4; *b* 1970; *educ* Marian College Dublin, National College of Art and Design, BA (Fine Art); *single;* Lecturer, Dun Laoghaire Institute of Art, Design and Technology, 1993-98; Creative Director, Multimedia, Agtel Communications, 1995-97; Director, 44k, DV4; Ireland's leading digital broadcasting and DVD companies; hobbies, music, clubbing, reading. Contact: 44k, 30 East Essex Street, Dublin 2. Tel: 01 670 3344.

DUNNE, Rachel, SENIOR CONSULTANT, PPG COMPUTING; *b* 1969; *educ* Sion Hill, Blackrock, Co. Dublin; University College Dublin, B.Soc.Sc.(First Class Hons.), MA, Women's Studies; *single*; Management Consultant, Andersen Consulting, implementing IT systems in Buenos Aires, Amsterdam, Dusseldorf, London, 1991-95; IT Recruitment Consultant, CPL, 1996-99; Senior IT Recruitment Consultant, PPG Computing, 1999 to date; hobbies, travelling, music, clubbing. Contact: PPG Computing, 37, College Green, Dublin 2. Tel: 01 609 8868.

EAST, Louise; JOURNALIST; *b* 1973; *educ* Newpark Comprehensive School, Blackrock; Trinity College Dublin, BA; *single;* Voluntary Aid Worker, Guatemala, 1996-97; Freelance Journalist, *The Irish Times*; *On The Town,* 1997-98, *Winging It,* 1999; Contributor, *Image Magazine, Food & Wine,* 1997 to date; Contributor to arts programmes on Irish, English and German television, 1998 to date; Panellist, *Entertainment Today,* Today FM, 1997-98; one of the most widely read young columnists in Irish journalism; hobbies, travel, reading, drawing, good food. Contact: The Irish Times, D'Olier Street, Dublin 2. Tel: 01 679 2022.

EGAN LANGLEY, Tara; SINGER; *b* 1975; *educ* Newtown School, Waterford; Portobello College, Dublin; *single;* sang with The Wilde Oscars, 1994-97, Igloo, 1996-97; completed acting course and has subsequently appeared in TV commercials; currently lead singer, Kaydee; has released debut album, *Stop I'm Doing It Again,*1998, and enjoyed Irish chart success with *Mister Sweeney, Cradle,* and *Seven Days*; hobbies, painting, drawing, chess; Contact: Jed Parle, Cradle Music Management, Unit 7, Abbey Business Centre, Abbey Road, Kilkenny. Tel: 056 23103.

EGAN, Emily; BARRISTER; *b* 1969; *educ* Alexandra College, Dublin; Trinity College Dublin, LLB (First Class Hons.); Millennium Scholarship, Oxford University, Masters, Commercial Law; Kings Inns, Dublin; *single;* worked in The Law Reform Commission and lectured in Commercial Law, University College Dublin, while at the Kings Inns; currently lecturing at the Dublin Institute of Technology and in her fifth year practising as a Barrister; Member, The Bar Council; Junior Counsel for the public interest in the Moriarty Tribunal; a brilliant legal mind, whose practice handles everything from commercial to constitutional law; hobbies, theatre, travelling, scuba diving; Contact: The Law Library, The Four Courts, Dublin 7.

EVERS, Peter; PHOTOGRAPHER, ARTIST; *b* 1973; *educ* St. Paul's College Raheny; St. Patrick's College, Maynooth, BA; *single;* worked as a model from the age of thirteen; trained as an advertising photographer under Walter Pfeiffer, 1994-95; began working as a fashion photographer, grooming Ireland's most successful international models, commissioned by top designers and fashion houses, 1995 to date; work has been published in *The Irish Times, The Sunday Tribune, The Sunday Independent, U Magazine, dSide Magazine, In Dublin;* began exhibiting as a fine art photographer, 1997; has already had five exhibitions, including Pop In, Force, both Arthouse, Temple Bar, Dublin, Invidi, Meeting House Square, Temple Bar, Dublin; currently working as curator and an exhibiting artist "continuing the advance of photography in latitude and form. After fifteen years of exhibiting, I want to leave a body of work that will contribute to the evolution of our species!" hobbies, reading, nature, photography. Contact: Morgan The Agency, 13, Herbert Place, Dublin 2. Tel: 01 661 4572.

EYRE, Aisling; MAKE UP ARTIST; *b* 1970; *educ* Holy Child, Killiney; Bronwyn Conroy Beauty School; Freelance Make Up Artist 1989-99; work has appeared in *Image Magazine, U Magazine, IT, Social & Personal, Himself Magazine, dSide, In Dublin, Vanity Fair, Elle, GQ, L'Homme Vogue, Vogue;* Make Up Artist, music videos for Boyzone (1996), Luka Bloom (1998); has worked with Vivienne Westwood, Blondie, Snowdon, Sarah Moon, Andy Earl, The Cranberries, Pulp, West Life, Philip Treacy, Bella Freud; the official Make Up Artist during Mary Robinson's Presidency, also a partner with sister Aveen in Candleberry, Westbury Mall, Dublin, 1993 to date; hobbies, going to the gym, being creative; Contact: Candleberry, Westbury Mall, Dublin 2. Tel: 01 671 8441.

FARRELL, Damien; CREATIVE DIRECTOR, PROPRIETOR, CABOOM LTD.; *b* 1971; *educ* St. Vincent's Glasnevin; Ballyfermot Senior College, Animation; *single;* Animator, Emerald City Productions; Animator, Don Bluth Entertainment, working on *Thumbellina,* and *The Pebble and the Penguin;* Freelance Animator, Murakami Wolf, working on various television projects, including *Teenage Hero Mutant Turtles*; Animator, *The Den,* RTE; directed Dustin The Turkey's music videos; Director, *A Scare At Bedtime with Podge & Rodge,* RTE; founded Caboom in his bedroom to produce an animated Colgate commercial, moving to an office to provide and produce animation and computer graphic sequences for television and advertising; Clients include: Guinness, Barry's Tea, AIB, Opera Ireland, Holsten Pils, Bord Gais, Shell, Mars; the company has also been involved in a number of special projects, including the revamp of Joe Dolan's image; hobbies, cinema, magic, puppeteering. Contact: Caboom, 10, St. Stephen's Green, Dublin 2. Tel: 01 672 7077.

FAY, James "Jimmy"; DIRECTOR, BEDROCK THEATRE COMPANY; *b* 1969; *educ* Old Bawn Community School, Tallaght; Liberties VEC, Performance Arts; *single;* co-founded Bedrock Theatre Company, 1993; co-founded Dublin Fringe Festival,1995; Staff Director, Abbey Theatre, 1996; Director, Bedrock Theatre Company 1993 to date; Freelance Theatre Director,1997 to date; productions include: *East* (Steven Berkoff), 1993; *Unidentified Human Remains and The True Nature of Love* (Brad Fraser), 1994; *The Resistible Rise of Arturo Ui* (Bertold Brecht), 1995; *Melon Farmer* (Alex Johnston), 1997; *At Swim Two Birds* (Flann O'Brien),1998; hobbies, digital filmmaking, swimming. Contact: Bedrock Theatre Company, 36-37, Lower Ormond Quay, Dublin 1. Tel: 01 872 9300.

FEARON, Patrick; HEAD OF TREASURY, ABN AMRO BANK; *b* 1968; *educ* St. Benildus' College, Kilmacud, Dublin; University College Dublin, B.Comm, MBS; *single;* Joined ABN AMRO as Management Trainee, 1989, Head of Trading, 1993, Head of Treasury, 1997; responsible for ABN trading and sales activity in treasury products; ABN Amro is one of the top three Euro banks in Ireland; hobbies, golf, tennis, soccer; Contact: ABN Amro, ABN Amro House, IFSC, Dublin 1. Tel: 01 609 3818.

FITZGERALD, Michael; ACTOR; *b* 1979; *educ* Gonzaga College, Dublin; The Samuel Beckett Centre, Trinity College Dublin; *single;* although studying Drama and Theatre in Trinity has already appeared to some acclaim in *Arcadia* (Gate Theatre); hobbies, football, singing, violin, film. Contact: Theresa Nolan Enterprises, 14 Beech Grove, Booterstown, Co. Dublin. Tel: 01 288 1537.

FITZGERALD, Michael

FITZHARRIS, Robert; CHEF; *b* 1977; *educ* Presentation College, Bray; DIT Cathal Brugha Street; Roslyn Park; *single;* nominated, National Apprentice of the Year, 1998, second place, 1999; awarded Gold and Bronze Medals, Ireland West Competition; chosen for Irish team in Euroskills Competition, Holland; unable to travel as it clashed with his travel to Providence, Rhode Island on the prestigious Johnson Wales Scholarship, 1998; chosen to represent Ireland once again, 1999; again refused because he is currently Head Chef in Tree of Idleness, Bray, Co. Wicklow; Contact: 8, Sidmonton Gardens, Bray, Co. Wicklow. Tel: 01 286 8123.

FITZSIMONS, Uaneen; BROADCASTER; *b* 1971 *educ* Assumption Grammar School, Ballynahinch; Down College of Further Education, Downpatrick; Dublin City University, B.Comm; *single;* worked with BBC Northern Ireland on Mike Edgar's *Across the Line* radio show, 1991-92; during university appeared regularly on *Jo-Maxi,* RTE, and worked with Frontier Films, stage managing *Megazone* and working as researcher on *Blackboard Jungle*; Press and Promotions Manager, the Ormond Multi Media Centre, Co-producer *Celtic Vision* music show, 1995-97; Press Officer, The Temple Bar Music Centre, 1996; Presenter, Researcher, *No Disco* music show, RTE 1997 to date; recently started her own radio show on 2FM; has compered concerts at Slane, presented the Heineken Green Energy documentary, The Big Day Out documentary and a six part series on the Liss Ard music festival; a confident, steadily rising broadcaster, has the determination and passion to rise to the top of her profession; hobbies, attending concerts, cinema, horse riding, cycling, socialising. Contact: RTE, Donnybrook, Dublin 4.

FLANNERY, Sarah

FLANNERY, Sarah; SCIENTIST; *b* 1982; *educ* Scoil Mhuire gan Smal, Blarney, Cork; *single;* has been acquainted with computer technology since her childhood; currently studying for her Leaving Certificate, has recently become the Esat Young Scientist Of The Year, 1999; her winning project revolved around Cryptography, the science of secrecy with a particular focus on encryption methods, making electronic transactions ten times faster; hailed as a mathematical genius, has been inundated with offers of jobs and scholarships from international computer companies and universities; hobbies, showjumping, basketball, cross country running, football, karate, playing the piano; Contact: FCC, 2-4 Clanwilliam Terrace, Grand Canal Quay, Dublin 2. Tel: 01 676 0168 Fax: 01 676 5241.

FOX, Mildred; POLITICIAN; *b* 1971; *educ* St. Kilian's Community School, Bray, Co. Wicklow; University College Dublin, BA, English, Psychology; *single;* Secretary, Dáil Eireann, 1992; worked in U.S.A. as a Hotel Manager and for a Stockbroker, before returning to Ireland on the death of her father, Johnny Fox, T.D., M.C.C., 1995; co-opted to his Council seat on Wicklow County Council, 1995; contested the Wicklow/East Kildare by election for her father's seat as an Independent Candidate, elected to Dáil Eireann, 1995; contested the General Election under the Wicklow/ East Carlow constituency, and was re-elected in1997; recently contested the local elections for the Bray ward of Wicklow County Council; hobbies, reading, ladies football (GAA), music. Contact: Dáil Eireann, Kildare Street, Dublin 2. Tel: 01 618 3333.

GALLAGHER, Alannah, EDITOR, IN DUBLIN MAGAZINE; *b* 1968; *educ* Loretto College, Milford, Donegal; Our Lady's Templeogue, Dublin; Esmod Fashion School, Paris; Grafton Academy of Dress Design, Dublin; Accountancy and Business School, Aungier Street; *single;* Menswear Buyer, Penneys, 1990-91; Freelance Journalist, *Dublin Diary, In Dublin, dSide, Ireland on Sunday, The Sun, The Independent*; 1991-97; Presenter, *Twelve to One*, RTE, 1994-97; Researcher, Contributor, *Fandango,* RTE Radio, 1996-97; Stylist, *Head To Toe*, RTE, 1996-97; Researcher, Contributor, *The Cliona Show*, Radio Ireland, 1997, *The Gerry Ryan Show*, RTE Radio,1996-98; Freelance Stylist *Image Magazine*, 1998; Researcher, Contributor, *Beyond The Hall Door*, RTE, *The Right Side*, RTE Radio; Producer, Presenter, *Cork's Big Breakfast*, Producer, Researcher, *Neil Prenderville Show*, 96FM, Cork, 1998; Editor, *In Dublin Magazine*, 1998 to date; an editor with a wide range of experience in print and broadcast media; hobbies, cinema, theatre, reading, music; Contact: In Dublin Magazine, 3-7 Camden Place, Dublin 2. Tel: 01 478 4322.

GANNON, Dermot; CHEF; *b* 1971; *educ* Clifden Secondary School; *single;* worked during the school holidays in the kitchens of Renvyle House Hotel; apprenticed to Paddy Foyle,

(Proprietor of Destrys, The Quay House in Clifden, co-owner of Rossleague Manor) in the kitchens of Rossleague Manor in Letterfrack; never opened a cookery book in his life, but has learned from Paddy Foyle and working in kitchens during winters spent travelling the world; currently renting and running Destrys Restaurant, Clifden; hobbies, travel, films. Contact: Destrys, Clifden, Co. Galway. Tel: 095 21722.

GANNON, Laura; ARTIST; *b* 1972; *educ* Gortnor Abbey, Mayo; University of Ulster at Belfast, BA (Hons), Fine Art; Ecole Nationale Des Beaux Arts, Cergy-Pontoise, Paris, France; *single;* Residencies include: Villa Montalvo Arts Centre, California, U.S.A., Le Pic Ronsenac, France, Irish Museum of Modern Art, Dublin, Irish Arts Council, Project Studio, Temple Bar Studios; solo exhibitions include: The Blue Nerve, The Context Gallery, Derry, The Spinning Room, The Jo Rain Gallery, Dublin, Temple Bar Gallery, Dublin; group exhibitions include: Art Rebels, Catalyst Arts, Belfast, Absolution, Temple Bar Music Centre, Dublin, Seed, Skin Up, Arthouse, Dublin, EV+A, Limerick, has exhibited in the U.K. and France; public collections include: Irish Arts Council, Principle Management, Office of Public Works, Founder Member, Crosstown Productions, Board of Directors, Sculpture Society of Ireland; has received numerous awards including The Thomas Damann Memorial Travel Award; hobbies, playing tennis, cinema, partying. Contact: Temple Bar Gallery and Studios, Temple Bar, Dublin 2. Tel: 01 671 0073.

GANNON, Laura

GERRARD, Joy; ARTIST; *b* 1971; *educ* Alexandra College, Dublin; Crawford College of Art, Cork, Dip. Painting; National College of Art and Design, BA, Printmaking; Il Besonte International Centre of Graphic Art, Florence; *single;* Exhibitions include: Taylor Art Awards, Royal Dublin Society, Dublin, 1995, Temple Bar International Print Show , Temple Bar Gallery, Dublin, 1996,Three Printmakers, University College Cork, 1998, Temple Bar International Print Show, Original Print Gallery, Dublin, Ormeau Baths Gallery, Belfast,1998, Scoíp 99, Siamsa Tire, Tralee Arts Centre, 1999, Print 99, Royal Hibernian Academy, Dublin, 1999; has exhibited in Scotland and Italy; has won numerous awards, most recently European Artists Pepinieres Award, Jyvaskyla, Finland, 1999; collections include: Office of Public Works, University College Cork, Il Bisonte, Florence, Italy; Private Collections in Ireland, Europe and the U.S.A.; an internationally renowned artist; hobbies, hillwalking, cinema, writing, literature, travel; Contact: Graphic Studio Gallery, Cope Street, Temple Bar, Dublin 2. Tel: 01 677 2288.

GOGAN, Nicola, "Nicky"; DIRECTOR, SINK DIGITAL MEDIA, DARKLIGHT FILM FESTIVAL; *b* 1969 *educ* Santa Maria College, Ballyroan, Dublin; National College of Art and Design, Degree, Sculpture; *single;* Entertainments Officer, NCAD, responsible for organising college events, 1991; Performance and Video Artist, 1991-93; travelled and worked around America for three years, returning to Ireland in 1996; co-founded Sink Digital Media, 1997, an Internet design company, which also focuses on creative, cultural projects; Sink recently organised the first digital film festival in Ireland, Darklight; hobby, music; Contact: Sink Digital Media, 19 Clare Street, Dublin 2. Tel: 01 662 9930 Fax: 01 662 6980

GOODBODY, Richard; DIRECTOR OF STOCKBROKING, BCP STOCKBROKERS; *b* 1971; *educ* Wesley College Dublin; Griffith College, ACCA; *m* Gillian Mulvin; Equity Dealer, BCP Stockbrokers, 1993, Director of Stockbroking, 1997 to date; heads up the dealing desk and is responsible for ongoing sales development; BCP Stockbrokers is one of the largest independent private client stockbroking firms in Ireland; hobbies, yacht racing and sailing, skiing, tennis; Contact: BCP Stockbrokers, 71-72 Upper Leeson Street, Dublin 4. Tel: 01 668 4688 Fax: 01 668 4246.

GRENNELL, Robert, "Rocky"; ART DIRECTOR, dSIDE MAGAZINE; *b* 1972; *educ* Blackrock College, Dublin; University College Dublin, BA, Philosophy, English; FAS Course, Graphic Design; *single;* on completing training course worked in a Repro House, 1996-97; Designer, Grafotone, 1997-98; Designer, *dSide Magazine*, 1998, Art Director, 1999; Freelance Designer under the *Rock Star* alias, designing flyers, logos, identities, brochures, 1996 to date; a clean, clinical style has ensured *dSide* remains fresh and engaging; hobbies, music, football. Contact: dSide Magazine, The Factory, 35a Barrow Street, Dublin 4. Tel: 01 668 4966.

GROGAN, Garret, DEALER, AIB GROUP TREASURY; *b* 1974; *educ* Belvedere College,

Dublin; Maynooth, BA, Economics, Finance; *single;* Settlements Official, AIB Security Services, 1996-98; Dealer, AIB Group Treasury,1998 to date; hobbies, agriculture, equestrian sports; Contact: Group Treasury AIB International Centre, IFSC, Dublin 1. Tel: 01 679 5776.

HANLY, Cuan; FASHION DESIGNER; *b* 1966; *educ* High School, Rathgar; The Grafton Academy, Diploma, Fashion Design; *single;* Stock Controller for the UK, Paul Smith Ltd, 1988, Retail Co-Ordinator for Europe, UK, U.S.A, opening Paul Smith outlets in Paris, London, Tokyo, 1990; started R. Newbold, the workwear division of Paul Smith, opening shops under the label in London and Japan, 1992-93; worked with John Rocha, A-Wear and Brown Thomas, developing the label, 1994; assisted in the setting up of Glibro Design for John Rocha; Launched own label, Cuan Hanly, 1996, with plans to export to UK, Europe and the Far East; recently worked with shirt manufacturer Clubman to develop shirt collection, is also offering tailoring services under the Cuan Hanly Bespoke name; has received wide media coverage in print and on television in Ireland, the UK and France, is established as one of Ireland's leading menswear designers; recently opened his own retail outlet, Cuan Hanly in Dublin's city centre; hobbies, cricket, architecture, photography; Contact: 6-7 Newmarket Square, Dublin 8. Tel: 01 454 4361 Fax: 087 347 6397 E-mail: cah@iol.ie.

HAYES, Brian

HAYES, Brian; POLITICIAN; *b* 1969; *educ* Garbally Park, Ballinasloe, Co. Galway; St. Patrick's College, Maynooth, BA; Trinity College Dublin, HDip.Ed; *m* Geneviere Deering; formerly a secondary school teacher and Fine Gael National Youth & Education Officer, currently Fine Gael spokesperson on Housing, House Prices & Urban Renewal; a candidate in the by-election for the constituency of Dublin South Central, 1994, elected to the Dáil, 1997, the first general election he contested; Former Secretary to the Fine Gael Group at the Forum for Peace & Reconciliation; member, South Dublin County Council, South Dublin Enterprise Board, Irish Council for the European Movement; Boards of Management of St. Aidan's & St. Mark's, and The Virginia House Arts Centre. Contact: Dáil Eireann, Kildare Street, Dublin 2. Tel: 01 618 3333.

HAYES, Rhonwen

HAYES, Rhonwen; MULTI MEDIA ARTIST; *b* 1970; *educ* Brigidine Convent, Abbeyleix; Ballyfermot Senior College; Dun Laoghaire College of Art and Design; National College of Art and Design, BA; Irish World Music Centre, Limerick, MA Ethnamusicology; has worked in a variety of jobs including waitress, record shop assistant, Bunratty singer; painted murals for bars in S Africa, Singapore and throughout Europe; currently working part-time in decorative art work, full time career jazz singer with Galway based group (yet to be named); a bright star, fame could be around the corner. Contact: 27 Nuns Island, Galway.

HEANEY, Catherine; NOTICES EDITOR, IMAGE MAGAZINE;*b* 1973; *educ* Pembroke School, Dublin; Trinity College Dublin, BA, M.Sc; *single;* Curatorial Assistant, Douglas Hyde Gallery, Dublin,1995-96; Freelance Journalist, *Image Magazine*, 1997, Editorial Assistant, 1998, Notices Editor, 1999; hobbies, reading, travel, music, fashion, visiting art galleries; Contact: Image Magazine, 22, Crofton Road, Dun Laoghaire, Co. Dublin. Tel: 01 280 8415.

HICKEY, Joby; ARTIST; *b* 1971; *educ* Newpark Comprehensive School, Dublin; Dun Laoghaire College of Art and Design; *single;* group exhibitions include: Annual Exhibition, RHA Gallery, 1997; World of Watercolours and Drawings, London, 1996; solo exhibitions include; Gallery of Schnowitz, Dallas, Texas, U.S.A, 1998, Fifth Floor, Harvey Nichols Exhibition, London, Leeds, 1996; work has been commissioned by Dáil Eireann, Dermot Desmond, Bono; hobbies, history, astronomy; Contact: New Apollo Gallery, Duke Street, Dublin 2. Tel: 01 671 2609.

HILL, Johanna; CATERING CONSULTANT; *b* 1968; *educ* Newtown School, Waterford; Ballymaloe, Cork; *m* Patrick Flynn; catering on Shannon cruisers was followed by six months in Becketts (Westbury Mall); next came a season as a chalet girl, a short stay in the Butlers Pantry (Merrion Avenue), then a trip to Australia; Head Chef, Avoca Handweavers (Enniskerry) 1993-99; currently running Johanna Hill Catering Consultants, re-designing kitchens, dining rooms and menus; hobbies, cooking, eating out, exercise and travel. Contact: 35 Taney Avenue. Goatstown, Dublin 14. Tel: 01 298 0220.

HOLMES, David; MUSIC PRODUCER, DJ; *b* 1970; *educ* St. Augustine's Ormeau Road,

Belfast; *single;* a former Hairdresser of The Year, subsequently turned his attention to music, promoting and DJing at the Sugarsweet and Shake Yer Brain club nights, Belfast; is now one of the most in demand DJs in the world; has released two albums, *This Film's Crap, Let's Slash The Seats,* (1996), *Let's Get Killed* (1998); provided the musical scores for Lynda La Plante's *Supply and Demand* and *Net Killer* television drama series on Channel 4; has turned his attention to working on film soundtracks, providing the scores for *Resurrection Man* and *Out of Sight,* featuring George Clooney and Jennifer Lopez; was the subject of a BBC documentary, *Gritty Shaker,* 1997, has also featured in countless magazine and newspaper articles in the international press; representing the new breed of pop stars, is fast becoming one of Ireland's most valuable musical exports; Contact: Influx Records and Productions, 3, Princes Court, Princes Street South, Dublin 2. Tel: 01 670 3771.

HOURICAN, Emily, ASSISTANT EDITOR, HIMSELF MAGAZINE; *b* 1971; *educ* European School, Brussels, Belgium; University College Dublin, BA, MA English; *single;* Production Assistant, aka Java Films 1995-97; Assistant Editor, *Himself* Magazine, 1997 to date; hobbies, Tae Kwan Do, hunting, reading, theatre, cinema, walking. Contact: Himself Magazine, 22, Crofton Road, Dun Laoghaire, Co. Dublin. Tel: 01 280 8415.

JANSEN, Simone; MANAGING DIRECTOR, SNICKERS WORKWEAR; *b* 1969; *educ* Loreto Convent, Foxrock; College of Marketing and Design, Dublin, Diploma and Certificate; *m* Matti Viio; founded Snickers Workwear, 1992, Managing Director, 1992 to date; Snickers Workwear currently employs ten staff; hobbies, hockey, travelling, skiing; Contact: 6, Upper Grand Canal Street, Dublin 4. Tel: 01 660 6748 Fax: 01 660 4507.

JONES, Melissa Jane; CATERER; *b* 1970; *educ* Mount Anville, Dublin; University College Dublin, B.Comm; *single;* started catering career as waitress, later manager, Break for the Boarder restaurant; formed Jackson Jones Ltd. with Paul Jackson, 1993; the company consists of an outside catering company, Jackson Jones Catering, and an independent cafe, Cafe Coombe; in-house caterers for The Chocolate Bar and PoD nightclub; opened Cafe Coombe, attached to Coombe Hospital, 1997, a highly successful venture, offering contemporary style food to hospital users and the residents of the South Circular Road area; member, Small Firms Association; club, Equinox, Sandymount; hobbies, keeping fit, reading, eating out, roller blading. Contact: Cafe Coombe, Coombe Hospital, Dublin 8.

JONES, Melissa Jane;

KEAVENEY, Cecilia; POLITICIAN; *b* 1968; *educ* Carndonagh Community School; University of Ulster, Jordanstown, B.Mus. (Hons), MPhil, P.G.C.E. Music, L.T.C.L. (Performers); *single;* Piano Teacher, University of Ulster, 1989-91; Head of Music, St. Joseph's High School, Coleraine, Derry, 1992; Music Director, The Igbinedion Education Centre, Benin City, Nigeria,1992-93; Licensed Teacher, Thomas Beckett School, Northampton, England, 1993-94; Music Teacher, St. Mary's Secondary School, Creggan, Derry, 1995-96; Member, Donegal County Council, 1995; Elected to Dáil Eireann, 1996, re-elected in the General Election, 1997; has been involved in the repatriation of political prisoners from England; member, Guildhall Chamber Orchestra, Derry, University of Ulster Choir, Chamber Choir and Orchestra, Moville, Donegal North East Ogra, Moville Fianna Fáil Cumann, North Inishowen Comhairle Ceantair; sits on a number of council committees; hobbies, horse racing and riding, camogie, swimming, canoeing, attending concerts, walking, music perfoming; Contact: Dáil Eireann, Kildare Street, Dublin 2. Tel: 01 618 4045 Fax: 01 618 3569.

KEAVENEY, Colm; INDUSTRIAL OFFICIAL, SIPTU; *b* 1971; *educ* St. Jarlath's College, Tuam, Co. Galway; Letterkenny RTC, Diploma, Computer Science; *single;* President, Letterkenny RTC Student's Union; Union Development Officer, Deputy President, President, Union of Students in Ireland; Policy Development Officer, National Youth Council of Ireland, European Commission Programme, Brussels, Dublin; Labour Candidate, Galway East, General Election,1997; Industrial Official, SIPTU, 1998 to date; one of the leading young socially conscious political minds in the country; hobbies, music, current affairs, travelling, socialising; Contact: SIPTU, Galway Number 2, Branch, Forster Court, Galway. Tel: 091 567246.

KELLY, Paul

KELLY, Paul; ARTIST; *b* 1968; *educ* St. Joseph's School, Rush; *m* Deborah Ball; 3 *da*; self taught artist, worked in animation studios in Dublin and Phoenix Arizona with MGM and

20th Century Fox, 1986-97; now a full time artist, has exhibited at Royal Hibernian Academy, 1989, 1991, 1993, 1994, 1995; has also exhibited, at The National Portrait Exhibition, Boyle Arts Festival and The Gorry Gallery (Dublin); recipient, James Kennedy Memorial Award, R.H.A., 1991; work hangs in public and private exhibitions including National Self Portrait Collection, Fingal County Library, Bank of Ireland Collection and the Brian P. Burke Collection, U.S.A.; a traditional painter, a master technician; his timeless, lyrical paintings are creating a stir in the Irish art world; Contact: Gorry Gallery Ltd., 20 Molesworth Street, Dublin 2. Tel: 01 679 5319.

KELTY, Gavin

KELTY, Gavin; ACTOR; *b* 1977; *educ* Jobstown Community College; *single;* the lead in *Accelerator*, written and directed by Vinnie Murphy, also plays 'Tatoo' in the film *Though The Sky Falls*, loosely based on the life of Veronica Guerin; other film credits include: *The Mammy, The General, The Boxer, The Butcher Boy, Crush Proof, Spaghetti Slow*; television appearances include: *The Family, The Van, Soft Sand Blue Sea, Bolt, Room Mates*; with an extensive resumé belying his youth, his recent work has won him recognition globally; hobbies, swimming, football, horseriding, snooker. Contact: Lorraine Brennan Management, Unit 22, Greenmount Industrial Estate, Harold's Cross, Dublin 6. Tel: 01 453 4355 Fax: 01 453 4412.

KEMP; Domini

KEMP; Domini; RESTAURATEUR, CHEF, CATERER, FOOD WRITER; *b* 1971; *educ* Lyford Kay School, Nassau, Bahamas; Headfort School, Kells, Co. Meath; Alexandra College, Milltown, Dublin; Leiths School of Food and Wine, London; *single;* Founded Catering and Hamper Company, 1987-90; Showjumper, US, UK and Irish circuit, 1989-95; Owner, Sporthorse International, an import export company specialising in custom made equestrian equipment, 1991-95; Conrad Gallagher's business partner, opening Lloyds and Christopher's, 1996; currently setting up It's A Bagel company; Publications include *New Irish Cooking* (1997), Conrad Gallagher's first cookery book; hobbies, showjumping, travel; Contact: Tel: 086 260 6001.

KIRWAN, Robert, "Rob"; RECORD PRODUCER; *b* 1970; *educ* St. Columba's College; *single;* started working in Windmill Lane Studios, 1992; worked his way up to in house engineer, 1995; worked on U2's *Zooropa* album, 1995, subsequently working on the band's *Passengers* and *Pop* albums, 1995-97; Freelance Producer, working for international artists including Howie B, Elastica, P.J. Harvey, Barry Adamson, Bomb The Bass, Pelvis, The Frank & Walters, 1997 to date; an established producer, a leader in his chosen field. hobbies, football, beer. Contact: Nina Jackson. Tel: 0044 181 940 5750.

LEDDEN, Emma; TELEVISION PRESENTER, MTV; *b* 1977; *educ* Mount Sackville, Dublin; Ballyfermot Senior College, Diploma, Journalism; *single;* Model, Assets Model Agency, 1995; Presenter, *The Den*, RTE, 1996-98; Researcher, Journalist, *dSide*, 1997-98; Presenter, *Daily Edition*, MTV, 1998 to date; has described herself as "honest, ambitious and very, very, impatient;" a natural in front of the camera, is destined to become a major TV personality over the coming years; hobbies, reading, swimming, going out; Contact: MTV, UK House, Oxford Street, London W1, England.

LENNON, Sonya; FASHION STYLIST; *b* 1968; *educ* Loreto College, St. Stephen's Green; Coláiste Dhúlaigh, Foundation Course, Communications; National College of Art and Design, Pattern Cutting; DIT Rathmines, Certificate, Public Relations; *single;* worked in Kamouflage and Firenze, independent fashion retailers, 1989-95; Fashion Editor, *dSide,* 1995 to date; Freelance Stylist, *Image Magazine, IT, Social & Personal, U Magazine;* film work includes Costume Designer, *Accelerator,* 1998; television commercials include Coca Cola, Guinness, Telecom, 1996 to date; hobbies, photography, rollerblading, swimming; Contact: 086 252 6026.

LEWY MOORE, Justin; TALENT AND LITERARY AGENT *b 1968 educ* The High School, Rathgar, Newtown School, Waterford; *single;* Freelance Sports Video Editor, 1986-89; Bar Manager, TS McHugh's Seattle, U.S.A. 1989-94; Agent, ICM, Los Angeles, U.S.A., 1994 to date; currently Managing Director, ICM Ireland Ltd., representing Ireland's emerging screen and stage talent community; hobbies, squash, reading. Contact: ICM Ireland Ltd., The Barracks, 76, Irishtown Road, Dublin 4. Tel: 01 667 6455 Fax: 01 667 6474.

LIEBMANN, Michael; ACTOR; *b* 1969; *educ* Inst Methody, Belfast; London Theatre School; single; Stage appearances include *Oliver Twist, Macbeth,* Lyric Theatre, 1983-86; television appearances include *Scout,* BBC, 1986, *Painted Lady,* Granada, 1997, *Eureka Street,* BBC, 1999; film appearances include *Resurrection Man, Vicious Circle, Sunburn, Old New Borrowed Blue, Sunset Heights;* hobbies, guitar, writing, washing up. Contact: 12 Blackhall Court, Blackhall Place, Dublin 7.

LINEHAN, Conor; PIANIST, COMPOSER; *b* 1971; *educ* Gormanston College, Co. Meath; Trinity College Dublin, BA Mod. Music and English; *single*; studied under Peter Feuchtwanger, London; currently teaching at The Royal Irish Academy of Music, Dublin; has played in all major Irish venues and has worked extensively in the U.K., Italy and Germany; finalist, The Guardian International Piano Competition, 1997; has worked as theatre composer, particularly in the Abbey Theatre, Dublin; wrote the score for *The Colleen Bawn,* Abbey Theatre Dublin, touring to the National Theatre, London; hobbies, chess, swimming. Contact: The Royal Irish Academy of Music, 39, Westland Row, Dublin 2. Tel: 01 676 4412.

LOGUE, Antonia; NOVELIST; *b* 1972; *educ* Loretto College, Coleraine; European School, Brussels, Belgium; Methodist College, Belfast; Trinity College Dublin, BA, English; *single;* started writing during college for *The Sunday Independent, The Irish Times, The Guardian, The Times (UK), The Scotsman,* 1992 to date; First novel, *Shadow Box,* published, 1999; currently working on an as yet untitled second novel; hobbies, reading, films, walking the dogs; Contact: AP Watt, 20, John's Street, London, WC1N 2DR, England.

LOGUE, Antonia

LOWRY, Paul; BUSINESS DEVELOPMENT CONSULTANT, NORKOM TECHNOLOGIES; *b* 1972; *educ* St. Kieran's College, Kilkenny; University College Dublin, Computer Science; Trinity College Dublin, BA Mod.; Senior Account Manager, Business Development, Iona Technologies, 1995-97; Business Development Manager, L.P.S., 1997-99; Independent Business Consultant, Norkom Technologies, 1999 to date; hobbies, chess, golf, squash; Contact: Norkom Technologies, Norkom House, 43, Upper Mount Street, Dublin 2. Tel: 01 676 9333. Fax: 01 676 9099.

LOWRY, Paul

LUNNY, Cora Venus; VIOLINIST; *b* 1982; *educ* Second Level Correspondence Course; private tuition, London, Manhattan, Zurich, Stratford-Upon-Avon; *single;* studying the violin since the age of three, has given recital and concerto performances in Ireland, the UK, Italy, Austria, Switzerland, Germany, ranging in repertoire from early baroque to contemporary composers; awarded RTE Musician of the Future, 1998; television and radio appearances include: *The Late Late Show, Echo Island, Cursaí, Kelly Live,* RTE, *Children In Need,* BBC; has recently recorded with the pianist John Lenehan and the oboist Malcom Messiter; described as "driven by some mysterious force, playing of a truly inspirational order;" hobbies, Formula 1, computers, shopping, walking, eating, socialising, laughing, diving. Contact: c/o Storeys. Tel: 0044 1276 691170 Fax: 0044 1276 691170.

LUNNY, Cora Venus

LYNCH, Declan; NEWS EDITOR, TV3; *b* 1972; *educ* Templeogue College; Ballyfermot Senior College, Diploma Media Studies; *single;* Voluntary Worker, Romanian Children's Appeal Ireland (RCAI), 1993; Sound Assistant, Patrick Spence Thomas Studios, Toronto, Canada, 1993; Sound Operator, RTE, 1994; Sound Assistant, Oasis Television, London, U.K., 1995; Producer, Director, Sonic Productions, Bogota, Colombia, 1996; Sound Mixer, RTE, 1997; News Editor, TV3, 1998 to date; hobbies, music, sports. Contact: TV3, Westgate Park, Ballymount Industrial Estate, Dublin 24. Tel: 01 4193333.

LYNCH, Michael; GROUP MANAGING DIRECTOR, LYNCH HOTEL GROUP; *b* 1969 *educ* St. Flannan's College, Ennis, Co. Clare; University College Galway, B.Comm; University of Surrey, M.Sc.; Member, British Chartered Institute of Marketing; *m* Geraldine Clarke; worked with Coopers & Lybrand in the Business Services Division, Dublin; worked with the Principal Hotel Group, the UK based independent hotel chain, in the U.K. and Europe; returned to the family hotel business, as Business Development Manager,1993; Won Young Entrepreneur of the Year, Junior Chamber, 1994; since then has concentrated on developing the business, tripling group turnover since 1993, now at an estimated £14 million; currently Group Managing Director, Lynch Hotel Group; hobby, sports; Contact: Lynch Hotel Group, Head

Office, St. Flannan's View, Ennis, Co. Clare. Tel: 065 66665 Fax: 065 23759

LYNN, Theo

LYNN, Theo; CHIEF EXECUTIVE OFFICER, EDUCATIONAL MULTIMEDIA GROUP; *b* 1973; *educ* Belvedere College, Dublin; University College Dublin, Degree, Business & Legal Studies, MIS; PhD Candidate, Business Research Programme, Michael Smurfit Graduate School of Business, University College Dublin; *single;* Founded Educational Multimedia Group, 1997; Educational Multimedia Group is a private multi-national training company with headquarters in Dublin and operations in North America and Europe; EMG is the parent company to Educational Multimedia Corporation; now one of the largest independent and fastest growing multimedia developers in Ireland, EMG offers state of the art training solutions to customers in the corporate, government and academic markets; hobbies, reading, music, film, travel; Contact: EMG House, Deansgrange Road, Deansgrange, Co. Dublin. Tel: 01 289 9000 Fax: 01 289 9150

LYONS, Barry; SOLICITOR; *b* 1968; *educ* Belvedere College, Dublin; Clongowes Wood, Clane, Kildare; Greenwich High School, Greenwich, Connecticut, U.S.A; University College Dublin, BCL; Blackhall Place; *m* Sonia Reynolds; worked for Lavelle Coleman, developing media practice, 1996-98; set up independent practice, 1998; predominantly involved in entertainment law, with a particular emphasis on film and music; hobby, sailing; Contact: 01 672 8039.

MAGUIRE, Neven; CHEF; *b* 1973; *educ* St. Clare's Comprehensive School, Manorhamilton; Fermanagh College; *single;* an interest in cooking comes from his mother Vera, who introduced him to kitchens in the family restaurant, McNean House and Bistro, Blacklion, Cavan as a schoolboy; awarded Baileys Chef of the Year; worked with the renowned Chef Lea Lester (the only female to win the Becasse d'Or) in Luxembourg; currently working in McNeans Bistro, running his own cookery school and teaching at Fermanagh College; selected to represent Ireland at Becasse d'Or in 2001; hobbies, eating out, sport, socialising; Contact: McNean House and Bistro, Blacklion, Co. Cavan. Tel: 072 53022.

MAHER, Emily; ATHLETE; *b* 1981; *educ* currently studying for Leaving Certificate at St. Brigid's College, Callan; *single;* started running aged seven, winning the Community Games in Mosney; has yet to be beaten at national level; won gold medals in the last World Youth Olympics; currently training under Linford Christie and participating in the World Championships, Seville and the European Juniors, Riga; Contact: BLE, 11 Prospect Road, Dublin 9. Tel: 01-8308925.

MAHER, TJ; PRESIDENT, MACRA NA FEIRME; *b* 1968; *educ* Patrician Brothers, Fethard, Co. Tipperary; Rockwell Agricultural College, Cashel, Co. Tipperary; *single;* completed Certificate in Agriculture on John Sheehy's farm, Nenagh, Co. Tipperary; has worked on his own beef and dairy farm, Killenaule, Co. Tipperary, 1987 to date; Munster Vice President, Macra na Feirme, 1997-99, elected President, 1999; responsible for the implementation of policy and the public face of the biggest rural youth organisation in Ireland; hobbies, GAA, soccer; Contact: Macra Na Feirme, Irish Farm Centre, Bluebell, Dublin 12. Tel: 01 450 8000.

MAHOOD, Sonya; SENIOR CONSULTANT, CPL COMPUTER PLACEMENT; *b* 1969; *educ* The King's Hospital, Palmerstown; Trinity College Dublin, BESS; Treasury Management, LGT Asset Management Ltd., 1993-97; Consultant, CPL Computer Placement, 1997; Senior Consultant, 1997 to date; hobbies, yoga, cinema. Contact: CPL Computer Placement, 83 Merrion Square, Dublin 2. Tel: 01 614 6017 Fax: 01 614 6011.

MALONEY, Catherine,"Kitty"; PORTFOLIO MANAGER, DAVY STOCKBROKERS; *b* 1971; *educ* Muckross Park, Dublin; Trinity College Dublin, BA, Economics, Politics; University College Galway, MA, Economics; *single;* worked for AIB Security Services, 1995-97; Portfolio Manager, Goodbodys, 1997-98; Portfolio Manager, Davy Stockbrokers, 1998 to date; One of the most dynamic and in demand young stockbrokers in the country; hobby, golf; Contact: Davy Stockbrokers, 49, Dawson Street, Dublin 2. Tel: 01 679 7788.

MATHEWS, Gillian Avena; SALES MANAGER T.C. MATHEWS CARPETS LTD.; *b* 1970; *educ* Alexandra College; D.I.T. Rathmines, DBS; Trinity College Dublin, BBS; *single;* joined established family carpet business founded 105 years ago in Dunleer, Co. Louth, in 1993; established a new branch at Sir John Rogerson's Quay 1996; currently Sales Manager and Board Director, T.C. Mathews Carpets Ltd.; T.C. Mathews, with four branches, is the largest carpet company in the state, responsible for carpeting major businesses such as the Brown Thomas Group and Irish Racecourses; member, Iveagh Fitness Club; hobbies, socialising, travel. Contact: TC Mathews Carpets Ltd., 3 Sir John Rogerson's Quay, Dublin 2. Tel: 01 671 7233. Fax: 01 671 7453.

McCALL, Niamh; DIRECTOR, CLARENCE PICTURES; *b* 1971 *educ* St. Paul's Greenhills, Walkinstown; University College Dublin, BA, French, Economics; Newman College, Postgraduate, International Marketing; *single;* Marketing Manager, Clarence Pictures, 1994-97; Director, Clarence Pictures, 1997 to date; Clarence have released *Dancing at Lughnasa, The Usual Suspects, Trainspotting* and *Priest* onto the Irish market; hobbies, cinema, reading, travelling. Contact: Clarence Pictures, Denzille Lane, Dublin 2. Tel: 01 661 4022 Fax: 01 661 4186.

McCLOSKEY, Colm; MARKETING AND SALES EXECUTIVE, BOYNE VALLEY GROUP LTD.; *b* 1973; *educ* Franciscan College, Gormanstown, Co. Meath; Portobello College, Dublin, BA, Business Information Management; *single;* worked part time for his father's business in Boyne Valley, before joining Barings Bank, IFSC, 1998; moved to London, working in The National Bank of Kuwait, before returning to Ireland to work for Boyne Valley Group Ltd., 1998; currently working in the non-food sector of the business, developing new brands; hobbies, walking, reading, bowling, socialising; Contact: Boyne Valley Group Ltd. Headquarters, Platin, Drogheda. Tel: 041 70300.

McCOY, Tony; JOCKEY; *b* 1974; *educ* St. Oclean's, Co. Antrim; *single;* a jockey for over a decade; starting off riding ponies on his parent's land; served his apprenticeship with Jim Bolger,1990, and later trained racehorses for both him and Willie Rock; moved to England and started to race professionally, 1994; Champion Jockey, 1994 to date; the winner of over 850 races, has ridden 253 winners in one season, a world record in jump racing; hobbies, golf, football; Contact: Tel: 0044 1737 761369.

McGOWAN, James; BARRISTER; *b* 1968; *educ* C.B.S., Belfast; University College Dublin, BCL, LLM; Queens University, Belfast, LLM; King's Inns Dublin, Barrister-at-Law Degree; was involved in the Bula and Tara litigations, 1994-97 and more recently the Flood Tribunal, 1998-99; hobbies, old cars, travel, reading; Contact: The Law Library, The Four Courts, Dublin 7.

McGUIRE, Helen; COPYWRITER; *b* 1973 *educ* Mount Lourdes Grammar School, Enniskillen; Manchester Metropolitan University, BSc; DIT Aungier Street, Dipl. Advertising; *single;* Copywriter, The Helme Partnership, 1996-97; Copywriter, Grey Ireland, 1997 to date; one of the advertising industry's most regarded copywriters; hobbies, philosophy, neuro linguistic programming, yoga. Contact: Grey Ireland, 6-7 Adelaide Court, Adelaide Road, Dublin 2. Tel: 01 478 5488.

McILROY, James, Samuel; ATHLETE; *b* 1976; *educ* Ballyclare High School; Larne Grammar School; Northumbria University, Newcastle, England, B.Sc, Sport and Exercise Science; *single;* coached by Sean Kyle, only started athletics in 1997, running 800m in 1 minute 51.8 seconds at BMC, Watford, UK, 1997, progressing to 1.45.32 in 1998; honours to date include:winner, Europa Cup, 800m, 1998, Irish Champion, 1500m, 1998, winner, Debut Mile, 1998, Nice GPI, 1998, Brussels GPI, 1998, 4th, European Championships, 1998, Gateshead GP 2, 1998; hobbies, football - played U12, U16 for Northern Ireland Schoolboy Squad, Irish League for Larne Town, Professional Trials for Dumbarton FC, golf, Ulster U17 Squad, Scratch Cup Cairndhu Gold Club winner, 1994; Contact: BLE, 11 Prospect Road, Dublin 9. Tel: 01 830 8925.

McKIMM, Lesley; FILM PRODUCER; *b* 1969; *educ* Dominican Convent, Sion Hill, Blackrock; Trinity College Dublin, BA, Drama, English; EAVE course for European producers, 1998; *single;* Script Supervisor, short films, commercials, *Korea* feature film, 1991-95; Researcher, Scriptwriter, The Heritage Corporation, 1992; Worked full time with Temple Films in development, casting and administration, 1993-95; Production Co-ordinator, *Balcony Belles, Reaper,* 1993-94; Production Co-ordinator, Post Production Supervisor, *Ailsa, Guiltrip,* 1993-95; Producer, *81,* 1995-96; Line Producer, *Barabbas, Sweety Barrett* 1996-98; Producer, *Home,* 1997-98; Post Production Supervisor, *Sweety Barrett,* 1998; Producer, *Ireland & The Movies, Anytime Now, Growing Pains,* 1999; hobbies, reading, music, good food and wine; Contact: Comet Films, Shamrock Chambers, 1-2 Eustace Street, Dublin 2. Tel: 01 670 4286.

McNULTY, David; CONCERT PIANIST; *b* 1979; *educ* Our Lady and St. Patrick's College, Belfast; currently studying at The Royal Irish Academy, Dublin; *single*; started playing the piano aged seven; has performed at The National Concert Hall, The Holland Music Sessions, Amsterdam, Holland; awarded numerous Feis Ceoil prizes, 2nd Prize Boyle Piano Awards, 1997, 1st Prize, Blacktie National Piano Competition, 1998, Yamaha Foundation Scholarship, 1999; hobbies, collecting music, swimming, languages; Contact: The Royal Irish Academy, 36-38 Westland Row, Dublin 2. Tel: 01 676 4412.

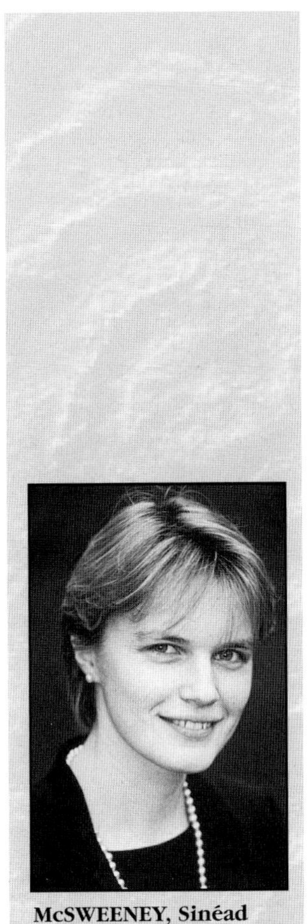
McSWEENEY, Sinéad

McSWEENEY, Sinéad; SPECIAL ADVISER TO THE ATTORNEY GENERAL; *b* 1971; *educ* St. Mary's High School, Midleton, Co. Cork; University College Cork, BCL; King's Inns Dublin; *single;* called to the Bar, 1993; worked as a Parliamentary Transcriber, House of the Oireachtas, 1992-96; Adviser to Bertie Ahern, the then Leader of the Opposition, 1996-97; Special Adviser to Michael Woods, Minister for the Marine and Natural Resources, 1997-98; Special Adviser to the Attorney General, David Byrne, SC, 1998 to date; a legal brain who made the move to the political arena; hobbies, cinema, theatre, reading, music; Contact: Office of the Attorney General, Merrion Street, Dublin 2. Tel: 01 661 6944.

MEEHAN, Alex; JOURNALIST, MEDIA CONSULTANT; *b* 1976; *educ* Blackrock College; Ballyfermot Senior College, HND Journalism; *single;* Freelance Journalist, *Irish Independent, Sunday Business Post, Himself, Business Plus, G4, Computer Scope,* 1997 to date; Freelance Media Consultant, 1998 to date; Awarded New Journalist of the Year, Irish Science Journalists Association, 1997; Resident DJ, Beauty Spot, Columbia Mills, 1997-98, *Strictly Handbag,* Ri-Ra, 1995 to date; hobby, martial arts. Tel: 087 236 5309.

MOHLICH, Sonja; FASHION STYLIST; *b* 1969; *educ* University of Ghent, Belgium, BA (CommSc); Exeter University, MA European Public Relations; *single;* Account Executive, Freud Communications, London, U.K.,1994-95; Journalist, Stylist *The Sunday Independent,* 1995-96, Stylist, Fashion Section, *The Sunday Independent,* 1996-97; Freelance Stylist, *Image Magazine, Sunday Independent, U Magazine, IT Magazine, Social & Personal,* 1997 to date; hobbies, fashion, interior design. Contact: First Option, 40, Dame Street, Dublin 2. Tel: 01 670 5233.

MOLONEY, "Elie"; EVENT RIDER; *b* 1978; *educ* Presentation College, Kilkenny; Leinster Business Institute, Dublin; *single;* works part time in Tattersalls (Ireland) Ltd.; Event rider, winner of class at Redim; has won numerous trophies at junior events in Ireland, U.K. and throughout Europe, riding mainly horses bred on the family stud, at Warrington, Kilkenny; member of three European teams, both young riders and juniors, now moving into the senior team; Awarded Silver Medal (Gottland), 1997; hobby, horses. Contact: Top Flight Equestrian Centre, Warrington Stud, Warrington, Kilkenny. Tel: 056 22682.

MOLONEY, Richard "Richie"; SHOWJUMPER; *b* 1981; *educ* Kilkenny College; *single;* started jumping family bred horses aged six; won numerous awards in the Pony Section, Horsemanship Award (UK), 1998; member, European Junior Team; won Bronze Medal, European Championships, placed 5th overall in Europe, riding *Speedy Flight,* bred at Warrington Stud; hobby, Manchester United; Contact: Top Flight Equestrian Centre, Warrington Stud, Warrington, Kilkenny. Tel: 056 22682.

MOONEY, James; HAIRDRESSER; *b* 1969; *educ* C.B.S. North Brunswick Street; *single;* Trainee, Paul's Hair Studio, Dublin, 1988; Stylist, Hannan's, London, 1991-92; Stylist, Jean Louis David, Paris, 1992; Stylist, David Marshall, 1993-94; Freelance Hair Stylist, *Company, B, Elle, Marie Claire, Marie Claire Bis, Italian Marie Claire, German Elle, Scene Magazine, Max International, The Times, The Independent* UK, *The Observer, The Daily Mail, Image Magazine, dSide Magazine, The Irish Times,* 1994 to date; film work includes *Michael*

Collins, 1996, *Accelerator*, 1999; a leading hair stylist on the international fashion scene, his work is visible on practically every catwalk and glossy magazine worldwide; Contact: First Option, 40, Dame Street, Dublin 2. Tel: 01 6705233.

MOORE, Hannah; DIRECTOR, KENNEDY PUBLIC RELATIONS; *b* 1973; *educ* Downside School, Somerset, England; Trinity College Dublin, BA (Hons.) Philosophy, Classics; *single;* Producer, Smirnoff International Fashion Awards, 1995-96; Account Executive, Kennedy PR, 1996, appointed Director, 1999; Clients include Debenhams, Clarks, Louise Kennedy, Marc O'Neill; hobbies, opera, shopping, breezy walks, travel. Contact: Kennedy PR, 1 Castle Street, Dublin 2. Tel: 01 667 0090 Fax: 01 667 1175.

MORAN; Gemma; SOLICITOR; *b* 1969; *educ* St. Mary's Convent, Nenagh, Tipperary; Trinity College Dublin, LL.B.; Blackhall Place; *single;* served apprenticeship with Lavelle Coleman, 1995-98; currently working for The Chief State Solicitor, specialising in criminal law; hobbies, sailing, travelling; Contact: The Chief State Solicitor's Office, Osmond House, Ship Street, Dublin 2. Tel: 01 417 6100.

MORRISSEY, Sinéad; WRITER; *b* 1972; *educ* Belfast High School, Trinity College Dublin, BA (Hons), English, German; currently studying at Queen's Belfast, MA in Modern Literary Studies; *single;* spent two years teaching English in Japan, travelling in New Zealand for one year; currently working for a HIV/AIDS charity, Belfast; Awarded The Patrick Kavanagh Award for Poetry, 1990 - the youngest poet ever to win the award - and The Eric Gregory Award, 1996; First collection of poetry, *There Was Fire in Vancouver*, published, 1996; work has appeared in journals and anthologies in Ireland, UK, America, New Zealand, Australia; work appears in the forthcoming *New Poetries 2* anthology; has been described as "a writer of rare intensity and talent. Her work was immediately striking and beguiling and suggests even greater things to come"; hobbies, writing, hill walking; Contact: Carcanet Press, 4th Floor, Conavon Court, 12, Blackfriars Street, Manchester M3 5BQ, England; Tel: 0044 161 8348730 Fax: 0044 161 8320084.

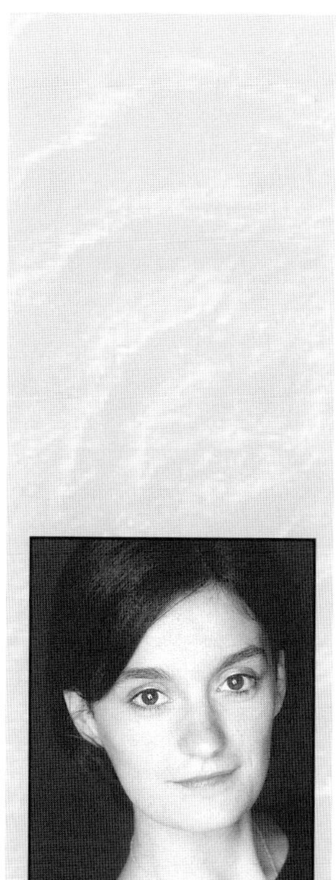
MOORE, Hannah

MOY, Johnny; DJ, PROMOTER, PRODUCER; *b* 1970; *educ* St. Laurence's College, Loughlinstown, Dublin; *single;* moved to England, working in Flying Records, London, 1990; returned to Dublin in 1991 to promote and DJ at The Beat Club; has subsequently become Ireland's best known DJ, working on the international circuit with residencies in New York, London, Barcelona, Madrid and Prague; has received numerous awards from publications including *The Face, i-D, Mixmag, DJ, Hot Press, Bassline*; Co-founded Influx Records and Promotions, a record label, club promotions agency and band management company, 1996; Influx is the biggest independent contemporary music organisation in Ireland, and has received numerous international awards for its contribution to music; has worked with and remixed U2, The Prodigy, David Holmes; hard work, determination and a passion for music point to even greater things to come. Contact: Influx Records and Productions, 3, Princes Court, Princes Street South, Dublin 2. Tel: 01-6703771.

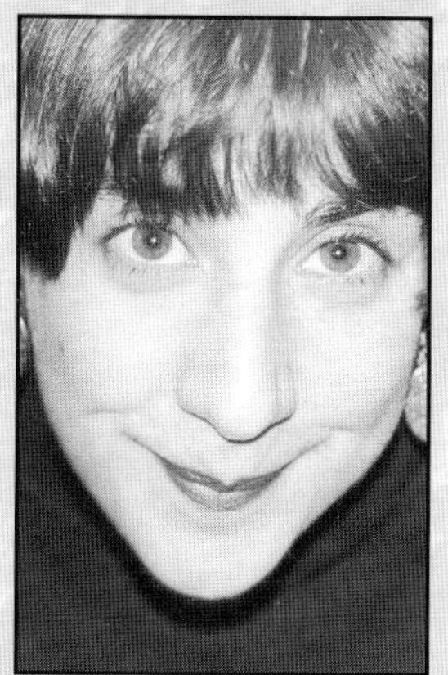
MORRISSEY, Sinéad

MURPHY, Mary; DIRECTOR, STOPWATCH TELEVISION; *b* 1969; *educ* Loretto Convent, Killarney, Co. Kerry; Dublin City University, B.Comm; *single*; Features Editor, *Aertel*, RTE, 1990-96; Founded stop.watch television with Tom Johnson, 1997; Series Co-Director, *@ last tv*, 1997-99; Producer, *What About The Children?* documentary, RTE, 1999; currently Director, Network 2's GAA series, *Breaking Ball*; an innovative, trend setting director, leading the national broadcaster's more experimental direction on Network 2; hobbies, cinema, theatre, sport (appreciation rather than participation); Contact: Stopwatch Television, Space 28, North Lotts, Dublin 1. Tel: 01 872 1882 Fax: 01 872 2086.

MURPHY, Tara; DIRECTOR, SOLOMON GALLERY; *b* 1971; *educ* St. Andrew's College, Booterstown, University College Dublin, BA(Hons.), Dip. Arts Administration; *m* Niall O hOisín; Gallery Assistant, Solomon Gallery, 1994-97, Gallery Director, 1997 to date; The Solomon is one of the most respected galleries in Ireland, representing Irish and international artists; hobbies, cinema, skiing, travel, food. Contact: Solomon Gallery, Powerscourt Townhouse, South William Street Dublin 2. Tel: 01 679 4237 Fax: 01 671 5262.

MURPHY, Tara

MURPHY, Tom

MURRIHY, Paula

NAUGHTEN, Denis

Ní CHIOSAIN, Fionnuala

MURPHY, Tom; ACTOR; *b* 1973; *single;* has worked in theatre for a decade, appearing in productions of *The Beauty Queen of Leenane, The Borstal Boy, Juno and the Paycock, True Lines, Upstarts* and *You Never Can Tell* among others; has also worked in television and cinema, appearing in *The Key, The Lost Hour, Fair City,* RTE, *Guest Of the Nation, The Bill,* Thames TV, *Michael Collins, The General*; awarded Tony Award for Best Actor for his role in *The Beauty Queen of Leenane.* Contact: The Agency, 47, Adelaide Road, Dublin 2. Tel: 01 661 8535 Fax:01 676 0052.

MURRIHY, Paula; SINGER; *b* 1978; *educ* Presentation Secondary School, Tralee, Co. Kerry; currently studying under Anne Marie O'Sullivan at the DIT Conservatory of Music and Drama, Dublin; performances include: Vivaldi's *Gloria,* Beethoven's *Mass in C,* Handel's *Messiah,* Bach's *Christmas Oratorio,* Tucapsky's *The Time of Christmas,* DIT Choral Society, Vivaldi's *Gloria,* Savaria Chamber Orchestra, Soloist in DIT's presentation of *An Evening of Lieder and French,* Schubert's *Der Hausliche Krieg,* RDS recital, *Spotlight on Youth* series, recorded for FM3; member, soloist, DIT Chamber Choir, 1996-98; has won numerous awards, including Feis Ceoil Dublin, 1999; Contact: Anne Marie O'Sullivan, School of Vocal, Operatic and Drama Studies, DIT Rathmines, Dublin 6. Tel: 01 402 3471 Fax: 01 402 3470.

NAUGHTEN, Denis; POLITICIAN; *b* 1973; *educ* St. Aloysius College, Athlone; University College Dublin, B.Sc (Hons.), Industrial Microbiology; University College Cork, M.Sc, Food Microbiology; *single;* the son of the late Liam Naughten, former Seanad Cathaoirleach; the youngest member of Dáil Eireann, the 1997 General Election was the first he contested; Senator, Agricultural Panel, 1997; Fine Gael Spokesperson on Youth Affairs, School Transport and Adult Education, responsible for liasing with Young Fine Gael and the promotion of young people within Fine Gael, 1997 to date; Member, Roscommon County Council, The Western Health Board, The Association of Health Boards; Contact: Dáil Eireann, Kildare Street, Dublin 2. Tel: 01 618 3333.

NELIS, Gillian; JOURNALIST; *b* 1974; *educ* St. Oliver's Community College, Drogheda; DIT Rathmines; *single;* Journalist, News and Features, *The Sunday Business Post,* 1994-95; Property Editor, 1995 to date; Health Columnist, 1998 to date; hobbies, reading, cinema; Contact: The Sunday Business Post, 80 Harcourt Street, Dublin 2. Tel: 01 679 9777 Fax: 01 6796498.

Ní BHEOLAIN, Sharon; NEWSCASTER, RTE; *b* 1971; *educ* Malahide Community School; Trinity College Dublin, Degree in Celtic Studies; *m* Kevin Cantrell; worked as a secondary school teacher and in public relations before turning to broadcasting; Contributor, *Combar, Anois,* 1992-96; worked for Radio Na Life as a Producer and Broadcaster; joined RTE as Irish Language Newsreader, 1994; currently News Reporter and Presenter *News 2* and the mainstream bulletins on RTE 1; regarded as "the natural successor to Ann Doyle"; hobby, animals. Contact: RTE, Donnybrook, Dublin 4.

Ní CHIOSAIN, Fionnuala; ARTIST; *b* 1966; *educ* St. Martin's London School of Art; National College of Art and Design, Dublin; solo exhibitions include shows at the City Centre Gallery, Dublin, 1991 and New York, 1993; has participated in group exhibitions at the Cornerhouse Gallery Manchester, The Irish Museum of Modern Art, Dublin, Itami City Museum of Art, Japan; took part in Idea Europa, Padua, Siena, Italy, 1994-95, l'Imaginaire Irlandais, l'Ecole des Beaux-Arts, Paris, 1996, A Century of Irish Painting, touring Japan, 1997; forthcoming exhibition, Irish Art Now, to tour U.S.A.; represented in the collections of The Irish Museum of Modern Art, The Municipal Gallery of Modern Art, Dublin, the National Self Portrait Collection of Ireland and Deutsche Morgan Grenfell, London, as well as many private collections in Europe and the U.S.A.; hobbies, music, film, literature, poetry. Contact: Kerlin Gallery, Anne's Lane, South Anne Street, Dublin 2. Tel: 01 670 9093 Fax: 01 670 9096.

NICOL, Tracey; CLIENT DIRECTOR, DRURY COMMUNICATIONS; *b* 1971; *educ* Rathdown School, Glenagearey, Co. Dublin; University College Dublin, BA, Psychology; College of Commerce Rathmines, Postgraduate Diploma, Public Relations; *single;* PR Executive, RTE Press and Information Office, 1993-94; Marketing Executive, Nat West Markets, Sydney, Australia, 1994-95; Client Executive, Drury Communications, 1995, Client Manager, 1997-98, Client Director, 1999 to date; clients include Dunnes Stores, Motorola, Campbell Bewley,

O'BRIAIN, Dara

O'BRIEN, Fergal

Jurys Hotel Group; hobbies, music, cinema, tennis; Contact: c/o Drury Communications, 1, Richview Office Park, Clonskeagh, Dublin 14. Tel: 01 260 5000.

NORMAN, Jake; STRATEGIC MEDIA PLANNER, MCM COMMUNICATIONS LTD. *b* 1974; *educ* Oatlands College, Mount Merrion, Dublin; University College Dublin, BCL; DIT Aungier Street, Dip., Advertising, winning the Conlon Gold Medal; *single;* travelled to Australia working for NEC and a publishing company, 1995-96; worked for Axicom PR, London, U.K, 1997; Junior Media Planner, McConnells, 1997, Strategic Media Planner, 1998 to date; responsible for the media strategy of some of Ireland's biggest brands, clients include Kellogg's, Dulux, Irish Distillers; McConnells is the largest advertising and communications group in Ireland; hobbies, socialising, football, reading, cinema, current affairs. Contact: MCM Communications, McConnell House, Charlemont Place, Dublin 2. Tel: 01 4781 544.

O'BOYLE, Alan, MUSIC PRODUCER; *b* 1970; *educ* Templeogue College, Dublin; DIT Kevin Street, Diploma, Electronic Engineering; *single;* Electronic Engineer, Ascom Timeplex, 1991-95; Music Producer, Member, In Motion, Decal, Ajax Disco Spanner, 1995 to date; work includes *The Language of Everyday Life, Ultramack 004, Lo Lite, Germ Rockit, 80s Funky, Endgame, Dublin Phunk City, Bleep;* Co-founder, Ultramack Record Label, 1993 to date; Promoter, *Sensoria, Soundclash, Rotation, Phunk City* nights, 1995 to date; Live and Studio Sound Engineer, 1995 to date; Music Columnist, *The Event Guide,* 1998 to date; one of the country's most experimental and passionate contemporary music producers; hobby, music. Contact: Ultramack Productions, PO Box 5417, Phibsboro, Dublin 7. Tel: 01 830 5507.

O'BRIAIN, Dara; COMEDIAN, TELEVISION PRESENTER; *b* 1972; *educ* Coláiste Eoin, Booterstown; University College Dublin, B.Sc., Mathematical Science; *single;* Co-founder, Editor, *University Observer,* 1994-95; Auditor, Literary and Historical Society, UCD; Winner, *The Irish Times* National Debating Competition in English and Irish, 1994; Presenter, *Echo Island,* Network 2; other presentation credits include *Eureka, Telethon* 1998, *Sporting Press Gang,* 1995-98; Columnist, *Get A Life, Sunday World,* 1995-98; Stand Up Comedian, 1995 to date: established as regular MC at Ireland's two largest comedy clubs; has performed shows at the last three Cat Laugh's Festivals and the last two Edinburgh Festivals; performed on BBC Radio 4 New Year's Special, 1998; Team Captain, *Don't Feed The Gondolas,* Network 2, 1998 to date; has been described as "stunningly accurate and uproariously funny"; hobbies, practically all popular culture, anything to do with science, especially physics. Contact: c/o ACME Management, 19-20, Fenian Street, Dublin 2. Tel: 01 661 7244.

O'BRIEN, Fergal; SNOOKER PLAYER; *b* 1972; *educ* Pobal Scoil Neasáin, Dublin; *m* Jean McGregor; member, Raphael's Snooker Club, Lucan; turned professional, 1991, currently ranked twentieth in the world; has notched up over forty centuries in professional snooker, and a highest tournament break of 143 at the Benson & Hedges Championship, Scotland, 1991; Tournament Highlights include Semi Finalist, Benson & Hedges Irish Masters, 1994, British Open Champion, 1999; has won over £300,000 in prize money during his career; hobbies, golf, tennis, football. Contact: Cuemasters, Kerse Road, Stirling FK7 7SG, Scotland. Tel: 0044 1786 462634 Fax: 0044 1786 450068.

O'BRIEN, Ronan; POLITICAL ADVISER; *b* 1968; *educ* Ard Scoil La Salle, Raheny; University College Dublin, BA, History, Politics; *single;* worked as Assistant to Derek McDowell, Labour TD, 1992-95; Labour Party Research Officer,1995-97; became political adviser to Ruairi Quinn, 1997 to date; has been dubbed "the new Fergus Finlay of the Labour Party"; hobbies, watching sport, reading; Contact: Dáil Eireann, Kildare Street, Dublin 2. Tel: 01 618 3333.

O'CINNEIDE, Dara; GAA FOOTBALL PLAYER; *b* 1975; *educ* Dingle C.B.S., Kerry; read Chemistry, University of Limerick, currently studying Education, Mary Immaculate College, Limerick; *single;* started to play Gaelic Football competitively at the age of eight, playing for An Gaeltacht, Dingle Kerry, progressing to the Kerry Minor team; currently playing for the Senior Kerry Team; a hard working forward, helping to shape The Kingdom's footballing future, has appeared in safe driving advertising campaigns; hobbies, collecting music, cinema; Contact: 087 294 7405.

O'CONNOR, Alan; PHOTOGRAPHER; *b* 1971; *educ* Rockbrook Park, Rathfarnham, Dublin; University College Dublin, BA; *single;* Freelance Photographer, 1993 to date; work has been published in *Time Magazine, The Guardian, Observer, Stern, The Irish Times, Magill, Sunday Tribune, Sunday Business Post, Cara;* book commissions include *The Long War, Dublin As A Work Of Art, Belfast Boy;* has covered stories in Bosnia, Lebanon, Eastern Europe and extensively in Northern Ireland; hobbies, running, cinema; Contact: The Irish Times, D'Olier Street, Dublin 2.

O'DONNELL, Barry; SOLICITOR; *b* 1969; *educ* Clongowes Wood College, Kildare; Blackrock College, Dublin; University College Galway BA; Incorporated Law Society, Blackhall Place; *m* Nicola Rooney; 1 da; apprenticeship with Rory O'Donnell, Solicitor, Dublin, 1991-94; worked with two legal firms in Sydney and Melbourne, Australia,1994-95; joined Giles J. Kennedy, Solicitors, Dublin, 1995-96; Associate Partner, Bruce St. John Blake, Solicitors, 1997 to date; member, Incorporated Law Society, Dublin Solicitors Bar Association, Society of Young Solicitors; hobbies, rugby (plays with Monkstown R.F.C.), GAA games, canoeing, flying. Contact: Bruce St. John Blake Solicitors, Serpentine Court, Ballsbridge, Dublin 4. Tel: 01 660 3122.

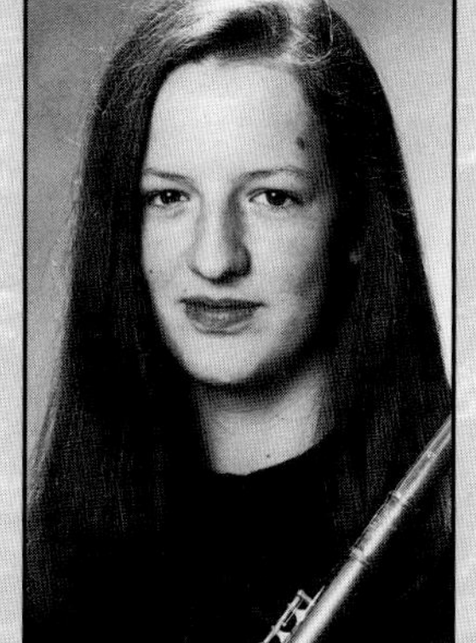

O'DUINNIN, Riona

O'DUINNIN, Riona; FLAUTIST; *b* 1975; *educ* Coláiste Rís, Dundalk, Co. Louth; Royal Irish Academy of Music, Degree in Music Performance; has studied under John O'Conor and William Dowdall of the National Symphony Orchestra; currently studying under Jeanne Baxtresser at The Manhattan School of Music, New York, U.S.A.; *single;* has played with The National Youth Orchestra of Great Britain, The Royal Irish Academy of Music Orchestra, The Hibernian Chamber Orchestra, The National Symphony Orchestra, Irish Youth Orchestra, The Manhattan School of Music Symphony Orchestra; has worked with the most acclaimed conductors, including Sir Colin Davis, Tadaki Otaka and Alexander Anissimov; has played with The Riverside Wind Quintet, Esposito Wind Quintent, Presburg Trio; solo appearances include Galway, Kilkenny Boyle Arts Festivals, Royal Irish Academy of Music, 1996, Royal Dublin Society, National Concert Hall, National Symphony Orchestra, Manhattan School of Music, 1998; awarded Fulbright Scholarship, Ulster Bank Music Foundation Award, 1998, Licentiate Diploma in Flute and Piano, Royal Irish Academy of Music, 1997; hobbies, walking, outdoor activities; Contact: Manhattan School of Music, 120 Claremont Avenue, New York, 10027, U.S.A.

O'HANLON, Jim

O'HANLON, Jim; THEATRE DIRECTOR, TELEVISION DIRECTOR; *b* 1970; *educ* Clonkeen College, Dublin; University College Dublin, BA; Balliol College, Oxford, U.K., M.Lit; *single;* Trainee Director, Gate Theatre, 1995; Lecturer, Performing Arts and Theatre, University of Hertfordshire, UK, 1995-96; Freelance Theatre Director, *In High Germany, Baby Jean,* 1996; Theatre Director, Miniature Theatre of Chester, Massachusetts, U.S.A., 1996; Storyliner, *Coronation Street,* Granada Television/ITV Television, 1996-98; Director, *Ready Or Not,* nominated for Manchester *Evening News* Theatre Award, 1998; Director, *Coronation Street* 1998-99; Director, *Bad Girls,* ITV Television, 1999; Director, *My Bonnie Lies,* Capital Theatre, Manchester,1999; Director, *I Am Of Ireland,* Miniature Theatre of Chester, Massachusetts, U.S.A., 1999; hobbies, playing tennis, football, badminton, guitar and bodhran; Contact: Lucid Productions, 152, New North Road, Islington, London N1 7BH, England.

O'HANLON, Shane, Bernard; COUNCILLOR; *b* 1971; *educ* Coláiste na Rinne, Dungarvan, Co. Waterford; Patrician High School, Carrickmacross, Co. Monaghan; College of Technology, Bolton Street, Diploma, Auctioneering, Valuation and Estate Agency; *single;* Self Employed Auctioneer, Valuer and Estate Agent; Agency Manager, EBS Building Society; Property and Agency Manager, Dublin, London; member, Carrickmacross Chamber of Commerce, Irish Auctioneers and Valuers Institute, Carrickmacross Fianna Fáil Cumann, 1986 to date, Fianna Fáil Northern Ireland Committee, 1999, Fianna Fáil Policy Committee on the Environment and Local Government, 1998 to date, Association of Municipal Authorities of Ireland, 1994 to date, Vice President, 1995-96, Carrickmacross Urban District Council, 1994 to date, National Youth Committee, 1997 to date, National Executive, Fianna Fáil, 1997 to date; hobbies, Gaelic football, golf, cycling, horse racing, travel, music; Contact: Convent Hill, Carrickmacross, Co. Monaghan. Tel: 042 966 2222.

O'hOISIN, Niall; 3D GRAPHICS ANIMATOR; *b* 1971; *educ* Coláiste Eoin, Booterstown, University College Dublin, BA; Ballyfermot Senior College, Computer Graphics; *m* Tara Murphy; Assistant Graphic Designer, Screen Scene,1995-97, 3D Graphics Animator, 1997 to date; hobbies, windsurfing, pool. Contact: Screen Scene, 41, Upper Mount Street, Dublin 2. Tel: 01 661 1501.

O'KANE, Deirdre; ACTRESS, COMEDIAN; *b* 1968; *educ* Loreto Abbey, Rathfarnham, Dublin; College of Marketing and Design, Mountjoy Square; Gaiety School of Acting; *single;* stage appearances include *At the Black Pig's Dyke,* Druid Theatre, Galway, Gate Theatre, Dublin, touring to London, Toronto, Canada, Australia, 1991-92; *Present Laughter,* Gate Theatre, Dublin, 1992; *Red Roses and Petrol,* Tivoli, Project Arts Centre, Dublin, London, 1995; *She Stoops to Folly,* Abbey Theatre, 1996; *Juno and the Paycock,* Abbey Theatre, 1997-98; Casting Director, *I Went Down,* 1996; Co-Casting Director, *Saltwater,* Conor McPherson's first film, 1999; Stand Up Comedian, various venues, Dublin, Cork, Galway, Kilkenny, Limerick, Belfast, London, Edinburgh, 1996-99; influenced by Dylan Moran, Rich Hall and Bill Hicks; a multi talented theatrical talent, currently working on two sitcoms for RTE and BBC, writing a screenplay and developing a drama, *Anytime Now,* for BBC; Contact: Marina Martin Associates, 12-13 Poland Street, London, England. Tel: 0044 171 734 4818.

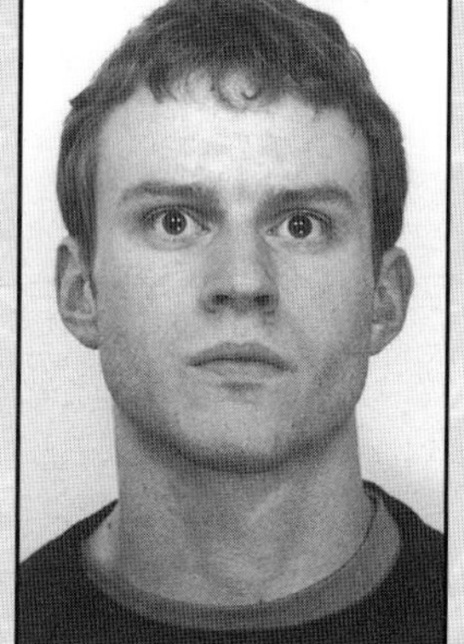

O'KANE, Eamon

O'KANE, Eamon; ARTIST; *b* 1974; *educ* National College of Art & Design, First Class Honours, Fine Art, Art History; University of Ulster, MA, Fine Art; *single;* solo exhibitions include Postcard Cities KoRaw Gallery, London, U.K., Koordinater MCMIC, Overgaden, Copenhagen; group exhibitions include Manifestatie Laurenskwartier, Rotterdam, Holland, The 12th Cleveland International Drawing Biennial, Middlesborough, U.K., Connect, Dublin, Belfast, Panorama, Athens, Greece, Perspective 98, Ormeau Baths Gallery, Belfast, Forest The Bull and Last, London, U.K., International Young Art, ArtLink@Sothebys, Chicago, U.S.A., Tel Aviv, Israel; has received numerous awards, including The Fulbright Award to study at Parsons School of Design in New York; his work is held in public and private collections including Microsoft WPGI, The Office of Public Works, UNIBANK Denmark, NKT Norway, Irish Contemporary Arts Society: The Butler Gallery and the collection of President Mary McAleese; currently Research Fellow in Painting at Cheltenham & Gloucester College of Higher Education, England. Contact: Tel: 0044 1242 532 283 Fax: 0044 1242 532 207.

O'KEEFFE, Rory; SINGER; *b* 1972; *educ* Newpark Comprehensive, Blackrock; *single;* formed first band during secondary school; travelled to France and Galway; returned and formed The Ultra Montanes, 1996; released debut album, *The Ultra Montanes,* 1998; the band has toured extensively in Ireland and the U.K., has played in the U.S.A. and Europe, appearing on television; has been the subject of much media attention recently, often compared to David Bowie and Blondie; have just completed recording their as yet untitled second album; hobbies, vodka, reading history; Contact: Lakota Records, 43, Donnybrook Manor, Donnybrook, Dublin 4. Tel: 01 283 9071.

O'MALLEY, Fiona; PUBLIC REPRESENTATIVE; *b* 1968; *educ* Laurel Hill School, Limerick; Trinity College Dublin, BA; City University, London MA (Museum and Gallery Management); awarded Thomas Damman Travelling Scholarship to research French Gothic Cathedrals 1989; *single;* Art Promoter (developing visual arts opportunities for audiences and artists in London region), London Arts Board 1994-98; PA (Constituency) for Liz O'Donnell, Minister of State, Department of Foreign Affairs 1998 to date; elected Progressive Democrat County Council member, Dun Laoghaire Rathdown (Stillorgan Ward) 1999; the politically astute daughter of the founder of the Progressive Democrats, Desmond O'Malley, holds promise of a career in national politics; hobbies, theatre, cinema, tennis, sailing, horse racing, bargain hunting at car boot sales. Contact: Dun Laoghaire Rathdown County Council, County Hall, Dun Laoghaire, Co. Dublin. Tel: 01 205 4700 Fax: 01 280 6969.

O'MEARA Peter

O'MEARA Peter; ACTOR; *b* 1969; *educ* Glenstal Abbey, Murroe, Co. Limerick; Trinity College Dublin, Dip. Theatre Studies; *single;* stage appearances include: *Philadelphia Here I Come!, How Many Miles to Babylon,* Lyric Theatre, Belfast, *The Colleen Bawn,* The Abbey Theatre, Dublin, National Theatre, London; Presenter, *It's Only Telly,* UTV, 1995-96; Presenter, *Echo Island,* RTE, 1996-97; television appearances include *Give My Head Peace,* BBC, 1998, the award winning *Two Ceasefires And A Wedding,* BBC, 1997, *Aristocrats,* BBC,

1999; Currently working with The Royal Shakespeare Company on *King Lear,* touring to Japan; an actor who can turn his hand with equal ease to comedy, drama and stage performances; hobbies, collecting world music, travelling; Contact: ICM Ireland Ltd., The Barracks, 76, Irishtown Road, Dublin 4. Tel: 01 667 6455 Fax: 01 667 6474.

O'NEILL, Barry; HEAD OF NEW MEDIA PUBLISHING, TELECOM EIREANN; *b* 1973; *educ* Ashton, Cork; *single;* worked for a period with Horizon Computers, Cork, before becoming a digital media consultant for Independent Pictures, Smurfit and other leading communication, computing and media companies; Head of Production & Training, Arthouse Multimedia Centre for the Arts, Temple Bar, 1995; Head of New Media Publishing, Telecom Eireann, 1997 to date, responsible for some of Ireland's most popular websites, including *The Doras Directory* and *MUSE,* the acclaimed online music magazine; Director, Arthouse, Ennis Information Age Town Ltd.; has lectured extensively on the subject of interactive media at NCAD, DLIADT, Trinity College, DIT and at numerous professional conferences, is regarded as one of the country's foremost experts in this field. Contact: Eircom, Block B, East Point Business Park, Fairview, Dublin 3. Tel: 01 701 0111

O'SHEA, Ken

O'NEILL, Paul; ARTIST, CURATOR; *b* 1970; *educ* Coláiste Phadraig, Lucan; National College of Art and Design, Degree, Fine Art (First Class Hons.); *single;* Residency, Museum of Modern Art, 1994-95, Polish National Sculpture Centre, Oronsko, Poland, 1995, Chateau Roux, Paris, France, 1996-97; group exhibitions include:*I* Love You, Temple Bar Gallery, 1995, Return to Sender, Hugh Lane Gallery, Dublin, various venues, Australia, 1998; solo exhibitions include: Gallery Marcel Du Champ, Paris, France, Project Arts Centre, Dublin; Curator, Passport, Arthouse, Temple Bar Gallery, Dublin, Musem of Modern Art, Warsaw, Poland, 1997-98, Inner Art, Public Art Project, 1998; founded Multiples X, 1998; Lecturer, MA, Fine Art Curating, Goldsmith University College, London, Dun Laoghaire School of Art and Design, Visiting Lecturer, National College of Art and Design, Crawford School of Art, Limerick School of Art and Design, 1998 to date; forthcoming shows in France, South London Gallery, London, UK, EV+A, Limerick, 1999; hobbies, reading, writing, soccer, travelling; Contact: Temple Bar Gallery and Studios, Dublin 2. Tel: 01 672 3322.

O'ROWE, Mark; PLAYWRIGHT; *b* 1970; *educ* St. Mark's Community School, Tallaght; *single;* worked in factories, shops, dabbled in electronics before starting to write in 1994; work includes *The Aspidistra Code,* 1996, *Anna's Ankle,* 1997, *From Both Hips* 1997, *Howie The Rookie,* 1999; work has been shown in London, Glasgow, Edinburgh, Dublin, with *Howie The Rookie* recently opening the Civic Theatre, Tallaght; inspired by Sam Peckinpah and lauded by many critics as the "Irish James Ellroy" for his dark, urban work; hobbies, movies, reading; Contact: Nick Marston, Curtis Brown, Haymarket House, 28-29 Haymarket, London SW1Y 4SP, England. Tel: 0044 171 396 6600 Fax: 0044 171 396 0110.

O'SHEA, Ken; REPORTER, RTE; *b* 1971; *educ* Deerpark C.B.S., Cork; Rathmines DIT, Dublin; *single;* Correspondent, *The Meath Chronicle,* 1990; Reporter, *The Sunday Tribune,* 1990-95; Reporter, *The Sunday World,* 1996-98; Reporter, *Primetime,* RTE, 1998 to date; One of RTE's youngest investigative reporters; hobbies, travelling, languages, Sino-Hiberno relations; Contact RTE, Donnybrook, Dublin 4.

O'SULLIVAN, Tara

O'SNODAIGH, Rossa; MUSICIAN; *b* 1971 *educ* Coláiste Eoin, Booterstown, Co. Dublin; *single;* busked in Dublin, forming the traditional band Kila during secondary school; Kila has played extensively in Ireland, Sweden, France, Belgium, Germany, Austria, Switzerland, Spain, Japan, New Zealand, Australia, Canada, U.S.A.; Albums include *Éist,* 1990, *Groovin'* 1991, *Kila,* 1992, *Mind The Gap,* 1995, *Tóg É Go Bog É,* 1997; have just released their sixth album; Awarded Kilkenny Cream of Irish Awards 1999; has composed and worked for The Irish Modern Dance Theatre, The Gallow Glass Theatre Company, The Machine, Amharclann de hIde; composed scores for *Gold on the Streets,* TnaG, *Hidden Treasures,* RTE; Presenter, *Nuachas an Dúchas,* Radió Na Life; has carried out studies on Irish and Quebec traditional music; has written an as yet unpublished book; hobbies, poetry, reading, clowning; Contact: Key Management, Stephen's Street, Dublin 2. .

O'SULLIVAN, Tara; ASSOCIATE VICE PRESIDENT, MARKETING, IONA TECHNOLOGIES; *b* 1969; *educ* Malahide Community School; Trinity College Dublin, BESS; University College

*O*ur Days Are often Soft, Our Malt Is always Mellow.

Close by the stunning Antrim coast, nestles the time-touched village of Bushmills.

There, in a distillery licenced since 1608, we first ferment and then triple-distil Irish malted barley. Ten maturing years follows in American oak bourbon barrels and European oak sherry casks creating the unique mellowness that characterises Bushmills Single Malt Irish Whiskey.

In just one smooth sip, you'll discover why Bushmills Malt was a Gold Medal Winner at the World Spirits Championships and noted as having:

"A silky mouthfeel; a soft, elegant finish with expanding warmth."

Above all, you'll savour a rare softness and mellowness that reflects a quiet land and a warm people.

Come softly to Bushmills Malt.
Come softly.

Dublin, MBS; *m* Mike Frazer; worked as Senior Marketing Adviser, Irish Life, while completing postgraduate degree, 1990-94; travelled extensively throughout South East Asia, 1995; Lecturer, LSB College, Dublin Business School, 1994-96; Marketing Executive Iona Technologies, 1996, Senior Marketing Manager, 1997, Associate Vice President, Marketing, 1998; Iona are world leaders in making software work together and is listed on Nasdaq; has recently been appointed Director of Marketing at ESAT Telecom, hobbies, cinema, the Internet; Contact: ESAT Telecom, The Malthouse, Grand Canal Quay, Dublin 2. Tel: 01 6616010

O'TOOLE, Gary; FORMER SWIMMER, DOCTOR; *b* 1969 *educ* Presentation College Bray; University College Dublin, B.Sc., MB, BAO, BCh, Royal College of Surgeons, AFRCSI; *m* Sorcha MacGabhann; European Silver Medalist, 200 metres breastsroke, Bonn, 1989; World Student Games, Gold Medallist, 200 metres breaststroke, Sheffield,1991; Participant, Irish Team, 200 metres breaststroke, Olympic Games, Barcelona, 1992; retired from competitive international swimming, 1994; Television Commentator, Olympic Games, 1996, RTE; Co-Presenter, *Pulse*, RTE, 1997-98; Practising orthopaedic non consultant hospital doctor, Cappagh Orthopaedic Hospital, Finglas,1999; hobbies, sports, cinema; Contact: Cappagh Orthopaedic Hospital, Cappagh, Finglas, Dublin 11.

OWENS, Eamonn

O'TOOLE, Laurence, "Leagues"; JOURNALIST; *b* 1972; *educ* Pobail Scoil Neasáin, Baldoyle; Ballyfermot Senior College, Diploma, Music Management and Information Agencies; *single;* Freelance Journalist, *The Event Guide, dSide, Sunday Times, Magnet, U Magazine,* 1995 to date; Music Editor, *The Event Guide*, 1998 to date; Assistant Editor, *Muse,* 1998 to date; An articulate, unsung supporter of the Irish music scene; hobbies, music, cinema, soccer, snooker; Contact: The Event Guide, 7, Eustace Street, Dublin 2. Tel: 01 671 3377.

OWENS, Eamonn; ACTOR; *b* 1983; *educ* currently attending St. Patrick's Secondary School, Cavan; *single;* first came to prominence with his role in *The Butcher Boy*, written by Pat McCabe and directed by Neil Jordan; has subsequently starred as the young Martin Cahill in *The General*, directed by John Boorman and has played a cameo role in *Angela's Ashes*; television work includes: *Amongst Women*, BBC, and *St. Patrick,* a TV film for Fox Channel U.S.A.; awarded the Silver Bear award at the Berlin Film Festival for his portrayal of Francie Brady in *The Butcher Boy*; hobbies, Gaelic football, hurling, soccer, snooker. Contact: Lorraine Brennan Management, Unit 22, Greenmount Industrial Estate, Harold's Cross, Dublin 6. Tel: 01 453 4355 Fax: 01 453 4412.

PAIC, Nives; TEAM LEADER, HANSARD EUROPE LTD.; *b* 1970; *educ* Gisela Gymnasium, European Management Academy, Degree, European Business and Languages, Munich, Germany; NCIR, Diploma in Human Resource Management; *single;* European Student Officer, Hibernia Learning Partnership, 1994-97; Team Leader, Hansard Europe, 1997 to date; hobbies, cinema, theatre, reading. Contact: Hansard Europe Ltd., PO Box 43, Enterprise House, Frascati Road, Blackrock, Co. Dublin. Tel: 01 211 2800 Fax: 01 211 2850.

PEARSON, Leo; MUSIC PRODUCER; *b* 1973; *educ* Newpark Comprehensive, Blackrock, Dublin; *single;* on leaving school set up his own fully professional studio and record label, Peak Records; has recorded under a number of guises, including Romin, Inevidence, Source, Invisible Armies and Resinated; has worked with U2, Howie B., David Holmes, Bush, Jon Carter and Johnny Moy to name but a few; has been commissioned by RTE to record music for videos and television programmes; an unassuming and as yet unrecognised musical talent; hobby, music. Contact: Influx Records and Productions, 3, Princes Court, Princes Street South, Dublin 2. Tel: 01 670 3771.

PHELAN, Suzanne Mary "Sue"; BRANCH MANAGER, GLANBIA; *b* 1970; *educ* Teresian School; Pembroke School; University College Dublin, BAgr.Sc.; *single;* joined Waterford Foods, now Glanbia, as Sales Executive 1994, appointed Gaultier Branch Manager in Dunmore East 1995; work involves liaising with local farmers on all aspects of agriculture; completed two year Management Course (NCR (Ranelagh) 1999; member, Agricultural Science Association; member, Kilotteran Riding Club (Hon. Sec.); hobbies, horses and travel. Contact: Gaultier, Dunmore East, Co. Waterford. Tel: 051 383 124.

REYNOLDS; Sonia

PLANT, Samantha; DIRECTOR, MARLBOROUGH PLC; *b* 1971; *educ* Alexandra College, Milltown; University College Dublin, B.Soc.Sc., NBS; *single;* worked for Relations with the Parliament, European Commission, Brussels, 1993-94, before returning to Ireland and joining The Marlborough Group as Consultant, 1994; on flotation of Marlborough Group in 1997 became Director of the newly formed plc; Marlborough is the biggest recruitment consultancy in Ireland, with offices in the U.K., Sydney and Melbourne, Australia; hobbies, hill walking, running. Contact: The Marlborough Group, 111-113 Grafton Street, Dublin 2. Tel: 01 617 3800.

PURCELL, Darragh; TELEVISION PRESENTER, TV3; *b* 1973; *educ* St. Joseph's College, Garbally, Ballinasloe, Galway; University College Dublin, BA, Politics, Sociology; *single;* Entertainments Officer, University College Dublin, 1996-97; Music Columnist, *Irish Independent,* 1997-98; Booking Agent, The Mean Fiddler Organisation, 1997-99; Presenter, Researcher, *Pop On 3,* TV3; Promoter, *Zeitgeist,* 1999; A highly individual style ensures that, as TV3's profile grows, so undoubtedly will his own; hobbies, music, cinema, playing darts; Contact: TV3, Unit 5, Westgate Business Park, Ballymount Industrial Estate, Dublin 24. Tel: 01 419 3333.

REDDY, Peter; GRAPHIC DESIGNER; *b* 1971; *educ* De La Salle Churchtown; Screen Printing Course FAS,1991; *single;* Trainee, Cuspal Signs, Dublin, 1991-92; Designer, Paintbox, 1993; Graphic Designer, The Kitchen, The PoD, Mean Fiddler, MCD, 1994 to date; Graphic Designer, Influx Records, 1996 to date; Freelance Designer Sony Records, 1997, Acid Jazz Records, 1996, Shadow Records, 1996; Winner, International Corel Draw Design Competition, 1995-97; Art Director, Fashion Consultant, Hobo Clothing Company, 1995 to date; Art Director, Cuba Clothing Company, 1998 to date; an iconoclastic, influential graphic designer; hobbies, Lambretta scooters, tailored clothes, music; Contact: Redman, 13, Trinity Street, Dublin 2. Tel: 01 677 9316.

REGAN, Paul; ARTIST; *b* 1970; *educ* C.B.S. Lucan; The College of Marketing and Design, Dip. Visual Communication Design; Painter, 1993 to date; *single;* Solo Exhibitions include Solo Works, City Arts Centre, Selected Works, The Globe, Big Money, The Front Lounge, Spiritual Dentist, The Bank of Ireland Arts Centre, From New York to L.A., The Front Lounge; Group Exhibitions include Expressions, Gallery 101, Imago, Irish Life Exhibition Centre, Human Rights Stamp Exhibition, Tokyo Postal Department, Tokyo, Japan, Zodiac Show, Gallery 101, Irish Commission for Prisoners Overseas - Poster Exhibition, Irish Museum of Modern Art, Fourth Bienniale of European Academies; has exhibited in Holland, Argentina, U.S.A., U.K., Belgium, Australia, Canada, Denmark, Russia; awarded numerous Arts Council grants; reviews include: *The Irish Times, The Sunday Times, Circa, The Sunday Business Post, Art Bulletin Magazine;* hobbies, surfing, cycling. Contact: 67 Main Street, Leixlip, Co. Kildare. Tel: 087 226 4384.

REYNOLDS, Robbie; DIRECTOR OF PHOTOGRAPHY, MacINNES; *b* 1971; *educ* St. Mary's, C.B.S., Drogheda; *single;* Senior Photographer, MacInnes, 1993-98; Freelance Photgrapher, *Irish Independent,* 1998-99; Director of Photography, MacInnes, 1999 to date; has worked in photography for twelve years, a combination of talent and determination has ensured recognition in his chosen area; hobbies, swimming, rowing. Contact: Tel: 01 661 0215.

REYNOLDS; Sonia; MODEL, EVENT MANAGER, AMPLIFY; *b* 1967; *educ* St. Michael's Grammar School, Lurgan, Co. Armagh; *m* Barry Lyons; Fashion Model, working extensively in Dublin, New York, Tokyo, Milan, Paris, Germany, Spain; has worked with Helmut Newton and Koto Bolfo; clients include: Romeo Jigli, Ghost, Jasper Conran, Arabella Pollen, Red Or Dead, Bella Freud, Philip Treacy, John Rocha, Paul Costello, Guess Jeans; has appeared in *Marie Claire, 17, Elle, Donna, Max, Country Living, Woman's Journal, Image Magazine, dSide, U Magazine, IT, Social & Personal, In Dublin*; television commercials include Guinness, Irish Tourist Board, Siucra, Master Card, Knorr Soup, Clairol; newspaper and magazine articles include: *Madison, Image Magazine, Irish Times, Irish Independent, Food & Wine Magazine, Northern Woman, IT Magazine;* television appearances include *The Gerry Ryan Show, Pat Kenny Show*; Co-founded Amplify, event management and representation of clients including Red Bull, Marc O'Neill, Barretstown, Angel Quest, Irish Cancer Society,

Cuan Hanly; hobbies, walking, sailing; Contact: Amplify, 46, Fitzwilliam Square, Dublin 2. Tel: 01 662 5652 Fax: 01 662 5654.

ROGERS, Deirdre; GLASS ARTIST, DESIGNER; *b* 1971; *educ* Loreto College, St. Stephen's Green, Dublin; National College of Art and Design, Degree in Craft; Orreforf Glass School, Sweden, Postgraduate, Glass Techniques; *m* Eugene Larkin; Designer, Sculpture Department, Waterford Crystal, 1995; Commissions include Heineken Colour In Your Life Fashion Award, 1995; *Hot Press* Rock Awards, 1997-98; Telecom Eireann/ *Irish Independent* Business Today Awards, 1999; Derry Verbal Arts Centre, 1999 to date; Work under Various Vessels range sells in Ireland, U.K. and U.S.A.; has featured in *Sunday Tribune, Image Magazine, Image Interiors, The Irish Times, The Irish Independent, House and Home Magazine, dSide, Glamour, Sunday Business Post, U Magazine, Gifts International, Select Magazine, Northern Ireland Homes, Interiors and Living, Irish Wedding and New Home Magazine;* Work has appeared on *Nationwide, The Pat Kenny Show, Beyond The Hall Door, Live at 3,* RTE; Exhibitions include NCAD - Celebrating 200 Years, RDS, Dublin, 1996; believes that "the most satisfying aspect about designing is creating with your own hands and seeing people appreciate and admire it as much as you do." hobbies, gardening, reading; Contact: The Garage Studios, Space 28, 28, North Lotts, Dublin 1. Tel: 01- 872 1882.

ROSS-MURPHY, Hilary; BUYER, DIRECTOR, CUBA CLOTHING LTD; *b* 1977; *educ* Wesley College, Ballinteer, Institute of Education, Leeson Street; read French, Italian, Economics, University College Dublin; *single;* Manager, Hobo Clothing, Dublin, 1997-98; Manager, Calypso, Long Island, U.S.A., a boutique frequented by stars and supermodels alike, 1998; currently Buyer and Director, Cuba Clothing Ltd.; hobbies, tennis, badminton, shopping; Contact: Cuba Clothing Ltd., 13 Trinity Street, Dublin 2. Tel: 01 672 7489.

ROWEN; Peter; PHOTOGRAPHER; *b* 1974; *educ* Mount Temple, Malahide Road, Dublin; *m* Carol Hanna; featured on the covers on U2's *Boy* and *War* albums as a child; on leaving school, worked for his father's business, before becoming involved in photography; Assistant to Eugene Langan, 1993-96; Freelance Photographer, *Food & Wine Magazine, World of Hibernia, Checkout Ireland, Himself Magazine;* Clients include Toyota, Irish Biscuits, Ericsson, Setanta Records, Silver Hill Foods, Boyne Valley Foods, The Morgan Hotel, O'Sullivan Ryan Advertising; a commercial photographer who can also turn his lens to the art of portraiture; cites Richard Avedon and Anton Corbijn as sources of inspiration; hobbies, playing golf, motorcycle racing, art; Contact: 63, Pleasants Place, Dublin 8. Tel: 01 475 5765.

ROWEN; Peter

ROWLAND, Robert, "Rob"; MUSIC PRODUCER; *b* 1973; *educ* Blackrock College, Dublin; Coláiste Dhulaigh, Coolock, Dublin; *single;* has been making and playing music since his teenage years; released his first record, *MFN,* 1994; has subsequently released eight records on Dublin's D1 label and U2's new Kitchen Recordings; has performed live extensively in Ireland, Spain, UK, Norway, Finland; currently setting up his own record label; hobbies, music, playing soccer; Contact D1 Records, 147 Parnell Street, Dublin 1. Tel: 01 874 9804.

SAXE, Róisín; TELEVISION, RADIO PRESENTER; *b* 1972; *educ* Coláiste Iosagáin, Maynooth College, BA; DIT Aungier Street, Dip., Public Relations; *single;* Researcher, Presenter, Radio na Life, 1994-95; Researcher, Reporter, *Popscene,* Network 2, 1997, Presenter, 1998-99; Researcher, Presenter, *Totally Irish,* 98FM, 1999 to date; hobbies, music, dancing; Contact: 98FM, South Block, The Malthouse, Grand Canal Quay, Dublin 2. Tel: 01 670 8970 Fax: 01 670 8969.

SCANNELL, Donal; TELEVISION PRODUCER, MUSIC ENTREPRENEUR; *b* 1972; *educ* Garbally College, Ballinasloe, Co. Galway, Dublin City University, B.Comm; *single;* Editor, *DropOut* Magazine, 1991-93; DJ, Promoter, 1992 to date; Researcher, *JMTV,* RTE, 1992-94; Researcher, *Late Late Show,* 1994-97; Associate Producer, *Moving People,* Channel 4, 1997; Associate Producer, *Gael Force,* Tyrone Productions, 1997-98; Co-ordinator, *Telethon,* RTE, 1998; Production, *2 Phat,* 1998-99; Segment Producer, Director, *@ last tv,* 1998; Producer, Director, *Something for the Weekend,* 1999; Director, music videos for Johnny Moy, David Gray, The Frames, Bass Odyssey, 1991 to date; Editor, *Shenanigans,* 1999; Journalist, *Irish Times, Hot Press, Sunday Independent, RTE Guide,* 1994-97; Manager, Quadraphonic Records, 1997 to date; Promoter, Quadraphonic, Stereophonic, Brown Sugar, Electronic club nights, 1996 to date; a media savvy figure with a thorough understanding of Irish youth culture; hobbies, DJing, cinema, walking, travelling, swimming. Contact: PO Box 5952, Dublin 1.

SCURRY, William, "Billy"; DJ; *b* 1971; *educ* C.B.S. North Brunswick Street; *single;* has been DJing since the early nineties, starting off in Leeson Street, before taking up residencies at Sides and The Temple of Sound, and more recently The PoD and U2's Kitchen nightclub; has performed extensively in Ireland and the U.K., Portugal, Holland, U.S.A.; a distinctive style and unmatched technical skills have ensured he has gained a reputation as Ireland's most respected DJ. Contact: Influx Records and Productions, 3, Princes Court, Princes Street South, Dublin 2. Tel: 01 670 3771.

SEOIGE, Gráinne; NEWSREADER, TV3; *b* 1973; *educ* Coláiste Croí Mhuire, Spiddal, Co. Galway; National University of Ireland, BA, Higher Diploma in Applied Communications; *single;* News Presenter, Video Journalist, TnaG, 1996-98; TV3 News Anchor, 1998 to date; a glamorous broadcaster, one of the mainstays of Ireland's third channel; hobbies, socialising, swimming, cinema; Contact: TV3, Unit 5, Westgate Business Park, Ballymount Industrial Estate, Dublin 24. Tel: 01 419 3333.

SEXTON, Sarah; VIOLINIST; *b* 1977; *educ* Christ the King Secondary School, Cork; Cork School of Music; currently studying at The Royal Academy of Music, London; *single;* has been playing the violin for twelve years; Leader of The National Youth Orchestra, has played with The National Youth Orchestra Under18s in Denmark, participated in festivals in France, Germany, Belgium, England, Spain and the U.S.A.; Member, The European Youth Orchestra; winner of all senior violin competitions at Feis Ceoil Dublin and Sligo, including both string bursaries; hobbies, swimming, cinema, theatre; Contact: Royal Academy Of Music, Marylebone Road, London MW1 5HT, England.

SEXTON, Tomás; ARCHITECT; *b* 1972; *educ* Clonakilty Community College, Cork; DIT Bolton Street, Degree (Hons.) Architecture; *single;* since graduating worked as an architect for Jim Coady & Associates, a practice with a varied portfolio for private and public clients; project work to date includes a £5 million four star hotel in Cork, health clinics, house designs and interior fit outs for private clients; currently working as project architect on £3.5 million Innovation and Business Centre for Dublin University; involved in consultancy work for building projects for a Kenyan based missionary; member R.I.A.I.; hobbies, snowboarding, canoeing and landscape design. Contact: Jim Coady & Associates, Trinity House, Charleston Road, Dublin 6. Tel: 01 497 6766 Fax: 01 497 0927.

SHEEHY, Ciara ATHLETE; *b* 1980 *educ* St. MacDara's Community College, Templeogue; Rathmines Senior College, Dip. Information Technology; *single;* started running aged ten, joined West Dublin Athletic Club; silver medalist, U17 200m AAA's of England, 1995; winner, 60m and 200m, National Bloe, Nenagh; winner, 100m and 200m Outdoor National BLOE Championships, 1995-97; competed in Slovenia, Latvia, Estonia, Cork at Senior Internationals for Ireland, 1997; winner, 200m, European Youth Olympics, Lisbon, becoming the first Irish female athlete to win gold at this event, 1997; winner, Scottish Junior 200m title, 1998; silver medallist, 200m, AAA's of England, 1998; winner, 60m and 200m, National Senior Indoor Championships, 1999; winner, 60m and 200m, AAA's of England, becoming the first Irish woman athlete to break 24 seconds indoor, a new Irish national record; recently achieved a new personal best of 23.74 seconds, plans to represent Ireland at the Sydney Olympics, 2000; Contact: BLE, 11 Prospect Road, Dublin 9. Tel: 01 830 8925.

SHERIDAN, Kirsten; FILM WRITER, DIRECTOR; *b* 1976; *educ* Mount Temple, Malahide Road, Dublin; Dun Laoghaire Institute of Art, Design and Technology; *single;* Work includes *The Bench*, 1995; *Patterns,* 1998, awarded Best Short Film, Cork Film Festival, Galway Film Fleadh, the Jesuit Film and Video Awards, Aspen Shorts Fest, U.S.A, Clermont-Ferrand Film Festival, France, Dresden Short Film Festival, Germany; European and Mediterranean Short Film Festival, Spain, Guinness Newcomer, 1998 ; Co-wrote *Honor Bright* with Audrey O'Reilly, awarded Miramax Screenplay Award, 1998; The daughter of Jim Sheridan, causing a stir on the international film scene with her award winning work; Currently working on *Majella McGinty*; hobbies, singing, playing the piano; Contact: 087 226 1218.

SHERIDAN, Sarah; WRITER; *b* 1968; *educ* St. Denis and Cranley School for Girls; The Edinburgh Academy; Trinity College Dublin; *single;* novels include *Truth or Dare*, 1998; *Ma Polinski's Pockets*, 1999, *The Pleasure Express* 2000; short films include *The Window Bed*, 1998; touted as one of GQ's Britlit talents of 1997 and nominated for a Young Achiever of Scotland Award, 1999; hobbies, swimming, yoga, cinema, travel; Contact: Random House, 20, Vauxhall Bridge Road, London, SW1V 2SA, England. Tel: 0044 171 840 8400.

SHERRY, RACHEL; PUBLIC RELATIONS EXECUTIVE; *b* 1969; *single; educ* Mount Sackville Convent, Dublin; College of Commerce, Rathmines; Chartered Institute of Marketing, Newman College, Dublin; worked as a tax consultant with Taxback, London, 1990-'95; joined public relations firm, Charles Barker BSMG, specialising in travel leisure accounts, 1995-'98; returned to Ireland as Senior Account Manager with Gilmore Communications Ltd. 1998 to date; an attractive and focused career woman, seen as a future leader in her fields; likely to head her own company in time. Hobbies, golf, swimming, theatre, reading. Contact: Gilmore Communications Ltd., 27 Sydney Parade Avenue, Dublin 4. Tel: 01 283 0088. Fax: 01 283 0119

SLATTERY, David; BUSINESS DEVELOPMENT MANAGER, SLATTERYS LTD.; *b* 1972; *educ* The Green, Tralee, Kerry; Trinity College Dublin, BESS; St. Patrick's College, Maynooth, Postgraduate, Information Technology; *single;* moved to England, Project Manager, British American Tobacco, working in London, Rome, Hamburg, Geneva, 1995-98; moved back to Ireland, working for the family business, Slatterys Ltd. as Business Development Manager; Slatterys is a long established independent travel and tour operator company, with offices in Ireland and the U.K.; the company also has property interests; hobbies, skiing, driving, local affairs. Contact: Slatterys Ltd., 1-4 Russell Street, Tralee, Co. Kerry. Tel: 066 712 4088 Fax: 066 712 5981.

SMURFIT, Victoria, "Vicky"; ACTRESS; *b* 1973; *educ* Prep School, Aravon, Bray; St. Columba's, Rathfarnham; St. George's Ascot, England; Bristol Old Vic Theatre School, England; *single;* Television appearances include *Ivanhoe, Berkeley Square, Ballykissangel*, BBC; film appearances include: *Run of the Country, Leading Man, The Beach*, with Leonardo Di Caprio; stage appearances include Brian Friel's *Translations*, Bristol; the daughter of Irish millionaire businessman Dermot Smurfit, has been described as a mixture of Meryl Streep and Shirley Maclaine; hobbies, painting, decorating, walking, reading; Contact: ICM Ireland Ltd., The Barracks, 76, Irishtown Road, Dublin 4. Tel: 01 667 6455 Fax: 01 667 6474.

STOKES, Christian

SPOLLEN, Brian; MUSIC PROMOTER, RECORD LABEL OWNER; *b* 1971; *educ* St. Michael's, Dublin; Ballyfermot Senior College, Sound Engineering Diploma; Freelance Sound Engineer, 1989-90; Tour Manager, The Frames, 1991, Manager, 1991-95; Freelance Music Consultant, MCD, 1994; Freelance Promoter, MCD, responsible for the Heineken Weekender, Bud Thud, Heineken Green Energy, Guinness Global Gathering festivals, 1995 to date; Promoter, Quadraphonic, Stereophonic, Brown Sugar, Electronic, 1996 to date; Owner, Quadraphonic Records; the brains behind some of the biggest music festivals in Ireland; hobbies, music, movies; Contact: The Factory, 35a Barrow Street, Dublin 4.

STOKES, Christian; RESTAURANT MANAGER, OWNER; *b* 1975; *educ* Sandford Park, Ranelagh; Wesley College, Ballinteer; LSB College, Diploma in Marketing, Advertising; *single;* has worked together with twin brother Simon in The Unicorn, becoming co-manager; recently purchased the old Pierre Victoire restaurant on Merrion Row with his brother and father Jeff Stokes, now opened as Bang; hobbies, weight training, tennis, travelling; Contact: 12B, Merrion Court, Merrion Row, Dublin 2. Tel: 01 662 4757.

SWEENEY, Eamonn

SWEENEY, Eamonn; WRITER; *b* 1968; *educ* Mary's College, Boyle, Co. Roscommon; *single;* Journalist, *The Roscommon Champion*, 1986-87; Journalist, Echo Newspapers, Basildon, Essex, UK, 1988-92; Returned to Ireland, worked as a freelance journalist, 1992-96; Published first novel, *Waiting for the Healer*, "an existential thriller based in the Midlands" and the non-fiction, *There's Only One Red Army*, 1997; has finished working on his second novel, *The Photograph*, "an Irish saga", to be published in March 2000; hobbies, football, reading, cooking; Contact: Peters Fraser & Dunlop, 503, The Chambers, Chelsea Harbour, Lots Road,

London, SW10 OXF, England.

SWORDS, Brian

SWORDS, Brian; DEPUTY MANAGING DIRECTOR, CAWLEY NEA LTD.; *b* 1970; *educ* Ard Scoil Rís, Limerick; University of Limerick, Degree, Business Studies; University College Galway, Postgraduate Degree, Marketing; single; worked in the marketing department of Cantrell & Cochrane while in college; Joined Dimension Advertising as Account Manager, 1992-93; Account Manager, Cawley Nea, 1993, Account Director, 1995, Director, 1995, Deputy Managing Director, 1999; Cawley Nea are the fast rising stars of the Irish advertising industry, successively making it into the top three in the Advertising Agencies of the Year Award in recent years; hobbies, football, surfing; Contact: Cawley Nea, 41a, Blackberry Lane, Rathmines, Dublin 6. Tel: 01 496 6920 Fax: 01 496 6923

SYNOTT, Shane; ARTIST; *b* 1971 *educ* Belvedere College, Dublin; National College of Design, BA, Fine Art Painting; *single;* Residency, The Cap Foundation, Dublin, 1997-98; Group Exhibitions include: Quadrant, The Belltable Arts Centre, Limerick, 1998; Iontas, RHA Gallagher Gallery, Dublin, Belfast, Sligo, 1998; residency, Artists Work Programme, Irish Museum of Modern Art, 1999; awarded Travel Award, The Arts Council, 1997, Materials Grant, The Arts Council, 1998; has won a scholarship to study at The Royal College of Art, London; Contact: c/o The Royal College of Art, London.

TUCKER, Liz

TOWNSEND, Stuart; ACTOR; *b* 1972; has starred in a number of films including *Trojan Eddie, Shooting Fish,* 1996, *Under The Skin, Resurrection Man,* 1997, *Simon Magus, Wonderland, The Wrong Blonde,* 1998, *All About Adam,* 1999; has worked with Gerry Stembridge and Stefan Schwarz amongst others; hobby, photography. Contact: Vanessa Pereira, The William Morris Agency, 1, Stratton Street, London, W1X 6HB, England. Tel: 0044 171 3558500 Fax: 0044 171 3558600.

TRITSCHLER, Robin; TENOR; *b* 1977; *educ* St. David's Greystones; Dublin City University/Royal Irish Academy of Music, BA, Music Performance; *single;* has performed extensively throughout Ireland, with all the major orchestras; has performed in London, Germany, Switzerland; Resident Tenor, Bach Festival, Dublin; Awarded Ulster Bank Music Foundation, 1999, RTE Singer of the Future, 1998; winner of most of the major prizes in Feis Ceoil; was recently accepted for the Britten Pears School for Bach Singing and The Royal Academy of Music, London; hobby, tennis; Contact: The Royal Academy of Music, Marylebone Road, London MW1 5HT, England.

TUOHIG, Cara

TUCKER, Liz; MODEL; *b* 1978; *educ* Loretto, Dalkey; joined 1st Option Model Agency, 1998; *single;* has appeared in *Image Magazine, U Magazine, dSide*; shows include Smirnoff Fashion Awards, 1998, Arnotts, 1999, Peter Mark, 1999; shoots include Kookai,1998; has been tipped for international success; hobbies, walking, reading. Contact: First Option, 40, Dame Street, Dublin 2. Tel: 01 6705233.

TUOHIG, Cara; PR MANAGER; *b* 1972; *educ* Loretto College, St. Stephen's Green; Loreto, Rathfarnham; University College Dublin, BA; *single;* Junior Account Executive, Drury Communications, 1992; Account Manager, 1994; Press Co-ordinator, American Embassy, Presidential Visit to Ireland, 1995; Fundraiser, Children's Hospital, Temple Street, 1996-98; currently PR Manager, *Hot Press* Irish Music Hall of Fame; hobbies, acting, horse riding, singing; Contact: Hot Press Irish Music Hall of Fame, 57, Middle Abbey Street, Dublin 1. Tel: 01 878 3345.

TYRANSEN, Olaf

TYRANSEN, Olaf; JOURNALIST, WRITER; *b* 1971; *educ* St. Enda's, Salthill, Galway; *single;* Freelance Journalist, *Galway Advertiser,* 1987-89; Editor, *The Word,* 1992-94; published his first book of poetry, *The Consequences of Slaughtering Butterflies,* 1992; Manager, The Far Canals, 1992-94; Freelance Journalist, *Hot Press Magazine, Magill, Mojo, Dazed & Confused, Sunday Times, Sunday Independent, Himself,* 1992 to date; ran as an independent candidate in the 1997 General Election; has read extensively at literary festivals worldwide; has contributed to countless poetry and literature journals, most recently the *Shenanigans* short story collection, 1987 to date; plans to publish an anthology of his journalism at the end of this year, and an anthology of poetry in 2000; hobbies, reading, writing, movies, music, travelling. Contact: Hot Press Magazine, 13 Trinity Street, Dublin 2. Tel: 01 679 5077.

WELD, Mark D.; RACEHORSE TRAINER; *b* 1975; *educ* Newbridge College; *single;* currently assistant trainer to father, Dermot Weld, having gained experience in the U.S.A. and Australia; hobbies, singing and playing music, sports, aviation. Contact: Rosewell House, Curragh, Co. Kildare. Tel: 045 441 273 Fax: 045 441 119.

WHELAN, Deirdre; INTERIOR DESIGNER; *b* 1966; *educ* St. David's Greystones; College of Marketing and Design, Degree, Interiors and Textiles; *m* Paul Kelly; worked with Richmond Interiors, London, Keane Murphy Duff Architecture, Dublin, Scott Tallon Walker Architects Dublin; set up own practice, 1996; projects include Ritz Casino, Mitsubishi Electric, Barings Bank, Telecom Eireann Headquarters, Stephen's Green, Unicorn Restaurant and Apartments, Silicon and Software Systems Offices, Arthur Cox Solicitors Offices, studio set for *Beyond the Hall Door*, RTE; awarded second prize, Japanese Competition, To Fulfil a Woman's Dream, 1994, special mention, Japanese Competition, Blossoming of a Woman's Vision, 1995, special mention, The Architectural Association of Ireland Awards, 1995; work has featured in *Japan Architect, Evening Press, The Sunday Independent, The Irish Times, Select Magazine, Beyond the Hall Door*, Member, Architectural Association of Ireland, Kilternan Sports Hotel; hobbies, working out, tennis, art, cooking and "all the good things life has to offer"; Contact: The Studio, 15, Upper Baggot Street, Dublin 2. Tel: 01 667 7277 Fax: 01 667 7278.

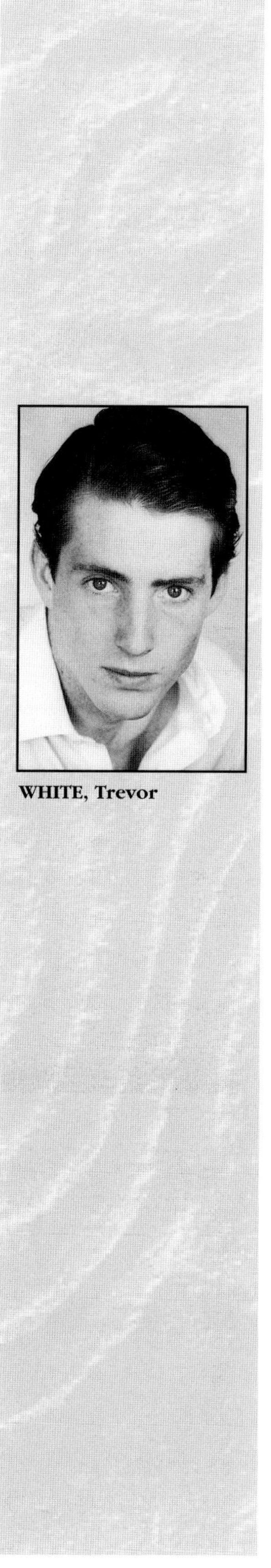

WHITE, Trevor

WHITE, Trevor; SENIOR EDITOR, CADOGAN PUBLICATIONS; *b* 1972; *educ* St. Columba's College, Rathfarnham; Trinity College Dublin Diploma, Theatre Studies; *single;* Features Editor, *Food & Wine Magazine,* 1997-98; Contributing Editor, *Europe's Elite 1000*; the definitive record of Europe's best luxury goods, 1998; Senior Editor, *America's Elite 1000,* 1999; a *bon viveur*, an excellent host and a keen sportsman; Member, Fitzwilliam Lawn Tennis Club; hobbies, tennis, cricket, playing pool; Contact: Cadogan Publications, 27 West 24th Street, New York, NY 10010,U.S.A. Tel: 212 414 8776 Fax: 212 414 8779

WILLS, Grainne; PORTFOLIO ANALYST, IRISH LIFE INVESTMENT MANAGERS; *b* 1971; *educ* Alexandra College, Milltown; University College Dublin, BA, Spanish, Economics; Michael Smurfit Graduate School of Business, DBS, MBS; *single;* Foreign Settlements Supervisor, AIB, 1996-98; Portfolio Analyst, Irish Life Investment Managers, 1998 to date; hobbies, photography, travel. Contact: Irish Life Investment Managers, Beresford Court, Abbey Street, Dublin 1. Tel: 01 704 2339.

YOURELL, Jade; ACTRESS; *b* 1978; *educ* Taylor's Hill, Galway; Loreto Abbey, Rathfarnham; *single;* studied at the Ann Kavanagh School of Drama; theatre credits include *Arcadia* (Gate Theatre), *Ideal Husband* (Gate Theatre); a young fresh talent who has already made her mark. Contact: Teri Hayden, The Agency, 47 Adelaide Road, Dublin 2. Tel: 01 661 8535.

INDEX

I N D E X

I N D E X

I N D E X

INDEX